BARRON'S

AP®

Advanced Placement Exam

SPANISH
2007

5TH EDITION

Alice G. Springer, Ph.D.
Professor of Spanish
Montgomery Bell Academy
Nashville, Tennessee

BARRON'S

Acknowledgments

Special thanks are due to John, my students at MBA, my editor at Barron's, Dimitry Popow, and Cristina Tarazona Marín.

All inquiries should be addressed to:
Barron's Educational Series, Inc.
250 Wireless Boulevard
Hauppauge, New York 11788
http://www.barronseduc.com

Library of Congress Control Number 2006041777

ISBN-13: 978-0-7641-7943-3
ISBN-10: 0-7641-7943-8

Library of Congress Cataloging-in-Publication Data

Springer, Alice G.
    AP advanced placement examination. Spanish / Alice G. Springer.—
5th ed.
        p. cm.
    Rev. ed. of: How to prepare for the advanced placement exam.
Spanish / Alice G. Springer.
    Includes bibliographical references.
    ISBN-13: 978-0-7641-3486-9 (book only : alk. paper)
    ISBN-10: 0-7641-3486-8 (book only : alk. paper)
    ISBN-13: 978-0-7641-7943-3 (book and CDs : alk. paper)
    ISBN-10: 0-7641-7943-8 (book and CDs : alk. paper)
    1. Spanish language—Examinations, questions, etc. 2. Advanced
placement programs (Education)—Examinations—Study guides.
I. Title: Barron's How to prepare for the AP advanced placement exam.
Spanish. II. Springer, Alice G. How to prepare for the advanced
placement exam. Spanish. III. Title.

PC4119.S7 2006
468.0076—dc22   2006041777

Printed in the United States of America
9 8 7 6 5 4 3 2 1

CONTENTS

PART ONE INTRODUCTION

Preparing for the Advanced Placement Spanish Language Examination

GENERAL CONSIDERATIONS

The Advanced Placement Spanish program consists of two areas: (1) Spanish Language, and (2) Spanish Literature. Each area is substantially different in terms of the content and the format of the respective examinations. While the Advanced Placement Spanish Literature Exam tests reading comprehension, and has an analytical writing component dealing with reading selections and works from a specified reading list of Spanish authors, the Spanish Language Exam tests ability to communicate in Spanish in four skill areas: listening, reading, writing, and speaking. There is no prescribed curriculum of material to be considered before the student takes the Spanish Language Examination. However, the difficulty of the exam roughly corresponds to material appropriate for most third year college Spanish courses. A dedicated, well motivated high school student can earn the highest score on the exam by demonstrating strong ability in both receptive and productive language skill areas. The student should be able to understand spoken and written Spanish at a very sophisticated level. In the productive skill areas, the student must demonstrate the ability to communicate fluently and accurately in speaking and writing Spanish. In the oral portion of the exam students are required to record their responses and submit the samples for evaluation. In the final analysis, results of the Spanish Language Exam evaluations are expressed in terms of a five point scale: 5—Extremely well qualified, 4—Well qualified, 3—Qualified, 2—Possibly qualified, 1—No recommendation.

DESCRIPTION OF THE EXAM FORMAT BEGINNING IN 2007

The four skill areas tested in the Advance Placement Spanish Language Exam are divided into two sections. Section I, which tests listening and reading comprehension, has multiple choice questions. Section II, which consists of a test of writing and speaking skills, comprises free-response tasks. Answers for the multiple choice questions of Section I are written on a standard multiple choice answer sheet. The free-response written part of Section II is provided in a test booklet. Speaking samples are recorded and submitted on a compact disc or on a cassette. College Board is moving as quickly as possible toward requiring compact discs for recordings of speech samples in response to the prompts on the exam.

**Structure of
the Exam**

Section I: Multiple Choice Questions
    Part A—Listening Skills
        Short and Long Dialogues and Narratives
    Part B— Reading
        Reading Comprehension
Section II: Free Response
    Part A—Paragraph Completion (with root words)
        Paragraph Completion (without root words)
        Informal Writing
        Formal Writing (integrated skills)
    Part B—Speaking
        Informal Speaking (simulated conversation)
        Formal Oral Presentation (integrated skills)

**Section I: Listening
and Reading**

Listening comprehension has two parts; one is short dialogues and narratives, and the other consists of two longer selections. The whole listening comprehension part of the exam amounts to 20 percent of the total score, and comprises about 30 to 35 multiple choice questions. You are to select the best answer from among the four choices to questions asked in the audio selections. The questions are not printed in the test booklet and are played only once. The second part of listening comprehension consists of two longer selections. The questions are printed in the test booklet, and there is time to read the questions before listening to the audio selections. This section is the same as in past exams.

For short dialogues and narratives, you can get some ideas about the context, such as where the speakers are, who they are, what the purpose of their conversation is, and some other details that may be essential. The dialogues may have been obtained from any type of audio medium, such as radio, television, films, podcasts, or streaming video. They could be casual conversations, or formal interviews, dialogues taken from soap operas, or two friends discussing life. Questions generally go from general to specific, from getting the main idea to details about time and place, for example. Some questions may be a portion that is replayed, followed by a question asking for an interpretation of that specific portion. Or the question may ask for a literal interpretation of a phrase or word. Other questions may deal with an inferred meaning of specific utterances found in the audio selection. For example, there could be a conversation between two people who are discussing going to a movie and trying to decide on when to go. In such a scenario, pay attention to the numbers expressing the hour, to the name of a movie selected from a list of movie names (which is the one they go to see), or the location of the theater.

The two longer selections, each about 5 minutes long, could be interviews, broadcasts, instructions on how to do or use something, stories, or any other kind of spoken material. There will be space to take notes while listening in order to refer to specific information in answering the questions. In some cases there may be some sort of visual material to help put the conversation in context, or an image that will help visualization of what is heard when the audio selection is played. There are no changes to the format of the two long selections of the exam.

Section II: Writing and Speaking

The exam has become more interactive, because you read and listen to source materials before writing and speaking. For both reading and speaking you need to be able to summarize and synthesize print and audio information related to a general question. The responses to the questions require analysis and critical thinking.

Part A of Section II (free response) includes four parts (1) paragraph completion (with root words), (2) paragraph completion (without root words), (3) informal writing, and (4) formal writing. The paragraph completions, with and without root words, are not much different from what has been on the exam in the past. These are the parts where a thorough knowledge of grammar is essential. Even though the paragraph completions only take 15 minutes and account for 5 percent of the score, they are important. The informal writing part takes about 10 minutes and is worth 5 percent in the calculation of the score. The formal writing consists of one prompt, for which 55 minutes are allotted to write a response. Formal writing amounts to 20 percent of the raw score.

Paragraph completion with root words means that there are paragraphs with numbered blanks in one column. In another column to the side you will see correspondingly numbered blanks with a word beneath each line. The word could be any part of speech: adjective (including definite and indefinite articles), adverbs, verbal tenses (including past and present participles), or other items relating to syntax and grammar. Each root word may need to be changed to a correct form, or, if no change is necessary, the given root word is to be written in the blank. If more than one form is correct, credit is given for all the possible correct forms. There are 10 questions for the paragraph completions. Note that for each blank more than one word may be needed. The paragraph or paragraphs provide the context for the response to be written in the blank. Therefore, what is contained in the rest of the paragraph needs to be clearly understood, because it often contains clues about the gender and number, or verbal tense required in the change of the root word. In this free-response part, there is no substitute for knowing correct verb forms, rules of agreement of adjectives and nouns, and many other points of grammar.

The informal writing sample is new on the 2007 exam. In response to one prompt, you are to write a short piece, similar to what would be written in an e-mail, a postcard, a journal entry, a telephone message, or a thank-you note. Here you will encounter a wide variety of possible contexts requiring a recognition of cultural aspects of communication, such as whether to use second person *tú*, or third person *usted*. The focus of the informal writing is the expression of personal attitudes or reactions. Instructions in the prompt are explicit about the topic. For example, if you are to write a postcard, there might be instructions to comment on a personal reaction to something seen or heard in the given place or situation, such an impression of the food at a restaurant in Barcelona that you have visited.

The last task in Part A is formal writing, which is different from past exams. The new format calls for integrating reading and listening skills into the writing task. Instead of simply writing an essay about a given topic, you need to gather information from something read and heard, and then you have to respond using an analytical or persuasive essay to communicate your reaction to that information. The process requires that you synthesize that information, and then interpret it. The topics can range from academic to cultural and social issues.

The formal writing prompt consists of print and audio material to be used in the response. About 7 minutes are allotted to read a short piece about some topic. The audio information will provide a short narrative or dialogue lasting about 3 minutes. Taking notes while listening is strongly recommended in order to cite information accurately from the sources when the essay is written. Five minutes are alloted to plan your essay. After reading and listening to the sources, 40 minutes are allotted to write a response, making sure to make reference to all of the sources, but without simply summarizing what each one said. There is no requirement to write any specific number of words.

Part B of Section II is the speaking skill area. Once again, there are significant changes in the format that require a different kind of practice in order to do well. There are two parts (1) informal speaking, which consists of a simulated conversation, and (2) a formal oral presentation, which requires integrating reading and listening into the speech response. There are no more directed response questions, nor is there a story based on a series of pictures. Context is very important, as is an understanding of cultural topics, because the information provided in the reading and listening parts of the prompt are usually based on some aspect of life in the Spanish-speaking world

Simulated conversations are structured with distinct parts, to give the impression that you are participating in an actual conversation. Within a given context and topic, a speech sample of what one person would say in the conversation is provided as a recorded prompt. After hearing each speech sample, you are given 20 seconds to continue the conversation in a logical manner. For example, the conversation might feature two friends making plans to go to a movie together. There would be a recording providing directions and the context of the conversation. The speaker would greet you and propose going out. There would be a 20-second pause for your response. After 20 seconds the recorded prompt would elaborate on the idea. You would have another 20 seconds to react to the idea. The conversation would continue in that interactive manner for the duration of the five or six opportunities given to you to speak. The general outline of the script is supplied, with directions for you to greet someone, explain a situation, express an opinion, invite, say good-bye, and so on.

The formal oral presentation is much more complex than simply telling a story. The reading prompt source may be articles from newspapers, magazines, brochures, or even contemporary literature. The speaking sources could be from any broadcast medium (radio, film, television, etc.). In the response to the information contained in the sources you have to find and report main points and important details in the information, so a personal interpretation, reaction, opinion, or analysis can be offered concerning what you have learned from the print and audio sources in the prompt. Two minutes are allotted to speak, using all the appropriate vocabulary and correct grammar possible.

Scoring the Samples

Although the exam contains a certain amount of new material each year, such as the prompts on the free-response sections, the scoring standards (rubrics) remain constant from year to year. A substantial command of Spanish reflected in well-developed ideas, structural accuracy, syntactical control, and fluency is very important. Each sample is evaluated on the merits of the language you use as a whole. The scoring of each writing and speech sample is holistic; that is, the language is considered a single entity and its elements are not analyzed separately. Points are not deducted for errors. Individual samples are not compared with other samples, nor are the faculty consultants (the people who evaluate the speaking and writing samples) aware of scores on other parts of the exam. You do not have to be a native speaker of Spanish to receive a top score on the examination.

Because the format is so different, instead of ranking the responses on a scale from zero to nine, broader categories for rating the samples provided in the responses are used. For the purposes of evaluating samples in this book, three major categories representing proficiency as well as competence are employed: low, medium, and high. In the speech samples, both informal and formal, the rubrics (scoring standards) still require the same linguistic basics, that is, adequate pronunciation, fluency, good range of vocabulary, correctness of grammatical and syntactic elements, ease of expression, awareness of register, and understanding of other cultural aspects. In the writing samples, both informal and formal, the same elements are necessary. Here, considering the additional time you are given to think about what is communicated, you should use every available opportunity to check organization, grammar, and orthography (the use of accents and other diacritical marks).

Scoring Writing Samples

For the informal writing sample, special attention is given to register (the appropriate use of *tú* and *usted*), syntax, and grammar. For formal writing, the 40 minutes allotted for writing the essay means that there is time to organize thoughts and to think through the same lexical, syntactic, and grammatical points that are evaluated in the informal writing part. Instead of a composition about a general topic, however, there is information from the reading audio sources that should be incorporated into the essay. For that reason, the language writing sample has some additional elements that are taken into consideration in the categories of low, medium, and high.

Each category is defined below.

Low: Language used that falls into this category is characterized by frequent lapses in several areas, such as inadequate knowledge of correct verbal forms (subjects and verb endings do not agree), use of the incorrect form for irregular, stem-changing, or spelling-change verbs, use of incorrect pronouns and misplaced pronouns, lack of adjective and noun agreement, incorrect use of verbs meaning "to be" in Spanish, incorrect use of the two past tenses, incorrect use of the subjunctive, and the use of English or Anglicized words instead of proper Spanish vocabulary. The selection of register is inappropriate. There is incorrect syntax, including translation of words into Spanish from English when they are not correct in an expression. Sentence fragments are used instead of fully formed ideas, verbal tenses are limited mostly to the present, with perhaps one or two incorrect attempts at the preterit or imperfect. There is a general inability to communicate thoughts and ideas intelligibly in Spanish.

Medium: Although some of the problems listed above may be in evidence, the student selects the appropriate register, observes the conventions of greetings and closings in informal written communications, uses a variety of verbal tenses, uses correct verbal forms (often knows how to use the subjunctive correctly), and employs appropriate vocabulary, including *modismos* or expressions that have no literal translation. The student shows some logical progression of the main idea in writing Although the organization of ideas in sentences may reveal some grammatical or lexical problems, the errors are random instead of systematic. Communication can be categorized as appropriate.

High: In this category the response shows language that is well developed and coherent. The student communicates thoughts and ideas clearly, uses a large and varied vocabulary, responds fully and with appropriate elaboration, goes beyond the basic requirements of the response, clearly demonstrates superior grammar and syntax, uses more complex grammatical structures, employs the subjunctive very effectively, uses the appropriate register, and organizes thoughts in a logical manner.

Scoring Speaking Samples

For **informal speaking**, in which there are five or six responses to supply within the framework of the given conversation, the following rubrics are used when scoring the sample.

Low: The responses are often difficult to understand because they consist of sentence fragments or unconnected phrases. The pronunciation makes Spanish words hard to recognize, with such errors and voicing the letter "h" or mispronouncing the letter "g," for example. There are frequent syntactical and grammatical errors. Verbs are often not conjugated correctly. Vocabulary is limited, and words often do not mean what the student thinks they mean. There are pauses, such that there is not much of a speech sample to score. Although the speech sample is appropriate at times, more often it is not sufficient to respond appropriately to the recorded prompts, and the response clearly shows a limited understanding of the recorded prompts that direct the flow and logic of the conversation.

Medium: There may be frequent errors; however, these do not seriously impair understanding. The responses show some ability to maintain a conversation, because the sample shows that the student understood what was said, and have supplied basic responses in the appropriate places. There are some difficulties with correctness of syntax and grammar. There is not much elaboration in the response, which is generally vague, with important information missing because of limited vocabulary. Pronunciation is clear, but delivery is halting at times. There is limited development of ideas, but the response as a whole is understandable.

High: Although there may be some errors, the overall response shows a speech characterized by ease of expression and fluency, making the sample seem like a natural conversation. Pronunciation is very clear and correct. Grammar and syntax are correct for the most part. Sentences contain varied structures, such as the use of adverbial clauses, or noun clauses that demonstrate a good command of the use of the subjunctive, for example. There is successful self-correction, such as backtracking to place a pronoun in front of a conjugated verb instead of after the verb, which would be typical of English. There is a logical development of thoughts or ideas in the conversation, and the response successfully fulfills what is required in the task.

Formal speaking draws on your ability to gather information using reading as well as audio sources, and then to process the information and to incorporate it into the response. The task requires much more that simply telling a story based on pictures for prompts. Therefore, the scoring categories generally consist of the following rubrics.

Low: In response to the reading and audio material provided and the topic question asked, the sample shows that the student relies heavily on one source (reading or audio instead of both). The student does not organize thoughts and ideas into a logical order in response to the question. There are long pauses while he/she thinks about what to say, which often is an indication of an effort to translate what is said from English to Spanish. Long pauses are heard, caused by a lack of appropriate vocabulary and/or a lack of knowledge of basic grammatical structures and syntax. There are continuous problems with pronunciation (such as pronouncing the letter "h" or "g") and intonation. Expressions that confuse and obscure coherent meaning, and unconnected sentence fragments make it difficult for the listener to follow the idea that the student is trying to communicate.

Medium: In this category the responses show that the student understood the material from both sources and could use it in relevant and appropriate ways. There still may be some pauses, or the delivery may be halting, even though what is said is coherent. The grammar is basic, and the range of vocabulary is limited. Sentence structures are basic, lacking appropriate use of noun, adjective, or adverb clauses. There may be confusion regarding the information obtained from the two sources. There is evidence of adequate expression and fluency, even though there are still some problems. Self-correction is shown at times, when a mistake is recognized in time to remedy the error. The student generally answers the questions appropriately.

High: This category shows superior command of the language, because the student makes full use of information from both printed and audio sources in answering the questions. He/she demonstrates a natural ease in the delivery of the speech sample, pronounces words correctly, uses complex sentences structures, employs correct grammar and syntax, including correct prepositions, pronouns, verb forms, verb tenses and moods. The student uses a wide range of words and expressions, utilizes original words to express thoughts (instead of borrowing heavily from the words and expressions used in the print and audio source materials), and, in spite of some random errors, clearly demonstrates a superior command of the language.

In many ways the new format of the exam makes it a more difficult test of ability. The emphasis has shifted from memorizing particular words to recognizing and using Spanish in more contexts. It is as important as ever to know the fundamentals of Spanish, such as correct verb forms, correct use of the preterit and imperfect, correct use of the subjunctive, correct adjective usage, as well as correct use of accent marks and question and exclamation marks. All the knowledge about correct language usage is to come purely from memory, without the prompts from sections testing specific points of grammar that used to be on the exam.

Reviewing or learning appropriate vocabulary to use in speaking, and then practicing as much as possible is essential. Use the chapter in this book dealing with grouped vocabulary to review and learn as many new words as possible, paying special attention to the suggested situations for oral practice. Because spelling, accents, verb forms, and all the other aspects of written language are still as important as ever, pay attention to the section on writing skills. Visual learners still find it easier to go from written to spoken words. Audio learners still find it useful to go from audio to visual exercises.

The rationale for making the changes to the exam are important to keep in mind when preparing for it. Besides making the exam test more of the abilities expected of students in the fifth and sixth semester of college Spanish, the exam also requires more knowledge of Spanish and awareness of cultural aspects of the Spanish-speaking world by requiring more sophisticated processing of the language. With integrated skills used in the speaking and writing questions, students are required to assimilate, analyze, and articulate thoughts in a more complex manner. Therefore, in addition to studying the exercises in this book, every opportunity should be taken to listen to Spanish speakers, to speak Spanish as often as possible and with as many native speakers as possible, and to read and write as much Spanish as you can. Study the material in this book, then put it in practice. There is absolutely no substitute for practice.

THE ADVANCED PLACEMENT SPANISH LANGUAGE STUDENT

This book is intended for English-speaking students who are preparing for the Advanced Placement Spanish Language exam, although native speakers will benefit from the description of the exam structure and the discussions of how the evaluation scales are applied. For most Spanish-speaking students, the vocabulary is not a major consideration in preparation, but it is for English-speaking students learning Spanish. Also, most Spanish-speaking students will have no difficulty with the listening comprehension and speaking portions of the exam. The preparation for the writing and reading sections of the exam should be helpful to both English- and Spanish-speaking students, however.

Because there are so many regional differences among Spanish-speaking people, there are many ways of communicating in the Spanish language. In spite of the wide variation in expression in Spanish, however, there are some aspects of expression that are more or less universal. The objective on this examination is for the student to express himself or herself as clearly, accurately, articulately, and fluently as possible in Spanish. The level of proficiency should be sophisticated enough for the student to carry on any nontechnical conversation. There is a basic grammar at the back of this book to help the student correct any persistent errors. Since the Advanced Placement course is intended to be college-level work taught at the high school level, both the vocabulary and grammatical aspects in this book are intended to represent an advanced level of communication. The course is designed to be a demanding and intensive program of language study. In order to succeed, the student must demonstrate a commitment to learning as much Spanish as possible. The successful student on this exam is also one who will take the initiative and responsibility for learning as much as possible.

The Advanced Placement course is designed to prepare a student to study Spanish in college at an intermediate to advanced level. The precise point at which a student would enter depends on the score that the student receives on the exam and the credit that will be given by the college or university. Up to date information about how much credit is given by colleges and universities is available from the College Board. *The College Handbook* is a publication listing over 3,000 two- and four-year institutions and the credit that each gives for AP scores. Information about credit given for the AP courses by various colleges and universities is provided by the College Board on their web site: *www.collegeboard.com.* (basic information about the exam can be found at *www.apcentral.collegeboard.com*).

Preparation for the Exam

The best preparation for taking the Spanish Language Examination is one that stresses oral skills, composition, and grammar study. Now that different skill areas are integrated into almost all of the tasks on the exam, it is more important than ever to practice all the skill areas. The reading and writing parts are 30 percent apiece (60 percent of the total score), and even these parts require understanding of spoken Spanish and the ability to read printed material in the source material for the prompts. You should use Spanish as much as possible in all four skill areas: speaking, listening, writing, and reading. You will find that the language in this guide reflects the wide range of expression found among Spanish-speaking people, from peninsular Spanish to Latin American. Samples of formal and informal discourse are also presented. The samples in the grammatical section are taken from a very wide range of sources—from newspapers, magazine articles, advertisements, short stories, and transcripts of interviews. Some are adaptations from these above sources.

OBJECTIVES IN THE FOUR SKILL AREAS

Listening Comprehension

You should be able to understand short conversations, narratives, interviews, or other material of a nontechnical nature. Listening to as much Spanish from as many different sources as possible, such as radio, television, taped songs, stories, and lectures is the best preparation for the listening comprehension section.

Reading Comprehension

You should be able to read any sort of nontechnical material that you might encounter in everyday situations—newspapers, recipes, instructions, any printed material that accompanies merchandise from or is intended for use by Spanish-speaking people, and short literary pieces. The more reading you do, the better prepared you will be.

Writing

You should have sufficient vocabulary and control of grammatical structures to permit you to express your thoughts clearly in writing. Practice in writing essays is especially important so that you can easily provide an informal writing sample, such as what you would write in an e-mail message, a memo, a postcard, a short personal note, or some other form of personal correspondence in the 10 minutes allotted. Familiarity with a wide range of words and expressions is also essential to the expository or persuasive essay that you will write based on the print and audio sources in the prompt. In the 40 minutes allowed for the essay there is not a lot of time to spare in thinking what words should you use. You should know enough vocabulary that you do not have to rely on repeating words seen or heard in the source material.

Speaking

You are asked in the speech samples to participate in a simulated conversation, and then to present a two-minute sample. Both tasks require that you understand audio and print source material to use as you speak in response to the prompts.

You will notice that vocabulary is not mentioned in any one skill area, but it is crucial in all of them. Vocabulary is tested before the reading comprehension but your ability to express yourself and to understand others is defined by what words and expressions you know. You should learn as much vocabulary as you can.

Cultural material is not tested in a separate part of the exam, but is integral to all of it. The more you know about geography, customs, traditions, institutions, history, and people in Spanish-speaking countries, the more vocabulary you are likely to know. Also you will find that some of the material used to test the skill areas is about cultural topics. If you are familiar with cultural material, you will be comfortable with those parts of the exam.

You should try to learn as much as possible about cultural topics by reading, watching, and listening to programs about Spanish-speaking countries and by talking to Spanish-speaking people. You can find information of a cultural nature in practically any kind of audio or print material in Spanish. Another good source is the Internet. Topics you have heard or read about are today easily accessible via Google or Yahoo.

USING THIS BOOK

In the absence of a formal Advanced Placement Spanish Language class, you can prepare for the examination by becoming familiar with the examination format and studying all the materials available. This guide to the Spanish Language Examination is designed to help you understand the structure of the exam and its grading. It also contains strategies for preparing for each of the skill areas, practice exercises in each of the skill areas, answer keys so that answers can be checked, and commentaries to help you understand why some answers are better than others. The practice exam and the answers will provide additional preparation for the actual exam.

The following pages are designed to help you prepare for the Spanish Language Examination by:

1. presenting material (vocabulary, grammatical structures and conversation topics) that are likely to be covered on the exam,
2. providing exercises for you to practice and master language in the different skill areas, and
3. providing one complete practice exam.

This book is divided into the four skill areas addressed on the exam: listening, reading, writing, and speaking. Each chapter is devoted to only a single skill area, but also contains information that will be useful in other skill areas. Vocabulary study is integrated into discussion topics and questions, explanations, and practice exercises for each skill area. There is some redundancy built into the vocabulary to reinforce some words that may be particularly useful. You will notice that different skill areas feature different kinds of vocabulary.

The listening comprehension vocabulary may seem difficult. But the commentaries should help you understand the taped material, and help you learn some useful vocabulary as well. The material does not contain slang, which tends to change rapidly and vary considerably from one region to another.

The vocabulary you use when listening is much larger than the vocabulary used when speaking, because in the former case you are able to recognize cognates of words that you may not recall without prompting. In many cases your ability to recognize cognates (words that sound alike in both English and Spanish) really depends on your vocabulary in English. Even conversational Spanish contains many words that have almost dropped from conversational English, so Spanish may seem more difficult to understand because of the range of vocabulary. If you have a large English vocabulary, you will recognize many cognates. If your vocabulary in English is small, you will need to learn words in order to feel comfortable in Spanish.

The reading vocabulary is the most difficult for many students but there are advantages to reading that you do not have with listening. Seeing a word on a page gives you time to try to remember it, and also gives you a context so that you can go back and reread what is said. You will find suggestions for how to understand vocabulary in the context of written passages.

Reading requires the largest vocabulary, which is why people who read a lot usually know the words they need to say exactly what they want to say. In this section of this book most of the vocabulary focuses on verbs. Frequently you can guess the meaning of nouns, but the verbs often are not cognates. Also in this section the interpretation of structures as well as meanings of words becomes important. There is a section of multiple-choice vocabulary and grammatical structures to show you some strategies.

Beginning students often write using the same vocabulary and syntactical constructions that they use in speech. In both skill areas you have to use only those words you have stored in memory in your mind. You cannot use a dictionary to look up words as you write your essay. But, by the same token, since you have time to think about what you are going to say, your written language should be more articulate than spoken language. You should have a somewhat better vocabulary when you write. In the written exercises, you need to use words and expressions that you learned in other chapters. This book will focus on helping you develop ways of organizing your thoughts, expressing them accurately and using the best vocabulary. Usually in writing, the sentence structures are more complex and your thoughts are more organized than when you speak.

Speaking vocabularies usually will not be as sophisticated as the vocabulary needed for reading or listening. When you are trying to remember the meaning of words, you do not have the advantage of seeing the word or expression on a page or screen to jog your memory; you have to recall the words without prompting. Because it is important to know a wide range of vocabulary, there is a section containing some words that may be useful to know for the exam. Speaking requires a vocabulary that includes a wide range of names of things, people, and places, as well as the adjectives to describe the named items. In conversation we tend to use more common irregular verbs. Make sure that the verb forms you use are correct, especially the common irregular verbs. You will find these verbs listed in the back of this book.

With each new skill area, more words are added so that you can learn as many as possible and add to the basic level. Some vocabulary that you remember from this book may make a great difference in your responses. Although all aspects of language are important, probably none is more important than vocabulary study. No matter how much grammar you know, if you do not know the words to communicate your thoughts, the grammar will not be useful.

STUDY STRATEGIES

Language comprehension and production is a complex process that uses a variety of skills simultaneously. There is usually a very strong correlation between different skill areas such as speaking and writing abilities, and between the reading and listening abilities on the exam. Improvement in any one area usually affects and enhances ability in other skill areas.

Suggestions for Studying for the Exam

1. Study when your mind is fresh and you can concentrate on the material.
2. Practice speaking and listening to Spanish whenever possible. Listen to Spanish language radio or television programs, Spanish movies or videotapes, or books on tape. Find friends or acquaintances who speak Spanish—anyone who can provide a native model for pronunciation, intonation, and fluency.
3. Do not attempt to learn too much at a time, since trying to cram too much material into a study period is counterproductive. You will have difficulty remembering material if you try to do too much. Study until your concentration begins to decrease, then take a break.
4. Review material from previous study sessions frequently.
5. Take the practice test in one sitting so you can get used to the length of time required to take the actual exam.
6. Practice recording your own voice so that the process will not feel strange or intimidating when you take the exam.
7. Find a comfortable place to study.
8. Find someone who can answer questions about things you do not understand.
9. Do not be afraid to try to speak Spanish whenever possible.
10. Read as much as possible to learn vocabulary and to practice reading comprehension strategies suggested in this book. Read from a variety of sources—newspapers, literature, novels and short stories, letters from Spanish-speaking friends, menus, schedules, tour guides, essays, the Internet, and anything printed or written in Spanish that you can find. There are also some computer software programs that contain reading material.

11. Find a good dictionary to look up things you want to say. Be sure to look up words from English to Spanish, then check the correctness of meaning by looking up the Spanish to English to make sure that you have selected the most appropriate word for what you want to say. Remember that the use of dictionaries on the exam is prohibited.

12. You will be surprised at how much you can say if you learn how to rephrase your thoughts when you do not remember a specific word. Do not simply memorize questions and answers, but learn to communicate information and ideas. You will never know all the words you may want to use on an exam, but you can learn to communicate thoughts if you know how to rephrase. You want to communicate ideas in Spanish, not translate your thoughts literally from English to Spanish.

13. Learn as much grammar as you can. Especially make sure you know how to use verb tenses and moods correctly.

These recommendations are intended to help you feel confident about taking the exam. The more confident and comfortable you are using the Spanish language, the better your chances are of doing well on the examination.

PART TWO LISTENING COMPREHENSION

GENERAL CONSIDERATIONS

The listening comprehension part of the Advanced Placement Spanish Language Examination consists of two parts. The first deals with short dialogues and narratives, and the second with two longer selections. The questions for the first part, which will not be printed in your test booklet, will be read only once. Some of the questions may ask for standard information, such as the general topic of the selection, or some information that you can infer about the selection, such as where does it take place, or what is going to happen later. Other questions may ask for an interpretation of a specific phrase, which will be replayed when you hear the questions after the selection. Other questions may ask for an interpretation of a specific idiomatic phrase, the meaning of which can be inferred from the context in which you hear it. You may also hear information about the source of the selection, which will help you put what you hear in context.

The questions for the longer selections are printed in the test booklet. There is also room for you to take notes on what you hear. You will have time to read the questions before listening to the longer selections, so you can focus on the information you need to extract from what you hear. The longer selections may be an interview taken from broadcast media, news reports, a lecture, or a dialogue from a film, or it may simulate an everyday conversation. The topics will be taken from any topic related to the Spanish-speaking world. The questions on the longer selections will ask you to identify and summarize main points, understand some detailed information, and draw conclusions about what you hear based on what you know about Spanish culture and customs.

The exercises in the following short dialogues and narratives should help you focus on learning to listen for the main idea and then for details that relate to time, place, and activity. If some parts are difficult to understand, the exercises will help you learn to work round unfamiliar phrases. On the exam it is not unusual to hear some words you do not recognize. In such cases you should not focus on what you do not know, but rather work with what you do know. Practicing with difficult passages helps you learn to listen carefully, and good concentration helps every time. The secret is not to get frustrated when you do not understand something. Focus on listening for phrases.

SHORT DIALOGUES

In listening to the dialogues, be sure to notice any nonverbal cues that communicate information such as where the dialogue takes place. If you hear a bell in the background, jet engines, train whistles, traffic sounds, or other such indicators, use the information to provide a context for the dialogue. You should also listen for the tone of voice to determine the attitude of the speakers. This information can help you understand what is being said; if you know the attitude, you can form an idea of what kind of vocabulary and information to listen for in the dialogue. Knowing what to expect to hear is very important since it helps you narrow the range of vocabulary.

You need to listen for information that tells where the dialogue takes place, who is speaking and what their relationship is, what the topic of conversation is, and why they are having that conversation. At other times you need to deduce information from the words and tone of voice of the speakers. Who the speakers are and their relationship to each other often is revealed simply by the gender of the speakers (whether one is male or female), young or old, whether they are good friends (whether they use *tú* or *usted*), and other such differences. When there is a noun you do not know, you can figure its meaning out by looking at what all the other nouns you understand have in common. For example, if the selection contains the words *tren, el metro, la estación, la oficina, pasajeros,* and *maletín*, then you may figure out that *andén* has something to do with trains, commuting, travel, or something related to travel to work. Listen especially for noun and verb selection to determine the topic of conversation. The most difficult part of understanding the dialogues is understanding why the two speakers are talking. This information is revealed by mood selection (listen for the subjunctive), and especially by adjectives and adverbs. In the following section, listen to the selections and try to answer the questions. Be sure to try to answer all of the questions. When you have finished, check your answers. Then go to the transcript of the conversation to look up the words that you did not understand. Listen to the selections again to make sure that you could recognize the words if you heard them again.

SHORT NARRATIVES

The short narratives you will hear can be about any topic. In this type of listening comprehension, you are listening for information of a different sort than in the dialogues. In these narratives, listen for words that indicate the topic or theme of the narrative. By knowing the main idea, you can once again narrow the range of vocabulary you can expect to hear. Most of the questions in the narrative section will deal with who, what, when, where, why kinds of information. Interpretation of narratives is different from dialogues in that you listen to one speaker who talks about a given topic.

LONGER SELECTIONS

The last portion of the listening comprehension part consists of two selections that will be either longer narratives, interviews, short lectures, instructions, or some other type of speech sample. These two selections will each be about five minutes long. You may take notes on this section if you wish. You should practice before taking the exam to see if you do better taking notes or if you do better simply trying to recall information from memory. The advantage of notes is that you have a cue to jog your memory about the content of the narrative. You may have trouble listening and writing at the same time, however, and find that taking notes distracts you so much that you do not hear what is being said while you write. Remember that there is a great deal of repetition in the selections and you should be able to retain almost everything you hear if you concentrate while you listen.

TEST-TAKING TIPS

Here are some suggestions to help improve your listening comprehension.

1. *Concentrate while you listen.* Block out other thoughts and make sure your mind does not wander as you listen. If you have difficulty listening without being able to focus, develop some strategies. Jotting down key words sometimes helps on the longer passages. Or make a doodle that represents some aspect of what you are hearing to help you visualize the selection.

2. *Try to visualize in your mind what you are hearing.* Picture the setting and objects or people. If the dialogue is between or about two young people standing on a street corner, visualize the images. In some cases a visual aid may be provided, such as a map, or a picture of a person or place.

3. *Learn to organize and categorize information that you hear.* When you hear information, file it in your memory according to what kind of information it is. When you hear a speaker talk about classes at the university, file the information under location or setting of the conversation or purpose, since it may deal with future events. If you hear the speaker say that he or she is going to class, in addition to revealing future plans, the information also tells you what the speaker may be—a university student or teacher.

4. *Take notes if necessary.* Practice beforehand to discover if you do better taking notes or listening without taking notes.

5. *Listen to as much Spanish as you can.* Listen to tapes, radio programs, videos, movies, and other people speaking Spanish.

6. *Learn to make educated guesses.* You may hear words you do not recognize, so learn to make educated guesses about what words mean. Learn to depend on the context of words to give you a clue about their meanings.

7. *Learn not to translate every word of what you hear as you listen.* Translating as you listen slows down comprehension, because as you think about the literal meanings, your mind does not listen to the rest of what is being said.

8. *Learn to recognize as many cognates as possible.* Remember, cognates are words that sound alike in both languages. To recognize cognates, try to visualize what the word looks like on paper.

9. *Know the endings of different parts of speech.* You need to listen particularly for verbs and identify their subjects. Then fill in information provided in adjective or adverb phrases.

10. *Try to understand the ideas* you hear instead of precise translations, unless the question asks for the specific meaning of a phrase or word.

CHAPTER 1: Answer Sheet for Short Dialogues

Dialogue One
1. Ⓐ Ⓑ Ⓒ Ⓓ
2. Ⓐ Ⓑ Ⓒ Ⓓ
3. Ⓐ Ⓑ Ⓒ Ⓓ

Dialogue Two
1. Ⓐ Ⓑ Ⓒ Ⓓ
2. Ⓐ Ⓑ Ⓒ Ⓓ
3. Ⓐ Ⓑ Ⓒ Ⓓ

Dialogue Three
1. Ⓐ Ⓑ Ⓒ Ⓓ
2. Ⓐ Ⓑ Ⓒ Ⓓ
3. Ⓐ Ⓑ Ⓒ Ⓓ

Dialogue Four
1. Ⓐ Ⓑ Ⓒ Ⓓ
2. Ⓐ Ⓑ Ⓒ Ⓓ
3. Ⓐ Ⓑ Ⓒ Ⓓ

Dialogue Five
1. Ⓐ Ⓑ Ⓒ Ⓓ
2. Ⓐ Ⓑ Ⓒ Ⓓ
3. Ⓐ Ⓑ Ⓒ Ⓓ

Dialogue Six
1. Ⓐ Ⓑ Ⓒ Ⓓ
2. Ⓐ Ⓑ Ⓒ Ⓓ
3. Ⓐ Ⓑ Ⓒ Ⓓ

Dialogue Seven
1. Ⓐ Ⓑ Ⓒ Ⓓ
2. Ⓐ Ⓑ Ⓒ Ⓓ
3. Ⓐ Ⓑ Ⓒ Ⓓ
4. Ⓐ Ⓑ Ⓒ Ⓓ

Dialogue Eight
1. Ⓐ Ⓑ Ⓒ Ⓓ
2. Ⓐ Ⓑ Ⓒ Ⓓ
3. Ⓐ Ⓑ Ⓒ Ⓓ
4. Ⓐ Ⓑ Ⓒ Ⓓ

Dialogue Nine
1. Ⓐ Ⓑ Ⓒ Ⓓ
2. Ⓐ Ⓑ Ⓒ Ⓓ
3. Ⓐ Ⓑ Ⓒ Ⓓ

Dialogue Ten
1. Ⓐ Ⓑ Ⓒ Ⓓ
2. Ⓐ Ⓑ Ⓒ Ⓓ
3. Ⓐ Ⓑ Ⓒ Ⓓ

Dialogue Eleven
1. Ⓐ Ⓑ Ⓒ Ⓓ
2. Ⓐ Ⓑ Ⓒ Ⓓ
3. Ⓐ Ⓑ Ⓒ Ⓓ

CHAPTER 1 Short Dialogues (Section I, Part A)

CD 1 TRACK 1

The multiple choices are given on the following pages. You do not need to stop the disc after each dialogue since time is allotted to answer the questions. At the end of this section there is a transcript of the material and commentaries about the answers. Now get ready to listen to the short dialogues on the disc.

1. Have ready access to the answer sheet on page 23.
2. Turn to the multiple choice answers starting below.
3. Start the disc player and follow its instructions. If you wish to select a particular dialogue, look for its track number on the left column.

DIALOGUE NUMBER ONE

CD 1 TRACK 2

1. (A) Está en una estación de policía.
   (B) Está en una oficina en el centro.
   (C) Está en casa.
   (D) Está en la calle.

2. (A) La policía acompaña a un actor que está visitando a un vecino.
   (B) Hay una emergencia médica y ha venido una ambulancia.
   (C) Un vecino está llamando para apaciguar a un amigo enojado.
   (D) La policía viene con una persona famosa que ha venido a la casa vecina.

3. (A) Está alegre.
   (B) Parece enojado.
   (C) Está temeroso.
   (D) Parece celoso.

DIALOGUE NUMBER TWO

CD 1 TRACK 3

1. (A) Cereal cuya mascota es Toni el Tigre.
   (B) Productos que no sean tan dulces como Toni el Tigre.
   (C) Un cupón para azúcar.
   (D) Un juguete nuevo para la niña.

2. (A) Es muy ameno.
   (B) Es muy terco.
   (C) Es muy quejoso.
   (D) Es muy avaro.

3. (A) Quiere que ella pague su cuenta.
   (B) Quiere que ella pruebe el cereal antes de comprarlo.
   (C) Quiere que ella compre azúcar.
   (D) Quiere que ella dé el cupón a la niña.

DIALOGUE NUMBER THREE

CD 1 TRACK 4

1. (A) Una huelga.
   (B) Un carnaval.
   (C) Una fiesta.
   (D) Una feria.

2. (A) Los dos hombres piensan que no pueden mejorar su situación.
   (B) Ellos opinan que merecen más pago.
   (C) La empresa está por quebrar y no puede pagarles.
   (D) Los otros empleados no desean cooperar con su plan.

3. (A) Proponen que la compañía les permita trabajar la semana que viene.
   (B) Proponen que la compañía les reembolse por el tiempo perdido del trabajo.
   (C) Recomiendan que la compañía acepte el ascenso de cincuenta dólares al mes.
   (D) Sugieren que el árbitro les permita regresar al empleo sin contrato para que puedan mantener la producción.

DIALOGUE NUMBER FOUR

`CD 1 TRACK 5`

1. (A) Son hombres de negocios, discutiendo expansión industrial.
   (B) Son viejos amigos discutiendo un nuevo negocio.
   (C) Son políticos planeando la modernización de su país.
   (D) Son ingenieros de una compañía con una fábrica nueva en otro país.

2. (A) Necesita contratar al señor Martínez por servicios necesarios.
   (B) Necesita arreglar el permiso necesario para poder construir la fábrica.
   (C) Necesita negociar con el señor Martínez para arreglar todo.
   (D) Necesita ponerse en contacto con el señor Martínez.

3. (A) No reacciona de manera muy complaciente.
   (B) Parece tratar de postergar todos los planes.
   (C) Favorece la propuesta del señor Gómez.
   (D) Se niega a ayudarle a realizar el plan.

DIALOGUE NUMBER FIVE

`CD 1 TRACK 6`

1. (A) Tienen hambre y desean almorzar en el centro.
   (B) Van de compras para preparar para una fiesta.
   (C) Necesitan ir al banco en la Calle Central.
   (D) Necesitan comprar un regalo para el cumpleaños de una prima.

2. (A) Tienen sólo cinco minutos.
   (B) Tienen once minutos.
   (C) Tienen quince minutos.
   (D) Tienen mucho tiempo.

3. (A) Tiene que arreglarse el pelo.
   (B) Tiene que preparar el almuerzo.
   (C) Tiene que preparar una lista.
   (D) Tiene que hallar un vestido.

DIALOGUE NUMBER SIX

`CD 1 TRACK 7`

1. (A) Está en primavera.
   (B) Está en verano.
   (C) Está en otoño.
   (D) Está en invierno.

2. (A) Él tiene familia en Miami a la cual quiere visitar.
   (B) Era marinero y visitaba muchos lugares fantásticos.
   (C) Él enseñaba el buceo cuando vivía allí.
   (D) Él pasaba mucho tiempo en el agua cuando vivía allí.

3. (A) Piensan ir a la playa para correr las olas.
   (B) Piensan hacer unas excursiones submarinas.
   (C) Piensan visitar un acuario.
   (D) Piensan visitar con familia.

**DIALOGUE
NUMBER SEVEN
CD 1 TRACK 8**

1. (A) Hablan de una pareja que se ha divorciado.
   (B) Hablan de los amores de una amiga.
   (C) Hablan de una fiesta en un disco.
   (D) Hablan de sus preparativos para un fin de semana.

2. (A) Su novio acaba de abandonarla por otra.
   (B) Ella acaba de abandonar a su novio.
   (C) Sus amigas acaban de abandonarla.
   (D) Ella no recibió una invitación a un baile al disco.

3. (A) Ellas saben que Raquel y Enrique no eran buenos amigos.
   (B) Saben que Raquel sabía que su novio había salido con otra.
   (C) Saben que Enrique no era confiable.
   (D) Saben que hacía mucho tiempo que los dos eran amigos.

4. (A) Ellas van a llamar a María por teléfono para preguntarle del asunto.
   (B) Ellas lo averiguarán cuando vean a todos en el baile.
   (C) Ellas llamarán a Raquel para preguntarle.
   (D) Ellas van a hablar con Enrique y Ramón sobre esto.

**DIALOGUE
NUMBER EIGHT
CD 1 TRACK 9**

1. (A) La noche anterior lanzaron muchos cohetes.
   (B) La noche anterior sufrieron un bombardeo.
   (C) La noche anterior hubo una plaga de insectos.
   (D) La noche anterior hizo muy mal tiempo.

2. (A) No tiene chicos en casa.
   (B) Sus hijos son nenes.
   (C) Los chicos son más crecidos.
   (D) Los chicos son pequeños, también.

3. (A) No tienen electricidad en la casa.
   (B) No tienen agua corriente en la casa.
   (C) No tienen plantas en el huerto.
   (D) No tienen ningunas gotas.

4. (A) Ella arreglará todo pronto, ese mismo día.
   (B) El ayuntamiento le ha prometido hacer reparaciones mañana.
   (C) Ella esperará hasta que brille el sol para colgar la ropa al aire.
   (D) No hay remedio, tendrá que esperar mucho tiempo.

**DIALOGUE
NUMBER NINE**

CD 1 TRACK 10

1. (A) Hay un problema con el agua en la casa.
   (B) La chica no tiene bastante tiempo para bañarse.
   (C) Ella quiere que le diga a su hermano que espere.
   (D) Él es plomero y está reparando la tubería.

2. (A) Porque ella abrió el grifo.
   (B) Porque hay aire en la tubería.
   (C) Porque los obreros no saben dónde están las líneas.
   (D) Porque Enrique está bañándose al mismo tiempo.

3. (A) Porque cerrarán el servicio de agua a la casa mientras reparan las líneas.
   (B) Porque su papá quiere bañarse también.
   (C) Porque ella tiene miedo del ruido.
   (D) Porque su hermano tendrá que bañarse pronto.

**DIALOGUE
NUMBER TEN**

CD 1 TRACK 11

1. (A) Parece que sufre de un mero resfriado.
   (B) Parece que sufre principalmente de insomnio.
   (C) Parece que tiene neumonía.
   (D) Este paciente es adicto a drogas peligrosas.

2. (A) Le sugiere que no más guarde cama y descanse.
   (B) Le sugiere unas pastillas.
   (C) Le da un producto nuevo.
   (D) Le recomienda que tome dos pastillas y que lo llame por la mañana.

3. (A) El paciente estará mejor el próximo día.
   (B) Podrá respirar mejor el próximo día.
   (C) Espera que le ayude pero no sabrá por dos días.
   (D) Espera que se mejore, porque sabe que la medicina es buena.

**DIALOGUE
NUMBER ELEVEN**

CD 1 TRACK 12

1. (A) Hablan de un programa sobre la astronomía.
   (B) Hablan de programas documentarios en la televisión.
   (C) Hablan de un personaje en un libro que han leído.
   (D) Hablan de una actriz famosa que vieron la noche anterior.

2. (A) Están de acuerdo que los dos papeles eran muy diferentes.
   (B) Les gustó una de las representaciones, pero no la otra.
   (C) No les gustó ninguno de los programas.
   (D) Opinan que una representación era inválida.

3. (A) La primera era fácil para la actriz porque era un documentario.
   (B) La primera le presentó un papel muy natural a la actriz.
   (C) La última no parecía requerir muchos cambios de la actriz.
   (D) La última era menos emocionante.

SCRIPTS AND ANSWERS

DIALOGUE NUMBER ONE

(Easy listening music, then sirens.)

NAR 1: Miguel, ¿qué pasará con todas las sirenas?

NAR 2: Pues, no estoy seguro. No vi nada por la ventana cuando me asomé por ella hace unos minutos. Parecía que había mucha luz en la calle para esta hora de la noche. ¿No te parece?

NAR 1: Sí, sí. Puede ser que haya un fuego. Y ya que me lo mencionaste, se huele humo por aquí.

NAR 2: Voy a llamar a nuestros vecinos para ver qué saben de esto.

(Sound of telephone dial.)

NAR 2: Hola, señor Rodríguez. Oiga, ¿sabe Ud. qué pasará? ... ¿No oye usted todas las sirenas? Parece que vienen calle abajo pero van a pasar por aquí. ¿Hay un fuego? ... ¿Ud. no puede ver nada? ¿Ni oye nada? ... Pues gracias, siento mucho haberle molestado por nada. Sólo me preocupé de... bueno.. sí, sí, ... sí, hasta luego.

NAR 1: Acabo de ver por la ventana que hay videógrafos del Canal 6 con un coche y la policía que se han parado delante de la casa al otro lado de la calle. Parece que filman una visita de una actriz a la casa de nuestro vecino.

NAR 2: Ya lo veo. Me imagino que si fuera un actor no vendrían todos los reporteros ni nada. ¡Qué molestia!

Número 1.

¿Dónde está la pareja que habla?

(A) Está en una estación de policía.

(B) Está en una oficina en el centro.

(C) Está en casa.

(D) Está en la calle.

Número 2.

¿Qué está pasando en esta escena?

(A) La policía acompaña a un actor que está visitando a un vecino.

(B) Hay una emergencia médica y ha venido una ambulancia.

(C) Un vecino está llamando para apaciguar a un amigo enojado.

(D) La policía viene con una persona famosa que ha venido a la casa vecina.

Número 3.

¿Cómo reacciona Miguel al saber qué pasa?

(A) Está alegre.

(B) Parece enojado.

(C) Está temeroso.

(D) Parece celoso.

Commentary

1. The first question asks about the setting of the dialogue. You should be able to determine this information by the sound of the telephone, the reference to looking out the window, and the reference to the neighbors. The answers that mention the police station, the office downtown, and the street are suggested by the background sounds, but the content of the dialogue with the references mentioned indicate that the only logical answer is the house as the setting. The correct answer is **C**.

2. The second question asks what is happening. The sound of the sirens suggests emergency vehicles, ambulances, policemen or firemen, and the dialogue refers to all of these possibilities. The dialogue also mentions famous people, however, so answer B is not a logical answer. The dialogue ends with Miguel complaining about the disturbance, but the telephone call does not indicate that somebody is being angry; it is only to find out what is happening. You need to distinguish between the gender of the person who is coming. Both actors and actresses are mentioned, but Miguel at the end is complaining about the difference of treatment actors and actresses get from the public. The correct answer is **D**.

3. How does Miguel react to the noise? That he is angry is indicated by his tone of voice with his last sarcastic remark about pretty actresses who get more attention than a man would get. The correct answer is **B**.

DIALOGUE NUMBER TWO

(Sound of cash registers.)

NAR 1: Mamá, mamá. Mira. Toni el Tigre. Mamá, mamá, cómprame este cartón de cereal...

NAR 2: Ya te dije que no voy a comprarte ese cereal. Mira. Aquí tienes éste que es mucho más sabroso.

(Sound of box opening.)

   Um-m-m. ¡Cuánto me gusta! Toma, prueba. ¿No te gusta también?

NAR 1: No, no, mamá. Me gusta Toni el Tigre, quiero comprar ése. Cómprame Toni.

NAR 3: Eh, señora, ¿qué hace abriendo el cereal aquí antes de pagarlo?

NAR 2: Oh, lo siento mucho, se me olvidó dónde estaba. Es que la niñita quiere comprar ese cereal que contiene tanto azúcar. Quiero que pruebe algo más saludable. ¡Qué difícil es convencer a los niños que se aprovechen más de comida sin tanto azúcar!

NAR 3: Ya lo entiendo. En casa mi chiquita también prefiere productos de ese tipo. Pero de veras debe usted de presentar un buen ejemplo y pagar la mercancía antes de abrirla. Si pudiera decirle a la cajera para que lo anote en la cuenta, y aquí tiene un cupón para un rebajo la próxima vez.

NAR 2: Muchísimas gracias. Usted es muy amable.

Número 1.

¿Qué quiere comprar la señora?

(A) Cereal cuya mascota es Toni el Tigre.

(B) Productos que no sean tan dulces como Toni el Tigre.

(C) Un cupón para azúcar.

(D) Un juguete nuevo para la niña.

Número 2.

¿Cómo es el comerciante?

(A) Es muy ameno.

(B) Es muy terco.

(C) Es muy quejoso.

(D) Es muy avaro.

Número 3.

¿Qué quiere el comerciante que haga la señora?

(A) Quiere que ella pague su cuenta.

(B) Quiere que ella pruebe el cereal antes de comprarlo.

(C) Quiere que ella compre azúcar.

(D) Quiere que ella dé el cupón a la niña.

Commentary

1. The first question asks what cereal the lady is buying. All of the alternatives contain words that appear in the dialogue. The fact that she wants to buy a nonsweetened product is indicated by the entire conversation she has with her child and the storekeeper, especially when the two adults commiserate about how hard it is to get little children to eat nutritious cereal. The correct answer is **B**.

2. This question asks what the storekeeper is like. He seems very understanding since he relates to the mother's problem, tells her about his own family and ultimately gives her a coupon to redeem later. Do not be misled by the simple repetition of words that appear in the dialogue. *Cupón* and *azúcar* are both mentioned, but the question asks what the shopkeeper wants the lady to buy. It does not refer to what he gives her. The correct answer is **A**.

3. What does the storekeeper want the shopper to do? He wants her to pay for the merchandise that the child has opened in the store. The correct answer is **A**.

DIALOGUE NUMBER THREE

(Sound of a crowd of people talking.)

NAR 1: Compadre. Escúcheme. Tenemos que organizar este grupo para ponernos en manifiesto contra esta administración.

NAR 2: Estoy de acuerdo. Hace seis meses que trabajamos sin contrato y no van a concedernos ningunos ascensos si no hacemos algo.

NAR 1: ¡Qué va! Siempre nos han tratado como si fuéramos esclavos. Mañana podremos mostrarles nuestra fuerza en un desfile por las calles del centro.

NAR 2: Pues, llamaré a todos los líderes del turno de la noche con quienes trabajo.

NAR 1: Y yo llamaré a los otros de mi turno. Podremos alcanzar cien hombres para una manifestación si llamamos a todos los que están con nosotros.

NAR 2: Con un poco de suerte podríamos negociar un contrato nuevo para el lunes si el árbitro tratara con nosotros de la manera que queremos. Pidamos un ascenso de cincuenta dólares al mes como mínimo, lo cual no es tanto como merecemos y veremos qué dicen.

NAR 1: Si nos lo otorgara, podríamos empezar de nuevo el martes por la mañana. Y de esta manera la empresa tendría la producción que desea sin perder mucho tiempo.

NAR 2: De acuerdo. Todo esto debería mostrarles que queremos que nos tomen en serio.

Número 1.

¿Qué están planeando estos hombres?

(A) Una huelga.
(B) Un carnaval.
(C) Una fiesta.
(D) Una feria.

Número 2.

¿Por qué están insatisfechos los dos?

(A) Los dos hombres piensan que no pueden mejorar su situación.
(B) Ellos opinan que merecen más pago.
(C) La empresa está por quebrar y no puede pagarles.
(D) Los otros empleados no desean cooperar con su plan.

Número 3.

¿Qué resolución proponen los dos?

(A) Proponen que la compañía les permita trabajar la semana que viene.
(B) Proponen que la compañía les reembolse por el tiempo perdido del trabajo.
(C) Recomiendan que la compañía acepte el ascenso de cincuenta dólares al mes.
(D) Sugieren que el árbitro les permita regresar al empleo sin contrato para que puedan mantener la producción.

Commentary

1. The first question asks you to identify the main idea of the conversation. These two are obviously planning a strike or some kind of demonstration, indicated by the repetition of words like *manifiesto, reunir, negociar, contrato, empresa,* and *ascenso.* The only word in the alternatives that fits with this sequence of grouped vocabulary is *huelga,* which is the correct answer, **A**.

2. This question asks why the two are planning work action. The answer is revealed in the reference to *esclavos,* which implies someone who works for nothing, and in the discussion about a raise in wages. Answer **A** is not a possibility because the workers think that they can work with the company and change their situation. Answers **C** and **D** are not indicated by the information in the dialogue. The two think that the company can pay them more, and that the other workers will cooperate. Answer **B** is the correct answer.

3. What is the likely outcome? Answer **C** is the only totally correct answer. The other answers are partially correct: they want to go back to work the next Tuesday, if their offer is accepted. Nothing is said about working if the offer is not accepted.

DIALOGUE NUMBER FOUR

NAR 1: Muy buenos días, señor Gómez. ¿Cómo está usted?

NAR 2: Muy bien, gracias, señor Martínez. ¿Y usted?

NAR 1: Bien. Y muy contento de poder hablar con usted debido al nuevo contrato que tenemos entre nuestros gobiernos.

NAR 2: El placer es mío. No ocurre todos los días que tengamos oportunidades como ésta. Nuestra empresa tiene muchos deseos de poder establecer una fábrica textil en su país este año.

NAR 1: Bueno, señor Gómez, nos interesa cualquier oportunidad que beneficie a todos.

NAR 2: Pues, como representante de mi compañía, me han dicho avisarles que proponemos poner la fábrica en las afueras de la ciudad con tal que podamos arreglar los servicios necesarios.

NAR 1: Esto, sí, sería muy interesante. Pero, ¿qué servicios en particular?

NAR 2: Específicamente necesitaríamos servicios de electricidad, agua, empleados, transporte ... todo lo normal, y buena fuerza de trabajadores, por supuesto.

NAR 1:   Esto requeriría negociaciones extensivas para poder realizarse, pero tiene posibilidades. Puedo ponerle en contacto con algunos de los agentes que hacen estos tratos para que lo discuta con ellos.

NAR 2:   Le agradezco mucho, señor Martínez. No más queremos la oportunidad de hablar con ustedes.

Número 1.
¿Quiénes son estos hombres?
(A) Son hombres de negocios, discutiendo expansión industrial.
(B) Son viejos amigos discutiendo un nuevo negocio.
(C) Son políticos planeando la modernización de su país.
(D) Son ingenieros de una compañía con una fábrica nueva en otro país.

Número 2.
¿Qué necesita el señor Gómez?
(A) Necesita contratar al señor Martínez por servicios necesarios.
(B) Necesita arreglar el permiso necesario para poder construir la fábrica.
(C) Necesita negociar con el señor Martínez para arreglar todo.
(D) Necesita ponerse en contacto con el señor Martínez.

Número 3.
¿Cómo reacciona el señor Martínez a la iniciativa del señor Gómez?
(A) No reacciona de manera muy complaciente.
(B) Parece tratar de postergar todos los planes.
(C) Favorece la propuesta del señor Gómez.
(D) Se niega a ayudarle a realizar el plan.

Commentary
1. Who are these two speakers? That they are businessmen is indicated by the words, *contrato, representante, compañía, fábrica, servicios,* and *fuerza de trabajadores.* This is a new business, but these speakers are not old friends, a fact indicated by the form of address of the two, the formal *usted.* The correct answer is **A**.
2. The second question asks what the first gentleman needs in order to set up business in the new country. Mr. Gómez does not know very much about the country in which he is hoping to estab-

lish a factory, nor business procedures. He does not need Mr. Martínez' permission, but he does need contacts and information about what that town has to offer. The correct answer is **D**.
3. How does Mr. Martínez react to Mr. Gómez? While Mr. Martínez cannot give Mr. Gómez the permission he is seeking, he does refer him to people who have the information. By providing the right contacts he shows his approval of the initiative. Be sure to learn the vocabulary in the incorrect responses. You may see it in other places. The correct answer is **C**.

DIALOGUE NUMBER FIVE
NAR 1:   ¿Dónde quieres almorzar hoy, Estela?
NAR 2:   No me importa. No tengo mucha hambre y todavía tendré que encontrar un vestido para el quinceañero de mi prima María.
NAR 1:   Esto puede ser difícil. Oye, hay una tienda nueva, muy pequeña que está a cincuenta metros de la esquina de la Calle Central y Balboa, junto al banco. Puede ser que puedas encontrar algo allí, y podemos almorzar después de visitarla.
NAR 2:   Ah, sí, la conozco. Bueno, visitémosla y almorzaremos después. Entonces tenemos que tomar el autobús de las once.
NAR 1:   Y ya son las once menos cuarto. Apúrate, Estela, y lo cogemos.
NAR 2:   Ya estoy lista. Sólo me falta peinarme y ponerme un suéter.

Número 1.
¿Qué piensan hacer estas chicas?
(A) Tienen hambre y desean almorzar en el centro.
(B) Van de compras para prepararse para una fiesta.
(C) Necesitan ir al banco en la Calle Central.
(D) Necesitan comprar un regalo para el cumpleaños de una prima.

Número 2.
¿Cuánto tiempo tienen antes de que venga el autobús?
(A) Tienen sólo cinco minutos.
(B) Tienen once minutos.
(C) Tienen quince minutos.
(D) Tienen mucho tiempo.

Número 3.
¿Qué tiene que hacer Estela antes de salir?
(A) Tiene que arreglarse el pelo.
(B) Tiene que preparar el almuerzo.
(C) Tiene que preparar una lista.
(D) Tiene que hallar un vestido.

Commentary
1. What are the speakers planning? They are obviously going downtown, and will take a bus. Although the words refer to the places downtown, they do not refer to the purpose of the trip, which is indicated by the words *vestido* and *quinceañero*. The *quinceañero* is a formal type of celebration of the fifteenth birthday, which means that the speaker is looking for a new dress to wear to that party. The correct answer is **B**.
2. The second question asks about schedules and how much time they have to catch the bus to go downtown. There are several numbers mentioned in the passage, *a las once, y son las once menos cuarto.* The answer is indicated by the word *cuarto*, which indicates fifteen minutes. The correct answer is **C**.
3. What does Estela need to do to get ready to go? *Arreglarse el pelo* means "to arrange one's hair," which is what she needs to do. Other alternatives mention activities that are incorrect or do not appear in the dialogue. The reference to the *vestido* relates to the purpose of the shopping trip, but not preparations for going downtown. The correct answer is **A**.

DIALOGUE NUMBER SIX
NAR 1: Mario, este junio mi familia y yo vamos de vacaciones en la Florida. Mis padres me han dicho que puedo invitar a alguien para acompañarme. ¿Quieres venir con nosotros?
NAR 2: ¡Hombre! ¡Qué hay de no querer! Vivía en Miami cuando era joven, antes de mudarnos aquí. Aunque actualmente no tengo ninguna familia allí, todavía conozco bien esa parte del estado. Puedo enseñarles algunos lugares fantásticos. Por supuesto, acepto.
NAR 1: ¡Estupendo! Les diré a mis padres que puedes. Si conoces a algunos lugares divertidos, seguramente los visitaremos. También he oído decir que el buceo es fantástico.

NAR 2: Ya lo creo. Cuando vivía allí íbamos todos los fines de semana a un arrecife cerca del parque nacional que hay allí. Es increíble la diversidad de la naturaleza submarina que se encuentra bajo las olas.
NAR 1: Bueno. ¡Qué venga pronto el junio! Pero antes de ir tenemos que aguantar seis meses más de tedio aquí en clases.

Número 1.
¿En qué estación están los chicos al momento de hablar en este diálogo?
(A) Están en primavera.
(B) Están en verano.
(C) Están en otoño.
(D) Están en invierno.

Número 2.
¿Por qué le gustaría a Mario acompañar a su amigo?
(A) Él tiene familia en Miami a la cual quiere visitar.
(B) Era marinero y visitaba muchos lugares fantásticos.
(C) Él enseñaba el buceo cuando vivía allí.
(D) Él pasaba mucho tiempo en el agua cuando vivía allí.

Número 3.
¿Qué piensan hacer durante las vacaciones?
(A) Piensan ir a la playa para correr las olas.
(B) Piensan hacer unas excursiones submarinas.
(C) Piensan visitar un acuario.
(D) Piensan visitar con familia.

Commentary
1. In which season does the conversation take place? Do not jump to the conclusion that the question asks what season they are talking about, which is the summer. In the dialogue at the end the speakers both lament having to wait another six months before going on vacation, *aguantar seis meses*, which means that it is still winter. The trip is planned for June. The correct answer is **D**, since six months before June is still winter.
2. Why would Mario particularly like to go with his friend? They talk about the fact that Mario lived in Miami before, and discuss his leisure activities there, but the speaker states that none of his family still lives there. The mention of the words *familia, lugares fantásticos,* and *buceo* can

mislead you if you do not pay attention to the verbs that accompany them. The correct answer is **D**, which sums up all the things that Mario did while he lived in South Florida.

3. The third question asks what they plan to do while on vacation. From the references to the beach and the sea, indicated by the words *buceo, arrecife, olas,* and *naturaleza submarina,* the venue is obviously a beach. And Miami is located on the coast. However, in the alternatives given, the words *playa, olas,* and *familia* are misleading. The word *submarina,* although it is mentioned in the dialogue, qualifies where they are going. The diving, and the marine life of the reef are the activities of choice. The word *submarina* in this case serves to define the place they are going to visit. The correct answer is **B**.

DIALOGUE NUMBER SEVEN

NAR 1: Gloria, ¿oíste lo de Raquel? María me dijo que la vio en el disco con Ramón. Y Enrique estuvo con otra.

NAR 2: ¡No me digas! ¿Cuándo supiste esto? Acabo de hablar con María y ella no me dijo nada.

NAR 1: Pues cuando hablé con ella anoche me lo dijo. Quizá no fuera Ramón sino otro el que la acompañaba. No puedo creer que la dejara por otra porque llevaban tantos años juntos.

NAR 2: Sí, sería una lástima si se hubieran separado. Parecía la pareja perfecta. Pero nunca se sabe. Nunca se puede confiar en los chismes ni rumores, pero la semana pasada no más lo vi a Enrique paseándose con Elena Ramírez por la plaza después de las clases.

NAR 1: ¿De veras? Entonces Raquel hubiera tenido buena razón para despedirse de él. Ella no soportaría que saliera con otra y ella no se quejaría de él porque es muy buena.

NAR 2: Tienes razón. Pues, sabremos por cierto este fin de semana cuando vamos al baile a la escuela. Si ella viene con Ramón otra vez entonces sabremos que se acabó con Enrique.

Número 1.

¿De qué hablan las chicas?

(A) Hablan de una pareja que se ha divorciado.

(B) Hablan de los amores de una amiga.

(C) Hablan de una fiesta en un disco.

(D) Hablan de sus preparativos para un fin de semana.

Número 2.

¿Qué le pasó a Raquel?

(A) Su novio acaba de abandonarla por otra.

(B) Ella acaba de abandonar a su novio.

(C) Sus amigas acaban de abandonarla.

(D) Ella no recibió una invitación a un baile al disco.

Número 3.

¿Por qué les sorprendió a las chicas que Enrique haya salido con otra?

(A) Ellas saben que Raquel y Enrique no eran buenos amigos.

(B) Saben que Raquel sabía que su novio había salido con otra.

(C) Saben que Enrique no era confiable.

(D) Saben que hacía mucho tiempo que los dos eran amigos.

Número 4.

¿Cómo averiguarán la verdad de la relación amorosa de su amiga?

(A) Ellas van a llamar a María por teléfono para preguntarle del asunto.

(B) Ellas lo averiguarán cuando vean a todos en el baile.

(C) Ellas llamarán a Raquel para preguntarle.

(D) Ellas van a hablar con Enrique y Ramón sobre esto.

Commentary

1. The first question asks what the topic of conversation is. The two friends are gossiping about another friend and her apparent breakup with a boyfriend. They have heard from a friend that Raquel's old boyfriend was at a party with another girl. They are trying to figure out what is going on with their friend Raquel. The correct answer is **B**. Although some of the choices are partially correct, partly correct information is not the best answer to the question. Throughout the whole conversation, the topic is who Raquel is dating, or who her old boyfriend is dating. **B** is the only answer that deals with the topic of the whole conversation, not just part of it.

2. The answer to the second question is **A**. What really happened with Raquel is only conjecture on the part of the two who are speaking. The use of the conditional in the choices of answers is a clue. Nowhere in the conversation do the two girls indicate that they really know what has happened with Raquel. The only thing that they know for certain is that Enrique and Raquel had been friends for a long time.

3. Relating to the third question, one of the speakers mentions at the beginning that Raquel and Enrique had dated for a long time. Later in the conversation one of the speakers speculates that Raquel would not put up with Enrique going out with someone else. That they spent the whole conversation talking about the topic also means that they do not know what to make of the situation. The correct answer is **D**.

4. The two finally decide that the only way to really know is to go to a party that weekend and see who comes with whom. Do not be mislead by the repetition of some parts of dialogue, such as *dance that weekend*, which can be combined with other erroneous information in incorrect responses. The correct answer is **B**; the two are going to go to the party to see if Enrique comes with another girl. Then they will know that their friend, Raquel, and Enrique are no longer seeing each other.

DIALOGUE NUMBER EIGHT

NAR 1: Esa tormenta que pasó por aquí anoche fue la más espantosa que jamás he visto en la vida. Perdimos toda la electricidad y llovió a cántaros con un rato de granizos que destruyeron todo, todo lo que tuvimos en el huerto. ¿Sufrieron ustedes mucho daño?

NAR 2: Era igual con nosotros. Y lo peor sucedió cuando tratamos de abrir los grifos en la cocina y no salió nada, ni una gota de agua. Pasamos una noche muy mala.

NAR: 1 ¡Ya lo creo! Y con todo el tronar y relampaguear los pobres niñitos se agarraron de mi esposo y de mí toda la noche por el susto que tuvieron.

NAR 2: Gracias a Dios los míos tienen bastante edad para no temer tanto el ruido. De veras fue el mayor espectáculo pirotécnico que jamás hayamos visto. Y esta mañana ¡fíjate cuánto brilla el sol, como si no hubiera pasado ni una nube por el cielo!

NAR 1: Sí, se siente la limpieza del aire esta mañana. ¿Y ahora? ¿Les han restablecido el agua?

NAR 2: Llamamos al ayuntamiento para decirles de nuestro problema y nos prometieron volver a ponérnosla esta misma mañana. Sería en buena hora porque hoy tengo que lavar mucha ropa sucia.

Número 1.
¿Qué acontecimiento comentan estas mujeres?
(A) La noche anterior lanzaron muchos cohetes.
(B) La noche anterior sufrieron un bombardeo.
(C) La noche anterior hubo una plaga de insectos.
(D) La noche anterior hizo muy mal tiempo.

Número 2.
¿De qué edad son los hijos de la segunda narradora?
(A) No tiene chicos en casa.
(B) Sus hijos son nenes.
(C) Los chicos son más crecidos.
(D) Los chicos son pequeños, también.

Número 3.
¿Qué molestia adicional ha sufrido la segunda narradora?
(A) No tienen electricidad en la casa.
(B) No tienen agua corriente en la casa.
(C) No tienen plantas en el huerto.
(D) No tienen ningunas gotas.

Número 4.
¿Qué remedio hay para el problema de la segunda narradora?
(A) Ella arreglará todo pronto, ese mismo día.
(B) El ayuntamiento le ha prometido hacer reparaciones mañana.
(C) Ella esperará hasta que brille el sol para colgar la ropa al aire.
(D) No hay remedio, tendrá que esperar mucho tiempo.

Commentary

1. The first question essentially asks what happened the night before. From the comments that the two speakers make, it is apparent that there was a tremendous storm, with much damage from hail. The first speaker tells about what happened in her house with the small children. The thunder and lightning (*trueno* and *relámpago*), frightened the children because they are small. The second speaker remarks that it reminded her of a fireworks display. (*Pirotécnica* refers to fireworks.) The answers that contain references to happenings that make loud noises are misleading. The topic of the whole conversation is the storm. The correct answer is **D**.

2. What are the ages of the second speaker's children? Part of the contrast between the two speakers and how they react to the storm has to do with how their children react. As you listen, create in your mind a profile of each speaker. For the first one you would notice that she has younger children, and her experience was more stressful because the little children were so frightened that they clung to their parents all night. The second speaker has children who are older, so they were not so frightened, but she was similarly inconvenienced by the storm although for different reasons. Her says her children were not frightened. In the possible answers, if you do not recognize the word *nene*, you can deduce that **C** is the right answer anyway, because none of the other answers is correct. Sometimes you need to use the process of elimination to arrive at a correct answer.

3. The third question asks for specific information about what happened to the second speaker. She answers this question at the beginning of the conversation, and at the end. The worst part of the storm was the loss of water in the house. She indicates that they still do not have water when she says that she has called the city and that she has washing to do. The correct answer is **B**.

4. When can the second speaker expect to have her service restored? The answer is in the expression, *esta misma mañana*. One choice contains the word, *misma*, and another contains the word *mañana*. The dialogue says *this very morning*, which means that choice **A** is correct. (One of the words to remember from this dialogue is *grifo*, which means *faucet*.)

DIALOGUE NUMBER NINE

NAR 1: Papá, ¿qué pasa? Hace unos minutos cuando iba a ducharme, abrí el grifo y oí grandes ruidos de la tubería.

NAR 2: Parece que había aire en los tubos porque, cuando no hay buena presión en el sistema, entra el aire en los tubos y suena al abrirse el grifo.

NAR 1: ¿Entonces no hay problema y puedo ducharme?

NAR 2: Claro, niña. No te hace daño alguno. Y no te espantes del ruido. Sólo significa que están trabajando en las líneas del servicio por alguna parte.

NAR 1: Gracias, papá. Estaba segura de que sabrías algo. Ya voy a ducharme antes de que Enrique venga para usar el baño.

NAR 2: Pues ten prisa, chica, porque ya son las siete y tu hermano se levanta a esta hora.

Número 1.
¿Por qué habla la chica con su papá?
(A) Hay un problema con el agua en la casa.
(B) La chica no tiene bastante tiempo para bañarse.
(C) Ella quiere que le diga a su hermano que espere.
(D) Él es plomero y está reparando la tubería.

Número 2.
¿Por qué suenan los tubos?
(A) Porque ella abrió el grifo.
(B) Porque hay aire en la tubería.
(C) Porque los obreros no saben dónde están las líneas.
(D) Porque Enrique está bañándose al mismo tiempo.

Número 3.
¿Por qué tendrá ella que tener prisa?
(A) Porque cerrarán el servicio de agua a la casa mientras reparan las líneas.
(B) Porque su papá quiere bañarse también.
(C) Porque ella tiene miedo del ruido.
(D) Porque su hermano tendrá que bañarse pronto.

Commentary

1. The first question asks the general topic, which is why there is so much noise in the pipes when the first speaker takes a shower. She does not know what to make of all the noise. Her father explains the reason and tells her not to worry. She will have to hurry, but that is not the main idea of the conversation. Choice **B** is not the correct answer. The other choices repeat words from the dialogue, but not in an answer to the question. Her father is not a plumber, nor is she asking her father to tell her brother to wait. The correct answer is **A**.

2. The second question asks for specific information about the problem. Her father explains the reason for all the noise that has frightened the girl. The correct answer is **B**. Other phrases are misleading in these choices, such as *tubería, grifo,* and *obreros.*

3. Why does she have to hurry? *Tener prisa* is a key expression here. Even if you do not know the expression, when she says that Enrique is getting up soon and will want to bathe, too, she is really saying that she will have to hurry. Her father reiterates the idea when he notices that it is time for Enrique to get up. The correct answer is **D**.

DIALOGUE NUMBER TEN

NAR 1: Estas pastillas que me recetó usted no aliviaron los síntomas. Pasé toda la noche con tos y dormí muy mal.

NAR 2: Ya veo que tiene temperatura elevada. A ver qué oigo en los pulmones mientras ausculto la respiración. Ahora, respire despacio, por favor.

(Sound of deep breathing.)

Em-m-m. Parece que todavía tiene mucha congestión. Tratemos otro remedio. Hay una marca nueva de jarabe que quizá le ayude. Tome Ud. dos cucharadas antes de acostarse esta noche y mañana cuando se levante tome dos más.

NAR 2: Se lo agradecería si pudiera darme algo para que pudiera dormir esta noche. Estoy tan cansado por no dormir bien. Y la otra medicina produjo alucinaciones espantosas.

NAR 1: Probemos ésta, entonces, y veremos si usted se mejora mañana. Si no se mejora

dentro de dos días, llámeme otra vez. Con el jarabe le recomiendo mucho descanso y muchos líquidos.

Número 1.

Dados los síntomas, ¿qué tendrá el paciente?

(A) Parece que sufre de un mero resfriado.

(B) Parece que sufre principalmente de insomnio.

(C) Parece que tiene neumonía.

(D) Este paciente es adicto a drogas peligrosas.

Número 2.

¿Qué le sugiere el médico que haga el paciente?

(A) Le sugiere que no más guarde cama y descanse.

(B) Le sugiere unas pastillas.

(C) Le da un producto nuevo.

(D) Le recomienda que tome dos pastillas y que lo llame por la mañana.

Número 3.

¿Qué resultado espera el médico de la nueva receta?

(A) El paciente estará mejor el próximo día.

(B) Podrá respirar mejor el próximo día.

(C) Espera que le ayude pero no sabrá por dos días.

(D) Espera que se mejore, porque sabe que la medicina es buena.

Commentary

1. There are probably some unfamiliar words in this dialogue. But from the words that are familiar, you know that a doctor is talking to a patient who has returned because the doctor gave him something the first time that did not work. The man says that he is still sick, and the doctor listens to his lungs again. There are enough cognates in the dialogue, such as *pulmones, temperatura, respiración,* and *líquidos,* that you get the general idea. The doctor listens to his lungs, which can be deduced from the words *respirar* and the sound of the man breathing deeply. Remember to listen for clues that are nonverbal in the dialogues. They will help fill in gaps where there are words you may not know, such as *auscultar.* The correct answer is **C**.

2. The second question asks what the doctor's recommendation is. You need to listen carefully for the subjunctive in this dialogue. The doctor uses it when he tells the patient what to take for his illness. He uses it in the first person plural: *tratemos* and *probemos*. The doctor suggests a new cough syrup, then tells the man to rest and drink plenty of liquids. Phrases from the dialogue are combined with other phrases to give incorrect choices. The new product is a *jarabe*. The man is supposed to rest, but that is not all there is to the recommendation. The correct answer is **C**.

3. The answer to the third question is that the man should get some relief by the next day, but that if he is not much better after another two days, he is to call back. This is essentially what is stated in **C**, the correct answer. The other choices mention the next day, but the doctor uses the future to express a "wait and see" attitude.

DIALOGUE NUMBER ELEVEN

NAR 1: ¿Qué tal te parece la nueva estrella del programa *La Vida Secreta de Pepita Jiménez,* Isabel?

NAR 2: ¿El que estrenó anoche? Me sorprendió que le dieran ese papel a ella. Antes la había visto en otro programa documental. Lo interpretó bien pero era otro tipo de personaje que el que hizo anoche.

NAR 1: Concurro por completo. Se esforzó mucho para lograr una representación válida. No obstante, dio una interpretación muy emocionante.

NAR 2: De acuerdo. Este papel era mucho más difícil que el otro por ser tan distinto de su tipo. Aun con todo el maquillaje y las pestañas postizas y todo, en mi opinión no logró el efecto deseado. También la producción carecía de redacción, con tantas escenas tan lentas.

Número 1.

¿De qué hablan estas jóvenes?

(A) Hablan de un programa sobre la astronomía.

(B) Hablan de programas documentarios en la televisión.

(C) Hablan de un personaje en un libro que han leído.

(D) Hablan de una actriz famosa que vieron la noche anterior.

Número 2.

¿Qué comparación hacen?

(A) Están de acuerdo que los dos papeles eran muy diferentes.

(B) Les gustó una de las representaciones, pero no la otra.

(C) No les gustó ninguno de los programas.

(D) Opinan que una representación era inválida.

Número 3.

¿Cómo se diferencia la última interpretación de la primera?

(A) La primera era fácil para la actriz porque era un documentario.

(B) La primera le presentó un papel muy natural a la actriz.

(C) La última no parecía requerir muchos cambios de la actriz.

(D) La última era menos emocionante.

Commentary

1. The first question asks about the topic. There are references to documentaries, stars, shows, programs, productions, and scenes. There are several false cognates in the dialogue, also, such as *interpretación, papel, personaje, emocionante,* and *representación.* Nevertheless, the topic throughout is the acting ability of a certain actress. The correct answer is **D**.

2. The second question asks about the comparison that the speakers make between the two shows in which they have seen this actress. The first is a documentary and the second is a drama of some sort that has required a lot of makeup, even false eyelashes. They both agree that the first program, which was a documentary, was more convincing, but they agree that the second was very moving. They also agree that the roles were very different. Notice that *papel* in this context means *role,* or *part* in a play or film. From the choices that are given, **A** is the only correct one.

3. The third question asks for specific information about the last program and what characterized it and distinguished it from the first one. All the information at the end of the conversation indicates that the second program was more difficult probably because the actress had to make more changes in the way she looked. The correct answer is **B**. Be sure to notice the negatives and do not be misled by looking for the repetition of exact words.

CHAPTER 2: Answer Sheet for Short Narratives

Group One, Narrative One
1. Ⓐ Ⓑ Ⓒ Ⓓ
2. Ⓐ Ⓑ Ⓒ Ⓓ
3. Ⓐ Ⓑ Ⓒ Ⓓ
4. Ⓐ Ⓑ Ⓒ Ⓓ

Group One, Narrative Two
1. Ⓐ Ⓑ Ⓒ Ⓓ
2. Ⓐ Ⓑ Ⓒ Ⓓ
3. Ⓐ Ⓑ Ⓒ Ⓓ
4. Ⓐ Ⓑ Ⓒ Ⓓ

Group Two, Narrative One
1. Ⓐ Ⓑ Ⓒ Ⓓ
2. Ⓐ Ⓑ Ⓒ Ⓓ
3. Ⓐ Ⓑ Ⓒ Ⓓ
4. Ⓐ Ⓑ Ⓒ Ⓓ

Group Two, Narrative Two
1. Ⓐ Ⓑ Ⓒ Ⓓ
2. Ⓐ Ⓑ Ⓒ Ⓓ
3. Ⓐ Ⓑ Ⓒ Ⓓ
4. Ⓐ Ⓑ Ⓒ Ⓓ

Group Three, Narrative One
1. Ⓐ Ⓑ Ⓒ Ⓓ
2. Ⓐ Ⓑ Ⓒ Ⓓ
3. Ⓐ Ⓑ Ⓒ Ⓓ
4. Ⓐ Ⓑ Ⓒ Ⓓ

Group Three, Narrative Two
1. Ⓐ Ⓑ Ⓒ Ⓓ
2. Ⓐ Ⓑ Ⓒ Ⓓ
3. Ⓐ Ⓑ Ⓒ Ⓓ
4. Ⓐ Ⓑ Ⓒ Ⓓ

Group Four, Narrative One
1. Ⓐ Ⓑ Ⓒ Ⓓ
2. Ⓐ Ⓑ Ⓒ Ⓓ
3. Ⓐ Ⓑ Ⓒ Ⓓ
4. Ⓐ Ⓑ Ⓒ Ⓓ

Group Four, Narrative Two
1. Ⓐ Ⓑ Ⓒ Ⓓ
2. Ⓐ Ⓑ Ⓒ Ⓓ
3. Ⓐ Ⓑ Ⓒ Ⓓ
4. Ⓐ Ⓑ Ⓒ Ⓓ

Group Five, Narrative One
1. Ⓐ Ⓑ Ⓒ Ⓓ
2. Ⓐ Ⓑ Ⓒ Ⓓ
3. Ⓐ Ⓑ Ⓒ Ⓓ
4. Ⓐ Ⓑ Ⓒ Ⓓ

Group Five, Narrative Two
1. Ⓐ Ⓑ Ⓒ Ⓓ
2. Ⓐ Ⓑ Ⓒ Ⓓ
3. Ⓐ Ⓑ Ⓒ Ⓓ
4. Ⓐ Ⓑ Ⓒ Ⓓ

Group Six, Narrative One
1. Ⓐ Ⓑ Ⓒ Ⓓ
2. Ⓐ Ⓑ Ⓒ Ⓓ
3. Ⓐ Ⓑ Ⓒ Ⓓ
4. Ⓐ Ⓑ Ⓒ Ⓓ

Group Six, Narrative Two
1. Ⓐ Ⓑ Ⓒ Ⓓ
2. Ⓐ Ⓑ Ⓒ Ⓓ
3. Ⓐ Ⓑ Ⓒ Ⓓ
4. Ⓐ Ⓑ Ⓒ Ⓓ

Group Seven, Narrative One
1. Ⓐ Ⓑ Ⓒ Ⓓ
2. Ⓐ Ⓑ Ⓒ Ⓓ
3. Ⓐ Ⓑ Ⓒ Ⓓ
4. Ⓐ Ⓑ Ⓒ Ⓓ

Group Seven, Narrative Two
1. Ⓐ Ⓑ Ⓒ Ⓓ
2. Ⓐ Ⓑ Ⓒ Ⓓ
3. Ⓐ Ⓑ Ⓒ Ⓓ
4. Ⓐ Ⓑ Ⓒ Ⓓ

Group Eight, Narrative One
1. Ⓐ Ⓑ Ⓒ Ⓓ
2. Ⓐ Ⓑ Ⓒ Ⓓ
3. Ⓐ Ⓑ Ⓒ Ⓓ
4. Ⓐ Ⓑ Ⓒ Ⓓ

Group Eight, Narrative Two
1. Ⓐ Ⓑ Ⓒ Ⓓ
2. Ⓐ Ⓑ Ⓒ Ⓓ
3. Ⓐ Ⓑ Ⓒ Ⓓ
4. Ⓐ Ⓑ Ⓒ Ⓓ

Group Nine, Narrative One
1. Ⓐ Ⓑ Ⓒ Ⓓ
2. Ⓐ Ⓑ Ⓒ Ⓓ
3. Ⓐ Ⓑ Ⓒ Ⓓ
4. Ⓐ Ⓑ Ⓒ Ⓓ

Group Nine, Narrative Two
1. Ⓐ Ⓑ Ⓒ Ⓓ
2. Ⓐ Ⓑ Ⓒ Ⓓ
3. Ⓐ Ⓑ Ⓒ Ⓓ
4. Ⓐ Ⓑ Ⓒ Ⓓ

CHAPTER 2 Short Narratives (Section I, Part A)

For practice on this part of listening comprehension, you will be asked to listen to two short narratives, lasting a few minutes. After each narrative there will be some questions about what you have just heard. The narratives will cover a wide range of topics, many of them about a cultural topic.

Some strategies for you to use on this section are:

1. Listen for words that indicate the topic in the first sentence. The word may be a noun or verb that indicates the name of the topic, or what is happening.
2. Once you have the topic in mind, listen for details about place, time, and characters. If you can sort and file this information as you hear it, you will remember it better. Listen for information that answers the questions: *who, what, when,* and *where.*
3. Listen for information about how something is done, reasons why something is happening, or what purpose is served. This information answers the questions *how, what for,* and *why.*
4. Draw conclusions based on the information you hear.

After each question, you will have about twelve seconds to select an answer from among the choices printed in your test booklet.

Listen to the narrative and answer the questions. Then, if you have difficulty understanding the narrative because of vocabulary, check the commentary that accompanies each narrative to see what vocabulary you need to know. Check the short list of words before looking at the transcript for the passage. You should not translate the whole selection, but instead focus on the ideas that the words communicate. You need to learn how to work around words you do not know because there will inevitably be some on the exam. Use these short narratives for listening practice to learn more vocabulary. Many of these words may appear in other sections to give you more chances to learn them.

There are eighteen short narratives arranged in groups of two for practice in this part of the book. Remember that you will not see the questions printed in the multiple choice answer section of your book. You will not need to stop the disc between questions since time to select your answer is allotted on the disc.

Now get ready to listen to the selections and answer the questions.

1. Have ready access to the answer sheet on page 39.
2. Turn to the multiple choice answers on pages 42–49.
3. Begin the disc and follow its instructions. If you wish to select a particular narrative, look for its track number on the left column beginning with page 42.

**GROUP ONE,
NARRATIVE ONE**

CD 1 TRACK 13

1. (A) Las visitas de viajeros a los Estados Unidos.
   (B) El sentido de humor de los estadounidenses.
   (C) Las noticias en los periódicos.
   (D) Las faltas de algunos diarios.

2. (A) Los redactores de los periódicos.
   (B) Viajeros que llegan de otros países.
   (C) Ciudadanos de Nueva York.
   (D) Los historiadores de periódicos.

3. (A) El hecho de que sólo tres de los mayores periódicos no la tiene.
   (B) El hecho de que los domingos hay una sección mucho más amplia.
   (C) El hecho de que una vez a la semana se imprimen en colores.
   (D) Todas estas razones.

4. (A) La fantasía tiene más atractivo que la realidad.
   (B) Los lectores sólo compran los diarios con historietas.
   (C) A los lectores les gusta leer páginas frívolas.
   (D) Los lectores de periódicos no tienen ningún interés en la historia.

**GROUP ONE,
NARRATIVE TWO**

CD 1 TRACK 14

1. (A) El papel de las mujeres en las corridas.
   (B) La historia de algunas "figuras" en las corridas.
   (C) La cuestión de qué país tiene los mejores toreros.
   (D) Por qué son tan populares las corridas.

2. (A) Las mujeres vinieron desde el principio.
   (B) Las mujeres podían venir con tal que se disfrazaran.
   (C) Las mujeres no asistieron a las corridas.
   (D) Si los hombres las llevaban, podían asistir.

3. (A) Hoy las mujeres tienen que disfrazarse.
   (B) Hoy las mujeres son algunas de las "figuras" más ilustres.
   (C) Hoy las mujeres participan plenamente en el espectáculo.
   (D) Hoy al público le da igual si el torero es hombre o mujer.

4. (A) A todos los aficionados les gusta que haya mujeres-toreros.
   (B) Muchos aficionados creen que una corrida con mujer-torero no es corrida.
   (C) A los del hemisferio occidental les gusta ver mujeres en la corrida.
   (D) Los aficionados se dan cuenta de que el cambio significa un avance.

**GROUP TWO,
NARRATIVE ONE**

CD 1 TRACK 15

1. (A) Era gran dibujante.
   (B) Era sociólogo muy importante.
   (C) Era periodista.
   (D) Era gran cómico.

2. (A) Retrató a todas las calaveras.
   (B) Pintó retratos de personas ricas.
   (C) Dibujó diseños de todas las clases étnicas y sociales.
   (D) Pintó a mexicanos extraordinarios.

3. (A) Los hombres y las mujeres que le rodeaban le pidieron que los pintase.
   (B) Vivía en un pueblo pequeño y no vio a otra gente.
   (C) Lo diario era lo que vio todos los días, lo que conocía mejor.
   (D) Publicó sus diseños en varios tipos de publicaciones.

4. (A) En las calaveras vio su propio destino, el cual lo alcanzaría si lo quisiera o no.
   (B) Representan una actitud dinámica hacia la vida y una resignación hacia la muerte.
   (C) Las figuras bailando menosprecian la muerte.
   (D) Los mexicanos no se preocupan por la muerte, sólo enfocan la vida.

GROUP TWO,
NARRATIVE TWO
CD 1 TRACK 16

1. (A) Diseño de ropa.
   (B) Fabricación de ropa a mano.
   (C) Producción de diseños interesantes.
   (D) Tejeduría de diseños.

2. (A) Usaron materias vegetales principalmente.
   (B) Utilizaron cualquier materia que se encontraba en su región.
   (C) Emplearon material de animales en su mayoría.
   (D) Usaron lo que les trajeron los turistas.

3. (A) Mostraban el tipo de animal que había en la región.
   (B) Mostraban quién era el fabricante.
   (C) Mostraban de dónde era el que los produjo.
   (D) Mostraban la riqueza del fabricante.

4. (A) Los turistas pueden comprarlos muy barato.
   (B) La manera de producir los diseños es muy antigua.
   (C) Algo hecho a mano es de mejor calidad que algo hecho a máquina.
   (D) La elaboración de diseños revela la tradición indígena del artista.

GROUP THREE,
NARRATIVE ONE
CD 1 TRACK 17

1. (A) Se ve su nombre por todas partes: de la emisora de radio de La Habana al aeropuerto.
   (B) Llegó a ser presidente de Cuba.
   (C) Soñó con la libertad de Cuba de la dominación de los españoles.
   (D) Viajaba por muchos países para visitar a los cubanos en el extranjero.

2. (A) No se relacionaba bien con otras personas.
   (B) Era gran poeta.
   (C) La policía lo odiaba.
   (D) Los españoles lo acusaron de traición.

3. (A) Quería ver el país de sus antepasados.
   (B) Tenía que salir de Cuba porque los españoles lo temían.
   (C) Necesitaba terminar sus estudios en España.
   (D) Porque era poeta famoso, todos lo invitaron a visitar.

4. (A) Los españoles lo mataron en Cuba.
   (B) Martí mató a unos españoles.
   (C) Publicó poesía patriótica en Cuba.
   (D) Los españoles lo invitaron a volver a Cuba.

**GROUP THREE,
NARRATIVE TWO**

CD 1 TRACK 18

1. (A) Es una zona del campo.
   (B) Es una república indígena.
   (C) Es un idioma indígena.
   (D) Es un tipo de poesía.

2. (A) Los españoles se veían sometidos lingüísticamente por los indios.
   (B) En este país todavía se usa el guaraní entre la gente.
   (C) Los españoles insistieron en que todos los indios aprendieran su lengua.
   (D) Los indios aprendieron a hablar el español principalmente.

3. (A) El guaraní es alto y colorado, y habla bien.
   (B) El guaraní es muy lírico y suena bien.
   (C) El guaraní es muy abstracto.
   (D) Se usa el guaraní para la actuación de leyes nacionales.

4. (A) Los indios no lo usan mucho corrientemente.
   (B) Los españoles no aprecian sus características buenas.
   (C) El español es más poético a causa del uso de vocablos guaraníes.
   (D) Se usa más y más el español por falta de palabras indígenas para expresar algunas cosas nuevas.

**GROUP FOUR,
NARRATIVE ONE**

CD 1 TRACK 19

1. (A) Los últimos días del imperio incaico.
   (B) El descubrimiento de la ciudad perdida del último rey de los incas.
   (C) La vida diaria de los indios de Machu Picchu.
   (D) La misteriosa historia de una ciudad abandonada.

2. (A) Creía que había encontrado el refugio de Manco Capac.
   (B) Creía que había descubierto un emplazamiento fortificado de los incas.
   (C) Creía que había encontrado un centro de un gobernador.
   (D) Creía que había encontrado un centro agrícola muy grande.

3. (A) Había muchas noticias de visitas por los españoles.
   (B) No se sabía absolutamente nada de la ciudad antes de 1911.
   (C) Había mención del lugar unas pocas veces en archivos.
   (D) Hiram Bingham sabía por investigaciones suyas en los archivos.

4. (A) Fue una ciudad muy próspera en su época.
   (B) Fue una ciudad situada en un lugar peligroso, por eso fue abandonada.
   (C) Definitivamente fue una ciudad fortificada, el último refugio de Viracocha.
   (D) Fue un jardín puesto en la cumbre de una montaña.

**GROUP FOUR,
NARRATIVE TWO**

CD 1 TRACK 20

1. (A) Era creador de un movimiento literario.
   (B) Era embajador nicaragüense a muchos otros países.
   (C) Era periodista que viajaba para escribir de sus visitas a otros países.
   (D) Era sacerdote nicaragüense.

2. (A) Después de cambiar su nombre, salió de Metapa.
   (B) Cuando había escrito unos libros de poesías, salió.
   (C) Cuando ya era famoso empezó a viajar.
   (D) Cuando otros poetas lo invitaron a visitarlos, salió de Nicaragua.

3. (A) Era *Azul*.
   (B) Era un grupo de hombres que creían en el progreso.
   (C) Era una nueva manera de escribir literatura.
   (D) Era un libro de poemas que escribió Darío.

4. (A) Era el vehículo por el cual Darío se hizo famoso.
   (B) Era para estimular interés en la literatura otra vez.
   (C) Era para promover la industrialización de los países del hemisferio.
   (D) Era una manera de estrechar las relaciones entre países.

**GROUP FIVE,
NARRATIVE ONE**
CD 1 TRACK 21

1. (A) Ciudad y campo.
   (B) Baile y vaquero.
   (C) Tango y gaucho.
   (D) Martín y Fierro.

2. (A) Estas imágenes tienen raíces en la época colonial.
   (B) Estas imágenes brotan de la cultura popular del país.
   (C) Estas imágenes vienen de la aristocracia.
   (D) Unos autores argentinos las crearon.

3. (A) Martín Fierro era tanguero famoso.
   (B) Martín Fierro era un gaucho ficticio.
   (C) Martín Fierro era una persona verdadera.
   (D) Martín era un símbolo de la vida civilizada de la ciudad.

4. (A) Actualmente los gauchos auténticos no existen.
   (B) Ahora las dos instituciones son estereotipos de lo que antes eran.
   (C) Hoy en día se encuentran muchos gauchos y clubs de tango.
   (D) El tango es tan popular como antes.

**GROUP FIVE,
NARRATIVE TWO**
CD 1 TRACK 22

1. (A) Los olmecas eran de Vera Cruz.
   (B) Los olmecas eran de La Venta.
   (C) No se sabe precisamente de dónde eran.
   (D) Se sabe que viajaban mucho en el sur de México.

2. (A) Dejaron unas esculturas enormes y enigmáticas.
   (B) En La Venta había un mercado.
   (C) Hay enormes cabezas labradas en jade.
   (D) Dejaron folletos con fotografías de sus monumentos.

3. (A) Las imágenes de las cabezas aparecen en muchas publicaciones.
   (B) En el mercado los mexicanos muestran sus esculturas,
   (C) Los restos de los olmecas se ven por muchas partes.
   (D) Los olmecas promovieron el turismo.

4. (A) Los llamamos por el nombre usado entre los indios antiguos.
   (B) Sin saber cómo se llamaban, los llamamos olmecas.
   (C) Los llamamos por el nombre de su lugar original históricamente.
   (D) Los llamamos olmecas porque se llamaban a sí mismos por este nombre.

GROUP SIX, NARRATIVE ONE
`CD 1 TRACK 23`

1. (A) Un grupo de mujeres con interés en política.
   (B) Un grupo de mujeres en el Congreso Nacional.
   (C) Un grupo de mujeres que quería conquistar una asamblea.
   (D) Un grupo de mujeres reunidas para promover cambios sociales.

2. (A) Por menos de medio siglo.
   (B) Por unos treinta años.
   (C) Por unos cuarenta años.
   (D) Por unos sesenta años.

3. (A) Que las mujeres tengan los derechos de cualquier ciudadano.
   (B) Sólo que las mujeres tengan el derecho de votar.
   (C) Que las mujeres tengan oportunidades económicas.
   (D) Que las mujeres puedan andar por cualquier camino.

4. (A) La Comisión ha realizado todos los sueños de las mujeres.
   (B) La Comisión ha eliminado la discriminación por todas partes.
   (C) Todas las mujeres del continente pueden participar en las elecciones.
   (D) Ahora las mujeres pueden trabajar dondequiera lo deseen.

GROUP SIX, NARRATIVE TWO
`CD 1 TRACK 24`

1. (A) Los españoles querían colonizar la Florida.
   (B) Los españoles necesitaban el territorio para protegerse.
   (C) Los españoles querían conquistar el territorio.
   (D) Los españoles esperaron encontrar riquezas.

2. (A) El poder se trasladaba de un lado a otro varias veces.
   (B) Las dos casi siempre han mantenido gran competencia.
   (C) Las dos nunca se llevaron bien.
   (D) Las dos esperan estrechar las relaciones más en el futuro.

3. (A) Los indios inmigraron a Cuba de la Florida.
   (B) Los españoles inmigraron a la Florida de Cuba.
   (C) Los españoles inmigraron de la Florida a Cuba.
   (D) Los ingleses inmigraron a Cuba de San Agustín.

4. (A) Como si fueran extranjeros en la Florida.
   (B) Como si fueran los nuevos conquistadores.
   (C) Como si fueran dueños de la propiedad.
   (D) Como si estuvieran volviendo a sus raíces.

GROUP SEVEN, NARRATIVE ONE
`CD 1 TRACK 25`

1. (A) Eran una gente indígena de Centroamérica.
   (B) Eran unos dioses guatemaltecos.
   (C) Eran un grupo de bailadores.
   (D) Eran figuras literarias del *Popol Vuh*.

2. (A) Se cuenta la literatura precolombina.
   (B) Se cuenta una narración de la creación de unos programas.
   (C) Se cuenta la geografía de las altiplanicies guatemaltecas.
   (D) Se cuenta el origen de la raza.

3. (A) Se ha creado un libro de extraordinaria popularidad.
   (B) Se han creado varias representaciones artísticas.
   (C) Se ha creado un cuerpo humano.
   (D) Se ha producido una serie de programas para la televisión.

4. (A) De tierra y alimentos.
   (B) De carne de animales.
   (C) De materia vegetal.
   (D) De barro y madera.

GROUP SEVEN,
NARRATIVE TWO
CD 1 TRACK 26

1. (A) La historia de una casa.
   (B) La historia de los amores de Bolívar.
   (C) La historia de un hotel.
   (D) La historia del héroe nacional de Colombia.

2. (A) Menos de cinco años.
   (B) Diez años.
   (C) Veinte años.
   (D) Toda su vida.

3. (A) Representaba un refugio de los que querían matarlo.
   (B) Representaba un lugar muy agradable para descansar.
   (C) Representaba la escena de gran felicidad doméstica.
   (D) Representaba un regalo para José Ignacio París.

4. (A) José Ignacio París la heredó por sus años de servicio a Bolívar.
   (B) Doña Matilde Baños recibió el título de Simón Bolívar.
   (C) Doña Manuela Sáenz la recibió por ser compañera de Bolívar tantos años.
   (D) Después de muchos años, pasó al uso público.

GROUP EIGHT,
NARRATIVE ONE
CD 1 TRACK 27

1. (A) Gonzalo Fernández de Oviedo.
   (B) Vasco Núñez de Balboa.
   (C) Bernardino de Sahagún.
   (D) Un novelista que presenció la exploración.

2. (A) Fernández había exagerado la historia.
   (B) Vasco Núñez de Balboa no quería compartir el tesoro.
   (C) La naturaleza reveló lo que la historia había olvidado.
   (D) Balboa se interesó más de su descubrimiento del mar.

3. (A) Que los historiadores no mienten.
   (B) Que los españoles tenían buena imaginación.
   (C) Que los indios eran fantásticos.
   (D) Que no quedan tesoros escondidos en ese momento.

4. (A) Reveló que los ríos son importantes para ayudar a descubrir tesoros.
   (B) Reveló que los historiadores no decían todo lo que sabían.
   (C) Reveló que Balboa era muy avaro.
   (D) Reveló que los indios poseían una civilización avanzada.

**GROUP EIGHT,
NARRATIVE TWO**
CD 1 TRACK 28

1. (A) Descubrió un nuevo tipo de café.
   (B) Descubrió características beneficiosas al café.
   (C) Descubrió un polvo en su café.
   (D) Descubrió una taza de café desecado.

2. (A) Después de unos días todo el agua se había evaporado.
   (B) Puesto que lo dejó en el jardín, alguien se había bebido todo el café.
   (C) Alguien había derramado el café, dejando nada más que polvo en la taza.
   (D) Descubrió todo el líquido en la taza cubierto con una capa de polvo.

3. (A) Añadió el polvo a un residuo para reconstituirlo.
   (B) Puso los residuos en agua muy caliente.
   (C) Mezcló el polvo con otros residuos.
   (D) Mezcló agua con granos de café.

4. (A) El café al instante es tan popular como antes.
   (B) El café soluble todavía se hace de granos de café.
   (C) Se produce el café soluble en jardines, secándose al sol.
   (D) Todavía se hace mezclando agua y polvo.

**GROUP NINE,
NARRATIVE ONE**
CD 2 TRACK 1

1. (A) Pidió una audiencia con el rey.
   (B) Pidió que le dejara estudiar las ciencias sociales en América.
   (C) Pidió que le diera dinero para explorar las Américas.
   (D) Pidió que el rey le otorgara permiso para explorar en América.

2. (A) Exploró la topografía del continente.
   (B) Se especializó en el estudio de los sistemas fluviales.
   (C) Exploró todos los aspectos de la naturaleza americana.
   (D) Investigó cuántos tipos de plantas desconocidas había en América.

3. (A) La falta de mapas e información del territorio era un obstáculo.
   (B) Las selvas eran impenetrables.
   (C) Las autoridades americanas le impidieron que continuara.
   (D) Le costó mucho transportar tantas plantas.

4. (A) Encontró doce mil tipos de plantas en el territorio del Amazonas.
   (B) Pasó treinta años en viajes de exploración en las Américas.
   (C) Escribió de todos sus descubrimientos en cartas al rey Carlos IV.
   (D) Contribuyó más al conocimiento de la naturaleza que cualquier otro científico previo.

**GROUP NINE,
NARRATIVE TWO**
CD 2 TRACK 2

1. (A) La construcción del *Metro* mexicano.
   (B) Los resultados de las excavaciones para el *Metro*.
   (C) La recuperación del pasado por la tecnología.
   (D) La muerte de aves y gente en los tiempos precolombinos.

2. (A) Solamente artefactos religiosos.
   (B) Piezas de todo tipo.
   (C) Estatuas extraordinarias.
   (D) Ejemplos de arquitectura azteca.

3. (A) El alto nivel y variedad de producción artística azteca.
   (B) La vida cotidiana que se veía representada artísticamente.
   (C) La variedad de especies de aves que representaban las ofrendas.
   (D) El aspecto puramente religioso de la vida azteca.

4. (A) Revelaron el carácter esencialmente religioso de la vida precolombina.
   (B) Revelaron la difusión de la práctica del sacrificio humano.
   (C) Revelaron aspectos antes desconocidos sobre la vida y religión aztecas.
   (D) Revelaron la dificultad de construcción en zonas metropolitanas.

SCRIPTS AND COMMENTARIES

GROUP ONE, NARRATIVE ONE

En cuanto al fenómeno de las historietas cómicas, se llaman de este modo aunque a veces no son ni cómicas ni tienen nada que ver con historietas. Pero no hay visitante de los Estados Unidos que comprenda la mágica fascinación que ejercen las historietas cómicas, o tiras cómicas, sobre millones de personas. Con las excepciones del *New York Times*, *Wall Street Journal*, y *USA Today*, no hay diario neoyorquino que olvide sus correspondientes historietas. Los diarios presentan múltiples historietas por pequeñas entregas y dedican a ellas tres o cuatro páginas. Los domingos las historietas se imprimen en colores y ocupan las primeras páginas de los periódicos ya que, en fin de cuentas gracias a las historietas se venden las publicaciones. Lejos de ser páginas frívolas, para muchos estas páginas son las únicas que les interesan.

Número 1   ¿Qué comenta esta selección?
Número 2   ¿Quiénes han notado este fenómeno?
Número 3   ¿Cómo se mide la popularidad de esta sección?
Número 4   ¿Cómo se explica esta fascinación?

Vocabulary:

historietas cómicas = comics	*ejercer* = to hold over, to work upon
diario = newspaper	*entregas* = inserts
imprimir = to print	*fin de cuentas* = in the end
frívolas = frivolous	*neoyorquino* = New Yorker

Commentary

Understanding this passage depends on recognizing negatives and the ironic tone set by the first sentence where the authors uses the negative, *no son ni ... ni.* The negative phrases are repeated throughout the passage: *no hay visitante que comprenda*, *no hay diario*, and *lejos de ser*. These negative phrases indicate a foreigner's point of view; the opposites represent the public's view. Listen to the narrative again to pick up on the structures. In the questions the vocabulary you need to know is:

notar = to note   *medir* = to measure

If you did not understand the questions, listen to them again now. Perhaps you could have guessed that *notar* was a cognate from the interrogative pronoun, *quién*, and the word *fenómeno.* In the next question, you perhaps could have guessed that *medir* means to measure by associating *popularity* with the answer choices.

GROUP ONE, NARRATIVE TWO

En España, con su historia de siglos de toreo, ha habido épocas en que a las mujeres se les prohibía hasta asistir a las corridas; luego se convirtieron en las principales aficionadas. Hay casos rarísimos de mujeres intentando torear. Cuando en el siglo XVIII, siglo de auge taurino, se veían mujeres en la plaza, enfrentándose a los toros, solía ser caso de hombres disfrazados. Eran estoqueadores vestidos de mujer, para risa y chacota de quienes se engañaban con aquella carnavalada. Pero hoy en día las mujeres han decidido, en el mundo entero, que no les quede vedada ninguna parcela de las actividades humanas, ni el toreo. En naciones taurófilas como Perú, Colombia, México, Venezuela, y hasta en España no faltan mujeres con grandes aficiones para convertirse en "figuras" al nivel de los maestros, aunque digan algunos españoles castizos que la mera presencia de la mujer-torero indudable e irevocablemente cambiará el espectáculo en su sentido fundamental.

Número 1   ¿Qué aspecto de la corrida comenta esta selección?
Número 2   ¿Cuál era antiguamente la actitud hacia las mujeres en la plaza de toros?
Número 3   ¿Cómo ha cambiado la corrida?
Número 4   ¿Cómo han reaccionado los aficionados?

Vocabulary:

torear = to fight bulls	*épocas* = eras
corridas = bullfights	*convertirse en* = to become
aficionados = fans	*auge* = peak, climax
taurino = taurine	*enfrentarse* = to confront
engañar = to deceive	*disfrazar* = to mask
risa = laugh	*castizos* = purists
vedar = to ban	

Commentary

This passage talks about the ways in which the role of women at a bullfight has changed. There are three stages indicated by the words, *hombres dizfrazados, ni el toreo, no faltan mujeres, aunque digan, la presencia cambiará.* Now listen again to see if you can identify the context for theses phrases. The only word in the questions that may be a problem, even though it is a cognate is *reaccionar*, which means *to react to*. In the possible responses, some useful words to know are: *constar* = to constitute, *darse cuenta* = to realize, *darle igual* = to be all the same to one.

GROUP TWO, NARRATIVE ONE

Tal vez ningún artista haya capturado mejor la esencia del mexicano que José Guadalupe Posada, el genial grabador de la vida mexicana, nacido en 1852 y muerto en 1913. Como artista popular, trataba la vida cotidiana del hombre y la sociedad que lo rodeaban con toda la agudeza del sociólogo. Lo que destaca en sus diseños era la expresión de los rostros, la variedad de composición, aunque es más conocido por las series de las calaveras, y la naturalidad de las actitudes. Posada trabajó en toda clase de publicaciones, especialmente las de jaez popular. Por eso era natural que en éste lo plebeyo ocupase el primer lugar, numéricamente hablando, en su producción. Las series de las calaveras especialmente llaman la atención porque parecen reflejar la extraordinaria fascinación de los mexicanos con la muerte. Pero la muerte, vista en caricatura, como si fuera el chiste más grande del mundo. La muerte danzante, la muerte que baila, que participa en el gran fandango para celebrar la vida vivida sin remedio, tal como la muerte experimentada sin remedio también.

Número 1   ¿Por qué es tan famoso José Guadalupe Posada?
Número 2   ¿A quiénes observó este hombre?
Número 3   ¿Por qué se enfocó más en lo cotidiano?
Número 4   ¿Qué importancia tiene el enfoque en las calaveras?

Vocabulary:

grabador = recorder	*cotidiana* = daily
rodear = to surround	*agudeza* = sharpness
destacar = to stand out	*diseños* = designs
calaveras = skeletons	*reflejar* = to reflect
chiste = joke	*experimentar* = to experience

Commentary

The word *artista* should give you a hint about the theme of the passage. Artists paint or draw pictures about things that they see around them. Use this knowledge to anticipate what kind of information you will hear. *Calaveras* should be apparent from the phrase *fascinación con la muerte*. The sense of the artist's work is indicated in the phrases, *vida sin remedio... muerte sin remedio*. In the questions the only vocabulary you may need to know is:

enfocar = to focus

In the choices, the vocabulary is:

retratar = to paint a portrait   *dibujar* = to draw

Now listen to the questions again to see if you understand them.

GROUP TWO, NARRATIVE TWO

La arqueología ha descubierto indicios de un alto nivel de trabajos textiles por todas partes de Hispanoamérica, desde las ruinas incaicas más antiguas hasta más recientes escombros de templos mesoamericanos. La principal materia prima de la industria textil precolombina fue el fino algodón nativo. La sedosa lana de la llama, el guanaco, la alpaca y la vicuña, fue también utilizada en el Perú. Plumas de brillantes aves tropicales fueron hábilmente aplicadas a las telas, y las pieles de jaguar y otros animales salvajes se emplearon como elementos decorativos. Hoy la mujer guatemalteca todavía teje en el antiguo telar de banda o correa posterior dentro de una variedad de completas técnicas que se remontan a los tiempos precolombinos. Durante la década de 1930, el trabajo de las distintas regiones, algunas veces aun tratándose de pueblos vecinos, se caracterizaba por sus diferentes diseños, estilizaciones y tejidos. Hoy se intercambian los diseños que se consideran más atractivos para el comprador, que es el turista. Es que este arte popular, hecho a mano, contiene algo de que carece nuestro arte superintelectualizado: el encanto que nos subyuga y el latido vital de la mano humana.

Número 1   ¿De qué arte se trata en esta selección?
Número 2   ¿Qué materias emplearon los artesanos?
Número 3   ¿Qué significación tenían los diseños?
Número 4   ¿Por qué les gustan tanto a los turistas estos productos?

Vocabulary:

incaicas = Incan	*escombros* = ruins, debris
materia prima = raw material	*algodón* = cotton
sedosa = silky	*telas* = cloth
tejer = to weave	*remontar* = to date back to
encanto = enchantment	*analfabeto* = illiterate

Commentary

You should be able to understand the cognate *textile*, which indicates the topic of the passage. The listing of animals and cotton all refer to sources of material for making fine cloths. The jump from the time indicated by the adjective *incaica* to the date, 1930, should indicate that this passage will be making comparisons between a centuries old tradition and modern times. The last part of the selection makes just such a comparison, which is indicated by the word *turista*. A vocabulary word that is useful in the questions is:

el artesano = the artisan

GROUP THREE, NARRATIVE ONE

José Martí llegó a ser el apóstol reconocido de la independencia de Cuba de España. Nacido en Cuba en 1853, hijo de españoles, Martí dedicó su vida por entero a su país. Ya a los quince años de edad publicaba el periódico escolar *La patria libre* en apoyo de los sublevados que habrían de luchar por diez años, sin éxito, por la independencia de Cuba. A los dieciséis fue arrestado por sospecha de deslealtad a España y, habiendo asumido la plena responsabilidad de sus actos en una muestra de oratoria patriótica durante su juicio, Martí fue condenado a trabajos forzados por desafiar a la autoridad del poder colonial. Pero, considerando su edad, las autoridades decidieron por desterrarlo a España en vez de encarcelarlo en Cuba. Así Martí cumplió su educación en la tierra de sus antepasados y llegó a ser poeta y artista bien conocido. Viajó por México y Estados Unidos, promoviendo la revolución entre los cubanos en exilio hasta que por fin, a los cuarenta y dos años de edad, volvió a Cuba. Los españoles lo mataron, sin que él jamás disparara un tiro contra los españoles. Presentó a todos los cubanos la inspiración para realizar su sueño de libertad.

Número 1   ¿Por qué es tan famoso el nombre de José Martí?
Número 2   ¿De joven, ¿qué problemas tuvo Martí?
Número 3   ¿Por qué viajó Martí por España y los Estados Unidos?
Número 4   ¿Qué le pasó cuando tenía cuarenta y dos años?

Vocabulary:

apóstol = apostle	*apoyo* = support
sublevados = insurrectionists	*éxito* = success
luchar = to fight	*desleadtad* = disloyalty
sospechar = to suspect	*desterrar* = to exile
desafiar = to defy	*disparar* = to shoot
promover = to promote	*antepasados* = ancestors
realizar = to fulfill	

Commentary

This passage deals with a national hero in Cuba, whose name, although he lived over a hundred years ago, still appears in numerous places. The words that indicate the topic are: *independencia, arrestado, oratoria patriótica, condenar, España, revolución, mataron,* and *inspiración.* From the words that are cognates, you should have some idea about what the passage discusses. Since this selection is mostly biographical, the questions deal with specifics about Martí's life and death.

Notice in the choices, in number 4, Choice C, the word is *publicó,* a verb, not *público,* which is a noun. The fact that this national hero was a revolutionary leader and a poet makes Martí an especially famous person in Cuban history and letters.

GROUP THREE, NARRATIVE TWO

La lengua aborigen, el guaraní, es usada corrientemente en el Paraguay tanto como el español—y aún más en las zonas del campo. Esto convierte a este país en el único bilingüe entre las repúblicas americanas. La razón histórica de este hecho radica en la fusión armoniosa de los elementos étnicos que integran al hombre paraguayo: mezcla que por su regularidad equiparó a ambos idiomas sin menoscabar el valor de ninguno. El guaraní se convirtió en lengua corriente durante la colonia, reservándose exclusivamente el español para la actuación oficial. Así se dio el caso de un pueblo conquistador que lingüísticamente es conquistado. Este idioma indígena es maleable y colorido, muy metafórico por razón de su primitivismo, que lo obliga a emplear la figura para la obtención del concepto; por ello mismo es propicio para la poesía, mas no para el concepto abstracto. Pero fácilmente se ven las influencias de una lengua en la otra, o en los vocablos o la pronunciación. No obstante, el desarrollo de la sociedad hispana va a paso rápido e influye en su idioma, lo cual difiere del estado del guaraní.

Número 1   ¿Qué es el guaraní?
Número 2   ¿Cómo es único Paraguay entre los países hispanoamericanos?
Número 3   ¿Cuáles son algunas características del guaraní?
Número 4   ¿Al transcurrir el tiempo, ¿qué cambios se han visto en cuanto a los idiomas?

Commentary

The word *lengua* tells you that the topic is languages. You should also know that *idioma* means the same thing. From there you should associate *guaraní* with language in Paraguay.

Vocabulary:

radicar = to be situated in	*mezcla* = mixture
corriente = present	*actuación* = enactment
propicia = favorable	*vocablos* = words
transcurrir = to pass	

Listen again to the passage. The topic is how *guaraní* fits into the linguistic scheme of the country and some of the subtleties of how the language is used. In the choices notice that *apreciar* means *to appreciate* and that *a causa de* means *because of*. You should also notice the difference between *conquistador* and *conquistado* and make the connection between who were the conquerors and who were the conquered. In Paraguay, because of the language, there was a strange twist to the relationship.

GROUP FOUR, NARRATIVE ONE

Según la tradición, el primero de los gobernantes incas, Manco Capac, llegó al Cuzco proveniente de una legendaria tierra alrededor del año 1200 de la era cristiana. Algunos siglos después, Viracocha, octavo en la línea dinástica, perseguido por otros indios enemigos que le atacaban, huyó del Cuzco hacia un invulnerable baluarte en la cresta de una montaña. Durante la era incaica, las cumbres de muchas colinas y montañas sirvieron de emplazamientos a pueblos y ciudades fortificadas. Fue una de esas ciudades, ya desde tiempo atrás invadida por el monte y arruinada, la que pensó el profesor Hiram Bingham que había descubierto en 1911. Esa ciudadela, nombrada Machu Picchu por los indios, parece no haber sido nunca conocida ni visitada. Ciertas frases ocasionalmente halladas en viejos archivos españoles sugirieron la posibilidad de que acaso uno o dos anticipados europeos hubieran visitado Machu Picchu, pero nada cierto se sabía con anterioridad al descubrimiento de Bingham. Los pobladores de Machu Picchu, adaptados a la enrarecida atmósfera, cultivaron sus muchas terrazas, dotaron de regadío sus jardines y criaron rebaños de llamas. Fue difícil identificar como tales las viviendas, pero es obvio que fueron numerosas.

Número 1   ¿Cuál es el tema de esta selección?
Número 2   ¿Qué pensaba Hiram Bingham que había descubierto?

Número 3   ¿Qué se sabía de Machu Picchu antes de 1911?
Número 4   ¿Qué tipo de lugar fue Machu Picchu?

Commentary

In passages like this one that contain several names, it is important to keep track of the names. When the names are in another language, there is a tendency sometimes not to differentiate between them by really remembering what they were, but what the first syllable sounded like. In this passage there is enough difference between *Manco Capac, Viracocha,* and *Machu Picchu* that you should not have any difficulty remembering the names, only which place is associated with which name. But you do need to be aware that when you listen to foreign names, there is a tendency to hear them and classify them all under the general heading of "foreign name" in your mind and not to distinguish one from the other. Practice noticing and associating names with specific information in passages such as this one where the differences are noticeable.

Vocabulary:

proveniente = coming from   *huir* = to flee
baluarte = bastion   *incaica* = Incan
cumbres = peaks   *hallar* = to find
dotar = to endow, to provide   *regadío* = irrigation
archivos = archives, libraries   *con anterioridad* = previously
rebaños = flocks   *viviendas* = housing
criar = to raise

Some words, such as *incaica,* may be words you do not recognize when you hear them, but that you would recognize if you were to see them on paper. With some words you may want to try to visualize them in writing to help you understand them. But remember that when you take the time to try to do this while taking the test, you may run the risk of missing some of the passage. You can also try to remember the sound, then when the passage is done, the meaning will probably become clear. Since you already knew from earlier in the passage that the topic was Incan ruins, you should have made the association between *inca* and *incaica.*

GROUP FOUR, NARRATIVE TWO

El vasto movimiento literario llamado *modernismo*, alcanza su máxima trascendencia en la figura central del poeta nicaragüense, Rubén Darío, cuya obra marca el momento culminante y abre el capítulo más significativo de nuestra historia literaria. Félix Rubén García Sarmiento (que era el nombre completo de Rubén Darío) nació en Metapa, Nicaragua. Aun antes de los veinte años era poeta publicado y autor de varios otros libros inéditos. Cuando tuvo veinte años empezó sus viajes por el continente, primeramente visitando Chile, Argentina, los Estados Unidos, luego, Francia y España. Su periódico *Azul* llegó a ser palabra sagrada, o sea, la *Biblia*, de poetas que quisieron publicar sus poemas modernistas. El *modernismo*, según el criterio del periódico de Darío, se distingue por el aprecio de la idea de belleza clásica, la fugacidad del placer y de la vida, referencias a la naturaleza, colores y sonido suave entre otras características. Todo lo hacía con el propósito de renovar la literatura poética de su época.

Número 1   ¿Quién era Rubén Darío?
Número 2   ¿Cuándo empezó sus viajes?
Número 3   ¿Qué era el *modernismo*?
Número 4   ¿Cuál era el propósito del *modernismo*?

Commentary

The vocabulary in this passage is fairly simple, but the way that it is put together may give you problems. The topic also is probably unfamiliar. *Modernismo* is a term used to designate a particular type of literature. It has certain characteristics that distinguish it from other types, and it has a particular author who was instrumental in its development. That is the topic of this passage. The author who was very important in the movement was Rubén Darío, a Nicaraguan.

Vocabulary:

inédito = unpublished
fugacidad = the fugacity (the quality of being ephemeral or fleeting)
propósito = the purpose
belleza = beauty

In the choices the words you may need to know are:

embajador = ambassador	*sacerdote* = priest
promover = to promote	*estrechar* = to bring together

GROUP FIVE, NARRATIVE ONE

Gaucho y tango son, probablemente, las dos palabras alusivas a la Argentina de mayor resonancia en el extranjero. Más que auténticas realidades, han llegado a adquirir el carácter de instituciones tradicionales; sin embargo, ambas palabras siguen constituyendo las dos expresiones más representativas de ese país. El tango es la música de la ciudad: provocativa, sentimental, ingeniosa y sensual, que tiene raíces en los bares de los barrios pobres y luego se convirtió en baile elegante del salón. El gaucho es el hombre de la pampa. Él encarna el verdadero campo que envuelve la ciudad, pero que permanece alejado de ella. Era experto jinete y vaquero, profundamente enraizado en la tierra, de sencillez de vida y decir sentencioso. Y el gaucho arquetípico, héroe del popular canto épico convertido en el poema nacional argentino, es Martín Fierro. Pero actualmente, el gaucho parece ser más institución para el turista, mientras el tango sigue como baile popular entre toda la gente.

Número 1   ¿Cuáles son las dos expresiones más representativas de Argentina?
Número 2   ¿De dónde proceden estas imágenes?
Número 3   ¿Quién era Martín Fierro?
Número 4   ¿A qué han llegado estas imágenes?

Commentary

The topic for this passage should be easily discernable: the *tango* and the *gaucho*. Both words have become recognizable in their Spanish form to most English-speaking people.

Vocabulary:

alusivas = alluding to
ingeniosa = ingenious
encarnar = to embody
alejado = distant
vaquero = cowboy
sencillez = simplicity
actualmente = presently

en el extranjero = abroad
raíz = root (plural: *las raíces*)
envolver = to wrap around
jinete = horseman
enraizado = grounded
sentencioso = terse
arquetípico = primary and original
    model, prototype

There are other words that you may not recognize immediately without thinking about them, such as *héroe*, which is easily recognizable when you remember that the *h* is never pronounced in Spanish. You need to know that the *pampas* are a geographical region of Argentina noted for being wide, open, sparsely populated range land. The word *turista* should also catch your ear and help you make the connection between the archetypal *gaucho* and what a *gaucho* is today.

GROUP FIVE, NARRATIVE TWO

Los arqueólogos de antigüedades mexicanas todavía disputan quiénes eran los olmecas, gente misteriosa cuyos monumentos en el sitio de La Venta primeramente dieron noticias de su existencia. Para la mayoría, los olmecas son conocidos por sus notables esculturas en piedras de las colosales cabezas pétreas, que varían en tamaño entre un metro y medio y tres metros. En muchos folletos de promoción turística a México han aparecido fotografías de estas cabezas enigmáticas. Pero hay otros artefactos, como altares, estelas, y tumbas con ricas ofrendas de jade para conservar los restos de personas importantes. Ignoramos qué nombre se daban a sí mismos los olmecas, ni de dónde provenían. La palabra olmeca significa *pueblo del caucho,* es decir, de la tierra donde éste se produce. Era el nombre de un grupo que vivía cerca de Vera Cruz en tiempos históricos. Actualmente se duda que los olmecas procedieran de esta región.

Número 1   ¿De dónde procedían los olmecas?
Número 2   ¿Qué señales dejaron de su presencia?
Número 3   ¿Cómo los conocen muchos visitantes a México?
Número 4   ¿Qué nombre les hemos dado?

Commentary

From the cognate *arqueólogos* you should have an idea about the topic. If you have heard of the Olmec culture, you know that this passage is about an ancient Mexican-Indian culture. It is somewhat enigmatic to most archaeologists because the only evidence is mute stone.

Vocabulary:

pétreas = stone
estela = stele (a carved
    stone pillar or slab)
ofrenda = offering
ignorar = to not know

folletos = pamphlets
proceder = to come from

restos = remains (bones)
provenir = to come from

The two false cognates in this passage that may mislead you are *ignorar*, which does not necessarily mean *to ignore*, but implies that one knows but chooses to not recognize, and *to not know*, which means that one does not recognize because one does not know. The other false cognate is *los restos*, which refers in this case to physical remains, or *bones*. In the choices for the questions, this distinction in meaning is particularly important because one does not see Olmec bones all over Mexico. In the passage, notice that the bones were in the *tumbas*, which is a cognate.

One other problem in this passage is that archaeologists do not agree on the geographic point of origin. For many years it was thought that the Olmec lived on the coast around the area of Vera Cruz. But newer investigations have placed their origin inland. If you have access to dated material, you may have contributed old information to your understanding of the passage. Listen to what the passage says, and do not necessarily rely totally on what you may already know.

GROUP SIX, NARRATIVE ONE

La Comisión Interamericana de Mujeres fue creada hace más de medio siglo con el propósito de luchar por la conquista de los derechos femeninos. Cumplió su primera función cuando, en 1961, el último país de América que faltaba reconoció su derecho de voto. La labor constante y sin interrupción de la CIM a partir de 1928 presenta un balance positivo de resoluciones aprobadas en sus asambleas. Su contribución ha sido valiosa en la conquista de la igualdad de derechos para hombres y mujeres, la eliminación de la discriminación por razón de sexo, así como los artículos que aparecen en los códigos de trabajo, instrumentos jurídicos de enorme alcance para beneficio de la mujer. No se puede decir que todos estos acuerdos tengan vigencia y se apliquen en la práctica, pero la acción de la CIM se encaminó en el sentido de lograrlo. Las mujeres todavía están reclamando sus derechos ahora a fines del siglo.

Número 1   ¿De qué tipo de organización es la CIM?
Número 2   ¿Desde cuándo está trabajando este grupo?
Número 3   ¿Qué propósito elemental tiene esta organización?
Número 4   ¿Con qué razón se sentiría orgulloso este grupo?

Commentary

The cognate *comisión* tells you that the group has an official function. A commission is a group that is organized to promote, enact, or study something and make a decision. You also can tell from the words you know and the cognates that this commission, the CIM, has an agenda that includes a number of things. The end of the passage gives the results of the work of the commission.

Vocabulary:

derechos = rights	*cumplir* = to fulfill
balance = balance sheet	*aprobar* = to approve, pass
por razón = because of	*códigos* = codes
jurídico = judicial	*el alcance* = achievement
acuerdo = agreement	*vigencia* = in practice
reclamar = to demand	*a fines de* = at the end of

In this passage there are several numbers that you will have to remember. You do not have to know exactly how many years passed between events, but you need a general idea. As you hear the numbers, mentally place them on a line by decades from past to present. Remember what to associate with each general time. Then when you need to remember time, refer to your visual image of when things happened. The rest of the information you can probably guess because the issues have not changed much over time, except for the right to vote.

GROUP SIX, NARRATIVE TWO

Quizás ninguna otra región de los Estados Unidos está más ligada por más tiempo a Hispanoamérica que la extensa península que proyecta hacia el sur: la Florida. A pesar de habitantes y topografía hostiles, los españoles se empeñaban en sus exploraciones en el siglo XVI. A partir de entonces la suerte del imperio dependería de unas cuantas plazas militares que servirían de bastiones defensivos. Así Cuba y la Florida comenzaron una hermandad de relaciones históricas de recíproco interés, y entre ambas se establecieron una forma de interdependencia cuyo centro de gravitación vacilaba entre las dos. Contrariamente a lo que con el tiempo llegaría a ser lo normal en los años 60, el primero de los exilios en masa procedió de la Florida a Cuba y tuvo lugar en el siglo XVIII cuando los ingleses capturaron San Agustín. El éxodo más grande ocurrió cuando los Estados Unidos tomó posesión en 1819. Pero a partir de principios de los 60, los cubanos han regresado a la Florida para restablecerse. En muchas partes del estado predominan los cubanos, que se encuentran "en su casa" en la Florida.

Número 1   ¿Por qué se establecieron los españoles en la Florida?
Número 2   ¿Cómo seguían las relaciones entre Cuba y la Florida?
Número 3   ¿De dónde proceden los primeros exilios?
Número 4   Actualmente, ¿cómo se sienten los cubanos en la Florida?

Commentary

Florida and Cuba have had a long and close relationship, ever since the Spaniards arrived to explore the peninsula. This topic of the migration of people between Florida and Cuba has a new twist in this passage. Although most of the words are cognates, some of the words you may need to know to understand it are:

Vocabulary:

ligar = to tie	*empeñarse* = to persist
hacia = toward	*a pesar de* = in spite of
hermandad = kinship	

You should make sure that you distinguish *hacia* from *hacía*. The first word is an adverb, meaning *toward*. The second is a verb, the imperfect indicative of *hacer*. There are several phrases in this passage that are useful to recognize, including *a pesar de, a partir de, estrechar las relaciones,* and *en su casa*. The expression *en su casa* means that they feel at home. The other aspect of this passage to notice is that there are several examples of the conditional tense to describe what the Spaniards planned to do with the territory. It may be helpful to know that St. Augustine, originally a Spanish community, is the oldest continuously inhabited city in the state of Florida.

GROUP SEVEN, NARRATIVE ONE

Los quichés, rama de los antiguos mayas, fueron la nación más poderosa de las altiplanicies de Guatemala en los tiempos precolombinos. Su libro sagrado, el *Popol Vuh,* ha sido caracterizado como el más distinguido ejemplo de literatura nativa americana que ha sobrevivido a través de los siglos. Contiene una extensa y refinada narración del mito maya de la creación. Los dioses antiguos crearon primero la tierra, luego los animales. Pero, viendo que éstos no podían hablar, se dieron a la obra de crear al hombre. Seres hechos de barro, y luego de madera, resultaron inaceptables y fueron destruidos. Y al fin los dioses hicieron la carne del cuerpo humano con alimentos vivos—mazorcas de maíz amarillo y blanco—y estos hombres fueron buenos. Esta visión cosmológica ha servido de inspiración recientemente a una gran variedad de programas, de un ballet de notable estilo y animación hasta un programa de dibujos animados para la pantalla televisora.

Número 1 ¿A qué o quiénes se refieren los quichés?
Número 2 ¿Qué se cuenta en el *Popol Vuh*?
Número 3 ¿Qué se ha hecho con el texto?
Número 4 Últimamente ¿de qué se hicieron los hombres?

Commentary

The topic is about the *Popol Vuh*, an ancient story of the Quiché Indians, who are descendants of the Maya. If you know about this book, this passage will be fairly easy because you can guess what the answers are based on what you already know.

Vocabulary:

la altiplanicie = highland	*rama* = branch
sagrado = sacred	*sobrevivir* = to survive
dibujos animados = cartoons	*pantalla* = screen
darse a = to set about	*barro* = mud
madera = wood	*mazorca* = ear of corn

This passage focuses on the fact that even though this is an ancient text, the story remains enchanting because it is a creation story. There are many ways to tell a creation story, but they all show how a group of people sees itself in the grand scheme of life.

GROUP SEVEN, NARRATIVE TWO

La Quinta de Simón Bolívar, como el Montecello de Jefferson y el Mount Vernon de Washington, es algo más que un monumento nacional; es el lugar donde la historia se ha detenido a través de los años. *La Quinta* se construyó originalmente en 1800. Bolívar vivió allí unos cuantos meses en 1826, después a fines de 1827 y de nuevo tras el atentado contra su vida en septiembre de 1828. Durante la mayor parte del tiempo que pasó Bolívar en la villa disfrutó de la compañía del más grande de sus amores, Doña Manuela Sáenz, la dama quiteña que había conocido en Perú. De tal modo, sus majestuosos aposentos, sus encantadores senderos de piedra y los viejos árboles que dan sombra a los jardines están inextricable e íntimamente ligados al gran romance que ha pasado a ser casi una leyenda. En 1830, unos pocos meses antes de su muerte, Bolívar cedió título de la estancia a su fiel amigo, Don José Ignacio París, el cual luego la transfirió a Doña Matilde Baños, para uso de educación pública, aunque tardaron muchos años antes de que ésta pudiera disfrutar de esta herencia.

Número 1   ¿Cuál es el tema de este trozo?
Número 2   ¿Cuánto tiempo vivió allí Bolívar?
Número 3   ¿Qué representaba esta residencia para Bolívar?
Número 4   ¿Qué disposición hicieron de la Quinta últimamente?

Commentary

At first you may not realize that *La Quinta* refers to a house, but when you hear the references to dates when Bolívar was there, you should be able to figure out that the selection is about a house. There are some words in the passage that specifically refer to a house, but if you do not recognize them, words such as *se construyó* and *jardín* should provide clues. Also, where else would a person spend time at the end of his life except in a residence with his favorite people nearby?

Vocabulary:

detenerse = to stop	*atentado* = attempt
disfrutar = to enjoy	*quiteña* = from Quito
aposentos = rooms	*encantadores* = enchanting
senderos = paths	*ligados* = tied
ceder = to give over	*tardar en* = to take a long time

Another word that you might not recognize when you hear it, but would easily understand when you saw it, is the word *herencia*. Remember the silent *h* at the beginning of words when you are trying to think of cognates. Another word that has a variety of meanings is *estancia*. In some countries an *estancia* is a large country house, an estate. In other contexts the word means *a stay*. *La quinta* is also a word for a country dwelling. One common expression in this passage is *tardar en*, which is used in such a way that it is awkward to translate literally. *Aunque tardaron mucho años antes de que ...* would mean *many years went by before....* The expression *tardar en* is found whenever you would comment about how long it took for something to happen, such as the time it took a letter to arrive.

GROUP EIGHT, NARRATIVE ONE

Se observa que los hechos históricos son a menudo más extraordinarios que las creaciones ficticias del novelista. Tal fue el caso de los tesoros de Coclé, cuya riqueza había narrado Gonzalo Fernández de Oviedo, el historiador real que describió lo que había descubierto Vasco Núñez de Balboa en sus campañas en Panamá. Toda la cultura parecía haber desaparecido de la tierra con sólo las referencias en los libros olvidados para marcar su existencia. El descubrimiento de Coclé fue un acontecimiento fortuito. El sitio habría permanecido escondido de vista si no se hubiera desviado el Río Grande, revelando el brillo del tesoro fabuloso. Una comparación entre la historia y la excavación arqueológica reveló que el fiel historiador no exageró ni el detalle más pequeño. Fácilmente se ven las técnicas descritas por un contemporáneo de Oviedo, el padre Bernardino de Sahagún, en la manera de labrar el oro. El conocimiento de la realidad de las historias y la esperanza de encontrar más tesoro enterrado todavía inspiran a muchos en una búsqueda fantástica.

Número 1   ¿Quién vio las riquezas de Coclé primero?
Número 2   ¿Por qué fue fortuito el descubrimiento del sitio?
Número 3   ¿Qué ha revelado el descubrimiento?
Número 4   ¿Qué importancia tiene el descubrimiento?

Commentary

There are many names in this passage that you need to keep straight. You will not need to remember the full name of each one, so remember the last names, *Balboa, Oviedo,* and *Sahagún.* Then attach a label to each one to help you remember what he did. Remember that Balboa was the first European to see the Pacific Ocean; he was an explorer. Associate *historiador* to the name Oviedo. Then remember the word, *padre,* Sahagún. They all did different things. Now you should be able to answer the questions.

Vocabulary:

a menudo = often	*ficticias* = not true
tesoro = treasure	*campañas* = campaigns
acontecimiento = event	*detalle* = detail
labrar = to carve	*conocimiento* = knowledge
enterrado = buried	*escondido* = hidden

In the choices, the words *poseer* means *to possess*, *avaro* means *greedy*, and *presenciar* means *to witness*.

This passage essentially talks about a comparison of historical records and archeological records in the search for buried treasure. The conclusion is that although historical records may seem more incredible than fiction, treasures are often even more fantastic than recorded history indicates. You should be sure not to confuse the word *enterrado*, from the infinitive *enterrar*, with a similar verb, *enterar*, which means *to inform*.

GROUP EIGHT, NARRATIVE TWO

Nada agrada como el aroma del grano recién secado, tostado, y remolido. Pero el café soluble ofrece la posibilidad de gozar de una taza sin que deba pasarse tanto tiempo preparando los granos. El café soluble fue descubierto por casualidad por cierto médico guatemalteco, Federico Lehnhoff Wyld. Cierto día le fue servida una taza de café. Debido a sus múltiples ocupaciones, dicha taza quedó olvidada intacta en el jardín de su residencia. Días más tarde, el buen doctor encontró en el mismo sitio aquella taza ya sin líquido y con residuos de fino polvo en el fondo. Su inclinación de investigador hizo que vertiera agua hirviendo sobre aquel residuo seco y al instante, ante sus asombrados ojos, obtuvo una nueva taza de café que conservaba su tinte y su sabor. La tecnología ha transformado el proceso de deshidratación, pero el efecto es igual. Todavía se añade agua hirviendo al polvo para gozar de una simple taza de café al instante, pero se ha mejorado el producto. Ahora tiene aun mejor sabor y tinte.

Numero 1   ¿Qué descubrió el médico?
Número 2   En efecto, ¿que había ocurrido a la taza de café?
Número 3   ¿Cómo podía el médico reconstituirlo?
Número 4   ¿Qué no ha cambiado en el proceso?

Commentary
Obviously this piece is about instant coffee and its accidental discovery.

Vocabulary:

agradar = to please	*soluble* = soluble
por casualidad = accidentally	*verter* = to pour
polvo = dust	*seco* = dry
hirviendo = boiling	*añadir* = to add
deshidratar = to dry	*tinte* = color
mejorar = to improve	

One other word that you may not recognize when you hear it, but probably can read, is *líquido*. Remember that the *qu* in Spanish sounds like *k* in English. Another word in the choices that you may need to know is *desecar*, which means *to dry out*. Another verb that means about the same thing is *deshidratar*, although the latter refers to a process in which the water is removed, instead of simply leaving the liquid to evaporate. As a point of grammar about this vocabulary, you will notice that *hirviendo* is a present participle and it describes a noun. It is one of only two present participles that can be used in this way in Spanish. The verb *mezclar* means *to mix*.

Since you now can deduce the process for making instant coffee from a liquid, you can probably figure out the words you do not know as you listen.

GROUP NINE, NARRATIVE ONE

Pocas figuras de Europa pertenecen tanto al Nuevo Mundo como Alejandro von Humboldt, joven aristócrata, cuyos mejores treinta años fueron dedicados casi totalmente al estudio de las ciencias naturales y sociales en América. En marzo de 1799, el Rey Carlos IV, en una audiencia, le dio autorización para trabajar en el campo de las ciencias naturales en los reinos españoles de ultramar. Con buen afán de científico alemán de su época, emprendió su trabajo. Una vez en América, lo impresionó la exuberancia extraordinaria de la vegetación tropical, y muchas formaciones geológicas le recordaron sus estudios anteriores. En uno de sus viajes, hecho a pie, comprobó la unión entre el río Orinoco y el Amazonas. Este recorrido, casi todo por selvas vírgenes, fue una hazaña de incalculable valor para la ciencia por la fabulosa cifra de doce mil plantas que coleccionaron él y sus compañeros. De este número, 3.500 eran totalmente desconocidas. Por otra parte, el viaje fue de lo más penoso debido a los peligros y obstáculos. Ningún aspecto de la geografía escapó su atención en las exploraciones que le costaron no sólo toda su dedicación sino su fortuna también.

Número 1   ¿Qué pidió Humboldt al rey Carlos IV?
Número 2   ¿Qué hizo en estos viajes?
Número 3   ¿Por qué eran tan difíciles estos viajes?
Número 4   ¿Cual fue el valor de sus viajes?

Commentary

Alexander Humboldt was truly one of the most remarkable naturalists to visit the Americas. His travels and monumental notes of his trips are invaluable sources of information about the land and people. His work is the topic of this passage. At the beginning the words *alemán, español,* and *Américas* should let you know that he has to travel to get to America. Later in the passage, the word *viajar* should confirm what you thought. There are a number of adjectives that you may not know, but are not necessary to understand the passage. There are many others that are cognates, such as *incalculable.* Other cognates should help you understand the topic, such as *ciencias naturales* and *estudios.*

Vocabulary:

emprender = to undertake	*comprobar* = to prove
hazaña = feat	*cifra* = number
selva = jungle	*peligro* = danger
(in some places, a plain)	

This passage contains a general introduction about who Humboldt was, where he went, and why. Included are a specific example of the type of trip he took and a conclusion about what it cost him. The example does not discuss every trip he took, only the ones in the jungles. The last sentences say that no aspect of geography escaped his notice, which can be taken to mean that he went other places, too.

In the choices, some words that you may want to know are: *otorgar,* which means *to grant, to authorize,* and *sistemas fluviales,* which means *river systems. Fluvial* is a fairly common word in areas where rivers are important for transportation.

GROUP NINE, NARRATIVE TWO

La construcción del *Metro* en la Ciudad de México proporcionó al mundo un vistazo de la vida precolombina a medida que excavaron los túneles. La arquitectura religiosa, la más abundante, fue hallada casi toda ella en dos zonas: en el centro ceremonial Pino Suárez y en la zona próxima a la catedral metropolitana. Dentro de estas ruinas excavadas había una gran cantidad de ofrendas, especialmente de aves, en Pino Suárez, y de sacrificios humanos en el centro metropolitano. Entre las aves se contaban pericos, guajolotes, patos silvestres, una especie de grulla y muchos loros. Sobresalían las aves acuáticas. También se han recuperado muchas piezas excepcionales de escultura. Entre ellas se destaca la llamada Coatlicue que fue encontrada formando parte de los cimientos de un edificio colonial. Otra pieza era el llamado Ehecatl-Ozomatli, de un formidable movimiento barroco que la aleja completamente de la severidad y rigidez azteca. Todo lo encontrado en la construcción sirvió para aumentar con objetos tangibles los escasos conocimientos de la vida precolombina de Tenochtitlán y la región del Lago Texcoco.

Número 1   ¿De qué acontecimiento trata este trozo?

Número 2   ¿Qué tipos de artefactos encontraron?

Número 3   ¿Qué revelaron muchos de los artefactos de Pino Suárez?

Número 4   ¿Por qué son tan importantes estos artefactos?

Commentary

The first and last sentences make clear that this passage deals with construction of a subway system. The artifacts mentioned were uncovered in the process of digging the tunnels. Many words are cognates, but there also some Indian names, such as those of gods and place names, that you will need to remember. The words *escultura, centro ceremonial, ruinas excavadas,* and *sacrificios humanos* should indicate the theme of the passage.

Vocabulary:

proporcionar = to furnish, provide   *catedral* = cathedral
ofrenda = offering   *aves* = birds
destacarse = to stand out   *cimientos* = foundations
alejar = to distance   *lago* = lake

The Indian names are: *Coatlicue, Ehecatl Ozomatli, Tenochtitlán,* and *Texcoco.* The names of the various kinds of birds are: *pericos, guajolotes, patos silvestres, grullas,* and *loros,* meaning *parakeet, turkeys, wood ducks, cranes,* and *parrots.* All you really need to remember, however, is that most birds were aquatic. There were two kinds of artifacts mentioned in this passage, evidence of human sacrifices and statues in ruins of buildings that were excavated.

The passage mentions two principle places where excavations were carried out: in Pino Suárez and near the cathedral in the central part of the city.

Answers for Short Narratives

Group One, Narrative One
1. B 2. B 3. D 4. A

Group One, Narrative Two
1. A 2. C 3. C 4. B

Group Two, Narrative One
1. A 2. C 3. D 4. B

Group Two, Narrative Two
1. D 2. B 3. C 4. D

Group Three, Narrative One
1. C 2. D 3. B 4. A

Group Three, Narrative Two
1. C 2. A 3. B 4. D

Group Four, Narrative One
1. D 2. B 3. C 4. A

Group Four, Narrative Two
1. A 2. B 3. C 4. B

Group Five, Narrative One
1. C 2. B 3. B 4. B

Group Five, Narrative Two
1. C 2. A 3. A 4. B

Group Six, Narrative One
1. D 2. D 3. A 4. C

Group Six, Narrative Two
1. B 2. A 3. C 4. D

Group Seven, Narrative One
1. A 2. D 3. B 4. C

Group Seven, Narrative Two
1. A 2. A 3. C 4. D

Group Eight, Narrative One
1. B 2. C 3. A 4. D

Group Eight, Narrative Two
1. D 2. A 3. B 4. D

Group Nine, Narrative One
1. D 2. C 3. A 4. D

Group Nine, Narrative Two
1. B 2. B 3. C 4. C

CHAPTER 3: Answer Sheet for Longer Selections

Narrativa Número Uno
1. Ⓐ Ⓑ Ⓒ Ⓓ
2. Ⓐ Ⓑ Ⓒ Ⓓ
3. Ⓐ Ⓑ Ⓒ Ⓓ
4. Ⓐ Ⓑ Ⓒ Ⓓ
5. Ⓐ Ⓑ Ⓒ Ⓓ
6. Ⓐ Ⓑ Ⓒ Ⓓ
7. Ⓐ Ⓑ Ⓒ Ⓓ

Narrativa Número Dos
1. Ⓐ Ⓑ Ⓒ Ⓓ
2. Ⓐ Ⓑ Ⓒ Ⓓ
3. Ⓐ Ⓑ Ⓒ Ⓓ
4. Ⓐ Ⓑ Ⓒ Ⓓ
5. Ⓐ Ⓑ Ⓒ Ⓓ
6. Ⓐ Ⓑ Ⓒ Ⓓ
7. Ⓐ Ⓑ Ⓒ Ⓓ
8. Ⓐ Ⓑ Ⓒ Ⓓ

Narrativa Número Tres
1. Ⓐ Ⓑ Ⓒ Ⓓ
2. Ⓐ Ⓑ Ⓒ Ⓓ
3. Ⓐ Ⓑ Ⓒ Ⓓ
4. Ⓐ Ⓑ Ⓒ Ⓓ
5. Ⓐ Ⓑ Ⓒ Ⓓ
6. Ⓐ Ⓑ Ⓒ Ⓓ
7. Ⓐ Ⓑ Ⓒ Ⓓ
8. Ⓐ Ⓑ Ⓒ Ⓓ

Narrativa Número Cuatro
1. Ⓐ Ⓑ Ⓒ Ⓓ
2. Ⓐ Ⓑ Ⓒ Ⓓ
3. Ⓐ Ⓑ Ⓒ Ⓓ
4. Ⓐ Ⓑ Ⓒ Ⓓ
5. Ⓐ Ⓑ Ⓒ Ⓓ
6. Ⓐ Ⓑ Ⓒ Ⓓ
7. Ⓐ Ⓑ Ⓒ Ⓓ
8. Ⓐ Ⓑ Ⓒ Ⓓ
9. Ⓐ Ⓑ Ⓒ Ⓓ
10. Ⓐ Ⓑ Ⓒ Ⓓ

Narrativa Número Cinco
1. Ⓐ Ⓑ Ⓒ Ⓓ
2. Ⓐ Ⓑ Ⓒ Ⓓ
3. Ⓐ Ⓑ Ⓒ Ⓓ
4. Ⓐ Ⓑ Ⓒ Ⓓ
5. Ⓐ Ⓑ Ⓒ Ⓓ
6. Ⓐ Ⓑ Ⓒ Ⓓ
7. Ⓐ Ⓑ Ⓒ Ⓓ
8. Ⓐ Ⓑ Ⓒ Ⓓ
9. Ⓐ Ⓑ Ⓒ Ⓓ

Entrevista Número Uno
1. Ⓐ Ⓑ Ⓒ Ⓓ
2. Ⓐ Ⓑ Ⓒ Ⓓ
3. Ⓐ Ⓑ Ⓒ Ⓓ
4. Ⓐ Ⓑ Ⓒ Ⓓ
5. Ⓐ Ⓑ Ⓒ Ⓓ
6. Ⓐ Ⓑ Ⓒ Ⓓ
7. Ⓐ Ⓑ Ⓒ Ⓓ
8. Ⓐ Ⓑ Ⓒ Ⓓ

Entrevista Número Dos
1. Ⓐ Ⓑ Ⓒ Ⓓ
2. Ⓐ Ⓑ Ⓒ Ⓓ
3. Ⓐ Ⓑ Ⓒ Ⓓ
4. Ⓐ Ⓑ Ⓒ Ⓓ
5. Ⓐ Ⓑ Ⓒ Ⓓ
6. Ⓐ Ⓑ Ⓒ Ⓓ
7. Ⓐ Ⓑ Ⓒ Ⓓ
8. Ⓐ Ⓑ Ⓒ Ⓓ
9. Ⓐ Ⓑ Ⓒ Ⓓ
10. Ⓐ Ⓑ Ⓒ Ⓓ

Entrevista Número Tres
1. Ⓐ Ⓑ Ⓒ Ⓓ
2. Ⓐ Ⓑ Ⓒ Ⓓ
3. Ⓐ Ⓑ Ⓒ Ⓓ
4. Ⓐ Ⓑ Ⓒ Ⓓ
5. Ⓐ Ⓑ Ⓒ Ⓓ
6. Ⓐ Ⓑ Ⓒ Ⓓ
7. Ⓐ Ⓑ Ⓒ Ⓓ
8. Ⓐ Ⓑ Ⓒ Ⓓ
9. Ⓐ Ⓑ Ⓒ Ⓓ
10. Ⓐ Ⓑ Ⓒ Ⓓ

Entrevista Número Cuatro

1. Ⓐ Ⓑ Ⓒ Ⓓ
2. Ⓐ Ⓑ Ⓒ Ⓓ
3. Ⓐ Ⓑ Ⓒ Ⓓ
4. Ⓐ Ⓑ Ⓒ Ⓓ
5. Ⓐ Ⓑ Ⓒ Ⓓ
6. Ⓐ Ⓑ Ⓒ Ⓓ
7. Ⓐ Ⓑ Ⓒ Ⓓ
8. Ⓐ Ⓑ Ⓒ Ⓓ
9. Ⓐ Ⓑ Ⓒ Ⓓ
10. Ⓐ Ⓑ Ⓒ Ⓓ

Entrevista Número Cinco

1. Ⓐ Ⓑ Ⓒ Ⓓ
2. Ⓐ Ⓑ Ⓒ Ⓓ
3. Ⓐ Ⓑ Ⓒ Ⓓ
4. Ⓐ Ⓑ Ⓒ Ⓓ
5. Ⓐ Ⓑ Ⓒ Ⓓ
6. Ⓐ Ⓑ Ⓒ Ⓓ
7. Ⓐ Ⓑ Ⓒ Ⓓ
8. Ⓐ Ⓑ Ⓒ Ⓓ
9. Ⓐ Ⓑ Ⓒ Ⓓ

Entrevista Número Seis

1. Ⓐ Ⓑ Ⓒ Ⓓ
2. Ⓐ Ⓑ Ⓒ Ⓓ
3. Ⓐ Ⓑ Ⓒ Ⓓ
4. Ⓐ Ⓑ Ⓒ Ⓓ
5. Ⓐ Ⓑ Ⓒ Ⓓ
6. Ⓐ Ⓑ Ⓒ Ⓓ
7. Ⓐ Ⓑ Ⓒ Ⓓ
8. Ⓐ Ⓑ Ⓒ Ⓓ
9. Ⓐ Ⓑ Ⓒ Ⓓ

Entrevista Número Siete

1. Ⓐ Ⓑ Ⓒ Ⓓ
2. Ⓐ Ⓑ Ⓒ Ⓓ
3. Ⓐ Ⓑ Ⓒ Ⓓ
4. Ⓐ Ⓑ Ⓒ Ⓓ
5. Ⓐ Ⓑ Ⓒ Ⓓ
6. Ⓐ Ⓑ Ⓒ Ⓓ
7. Ⓐ Ⓑ Ⓒ Ⓓ
8. Ⓐ Ⓑ Ⓒ Ⓓ
9. Ⓐ Ⓑ Ⓒ Ⓓ

CHAPTER 3 Longer Listening Selections
(Section I, Part A)

In this part of the exam, you will hear two selections consisting of either a narrative, an interview, or a broadcast. Each piece will be about five minutes long. If you know something about the topic, you will be able to understand more than if the subject matter is completely new to you. These topics will be about a wide variety of aspects of Spanish culture, including music, art, history, food, customs (such as the *posadas*, or bullfighting), traveling in Spanish American countries, daily routines, business, shopping, entertainment, television, ethnic differences, the roles of men and women in society, schooling for children, higher education, finding jobs, family traditions, family relationships, national institutions (such as ONCE in Spain, that runs the national lottery), dating customs etc. The more you can find out about these and other topics from sources such as magazines, television programs, radio programs, Spanish-speaking people, or literature, the better prepared you will be.

Some strategies for you to use to do well on this section are:

1. *Listen for repeated words.* These may tell you what the main topic will be. If you do not know the vocabulary used for the main topic, listen for other clues, such as descriptions of places, people, or things. These descriptions could also indicate what the topic is.
2. In an interview the *host will ask questions* usually and the *person being interviewed will answer.* The format of questions and answers has repetition built in. Sometimes the person being interviewed will repeat the question, or the essential information, but at other times, the person will simply give the response. The information is spaced out between the two speakers, though, which will give you more time to assimilate what is being said.
3. *Listen for direction* in the conversation or in the narrative. Usually the topic will be presented with some generality, then go in a specific direction or directions.
4. *Listen for cognates.* You will recognize more words if you have a good vocabulary in your native language. Use that knowledge to help you figure out the words. It also helps to have a good understanding of Spanish phonetics. Then remember that there are some rules about pronunciation that will help. Spanish uses the letter *e* before consonant groupings such as *str-, spr-, sch-,* making words like *estructura* or *especial.* The English sounds of *k* and *ch* in Spanish are *qu-,* as in the word *parque.* In Spanish the English *th-* does not exist, so if you visualize words you hear, you may need to remember to use a *t* for the *th,* as in words like *teatro* for *theater,* or *tema* for *theme.*
5. *Learn numbers well.* If you hear numbers in the selection, try to visualize the numerals instead of the words. Practice words for tens and hundreds so that you do not have to waste time translating words as you listen.

6. Once you know what people are talking about in the conversation, *anticipate where the conversation will go.* Being able to anticipate what will be said will help you understand what you hear. As you listen, think ahead. Then you can check what you *expect* to hear with what you *actually* hear, which will increase your comprehension. Pay attention to details once you have gotten the main idea and constantly compare what you hear with what you know about the topic.

7. As you listen, *make mental notes.* Under the general heading of the main idea, make categories for subtopics that are discussed. If you have some way of mentally sorting the information you hear, you will remember it better.

8. If you do not know much about the topic, *imagine what it would be like.* A good imagination can help you anticipate what to expect to hear.

9. If possible *visualize the selection* as you hear it. If the piece is an interview, think about where it is taking place. One of the problems with visualization is the difficulty of imagining or visualizing places, people, and things you have never seen. In such cases think about the characteristics of other similar places, people, or things that you may know.

10. You can remember a lot of information for a short time if you know how to *concentrate well as you listen.* Practice listening to develop your ability to concentrate. You can do this in any language, not just Spanish. Practice on anything that is about five minutes in length so you develop a good idea of how long you will have to really focus on this part of the exam.

11. Make sure you *read the questions well.* You need especially to know the interrogative pronouns. If the question asks, *¿de quién?* you should answer *about whom?...* and not just *who?*

12. *Jot down notes if needed,* but do not wait until you take the actual exam to find out if you do better taking notes or not.

13. *It is not necessary to read the questions before listening* to the selection. In fact, you may lose a portion of the selection by thinking about the questions instead of thinking about what you are hearing. On longer selections it is probably better to focus on remembering what you hear instead of trying to listen for specific information that you want to get out of the selection.

You will find the answers on page 98. When you have finished listening to each selection and answering the questions, check your responses. If you have missed some questions, listen to the selection again. If you have listened to the selection twice and still do not understand some parts of it, check the transcript at the end of this section. Remember that you will hear each longer selection only once on the AP Exam.

The multiple choices are printed on the following pages. The scripts start on page 85.

Now get ready to listen to the disc.

1. Have ready access to the answer sheet on pages 67–68.
2. Turn to the multiple-choice answers on pages 71–85.
3. Begin the disc and follow its instructions.

LONGER NARRATIVES

**NARRATIVA
NÚMERO UNO**

CD 2 TRACK 3

1. ¿Cuándo se inauguró el servicio?
   (A) En el año 1913
   (B) En el año 1917
   (C) En el año 1919
   (D) En el año 1970

2. ¿Qué servía de transporte de materiales para la construcción?
   (A) El Metro.
   (B) Animales.
   (C) Carros.
   (D) Los hombres los llevaron.

3. ¿Dónde tuvo lugar la primera celebración?
   (A) En la estación Rufino Blanco.
   (B) En la estación Alfonso XIII.
   (C) En la estación Cuatro Caminos.
   (D) En la estación el Metro de Madrid.

4. ¿Cuánto tiempo transcurrió en el primer recorrido del Metro?
   (A) Siete minutos y pico.
   (B) Trece minutos.
   (C) Quince.
   (D) Sesenta minutos.

5. ¿Cómo ha cambiado el Metro?
   (A) Ahora más personas desesperadas lo usan.
   (B) Ahora hay músicos que entretienen a los pasajeros en los carros.
   (C) Actualmente es demasiado peligroso para usar.
   (D) Actualmente es usado por una gran variedad de personas.

6. ¿Qué suelen oír los que usan el Metro?
   (A) Un anuncio advirtiéndoles tener prisa.
   (B) Anuncios con sugerencias para la cortesía.
   (C) Anuncios para ayudar a los desesperados que lo usan.
   (D) Anuncios recomendando mayor seguridad y eficiencia.

7. Hoy en día ¿cuántos coches hay en el sistema?
   (A) 155.
   (B) 555.
   (C) 984.
   (D) 6.434.

**NARRATIVA
NÚMERO DOS**

CD 2 TRACK 4

1. ¿Qué tipo de servicio ofrece RENFE?
   (A) RENFE parece ofrecer servicio ferrocarrilero.
   (B) RENFE es una agencia de turismo.
   (C) RENFE ofrece giras por autobús.
   (D) RENFE es una cadena de hoteles.

2. ¿Con qué propósito se está hablando de ciertas líneas en esta selección?
   (A) RENFE quiere volver al pasado recreando viajes del pasado.
   (B) RENFE quiere que más pasajeros viajen en tren.
   (C) RENFE quiere que todos estén más confortables en sus habitaciones.
   (D) RENFE quiere que más personas sepan la historia de España.

3. ¿En qué parte de España se ofrece este servicio principalmente?
   (A) Se está ofreciendo en el sur.
   (B) Las líneas circulan principalmente en el suroeste.
   (C) Las líneas circulan por casi todas las partes de España.
   (D) Se está ofreciendo servicio al oeste de España.

4. ¿Qué hay de nuevo en este servicio?
   (A) Hay más atracciones en las ciudades.
   (B) Los servicios son más lujosos y modernos.
   (C) Rodan películas de vaqueros en estos viajes.
   (D) Los trenes van a nuevos lugares.

5. ¿Cómo es el nuevo servicio del Al-Ándalus?
   (A) En este tren imitan fielmente los grandes trenes del pasado.
   (B) Este tren es moderno pero no muy cómodo.
   (C) Este tren está encantado.
   (D) Este tren es una buena mezcla del presente y el pasado.

6. ¿Por qué se han hecho estos cambios?
   (A) RENFE quiere atraer la industria cinematográfica norteamericana a España.
   (B) Las ciudades quieren disponer de vagones viejos.
   (C) RENFE quiere que todos se diviertan en sus viajes.
   (D) RENFE quiere aumentar la competencia por turistas entre ciudades.

7. ¿Por qué necesitaría un pasajero valor para montarse en el tren que va a las Cuevas de Guadix?
   (A) Ese tren pasa por paisaje muy peligroso.
   (B) Fácilmente puede perderse en las cuevas.
   (C) En esa ruta hay peligro de ataques por bandidos.
   (D) En ese viaje hay una reproducción de un asalto como en el Viejo Oeste estadounidense.

8. ¿Qué tipo de selección parece ser ésta?
   (A) Parece un reportaje para un periódico.
   (B) Parece un anuncio para la radio.
   (C) Parece ser un reportaje para la televisión.
   (D) Parece ser un anuncio de servicio público por RENFE.

**NARRATIVA
NÚMERO TRES**

CD 2 TRACK 5

1. ¿Cuál es el tema de esta selección?
   (A) Noticias de interés nacional.
   (B) El papel de un periódico.
   (C) Un discurso sobre política nacional.
   (D) Una crítica de la prensa.

2. ¿Qué importancia lleva este acontecimiento?
   (A) Revela que los españoles están leyendo más ahora que antes.
   (B) Revela que la prensa ha alcanzado un nuevo nivel de profesionalismo.
   (C) Revela que la monarquía está ligada firmemente con la prensa.
   (D) Revela que este periódico tiene en su poder cambiar la vida nacional española.

3. ¿Cómo se ha transformado España en los últimos treinta años?
   (A) Menos españoles son analfabetos ahora que antes.
   (B) Los españoles aprecian al rey más ahora que antes.
   (C) El gobierno actual permite más libertad de expresión que antes.
   (D) La sociedad española goza de más opciones políticas, sociales, y económicas.

4. ¿Cuál es la misión de *El País*?
   (A) *El País* tiene por misión informar al público de su historia.
   (B) Este periódico sirve los propósitos del rey.
   (C) El diario se esfuerza para estar al tanto de las noticias.
   (D) El periódico necesita servir los intereses de todo el público.

5. ¿Por qué comentó el Rey Juan Carlos las aportaciones del periódico?
   (A) Él sabe que sin la prensa libre no hay una sociedad libre.
   (B) *El País* promovió el fin de la época de Francisco Franco.
   (C) El rey sabe que el apoyo de la prensa es indispensable para su reino.
   (D) Juan Carlos reconoce que la imparcialidad de este diario es notable.

6. ¿A qué coincidencia histórica se refiere en la selección?
   (A) Empezó a publicarse cuando estalló la guerra en el Golfo Pérsico.
   (B) Empezó a publicarse dentro de unos meses de la muerte de Franco.
   (C) Empezó a publicarse cuando el rey empezó su reino.
   (D) Empezó a publicarse hace cinco años.

7. ¿Cómo notó *El País* la ocasión de la venta de cinco mil números?
   (A) El diario publicó una carta de felicitaciones de Franco.
   (B) El diario no publicó ningún número ese día.
   (C) El diario incluyó una sección adicional.
   (D) El diario publicó un extra ese día.

8. ¿A qué asunto se dirige *El País* actualmente?
   (A) Se dedica al repaso del pasado.
   (B) Se decide a presentar nuevas direcciones.
   (C) Se esfuerza por presentar a España en el mundo moderno.
   (D) Presenta las posibilidades del futuro basadas en los hechos históricos.

**NARRATIVA
NÚMERO CUATRO**

CD 2 TRACK 6

1. ¿En qué estación están?
   (A) Están en el último mes del año.
   (B) Están preparando para las Pascuas.
   (C) Están en el año 1847.
   (D) Están en el verano.

2. ¿Qué es *El Indio*?
   (A) *El Indio* es el nombre del propietario de una tienda.
   (B) *El Indio* es apodo del hombre con quien habla el interlocutor.
   (C) *El Indio* es un pequeño taller que elabora cierto tipo de dulce.
   (D) *El Indio* es la marca de un producto que fabrican en la tienda.

3. ¿Quién es el dueño de la tienda donde hablan estas personas?
   (A) La familia de José María.
   (B) José María Pinaqui.
   (C) Francisco Pinaqui.
   (D) La familia Ruiz de Diego.

4. Principalmente, ¿con qué está encargado José María?
   (A) Está encargado de ser guía por la fábrica para mostrársela al público.
   (B) Está encargado de la producción de chocolate en forma artesanal.
   (C) Está encargado de probar el producto al fin del proceso de elaboración.
   (D) Está encargado de vender el producto al público.

5. ¿Cómo empieza y termina el proceso de elaboración en *El Indio*?
   (A) Empiezan con un polvo, el cual luego se calienta para poder trabajarlo.
   (B) Empiezan con el cacao crudo y terminan con el dulce en moldes.
   (C) Empiezan con la masa de chocolate, la cual luego se reparte entre moldes.
   (D) Empiezan con polvo de cacao y terminan con tabletas.

6. ¿Por qué es tan notable este lugar en Madrid?
   (A) Tienen una nueva manera de elaborar el chocolate que es mejor que la vieja.
   (B) Venden tres tipos de chocolate en el mismo lugar donde lo producen.
   (C) Venden chocolate de un pueblo en las montañas donde lo producen a mano.
   (D) Conservan todo el proceso antiguo para producir y vender chocolate.

7. ¿Para qué es una refinadora?
   (A) La refinadora muele y pulveriza la pasta de cacao.
   (B) La refinadora muele el azúcar para poner en la masa.
   (C) Ponen la masa en la refinadora para mantenerla a cierta temperatura.
   (D) Se muele el azúcar en ella para hacerlo más fino para poner en el chocolate.

8. ¿Qué opina José María Pinaqui de lo que hace?
   (A) No le gusta tener que probar el chocolate.
   (B) Se pone melancólico porque ya está muy viejo.
   (C) Se está engordando demasiado porque prueba tanto chocolate.
   (D) Está triste que no haya más personas que quieren aprender el proceso.

9. ¿Qué señal le da al interlocutor de lo que piensa de su trabajo?
   (A) Dice que lo cambiaría si pudiera pero tiene demasiado años para cambiar ahora.
   (B) Dice que no comería tanto chocolate si no le gustara tanto el producto.
   (C) Dice que le gustaría trabajar en otra fábrica si le pagara más.
   (D) Dice que no cambiaría porque por muchos años le ha gustado mucho.

10. ¿Qué pronóstico tiene el interlocutor de esta tradición?
    (A) Parece que esta tradición está para desaparecer por falta de artesanos.
    (B) Se conservará mientras haya una aldea en las montañas.
    (C) Se conservará cincuenta años más en lugares como éste.
    (D) Mientras quiera el público esta confección, habrá chocolaterías como ésta.

**NARRATIVA
NÚMERO CINCO**
CD 2 TRACK 7

1. ¿Por qué es tan famoso Montserrat?
   (A) Hay allí una bella estatua de la Virgen.
   (B) Hay una iglesia allí.
   (C) Hay una ermita allí.
   (D) Napoleón visitó a Montserrat.

2. Históricamente ¿cuándo establecieron el monasterio allí?
   (A) Los primeros monjes establecieron el monasterio a fines del siglo XII.
   (B) Napoleón mandó que lo establecieran en el siglo XIV.
   (C) Los monjes de Ropill vinieron en el siglo XI.
   (D) Después del saqueo por Napoleón construyeron un nuevo monasterio.

3. ¿Por qué establecieron el monasterio allí?
   (A) A Napoleón le gustó el sitio.
   (B) A los monjes de Ropill les gustó el sitio.
   (C) A todos los peregrinos que vinieron les gustó.
   (D) Les gustó el sitio a los que vinieron del centro de Europa.

4. ¿De dónde eran procedentes los peregrinos que vinieron durante los siglos XII a XIV?
   (A) Vinieron de Cataluña.
   (B) Vinieron de Santiago de Compostela.
   (C) Vinieron de Europa.
   (D) Vinieron de Montserrat.

5. ¿Cómo se explica el color de la Virgen?
   (A) Se dice que el escultor la hizo así, porque dice la Biblia que la Virgen era negra.
   (B) Se dice que a causa de una reacción química ella es negra.
   (C) Se dice que el humo de velas por tantos siglos cambió el color.
   (D) Todas las razones indicadas arriba son correctas.

6. Además del monasterio, ¿qué otras funciones realizan los monjes de Montserrat?
   (A) Tienen que explicarles a los visitantes por qué no pueden usar el santuario.
   (B) Tienen que atender a los turistas que vienen para visitar las tiendas.
   (C) Tienen que hacer peregrinaciones recíprocas a otras ermitas.
   (D) Tienen que preocuparse de todo, hasta de los trabajos diarios del lugar.

7. ¿Cuál es el trabajo del grupo encargado del monasterio?
   (A) Mantiene todas las actividades del santuario y el monasterio.
   (B) Pasa mucho tiempo estudiando en el monasterio y dando clases.
   (C) Vende cerámica a los turistas al monasterio, entre otras mercancías.
   (D) Publica música del monasterio para vender a los turistas.

8. ¿Quiénes vienen a Montserrat ahora?
   (A) Principalmente peregrinos en camino a Santiago de Compostela.
   (B) Turistas de todo el mundo, de todas las religiones.
   (C) Monjes de muchos otros monasterios.
   (D) Principalmente peregrinos del centro de Europa.

9. ¿A qué actividad se dedican algunos monjes?
   (A) Algunos se dedican a estudios religiosos.
   (B) Algunos enseñan clases de música en la Escolanía.
   (C) Algunos se dedican a la construcción de nuevos monasterios.
   (D) Algunos están escribiendo historias del lugar.

INTERVIEWS

**ENTREVISTA
NÚMERO UNO**

`CD 2 TRACK 8`

1. ¿Qué ha hecho Ana Belén que están comentando en esta entrevista?
   (A) Ha escrito un libro en el que fue basada una nueva película.
   (B) Acaba de estrenarse como estrella de una nueva película.
   (C) Acaba de dirigir el rodaje de una película de un libro muy popular.
   (D) Acaba de entrevistar a la autora Carmen Rico-Godoy.

2. ¿Qué calificaciones tiene Ana Belén para esta película?
   (A) Ana Belén ha gozado de mucho éxito como actriz y cantante.
   (B) Ana Belén es una crítica de los hombres en el seno de la familia.
   (C) Ana Belén conoce bien a Carmen Rico-Godoy.
   (D) Ana Belén está dispuesta a seguir aprendiendo en su vida.

3. ¿Cuál es el tema de la película?
   (A) Los hombres no saben llevarse bien con las mujeres.
   (B) En las relaciones, ni los hombres ni las mujeres juegan limpio.
   (C) La mujer determinada siempre triunfará.
   (D) Los hombres no se portan bien ni con la esposa ni con la familia.

4. ¿Cómo reaccionaron los actores a los papeles que interpretaron?
  (A) Todos tenían mucha simpatía para con sus personajes.
  (B) Asemejan mucho a los papeles en sus propias vidas.
  (C) Los actores se sentían muy diferentes de los personajes.
  (D) Creían que todos los hombres son estereotipos.

5. ¿Qué nuevas habilidades ha demostrado Ana Belén en esta obra?
  (A) Que es buen intérprete de la escena contemporánea.
  (B) Que es buena actriz.
  (C) Que tiene buen sentido de humor.
  (D) Que puede mandar sin ofender.

6. ¿Qué observaciones de su estilo le han notado sus colegas?
  (A) Dicen que les gusta porque tiene buen sentido de humor.
  (B) Dicen que Ana Belén no sabe mucho de rodar una película.
  (C) Dicen que les trató como si fueran sus hijos.
  (D) Dicen que tenía un combate constante entre todos.

7. ¿Qué comparación hacen los actores en cuanto a lo que hace?
  (A) Dicen que ella sabe menos que otros y no hizo bien.
  (B) Dicen que ella mantiene una actitud abierta hacia el trabajo.
  (C) Dicen que ella era la mejor en cuanto a la técnica de rodar.
  (D) Dicen que es la más honesta de todos con quienes han trabajado.

8. ¿Qué actitud hacia la vida muestra esta señora en esta entrevista?
  (A) Ella está divirtiéndose muchísimo en todo lo que hace.
  (B) Ella parece no poder tomar nada en serio.
  (C) Ella parece no tener mucha confianza en sus habilidades.
  (D) Ella reconoce sus limitaciones técnicas, y no se preocupa de eso.

ENTREVISTA
NÚMERO DOS
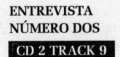

1. ¿Qué teoría, ahora casi certeza, proclama Juanjo Benítez?
  (A) En el futuro los seres humanos viajarán a otros planetas.
  (B) Hay extraterrestres disfrazados como seres humanos que habitan en España.
  (C) La Guardia Civil está controlada por unos humanoides de más allá de las estrellas.
  (D) Hay un ejército de marcianos que planea una invasión de la Tierra.

2. ¿Por qué cree este autor que puede declarar con tanta seguridad esta teoría?
  (A) Ha escrito un libro proclamando la verdad.
  (B) Este autor ha visto los extraterrestres visitando el planeta.
  (C) Ahora tiene testigos que pueden corroborar lo que dice.
  (D) El gobierno ahora reconoce que hay visitantes al planeta.

3. ¿Qué es un OVNI?
  (A) Es un coche de tipo turismo.
  (B) Es un tipo de nave espacial.
  (C) Es un extraterrestre.
  (D) Es un grupo de turistas.

4. ¿Qué tiene la Guardia Civil que hacer con este tema?
   (A) Algunos de la Guardia detuvieron a un grupo de extraterrestres.
   (B) Algunos de la Guardia hablaron con unos españoles que vieron a los tripulantes.
   (C) La Guardia tiene un coche que unos visitantes habían usado.
   (D) La Guardia alega que los seres de un OVNI capturaron a algunos de la Guardia.

5. ¿Dónde tuvo lugar uno de estos descubrimientos?
   (A) Tuvo lugar en varios pueblos alemanes.
   (B) Aparecen solamente en el sur de España.
   (C) En Jerez donde unos de ellos viven.
   (D) Los han visto en caminos y carreteras españoles.

6. En el citado incidente, ¿qué pasó?
   (A) Una nave aérea volaba a altura baja encima de la ciudad de Jerez.
   (B) Un grupo de turistas vieron un plato volador encima de la carretera.
   (C) La Guardia Civil persiguió una nave espacial, la cual se transformó en coche.
   (D) La Guardia Civil vio a un grupo de seres volando por la carretera.

7. ¿Por qué no capturaron ninguna prueba en el citado incidente?
   (A) Estos visitantes tienen poderes extraordinarios para transformarse.
   (B) Los seres se convierten en coches cuando se encuentran con seres humanos.
   (C) Los seres se inscriben en hoteles cuando piensan que alguien está persiguiéndolos.
   (D) La Guardia Civil tiene miedo de estos seres humanoides.

8. Según la historia ¿cómo acabó el episodio?
   (A) El grupo desapareció y no los vio nadie.
   (B) Los del OVNI transformaron a la Guardia Civil en humanoides.
   (C) Los seres embarcaron y salieron inmediatamente.
   (D) Los extraterrestres se mutaron por completo para disimular.

9. ¿Cuál parece ser la actitud del interlocutor hacia el autor?
   (A) Lo toma muy en serio.
   (B) Parece creer todo lo que le dice el experto, Juanjo Benítez.
   (C) Se ríe por lo bajo para no ofenderlo.
   (D) Piensa que sería una posibilidad muy sorprendente.

10. ¿Parece ser Juanjo Benítez una persona muy cuerda?
    (A) Habla como si supiera que muchos no le creyeran.
    (B) Habla como si hubiera sido transformado en humanoide.
    (C) Habla como si hubiera visto con sus propios ojos todo esto.
    (D) Habla como si llevara muchos años creyendo estas historias.

**ENTREVISTA
NÚMERO TRES**
CD 2 TRACK 10

1. ¿Qué pasó con los extraterrestres en el primer episodio?
   - (A) Se transformaron en dos parejas.
   - (B) Se mutaron en otros seres extraterrestres.
   - (C) Salieron en un OVNI que volaba cerca de Jerez.
   - (D) Se transformaron en un gran coche turismo.

2. ¿Qué pidieron a los extraterrestres?
   - (A) Ni hablaron con ellos para pedirles nada.
   - (B) Les pidieron la matrícula.
   - (C) Les pidieron que les acompañaran a la estación.
   - (D) Les pidieron identificación.

3. ¿Por qué hubiera sido buena idea pedirles la identidad?
   - (A) Necesitan datos sobre estos señores para poder localizar sus domicilios.
   - (B) Necesitan hablar con el banquero con quien viven.
   - (C) Para convencer al público sería ideal entrevistarlos.
   - (D) Necesitan saber su dirección en Madrid.

4. ¿De qué principio habla el buen autor?
   - (A) Se sabe que los extraterrestres habitan con un banquero en Madrid.
   - (B) Se sabe que no viven entre seres normales.
   - (C) Se sabe que sólo Dios sabe con qué intención están entre nosotros.
   - (D) No se sabe por qué están, pero nada tiene que ver esto con ningún banquero.

5. Según este señor, ¿para qué sirve el Ejército?
   - (A) El Ejército es para defender al país de las invasiones extraterrestres.
   - (B) Defendería la patria pero no puede revelar los planes.
   - (C) Sirve para guardar todos los datos en secreto.
   - (D) No sirve para nada porque rehusa reconocer los testimonios.

6. ¿Cuál es la actitud de los gobiernos?
   - (A) Los gobiernos quieren saber todo sobre estos fenómenos.
   - (B) Quieren descubrir la verdad de estos episodios.
   - (C) Quieren ocultar estas actividades porque no quieren confesar su impotencia al público.
   - (D) Saben que estas noticias aterrorizarán al público y quieren protegerlo.

7. ¿Qué otro ejemplo tiene el autor de la existencia de los extraterrestres?
   - (A) Dice que un grupo de extraterrestres apareció en el pueblo de Burgos.
   - (B) Dice que un grupo apareció en una viña en Briones.
   - (C) Dice que un grupo de extraterrestres habló con los habitantes de un pueblo remoto.
   - (D) Dice que otro grupo de extraterrestres se apareció a unos terroristas.

8. ¿Dónde tuvo lugar este episodio?
   - (A) En un castillo abandonado en la provincia de León.
   - (B) En una viña en Briones.
   - (C) En un castillo en el pueblo de San Vicente de la Sonsierra.
   - (D) En un proceso de Burgos.

9. ¿Por qué no podría este autor identificar a los ex miembros de ETA?
   (A) Porque otros testigos querrán matarlos.
   (B) Ahora los extraterrestres los buscan para asesinarlos.
   (C) Entre los terroristas es peligroso ser ex miembro del grupo.
   (D) Las autoridades los buscan para encarcelarlos.

10. ¿Qué significa cuando el interlocutor se corrige para decir "historias" en vez de "datos"?
    (A) Indica que cree que todo es pura historia, y así es pura verdad.
    (B) Significa que no cree ni una palabra porque no hay testigos.
    (C) Significa que una historia no corresponde a la verdad necesariamente.
    (D) Quiere decir que todo esto todavía es rumor sin testigo irrefutable.

ENTREVISTA NÚMERO CUATRO

CD 2 TRACK 11

1. ¿Cuál es la profesión del hombre con quien habla el interlocutor?
   (A) Pedro Almodóvar es estrella del cine.
   (B) Pedro Almodóvar es crítico de cine.
   (C) Pedro Almodóvar es director de cine.
   (D) Pedro Almodóvar es novelista.

2. ¿Qué reacción inspiró la película?
   (A) Les gustó mucho a los toreros en la Maestranza.
   (B) El público la recibió bien, pero a los críticos no les gustó.
   (C) A los críticos les gustó tanto como al público.
   (D) Al crítico de *El País* le gustó más.

3. ¿A quién prefiere Pedro Almodóvar satisfacer más?
   (A) A los críticos.
   (B) Al público.
   (C) A los dos igualmente.
   (D) A sí mismo solamente.

4. ¿Qué opina Almodóvar de los críticos?
   (A) Cree que desempeñan un papel muy importante en la industria cinematográfica.
   (B) Con tal que les guste la película, cree que son buenos.
   (C) No cree que merezca la reacción que muchas veces recibe de ellos.
   (D) Con tal que pueda comprenderlos, le gustan.

5. ¿Por qué era diferente la crítica de *El País*?
   (A) A este crítico no le gustó la película.
   (B) El elogio de este crítico era más grande que los otros.
   (C) Esta crítica no apareció al mismo momento que las otras.
   (D) Esta crítica contrastaba con las demás críticas.

6. ¿Cómo reaccionó Almodóvar a esa crítica?
   (A) No le importaba.
   (B) Se enfadó.
   (C) No la leyó.
   (D) Quedó confundido.

7. ¿Cómo define Almodóvar a un buen crítico?
   (A) Debe informar al público sobre todo.
   (B) Debe poder revelar algo que ve, tanto bueno como malo.
   (C) Debe siempre tener razón en lo que dice.
   (D) Debe indicar a la gente qué debe ésta ver.

8. ¿Cómo sabe Almodóvar si ha hecho bien esta película?
   (A) Si la gente sale toreando de las corridas, habrá hecho bien.
   (B) Si la gente sale hablando de la película, la ha hecho bien.
   (C) Si la gente se atreve a hablar de la verdad de las relaciones, fue un éxito.
   (D) Si la gente sale hablando de la guerra, fue un éxito.

9. ¿Qué le interesa más a Almodóvar?
   (A) Ser reconocido por toda la gente.
   (B) El proceso de crear una obra de arte.
   (C) Ser amado de toda la gente.
   (D) Gozar de toda la atención en el momento del estreno.

10. ¿Qué característica de gran hombre le distingue a este señor?
    (A) Tiene más interés en el trabajo que la ganancia del trabajo.
    (B) Le gusta el reconocimiento que le da el público.
    (C) Es un hombre solitario.
    (D) Todavía está abierto a lo que le lleve el momento u ocasión inesperado.

ENTREVISTA NÚMERO CINCO
`CD 2 TRACK 12`

1. ¿Cuál es el propósito del programa "Viajes para las personas mayores"?
   (A) Es para que puedan ir de vacaciones las personas que viven en el centro de España.
   (B) Es para que tengan unas vacaciones personas viejas que nunca han viajado.
   (C) Es para que los que viven en ciudades históricas puedan visitar las costas españolas.
   (D) Es para mejorar la economía de regiones costeñas de España.

2. ¿Qué oportunidad les proporciona este programa a los mayores de edad?
   (A) Ellos pueden saber que su pueblo es el mejor lugar.
   (B) Ellos sabrán que hay otros mundos fuera de sus propios pueblos.
   (C) Ellos tendrán la oportunidad de conocer a otras personas.
   (D) Ellos podrán escapar de su esclavitud económica.

3. ¿Cómo será diferente la vida para estas personas?
   (A) Ellas estarán insatisfechas con la vida rural después de viajar.
   (B) Ellas se sentirán defraudadas por haber pasado la vida en su pueblo.
   (C) Ellas tendrán otro punto de vista después de visitar otros lugares.
   (D) Ellas querrán mudarse a nuevos lugares y explorar nuevos horizontes.

4. ¿Qué calificación se necesita para poder aprovecharse de la oportunidad?
   (A) No hay ningunos requisitos.
   (B) Hay que tener pasaporte.
   (C) Sólo hay que presentarse para hacer reservas.
   (D) Hay que presentar identificación.

5. ¿Adónde van estos mayores?
   (A) Van donde no hace mucho calor.
   (B) Van a lugares donde pueden encontrar muchas ventas especiales.
   (C) Van a lugares donde haya clima cálido.
   (D) Van al campo para descansar.

6. ¿Por cuánto tiempo durará el viaje?
   (A) Durará veinte días
   (B) Durará medio mes.
   (C) Durará dieciséis días.
   (D) Durará diecisiete días.

7. ¿Cuánto costará?
   (A) No costará mucho.
   (B) Costará diecisiete mil pesetas.
   (C) Costara dieciséis mil pesetas.
   (D) Costará quince mil pesetas.

8. ¿Por cuál casualidad hay una póliza de seguro?
   (A) En caso de emergencia médica.
   (B) En caso que se ponga enfermo.
   (C) En caso que alguien muera.
   (D) En caso que se decida volver a casa.

9. ¿Qué tal le parece este programa al interlocutor?
   (A) Le parece increíble que fuera tan caro.
   (B) Le parece que entusiasmará mucho a los televidentes.
   (C) Le parece milagroso que sea tan económico.
   (D) Está seguro de que les gusta a los viejos.

ENTREVISTA NÚMERO SEIS
CD 2 TRACK 13

1. ¿Qué hace Marcos en Nueva York?
   (A) Es farmacéutico.
   (B) Es policía.
   (C) Es psiquiatra.
   (D) Es narcotraficante.

2. Para Marcos, ¿cómo se comparan las dos ciudades?
   (A) Marcos cree que los neoyorquinos son más locos que los sevillanos.
   (B) Le gustan mucho los sevillanos porque le invitan a sus casas.
   (C) Las dos ciudades tienen sus problemas y no son tan diferentes.
   (D) La manera de mostrarse la locura en las dos poblaciones es diferente.

3. ¿Por qué está Marcos en Sevilla?
   (A) Está para asistir a una reunión de psiquiatras.
   (B) Asiste a una competencia de bicicletismo.
   (C) Asiste a una conferencia sobre el abuso de sustancias tóxicas.
   (D) Habla en una conferencia sobre el tema de la salud mental en Nueva York.

4. ¿Cuál es la diferencia entre el problema de las drogas en las dos ciudades?
   (A) Cree que el problema de las drogas en Nueva York es peor que el de Sevilla.
   (B) Cree que el problema en Nueva York está aumentando más que en Sevilla.
   (C) Cree que en Sevilla actualmente se ve un aumento del problema más que en Nueva York.
   (D) Cree que hay tanto problema en Sevilla que en Nueva York.

5. ¿Qué diferencia hay entre el uso de drogas actualmente en Estados Unidos y el de hace veinte años?
   (A) Antes el uso de drogas se asoció con grandes movimientos de población.
   (B) Actualmente el uso no parece estar relacionado con la presión emocional de la vida moderna que existió hace veinte años.
   (C) Antes el uso de drogas se basó en los motivos filosóficos y sociales de esa generación.
   (D) Antes los tipos de drogas eran más nefastos.

6. ¿Qué optativas tienen en Nueva York para resolver el problema?
   (A) Una es el establecimiento de clínicas.
   (B) Una optativa es la encarcelación del adicto.
   (C) Están considerando la despenalización de algunas drogas.
   (D) Están investigando maneras de aliviar la tensión de la vida para los adictos.

7. ¿Por qué no le gusta a Marcos la idea de legalización?
   (A) Opina que los adictos no buscarán la ayuda que necesitan.
   (B) Cree que habrá demasiada demanda para poder satisfacer a todos.
   (C) Teme una epidemia de varias enfermedades asociadas con el uso.
   (D) Si fuera legal, no sabrían cuántos adictos había.

8. ¿Qué propone Marcos para los profesionales que tratan con los adictos?
   (A) Sugiere que los profesionales cambien la manera de considerar el problema.
   (B) Recomienda que la gente se relaje un poco para mantener buena salud mental.
   (C) Propone que los profesionales consideren a los adictos como los enfermos que son.
   (D) Será preciso cambiar la sociedad tan hipercompetitiva a una más tolerante.

9. ¿Cómo debiera ser el tratamiento, según Marcos?
   (A) Cuidadosamente controlado pues de lo contrario el tratamiento matará más de lo que curará.
   (B) Es necesario que el tratamiento se ajuste a las necesidades del drogadicto.
   (C) La generalización del problema es útil para describir casos individuales de drogadicción.
   (D) Hay que adaptar a los drogadictos al tratamiento en vez de lo contrario.

**ENTREVISTA
NÚMERO SIETE**

CD 2 TRACK 14

1. ¿Dónde están estas personas que hablan?
   - (A) Están en North Carolina.
   - (B) Están en la Argentina.
   - (C) Están en Barcelona.
   - (D) Están en Italia.

2. ¿Qué hace la mujer que están entrevistando?
   - (A) Ella es campesina.
   - (B) Ella es dependiente de una tienda.
   - (C) Ella vende flores.
   - (D) Ella vende frutas de su huerto.

3. ¿Cuánto tiempo hace que está en este lugar?
   - (A) Ella está en su puesto hace cien años.
   - (B) Su puesto está en el mismo lugar hace ciento cincuenta años.
   - (C) Ella lleva cincuenta años allí.
   - (D) Hace treinta años que está allí.

4. ¿Por qué le gusta a Carolina lo que hace?
   - (A) Todos los días ella puede hablar con reyes, príncipes y gente muy importante.
   - (B) Le encanta a ella la diversidad de personas con quienes se encuentra.
   - (C) Le gustan los varios tipos de flores.
   - (D) A ella le gusta la tradición de ser dependiente en una tienda.

5. ¿Quiénes compran?
   - (A) Por la mayor parte son jóvenes.
   - (B) Generalmente son personas que llevan muchos años visitándola.
   - (C) Personas que no quieren compran los productos en otras tiendas.
   - (D) Señoras que pasan en la calle en camino a casa del mercado.

6. ¿Cómo son diferentes los clientes que tiene?
   - (A) Los jóvenes no gastan tanto como los viejos.
   - (B) La vieja clientela gasta menos que los jóvenes.
   - (C) Los enamorados gastan más que nadie.
   - (D) Los viejos gastan tanto como los jóvenes.

7. ¿Qué tipo de consejos le da esta señora a su clientela?
   - (A) Aconseja violetas en invierno y rosas en verano.
   - (B) Lo que sugiere depende de la estación.
   - (C) Cuando quieren algo inapropiado, se lo dice.
   - (D) No da consejos a la gente que viene con idea fija.

8. ¿Qué es un ramo de señora?
   - (A) Consiste en violetas en el invierno.
   - (B) Consiste en rosas en verano.
   - (C) Consiste en una mezcla de varios tipos de flores.
   - (D) Consiste en un ramo de flores grande.

9. ¿Cuánto tiempo se dedica a este trabajo?
   (A) Todos los días menos los días de fiesta.
   (B) Todo el tiempo menos los días feriados.
   (C) Solamente se descansa el domingo por la tarde.
   (D) Desde antes de la madrugada hasta el anochecer.

SCRIPTS

NARRATIVA NÚMERO UNO

Vemos el presente e intentamos incluso asomarnos un poco al futuro, pero lo que ahora les proponemos es un viaje al pasado, o un regreso al tiempo en que todo era diferente, aunque estemos sin embargo sobre el mismo escenario. El Metro de Madrid tiene setenta años, y estos datos curiosos nos permiten reconstruir el primer día del Metro de Madrid: diecisiete de octubre de 1919, hace setenta años. A las tres y media de la tarde, en la estación de Cuatro Caminos, el rey Alfonso XIII inauguraba la línea 1 del Metro de Madrid. Fue el acontecimiento del día, naturalmente. Acudieron todos aquellos que eran alguien en el Madrid de entonces. Siete minutos y cincuenta y seis segundos tardó el rey en recorrer todo el trayecto, según el cronómetro del periodista y escritor Rufino Blanco. Han pasado muchos otoños ya de aquella efemérides. Atrás quedó la carreta de bueyes que transportó una noche de julio de 1917 los primeros materiales de construcción para la Compañía Metropolitana de Alfonso XIII. Los madrileños de 1919 pagaron por el primer viaje por los túneles del Metro quince céntimos. Ha pasado mucho tiempo, han pasado setenta años, y el Metro de Madrid, que es el décimo del mundo, por orden de antigüedad, ha dejado de ser un simple medio de transporte. Ahora, como ocurre en todos los metros de las grandes capitales del mundo, se ha convertido en refugio de mendigos, mural de grafistas, escenario musical, centro comercial, alternativa a los atascos, final de desesperados. Los túneles de las diez líneas que actualmente existen son todo un mundo por el que diariamente transita un millón de personas que se conocen de memoria eso de *Antes de entrar, dejen salir* o *Cuidado para no introducir el pie entre coche y andén*. Ciento cincuenta y cinco estaciones repartidas por la ciudad por las que circulan novecientas ochenta y cuatro unidades, o vehículos, en las que trabajan seis mil cuatrocientas treinta y cuatro personas son los datos del Metro de hoy. Setenta años hace ya de la inauguración, del día 17 de octubre de 1919.

NARRATIVA NÚMERO DOS

RENFE: La compañía del ferrocarril español, organiza una serie de servicios turísticos que ayudan a conocer mejor las tierras de nuestro país y que además resultan muy, pero que muy divertidos. Os hablamos del tren Al-Ándalus, del Sureste Exprés, del Tren de la Fresa y de muchas otras líneas con las que se puede visitar el Monasterio de Piedra, la Ciudad Encantada de Cuenca, Toledo, las Murallas de Ávila, y Sigüenza. La oferta de RENFE no finaliza aquí. También hay trenes con los que podemos recorrer al noroeste el Camino de Santiago, el Camino de Soria, o acercarnos hasta la Ciudad Monumental de Cáceres. De todos estos servicios, claramente turísticos, hay que destacar los trenes Al-Ándalus y Sureste Exprés. El recorrido del Al-Ándalus comienza en Sevilla para recorrer después Córdoba, Granada, Málaga y Jerez. Al embrujo de Andalucía, zona que visitamos con el Al-Ándalus, hay que sumar el encanto de este tren, decorado y ambientado como aquellos antiguos ferrocarriles refinados de principios de siglo. Este retroceso en el tiempo no impide el confort: aire acondicionado, sala de juegos, piano bar, videoteca, duchas en los compartimientos, restaurantes con exquisitas comidas. No será difícil imaginar y vivir mil y una historias durante los días en los que dure el trayecto. El Sureste Exprés reproduce un viaje del año 1911, entre Almería y Guadix, en el que no falta, naturalmente, la máquina de vapor. Concursos y música amenizan este viaje que depara a los viajeros otra sorpresa: un asalto al tren por un grupo de cuatreros dignos del Oeste americano (no olvidemos que en Almería se ruedan muchas de las películas de vaqueros). Los datos sobre estos servicios de RENFE se pueden obtener en cualquier oficina de información al viajero de las estaciones. Allí pueden concretaros horarios, precios y dónde comprar los billetes. Una última recomendación: si sois suficientemente valientes para montaros en este tren, visitad las cuevas de Guadix.

NARRATIVA NÚMERO TRES

Y decíamos que un periódico extraordinariamente importante en España, *El País*, había llegado al número cinco mil. El diario *El País* había nacido el día 4 de mayo del año 1976, y el día 28 de diciembre cumplió sus primeros cinco mil números. Un acontecimiento más que periodístico y más que editorial: político y social, diríamos, dado el papel que *El País* ha jugado en estos años en la España que se transformaba a gran velocidad. En el número que recordaba el cumpleaños, el "cinco mil números de libertad", decía el diario *El País*: *Este periódico reitera lo que ya escribía en su primer número, el 4 de mayo del 76. Este periódico ha sido posible porque hay cientos de miles de españoles que piensan que no son de derechas ni de izquierdas o, mejor dicho, que son de derechas y de izquierdas, pero que no optan por expender patentes de patriotismo, ni piensan que la mejor manera de convivir sea la que, desgraciadamente, se nos ha querido enseñar en el pasado: la supresión del adversario.* Esto es lo que decía *El País* el día que nacía y reiteraba el día que cumplía cinco mil números. Ese día, en ese número, el periódico publicaba una carta de felicitación remitida por el Jefe del Estado, el Rey Don Juan Carlos. *No sería justo pasar por alto*—decía el Rey—*el papel desempeñado por la prensa española en la transición política y en la consolidación de la normalidad constitucional. Siempre he estado seguro de que, como Rey, podría contar con* El País, *en cada ocasión en que la historia reciente lo requería: es decir, cotidianamente, en los momentos más graves y en los más livianos. Por cumplirse aquel aniversario de* El País, *saludo y felicito al director, a la redacción y a sus lectores, como saludo también en él a toda la prensa española.* Palabras del Rey en el aniversario de *El País* que, como decimos, nació el 4 de mayo del 76, unos meses después de que falleciera el anterior Jefe del Estado, el general Franco, y se inaugurara un tiempo histórico nuevo en España. Con motivo del número cinco mil, el diario *El País* ofrecía a sus lectores un "Extra" de 64 páginas con un repaso pormenorizado de todos los sectores de la vida española y al mismo tiempo se preguntaba: *¿Qué nos traerá el fin del siglo? Se puede atisbar que una Europa unida, en la que España pondrá fin a siglos de aislamiento exterior y de tenebrismo, está naciendo. Pero, ¿qué ocurrirá en el nuevo milenio?* El diario *El País* se preguntaba esto menos de un mes antes de que estallara el conflicto del Golfo Pérsico.

NARRATIVA NÚMERO CUATRO

En Madrid cuando se está en Navidad hay un lugar particular en donde un aroma extraordinario le espera al cliente. El Indio es probablemente uno de los pocos establecimientos que quedan en España especializados en realizar el chocolate de forma artesanal. Fundado en 1847, los sucesores de aquellos primeros Ruiz de Diego han mantenido a lo largo del tiempo las recetas de sus abuelos. No han sido las recetas lo único que ha perdurado: los utensilios, el mostrador de nogal, los estantes de caoba, las viejas cajas de hojalata donde se guardaba el café y el té llegado de las Américas, incluso el papel con el que se envuelven las tabletas de chocolate—todo ha soportado el paso de los años. Pero si algo ha sobrevivido para dar personalidad y calor a esta tienda cercana a la Gran Vía madrileña, ha sido el molino. Fundido en bronce, y rodeado de cuatro columnas salomónicas de caoba, aún muele el chocolate del que luego saldrán los bombones, las tabletas, o la variedad en polvo para cocinar. José María es el único obrero que tienen en la actualidad Francisco, Asunción, Josefa y María Ruiz de Diego, dueños de la tienda. En esos días tan cercanos a las fiestas de Navidad vale visitar la tienda para saborear un poquito los aromas que envuelven a José María Pinaqui justo en el momento en que va preparando una receta de la casa.

El chocolate se elabora en el establecimiento de la forma siguiente. Primeramente, se tuesta el cacao, que viene crudo. El cacao asemeja una almendra que viene de África o las Américas. Luego, una vez que está tostado, se limpian las semillas, y entonces hay que quitarles las cascarillas. Una vez que está eso limpio y está triturado, el cacao pasa de ahí al molino, que es el que lo muele. Entonces se mezcla con el azúcar, cereal o harina, en fin, la fórmula que lleve uno, y se hace una pasta, o sea, una masa.

Una vez que está hecha la masa hay que meterla a cierta temperatura en unos moldes. Esos moldes pasan luego después a un frigorífico, una cámara, y una vez que se enfrían, se envuelven, y se venden o se despachan.

En El Indio hay tres tipos o clases de chocolate producidos de esa manera tradicional. Uno que se hace polvo y dos que se cuecen para hacerlos, pero hay que espesarlos. En estos dos últimos hay uno que se espesa un poco y hay otro que se espesa menos. Cualquiera de éstos últimos dos se puede comer hecho o crudo.

Lo único de este establecimiento tan venerado en Madrid es que es el último en hacer chocolate de manera artesanal. En algunas aldeas de España hay otros lugares en que se dedican a hacer el chocolate artesanal para sus ciudadanos. No lo hacen para vender ni nada de eso, sino realmente es para las familias o para los mismos del pueblo que se lo reparten.

La maquinaria del establecimiento llama la atención por ser tan vieja. Para hacer el chocolate de la antigua manera se usan máquinas como la refinadora, las cuales en muchos casos son originales. La refinadora es para refinar. El cacao sale tan grueso al hacerse la pasta en el molino que se puede masticar. Para que sea más fino, se usa la refinadora para hacerlo polvo.

José María Pinaqui, como el establecimiento, lleva muchos años preparando el chocolate que tanto les gusta a los madrileños. Nunca ha pensado José María trabajar en otro sitio ni en otro tipo de fábrica de chocolate porque hay tantas ventajas del empleo. La más atractiva para él es que él prueba el chocolate todos los días. Por eso le ha gustado tanto seguir trabajando en ese lugar. Pero se pone melancólico al reflexionar que algún día va a desaparecer la antigua tradición del chocolate de elaboración casera.

NARRATIVA NÚMERO CINCO

El monasterio de Montserrat, cerca de Barcelona, es reconocido por todo el mundo por contener la Virgen Negra, "La Moreneta". La historia del monasterio posado en las alturas de las montañas es muy interesante. De hecho, el monasterio tuvo origen en el siglo XI, época en que se construyeron muchos otros monasterios que estaban también en lugares y sitios bonitos. En el caso del monasterio de Montserrat se escogió un sitio realmente fascinante. En realidad, no es que fuese escogido, sino que en el siglo XI, tres o cuatro monjes de un monasterio muy famoso en Cataluña, llamado Ropill, vinieron a Montserrat porque aquí había unas ermitas pequeñas que estaban en un terreno que dependía de ellos. Entonces empezó el monasterio allí en el siglo XI.

En seguida la comunidad fue creciendo. En el monasterio, a fines del XII, les monjes construyeron una nueva iglesia que duraría unos cuatro siglos. Para decir algún hito importante, a partir del siglo XII hasta XIV, empezaron bastantes peregrinaciones, muchas del centro de Europa, camino de Santiago. Otro hito importante pero triste fue que se destruyó prácticamente por completo el monasterio a principios del siglo XIV, con la guerra de Napoleón. Todo quedó muy saqueado.

Mucha de la fama del lugar se debe a la imagen de la Virgen tan venerada en Cataluña y todo el mundo. La leyenda cuenta que fue encontrada en una cueva a unos veinte minutos o veinticinco minutos del monasterio. Es una imagen románica de fines del siglo XII, o principios del XIII, que siempre ha estado venerándose en el santuario de Montserrat. Algunos visitantes preguntan a veces por qué es negra, porque popularmente se la llama "Moreneta", "Morenita" o "Morena". No se sabe exactamente la razón. Una de las explicaciones es por el humo a lo largo de los siglos, o a veces dicen que también fue por una reacción química de los barnices que ponían. Esto es posible. Hay algunos que creen que quizás el escultor que la realizó quizás la hizo negra, o un poco oscura, pensando en un texto bíblico del *Cantar de los Cantares*. En ese texto la protagonista, una mujer, dice que ella es morena pero hermosa. Este texto se ha aplicado a veces a la Virgen. Entonces, hay otros que dicen quizás algún autor o algún escultor hizo ya negra esta imagen pensando en este texto bíblico.

El trabajo de la comunidad es muy variado. Un trabajo muy principal es estar al servicio del santuario. Montserrat es, como se ha dicho, por un lado un monasterio, pero por otro también un santuario. Es decir que es un sitio adonde va mucha gente, no solamente del país, sino también de fuera. Y hay que atenderles, no solamente para las cuestiones de culto, sino también charlas, retiros, sacramentos, o bodas, por ejemplo. Entonces los monjes han reunido esos trabajos. Otro trabajo sería manual: cerámica o imprenta. También hay un trabajo más cultural, que es la editorial de publicaciones que tienen. Consiste en la impresión de revistas o libros que van editando los monjes. También hay algunos monjes que se dedican más al estudio ya a un nivel más alto: estudios bíblicos o teológicos o de historia, por ejemplo. No se puede olvidar también el trabajo al servicio de la Escolanía, como por ejemplo, las clases de música. Y también los trabajos cotidianos de la casa que también les ocupan a los padres cierto tiempo.

El monasterio de Montserrat es una parte fundamental en la historia de Cataluña. No solamente por la historia que encarna, sino por el descanso espiritual que imparte a los viajeros que pasan por sus puertas. La contemplación de la imagen de la Morenita, el coro de monjes en la misa y la belleza del lugar consuelan al viajero en busca de un momento de paz. Bien vale visitar Montserrat cuando uno esté cerca.

ENTREVISTA NÚMERO UNO

NAR 1: Hablamos ahora de una película que se convierte en noticia porque su directora es la mujer más famosa de España—pero no como directora, sino como actriz y como cantante. Ana Belén acaba de rodar para la pantalla del cine un libro de Carmen Rico-Godoy, titulado *Cómo ser mujer y no morir en el intento*, que constituye una crítica mordaz a los comportamientos de los hombres en el seno de la pareja y en el seno de la familia. Carmen Rico-Godoy se preguntaba: *¿Cómo ser mujer y no morir en el intento?* No parece demasiado fácil la respuesta. ¿La ha adivinado Ana Belén? ¿Sabe cómo ser mujer y no morir en el intento?

NAR 2: Pues, no lo sé muy bien, pero me parece que la vida diaria, por lo menos hace que aprendamos a serlo, ¿eh?

NAR 1: Sí. ¿Va a haber que ver la película como una especie de lectura panorámica del comportamiento de *los* hombres y del comportamiento de *las* mujeres? ¿O no? ¿O una historia de unos hombres y unas mujeres, sin más?

NAR 2: Yo creo que es una historia de—y además está contada en primera persona—de una determinada mujer. Es decir, de una mujer con una vida determinada, con un trabajo determinado y con una vida en pareja muy determinada. Lo que sí ocurre es que esta mujer nos cuenta unas situaciones por las que, de alguna manera, todos hemos pasado, en mayor o menor medida, porque incluso cuando Carmen y Antonio Resines y yo estábamos trabajando en el guión, el guión y tal, las primeras secuencias y tal, y un poco aclarando, ¿no? los personajes. Y fue muy gracioso, porque de repente dice Carmen: *¡Ay, no tiene nada que ver conmigo esta mujer!* Y yo le dije; *Conmigo, tampoco.* Y decía Resines: *Pues, anda, que el hombre conmigo, nada. Porque yo soy como todo lo contrario y ta, ta, ta.* Y sin embargo, muchas de las situaciones que retrataba, pues, nos eran conocidísimas.

NAR 1: Por un lado la película y la inevitable lectura desde la perspectiva hombre-mujer, una especie de combate perpetuo, pero por otro lado el debut de usted como directora de cine. ¿Cómo te has encontrado? Leemos esta mañana en una revista que acaba de salir a los quioscos, lo que dice Carmen de ti. Dice que está encantada contigo, que no te pareces a otros directores con los que ha trabajado, que le has dado muchas sorpresas. Por ejemplo, una capacidad de mando clarísima, mucha seguridad. Te has tomado las cosas con un enorme sentido del humor, se ha dicho. Y que las posibles carencias de conocimiento técnico te las tomabas con mucho humor. Cuando necesitabas ayuda la pedías, en vez de disimular, y dice: *Tampoco sabía yo...*—dice Carmen en el artículo, —*que Ana era tan tierna y tan cariñosa.* Bonito, ¿no?

NAR 2: Precioso. Sí, sí. Y además me gusta mucho que lo diga Carmen.

NAR 1: Claro.

NAR 2: Sí.

NAR 1: La mejor actriz de Europa, dicen.

NAR 2: Sí, y además, eh, sí, me gusta mucho, porque, hombre, siempre son como hijos. Ah, tengo un poco la sensación como de que todos han sido mis hijos y los he querido muchísimo durante el rodaje, muchísimo. Sé que ha habido una parte, como la parte buena que todos tenemos, que se ha potenciado mucho con el rodaje y ha ido en ese sentido estupendamente todo.

NAR 1: ¿Y cómo te has encontrado tú como directora de cine, Ana, después de estar tanto tiempo al otro lado de las cámaras, viéndote así...?

NAR 2: Pues, hombre, lo que dice Carmen es verdad. Yo, como no he intentado engañarme a la hora de hacer y de afrontar este trabajo, nunca dije: *Pues sí, lo podría hacer.* Dije: *Igual puedo hacerlo.* Hice, con miles de dudas, ¿no? lo afronté, y desde luego, sabiendo que carecía de unos conocimientos de los que todavía sigo careciendo y que si sigo trabajando en esta parte del cine, pues no sé, pues iré paliándolos, iré aprendiendo, y tal, porque—y además, creo que no se acaba nunca de aprender esto, ¿no?

ENTREVISTA NÚMERO DOS

NAR 1: Juanjo Benítez es el autor de los más importantes *best-sellers* de España y va a lograrlo también en esta ocasión, con su nuevo libro *La quinta columna*. Asegura Juanjo Benítez que en nuestro planeta conviven con nosotros personajes que han llegado de más allá de las estrellas, que se han disfrazado de humanos y que, confundidos con nosotros, viven entre nosotros. Inquietante tesis, ¿verdad? ¿Existen habitantes de otros planetas, y además viven entre nosotros?

NAR 2: Pues, ése es el "descubrimiento", entre comillas, que hemos hecho en los tres, cuatro, cinco últimos años. Que lo teníamos un poco como teoría, pero que ahora casi es una certeza. Tienen algunas civilizaciones, por lo que observan los testigos—por ejemplo, lo que ocurrió el año pasado a finales, en Conil, en Cádiz—la capacidad técnica, suponemos, de mutar o de transformar su aspecto original, que generalmente no es exactamente humano, en seres completamente normales e infiltrarse en la sociedad, pero tan tranquilos. Nosotros pudimos seguir el rastro de una pareja que se inscribió en un hotel, incluso con un nombre alemán, un hombre y una mujer alemanes.

NAR 1: ¿Podrías contarnos alguna de estas historias que, mejor que cualquier teoría, nos van a permitir entender lo que nos aguarda en este libro?

NAR 2: Bueno, hay otros casos anteriores, incluso protagonizados por la Guardia Civil, en que no solamente las personas, o los tripulantes o los humanoides, se mutan o se transforman en cuestión de segundos, casi instantáneamente, sino las propias naves. Es decir, hay un caso de un ovni posado en la carretera que es perseguido por la Guardia Civil, e instantáneamente se transforma, ante la visión de estos señores, en un coche tipo turismo, gran turismo, con tres personas dentro, absolutamente normales.

NAR 1: ¿Eso lo ha visto la Guardia Civil? ¿Figura en los informes de la Guardia Civil?

NAR 2: Sí, sí, sí. Exactamente.

NAR 1: ¿Habéis tenido vosotros los informes de la Guardia Civil que hablaban de este hecho?

NAR 2: Claro. Naturalmente. Y los testimonios directos de los propios testigos, de los propios guardias.

NAR 1: ¿Donde ha ocurrido esto?

NAR 2: Esto, en Jerez.

NAR 1: ¿Hace mucho?

NAR 2: No, hace escasamente cuatro o cinco años.

NAR 1: Entonces, ¿qué ocurrió? ¿La Guardia Civil localizó un objeto?

NAR 2: Un objeto que estaba volando en las proximidades de Jerez, a baja altura. Empezaron a perseguirlo porque evidentemente vieron que era una cosa muy extraña, en silencio, como casi todos los ovnis. Y de repente se posó en la carretera, en una carretera comarcal. La Guardia Civil se quedó a muy corta distancia, mirando, asombrada. Y de repente desapareció el objeto, y en su lugar, exactamente, apareció un gran coche. Se aproximó la Guardia Civil, y entonces, encontraron a dos hombres y una mujer bellísima; y los dos señores de una edad mediana, perfectamente trajeados, pulcramente vestidos. Y estos hombres, en castellano total, con acento de ningún tipo, les preguntaron a la Guardia Civil por dónde se iba a la Carretera Nacional IV. Bueno, la experiencia es bastante más larga, pero...

NAR 1: Pues, gracias por estas noticias tan asombrosas.

ENTREVISTA NÚMERO TRES

NAR 1: Estamos hablando con el autor renombrado como experto en todo tipo de experiencias con los ovnis. Nos ha contado una experiencia de la Guardia Civil en la que un ovni que volaba cerca de Jerez se transformó en gran coche turismo y los extraterrestres en dos hombres y una mujer bellísima. Señor,

¿Se quedó la Guardia Civil con los nombres y los apellidos de los turistas? ¿Les pidió la documentación, por ejemplo?

NAR 2: No, no, no, no.

NAR 1: ¿No?

NAR 2: La matrícula.

NAR.1: Por lo tanto, fue un fallo, porque si hubiera pedido la identidad, a lo mejor podríamos ahora averiguar dónde están esos señores, si habitan entre nosotros o no.

NAR 2: Por supuesto. Lo que pasa es que la Guardia Civil estaba sencillamente aterrorizada.

NAR 1: Aterrorizada. Y se quedó con la matrícula. ¿La matrícula se investigó? Correspondía...

NAR 2: Sí,

NAR 1: ...¿a qué correspondía?

NAR 2: Sí, correspondía a un banquero de Madrid, que no tiene nada que ver con el asunto.

NAR 1: Absolutamente nada que ver.

NAR 2: En, en principio.

NAR 1: Ya. "En principio." Ese "en principio", ¿qué quiere decir, señor?

NAR 2: Pues, que uno ya no sabe qué pensar. Porque si realmente estos casos son reales, y pensamos que lo son, significaría que desde Dios sabe cuándo se pueden estar infiltrando en la sociedad humana, en todos los testamentos, esta serie de civilizaciones no humanas, con objetivos que, la verdad, desconocemos.

NAR 1: Varias veces nos hemos aproximado a este tema y siempre nos ha sorprendido ese extremo. Cuando hablamos de estas cosas como de algo fantasioso, absurdo, ¿por qué se juega con tanto secreto con estos documentos oficiales, que nos consta que los tiene el Ejército, etcétera? ¿Por qué no se difunden abiertamente?

NAR 2: Probablemente porque afecta la defensa nacional de todos los países y porque llevan muchos años ocultando este asunto y porque no tienen argumentos para responderle al contribuyente para qué sirven los sistemas de defensa de cualquier país ante treinta, veinte o cincuenta violaciones anuales del espacio aéreo.

NAR 1: Historias, desde luego, impresionantes. Decías, entonces, que estos habitantes de otros planetas están aquí, habitan entre nosotros. Y además, aunque no tienen nuestra forma, se transmutan, se convierten en algo parecido a lo que somos nosotros. Cuéntanos algún, algún otro hecho, de los veinte que se recogen en tu libro, que nos acerque a otro aspecto de este asunto.

NAR 2: Bueno, hay uno sorprendente que a mí me dejó pasmado. Y es que yo nunca pude imaginar que los terroristas pudieran cambiar el salto y el giro de sus ideales después de haber visto tripulantes de ovnis. Esto es lo que ha ocurrido con dos comandos de ETA-militar, o con, digamos, una serie de miembros de esta banda terrorista.

NAR 1: ¿Qué pasó?

NAR 2: Eh, el primer caso, en la Rioja, en un pueblecito que se llama San Vicente de la Sonsierra. Un ex miembro de ETA, que había participado en el proceso de Burgos y toda aquella época histórica, tuvo un encuentro en el castillo de este maravilloso pueblo, a las dos de la madrugada, con tres seres enormes que estaban a unos ocho o diez metros, que no le hablaron, que no le dijeron absolutamente nada. Pero este hombre decía que ese silencio y los tres pares de ojos grandes y rojos como semáforos, que parpadeaban simultáneamente—cosa increíble—le provocaron tal pánico que salió corriendo del lugar. Perdió incluso la dirección, se fue hacia Briones. Se refugió hasta el amanecer en una viña. Y a partir de ese momento, cambió completamente el rumbo de sus ideas, porque se dio cuenta de que había alguna cosa más de lo que realmente llevaban entre manos. Y el segundo caso, en las montañas de León. Ya un grupo más numeroso también vio a un ser que empezó a formarse por la cabeza y que, de acuerdo con la disposición, me decían, mental, que teníamos entre nos-

otros de aceptación o no, iba terminando de formarse.

NAR 1: Y estos datos, quiero decir, estas historias, nos las cuentas en el libro, con la aportación de los testimonios, los datos, los nombres y los apellidos de los ciudadanos que las vivieron.

NAR 2: Sí, salvo en los casos de los ex miembros de ETA, que, por razones obvias no he podido dar los nombres, sí.

NAR 1: Muchísimas gracias.

ENTREVISTA NÚMERO CUATRO

NAR 1: A veces nos preguntamos qué pensará un director como Pedro Almodóvar, al estrenar una película. Y aquí estamos entrevistándolo. ¿Cómo estás, Pedro?

NAR 2: Pues, bien.

NAR 1: Bien, estás bien.

NAR 2: Sí, sí, muy contento.

NAR 1: Estás contento.

NAR 2: Sí.

NAR 1: ¿Has leído todas las críticas de la película *Átame*?

NAR 2: No, no todas, no creo que las haya leído todas, porque salen en todos los sitios, continuamente. Pero vamos, he leído bastantes, y sobre todo también, bueno, en estos tres días la película en Madrid sólo ha hecho ya cuatro millones, lo cual significa que están aforrando los cines, y eso es muy interesante.

NAR 1: Eso es muy importante. ¿Te importa más que la crítica? Aunque me imagino que te impresionará mucho, también, como creador, saber cómo está siendo visto tu trabajo, ¿no?

NAR 2: Sabes, impresiona mucho la letra impresa, yo le tengo mucho respeto a la letra impresa. Pero yo trato de pensar en el crítico como un individuo que escribe y también trato de pensar en el espectador como un individuo que va a ver la película y que también se manifiesta de otros modos. Entonces, no le doy más importancia a uno que a otro. La verdad es que, una vez estrenada la película, me interesa muchísimo más la respuesta del público, pero, sin embargo, un crítico puede herirte y muchísimo más que diez mil personas en un patio de butacas.

NAR 1: Comentábamos a la mañana siguiente del estreno que—salieron las críticas además a gran velocidad, a veces suelen hacerse esperar, pero éstas salieron todas juntas—que había habido una cierta reserva en el elogio por parte de un crítico de *El País*, y después un elogio enorme por parte de todos los demás.

NAR 2: Sí, no, yo creo que, yo leí cinco al día siguiente y cuatro eran excelentes y la de *El País* era muy mala, no era, no era una, jm, una crítica...

NAR 1: Muy mala, muy mala te pareció.

NAR 2: Sí, muy mala, pero bueno...

NAR 1: Sí, sí.

NAR 2: A mí me parece muy mala, no sólo porque dijera que era muy mala la película, sino porque yo no acababa de entenderla. Quiero decir, a mí las críticas malas siempre me informan de muchas cosas que están dentro también de la película, aunque el crítico pueda o no tener razón, pero sí que te dan una gran información sobre cómo se puede ver tu película... y la de ese crítico...

NAR 1: No entendiste la de él.

NAR 2: No. No. No, no. No sé qué película vio él.

NAR 1: Hay una cosa bastante clara. Dicen que de las grandes corridas en la Maestranza salía la gente toreando con el abrigo y de las películas de Pedro Almodóvar sale la gente, salimos, hablando de cosas que nunca solemos comentar los aficionados de infantería; determinados planos, determinadas escenas, determinadas iluminaciones.

NAR 2: Y también sale la gente hablando de sí misma, de cosas que no se atreven a hablar en otros momentos.

NAR 1: Eso también es verdad.

NAR 2: Sí, porque el día del estreno, incluso, que es un día básicamente muy vano, pero a mí lo que más me emocionó en la fiesta, y en todo lo demás, es que la gente se reconocía esa necesidad de ser amado y en esa gran aventura que signi-

fica el conocimiento de otra persona y, lo doloroso que a veces resulta conseguir de que otra persona te conozca. Y son cosas que yo creo que nos afectan a todos, y que normalmente no hablamos de ellas, no hablamos de ellas.

NAR 1: ¿No te cansas de discutir el proceso? Hay que andar explicando lo que emocionó hace mucho, ¿no?

NAR 2: Sí, la parte más importante, la parte en la que me va la vida es el momento del rodaje, básicamente. Aunque la escritura del guión también es esencial, y ésa, lo que pasa es que ésa es una aventura solitaria, mucho menos agradecida que, más abstracta que el rodaje, porque el rodaje todo es objetivo, todo está lleno de vida, todo explota ante tus ojos, incluso explota en una dirección que a lo mejor no es la que tú preveías, pero es una gran, gran aventura. Es como adentrarte en una selva y que no sabes lo que va a ocurrir al final. Entonces, para mí, la principal emoción la recibo en mi contacto con el equipo, que es cuando empiezas a ver que todo aquello que tú has soñado empieza a tener vida y empieza a crecer delante de tus ojos.

ENTREVISTA NÚMERO CINCO

NAR 1: Seguramente las personas mayores en España, por circunstancias históricas y las debilidades económicas de este país no han podido desplazarse mucho, ni siquiera por España. Durante generaciones ha sido mucho más frecuente que alguien naciera, creciera y muriera en su propio terruño o poco más. La iniciativa "Viajes para las personas mayores"— viajes para la tercera edad—adquiría en España un verdadero carácter sociológico, ¿verdad?

NAR 2: Claro, ésa es una de las virtualidades. El programa tiene muchas cosas interesantes, muchas cosas bonitas, pero una de ellas es ésa que usted dice, que hay personas, en un buen número, que es la primera vez, por ejemplo, que ven el mar, es la primera vez que conocen otras regiones. Se abre su horizonte, se abre su mente. Ellos creían que el centro del mundo era su pueblo, la esclavitud de su trabajo diario, nunca haber disfrutado de unas vacaciones. Y con este programa tienen esa oportunidad.

NAR 1: Otra cosa. Conocer gente. Porque no cabe duda que uno de los problemas de las personas mayores puede ser el de encerrarse mucho en su propio mundo, ¿verdad? En los viajes me imagino que se harán muchos amigos, ¿no?

NAR 2: Sí, efectivamente. Por eso yo creo que se podría sintetizar la riqueza del programa en relación con las personas que participan en él, en una frase siguiente: les da calidad de vida. Y eso es muy amplio. Les da calidad de vida porque su cultura se agranda, conocen otras personas, observan otros comportamientos, otros enfoques, otras actitudes ante la vida. Y seguro que, aparte de haber disfrutado, como cualquier ser normal, de lo que es ver parajes nuevos, ciudades nuevas, edificios nuevos, el mar, que algunos no lo han visto nunca, cuando vuelven a su pueblo de estas vacaciones—no digo todo el mundo, pero un porcentaje importante de la población que disfruta de estas vacaciones—vuelven renovados, vuelven viendo el mundo de otra manera, y vuelven con unas ideas distintas de, tal vez, aquéllas que tenían cuando se fueron de viaje.

NAR 1: Sí, vamos con los detalles. ¿Quiénes pueden ir?

NAR 2: Sí, los requisitos son sencillísimos: ser persona mayor de sesenta y cinco años, o ser pensionista, o ser una persona que esté unida a uno de esas dos características, la esposa o la compañera de esa persona. No hay más requisitos. Y presentarse en la agencia que está comercializando el viaje, que están repartidas por todo el país—un montón, treinta o cuarenta agencias—pero con puntos de venta del orden de los cuatrocientos o cuatrocientos y pico. Y no se exige ningún papel. Es sencillamente presentarse allí, hacer la reserva para su viaje. Allí

le explican y le cuentan: Pues mire usted, puede ir a estos sitios, que los sitios están en toda la costa de la Península, desde Cataluña hasta Huelva—porque es la zona más habitual de clima bueno, de clima cálido, que para las personas mayores eso es más agradable que no enfrentarse a zonas más duras, de temperaturas más bajas—o Mallorca, Baleares, Mallorca e Ibiza. Este año como experiencia primera. Y sencillamente eso, hacer el abono de su reserva de plaza, que es el veinte por ciento del costo, que el costo es diecisiete mil quinientas pesetas para cualquier persona de todo el ámbito del estado que quiera ir a la costa peninsular.

NAR 1: ¿Cuántos días?

NAR 2: Diecisiete mil, quince días.

NAR 1: Quince días.

NAR 2: Con todo incluido. Pensión, el viaje de ida y vuelta, a veces en avión, a veces en tren, a veces en autobús, todas esas cosas con los requisitos que decía.

NAR 1: Es muy barato eso.

NAR 2: Claro, muy barato.

NAR 1: Un precio muy económico.

NAR 2: Todo eso, le digo, que con los requisitos que desde el Ministerio de Asuntos Sociales exigimos para que haya garantía de que las cosas se hagan, se hagan bien y que ellos vayan confortablemente.

NAR 1: Ese precio que ha dicho usted, diecisiete mil pesetas, los quince días, ¿qué incluye exactamente?

NAR 2: Pues, incluye el transporte de ida y vuelta, como le decía, y estancia allí en régimen de pensión completa, es decir, alojamiento. En todos los hoteles hay un servicio médico, póliza de seguro contra determinadas contingencias que pueden ocurrir, como es el caso de fallecimiento o cualquier otro percance que pueda ocurrir. La póliza de seguro afronta después los gastos que se deriven de eso para la persona que, familiar, que tuviese que ir, porque se haya producido eso, que ojalá que no se produzca, pero que ocurre, ¿no?

NAR 1: Buen programa para los mayores de edad. Diecisiete mil quinientas pesetas, quince días. Gracias.

NAR 2: Ha sido un placer.

ENTREVISTA NÚMERO SEIS

NAR 1: Nos vamos a Sevilla, donde nos espera un psiquiatra eminente, que lleva un cargo de mucha responsabilidad en la ciudad de Nueva York y que viene a Sevilla para participar en este ciclo "Sevilla y la droga", del cual están saliendo algunos asuntos bien importantes en las últimas semanas, un ciclo organizado por el Pardio Andalucista. Doctor Marcos, muy buenos días.

NAR 2: Muy buenos días.

NAR 1: Me imagino que contento en casa, ¿no?

NAR 2: Pues sí, la realidad es que estoy muy contento en esta Sevilla tan maravillosa.

NAR 1: ¿Se adapta usted un poco o aún tiene la mente llena de Nueva York?

NAR 2: Bueno, realmente yo sólo llegué de ayer, luego todavía sigo con la mente llena de Nueva York.

NAR 1: Deben ser dos concepciones de la vida tan radicalmente diferentes que seguramente un loco neoyorquino es difícilmente imaginable para un loco sevillano, ¿no?

NAR 2: Pues sí, realmente son locuras diferentes, las dos interesantes.

NAR 1: Hablamos de la droga. ¿Usted cree que va a más, está detenido, formó parte de la moda de un tiempo atrás, o ya ha quedado instalado en nuestra sociedad para siempre el consumo de las drogas?

NAR 2: Bueno, yo creo que la droga siempre ha estado con nosotros y siempre estará porque básicamente el ser humano tiende a huir del dolor y le apetece el placer. La situación de la droga en Nueva York, por ejemplo, parece ser que desde hace aproximadamente un año se está manteniendo al nivel en que estaba, no parece que esté aumentando. Por lo que a mí me han dicho en España y, concretamente en Sevilla, parece ser que el problema de la droga es un problema en evolución.

NAR 1: Aumentando. Decíamos que hace algún tiempo, hace veinte años, por ejemplo, lo del consumo de las drogas se asoció torpemente a determinadas banderas de modernidad, diciéndose que está relacionado con el *Rock and Roll,* los movimientos de libertad sexual, etcétera, ¿no? Un prendido verdaderamente nefasto, ¿no?

NAR 2: Sí. Así es, así es. Hace veinte años, pues sí, sobre todo la marihuana, las anfetaminas, se asociaban a esos movimientos antibélicos o movimientos pacifistas, sobre todo en los Estados Unidos. Pero hoy hemos visto que sobre todo las drogas puras como la heroína, la cocaína, en la forma del *crack,* por ejemplo, son drogas que realmente no están relacionadas con ningún movimiento filosófico o político.

NAR 1: Sino tal vez con mecanismos de defensa en una sociedad muy difícil, para huir de la realidad.

NAR 2: Exactamente. Son mecanismos de fácil acceso para huir de una realidad que es básicamente dolorosa.

NAR 1: Aquí hay bastante tensión en puntos de vista discrepantes en relación con, por ejemplo, despenalización de la droga blanda, permiso o no de consumo o persecución del propio consumo, libertad de venta de la droga en las farmacias. De todo se ha dicho, incluso en ese ciclo. ¿Qué opinión tiene usted sobre estas cosas?

NAR 2: Mi opinión, que es opinión personal pero también es la opinión, en este momento de Sanidad Pública en la ciudad de Nueva York y en los Estados Unidos en general, es que la despenalización de la droga es un error. Básicamente por dos razones: una, es que el consumo de la droga se dispararía en el caso en que la droga no fuera ilegal. La droga sería mucho más barata y mejor. Segundo, es que las consecuencias para la sanidad pública serían devastadoras. Hoy día, como sabes, los problemas como el SIDA, que están tan unidos a la droga, forman ya una epidemia de un costo no solamente económico, sino de un costo al sufrimiento humano.

NAR 1: ¿Cómo se cura a un drogadicto? ¿Están resultando eficaces las acciones que ustedes tienen en marcha, ahora mismo, para curar a los drogadictos? ¿O es imposible mientras la sociedad sea tan hipercompetitiva, tan hostil para la vida de muchos hombres?

NAR 2: Bueno, yo creo que para empezar, hay que considerar el problema de la droga como una enfermedad crónica. La idea de que un mes en un sanatorio, o tres meses en una granja van a solucionar el problema—esa idea no es ni realista ni es posible. Una vez que consideramos la drogadicción como una enfermedad crónica, digamos, como la esquizofrenia, como la diabetes—enfermedades que duran prácticamente toda la vida o por lo menos muchos años—entonces, ya nuestras expectativas empiezan a ser más razonables. En segundo lugar, es importante no adaptar el enfermo al tratamiento, no decir bueno, todos los drogadictos van a ir a una granja o todos van a recibir metedona. No, hay que adaptar el tratamiento al drogadicto. Los drogadictos, los que sufren de adicción a las drogas, son diferentes, no se puede generalizar de que todos tienen el mismo problema. Entonces, es fundamental analizar cada caso individualmente y adaptar un plan de tratamiento a cada caso.

ENTREVISTA NÚMERO SIETE

NAR 1: Hoy estamos en la Rambla barcelonesa y vamos a hablar con una florista de siempre, de toda la vida, aquí, en estos perennes puestos que hacen que la Rambla tome su nombre y se convierta en Rambla de las Flores. Sitio típico.

NAR 1: Hola, buenos días, Carolina.

NAR 2: Hola, buenos días.

NAR 1: A ver, ¿qué fue primero? ¿La Rambla o los puestos de flores?

NAR 2: Bueno, la Rambla antes era una ría, hace más de ciento cincuenta años. Hace ciento cincuenta y siete que hay puestos de flores. Antiguamente se dedicaban a vender los campesinos que venían a traer las flores que cultivaban en su campo, en su huerto y tal. Después fueron poniendo una especie como de paradas, primero de hierro, después de madera, y así han ido evolucionando.

NAR 1: ¿Es cierto que por aquí han pasado reyes, príncipes, gente muy importante a comprar sus flores?

NAR 2: Pues, sí, señor. Yo he tenido el gusto de servir a Fleming, por ejemplo, por decirle alguien. Y mi abuela servía a Alfonso XIII.

NAR 1: Mm. Interesante.

NAR 2: Y, bueno, podríamos estar enumerando así a un montón de personas.

NAR 1: ¿Cuándo se vendía más, antes o ahora?

NAR 2: Antes, indiscutiblemente.

NAR 1: ¿La gente era más romántica quizás, o...?

NAR 2: Bueno, yo creo que es que antiguamente, lo que pasaba es que no había tiendas de flores. Entonces, la gente, por fuerza, tenía que bajar a la Rambla. Y al tener que bajar a la Rambla, pues claro, todo se concentraba aquí.

NAR 1: ¿Desde cuándo se dedica usted?

NAR 2: Hace treinta años que me dedico a ello.

NAR 1: Hace treinta años, ¡madre mía! ¿Ha sido por algo especial, fue por algo especial, tradición, o algo así?

NAR 2: Sí, bueno, toda mi familia se ha dedicado siempre al mismo ramo y yo he seguido la tradición, y lo siguen mis hijos.

NAR 1: Una cosa, ahora, ¿qué tipo de público le compra a usted sus flores?

NAR 2: Bueno, yo, la verdad es que el público que a mí me compra es una clientela fija por la cantidad de años que llevo aquí.

NAR 1: Una cosa, ¿los enamorados vienen con una idea fija a comprar sus flores o es usted quien les aconseja un poco?

NAR 2: Normalmente vienen con una idea fija.

NAR 1: Vienen con una idea fija, ¡vaya! ¿Pero no les dice usted, por ejemplo, pues, esto va mejor con esto o con lo otro, o quizás, no?

NAR 2: Sí, lo hago. Ah, normalmente los enamorados suelen comprar en invierno.

Los enamorados jovencitos, me refiero, y de poco dinero...

NAR 1: Sí, sí...

NAR 2: ...en invierno violetas, y en verano las rosas.

NAR 1: Así que los señores mayores, quizá, es...eh...

NAR 2: Ya es distinto, entonces, ya es un ramo combinado, como decimos, un ramo de señora.

NAR 1: Ah, eso está muy bien. Es decir, que hay ramos para jovencitos y ramos para...

NAR 2: Exacto, y ramos para señoras, ¿eh?

NAR 1: Una pregunta, ¿se ha de tener una sensibilidad especial para dedicarse tanto tiempo a esto?

NAR 2: Yo creo que sí y muchísima fuerza de voluntad por la cantidad de horas que hacemos diariamente, y que no tenemos ni un día de fiesta a la semana.

NAR 1: ¿Ningún día de fiesta?

NAR 2: Ningún día, nada más que el domingo por la tarde.

NAR 1: Y hay que darle dedicación a esto, ¿eh?

NAR 2: Sí, nos levantamos a las tres y media de la mañana cada día para ir a comprar a Mercabarna el género y estamos aquí hasta las ocho y media de la noche, de un tirón.

NAR 1: Hasta las ocho y media de la noche, ¡madre mía! Bueno, eh, muchas gracias.

Answers for Longer Narratives and Interviews

Narrativa Número Uno
1. C   2. B   3. C   4. A   5. D
6. D   7. C

Narrativa Número Dos
1. A   2. B   3. C   4. B   5. D
6. C   7. D   8. D

Narrativa Número Tres
1. B   2. B   3. C   4. C   5. D
6. B   7. D   8. D

Narrativa Número Cuatro
1. A   2. C   3. D   4. B   5. B
6. D   7. A   8. D   9. D   10. A

Narrativa Número Cinco
1. A   2. C   3. B   4. C   5. D
6. D   7. B   8. B   9. B

Entrevista Número Uno
1. C   2. A   3. D   4. C   5. D
6. A   7. D   8. D

Entrevista Número Dos
1. B   2. C   3. B   4. A   5. D
6. C   7. A   8. D   9. D   10. D

Entrevista Número Tres
1. A   2. B   3. A   4. C   5. B
6. C   7. D   8. C   9. C   10. C

Entrevista Número Cuatro
1. C   2. C   3. B   4. D   5. D
6. D   7. B   8. C   9. B   10. D

Entrevista Número Cinco
1. B   2. B   3. C   4. C   5. C
6. B   7. B   8. C   9. C

Entrevista Número Seis
1. C   2. D   3. C   4. C   5. C
6. C   7. C   8. C   9. B

Entrevista Número Siete
1. C   2. C   3. D   4. B   5. B
6. A   7. C   8. C   9. C

PART THREE READING COMPREHENSION

GENERAL CONSIDERATIONS

Section I, Part B, comprises multiple choice questions related to reading comprehension. But before you get to the reading passages, you should consider other parts that test your understanding of specific vocabulary and grammatical structures.

In one part you will find passages of about a paragraph in length with several blanks. Corresponding to the numbers in the blanks, there are multiple choice answers. You will need to select the best answer from among the choices printed to complete the meaning of the sentences in the passage. Another part consists of discrete sentences in which four words or phrases are underlined. From among the underlined words or phrases, you must select the incorrect grammatical structure.

Doing these parts before the reading passages should help you focus on dealing with unfamiliar vocabulary and grammatical structures. By recalling vocabulary and grammatical structures first you should be better able to identify and interpret structures you will encounter in the passages. There is a grammar review in the Appendix of this book to refresh your memory on the basic rules of grammar before beginning the multiple choice practice exercises that follow.

The reading passages on the examination and in these practices are taken from a variety of sources, from newspaper articles to literary works. For each reading passage in Part B, there are from five to eleven questions. Each question will have four choices for answering the question or completing the sentence. Random guessing is penalized by deducting one point for every three incorrect answers. If you can eliminate one or two of the four choices, then you should make an educated guess from the remaining alternatives.

There are several things to keep in mind about the construction of multiple choice tests. First, the cues for the correct answers are given in the passage or in the sentence, whether they appear in the vocabulary, grammar, or reading comprehension questions. Second, the distractors, or incorrect choices, are sometimes based on words that are false cognates, or words that are based on common misconceptions or errors that teachers know students make. The distractors are not the complete opposite of the correct answer, nor are they nonsensical or ungrammatical. They may be only partly incorrect or correct, and they all are plausible. By the same token, the correct answer does not stand out because it is different in length, complexity, or vocabulary, or has any other distinguishing feature.

With regard to reading comprehension questions specifically, there are some additional points to consider. The question clearly states whether it is about what is stated in the text, indicated by phrases like *Según el autor,* or *Según el pasaje,* or whether you are being asked to make some inference. Inferences are indicated by phrases such as *Se puede decir* or *El autor implica que...,* meaning that you should make a determination about what you think the passage says. Remember that the correct answer, as well as the distractor, paraphrase what the text says. Any time that a line seems to be copied directly from the text, be careful, because it is almost always a wrong choice. Choices are arranged in a logical order, so use logic when you sort through them. If there is a pair of choices that are direct opposites, the correct answer is usually not one of the pair. Correct answers are not revealed in subsequent questions or choices.

In terms of the content of the questions, usually there is a question about the general idea of the passage. One question will deal with secondary information, or some detail. One question may well ask about when and where the event takes place in the passage. Sometimes an expression, a line, or a sentence is selected as the basis of the question. Finally, a question may be asked about some aspect that requires analysis of the text. Be advised that the literal translation of a phrase or a portion of a text is not the question, but rather, your interpretation of something about the text. The questions deal with your impressions about the tone of the passage, the style, or perhaps the author's intent as you understand it from the cues given in the text. On the following pages you will practice reading for the kinds of information you will be asked on the exam.

PREPARATION FOR READING COMPREHENSION

In this book, the reading part is divided into three chapters:

1. *Vocabulary and grammatical structures.* This chapter contains suggestions for dealing with unfamiliar vocabulary and hints for taking the multiple choice part of the examination that tests vocabulary and grammatical structures in context. You will find that, although there are not many questions that deal specifically with vocabulary, it is vitally important to learn how to figure out words you do not recognize. There is a glossary at the back of this book, but you should have your own dictionary. The more often you have to look up any particular word, the more likely you are to remember it. When you have finished the practice exercises, there are answers and explanations to help you recall grammar and learn some strategies for choosing the correct vocabulary to complete the meaning of the paragraph.
2. *Error recognition.* This chapter contains practice exercises consisting of sentences in which four words or phrases are underlined. You are to find the incorrect point of grammar.
3. *How to read.* This section has suggestions for reading more effectively. Included are some ideas about how to get the most out of what you read by learning to sort information contained in the passages. Also included are samples with detailed explanations of why some answers are considered correct, while others are deemed wrong. Then there are some reading comprehension passages that let you practice what you have learned.

VOCABULARY STUDY

You will notice that there is not an extensive amount of vocabulary that is specifically tested in this part of the examination. Of the few questions about vocabulary you will have to answer, all of the parts of speech will be the same kind, and for each question, you will mostly select from among four verbs, nouns, adjectives, or adverbs. Studying long lists of vocabulary probably will not greatly enhance your performance on this part of the examination, but an ample vocabulary will be essential to answer the few questions that are specifically devoted to vocabulary. As much as a test of how much vocabulary you already know, the examination tests your ability to deduce the meaning of words from the context in which they appear. The best way to prepare for the vocabulary questions is to read as much as you can. Look up words you think are vital to understanding the reading. Increasing your vocabulary will help you on all parts of the examination, not just on the reading.

Although all of the choices in the multiple choice vocabulary questions will be the same part of speech, it is helpful to remember that most often different parts of speech have the same root, or basic word. If you do not recognize a word, try to think of another part of speech that may have the same root and see if it can be changed to be meaningful in the new context. Frequently you can tell what part of speech a word is by the ending it has. For example, many adjectives are past participles of verbs, ending in *-ado* or *-ido*, such as in *sentado*, from *sentar*, meaning *seated*. By the same token, some infinitives contain adjectives embedded in them, such as *engordarse* (*to get fat*), from *gordo* (*fat*). Nouns and verbs also frequently have the same stem, such as *conocimiento* (*understanding*), from *conocer* (*to know*). The following closer look at some specific examples can give you a good idea about how to sort words out according to their parts of speech and function, while at the same time looking for the root that they have in common.

Study the following commonly used endings to learn to recognize how some words function in a sentence.

1. Many nouns have endings in Spanish that correspond to certain endings in English. The following endings always have indicated English endings: *-ción* (*-tión* and *-cion*), *-dad* (*-ly*), *-ería* (*-ery*), *-ancia* (*-ance*), and *-umbre* frequently correspond to *-ness*. Other common noun endings are *-miento*, *-aje*, and *-ío*. When you have to guess the meanings of these words, you can try adding the English ending to the stem to see if it makes sense. Also remember that the endings *-ista* and *-dor* indicate a person who does a particular job.

2. Words that end with *-oso* usually are adjectives whose English ending is *-ous*. Other adjective endings are: *-dizo, -ado, -ido, -ante,* and *-iente*. Adjectives will describe characteristics of a noun. Sometimes there are prefixes, such as *em-* or *en-*, that are used in making verbs out of adjectives. An example is *empobrecerse*, meaning *to get poor*, or *enriquecerse*, meaning *to get rich.* Look for adjectives like *pobre* and *rico* in the middle of a verb if you do not immediately recognize it.

3. Words that end with *-mente* are adverbs whose English ending is *-ly*. These words are adverbs and will describe the manner in which an action happens.

4. Infinitives end with *-ar, -er,* or *-ir.*

If you know a word in one form, such as in the infinitive (*correr*, for example), you can guess about other forms of the word if you can recognize what the endings mean. *Correr*, meaning *to run*, can appear in an adjective form, *corredizo*, meaning *running* or *sliding*. In its adjective form it is used to describe a kind of car door, or sliding glass door. In another adjective form, *corriente*, it means *running*, as in *running* water. In the adverbial form, *corrientemente*, the word would mean *usually* or *fluently*, which shows ongoing action. In the noun form, *corrimiento*, the word can commonly mean *landslide* or *slippage*.

Study the following groups of words and look for particular endings. Notice which endings indicate which part of speech, and how it is expressed in English. Use these examples as a guideline to help categorize words.

CONGREGAR	**TO CONGREGATE, TO GATHER** (infinitive)
congreso	congress, a gathering (noun)
congregado	congregated, gathered (adjective)
congregación	a congregation (noun)
congresista	a delegate to a congress (noun)
congregante	a member of a congregation (noun)
PESAR	**TO WEIGH** (infinitive)
pesado	weighty, heavy (adjective)
pesante	weighty, sad (adjective)
pesadamente	heavily, slowly, tiringly (adverb)
el pesador	weigher (noun)
el pesaje	weighing in (noun)
la pesadumbre	heaviness, sorrow (noun)
la pesa	weight (noun)
la pesadez	heaviness, weight (noun)
el pesacartas	letter-weighing scale (noun)
el pésame	condolences, literally, *it saddens me* (noun)
LA PERSONA	**PERSON** (noun)
personalizar	to personalize (infinitive)
personal	personal (adjective)
personalmente	personally (adverb)
la personalidad	personality (noun)
el personalismo	personalism (noun)
personarse	to appear in person (infinitive)
la personalización	personalization (noun)
el personaje	personage, character in a play (noun)
LA PLUMA	**FEATHER, FOUNTAIN PEN** (from times when quills were pens) (noun)
el plumero	feather duster (noun)
el plumaje	plumage (noun)
la plumada	stroke of a pen (noun)
plumear	to write (American) (infinitive)
la plumilla	little feather, nib of a pen (noun)
desplumar	to pluck (infinitive)
la desplumadura	the plucking (noun)
desplumado	plucked (adjective)

In the last example, *desplumar*, notice that the prefix *des-* makes a word negative. *Desplumado* means *not feathered*. Other prefixes meaning *not* are *a-*, *-in*, *-im*, and *-ad*. For example, *pegar* means *to stick to* or *to strike. Despegar*, however, means *to take off, to remove from*. With some imagination, you can guess that *despegar* also refers to an airplane taking off from the ground. Likewise, *desesperar* means the opposite of *esperar*. The opposite of *to hope* is *to despair*, or *to not hope*.

Of course, the better your English vocabulary, the more words you will recognize as cognates. (Cognates are words that sound alike in Spanish and English.) Sometimes you need to think of synonyms in English to help you arrive at the meaning of a word. For example, when you *know* something, you *understand* it. *Knowing* and *understanding* are similar in meaning. When you are trying to make sense out of how a word would work in a sentence, think of synonyms.

Sometimes a word will look familiar, but is slightly different. Remember that frequently in Spanish, a *y* in English will be an *i* in Spanish. For example, the word *sinónimo* is the word for *synonym*. Other rules of phonics to remember are that in Spanish there are no *th* combinations. This should help you recognize *atletas,* or *teatro.* Also, in Spanish, any beginning consonant combination of *spr-, str-, scr-,* or *sch-,* will have an *e* as the first letter. An example is *especial*, meaning *special.*

You can figure out other words if you think about the English cognates. For example, the word *incorporarse* means *to gather oneself together* or *to collect oneself to get up.* The word is like the word *incorporate* in English, but the meaning is one you may not have recognized. In English you see the word after the names of companies or after the names of towns on road signs. The word in those English contexts means that the communities or the businesses have organized themselves; they have pulled together. Another example is the word *funcionar.* The literal translation is *to function.* But when you hear it in the sentence, *Mi coche no funciona*, it does not sound like something English-speaking people would say. A synonym would be *is not working.* To function and to work are similar activities.

With practice, you can learn many new words by learning one of their forms as a part of speech.

GRAMMATICAL STRUCTURES

The other kinds of questions contained in this section pertain to grammar. You will need to study the choices you have in each question and determine what kind of information the question is testing. You can tell the information being tested by comparing what all the choices have in common; for example, if they are all relative pronouns, adjectives, verbal tenses, or the like. Then you will need to look at the context in the paragraph and determine which is the correct answer from among the multiple choices. If you can isolate your weak points in grammar from doing these practice exercises, then you can correct your mistakes and improve your grammar. Cleaning up grammatical mistakes improves your abilities in all the skill areas and betters your reading comprehension.

To help you identify problems you may have with vocabulary and grammar, there are twelve practice passages in this chapter, with explanations for the answers to help you understand what is meant in each case. After a while you should be able to see if your errors are random (for example, you may occasionally miss a pronoun, or perhaps incorrectly use the preterit and imperfect), or systematic. If your mistakes are systematic, that means that you make the same kind of mistake all of the time because of something you have not yet understood. Random errors usually result from mental lapses and are harder to correct because each mistake is an isolated occurrence. For example, you may have to relearn the gender of a noun such as *el problema.* But if you can remember that *problema* is like many other nouns that end in *-ema, -ama,* or *-ima* that are masculine even though they end in *-a,* you will have less difficulty remembering that *problema* is masculine. In many cases correcting systematic errors can quickly improve your ability to communicate with a minimum of effort.

In the event that you need more refresher material on the grammar than is offered at the end of each exercise, refer to the grammar review in the appendix of this book. It may even be helpful for you to study that grammar review before you begin these practice exercises. Then, when you read the explanations after each practice exercise, perhaps the connection between isolated examples and the larger subject of grammatical structure will become clearer. Remember that there are many grammatical variations of expression in Spanish, but for the purposes of the Advanced Placement Spanish Language Examination, there is a standard, textbook grammar.

STEPS FOR PRACTICING MULTIPLE-CHOICE GRAMMAR QUESTIONS

1. Review the basic grammar in the appendix of this book.
2. When doing an exercise, read the whole passage before beginning to select answers in order to get a general idea about the subject matter and time frame of the selection.
3. Go back and reread the passage. For each question determine if the item tests vocabulary or grammar.
4. For the vocabulary items, select the word that best completes the meaning.
5. Be wary of obvious cognates, or words that sound and look alike in English in Spanish. Words such as *embarazada* frequently have different meanings in Spanish.
6. If you do not immediately recognize any of the words, see if you can identify prefixes and suffixes that obscure a root word you may recognize, such as *intervenir,* meaning to *intervene* or *interfere.*
7. If you still cannot recognize the word, try to find an English word that may be similar. It may have a slightly different, but related meaning, such as *elaborar,* meaning *to work up* or *to manufacture.* Naturally, the better your vocabulary in English, the more words you may be able to recognize using this strategy.
8. Many of the questions are about verbal tenses. Study the context to see if the verb should be in the indicative or the subjunctive. All of the choices will be in the correct person and number, so you need to focus on the correct tense only.
9. If the question asks about relative pronouns, identify the noun that the pronoun replaces in order to select the correct person and number.
10. If the question asks about conjunctions, look at the content of each clause and study the relationship between them to determine which conjunction to use.
11. For questions about demonstrative adjectives and pronouns, be sure you remember the correct forms for each gender and number.

12. Be sure you review which prepositions come after which verbs, such as *depender de,* meaning *to depend on.*

13. For adjectives, remember that you do not really need to know what a word means to make sure it agrees in gender and number with the noun it modifies.

14. When you come to a question you cannot answer, go on to the next question.

15. After you have finished the whole passage, go back and think about the questions you left blank.

16. When you have finished one whole practice exercise, compare your answers with those at the end of the passage.

17. Notice what kind of mistakes you made and try to categorize your errors.

18. Study the explanations for the questions you missed and try to figure out where you made an error in your thinking.

19. If you still do not understand your mistake, make a note about the item and go on to the next section. Not all of the explanations are the same. You may make the same mistake on another passage and find a different explanation that makes sense to you.

CHAPTER 4: Answer Sheet for Multiple-Choice Vocabulary and Grammatical Structure Questions

Selección Uno
1. Ⓐ Ⓑ Ⓒ Ⓓ
2. Ⓐ Ⓑ Ⓒ Ⓓ
3. Ⓐ Ⓑ Ⓒ Ⓓ
4. Ⓐ Ⓑ Ⓒ Ⓓ
5. Ⓐ Ⓑ Ⓒ Ⓓ
6. Ⓐ Ⓑ Ⓒ Ⓓ
7. Ⓐ Ⓑ Ⓒ Ⓓ
8. Ⓐ Ⓑ Ⓒ Ⓓ
9. Ⓐ Ⓑ Ⓒ Ⓓ
10. Ⓐ Ⓑ Ⓒ Ⓓ
11. Ⓐ Ⓑ Ⓒ Ⓓ

Selección Cuatro
1. Ⓐ Ⓑ Ⓒ Ⓓ
2. Ⓐ Ⓑ Ⓒ Ⓓ
3. Ⓐ Ⓑ Ⓒ Ⓓ
4. Ⓐ Ⓑ Ⓒ Ⓓ
5. Ⓐ Ⓑ Ⓒ Ⓓ
6. Ⓐ Ⓑ Ⓒ Ⓓ
7. Ⓐ Ⓑ Ⓒ Ⓓ
8. Ⓐ Ⓑ Ⓒ Ⓓ
9. Ⓐ Ⓑ Ⓒ Ⓓ
10. Ⓐ Ⓑ Ⓒ Ⓓ
11. Ⓐ Ⓑ Ⓒ Ⓓ

Selección Siete
1. Ⓐ Ⓑ Ⓒ Ⓓ
2. Ⓐ Ⓑ Ⓒ Ⓓ
3. Ⓐ Ⓑ Ⓒ Ⓓ
4. Ⓐ Ⓑ Ⓒ Ⓓ
5. Ⓐ Ⓑ Ⓒ Ⓓ
6. Ⓐ Ⓑ Ⓒ Ⓓ
7. Ⓐ Ⓑ Ⓒ Ⓓ
8. Ⓐ Ⓑ Ⓒ Ⓓ
9. Ⓐ Ⓑ Ⓒ Ⓓ
10. Ⓐ Ⓑ Ⓒ Ⓓ
11. Ⓐ Ⓑ Ⓒ Ⓓ

Selección Diez
1. Ⓐ Ⓑ Ⓒ Ⓓ
2. Ⓐ Ⓑ Ⓒ Ⓓ
3. Ⓐ Ⓑ Ⓒ Ⓓ
4. Ⓐ Ⓑ Ⓒ Ⓓ
5. Ⓐ Ⓑ Ⓒ Ⓓ
6. Ⓐ Ⓑ Ⓒ Ⓓ
7. Ⓐ Ⓑ Ⓒ Ⓓ
8. Ⓐ Ⓑ Ⓒ Ⓓ
9. Ⓐ Ⓑ Ⓒ Ⓓ
10. Ⓐ Ⓑ Ⓒ Ⓓ
11. Ⓐ Ⓑ Ⓒ Ⓓ

Selección Dos
1. Ⓐ Ⓑ Ⓒ Ⓓ
2. Ⓐ Ⓑ Ⓒ Ⓓ
3. Ⓐ Ⓑ Ⓒ Ⓓ
4. Ⓐ Ⓑ Ⓒ Ⓓ
5. Ⓐ Ⓑ Ⓒ Ⓓ
6. Ⓐ Ⓑ Ⓒ Ⓓ
7. Ⓐ Ⓑ Ⓒ Ⓓ
8. Ⓐ Ⓑ Ⓒ Ⓓ
9. Ⓐ Ⓑ Ⓒ Ⓓ
10. Ⓐ Ⓑ Ⓒ Ⓓ
11. Ⓐ Ⓑ Ⓒ Ⓓ

Selección Cinco
1. Ⓐ Ⓑ Ⓒ Ⓓ
2. Ⓐ Ⓑ Ⓒ Ⓓ
3. Ⓐ Ⓑ Ⓒ Ⓓ
4. Ⓐ Ⓑ Ⓒ Ⓓ
5. Ⓐ Ⓑ Ⓒ Ⓓ
6. Ⓐ Ⓑ Ⓒ Ⓓ
7. Ⓐ Ⓑ Ⓒ Ⓓ
8. Ⓐ Ⓑ Ⓒ Ⓓ
9. Ⓐ Ⓑ Ⓒ Ⓓ
10. Ⓐ Ⓑ Ⓒ Ⓓ
11. Ⓐ Ⓑ Ⓒ Ⓓ

Selección Ocho
1. Ⓐ Ⓑ Ⓒ Ⓓ
2. Ⓐ Ⓑ Ⓒ Ⓓ
3. Ⓐ Ⓑ Ⓒ Ⓓ
4. Ⓐ Ⓑ Ⓒ Ⓓ
5. Ⓐ Ⓑ Ⓒ Ⓓ
6. Ⓐ Ⓑ Ⓒ Ⓓ
7. Ⓐ Ⓑ Ⓒ Ⓓ
8. Ⓐ Ⓑ Ⓒ Ⓓ
9. Ⓐ Ⓑ Ⓒ Ⓓ
10. Ⓐ Ⓑ Ⓒ Ⓓ
11. Ⓐ Ⓑ Ⓒ Ⓓ
12. Ⓐ Ⓑ Ⓒ Ⓓ

Selección Once
1. Ⓐ Ⓑ Ⓒ Ⓓ
2. Ⓐ Ⓑ Ⓒ Ⓓ
3. Ⓐ Ⓑ Ⓒ Ⓓ
4. Ⓐ Ⓑ Ⓒ Ⓓ
5. Ⓐ Ⓑ Ⓒ Ⓓ
6. Ⓐ Ⓑ Ⓒ Ⓓ
7. Ⓐ Ⓑ Ⓒ Ⓓ
8. Ⓐ Ⓑ Ⓒ Ⓓ
9. Ⓐ Ⓑ Ⓒ Ⓓ
10. Ⓐ Ⓑ Ⓒ Ⓓ
11. Ⓐ Ⓑ Ⓒ Ⓓ

Selección Tres
1. Ⓐ Ⓑ Ⓒ Ⓓ
2. Ⓐ Ⓑ Ⓒ Ⓓ
3. Ⓐ Ⓑ Ⓒ Ⓓ
4. Ⓐ Ⓑ Ⓒ Ⓓ
5. Ⓐ Ⓑ Ⓒ Ⓓ
6. Ⓐ Ⓑ Ⓒ Ⓓ
7. Ⓐ Ⓑ Ⓒ Ⓓ
8. Ⓐ Ⓑ Ⓒ Ⓓ
9. Ⓐ Ⓑ Ⓒ Ⓓ
10. Ⓐ Ⓑ Ⓒ Ⓓ
11. Ⓐ Ⓑ Ⓒ Ⓓ

Selección Seis
1. Ⓐ Ⓑ Ⓒ Ⓓ
2. Ⓐ Ⓑ Ⓒ Ⓓ
3. Ⓐ Ⓑ Ⓒ Ⓓ
4. Ⓐ Ⓑ Ⓒ Ⓓ
5. Ⓐ Ⓑ Ⓒ Ⓓ
6. Ⓐ Ⓑ Ⓒ Ⓓ
7. Ⓐ Ⓑ Ⓒ Ⓓ
8. Ⓐ Ⓑ Ⓒ Ⓓ
9. Ⓐ Ⓑ Ⓒ Ⓓ
10. Ⓐ Ⓑ Ⓒ Ⓓ
11. Ⓐ Ⓑ Ⓒ Ⓓ

Selección Nueve
1. Ⓐ Ⓑ Ⓒ Ⓓ
2. Ⓐ Ⓑ Ⓒ Ⓓ
3. Ⓐ Ⓑ Ⓒ Ⓓ
4. Ⓐ Ⓑ Ⓒ Ⓓ
5. Ⓐ Ⓑ Ⓒ Ⓓ
6. Ⓐ Ⓑ Ⓒ Ⓓ
7. Ⓐ Ⓑ Ⓒ Ⓓ
8. Ⓐ Ⓑ Ⓒ Ⓓ
9. Ⓐ Ⓑ Ⓒ Ⓓ
10. Ⓐ Ⓑ Ⓒ Ⓓ
11. Ⓐ Ⓑ Ⓒ Ⓓ

Selección Doce
1. Ⓐ Ⓑ Ⓒ Ⓓ
2. Ⓐ Ⓑ Ⓒ Ⓓ
3. Ⓐ Ⓑ Ⓒ Ⓓ
4. Ⓐ Ⓑ Ⓒ Ⓓ
5. Ⓐ Ⓑ Ⓒ Ⓓ
6. Ⓐ Ⓑ Ⓒ Ⓓ
7. Ⓐ Ⓑ Ⓒ Ⓓ
8. Ⓐ Ⓑ Ⓒ Ⓓ
9. Ⓐ Ⓑ Ⓒ Ⓓ
10. Ⓐ Ⓑ Ⓒ Ⓓ
11. Ⓐ Ⓑ Ⓒ Ⓓ

CHAPTER 4 Vocabulary and Grammatical Structures

Practice Exercises

Although grammar and vocabulary are no longer tested in the exam using the format in the following exercises, it is very important to know both the grammar and vocabulary contained in them. The exercises are excellent practice to ensure that you know appropriate language for the free response parts of Section II. In the informal writing, formal writing, informal speaking, and formal presentation parts, you will need to incorporate as much of the vocabulary and grammar into your writing and speech samples as you can. In the paragraph completion exercises at the beginning of the writing parts you will have to fill in blanks with correct responses. For half of the paragraph completion fill-ins there will be no words given, and you will have to decide what is appropriate based on your understanding of how parts of speech function in sentences. In the exercises that follow, you can study the sentence structures to make sure you understand the grammar. You can look up words you do not know in order to learn appropriate vocabulary. It may seem that it will be easier to get a higher score without the vocabulary and grammar multiple-choice questions, but in a sense, it can be harder. The free-response section of the exam can be more difficult because you have fewer prompts. There is nothing to jog your memory about words and structures you need to use. In the free response part, the only language you will hear or see before you have to write and speak is contained in the reading selections and the listening comprehension parts of the exam. It is a good idea to prepare thoroughly. The following exercises should help you with enough grammar and vocabulary to do well on the examination.

Before you begin this section of practice, it would be useful to review the brief grammar contained at the back of this book. In addition, there are several points of grammar and a couple of suggestions regarding the multiple choice section that you would do well to follow:

1. Verb endings agree in person and number.
2. Adjectives agree in gender and number with the nouns they modify.
3. Review common nouns that have a feminine ending, but are masculine.
4. Remember that numbers do not agree in gender and number.
5. After prepositions, always use an infinitive if you need to use a verb.
6. Always use the subjunctive after *antes de que, para que, a menos que, con tal que, a fin de que,* and *a no ser que.*

To do the practice exercises:

1. Read each passage through once to get the general idea of subject matter and time frame.
2. Determine what information is asked in the question.
3. Study the multiple choices for the correct answer.
4. Record your answer on the answer sheet at the end of this chapter.
5. Check your answers after each practice exercise.
6. Review the grammatical explanation if you made a mistake.
7. Learn grammar and vocabulary.

SELECCIÓN UNO

En ese contexto, la postura apolítica de *Soda Stereo* y sus

referencias musicales internacionales sugieren una reacción contra

lo que se ___(1)___ haber considerado políticamente correcto en ese

momento. "Había muchas bandas surgiendo a finales de la dictadura

y existía una necesidad de hablar de otras cosas (al margen de la

política), no porque no ___(2)___ lo que había pasado, ___(3)___

porque creíamos que había llegado el momento de avanzar", explica

Cerati.

Su enfoque, el sonido, indudablemente tocó ___(4)___ en las

audiencias fuera de Argentina. ___(5)___ 1986 el grupo andaba en

___(6)___ por Latinoamérica, y a su tiempo llegó a Chile, Perú,

Colombia, Ecuador y Venezuela, algo sin precedentes en el rock

latinoamericano.

1. (A) puede
   (B) podía
   (C) podría
   (D) pudo

2. (A) vemos
   (B) vimos
   (C) veíamos
   (D) viéramos

3. (A) pero
   (B) sino
   (C) sino que
   (D) y

4. (A) alguno
   (B) ninguno
   (C) algo
   (D) nadie

5. (A) Por
   (B) A
   (C) De
   (D) Para

6. (A) revoloteo
   (B) vía
   (C) gira
   (D) guión

"No estoy muy seguro de cómo pasó", dice Cerati.

"____(7)____ una mezcla de aventura y mercadeo. *Nada personal* (su

segundo álbum que salió a la venta en 1985) ____(8)____ explotó,

comenzó a venderse y el grupo ____(9)____ lo suficiente grande como

para atravesar fronteras. No ____(10)____ un gran estrategia tras

____(11)____ ".

7. (A) Es
   (B) Era
   (C) Fue
   (D) Sería

8. (A) súbitamente
   (B) cautelosamente
   (C) sigilosamente
   (D) largamente

9. (A) se hizo
   (B) llegó a ser
   (C) se puso
   (D) se convirtió

10. (A) hay
    (B) hubo
    (C) había
    (D) habría

11. (A) ese
    (B) eso
    (C) este
    (D) esto

SELECCIÓN DOS

Durante años, Aurora, Nana y Victoria Eugenia marcaron pasos de

baile en distinguidas compañías de su país. Retiradas del escenario,

siguen marcando pasos en el Ballet Nacional de España, donde el

triunvirato femenino ha sentado ____(1)____ contra viento y marea.

Desde los inicios de la compañía hasta 1984, Aurora fue la

profesora del ballet, luego de ____(2)____ laborado por 15 años como

primera bailarina del Teatro del Liceo de Barcelona.

1. (A) pauta
   (B) ajena
   (C) descalza
   (D) insólita

2. (A) habiendo
   (B) había
   (C) habido
   (D) haber

"Procuramos avanzar dentro del estilo, tal vez contemporáneo,

_____(3)_____ siempre muy español, la raíz no _____(4)_____ podemos

perder. La diferencia que se puede encontrar y que _____(5)_____

reflejado en las críticas, es que los bailarines son más ellos.

Dejamos que _____(6)_____ su personalidad".

En el repertorio actual del BNE se destacan dos estrenos: _Leyenda_

y Bolero, en los cuales trabajaron las tres. ¿ _____(7)_____ el trabajo de

equipo la clave del éxito de estas artistas? "Cada una llevamos un

departamento: son seis ojos y tres cabezas", apunta Nana. "Si no

_____(8)_____ puesto cada una de _____(9)_____ una parte, en el sentido de

adaptarnos a nuestras diferentes ideas y formas de trabajo, hubiera

sido un infierno. Hay discusiones, pero siempre llegamos a un

acuerdo para beneficio de la compañía".

"Tenemos un lujo de primeros bailarines que se reparten los

papeles entre todos. Cada ballet lo hacen parejas diferentes, es más

_____(10)_____ para el público que la misma coreografía la _____(11)_____

distintos bailarines".

3. (A) sino
   (B) sino que
   (C) pero
   (D) ya

4. (A) lo
   (B) la
   (C) se
   (D) nos

5. (A) ha
   (B) se ha
   (C) se había
   (D) hay

6. (A) sale
   (B) salió
   (C) salga
   (D) saliera

7. (A) Es
   (B) Será
   (C) Era
   (D) Sería

8. (A) hemos
   (B) habíamos
   (C) habríamos
   (D) hubiéramos

9. (A) ellos
   (B) ellas
   (C) nosotras
   (D) vosotras

10. (A) real
    (B) imprevisto
    (C) aliciente
    (D) pernicioso

11. (A) baila
    (B) bailen
    (C) bailará
    (D) bailaran

SELECCIÓN TRES

No _____(1)_____ duda de que el muerto decía la verdad. Su misma

muerte era la prueba. Sara estudió a _____(2)_____ pasajeros. ¿Cuáles

eran los bandidos? ¿Quién era el asesino? Si _____(3)_____ encontrar la

respuesta... Pero ninguno parecía culpable ni por asomo.

Los pensamientos de Sara se interrumpieron brúscamente cuando

la voz del piloto sonó por los altavoces situados sobre sus cabezas.

—Debido a un asesinato imprevisto, _____(4)_____ nosotros a toda

velocidad, siguiendo la ruta más corta a Tsetsé, con el fin de llegar

antes de lo previsto.

Sara consultó su reloj. Eran las tres y media, y _____(5)_____

tenían que encontrar las otras instrucciones del muerto. Consultó el

mapa que la azafata le había dado a Pío.

—¿Dónde estamos?—murmuró.

La azafata se le acercó y le dijo que estaban justo encima de la

_____(6)_____ del río Okracoke.

De repente, algo le vino a la memoria, y recordó dónde había

visto antes el frasco de veneno. Había estado en el carrito de servicio,

mientras todos se _____(7)_____ por las bebidas. ¡Qué fácil debió ser para

el asesino echar unas gotas de veneno en un vaso de zumo de

tomate! _____(8)_____ se hubiera fijado. Pero Pío se había fijado en las

manos que rodeaban el carrito. Y _____(9)_____ era más, se acordaba

claramente de todas ellas.

1. (A) cabe
   (B) cabía
   (C) cupo
   (D) cabría

2. (A) lo demás
   (B) los demás
   (C) las demás
   (D) más

3. (A) puede
   (B) podía
   (C) podría
   (D) pudiera

4. (A) volemos
   (B) vuelo
   (C) volaremos
   (D) volaría

5. (A) aun
   (B) aún
   (C) ya
   (D) justo

6. (A) embarcación
   (B) desembarque
   (C) embocadura
   (D) flotación

7. (A) pelean
   (B) peleaban
   (C) peleen
   (D) pelearon

8. (A) Alguien
   (B) Nada
   (C) Nadie
   (D) Ningún

9. (A) lo que
   (B) la que
   (C) el que
   (D) quien

Si pudiera encontrar a ____(10)____ pertenecían las manos, podría

hacer una lista de sospechosos. Y sería fácil ____(11)____ pasando una

caja de caramelos blandos.

10. (A) que
    (B) qué
    (C) quien
    (D) quién

11. (A) avergonzarlo
    (B) rendirlo
    (C) arrancarlo
    (D) averiguarlo

SELECCIÓN CUATRO

Aunque el estrés se describe como malo en cualquier caso, el

nuevo estudio sugiere que sus efectos ____(1)____ marcadamente entre

una persona y otra. Algunos sufren las frustraciones sin que se les

____(2)____ mucho la presión arterial, pero a otros les sube mucho.

Los expertos han sabido durante mucho tiempo que las

personas que padecen de hipertensión continua tienen ____(3)____

riesgo de desarrollar arteriosclerosis, que es la acumulación de

colesterol en los vasos sanguíneos que comúnmente se describe

como ____(4)____ de arterias. Por ____(5)____ unos investigadores de la

Universidad de Western Ontario se dispusieron a averiguar si con las

personas ____(6)____ lo mismo.

1. (A) varían
   (B) variarían
   (C) variarán
   (D) variaran

2. (A) altera
   (B) alterará
   (C) altere
   (D) alteraría

3. (A) mejor
   (B) mayor
   (C) menor
   (D) peor

4. (A) endurecimiento
   (B) embotellamiento
   (C) engordamiento
   (D) embuste

5. (A) lo que
   (B) qué
   (C) los cuales
   (D) lo cual

6. (A) ocurre
   (B) ocurriría
   (C) ocurra
   (D) ocurriera

Utilizaron un complicado juego de computadoras llamado "interferencia de colores y palabras" para estudiar las diversas reacciones de los 348 voluntarios al estrés. Se requería que los voluntarios ___(7)___ rápidamente los colores de las letras con que ___(8)___ escritas las palabras de los colores. Por ejemplo, la palabra "roja" puede estar escrita en letras amarillas, por lo tanto, la respuesta correcta es amarillo.

Para ___(9)___ las cosas, el juego estaba programado para ir progresivamente más rápido hasta que todo el mundo ___(10)___ errores el 17 por ciento del tiempo, no importa ___(11)___ se esforzaran. Y todo ese tiempo, tenían conectados los monitores de presión arterial.

7. (A) identifican
(B) identificaban
(C) identificaron
(D) identificasen

8. (A) están
(B) son
(C) han
(D) hay

9. (A) estremecer
(B) escampar
(C) estallar
(D) empeorar

10. (A) comite
(B) comiten
(C) comitían
(D) comitiera

11. (A) cuando
(B) cuanto
(C) cuánto
(D) cuánta

SELECCIÓN CINCO

Una mañana agitada vivió la dirigencia de la Universidad Católica para tomar una decisión final respecto a la situación del hasta ayer renunciado técnico cruzado Manuel y que derivó, finalmente, en la confirmación del DT en la banca del club estudiantil.

La jornada se ___(1)___ muy temprano, cerca de las 8.20 horas, cuando Manuel llegó a la casa de Germán, presidente de la Comisión del Plantel Profesional, ubicada en el sector oriente de la capital.

___(2)___ las 8.30 se inició la reunión. A las 10.20, Manuel abandonó la casa de Germán. Sólo atinó a señalar que " ___(3)___ todo dicho, no tengo más que ___(4)___ ".

1. (A) inicia
(B) iniciaba
(C) inició
(D) iniciaría

2. (A) Pasado
(B) Pasada
(C) Pasadas
(D) Pasados

3. (A) Es
(B) Fue
(C) Está
(D) Estaba

4. (A) aportar
(B) hurtar
(C) solicitar
(D) someter

Fue el dueño de la casa quien tomó la palabra: "Se resolvió la

confirmación de Manuel, hasta fin de año. Creemos que la baja del

equipo no ___(5)___ totalmente por el técnico, ___(6)___ también

por el plantel que no está jugando en un buen nivel". Germán agregó

que "aquí la responsabilidad pasa ___(7)___ todos, ya ___(8)___

entrenador, dirigentes o jugadores. Por eso, tenemos que unirnos

todos para revertir esta situación."

Consultado sobre si se pensó en algún momento en posibles

nombres para reemplazar a Manuel, el directivo comentó:

"Candidatos siempre hay. Pero pensamos que no ___(9)___

conveniente modificar la dirección técnica ___(10)___ de año.

¿Presiones externas? Creemos que un técnico siempre está expuesto

a ___(11)___ ".

5. (A) pasa
   (B) pasó
   (C) pasaba
   (D) pasaría

6. (A) sino
   (B) pero
   (C) sino que
   (D) ya que

7. (A) con
   (B) hasta
   (C) para
   (D) por

8. (A) es
   (B) era
   (C) sea
   (D) fuera

9. (A) es
   (B) era
   (C) fue
   (D) sería

10. (A) a medio
    (B) a mitad
    (C) en la mitad
    (D) a medianos

11. (A) ese
    (B) ése
    (C) esto
    (D) eso

SELECCIÓN SEIS

La propuesta del *V-chip* se complementará también con la exigencia de que las empresas dedicadas al entretenimiento ____(1)____ un sistema de calificación del contenido violento de sus programas, en el plazo de un año. De no hacerlo, sería la Federal Communications Commission (agencia federal que regula las telecomunicaciones en EEUU) ____(2)____ se encargaría de llevarlo a cabo.

Aunque nadie sabe con exatitud cómo ____(3)____ el *V-chip*—no deja de ser un proyecto aún en plena fase de estudio—se piensa que podrá ser programado por los padres para bloquear los programas calificados ____(4)____ violentos. Es decir, se podría definir como un *termostato electrónico* que, según el código que ____(5)____ de la señal de TV sintonizada, sea capaz de desconectarse de esta señal.

____(6)____ es una idea muy popular en EEUU, que cuenta con el apoyo al gabinete de Clinton y que ha terminado también por enrolar a la oposición republicana, porque oponerse a ella ____(7)____ con la defensa de los valores familiares que todos respaldan.

1. (A) desarrollan
   (B) desarrollen
   (C) desarrollarán
   (D) desarrollarían

2. (A) la que
   (B) las que
   (C) el que
   (D) los que

3. (A) funciona
   (B) funcione
   (C) funcionará
   (D) funcionaría

4. (A) de
   (B) tan
   (C) así
   (D) como

5. (A) recibe
   (B) reciba
   (C) recibirá
   (D) recibiera

6. (A) Esto
   (B) Ésta
   (C) Aquélla
   (D) Esa

7. (A) choca
   (B) choque
   (C) chocaría
   (D) chocara

_____(8)_____ , la entrada en vigor del uso del *V-chip* podría retrasarse,

ya que el presidente Bill Clinton quizá _____(9)_____ la ley general de

comunicaciones en que se incluye, puesto que no está de acuerdo

con algunos otros de sus apartados. Además, incluso si se aprobara,

sólo _____(10)_____ a los aparatos nuevos de televisión, mientras que los

_____(11)_____ tienen, al menos, vida para otra década.

8. (A) Por lo tanto
   (B) A propósito
   (C) Al contrario
   (D) No obstante

9. (A) veda
   (B) vede
   (C) vedará
   (D) vedaría

10. (A) afecta
    (B) afecte
    (C) afectaría
    (D) afectase

11. (A) reales
    (B) actuales
    (C) verdaderos
    (D) presentes

SELECCIÓN SIETE

Si a estas alturas, en que tan _____(1)_____ se lee, usted se pregunta

para qué puede servir un libro, puede responderse que para salvar la

vida de un hijo que se _____(2)_____ al desastre. El autor y poeta

mexicano Luis A. Rodríguez da fe a ese poder regenerador de la

literatura. Fue testigo de innumerables suicidios de sus compañeros

en "la vida loca", como se designa la existencia de los pandilleros.

"Una de las razones por _____(3)_____ se ingresa en las pandillas",

explica Rodríguez, de 41 años, "es para buscar respeto y algo de

poder para combatir la discriminación. Para muchos, entregarse a esa

vida brutal, no es una elección, sino una fatalidad. De joven,

_____(4)_____ los libros los que me mostraron que existían otras vidas

que _____(5)_____ tenían que ver con las pandillas", dijo Rodríguez.

"Así, el mundo se me fue _____(6)_____ en las bibliotecas.

1. (A) pequeño
   (B) poco
   (C) bien
   (D) mucho

2. (A) precipita
   (B) remonta
   (C) elude
   (D) proporciona

3. (A) el cual
   (B) la cual
   (C) las cuales
   (D) lo cual

4. (A) era
   (B) eran
   (C) fue
   (D) fueron

5. (A) mucho
   (B) nada
   (C) nadie
   (D) nunca

6. (A) abrir
   (B) abierto
   (C) abriendo
   (D) abriertas

_____(7)_____ transmitir a mi hijo esa experiencia y mostrarle que la

pandilla no era la única salida".

   "Lo que hago en mi libro", prosigue diciendo el escritor, "es tratar

de trascender la violencia por medio del arte". Pero es

imprescindible que se _____(8)_____ para poder superar la violencia y la

vida marginal y para ser sano.

   La ruptura de Rodríguez con el mundo de las pandillas fue un

duro y complejo proceso. _____(9)_____ primer término, supuso

enfrentar las consecuencias y peligros que pesan sobre los

"desertores" de un mundo delictivo con férreos códigos de lealtad.

"Por supuesto", recuerda Rodríguez, "tuve que enfrentar el rechazo,

pues no se rompe _____(10)_____ con un modo de vida y menos con 'la

vida loca'. Pero _____(11)_____ huí. Me quedé en el barrio latino".

SELECCIÓN OCHO

No le conozco _____(1)_____ él me conoce a mí y no sabe si soy

extranjero o paisano, turco o aragonés, chilote o tahitiano; sólo veía

en mí a alguien que se hallaba solo _____(2)_____ el trote largo de

cincuenta animales de tropa. No me resolvía a huir. Pero cuando los

animales _____(3)_____ a unos treinta pasos y el ruido de sus cascos y el

sonar de los metales se agrandó hasta hacérseme _____(4)_____ y cuando

miré la caballada y vi los sables y las astas de las lanzas, me di

cuenta de que de quedarme allí no habría esperanza alguna para

_____(5)_____ y que de nada serviría el ser extranjero o nativo, el tener o

no un certificado; mi espalda, mis manos y mi pie se

7. (A) Quiero
   (B) Quería
   (C) Quise
   (D) Quisiera

8. (A) esfuerza
   (B) esfuerzará
   (C) esfuerce
   (D) esforzará

9. (A) Al
   (B) En
   (C) Para
   (D) Del

10. (A) propiamente
   (B) impunemente
   (C) sumamente
   (D) malignamente

11. (A) siempre
   (B) por poco
   (C) también
   (D) jamás

1. (A) o
   (B) u
   (C) pero
   (D) ni

2. (A) hacia
   (B) ante
   (C) tras
   (D) próximo

3. (A) están
   (B) estaban
   (C) estuvieron
   (D) estarían

4. (A) insoportable
   (B) ineludible
   (C) inoportuno
   (D) inválido

5. (A) él
   (B) mí
   (C) mi
   (D) ello

_____(6)_____ contra el muro y me despidieron con violencia hacia

adelante; salté y toqué apenas el suelo, mirando de reojo al

escuadrón: uno de los policías venía _____(7)_____ hacia mí y

hasta me pareció ver que su mano buscaba una buena posición en el asta.

Estaba a una distancia ya muy pequeña y por un instante dudé de

que _____(8)_____ escapar. De no ocurrir algo imprevisto, el lanzazo, si

se _____(9)_____ a herirme con el hierro, o el palo, si quería ser

magnánimo, me enterraría de cabeza en el suelo. Giré en el aire y

empecé a correr y en el momento en que lo hacía los hombres que

me rodearon unos momentos antes y que después se alejaron de mí,

_____(10)_____ más allá, empezaron también a correr, como si _____(11)_____

esperado que lo hiciera primero. El hombre delgado y moreno gritó

de nuevo, ahora con energía, desafiante y _____(12)_____:

—¡Bravo, compañerito!

6. (A) apoyaba
   (B) apoyaban
   (C) apoyó
   (D) apoyaron

7. (A) exacto
   (B) erguido
   (C) derecho
   (D) claro

8. (A) podía
   (B) podría
   (C) pudo
   (D) pudiera

9. (A) decide
   (B) decidía
   (C) decidió
   (D) decidiría

10. (A) agruparse
    (B) agrupándose
    (C) se agruparon
    (D) se agrupó

11. (A) había
    (B) hubo
    (C) habría
    (D) hubiesen

12. (A) temeroso
    (B) mezquino
    (C) alentador
    (D) zozobroso

SELECCIÓN NUEVE

Al español le _____(1)_____ preguntar lo que se refiere a su _____(2)_____

porque, naturalmente, _tiene que saberlo todo_. Una vez tuve un coche

que tenía el defecto de escupir la gasolina que entraba a presión.

Cada vez que me _____(3)_____ en una estación de combustible lo

1. (A) avergüenza
   (B) avergüence
   (C) avergonzará
   (D) avergonzara

2. (A) deber
   (B) personal
   (C) oficio
   (D) técnica

3. (A) detengo
   (B) detenía
   (C) detuve
   (D) detendría

advertía, ____(4)____ y precisamente, al encargado: "Se trata de un

codo mal construido, ____(5)____ usted cuidado porque se sale, vaya

usted muy despacio..." Normalmene asentían con aire distraído; mi

advertencia les parecía totalmente innecesaria, y más de una vez me lo

recordaron: "No se preocupe..., llevo muchos años echando gasolina..."

"Pero es que en este caso es distinto—insistía yo—. Escupe mucho".

Con aire seguro colocaban la manga en el agujero de entrada y daban al

motor. La gasolina surgía violentamente, ____(6)____ por el suelo, y el

mecánico se volvía hacia mí, que seguía impertérrito porque lo esperaba.

"¡____(7)____!" "¡Pero escupe mucho!" No encontré ____(8)____ a un empleado

que me ____(9)____ : "Tenía usted razón." Parecía que en cada ocasión—y la

experiencia ____(10)____ en toda la geografía peninsular—hablábamos

lenguajes distintos. Cuando yo decía "escupe mucho," no era lo mismo que

cuando ____(11)____ decía él: las mismas palabras tenían distinto significado

al pasar por sus labios.

4. (A) lento
   (B) lenta
   (C) lente
   (D) lentamente

5. (A) tiene
   (B) ten
   (C) tenga
   (D) tendría

6. (A) derrumbándose
   (B) derramándose
   (C) agotándose
   (D) acongojándose

7. (A) Oigo
   (B) Oye
   (C) Oiga
   (D) Oíd

8. (A) nunca
   (B) siempre
   (C) alguna vez
   (D) antes

9. (A) dice
   (B) diría
   (C) diga
   (D) dijera

10. (A) se realizó
    (B) se dio cuenta
    (C) se cumplió
    (D) se transcurrió

11. (A) el
    (B) la
    (C) lo
    (D) las

SELECCIÓN DIEZ

Hasta muy entrada la tarde ignoré de qué se trataba, qué era

_____(1)_____ se pretendía subir a veinte y quiénes debían morir; en

aquel momento, por lo demás, no me interesaba averiguar nada: lo

único que quería era asegurarme de que la triple hilera de caballos y

policías, con sus lanzas y sables, había seguido corriendo y

desaparecido. Algunos vecinos se unieron a nosotros. Mientras

corría _____(2)_____ a mis compañeros; a juzgar por sus ropas eran

obreros y se les veía transpirando, _____(3)_____ , _____(4)_____ no

cansados. La pelea _____(5)_____ . El hombre desconocido, delgado y

moreno, corría al lado _____(6)_____ y me habló;

—¿Tuvo miedo?

Me encogí de hombros y sonreí, _____(7)_____ :

—¿De qué?

Hizo un gesto vago:

—¡Creí que el policía _____(8)_____ iba a alcanzar y ya me parecía

verlo caer de punta al suelo! ¿Por qué no corría?

Repetí el gesto: no _____(9)_____ explicar por qué no huí desde el

principio y por qué lo hice después; estaba fuera de mí, como estaba

fuera de mí el ir corriendo junto a ellos. La vanguardia del grupo

llegó al extremo del patio y los hombres, deteniéndose en la acera,

1. (A) quién
   (B) que
   (C) cual
   (D) lo que

2. (A) observaba
   (B) obserbaban
   (C) observé
   (D) observaron

3. (A) aniquilados
   (B) pululantes
   (C) entremetidos
   (D) anhelantes

4. (A) pero
   (B) sino que
   (C) aunque
   (D) hasta

5. (A) empieza
   (B) empezaba
   (C) empezó
   (D) había empezado

6. (A) mí
   (B) mío
   (C) suyo
   (D) cuyo

7. (A) asqueroso
   (B) jactancioso
   (C) chisposo
   (D) jubilado

8. (A) Vd.
   (B) él
   (C) lo
   (D) te

9. (A) he podido
   (B) había podido
   (C) habría podido
   (D) hubiera podido

gritaron, (levantando ___(10)___ brazos y cerrando los puños:

—¡ ___(11)___ los verdugos del pueblo!

10 (A) los
    (B) sus
    (C) mis
    (D) su

11. (A) Mueren
    (B) Mueran
    (C) Morirían
    (D) Murieron

SELECCIÓN ONCE

En cierta forma se puede decir que la presencia de la pobreza ___(1)___ un constante en la historia de la humanidad. Pero sólo en esta segunda mitad del siglo XX ha adquirido una importancia ecológica que la convierte en un problema de supervivencia de la civilización mundial. ___(2)___ , las guerras, las epidemias y las catástrofes naturales regulaban el ciclo de la población limitando el número de los pobres. Hoy en día, estos factores, por razones que no cabe analizar aquí, han reducido en mucho su eficacia reguladora de ___(3)___ suerte que al momento la población pobre ___(4)___ con un ritmo sostenido que termina ___(5)___ afectar el propio crecimiento económico reforzando así el incremento de la pobreza.

___(6)___ , la pobreza, además de ser un problema humano en sentido ético y sociológico es también un problema económico no sólo en el sentido obvio de que es causada por el sistema económico, ___(7)___ , sobre todo, porque su presencia indica el buen funcionamiento de la economía.

1. (A) está
    (B) ha estado
    (C) había sido
    (D) ha sido

2. (A) Anterior
    (B) Antaño
    (C) Después
    (D) Anteayer

3. (A) tanta
    (B) tan
    (C) tal
    (D) tanto

4. (A) crece
    (B) crezca
    (C) ha crecido
    (D) crecía

5. (A) por
    (B) para
    (C) en
    (D) con

6. (A) Al tanto
    (B) A continuación
    (C) Por lo tanto
    (D) Sin embargo

7. (A) pero
    (B) sin
    (C) sino
    (D) sino que

Un segundo problema ____(8)____ ofrece el concepto de capacidad

para general medios de satisfacción de las necesidades. ____(9)____

significa que el pobre es pobre porque es incapaz de producir sus

medios de satisfacción. Aquí lo fundamental es determinar si no los

produce porque no tiene la destreza para trabajar adecuadamente o

porque, aun teniéndola, no logra conseguir un empleo ____(10)____ . En

el primer caso, su incapacidad radicaría en su falta de habilidades

personales que le impiden ser empleado productivamente por el

sistema económico. En el segundo caso, es el propio sistema

económico ____(11)____ no puede absorberlo al margen de sus

habilidades personales.

SELECCIÓN DOCE

Si la originalidad es más amplia, si se extiende al género, al estilo,

a los supuestos que se dan por consabidos, la atención se desorienta,

se hace ____(1)____ , no se da cuenta ____(2)____ consiste la innovación.

   Hay casos desfavorables, y uno de ellos es la situación de la

cultura española de nuestro tiempo: cuando no se espera lo

inesperado, es improbable que se lo ____(3)____ si aparece. Esto

ocurrió desde el siglo XVIII, con una interrupción en la época

romántica, que pasó pronto—Galdós lo percibió ____(4)____ .

Cuando florecieron los autores del 98, ____(5)____ se contaba con que

de España ____(6)____ nada nuevo ni interesante.

8. (A) lo
   (B) la
   (C) le
   (D) se

9. (A) Esta
   (B) Ésta
   (C) Esto
   (D) Éste

10. (A) célere
    (B) eficaz
    (C) suministro
    (D) idóneo

11. (A) que
    (B) el que
    (C) la que
    (D) lo que

1. (A) brusca
   (B) calumniosa
   (C) egregia
   (D) borrosa

2. (A) de que
   (B) de qué
   (C) en qué
   (D) lo que

3. (A) ve
   (B) verá
   (C) vería
   (D) vea

4. (A) perspicazmente
   (B) vanamente
   (C) lozanamente
   (D) soberbiamente

5. (A) últimamente
   (B) apenas
   (C) además
   (D) por casualidad

6. (A) llega
   (B) llegará
   (C) llegaría
   (D) llegase

Y cuando hubiera sido posible que se ___(7)___ la percepción,

estimulada por la esperanza, como sucedió después de 1920, poco

después sobrevino la guerra civil, y entonces se decretó que en

España "no podía haber" nada interesante, valioso, no ___(8)___

original.

    Pero lo que me interesa señalar es que la originalidad que ha

germinado en España en este siglo ha sido de la variedad que no

suele verse. Responde a un cambio profundo de actitud, a una

necesidad de entrar en últimas cuentas con ___(9)___ mismo, de

descender al fondo de la propia persona y—no se olvide—de la

realidad a la que se pertence, de ___(10)___ está uno hecho. Si se

olvida esto, ¿se puede entender a Unamuno y a ___(11)___ más de

este siglo moderno?

7. (A) desarrolla
   (B) desarrollaró
   (C) desarrollaría
   (D) desarrollara

8. (A) digamos
   (B) decimos
   (C) dijimos
   (D) dijéramos

9. (A) el
   (B) lo
   (C) si
   (D) uno

10. (A) cual
    (B) el cual
    (C) la cual
    (D) lo cual

11. (A) tantos
    (B) tales
    (C) los
    (D) cuantos

Answers and Explanations

SELECCIÓN UNO

1. (C) *podría.* The conditional is used to communicate probability in the past, indicated by the use of *ese* before *momento,* and by additional information in the paragraph. Implied is a contrast between past politically correct attitudes and the normally apolitical group stance of the group *Soda Stereo.* None of the other tenses would indicate probability in the past. The present would not be the best answer, although it would be grammatically correct. Also notice that the indicative instead of the subjunctive is used following the verb *sugerir,* because there is no volition (meaning request or desire), implied in the statement.

2. (D) *viéramos.* The imperfect subjunctive is used in the sentence to express something contrary to fact. None of the other selections would communicate that the group had seen what was going on, even though they appear not to have seen.

3. (B) *sino.* This conjunction is used in comparisons. The speaker compares what appeared to have happened with a comment about what he really believed happened. *Sino que* is used when the conjunction is followed by a clause containing a verb. Although in this case there is a verb in the clause, the additional conjunction *porque* is used, which means that you do not need *que* following *sino. Pero* and *y* are not used because of the comparison

that is presented. The use of *no* before the verb in the previous clause indicates that the structure is *not because of...but rather because of*.

4. (C) *algo*. The affirmative indefinite pronoun for *something* is indicated by the context. *Ninguno* and *nadie* are not correct because the negative indefinite adjectives and pronouns that follow the verb need a negative before the verb. Remember that double negatives are required in Spanish. *Alguno* is an indefinite adjective that can be nominalized, but in this case would not make any sense since the antecedent is not clear and there is no personal *a*.

5. (D) *Para*. This preposition indicates destination in time in the future from the perspective of the time frame in the main clause. The group was to be taking a tour, and in due time arrived at the listed countries. *Por* is used to indicate duration of time, meaning *during*. The tense of the verb *andar* would normally be in the preterit in that case to indicate completed action. Neither *A* nor *De* makes sense in this context.

6. (C) *gira*. This is a vocabulary question. If you did not know the correct word, you should have been able to improve your chances of guessing the right one by eliminating some words. You could have recognized *vía* from other expressions having to do with *way* or *manner*, neither of which make sense in the context of this paragraph. You could also have recognized that the prefix *re-* means *again*, which, combined with the stem *vol-* suggests the verb *volar*. Although the noun form of this verb might make sense, it does not mean anything with a prefix on the front of it. The word *guión* suggests a word for *guide*, which does not make much sense either. The best alternative would be *gira*.

7. (C) *Fue*. The preterit is the best answer in the context of this paragraph because the speaker is referring to a specific action at a specific moment in the past that is completed. The speaker is not sure *how* it happened, but he knows it *was* a mixture of adventure and marketing. The preterit is the best choice.

8. (A) *súbitamente*. The ending *-mente* on the ends of these words tells you that they are all adverbs. If you do not recognize the correct word, identify what you can about some of them. From reading music, you may recognize *súbito*, which has a similar meaning in music to its meaning here: *suddenly*. Look for an adjective or noun that may give some clue about the meaning of the word. Remember that *largo* means *long*, not *large*. *Cauteloso* means *cautious* and *cautela* means *caution*. *Sigiloso* means *silently*. This word comes from *sigiliar* meaning *to seal* or *to hide*. What is the connection between *silent* and *to seal*?

9. (A) *se hizo*. This is a vocabulary question because all of these verbs mean *to become*. *Hacerse* is the best alternative, because it is the only one that means that the group became something in the sense that it made itself great enough to do whatever the members wanted to do. *Llegar a ser* implies that over time something becomes something else. *Ponerse* implies a change in emotional state of being or a physical change of some sort. *Convertirse* indicates a substantial conversion, from one state to another.

10. (B) *hubo*. This third person singular form of *haber* means *there was*. The preterit is the best selection here because the context is a specific moment in time in the past in which the action is completed. None of the other alternatives communicate this meaning.

11. (B) *eso*. This neuter demonstrative pronoun has no specific antecedent. *Eso*, meaning *that*, is used to refer to past time in which the speaker is reflecting on the early success.

SELECCIÓN DOS

1. (A) *pauta*. This is a vocabulary question, and all of these words are adjectives. You may recognize some of these adjectives, but if you do not, look for prefixes that may help. *Insólita* could remind you of the word *insolent*, which, with some creative thinking could yield its meaning: *unaccustomed* or *unusual*. In English *insolent* implies lack of respect, perhaps from lack of understanding or unfamiliarity. If you have to think too long about these meanings, however, it is best to skip the question and return to it if you have time later. The best preparation is to look up adjectives that you come across in reading, if you see the same one more than a couple of times.

2. (D) *haber*. Remember that after a preposition (such as *de, a, con, por, para, sin, en*), you should always use an infinitive, no matter what the English word would be in translation.

3. (C) *pero*. Since there is no verb in the clause introduced by the conjunction, *sino que* is not appropriate. *Sino* indicates a positive statement in direct contrast to a preceding negative. *Ya* is not appropriate, since the information contained in the clause qualifies the adjective *contemporáneo*. The conjunction *and* implies equivalencies.

4. (B) *la*. This is an example of the redundant use of a direct object pronoun, meaning that it is not necessary. The noun to which it refers is *raíz*. Remember that the pronoun can precede the conjugated verb, or it can be attached to the end of the infinitive *perder*.

5. (B) *se ha*. This is an example of the impersonal *se*, used when there is no specific subject of the verb, and is expressed in English as a passive voice construction. The subject is *la diferencia* and the present perfect is used because in the context of this paragraph, the speaker is talking about articles that have appeared in the recent past, just prior to the present moment.

6. (C) *salga*. The present subjunctive is used in a dependent noun clause after a main clause containing a verb of volition (granting permission, request, expressing desire, etc.). The present is used because in the sequence of tenses, the present subjunctive follows present tense verbs in the main clause.

7. (B) *Será*. To express probability in the present, use the future. Remember that this tense in English would be expressed with a phrase such as *Could teamwork be the key...?* Or sometimes, *I wonder what...?* or *I wonder who...?* This is a rhetorical question that is answered in the following sentence.

8. (D) *hubiéramos*. The past subjunctive is used in this case because this is an *if-then* statement. Notice that in the *then* portion of the sentence, the *-iera* form of the past subjunctive is used in place of the conditional tense. Be sure to scan the whole reading passage before going to the questions.

9. (C) *nosotras*. The rest of the sentence reveals that the speaker is talking about all three of the women who direct the group and the role that each one has in the dance company. Another indication is the use of the first person plural in the verb at the beginning of the sentence.

10. (C) *aliciente*. With a good English vocabulary you can recognize some of these adjectives, such as *pernicioso* (meaning *insidious, harmful*). However, you should be aware of false cognates, such as *real*, which can mean *royal*.

Two prefixes in front of *visto* mean *not* and *before*, giving *imprevisto* the meaning of *unforeseen*. By the process of elimination you can arrive at the correct answer, *aliciente,* which means *attractive, pleasing.*

11. (B) *bailen.* The present subjunctive is used in this dependent noun clause following an impersonal expression, *es más + adjective.* Do not be confused by unusual syntax, when the object of the verb comes before the verb in the place where you would ordinarily find the subject. If you take the time to identify the subject and object of each verb, you will not make careless mistakes.

SELECCIÓN TRES

1. (B) *cabía.* If you had read the whole passage first, you would have noticed that the whole selection is told in the past tense. The imperfect is used to relate background information in this case. An indicator of this tense is the imperfect in the verb *decía.*

2. (B) *los demás. Demás* is an adjective that is invariable, but the definite article, *los,* must agree with the noun it modifies, *pasajeros.*

3. (D) *pudiera.* To express contrary-to-fact information, or to communicate hypothetical situations, use the past subjunctive. This is an elliptical statement, meaning that part of it is omitted, which is indicated by the three dots at the end of the clause. The omitted part is a *then* clause, and the part that is expressed is the *if* portion. *Pudiera* is the only correct answer.

4. (C) *volaremos.* The future is used here. Although the simple present tense *volamos* could also be used, the future is probably the best choice. You should notice that this is dialogue embedded in the story, which is told in the past tense. Even though *nosotros* comes after the verb, it is the subject; it cannot be an object pronoun.

5. (B) *aún.* This adverb has the meaning of *as yet,* which is the best answer in this case. *Aún,* with an accent mark, should not be confused with *aun,* without an accent mark. Although the latter is an adverb, it is also a conjunction that means *even* or *still. Ya* usually means *already.*

6. (C) *embocadura.* Embedded in the first two choices is some form of the word *barco,* which can be associated with rivers. *Flotación* is also associated with water, but none of these refers to a part of a river, such as the mouth. *Boca,* in the middle of *embocadura* should give you a clue about its meaning. The suffix *-dura* indicates a noun.

7. (B) *peleaban.* The imperfect is used here to show something that was going on when something else happened. This is the only correct answer.

8. (C) *Nadie.* From the use of *pero* at the beginning of the next sentence and the context you can deduce that no one noticed except Pío. If you missed this question, you may want to review indefinite adjectives, pronouns, and adverbs.

9. (A) *lo que.* This relative pronoun refers to a concept or an idea, so the neuter form is used.

10. (D) *quién.* Since the person to whom this pronoun refers is unknown, the interrogative is used. The personal a before the verb should indicate an interrogative pronoun that refers to a person. Remember that all interrogative pronouns have an accent mark, even when they occur in declarative sentences.

11. (D) *averiguarlo.* This verb contains an English word that is related to the meaning of *averiguar, verify. Avergonzarlo* is the verb form of *vergüenza.*

SELECCIÓN CUATRO

1. (A) *varían.* This is the present indicative of the verb *variar.* Remember that verbs with a weak vowel next to the infinitive ending take an accent mark in the present on the *i.* Without the accent mark, the stress would not fall on the stem of the verb. In the first person plural, there is no accent mark, because the ending is a two syllable ending, and in the second person, there is an accent mark on the *a,* in *áis.* There are other verbs like this one, such as *enviar* and *esquiar.* If you see these verbs on the free response section, you need to remember the accents, because the verb form is incorrect without the accent mark.

2. (C) *altere.* After the adverbial conjunction *sin que,* you should always use the subjunctive. According to the proper sequence of tenses, you should use the present subjunctive after the present tense in the main clause. This is the only correct answer.

3. (B) *mayor.* Of all of these words, *mayor* is the only one that refers to greater size. *Menor* refers to size, also, but in the context of this paragraph does not make sense.

4. (A) *endurecimiento. Duro* is the adjective in the middle of this word, and is related to *hardening* of the arteries. *Botella* in the middle of *embotellamiento* does not make sense, nor does *engordamiento,* which contains the adjective *gorda.*

5. (D) *lo cual.* After the preposition *por, lo cual* is used to avoid any possibility of confusion with *por qué,* the interrogative pronoun. The neuter is used because the antecedent for this relative pronoun is the idea contained in the previous sentence.

6. (A) *ocurre.* The simple present indicative is used here because there is no need to use the subjunctive. Remember that most often the indicative is used after *si* if verbs are in the present tense. This is not an *if-then* statement, so the past subjunctive is not used. You should always look for the conditional tense in one of the clauses whenever you see *si,* because it frequently indicates an *if-then* statement.

7. (D) *identificasen.* The past subjunctive is used in this dependent noun clause after *requerir,* because it expresses volition (a command, request, desire, etc.). The other verbs in the paragraph are in past tenses, indicating the need for the past subjunctive. Remember that there are two sets of endings you can use for the past subjunctive, the *-ra* form, or the *-se* form. Review these endings in the appendix of this book if you do not remember the latter form.

8. (A) *están.* This question requires you to decide between some of the different verbs that mean *to be.* Since this is a description of a state of being, the verb *estar* is correct. *Ser* is used to describe inherent or definitive characteristics. *Ser* plus the past participle also frequently indicates the passive voice when the agent is expressed, which is not the case in this example. The verb *haber* also is frequently used with a past participle, but in compound tenses, which makes no sense in the context of this sentence. Also notice that in the following line the words *puede estar escrita* indicates the use of *estar.* Although this repetition would rarely occur on the examination, always be sure to look at the whole context, not just the words that immediately precede or follow the blank.

9. (D) *empeorar.* Once again, an adjective found in the middle of a word in a vocabulary question can reveal the correct answer. *Peor* relates to getting worse, which makes sense in this sample.

10. (D) *comitiera. Hasta que* is an adverb conjunction of time. In the sequence of tenses in this paragraph the action in the dependent clause has not already occurred from the perspective of the time in the main clause, so the subjunctive is used. Usually you will find the subjunctive in adverb clauses of time when the future is used in the main clause, or when the action has not yet happened (such as a command). If you are unclear about sequences of time and the subjunctive, review the appropriate section of the appendix of this book.

11. (C) *cuánto.* The neuter form of the interrogative is used here because the amount is unknown. Also notice the past subjunctive *esforzaran* in the dependent adjective clause because *no importa* is an impersonal expression.

SELECCIÓN CINCO

1. (C) *inició.* Since the specific hour is mentioned here, there is no doubt that the preterit here refers to a point in time when the action was begun and completed. The rest of the story is also told in the preterit, so this first verb is the beginning of a narrative.

2. (C) *Pasadas.* This adjective refers to *horas.* Although the noun is not mentioned, the article *las* indicates that the numbers refer to an hour of the day. Do not be confused by the singular verb form; the subject is *la reunión,* but the adjective does not refer to this noun.

3. (C) *Está. Estar* in this case refers to a resultant action, instead of definitive characteristics. Also notice that the present is used since the sentence is dialogue.

4. (A) *aportar.* If you do not know this verb, try to figure out others. If you know Latin, you could probably guess that *hurtar* means *to steal, to rob,* and you would recognize that often words in Spanish have an *h* where Latin uses an *f*. A word in English with a related meaning would be *furtive. Solicitar* means to *solicit* in the sense of petitioning or applying for something like a job. It is not exactly a cognate, but the meaning is close enough for you to figure out that it does not make sense in the context of this paragraph.

5. (A) *pasa.* There is no reason to use a past or conditional tense in this sentence. Other verbs in the sentence are in the present tense.

6. (A) *sino.* After a negative statement of what something is not, *sino* is used to introduce a positive statement. The verb in the subsequent clause occurs after another relative pronoun, *que.*

7. (D) *por.* Because this preposition indicates *through, among, between* in this sentence, *por* is the only answer in these choices that communicates that meaning. Remember that *por* most often refers to source, manner of action, or reciprocal action, while *para* pertains to destinations in time or space, and contrasts. *Para* will indicate a recipient of an action.

8. (C) *sea.* The subjunctive in this clause indicates uncertainty. Implied is a main clause stating that *it does not matter...,* which is an impersonal expression. The time frame is present, so a past tense is not correct.

9. (B) *era.* The imperfect here is correct because this impersonal expression is not limited in regard to time; it does not refer to a specific moment in past time that is completed. In the context of the whole sentence the present tense is not the best choice.

10. (B) *a mitad.* There are a number of expressions to communicate the concept of a half, or half way. The last two choices do not make sense, and *de* after the blank limits the possibilities to B.

11. (D) *eso*. The neuter form of *that* is used to refer to the whole preceding situation. Notice demonstrative pronouns have an accent mark, while demonstrative adjectives do not. If you have difficulty with demonstratives, review the grammar at the end.

SELECCIÓN SEIS

1. (B) *desarrollen*. Although the structure of this sentence is a little different, you can still recognize the expression of volition in the main clause, which means that you need the subjunctive in the dependent clause. The present tense is used because all the other verbs are present or future tense.

2. (A) *la que*. This relative pronoun is the subject of the verb *se encargaría*. The referent is *la comisión*.

3. (C) *funcionará*. There is no reason to use the subjunctive, and the future is the best choice because the action has not happened yet. It is not the immediate future, either, so the present tense instead of the future is not the best selection.

4. (D) *como*. This is the only alternative that means *as*, when it is not a conjunction.

5. (B) *reciba*. In this adjective clause, the referent is indefinite, so the subjunctive is indicated. Even though there are some verbs in the conditional, the time frame of the whole passage is present and future.

6. (B) *Ésta*. This demonstrative pronoun refers to *la idea*, so the feminine singular form is necessary.

7. (C) *chocaría*. The conditional is used because it will not necessarily happen. There is no reason to use the subjunctive, because the conjunction that begins the clause is *porque*.

8. (D) *No obstante*. This expression means *notwithstanding*, or *nevertheless*, which is the best alternative in the context of this paragraph. If you are not familiar with the transitional expressions in these alternatives, it would be helpful to learn them to use on other parts of the examination. You will find them again in the free response writing section of this book.

9. (B) *vede*. Even if you do not know what this verb means, you can eliminate some of these choices. Choice C tells you that the verb is an *-ar* verb, so the present subjunctive is alternative B. This verb also occurs in a main clause, but it follows the word *quizá*, which means that the subjunctive can be used. In the context of this paragraph, the subjunctive is correct to express the uncertainty about what the president will do.

10. (C) *afectaría*. This is an *if-then* statement and the conditional is needed in the *then* portion. Remember that *aceptase* would not be correct because you could only use the *-ara* form instead of the conditional.

11. (B) *actuales*. Be careful of some cognates, such as *actual*, which means *present* or *current*. There are other false cognates in this list of choice that you need to learn to recognize.

SELECCIÓN SIETE

1. (B) *poco*. *Pequeño* refers to size and *poco* refers to quantity. In this context *poco* is the best choice.

2. (A) *precipita*. Of all of the choices, this is the only one that makes any sense. *Precipitar* is a false cognate, since the word in English is associated with rain. But it means *to start toward* in Spanish, a meaning that is not readily apparent. In the adjective form, *precipitous*, the meaning is a little closer, meaning a sudden change. *Elude* has a related meaning, but in the context

of the paragraph, the meaning makes little sense, and can be eliminated. *Proporcionar* has a related meaning, too, although it is even more obscure. The word is relatively common in Spanish and means *to apportion, to supply, to provide.*

3. (C) *las cuales.* A relative pronoun referring to *razones* is needed in this blank. Do not be misled by the singular verb form; the subject of the verb is *una.* Also remember that after *por, cual* is used instead of *que* to avoid confusion with *porque.*

4. (D) *fueron.* Even though the subject comes after the verb in this case, you could figure out that the third person plural is needed because *los libros* has no meaning if it is not the subject. The preterit is necessary because the speaker is referring to a specific moment that is completed in the past.

5. (B) *nada.* Since *tener que ver* means *to have to do with*, there is no other choice that makes sense. Be sure not to confuse *nada* with *nadie* or *nunca.* Remember that if the negative indefinite pronoun comes before the verb, no other negative word is needed, but if it comes after the verb, a negative must be used before the verb.

6. (C) *abriendo.* After a verb of perception or motion, the present participle can be used as an adverb, which is the case in this sentence. *Se* indicates the *se* substitute for the passive voice, and *me* is an indirect object pronoun. The infinitive *abrir* is not correct because it makes no sense as the object of the verb. The past participles *abierto* and *abiertas* do not make sense because as past participles they would function as adjectives, describing a noun. There is no noun to which they could refer after the verb *ir.* And after the verb *ser* used with the pronouns, these participles do not make sense. If you are confused by the pronouns, review the grammar referring to the uses of pronouns in the appendix.

7. (C) *Quise.* The preterit in this instance is necessary to communicate the idea of effort on the author's part. Remember that there are several verbs that have different meanings in the preterit. *Querer* means *to attempt* or *to try.* *No querer* means *to refuse*, which is the logical translation of the preterit tense of *not wanting* in a specific moment in the past. Verbs with special meanings are listed in the appendix of this book.

8. (C) *esfuerce.* The present subjunctive is needed in this dependent noun clause after an impersonal expression in the main clause. Even if you do not recognize the word *imprescindible*, you can recognize the structure of *es* (*ser*), with no apparent subject, then an adjective. Words that end with *-ible* are frequently adjectives. The present is used because *es* is the present tense of *ser.* This is the only correct choice for this question.

9. (B) *En.* The difference between *en* and *a* is very subtle. One clue would be that *a* is used with an article. *En* is used to designate something that happens at a given moment. *A* is used to express a specific hour when something happens, or something that happens after a period of time, or things that happen at the same time (*al* + the infinitive). *Para* indicates a deadline, a time by which something has to be done or something is to happen. *Del* indicates a point in time from which subsequent time is measured. It would also help to understand that *término* is not readily translated in this example; the whole phrase means *In the first place....*

10. (B) *impunemente.* Perhaps the English word *impunity* could be a clue to the correct meaning of this adverb. The adjective *maligno* should be recognizable from the English word *malignant*, meaning *harmful.* *Sumamente* can

be deduced from the verb *sumar*, which means *to add up, to total up*. The adverb means *highly, exceedingly*. *Propiamente* comes from *propio*, meaning *own* or *proper*. It is a common expression used to say *properly speaking*, for example.

11. (D) *jamás*. The following sentence limits the choice to *jamás*, although *nunca* would also have been a correct response, if it had been offered. *Por poco*, meaning *almost*, is a possibility, but is not the best choice because the conjunction *pero* indicates that the speaker's response to his situation was directly contrary to what he could have done, which was flee the neighborhood.

SELECCIÓN OCHO

1. (D) *ni*. The correct conjunction here is the Spanish equivalent of *neither*. *Pero* is not a correct choice because the next part of the sentence states that the other man did not know anything about the speaker.

2. (B) *ante*. Be sure not to confuse *ante* and *antes*. *Ante* means *before, in the presence of*, and is related to how things are placed (spacial relationships). *Antes*, meaning *before*, refers to time (temporal relationships). If may be helpful to review those prepositions that describe the physical locations, such as *after, beside, above, over, alongside*, etc. *Hacia*, meaning *toward*, also is a preposition that you should be able to recognize. Do not confuse it with *hacía*, which has an accent mark and is a verb form.

3. (C) *estuvieron*. The third person plural preterit is used here because the speaker refers to an event that is completed in the past. The difference between the imperfect and the preterit is often stated as the difference between describing a past event and narrating an event. In the context of this passage, the narrator has used the imperfect up to this point to describe the scene, using the verbs *veía, hallaba, resolvía*. The conjunction *pero* indicates that the narrator is through describing the event; he is now narrating the moment when something took place. It began when the animals were right there, almost upon him. The verbs after *pero* are in the preterit, as the narrator relates the story of what happened. Remember that the preterit is used for actions that have a beginning or an ending at a specific moment in the past.

4. (A) *insoportable*. The verb *soportar* is a false cognate. Instead of *support*, it means *tolerable*. The prefix *-in* means *not*, so the adjective is *intolerable*. But since all of the prefixes are *-in*, you need other information to make a good guess if you do not recognize the words. *Oportuno* means *opportune*, but in the sense of *timely*. Most likely, to make a correct selection in this question you need to figure out that *agrandarse* means *to become greater* or *larger*.

5. (B) *mí*. After a preposition, *para*, a prepositional pronoun is used. Since all of the possessive adjectives and reflexive pronouns in the preceding phrase are first person singular, *mí* is the only correct answer in this case. Remember that *mi* is a possessive adjective because it has no accent mark.

6. (D) *apoyaron*. The plural preterit is used because the subjects are *pie* and *manos*. The preterit is used because the narrator is retelling what happened.

7. (C) *derecho*. All of the words meaning *right* or *straight* can be confusing. This is a vocabulary question that would be difficult to answer correctly unless you knew the words. The word *derecho* can have a variety of mean-

ings, depending on how it is used, from *right hand*, as an adjective, to *law* or *right* as a noun. In this choice, *exacto* and *claro* do not really fit, and can be eliminated. *Erguido* comes from the verb *erguir*, meaning to *erect, to set up straight.*

8. (D) *pudiera.* The past subjunctive is used here in a dependent noun clause after a verb expressing doubt in the main clause. There is no other correct choice.

9. (B) *decidía.* The imperfect is used here because the narrator is describing possible actions. Notice that the construction of *De no ocurrir* is used as a substitute for the past subjunctive in an *if-then* statement, and the conditional part of the sentence occurs after the *if* clauses that describe actions that would happen. This blank is for one verb in a parallel construction, with *lanzazo* as the subject of the first verb, and *palo* as the subject of the second verb, *quería.* By looking carefully at the structure of the sentence, you could see that this blank is not the *if* portion of the main *if-then* statement. It is quite possible to use the imperfect after *si* in the past, but use the past subjunctive after *si* in *if-then* statements.

10. (B) *agrupándose.* The present participle is used as an adverb in this case. Although it may seem that C is a possible choice, it is not because of a lack of a conjunction, such as *y* before the last clause, *empezaron también a correr.* None of the other choices makes sense grammatically.

11. (D) *hubiesen.* The past subjunctive is always required after *como si*, without exception. Remember to review the *-se* form of the past subjunctive if you do not recognize it.

12. (C) *alentador.* This is a vocabulary question. *Alentar* means *to breathe, to cheer, to encourage,* hence the adjective has to do with encouraging someone, or cheering them on. *Temeroso* can be deduced from *temor*, meaning *fearful. Mezquino* means *petty, miserly,* or *mean.*

SELECCIÓN NUEVE

1. (A) *avergüenza.* Do not assume that every blank will have to be filled with a subjunctive or preterit or imperfect verb form. If you read the whole selection before beginning you will notice that all the other verbs are in the present. You will also notice that there is no reason to use the subjunctive in the main clause at the beginning of this selection.

2. (C) *oficio.* This word is a false cognate; it means *office* only in the sense of *vocation, profession, duty.* But *deber* means *duty* in the sense of *obligation.* It helps to know that *avergonzar* means to *embarrass.* Knowing this verb, combined with the italicized words in the sentence should help you recognize that *oficio* is the correct choice.

3. (B) *detenía.* The phrase *cada vez* indicates ongoing action, so the imperfect is the only correct choice in this case. Look at other verbs in the sentence, also, to see that there is some correlation between the tense you choose for the blank and other tenses in the sentence.

4. (B) *lenta.* Remember that when there are two consecutive adverbs, the first one is shortened and ends in *a.* You might also want to review how to form adverbs from adjectives.

5. (C) *tenga.* Even if you did not realize that the third person command was the correct choice in this question, you should have noticed that the following clause contained *vaya*, which is another third person command. It occurs in a parallel construction.

6. (B) *derramándose.* This vocabulary question has some choices that you can easily eliminate. Although *gota*, meaning *drop*, appears in one of the options, the prefix *a* frequently, but not always, indicates negation. *Agotar* means *to drain off, to exhaust.* On the other hand, the prefix *de-*, indicates separation. Either of the first two choices would be better guesses than the last two, based on the prefixes.

7. (C) *oiga.* This is another third person singular command, required because in the context the speaker is expressing exasperation because the attendant does not listen to his advice about the problem he has with his car. The simple indicative would be a possibility, except that the attendant would not say the next sentence if he had understood what the speaker was saying. *Oíd* is the second person plural form, that is not appropriate here.

8. (A) *nunca.* The negative in front of the verb is a clue to the negative indefinite adverb, *nunca.*

9. (D) *dijera.* The past subjunctive is needed in this dependent adjective clause because the antecedent is nonexistent. All the other verbs in the sentence are in a past tense.

10. (A) *se realizó.* Remember that this verb is a false cognate. It means *to realize* in the sense of fulfilling a dream or coming into being. Students frequently confuse *realizar* and *darse cuenta de*, but do not assume that just because both vocabulary items are included, *darse cuenta* is the correct answer. *Transcurrir* does mean *to pass*, but only when talking about time.

11. (C) *lo.* The antecedent for this pronoun is the idea expressed in the words *escupe mucho.* If you cannot identify a noun that a pronoun would replace, always consider using the neuter form. You might also notice that *lo mismo*, meaning *the same thing*, uses a neuter article with an adjective. It also refers to the words *escupe mucho.*

SELECCIÓN DIEZ

1. (D) *lo que.* This relative pronoun is needed as the subject of the verb that follows it. *Que* is used to introduce dependent clauses, but needs an article to make it a relative pronoun in his sentence. If you have difficulty deciding when to use *lo que*, try using *that which* in determining the English meaning of the Spanish words.

2. (C) *observé.* The imperfect after *mientras* indicates ongoing action that is background information. The imperfect "sets the stage" for narrating something that happens, as is the case in this question. The personal *a* tells that *mis compañeros* is the object of the verb, not the subject.

3. (D) *anhelantes. Aniquilado* means *annihilated*, which is not exactly a cognate, but if you are guessing, perhaps could be enough of a clue to eliminate it in this question. You need an adjective that describes the attitude of a group of people who are watching something dramatic happen. *Pululante* has an English cognate, *pullulating*, but it probably will not help, unless you know its other meaning, *sprouting.* The prefix *entre-* on the next adjective should help you eliminate it; it means *between. Anhelante* means *eagerly, longingly;* which would be appropriate in this question.

4. (C) *aunque.* The adjective following this blank provides additional information about the state of being of the workers watching the scene the narrator describes. To make the correct selection in this question, you need to realize that *transpirar* means to *perspire.* In this case, the meaning implicit in *although* is the best choice. *In spite of the fact* that they could be seen per-

spiring, the workers were not tired. *Sino que* is not correct because the phrase that follows it does not contain a verb.

5. (B) *empezaba*. The imperfect is the best choice in this question because the narrator is describing the beginning of the fight. He does not just say that it began and continue his narration. Notice that only the verb *observé* is in the preterit, further indicating that the narrator is describing the action, not narrating what happened. This information is background for the conversation that follows, which is narrated, and the action that follows in the second part of the passage.

6. (B) *mío*. Since there is no preposition *de*, the longer form of the possessive adjective is correct when it follows the noun. The first person is indicated by *me* before the verb that follows the blank.

7. (B) *jactancioso*. This adjective comes from *jactar*, meaning *to boast*. Remember that *jubilar* means *to retire from work* and is a false cognate. *Asqueroso* means *detestable* and *chisposo* means *sparkling* or *sputtering*.

8. (C) *lo*. This direct object pronoun refers to the speaker, third person singular, masculine and is the only choice that makes sense grammatically. *Él* and *Vd.* cannot be the subjects because *el policía* is the subject. The second person singular is never used in this passage, and there is no reason to use it here.

9. (C) *habría podido*. The conditional expresses the narrator's attitude, to explain why he repeated his response to the question. Notice that you use the conditional in this clause; the sentence is not an *if-then* statement. The imperfect in the following clause explains why he would not be able to explain.

10. (A) *los*. With parts of the body and articles of clothing, possession is usually indicated with an indirect object pronoun. In other cases, where possession is indicated by the subject of the verb (*the men raised...*), the definite article is used.

11. (B) *Mueran*. This third person plural command is indicated by the noun, *verdugos*. Even if you do not recognize the noun that is the subject of the verb, you can assume that it is someone who oppresses the masses since the verb is *morir*. This whole scene describes a confrontation between two groups, the police and the workers. In the context of this setting, the command is correct.

SELECCIÓN ONCE

1. (D) *ha sido*. The present perfect is the best choice in this question because the speaker is referring to all time from past up to the present. The verb *ser* is correct because the characteristic *constante* is definitive.

2. (B) *Antaño*. From the rest of this paragraph, it is apparent that this speaker is talking about a long time ago. Of all of the choices, this one is the only one that would communicate that meaning. *Anterior* would usually have *-mente* on the end if it were used as an adverb in this case.

3. (C) *tal*. This adjective is used because it is the only choice that would mean *such*. *Tanta* is also an adjective, but it means *so much* used before a noun. Since there is no *como* in a following phrase, any form of *tanto* can be eliminated. If you are unclear about comparisons of equality or inequality, you may want to review them.

4. (A) *crece*. The present is indicated by the phrase *al momento*. Even though this is a rather lengthy sentence, there are not many verbs. When you come

across this kind of text, be sure you can correctly identify the subjects and objects, then look for adverbs that will reveal information about the frame of reference in time.

5. (A) *por.* When *por* is followed by an infinitive, it expresses impending action, or an action that is not yet completed, as is the case in this question. *Para* followed by an infinitive expresses purpose, indicated in English by *in order to* + the verb. *En* is a literal translation from English to Spanish that is not the best selection.

6. (C) *Por lo tanto. Therefore* is the best transitional phrase to introduce the next idea that the writer presents. It is a logical continuation of the thoughts already presented. *Sin embargo*, meaning *nevertheless*, implies a following statement in opposition to the previous one. *Al tanto* has no coherent meaning in this context; it means *up to date, current.* Similarly, a *continuación* means *following.*

7. (C) *sino.* The use of *además* then *no sólo* in the previous clauses indicates that *sino* is the best choice in this question. The logic of the selection is *moreover . . . not only . . . but (also) . . .*, even though *sobre todo* is used instead of *también.* In the following clause, *porque* is used, which means that *sino que* is not correct.

8. (A) *lo.* This direct object pronoun refers to *problema* and is used redundantly. The subject of the verb follows it. Notice that the noun that is the direct object also precedes the verb. With this inverted syntax, or word order, the pronoun functions as a marker.

9. (C) *Esto.* The neuter demonstrative pronoun is used here to refer to the idea presented in the preceding material. It is the only possible choice in this case. To test whether it would make sense, if you are unsure, try to identify the noun to which the pronoun would refer and see what it would mean in the context.

10. (D) *idóneo.* This adjective is used instead of *ideal.* From Latin, the meaning of *célere*, meaning *quickly* would be apparent. The word is related to the English word accelerate. *Eficaz* is a cognate, meaning *efficient. Suministro* means *supply.*

11. (B) *el que. El sistema económico* is the referent for this relative pronoun, that functions as the subject of the verb it follows. The word order in this sentence necessitates using *el que*, meaning *that which.*

SELECCIÓN DOCE

1. (D) *borrosa.* This adjective means *muddy, blurred.* All of the other words are cognates, but in order to recognize them, a good English vocabulary is necessary. Some of them also come from Latin, so knowledge of Latin roots may help. *Brusca* means *rude, rough*, which are similar to *brusk. Calumniosa* is *calumnious*, meaning *slanderous. Egregia* is *egregious*, meaning *extraordinary* or *scandalous.*

2. (C) *en qué.* Remember that the verb *consistir* is followed by the preposition *en. Qué* has an accent mark because it is an interrogative in this sentence.

3. (D) *vea.* The subjunctive is used in this sentence because it occurs in a dependent noun clause after an impersonal expression, *es improbable.* The present is used because *es* is present tense.

4. (A) *perspicazmente.* This adverb is a cognate for *perspicaciously*, meaning *with keen judgement*, or *wisely.* Although this may seem to be a rather unusual word, it is not as uncommon in Spanish as it is in English. *Vana-*

mente is also a cognate; you may recognize *vainly*, used to describe a futile effort. *Lozanamente* means *briskly, nimbly*. *Soberbiamente* comes from *soberbia*, which, although it looks like *sober* in English, really means *arrogant*. The adverb, then, means *haughtily* or *arrogantly*.

5. (B) *apenas*. This adverb means *scarcely*, and in the context of this passage is the best choice. With the sequence of tenses, *cuando florecieron* before, and *se contaba con* after the blank, choices A and C do not make sense. *Por casualidad* does not make any sense at all.

6. (D) *llegase*. The past subjunctive is used in this clause because it occurs in a dependent noun clause after a verb expressing hope. In this case *se contaba con que...*, using the *se* substitute for the passive voice means that the subject is *nada*. Even though the word order in this sentence is inverted and the dependent adverb clause comes first in the sentence, if you can locate the subject of the verb, you can figure out the correct answer.

7. (D) *desarrollara*. The past subjunctive occurs here in a dependent noun clause after an impersonal expression. Even though it is expressed using the pluperfect subjunctive, *hubiera sido*, it is still an impersonal expression because the subject, *it*, does not refer to any specific antecedent. Remember that the impersonal expression may not always be expressed in the simple present, preterit, or imperfect indicative tenses.

8. (A) *digamos*. There is no indication of the subject of this verb in this passage, but all the choices are first person plural. In trying to decide which tense to use, it is helpful to understand that this speaker is expressing an opinion, and appears to be inviting the reader to consider the topic from his point of view. This is an example of a first person plural indirect command: *let's not say original*. The idea at the end of this paragraph returns to the writer's point of view in the first sentence of the paragraph, where he states that from the time of the Spanish Civil War, people do not expect the unexpected.

9. (D) *uno*. *One's self* is what is meant in this sentence. There is no other antecedent to which any of the other choices could refer. Notice that *si* does not have an accent mark, which would be necessary if it were to come before *mismo*. *Lo mismo* does not make sense because *persona* in the following part of the sentence makes it clear that the writer is talking about a person reflecting on his own reality.

10. (C) *la cual*. The antecedent for this relative pronoun is *realidad*. *La cual* emphasizes that one particular reality is meant from a variety that present themselves to a person. A person exists within a particular reality. *Realidad* and *pertence* and *uno* at the end of the sentence all indicate the gender of the article to use with the relative pronoun.

11. (A) *tantos*. This adjective is nominalized; *autores* is understood. Even if you did not know that *Unamuno* was a *writer* of the *Generación de '98*, the context should strongly suggest that he was a writer. Since the topic is originality, you would think of a creative person, such as a writer. *Tales* would not precede *más*, and *cuantos* does not have an accent mark. *Los* is not used before *más*, but before *demás*.

CHAPTER 5: Answer Sheet for
Name-the-Error Exercises

Group One
1. Ⓐ Ⓑ Ⓒ Ⓓ
2. Ⓐ Ⓑ Ⓒ Ⓓ
3. Ⓐ Ⓑ Ⓒ Ⓓ
4. Ⓐ Ⓑ Ⓒ Ⓓ
5. Ⓐ Ⓑ Ⓒ Ⓓ
6. Ⓐ Ⓑ Ⓒ Ⓓ
7. Ⓐ Ⓑ Ⓒ Ⓓ
8. Ⓐ Ⓑ Ⓒ Ⓓ
9. Ⓐ Ⓑ Ⓒ Ⓓ
10. Ⓐ Ⓑ Ⓒ Ⓓ
11. Ⓐ Ⓑ Ⓒ Ⓓ
12. Ⓐ Ⓑ Ⓒ Ⓓ

Group Four
1. Ⓐ Ⓑ Ⓒ Ⓓ
2. Ⓐ Ⓑ Ⓒ Ⓓ
3. Ⓐ Ⓑ Ⓒ Ⓓ
4. Ⓐ Ⓑ Ⓒ Ⓓ
5. Ⓐ Ⓑ Ⓒ Ⓓ
6. Ⓐ Ⓑ Ⓒ Ⓓ
7. Ⓐ Ⓑ Ⓒ Ⓓ
8. Ⓐ Ⓑ Ⓒ Ⓓ
9. Ⓐ Ⓑ Ⓒ Ⓓ
10. Ⓐ Ⓑ Ⓒ Ⓓ
11. Ⓐ Ⓑ Ⓒ Ⓓ
12. Ⓐ Ⓑ Ⓒ Ⓓ

Group Seven
1. Ⓐ Ⓑ Ⓒ Ⓓ
2. Ⓐ Ⓑ Ⓒ Ⓓ
3. Ⓐ Ⓑ Ⓒ Ⓓ
4. Ⓐ Ⓑ Ⓒ Ⓓ
5. Ⓐ Ⓑ Ⓒ Ⓓ
6. Ⓐ Ⓑ Ⓒ Ⓓ
7. Ⓐ Ⓑ Ⓒ Ⓓ
8. Ⓐ Ⓑ Ⓒ Ⓓ
9. Ⓐ Ⓑ Ⓒ Ⓓ
10. Ⓐ Ⓑ Ⓒ Ⓓ
11. Ⓐ Ⓑ Ⓒ Ⓓ
12. Ⓐ Ⓑ Ⓒ Ⓓ

Group Ten
1. Ⓐ Ⓑ Ⓒ Ⓓ
2. Ⓐ Ⓑ Ⓒ Ⓓ
3. Ⓐ Ⓑ Ⓒ Ⓓ
4. Ⓐ Ⓑ Ⓒ Ⓓ
5. Ⓐ Ⓑ Ⓒ Ⓓ
6. Ⓐ Ⓑ Ⓒ Ⓓ
7. Ⓐ Ⓑ Ⓒ Ⓓ
8. Ⓐ Ⓑ Ⓒ Ⓓ
9. Ⓐ Ⓑ Ⓒ Ⓓ
10. Ⓐ Ⓑ Ⓒ Ⓓ
11. Ⓐ Ⓑ Ⓒ Ⓓ
12. Ⓐ Ⓑ Ⓒ Ⓓ

Group Two
1. Ⓐ Ⓑ Ⓒ Ⓓ
2. Ⓐ Ⓑ Ⓒ Ⓓ
3. Ⓐ Ⓑ Ⓒ Ⓓ
4. Ⓐ Ⓑ Ⓒ Ⓓ
5. Ⓐ Ⓑ Ⓒ Ⓓ
6. Ⓐ Ⓑ Ⓒ Ⓓ
7. Ⓐ Ⓑ Ⓒ Ⓓ
8. Ⓐ Ⓑ Ⓒ Ⓓ
9. Ⓐ Ⓑ Ⓒ Ⓓ
10. Ⓐ Ⓑ Ⓒ Ⓓ
11. Ⓐ Ⓑ Ⓒ Ⓓ
12. Ⓐ Ⓑ Ⓒ Ⓓ

Group Five
1. Ⓐ Ⓑ Ⓒ Ⓓ
2. Ⓐ Ⓑ Ⓒ Ⓓ
3. Ⓐ Ⓑ Ⓒ Ⓓ
4. Ⓐ Ⓑ Ⓒ Ⓓ
5. Ⓐ Ⓑ Ⓒ Ⓓ
6. Ⓐ Ⓑ Ⓒ Ⓓ
7. Ⓐ Ⓑ Ⓒ Ⓓ
8. Ⓐ Ⓑ Ⓒ Ⓓ
9. Ⓐ Ⓑ Ⓒ Ⓓ
10. Ⓐ Ⓑ Ⓒ Ⓓ
11. Ⓐ Ⓑ Ⓒ Ⓓ
12. Ⓐ Ⓑ Ⓒ Ⓓ

Group Eight
1. Ⓐ Ⓑ Ⓒ Ⓓ
2. Ⓐ Ⓑ Ⓒ Ⓓ
3. Ⓐ Ⓑ Ⓒ Ⓓ
4. Ⓐ Ⓑ Ⓒ Ⓓ
5. Ⓐ Ⓑ Ⓒ Ⓓ
6. Ⓐ Ⓑ Ⓒ Ⓓ
7. Ⓐ Ⓑ Ⓒ Ⓓ
8. Ⓐ Ⓑ Ⓒ Ⓓ
9. Ⓐ Ⓑ Ⓒ Ⓓ
10. Ⓐ Ⓑ Ⓒ Ⓓ
11. Ⓐ Ⓑ Ⓒ Ⓓ
12. Ⓐ Ⓑ Ⓒ Ⓓ

Group Eleven
1. Ⓐ Ⓑ Ⓒ Ⓓ
2. Ⓐ Ⓑ Ⓒ Ⓓ
3. Ⓐ Ⓑ Ⓒ Ⓓ
4. Ⓐ Ⓑ Ⓒ Ⓓ
5. Ⓐ Ⓑ Ⓒ Ⓓ
6. Ⓐ Ⓑ Ⓒ Ⓓ
7. Ⓐ Ⓑ Ⓒ Ⓓ
8. Ⓐ Ⓑ Ⓒ Ⓓ
9. Ⓐ Ⓑ Ⓒ Ⓓ
10. Ⓐ Ⓑ Ⓒ Ⓓ
11. Ⓐ Ⓑ Ⓒ Ⓓ
12. Ⓐ Ⓑ Ⓒ Ⓓ

Group Three
1. Ⓐ Ⓑ Ⓒ Ⓓ
2. Ⓐ Ⓑ Ⓒ Ⓓ
3. Ⓐ Ⓑ Ⓒ Ⓓ
4. Ⓐ Ⓑ Ⓒ Ⓓ
5. Ⓐ Ⓑ Ⓒ Ⓓ
6. Ⓐ Ⓑ Ⓒ Ⓓ
7. Ⓐ Ⓑ Ⓒ Ⓓ
8. Ⓐ Ⓑ Ⓒ Ⓓ
9. Ⓐ Ⓑ Ⓒ Ⓓ
10. Ⓐ Ⓑ Ⓒ Ⓓ
11. Ⓐ Ⓑ Ⓒ Ⓓ
12. Ⓐ Ⓑ Ⓒ Ⓓ

Group Six
1. Ⓐ Ⓑ Ⓒ Ⓓ
2. Ⓐ Ⓑ Ⓒ Ⓓ
3. Ⓐ Ⓑ Ⓒ Ⓓ
4. Ⓐ Ⓑ Ⓒ Ⓓ
5. Ⓐ Ⓑ Ⓒ Ⓓ
6. Ⓐ Ⓑ Ⓒ Ⓓ
7. Ⓐ Ⓑ Ⓒ Ⓓ
8. Ⓐ Ⓑ Ⓒ Ⓓ
9. Ⓐ Ⓑ Ⓒ Ⓓ
10. Ⓐ Ⓑ Ⓒ Ⓓ
11. Ⓐ Ⓑ Ⓒ Ⓓ
12. Ⓐ Ⓑ Ⓒ Ⓓ

Group Nine
1. Ⓐ Ⓑ Ⓒ Ⓓ
2. Ⓐ Ⓑ Ⓒ Ⓓ
3. Ⓐ Ⓑ Ⓒ Ⓓ
4. Ⓐ Ⓑ Ⓒ Ⓓ
5. Ⓐ Ⓑ Ⓒ Ⓓ
6. Ⓐ Ⓑ Ⓒ Ⓓ
7. Ⓐ Ⓑ Ⓒ Ⓓ
8. Ⓐ Ⓑ Ⓒ Ⓓ
9. Ⓐ Ⓑ Ⓒ Ⓓ
10. Ⓐ Ⓑ Ⓒ Ⓓ
11. Ⓐ Ⓑ Ⓒ Ⓓ
12. Ⓐ Ⓑ Ⓒ Ⓓ

Group Twelve
1. Ⓐ Ⓑ Ⓒ Ⓓ
2. Ⓐ Ⓑ Ⓒ Ⓓ
3. Ⓐ Ⓑ Ⓒ Ⓓ
4. Ⓐ Ⓑ Ⓒ Ⓓ
5. Ⓐ Ⓑ Ⓒ Ⓓ
6. Ⓐ Ⓑ Ⓒ Ⓓ
7. Ⓐ Ⓑ Ⓒ Ⓓ
8. Ⓐ Ⓑ Ⓒ Ⓓ
9. Ⓐ Ⓑ Ⓒ Ⓓ
10. Ⓐ Ⓑ Ⓒ Ⓓ
11. Ⓐ Ⓑ Ⓒ Ⓓ
12. Ⓐ Ⓑ Ⓒ Ⓓ

Error Recognition Exercises, Answers, and Answer Explanations

Like the exercises in the previous chapter, the error recognition exercises in this chapter can help you hone in on problem areas in grammar. Mistakes you may make here will reveal misconceptions you may have about what is correct grammar, syntax, and vocabulary. There is no better practice than finding the one word that makes no sense in a sentence. These exercises are particularly useful to learn the little details that reveal what makes a sentence confusing in Spanish. The explanations of the answers can help you clear up grammatical mistakes that you might have made on the paragraph completion exercises. Of special importance is to focus on identifying parts of speech, so that you can figure out what words are needed to be written in the blanks on the paragraph completion without root words section.

The exercises consist of sentences, each with four underlined words or phrases. Below each underlined element is a letter from A through D. Of the four words or phrases underlined only one choice is incorrect. You are to choose the **incorrect** word and write the corresponding letter on your answer sheet. The directions are given in English and in Spanish. This part of the exam is to check how well you understand the grammar. You can easily use a checklist of rules to determine the **incorrect** word. In some cases you do not even need to know what the words in the sentence mean if you can recognize parts of speech, make an educated guess about the gender of nouns, and remember basic rules of Spanish grammar.

Here is a checklist of grammatical points to remember:

1. Verbs need to be in the correct tense and mood. Check to see that the sequence of tenses is correct and that the subjunctive is used correctly in dependent noun and adjective clauses, and in subordinate adverb clauses. Most important, check the agreement of the subject and verb endings.
2. Pronouns need to be the correct kind.
3. Adjectives must agree with the nouns they modify in gender and number. Be especially careful to recognize nouns that end in -*a* that are masculine, and those that end in -*o* that are feminine, and to recognize compound forms such as *el rascacielos, el cumpleaños,* etc.
4. Watch for adjectives that need to be shortened before masculine singular nouns, such as *bueno, malo, primero, tercero, ciento, alguno, ninguno, uno,* and *santo* (unless *Santo* comes before a name that begins with *To-* or *Do-*). Also remember that the adjective *grande* is shortened before masculine and feminine singular nouns. Review when to shorten *ciento*.
5. The verb form that follows a preposition is always an infinitive.
6. All past participles that function as adjectives agree in gender and number with the nouns to which they refer.

7. All past participles that follow the auxiliary verb *haber* function as verb forms, and always end in *-o*.
8. Make sure you know which prepositions come after some verbs in idiomatic expressions.
9. Remember that when two or more adverbs are used, the first one or ones are shortened, and end in *-a*.
10. All present participles always end in *-o*.
11. Check that the conjunctions are correct, especially *pero, sino, sino que, y/e* and *o/u*.

Here are some strategies for taking this part of the exam:

1. Read the whole sentence before checking any of the grammatical points.
2. Identify the main verb and its subject.
3. Identify the objects of the verb.
4. Be especially careful of command forms that will require the subjunctive in the dependent clause. The hardest form to recognize is the familiar *tú* command, because it can appear to be a third person singular verb in a declarative sentence instead of a command. (For example: *Escucha a tu mamá, Juanito.*)
5. Look for the agreement of the indirect object pronoun and the subject of the verb in the dependent clause. (For example: *Pídanle a su profesor que les dé más tiempo.*)
6. Don't try to justify what you see; try to remember the rules of grammar that apply to each underlined word or phrase before making your choice of the incorrect part.
7. Use the process of elimination. If you know that three of the four points of grammar are correct, then assume that the fourth underlined word or phrase is the incorrect choice.
8. If you can eliminate two of the four possibilities, then make an educated guess.
9. Don't spend too much time on sentences where you cannot find the error; go on and finish what you can, and then go back to those sentences that are more difficult to do.

The following pages have 12 sets of sentences, with the answers and explanations following each set so that you can see why your answer was right or wrong. These exercises can be difficult if you are not very sure of your grammar. Remember that the grammar on the exam is precise. Although there are many ways of saying something in Spanish, there will always be only one correct answer. By the time you finish these exercises, you should feel a little more confident about your ability to recognize incorrect grammar. You should also have a better idea of what grammar points you are likely to see on the exam.

Directions: In the following sentence there are four words that are underlined. One of the four words is grammatically incorrect. You are to select the one incorrect word and write the corresponding letter of the word on your answer sheet.

Pídanle Vds. a <u>su</u> padre que <u>les</u> <u>da</u>   ○ ○ ● ○
        A   B C   A B C D
más dinero para el cine <u>esta</u> noche.
                    D

In the sample in the box, the incorrect word is *da*, which should be *dé*, because it occurs in a dependent noun clause after a verb of volition, *pedir. Su* is correct, because the possessive adjective, *your*, agrees with *padre*, not with *Vds. Les* is correct because it corresponds with the subject of *pidan*. Remember that *noche* is a feminine noun, so *esta* is correct.

This section of the exam requires you to think carefully about the rules for putting words together to make a coherent sentence. Use what you know about grammar, and some logic for eliminating some choices. Then make your decision based on a thought process, not on what you think sounds right. You can be very successful on this section if you are careful.

GROUP ONE

1. Me alegré que Vd. <u>habrá</u> <u>podido</u>
              A   B
comprender <u>lo</u> difícil que le <u>fue</u> admitir su
          C   D
error.

2. A los alumnos no <u>le</u> gusta <u>el</u> profesor
                A   B
que <u>le dé</u> demasiada tarea.
    C D

3. <u>Quien</u> sabe <u>qué</u> habría hecho el pobre con
  A   B
el premio si <u>lo</u> <u>habría</u> ganado.
        C   D

4. La casa, dentro de <u>la cual</u> pasamos <u>tantos</u>
               A   B
años felices, ahora <u>está</u> <u>destruido</u>.
               C   D

5. Ahora, <u>dígame</u>, <u>¿cómo</u> propones resolver
        A   B
<u>el</u> problema cuando <u>tienes</u> la oportunidad?
C   D

6. <u>Cualquier</u> maneras que <u>utilicen</u> Vds. <u>para</u>
    A   B   C
alcanzar su meta <u>serán</u> aceptables.
             D

7. No conocíamos a <u>ningún</u> pueblo que <u>era</u>
               A   B
más <u>lindo</u> que <u>aquél</u>.
   C   D

8. Tan pronto como <u>se</u> <u>vio</u> las noticias,
             A B
<u>supieron</u> lo triste que <u>fue</u> el suceso.
  C   D

9. <u>Ninguno</u> de los visitantes <u>habría</u> visto tal
  A   B
cosa en la vida si no <u>hubiera</u> sido <u>con ti</u>.
             C   D

10. No te <u>enojes</u> con tus amigos si no <u>le</u> dijiste
      A   B
que te <u>acompañaran</u> <u>al</u> programa.
     C   D

11. <u>Por</u> difícil que <u>ha</u> <u>sido</u>, hemos esperado
  A   B C
hasta que Vds. <u>vuelvan</u>.
         D

12. <u>Nos</u> recomendó que <u>habláramos</u> a los
  A   B
otros antes que <u>elegiríamos</u> <u>al</u> líder.
         C   D

Answers and Answer Explanations for Group One

1. (A) *hubiera, haya.* Either verb form would be correct in this case. After *alegrarse* the subjunctive is used in the dependent clause when there is a change of subject. After the auxiliary verb *haber*, the past participle *podido* is correct. The neuter article, *lo*, is used correctly with an adjective to mean *the difficult thing*. The preterite indicative *fue* is correct because there is no construction requiring the use of the subjunctive.

2. (C) *les*. The indirect object refers to *los alumnos*, so the pronouns should be third person, plural. *Les* is correct before *gusta* because *los alumnos* is the referent. *El profesor* is the subject of *gustar*, so the article without the personal *a* is correct. The verb *dé* is correct because the verb *gustar* has the meaning of a verb of emotion in this sentence.

3. (D) *hubiera*. The imperfect subjunctive is used in the *if-then* statement indicated by the use of the conditional in the *then* clause, and *si* at the beginning of the other clause. *Quien* is correct because it means *who*, and is not in an implied question. *Qué*, however, is an interrogative pronoun, so the use of the accent on the word is correct.

4. (D) *destruida*. This past participle functions as an adjective in this sentence, so it must end in *-a* to agree with *casa*. *La cual* refers to *casa*, also, and is the correct relative pronoun to use after a compound preposition such as *dentro de*. *Tantos* is correct because it means *so many*. It is masculine plural because it refers to *años*. The verb *estar* is correct because it is used to describe a state of the house.

5. (A) *dime*. The other verbs in the sentence reveal that the subject is *tú*, in which case the first verb should be the familiar, affirmative command form. *Cómo* is the correct interrogative pronoun to use in the question. Remember that *problema* is one of those words that ends in *-a* but is masculine. The indicative is correct after *cuando*, although a case could be made for the subjunctive, depending on the context in which the sentence occurs.

6. (A) *Cualesquier*. The noun to which this indefinite adjective refers is plural, so the correct form of *cual* is *cuales*. The end of the adjective does not change; the *-a* is still dropped before a noun of either gender or number. The subjunctive is correct in this adjective clause, because the subject of the verb in the adjective clause is indefinite or unknown. *Para* is correct because it indicates purpose, *in order to*. The future is correct because there are no structures that require the subjunctive.

7. (B) *fuera*. The subjunctive is used because this is an adjective clause and the noun that is the subject of the verb is an unknown, indefinite, or nonexistent referent. *Ningún* is correct because the final *-o* of *ninguno* is dropped before masculine singular nouns and an accent is written over the *-u*. *Lindo* refers to *pueblo*, so it is the correct gender and number. *Aquél* is the correct demonstrative pronoun. Remember that demonstrative pronouns have written accents on them to distinguish them from demonstrative adjectives.

8. (B) *vieron*. This verb should be plural because the subject is *noticias*. This sentence shows the *se* substitute for the true passive voice, so the verb will be third person singular or plural, depending upon the number of the noun that is the subject. *Supieron* is correct because it has the meaning of *they found out* or *they discovered*. The preterite indicative is correct in the last verb form because there is no construction that would require the subjunctive.

9. (D) *contigo*. Remember that after the preposition *con* in the first and second persons singular, the pronoun is combined with the preposition *conmigo* and *contigo*. *Ninguno* is the correct indefinite negative adjective to use to mean *none*. The conditional and the imperfect subjunctive are correct in the *if-then* statement.

10. (B) *les*. This pronoun refers to *tus amigos* and is the subject of the verb *acompañaran*. *Enojes* is the correct form of *enojar* because it is a negative,

second person singular command form. *Acompañaran* is correct because *decir* in this sentence has the meaning of a verb of volition. Remember that *programa* is one of those nouns ending with -*a* that is masculine.

11. (B) *haya.* In the adjective phrase *por* followed by an adjective and *que,* the subjunctive is correct. *Por* is the correct preposition to use in the phrase; it means *no matter,* and is an idiomatic expression. The verb *ser* is correct; the past participle is used after any form of the auxiliary verb *haber.* The subjunctive is correct in the adverbial clause after *hasta que* because the event has not happened. When the action after the adverbial conjunction of time is in the future, the subjunctive is used.

12. (D) *eligiéramos.* This verb should be in the imperfect subjunctive because it comes after *antes de que,* an adverbial conjunction that always requires the subjunctive. The imperfect subjunctive is used because the other verbs in the sentence are in the past tense. *Nos* is correct because it is indicated as the subject of the other verbs in the sentence. *Habláramos* is correct because it occurs in a dependent noun clause after a verb of volition in the main clause, *recomendar.* *Al* is correct because it is the contraction of *a* and *el,* the correct article for *líder.*

GROUP TWO

1. El fotógrafo <u>sacó</u> <u>la</u> foto sin que <u>ninguno</u>
         A   B   C
de los chicos se <u>dieran</u> cuenta del hecho.
            D

2. Te prestaré tanto dinero <u>que</u> <u>quieras</u>
                A   B
antes de que <u>salgas</u> <u>para</u> la reunión.
       C   D

3. Juan y Ana, <u>sentaos</u> en <u>sus</u> asientos para
         A   B
que <u>podáis</u> empezar <u>el</u> tema del día.
   C   D

4. Nos parecía extraño que <u>tantos</u> chicos de
                   A
<u>nuestra</u> edad <u>tenían</u> que <u>trabajar.</u>
  B   C   D

5. <u>Los</u> pies siempre me <u>parecía</u> <u>demasiado</u>
  A   B   C
grandes <u>para</u> un niño de diez años.
      D

6. <u>Pudiendo</u> <u>habérsela</u> dicho, se avergonzó
   A   B
<u>de</u> no haber <u>revelada</u> la verdad.
  C   D

7. Si no <u>tienes</u> otra cosa esta noche, <u>ven</u> al
      A   B
café y <u>pregunte</u> <u>por</u> mí.
     C   D

8. <u>Hace</u> siglos <u>los</u> indígenas de la
  A   B
selva <u>decían</u> el mismo mito cuando <u>lo</u>
     C   D
oímos por primera vez.

9. <u>Unos</u> programas que han <u>estado</u> <u>realizados</u>
  A   B   C
<u>por</u> los actores son formidables.
  D

10. <u>Fue</u> extraño que <u>desaparecieron</u> como
  A   B
si <u>fueran</u> fantasmas <u>pavorosos.</u>
   C   D

11. María <u>y</u> Inés, ahora <u>se</u> van vuestros
     A   B
abuelos; <u>despedíoslos</u> antes que <u>salgan.</u>
     C   D

12. <u>El</u> guía les aconsejó que <u>visitarían</u> los
  A   B
museos <u>que</u> les <u>gustaran.</u>
     C   D

Answers and Answer Explanations for Group Two

1. (D) *diera.* The subject of the verb is *ninguno*, which is singular, so the verb should be in the singular. The subjunctive is correct because *ninguno* in an indefinite referent. The verb *sacó* is the correct use of the preterite. *Ninguno* is the correct form of the indefinite negative adjective to mean *none.*

2. (A) *como.* In this comparative structure of equality, *tanto* and the noun are followed by *como* to mean *as (much money) as.* The subjunctive can be correctly used for *quieras* when the amount is indefinite, or not specified, as is the case in this sentence. The subjunctive is also correct to use after *antes de que.* The preposition *para* in this case indicates direction toward, and is correct.

3. (B) *vuestros.* The subject of the verb is the second person plural, so the possessive adjective should also be the second person plural form. *Sentaos* is the correct affirmative, second person plural command form when a reflexive pronoun is attached to the end of the verb form. The subjunctive is correct after *para que* for the verb *podamos.* Remember: *tema* is one of the nouns that ends with *-a*, but is a masculine noun.

4. (C) *tuvieran.* The subjunctive is correct because it occurs in a dependent noun clause after an impersonal expression, *nos parecía.* *Tantos* is the correct adjective to use to mean *so many* because *chicos* is masculine, plural. *Edad* is a feminine noun, so *nuestra* is correct. The infinitive is used after the expression *tener que.*

5. (B) *parecían.* The subject of the verb is *pies*, so the verb should be plural. *Pies* is a masculine noun, so the article, *los*, is the correct gender and number. *Demasiado* is used as an adverb in this sentence, so it ends with *-o*, and does not agree with *pies.* The preposition *para* is correct because of the comparison being made. The child is compared with others of his age.

6. (D) *revelado.* This past participle is a verb form after the auxiliary verb *haber*, so the form should always end in *-o.* The present participle *pudiendo* at the beginning of the sentence expresses cause or manner, and means *by being able.* *Habérsela* is the correct form of the verb to use after the verb *poder,* and the pronouns are properly added to the infinitive since they cannot be placed at the end of the past participle that follows *haber.* The preposition *de* is correct with *avergonzarse.*

7. (C) *pregunta.* The correct second person singular command form in the affirmative is the third person singular of the present indicative form of the verb. The subject of the verb is given in the other verbs, *tienes* and *ven.* Remember that you will probably not see the present subjunctive after *si* on this exam. If you thought that *ven* was incorrect, go back and review irregular second person affirmative command forms. *Por* is correct because a person is the object of the request.

8. (A) *Hacía.* This verb should be in the imperfect because the other verb in the sentence is in the imperfect. Remember: the present tense of *hacer* with the present tense in the following verb has the meaning of the present progressive to indicate time going by. *Hace dos meses que estudio español.* means *I have been studying Spanish for two months.* Remember that the present tense of *hacer* followed by the preterite has the meaning of *ago. Hace dos meses que estudié español.* means *I studied Spanish two months ago.* *Los* is the correct article for *indígenas* because it is one of those words that ends with *-a* that is masculine. *Lo* refers to *el mito* and is the correct masculine singular direct object pronoun.

9. (B) *sido.* Look for the true passive voice indicated by the construction of *to be*, followed by an adjective, followed by the preposition *por* and then by the agent doing the action. The correct verb to use in the true passive constructions is *ser.* Remember that *programas* is masculine, so *unos* and *realizados* are correct. *Por* is the correct preposition to use in the true passive to indicate the agent or person doing the action.

10. (B) *desaparecieran.* The subjunctive is used after an impersonal expression, such as *Fue extraño.* Remember: after *como si* the imperfect subjunctive is always used to express a condition that is contrary to fact. *Fantasmas* is another of those nouns that end in *-a* that is masculine.

11. (A) *e.* Remember that *y* changes to *e* before words that begin with a stressed *i* sound. *Se* is correct since *ir* is a reflexive pronoun; *se* agrees with the subject of the verb, *los abuelos. Despedíoslos* is the correct affirmative second person plural command form, with the appropriate second person reflexive pronoun and a direct object pronoun attached to the end. The subjunctive is always used after *antes de que.*

12. (B) *visitaran.* After the verb *aconsejar*, you should use the subjunctive in the dependent noun clause that follows. Also, the subjunctive in *gustaran* is correct because the subject of the verb, *los museos*, is indefinite.

GROUP THREE

1. No conozco a nadie más <u>inofensivo que</u>
                   A   B
ella ni a quien sus amigos <u>lo quieren</u> más.
             C   D

2. No me <u>digáis</u> que el profesor no os dijo
        A
<u>nada</u> antes de que <u>salió</u> él <u>por</u> el día.
 B   C   D

3. <u>Para</u> el fin de semana tendré <u>resueltas</u>
  A   B
<u>todos</u> sus problemas que <u>quedan</u> en
 C   D
cuanto al asunto.

4. Se <u>le</u> <u>hacen</u> falta unos pocos dólares a menos
  A B
que alguien le <u>presten</u> más <u>de</u> veinte más.
          C   D

5. Toma <u>una</u> decisión y no <u>espere</u> hasta que
     A   B
la situación <u>haya</u> <u>empeorado</u> aún más.
         C   D

6. Si <u>quieres</u> permiso <u>para</u> dirigirte a la
    A   B
clase, yo <u>se</u> lo <u>daré</u>.
     C   D

7. <u>Los</u> idiomas de la lengua común, incluido
  A
<u>aquél</u> del que <u>ésta</u> procede, son <u>antiguas</u>.
  B   C   D

8. La verdad pertenece a <u>los que</u> la <u>hacen</u>
                A   B
<u>suyas</u>, según los más sabios <u>del</u> mundo
 C   D

9. Es de esperar que todo el mundo <u>pueda</u>
                     A
vivir donde <u>el</u> agua <u>pura</u> <u>sale</u> al pedirla.
      B   C D

10. En <u>ese</u> planeta no le <u>habrían</u> sorprendido
   A   B
al astronauta si <u>hubieran</u> <u>aparecido</u> unos
          C   D
hombrecillos verdes.

11. No había creído que esa vez se <u>juzguen</u> a
                    A
quienesquiera <u>trataran</u> <u>de</u> resolver <u>el</u> dilema.
         B C   D

12. Te digo <u>una</u> vez más que no <u>coloque</u>
      A   B
en un pedestal a quien no se <u>lo</u> <u>merece</u>.
                  C D

Answers and Answer Explanations for Group Three

1. (D) *quieran*. The subjunctive, *quieran*, is correct because it occurs in an adjective clause with a nonexistent subject, *nadie*. Both *inofensivo* and *lo* refer to *nadie*, not to *ella*, so the masculine forms of the adjective and the pronoun are correct. Although *nadie* may be either masculine or feminine, when referring to people in general or mixed gender groups the masculine gender predominates. Since there cannot be two incorrect choices, you need to look for another grammatical error. *Que* is the correct comparative to use; it means *than*.

2. (C) *saliera*. The subjunctive must be used after *antes de que*. *Nada* is the correct negative pronoun to use to mean *nothing*, or *anything* in a double negative. *Por* is correct since it refers to the duration of time in the day. *Digáis* is the correct negative second person plural command form of *decir*.

3. (B) *resueltos*. The past participle functions as an adjective that refers to *problemas*, which is a masculine noun ending in *-a*. *Para* is correct since it refers to a deadline in time in the future. *Quedan* is correct since the subject is *problemas*, and it occurs in the main clause of the sentence, thus the indicative is correct.

4. (C) *preste*. The verb is used correctly in the subjunctive after the adverbial conjunction *a menos que*, but should be in the singular because *alguien* is the subject. Remember that in the expression *más que*, meaning *more than*, *que* changes to *de* before numbers, unless the expression is negative. *Alguien* is the correct indefinite pronoun to mean *someone*.

5. (B) *esperes*. The correct negative second person singular command form corresponds to the second person singular present subjunctive form. All words that end with *-ción* are feminine, so *una* is correct. The subjunctive is correct after *hasta que* because the action has not happened. *Empeorado* is a verb form after *haber*, so it must end with *-o*.

6. (C) *te*. The second person indirect object is indicated by the verb *quieres* and by the pronoun at the end of *dirigirte*. *Para* is correct because it indicates purpose. *Daré* is the correct first person singular future verb form, indicated by the pronoun *yo*.

7. (D) *antiguos*. The adjective refers to *idiomas*, which is masculine, in spite of ending in *-a*. *Aquél* refers to *idiomas*, also, while *ésta* refers to *lengua*.

8. (C) *suya*. *Los que* is the subject of *hacen*; it means *those who*. *Suyas* must agree with what is possessed, *la verdad*, not with those who possess something, so it is singular. In superlative constructions *in* is translated as *de*, which is combined with *el* to make *del*.

9. (D) *salga*. The subjunctive is correct because it is indefinite wherever that place, *donde*, may be. Remember that *agua* is feminine, but in the singular form takes a masculine article, *el*. Since the noun is feminine, *pura* is correct, also. The subjunctive form, *pueda*, is correct because it comes after an impersonal expression, *Es de esperar*. Not all impersonal expressions will begin with some form of *ser*, although they usually do.

10. (A) *habría*. The verb should be singular because *it*, referring to the fact that the little green men would appear, is the subject. *Hubieran* is in the subjunctive because it comes in the *if* portion of an *if-then* statement. The subject of *hubieran* is *hombrecillos*. *Planeta* is another word ending

in -*a* that is masculine. *Aparecido*, used as a past participle after *haber*, is invariable because it is a verbal form.

11. (A) *juzgaran*. The verb should be in the third person plural imperfect subjunctive because the subject is *quienesquiera*. *Trataran* is correct because the subject is *quienesquiera*. Look carefully to see that the plural form, *quienes* or *cuales,* is contained in the word, since the ending -*quiera* is invariable. *De* is the correct preposition to follow *tratar*. *Dilema* is another noun that ends in -*a* that is masculine.

12. (B) *coloques*. The subject of the verb is indicated by the indirect object pronoun in front of *digo* and is the second person singular. *Lo* is correct, referring either to an idea of putting someone on the pedestal, or referring to the pedestal itself. *Merece* is correct, although a case could be made for the subjunctive. However, since the indicative is not incorrect, the word cannot be the item that has to be changed.

GROUP FOUR

1. <u>Estaba</u> yo en el comedor cuando se <u>oyó</u>
   A   B
voces <u>altas</u> en la calle <u>gritando</u> la alarma.
      C   D

2. Las niñas, <u>cuyas</u> padres <u>acudieron</u> al
            A   B
espectáculo, no <u>quisieron</u> salir sin <u>verlo</u>.
            C   D

3. No se <u>supo</u> si fue <u>por</u> vergüenza o no que
       A   B
salió sin que nadie <u>se</u> <u>despidió</u> de él.
               C D

4. Sus actividades <u>fueron</u> meritorias <u>habiendo</u>
              A   B
antes <u>habido</u> toreros con valor y el arte
      C
<u>apropiada</u>.
  D

5. <u>El</u> lugar ideal <u>para</u> arreglar el jardín es un
  A   B
<u>gran</u> prado de flores <u>expuestas</u> al sol.
  C   D

6. <u>Recuerda</u> esto bien porque de las mil manos
   A
que <u>estreches</u> en tu vida quizás no <u>haya</u>
     C   D
diez que valgan más que <u>el suyo</u>.
                 D

7. Cuando <u>entraba</u> en el aula, lo <u>saludaron</u>
        A   B
como si <u>hubiera</u> entrado un rey <u>de</u> verdad.
      C   D

8. Te aseguro que <u>tendré</u> <u>hecho</u> toda la tarea
           A   B
si me <u>das</u> tiempo para que la <u>haga</u>.
     C   D

9. Quizás sería mejor que <u>dijera</u> que <u>empezó</u>
                A   B
<u>hacía</u> doce años cuando <u>vino</u> mi primo.
  C   D

10. La nave Colombia, <u>cuyo</u> sistema de
             A
navegación ya está funcionando, será
<u>puesto</u> en servicio a menos que se
  B
<u>encuentre</u> <u>un</u> problema.
  C   D

11. Si quieres leer un libro que <u>sea</u> interesante,
                   A
te sugiero que <u>busque</u> uno <u>por</u> <u>ese</u> autor.
         B   C D

12. El actor nos dijo que <u>el</u> día que no lo
             A
<u>viniera</u> a ver el público, se <u>jubilaría</u> si
  B   C
le <u>sería</u> posible hacerlo.
   D

Answers and Answer Explanations for Group Four

1. (B) *oyeron.* The plural verb form is needed because the subject is *voces.* *Estaba* is correct because the imperfect indicative is needed to describe background information, or continuing action when something else takes place. *Altas* is correct because *voces* is feminine. *Gritando* is a present participle used as an adverb.

2. (A) *cuyos.* This adjective must agree with the noun it modifies, *padres,* not with *niñas.* The preterite tenses in the verb forms are correct; the tense refers to a specific moment in the past. Remember that *querer* in the preterite means *to refuse. Sin* is a preposition and must be followed by the infinitive. *Lo* is the correct pronoun to refer to *el espectáculo.*

3. (D) *despidiera.* The subjunctive should be used after the adverbial conjunction *sin que. Supo* is correct, meaning *to find out* or *to discover.* In this sentence it would mean *It was never discovered. Por* is correct because it means *out of. Despedirse* is reflexive, so the pronoun *se* is correct.

4. (D) *apropiado. Arte* is always feminine in the plural form, *las bellas artes,* but is usually masculine in the singular form, except when followed by certain adjectives, such as *poética.* The preterite of *fueron* is correct since it occurs in the main clause of the sentence. *Habiendo* is the present participle used adverbially, to describe an ongoing situation. *Habido* is the past participle, following the present participle form of *haber,* and is used in the sense of *there having been.*

5. (D) *expuesto.* The adjective refers to *prado* so it must be masculine singular. *Lugar* is a masculine noun. *Gran* is shortened before singular nouns of either gender. *Para* is used in the sense of *in order to,* expressing purpose.

6. (D) *la suya.* Remember that *mano,* to which the adjective refers, is feminine, in spite of ending with *-o. Recuerda* is correct because it is the second person singular affirmative command form. The subjunctive of *estreches* is used because it occurs in an adjective clause with an indefinite subject. *Haya* is correct because it is used after *quizás,* expressing doubt or uncertainty by the speaker.

7. (A) *entró.* The preterite is correct in this sentence because it refers to a singular event in the past. The preterite in *saludaron* serves to limit the time to a specific moment. Remember that after *como si* you must use the imperfect subjunctive. *De verdad* is an idiom, an expression for which there is no literal translation.

8. (B) *hecha.* The feminine form is used because it refers to *tarea.* The verb *tener* is not an auxiliary verb, so *to have done* in this sentence does not require that you use an invariable past participle. After the verb *asegurar* there is no need to use the subjunctive, so the indicative is correct. After *si* you need to use the indicative if the verb is in the present. In some cases you can use the present subjunctive after *si,* but you will probably not see it on this exam. After *para que* you need to always use the subjunctive.

9. (C) *hace.* The preterite tense in the other verbs indicates that the time is over and done, meaning *ago,* so the present tense of *hacer* is indicated. After impersonal expressions, such as *sería mejor,* you must use the subjunctive.

10. (B) *puesta.* The adjective refers to *la nave,* so the past participle referring to the noun must agree in gender and number. Remember that *sistema* is

another noun that ends in -*a* that is masculine, and *cuyo* must agree with *sistema*. *A menos que* also requires the subjunctive since it is an adverbial conjunction of condition. *Problema* is also masculine.

11. (B) *busques*. The subject of the verb, indicated by the words *quieres* and *te*, should be in the second person singular. The subjunctive is correct because it occurs in a dependent noun clause after a verb of volition, *sugerir*. The verb *sea* is correct because it occurs in an adjective clause where the subject is unknown or indefinite. *Ese* is the correct masculine singular demonstrative adjective to agree with *autor*.

12. (D) *fuera*. The subjunctive is used in this *if-then* statement. Look for the conditional tense in the *then* portion of the sentence, then *si* in the portion of the sentence, communicating a hypothetical circumstance. The imperfect subjunctive is used in *viniera* because it occurs in an adjective clause where the subject of the verb is indefinite or not specified. Remember that *día* is masculine.

GROUP FIVE

1. Señora, si usted <u>es</u> <u>dispuesta</u> a alquilar la
                              A   B
   pieza, le diré cuánto le <u>ofrecería</u> por <u>ella</u>.
                                     C   D

2. Todo <u>esto</u> comenzó <u>hará</u> unos seis meses,
              A   B
   aquella mañana en que <u>llegó</u> un sobre <u>rosa</u>.
                                  C   D

3. Pero la pobre seguía <u>mudo</u> y <u>vigilando</u>
                                A   B
   las esquinas, como si <u>deseara</u> irse
                                  C
   <u>tan</u> rápido como fuera posible.
        D

4. Como buena dama, aquí me pareció

   <u>oportuno</u> <u>quedarse</u> a mi vez <u>callada</u> y
        A   B   C
   mirarlo <u>fijo</u>.
                D

5. —<u>Vete</u>, hijo mío,—dijo el médico. —Y
        A
   <u>tengas</u> buena fortuna, que bien <u>la</u> <u>merece</u>.
        B   C   D

6. —Ten cuidado, eh, —volvió a <u>decirme</u>. —Yo
                                        A
   <u>espero</u> que me <u>dirás</u> cuando <u>vuelvas</u> a verme.
        B   C   D

7. Y si tú y yo no <u>te</u> volvemos a ver, <u>acuérdate</u>
                        A   B
   de que no <u>os</u> <u>olvidaré</u> nunca a ti y a tus
                    C   D
   amigos.

8. Soy amigo de su hijo, señora, <u>la cual</u> me
                                          A
   <u>pidió</u> si <u>podría</u> pasar por aquí para <u>darle</u> esto.
        B   C   D

9. El jugador se <u>retiró</u> de la liga <u>hacía</u> dos
                        A   B
   años porque ya <u>había</u> ganado más <u>de</u>
                            C   D
   cuarenta millones de dólares.

10. Buscamos un artista que <u>reúna</u> los
                                    A
    requisitos y <u>esté</u> <u>dispuesta</u> a <u>viajar</u>.
                      B   C   D

11. Siempre será posible que el jefe <u>prohíbe</u>
                                              A
    la salida del grupo, <u>lo cual</u> no <u>le</u> <u>gustará</u>.
                                B   C   D

12. Cuando <u>recibimos</u> las gorras, <u>pongámonos</u>
                    A   B
    <u>las nuestras</u> al salir porque <u>hace</u> frío.
          C   D

Answers and Answer Explanations for Group Five

1. (A) *está*. The verb *estar* is used in the expression *to be willing* because it indicates a state of being. *Dispuesta* is correct because it refers to *señora*. There is no need to use the subjunctive, so the conditional is correct because it means *I would offer*. It is a portion of an *if-then* statement in which the *if* portion is omitted. *Ella* refers to *pieza* and is the correct pronoun to use after a preposition.

2. (B) *haría*. The conditional is used to express probability in the past tense, indicated by all the other past tense verb forms. The meaning is *it must have been*, followed by the time phrase. *Esto* is the correct neuter demonstrative pronoun because the referent for the pronoun is an idea or an event. *Llegó* is correct because of the specific moment referred to in the sentence. *Rosa* is an invariable adjective, so it will always end in *-a* even when it modifies a masculine noun.

3. (A) *muda*. The adjective refers to *la pobre*, so it must end in *-a*. Remember that adjectives can be made into nouns by adding an article in front of them, as is done in this case. The gender of the person or thing is indicated by the article, since the noun itself ends in *-e*. *Vigilando* is used as an adverb after the verb *seguir*, so it is correct. *Como si* requires the imperfect subjunctive, so *deseara* is correct. *Tan* means *so* and is correctly used before an adjective in the comparison of equality, *as fast as possible*.

4. (B) *quedarme*. Since the verb refers to what the speaker plans to do, the first person reflexive pronoun on the infinitive is necessary. *Oportuno* does not modify the noun *dama*, however, so it ends correctly in *-o*. *Callada* does refer to the subject who is speaking, *una buena dama*, so it agrees in gender and number with the subject. *Fijo* is an adjective used as an adverb, describing how she was looking, in which case the masculine form is correct.

5. (D) *mereces*. The subject of the verb is second person singular, indicated by the other verbs in the sentences, *vete* and *tengas*. *Ve* is the correct second person affirmative irregular command form. *Tengas* is part of an elliptical statement. The part that is omitted corresponds to *I hope that*, an expression that would require the subjunctive in the dependent clause containing *tengas*. *La* refers to *fortuna*.

6. (B) *digas*. After *espero que* the verb in the dependent clause should be in the subjunctive. The second person singular is indicated by the other verbs, *ten* and *vuelvas*. After the preposition *a* the infinitive is used in *decirme*. The subjunctive *vuelvas* is used after the adverbial conjunction of time, *cuando,* because the event has not happened. Always look for the future, or some other indication that the action is in the future. Remember that when *cuando* is used in the past tense, it is usually in the indicative.

7. (A) *nos*. The reflexive pronoun is used in this sentence to indicate reciprocal action, meaning *each other*. *Acuérdate* is the correct second person singular affirmative command form. Remember that pronouns go at the end of affirmative commands. *Os* is the correct direct object pronoun that is indicated by *a ti y a tus amigos*. There is no need to use the subjunctive after *acordarse de*, so the future tense is correct.

8. (A) *el cual*. This relative pronoun should be masculine because it refers to *su hijo*. *Su hijo* is also the subject of *pidió*, which is correct because it is in the main clause of the sentence. *Podría* is correct because there is

no *if-then* statement requiring the subjunctive. Remember that you need to find the conditional tense in the *then* portion of a statement in order to use the imperfect subjunctive after the conjunction *si*. It is correct to use the infinitive after a preposition, such as *para darle*.

9. (B) *hace*. This time expression is something that happened at a moment in the past, years *ago*. If you see the imperfect of *hacer*, the other verbs in the sentence are going to be in the imperfect also, not in the present or the preterite. The preterite of *se retiró* refers to a specific moment in the past, so the preterite is correct. *Había* is correct because the indicative is used after *porque*. Remember that *que* changes to *de* when it comes before numbers and means *than*, unless the expression is *no más que*.

10. (C) *dispuesto*. The noun to which the adjective refers is *un artista*. Even though the noun ends in *-a*, you can tell the gender of nouns that end in *-ista* by the article. The subjunctive of *reunir* and *ser* are correct because they occur in an adjective clause with an indefinite referent. Notice that there is no personal *a*, as there would be if the person were known to the speaker. After the preposition *a* the infinitive is the correct verb form to use.

11. (A) *prohíba*. The subjunctive is correct after the impersonal expression in *será posible*. Notice that there is an accent written on the verb form because of the silent *h*. To avoid making a diphthong of the vowels in the verb, the syllable with the *i* is accented, which separates it from the first syllable of the verb. *Lo cual* is correct because it refers to the whole idea. *Lo cual* is also the subject of *gustará*, so the verb is singular. *Le* is correct because collective nouns in Spanish always take the singular verb form. *El grupo* is singular, as are other collective nouns such as *familia* and *gente*.

12. (A) *recibamos*. The subjunctive should be used after the adverbial conjunction *cuando* if the action has not happened. The fact that the command form of *poner* is used in the main clause indicates that we have not yet received the caps. *Pongámonos* is the correct form of the reflexive, first person plural indirect command, meaning *let's put on*. Remember that, when the reflexive pronoun is added at the end of the first person plural form, the final *s* is dropped from the verb ending. *Las nuestras* is the correct possessive pronoun referring to *gorras*. *Hace* is the correct tense and form to mean *it is* (cold).

GROUP SIX

1. Quizás éste <u>será</u> el año en que se <u>gasta</u>
        A   B
más <u>de</u> lo normal para que se <u>mejoren</u>
    C   D
las escuelas.

2. Todavía se <u>descubría</u> en sus facciones
            A
que en su mocedad <u>habría</u> <u>estado</u> una
                B   C
mujer bonita a pesar de que no <u>tenía</u> pelo.
                          D

3. Hizo todo de tal modo como si <u>nadie</u>
                            A
<u>hubiera</u> que no <u>estuviera</u> previsto desde
    B   C
<u>hace</u> años.
   D

4. Me pareció como si no le <u>importara</u> a
                      A
él si <u>vivía</u> o no; <u>era</u> llorando <u>tan</u>
     B   C   D
amargamente.

5. Nadie nos <u>dijo</u> que la vida familiar del futuro
             A

  <u>sería</u> fácil, <u>sino</u> cada día nos <u>indica</u> lo
   B   C   D

  contrario.

6. Luego que <u>recibieran</u> las noticias, mi amigo
             A

  salió <u>corriendo</u> del cuarto para que él <u>se</u>
       B   C

  las <u>diera</u> a su mamá.
      D

7. Está preocupado que <u>haya</u> gente que <u>está</u>
                A   B

  cediendo sus derechos sin <u>saberlo</u> al <u>firma</u>
                       C   D

  su nombre.

8. El consejero prefirió que <u>busquen</u> ayuda
                    A

  legal <u>por</u> medio de una agencia sin <u>fines</u>
       B   C

  <u>lucrativa</u>.
   D

9. <u>Mucha</u> gente <u>pagan</u> una multa <u>pensando</u>
   A   B   C

  que <u>lo</u> va a solucionar sus problemas.
     D

10. De <u>haber</u> <u>agarrado</u> él los vasos con más
     A   B

  cuidado, no se <u>les</u> <u>habrían</u> caído al suelo.
              C   D

11. Dondequiera que <u>construye</u> su casa, no <u>deje</u>
                 A   B

  de utilizar tan <u>buen</u> arquitecto como <u>pueda</u>.
            C   D

12. Me <u>molestaba</u> que mis vecinos <u>permitieran</u>
      A   B

  que sus animales <u>vinieran</u> a mi jardín
              C

  porque siempre <u>la</u> deshacían.
           D

Answers and Answer Explanations for Group Six

1. **(B)** *gaste*. This verb is in the subjunctive in this adjective clause because the year when the money will be spent is indefinite. After *quizás* either the subjunctive or the indicative can be used, so the indicative of *será* is correct. *Más de* is the expression for *more than*. After *para que*, the subjunctive is always used. Once again, use the process of elimination to narrow the incorrect element down to one or two answers. If you know that you can use the indicative after *quizás*, then you should eliminate the verb after it as a possible incorrect word, because there is no rule stating that the subjunctive must be used after *quizás*. Other words that introduce both the subjunctive and the indicative are *tal vez* and *acaso*, both also meaning *perhaps*.

2. **(C)** *sido*. The verb *ser* is correct because it refers to a definitive characteristic of the subject. The impersonal subject of *descubrir*, and the impersonal subject communicated with the use of *se* are correct forms of saying *one could see*. The conditional in *habría* communicates probability or conjecture in the mind of the speaker. Remember that, in the present tense, the use of the future tense can communicate such probability, just as the conditional does in the past tense. After *a pesar* the indicative or the subjunctive can be used correctly, so the use of the imperfect in *tenía* is not incorrect.

3. **(A)** *nada*. The correct indefinite negative pronoun is *nada*, meaning *nothing*, a meaning determined from looking at the information contained in the rest of the sentence. *Hubiera*, an impersonal expression meaning *there was*, is correct because the imperfect subjunctive always

follows *como si. Estuviera* is correct because the subject is nonexistent, *nada. Hace* is correct because in the expression *desde hace*, used with the preterite tense or the imperfect subjunctive in the other verb form, it means *long ago*, or *from a long time back.*

4. (C) *estaba.* Remember that with the present participle in the progressive verb forms you must use the verb *estar.* The imperfect subjunctive after *como si* is correct. After *importarle* you would think that you needed the subjunctive after the impersonal expression. Notice, however, that although *si* introduces the verb, this is not an *if-then* statement so you do not need to use the subjunctive. Pay attention to small words. *Tan,* meaning *so,* is correct before adverbs; *tanto* comes before nouns.

5. (C) *sino que.* Since there is a conjugated verb after the conjunction, you need to use *que.* The indicative for *dijo* is correct because *nadie* is the subject of the verb in the main clause. Only use the subjunctive when *nadie* or *nada* are the subjects of the verbs in adjective clauses, in which case they become nonexistent referents. The conditional *sería* is correct because the verb *decir* in the sentence is not a verb of volition; no command is implied. The present tense, *indica,* is correct because the speaker is speaking in the present while remembering the past. When in doubt always look to see what the sentence says, so that you won't be misled into thinking that all verbs need to be in the same general time frame.

6. (A) *recibieron.* Although *luego que* is an adverbial conjunction of time, the action has already happened, so the verb should be in the indicative. Only use the subjunctive after adverbial conjunctions of time when the action has not already happened in relation to the tense of the verb in the main clause. *Corriendo* is used as an adverb, so it is correct. *Se* is the replacement of the third person indirect object, *le,* referring to *a su mamá.* Any combination of third person indirect and direct object pronouns results in the indirect object pronoun being changed to *se. Para que* always requires the use of the subjunctive.

7. (D) *firmar.* After *al* you must always use the infinitive verb form. When you see an item like this one, where the rules are so clear, you should not even have to bother looking at what the sentence says. After all prepositions and *al,* you must use an infinitive verb form. You can save time by looking for obvious errors, then use the time you save for more difficult sentences. *Sin* is also a preposition, meaning that *saberlo* is correct. After *estar preocupado* the subjunctive is correct for *haya. Cediendo* ends with *-iendo,* meaning that it is a present participle, so *estar* is correct.

8. (D) *lucrativos.* The adjective agrees in gender and number with *fines.* Even if you did not know the gender and number of *fines,* you should have observed that the noun is plural, meaning that *lucrativa* is not correct. The subjunctive after *preferir* is correct, and the present is not incorrect. Even though the present tense is used in the dependent clause after the preterite in the main clause, it is correct. When you see the combination of past and present tenses, translate the sentence to see if it makes sense. If it does, then you should look for the error in the other choices in the sentence. *Por* is the correct preposition because it expressed the idea of *by means of. Fines* is a noun that is the correct plural form of *fin.*

9. (B) *paga. Gente* is a collective noun, but always takes the singular verb form because the noun is singular. It is also a feminine noun, so *mucha*

is correct. *Pensando* is a present participle used as an adverb, so it always ends in *-o*, and is correct. *Lo* refers to a whole idea, so the masculine form of the direct object pronoun is used.

10. (C) *le*. Since the subject of the verb is indicated after the infinitive perfect construction in the first clause, the singular indirect object pronoun is used in this impersonal *se* structure. The infinitive perfect phrase *haber agarrado*, used after the preposition *de*, is used in place of the *if* portion of an *if-then* statement, leaving the conditional perfect verb form in the *then* clause, *habrían caído*. The verb *habrían* is plural because the subject, *los vasos*, is plural. Look for the phrases where the reflexive pronoun and the indirect object pronoun are used in constructions where the active voice is avoided, in situations where blame is shifted. The meaning of *no se le habrían caído* is *would not have fallen from his hands*, meaning that he did not drop the glasses intentionally.

11. (A) *construya*. The subjunctive should be used after *dondequiera* because it is an indefinite subject in the adjective clause. *Deje* is a command form, which is not incorrect. *Buen* is always shortened before masculine singular nouns. *Pueda* is correct because it is unknown in the speaker's mind what the subject can possibly pay for an architect, as indicated by the phrase *tan...como*.

12. (D) *lo*. The referent for the pronoun is *jardín*, a masculine singular noun, so the correct corresponding direct object pronoun is *lo*. The imperfect in *molestaba* is correct when it describes habitual, ongoing, or repeated action in the past. *Permitieran* is correct since it occurs in a dependent noun clause after a verb of emotion. *Vinieran* is correct, because it comes in another dependent noun clause after a verb of volition, *permitir*.

GROUP SEVEN

1. El sol <u>le</u> daba en <u>sus</u> ojos y tuvo que
       A   B
<u>taparlos</u> con <u>la</u> mano.
  C   D

2. <u>Nos</u> fue obvio que el resultado <u>dependía</u>
 A   B
<u>en</u> cómo se <u>aplicaban</u> las reglas.
 C   D

3. La pelota <u>se</u> dio <u>velozmente</u> <u>con</u> la pared
          A   B   C
de enfrente, causando no <u>poco</u>
                    D
desconfitura.

4. El profesor movía <u>la</u> cabeza como si se
              A
<u>negaba</u> dar crédito a <u>lo</u> <u>que</u> <u>oía</u>.
 B   C D

5. <u>Era</u> las tres <u>de</u> la tarde cuando <u>por</u> fin
 A   B   C
pudimos cruzar al río, <u>tal</u> era el desborde.
                 D

6. El capitán esperó a que todos <u>callasen</u> y
                            A
<u>decía</u>, —<u>Resignémonos</u> y quizás <u>salgamos</u>
 B   C   D
bien.

7. Unos hombres entraron <u>a</u> la lancha, pero
                   A
las olas <u>la</u> volcaron y dos de <u>ellos</u>
        B   C
<u>se perdieron</u>.
   D

8. Mario, <u>con</u> una voz que no parecía <u>la suya</u>
       A   B
<u>gritaba</u> a su amiga—¡<u>Te</u> doy mi sitio!
 C   D

9. <u>Para</u> mí, esa chica parecía <u>la</u> más
   A   B

   inteligente <u>en</u> todo el contorno,
                   C

   incluyendo <u>el mío</u>.
              D

10. En <u>esos</u> días se <u>veían</u> el chico y su perro,
       A   B

   <u>inseparable</u> caminando <u>por</u> el parque.
      C   D

11. <u>Para</u> asustar a la chica, el payaso abrió <u>la</u>
    A   B

   boca, como si <u>fuese</u> a <u>comérselo</u> por
               C   D

   complete.

12. Cuando el pobre papá de <u>los</u> Galgos se
                         A

   <u>empezaron</u> a <u>ahogar</u>, el niño fue <u>por</u> el
      B   C   D

   médico.

Answers and Answer Explanations for Group Seven

1. (B) *los.* The possessive adjective is not normally used in this case. The definite article is used in place of the possessive adjective, *sus,* when speaking of a part of the body or an article of clothing. Remember that *mano* is feminine, so *la* is correct. Also, the infinitive form of the verb with the pronoun *los* is correct, because it is the object of the expression *tener que.*

2. (C) *de.* The proper preposition after *depender* is *de,* even though in English another preposition is used. *Aplicaban* is correct since this is an example of the use of the third person plural in the *se* substitute for the passive voice.

3. (D) *poca.* This word describes *desconfitura,* so the ending needs to be feminine. The expression for *to hit against* is *darse con* so the other underlined words in the sentence describing what the ball did are correct.

4. (B) *negara.* The past subjunctive is always used after *como si. Lo que* is correct, because the antecedent of this relative pronoun is indefinite. *Oía* is correct, because the subject is *el profesor* and the time frame is indefinite past.

5. (A) *Eran.* The verb needs to be plural, because the hour is past one o'clock. Remember that the third person singular of *ser* is used only for one o'clock. *De* is correct, because a specific hour of the day is indicated. *Por* is correct, because it is part of the expression, *por fin. Tal* is correct because it describes *el desborde,* which is singular.

6. (B) *dijo.* The preterit should be used in this case, because the moment of time is specific, and the action is begun and completed in that specific moment in the past. *Callasen* is correct, because it is the past subjunctive and follows the adverbial conjunction *a que,* which indicates purpose. Remember that there are two forms for the past subjunctive and that in most cases both are correct. Usually when the past subjunctive is used for the conditional in *if-then* statements, the *-iera* or *-ara* form can be used, but not the *-iese,* or *-ase* form. *Resignémonos* is the correct first person plural indirect command. Remember that when the reflexive pronoun is added to the end of the first person plural form, that the final *s* is dropped. *Salgamos* is correct after *quizás,* to express uncertainty.

7. (A) *en.* The preposition *en* normally follows the verb *entrar. Ellos* is correct, because it refers to *los hombres. Se perdieron* is correct, because the reflexive form means *to become lost.*

8. (C) *gritó.* The preterit is needed here because the action is begun and completed at a specific moment in the past.

9. (C) *de*. The preposition that is used in superlative constructions is always *de*. Any other preposition is a direct translation of English to Spanish that is not correct. *Para* is correct, because the meaning of the preposition *for* in this case is *in my opinion*. *El mío* is correct, because this possessive pronoun refers to *el contorno*. *La* is correct, because it refers to *la chica* and is necessary to form the superlative construction.

10. (C) *inseparables*. The plural form of the adjective is necessary, because it refers to *el chico y su perro*. *Esos* is correct, because *días* is masculine. *Veían* is correct, because it is the *se* substitute for the passive voice. *Por* is correct, because the meaning of the preposition in this context is *through* the park.

11. (D) *comérsela*. The pronoun at the end refers to *la chica*, in which case the direct object pronoun needs to be feminine. Remember that *fuese* is correct after *como si*, because it is another form of the past subjunctive. *Para* is correct, because the meaning in the context of this sentence is *in order to*.

12. (B) *empezó*. The singular form of the verb is needed, because the subject is *el papá*. *Los* is correct, because it refers to all of the family members. *Ahogar* is correct because the infinitive is necessary after the preposition *a*. *Por* is correct, because the *médico* is the object of a search.

GROUP EIGHT

1. A <u>las</u> ocho <u>estábamos</u> todos en clase
    A   B
cuando <u>empezaban</u> a <u>llamarnos</u>.
        C   D

2. Cogí <u>aquella</u> mano fuerte y leal <u>por</u> debajo
      A   B
del banco, y <u>la</u> estreché entre <u>los míos</u>.
        C   D

3. El año <u>venidero</u> no estaréis ya <u>conmigo</u>,
        A   B
pero <u>les</u> veré de <u>cuando</u> en cuando.
    C   D

4. Nos dijo, —Si <u>alguna</u> vez me <u>ha</u> faltado la
          A   B
paciencia, sin <u>queriendo</u> ser así,
         C
<u>perdonadme</u>.
  D

5. Lo decía para que el otro <u>las mirara</u>, pero
                 A B
<u>éste</u> no <u>le</u> fijó en las botas nuevas.
  C   D

6. —<u>Dispénsame</u>—repitió nuestro maestro, —y
       A
no <u>dejéis</u> de <u>quererme</u> sólo porque os <u>dejo</u>.
    B   C   D

7. En un <u>parpardear</u> de los ojos, corrieron
      A
sueltos todos los chicos tan pronto como
<u>llegaran</u> <u>al</u> agua <u>fría</u> del lago.
 B   C   D

8. Entre <u>aquellos</u> acusados <u>de</u> complicidad
      A   B
con el cartel <u>están</u> un funcionario <u>y</u>
          C   D
inspector.

9. <u>La</u> agente nueva, que había <u>sido</u> <u>enviado</u>
  A   B   C
para perseguir <u>al</u> cartel, murió en el
           D
ataque.

10. <u>Se veía</u> salir <u>de</u> la casa dos camionetas
    A   B
<u>rojas</u> y una <u>verde</u>.
  C   D

11. <u>Lo que</u> quiere el director es que no
    A
   <u>luchemos</u> con armas <u>pero</u> que <u>dialoguemos</u>
     B   C   D
  primero.

12. Si usted <u>desee</u> que le <u>presenten</u> una copia
        A   B
  del documento, <u>pregúntele</u>, —¿Podría
              C
  <u>mostrármelo</u>?
    D

Answers and Answer Explanations for Group Eight

1. (C) *empezaron.* The preterit is necessary in this case because action is begun and completed at a specific moment in the past. The infinitive form of *llamarnos* is correct after a preposition, and the pronoun is correct because it refers to the subject of the verb *estábamos.*

2. (D) *las mias.* This possessive pronoun refers to *las manos,* so the form needs to be feminine. For the same reason, *aquella* and *la* are correct because they refer to *mano,* also. *Por* is correct because in the context of this sentence, the meaning of the word is *underneath* the table.

3. (C) *os.* The second person plural form is indicated by the second person plural ending on the verb in the first clause. The word *venidero* is the correct gender and number to agree with *año. Conmigo* is the correct form for the prepositional pronoun *mí* after *con,* and *cuando* is at times used in place of *vez* in the expression *de vez en cuando.*

4. (C) *querer.* The infinitive is necessary after the preposition *sin,* no matter what the English uses in this case. *Alguna* is correct because it refers to *vez,* which is feminine. *Ha* is correct because the subject of the verb is not *me* (which is not a subject pronoun), but *la paciencia. Perdonadme* is the correct form for the second person plural affirmative command.

5. (D) *se.* The correct pronoun to use in this case is the reflexive pronoun. *Las* is correct because the pronoun refers to *las botas. Mirara* is correct because the subjunctive is needed after the adverbial conjunction *para que.*

6. (A) *dispensadme.* The correct second person plural affirmative command is *dispensadme.* That the subject is second person plural is indicated by the ending of the verb *dejéis* and the indirect pronoun *os. Dejo* is correct because there is no reason to use the subjunctive; it does not occur in a noun clause after a verb of emotion, doubt, denial, volition, or an impersonal expression. *Dejéis* is the correct second person plural negative command form. *Quererme* is correct because it is the object of the preposition *de.*

7. (B) *llegaron.* The indicative is used here because the action has already happened. In the past, if the time frame of the action in the dependent adverbial clause has not happened in relation to time in the main clause, use the subjunctive. For example, *Luego nos dijo que hablaría tan pronto como llegaran. (He told us he would talk to them as soon as they arrived.)* The conditional tense indicates that the speaker had not already talked to them. If the action took place, use the indicative. *Les habló tan pronto como llegaron. (He spoke to them as soon as they arrived.).* They arrived and they talked. Notice that the preterit is used instead of the conditional to indicate something that really happened. Refer to the grammar review in the appendix of this book for a listing of the common adverbial conjunctions introducing time clauses. *Parpardear* is correct because the infinitive is used as a noun in this instance. *Al* is correct, because the preposition *a* is combined with the

article *el*. The masculine article is used, even though the noun is feminine because the word begins with a stressed *a*. Again, refer to the grammar review for a listing of common words that fall into this category. Because *agua* is feminine, the adjective *fría* is correct.

8. (D) *e*. Remember that when the word following the conjunction *y* begins with a stressed *i*- or *hi*- sound, that the conjunction changes to *e*. Notice that words that begin with *hie-*, however, do not require that the conjunction change because the *i* is not stressed. *Están* is correct since the subject is *un funcionario e inspector*. *Aquellos* is the correct demonstrative adjective to use with *acusados*.

9. (C) *enviada*. Since the adjective refers to *la agente*, this past participle used as an adjective should be feminine. *Sido* is part of the compound tense and is invariable. *La agente* is correct for the feminine form of *agente*. *Al* is a proper contraction of *a* and *el*.

10. (A) *Se veían*. The subject of the verb is *camionetas* so the verb should be in the third person plural form. *De* is the preposition that normally follows *salir* when the meaning is *to go out of*. *Rojas* is correct because the adjective describes *camionetas*. *Verde* is invariable.

11. (C) *sino*. The meaning of this conjunction is *but rather*, since the clause that follows is the opposite of what precedes it. *Lo que* is correct because it refers to the whole idea of not fighting, rather talking things over. *Luchemos* and *dialoguemos* are both correct because they occur in dependent noun clauses after a main clause in which the verb expresses a wish, request, or desire.

12. (A) *desea*. The present indicative is normally used after *si*, not the present subjunctive. Remember that the past subjunctive is used after *si* in *if-then* statements, but when the present or future is used in the *then* part of the statement, the indicative is used. *Presenten* is correct because it occurs in a dependent noun clause after a verb expressing a wish or a request in the main clause. *Pregúntele* is correct, although the pronoun can also be *les*, since the subject of *presenten* is plural. The sentence could also read *If you want them to present you a copy of the document, ask him*. *Mostrármelo* is correct because the infinitive completes the meaning of *poder* and the pronouns refer to the proper people. Notice the accent over the infinitive ending vowel when two pronouns are attached.

GROUP NINE

1. Nada existe en la democracia que no <u>está</u>
                                          A
   <u>sujeto</u> a la razón, <u>la cual</u> se halla
     B   C
   <u>difícilmente</u>.
      D

2. Para que la cosa <u>funciona</u>, <u>lo</u> esencial es
                       A   B
   contar <u>con</u> un actor o actriz <u>simpático</u>.
          C   D

3. Con esa actriz no <u>hay</u> término medio: <u>o</u> te
                       A   B
   <u>guste</u> o la <u>aborreces</u>.
      C   D

4. Es un <u>hermoso</u> melodrama con tintes casi
            A
   <u>fantásticos</u> que <u>hace</u> <u>agradable</u> esta pieza.
      B   C   D

5. Le era al pobre <u>mucho</u> doloroso <u>oírla</u>,
   A   B   C

como si fuera una voz que <u>viniese</u> del
                                    D

cielo.

6. Se lee de <u>cuando</u> en cuando de las
            A

ciudades secretas, <u>conocidas</u> <u>por</u> el
                     B   C

nombre de la más <u>cercano</u>.
                  D

7. Se estrena un negocio este fin de semana

en <u>el que</u> espera <u>consigue</u> 3,3 millones <u>de</u>
    A   B   C
oyentes <u>semanales</u>.
        D

8. El plan gozará <u>de</u> mucho éxito por dos
                A

razones; la música y la publicidad que <u>se</u>
                                 B

<u>ofrecerán</u> en <u>lo</u>.
  C   D

9. "<u>Cualquiera</u> se siente una estrella si se <u>le</u>
     A   B

<u>envían</u> una carta", era <u>el</u> lema final del
  C   D

anuncio.

10. <u>Éste</u> es mi <u>tercer</u> programa <u>cinematográfica</u>
    A   B   C

en <u>cuya</u> producción ha intervenido Tele 1.
    D

11. Cuando <u>descubras</u> este nuevo coche,
         A

<u>sabrás</u> <u>qué</u> has <u>conseguido</u> una maravilla.
  B   C   D

12. Cuando <u>llegue</u> podré decirle si a los otros
        A

pilotos <u>le</u> <u>molesta</u>, pero ahora no me
      B   C

preocupa lo que <u>piensen</u>.
              D

Answers and Answer Explanations for Group Nine

1. (A) *esté.* The subjunctive is needed in this clause because it occurs in an adjective clause and refers to a nonexistent antecedent. *Sujeto* is correct because it also refers to *nada*, which takes the masculine adjective. *Difícilmente* is the correct adverbial form to describe the verb *se halla.*

2. (A) *funcione.* The subjunctive is needed in this dependent adverb clause because it follows *para que,* an adverbial conjunction expressing purpose. *Lo* is used to mean *the essential thing.* The adjective *escencial* is nominalized, but does not refer to any specific noun. *Con* is correct because it is part of the expression *contar con,* meaning *to count on.* *Simpático* is correct because when there are two antecedents for an adjective, one of which is masculine and the other feminine, the masculine plural form of the adjective is used.

3. (D) *aborrezcas.* The subjunctive is used here because the adjective clause describes *término*, an indefinite antecedent. The subject of the verb is *tú*, which is indicated by the indirect object pronoun in front of *guste.* The subject of *guste* is *actriz.* *Hay* is correct because it occurs in the main clause.

4. (C) *hacen.* The subject of this verb is *tintes.* Even if you do not know the meaning of *tintes*, you can determine that it is the subject by looking at the structure of the sentence and the words you do recognize. Nouns are subjects of verbs and *tintes* is a noun. The preposition *con* indicates that the subsequent clause will describe *melodrama.* A melodramatic piece

does not make itself pleasant; there is some aspect of it that accomplishes that fact, and that aspect is *tintes.*

5. (B) *muy.* The adverb *muy* is needed here to modify the adjective *doloroso. Le* is correct even though it is used redundantly. *Oírla* is also correct because the infinitive is used as a noun in this sentence. The pronoun *la* could refer either to the noun *voz* in the next clause, or to some other noun not named in the sentence, such as *la muchacha. Viniese* is a correct use of the past subjunctive in an adjective clause, describing an indefinite or hypothetical antecedent, such as a mysterious voice.

6. (D) *cercana.* The adjective refers to *la ciudad,* not *el nombre.* The correct gender is feminine. Remember that *cuando* can be used in place of *vez* in this expression: *de vez en cuando.* Also, *conocidas* refers to *ciudades,* so it is feminine plural. *Por* means *by* in this sentence and is correct.

7. (B) *conseguir.* The infinitive is needed to function as the object of the verb *esperar. El que* is correct because it refers to *un negocio. De* is correct because it is the preposition that normally follows *millones. Semanales* is the correct form of the adjective to describe *oyentes.*

8. (D) *él. Lo* is not the correct masculine singular pronoun to use after a preposition. *Ofrecerán* is correct because *música* and *publicidad* are a compound subject. *De* is the correct preposition to use after *gozar.*

9. (C) *envía.* The third person singular form is needed because of the *se* substitute for the passive voice, by the indirect object pronoun *le,* and by the singular subject of the verb, *cualquiera. El* is correct because *lema* is masculine. *Cualquiera* is correct since either the whole form, *cualquiera,* or the shortened form, *cualquier,* is correct. It may be useful to remember that there is a plural form of this indefinite adjective: *cualesquiera.*

10. (C) *cinematográfico.* This adjective modifies *programa.* All of the other underlined words are correct. They all agree with the nouns they modify. Remember that *tercero,* like *primero,* drops the *-o* before masculine singular nouns.

11. (C) *que.* When *que* functions as a relative that introduces a dependent clause, there is no accent. Remember that writing the accent on the word changes what part of speech it is; *qué* becomes an interrogative pronoun with the written accent. *Descubras* is correct because the verb in the main clause is in the future, which means that the action in the dependent adverb clause is expressed in the subjunctive since it has not happened yet. *Sabrás* is correct if the subjunctive is correct in the dependent clause, and since you can only name one error, this one would not be it; you would have to change *descubras,* also. *Conseguido* is the correct past participle to use after *haber.*

12. (B) *les.* The plural indirect object pronoun is needed since the object is *a los otros pilotos. Llegue* is correct because it occurs in a dependent adverb clause, and the action has not happened yet. *Molesta* is correct because the present indicative is needed after *si. Piensen* is correct because it occurs in an adjective clause that refers to an indefinite antecedent, *lo que.* The subject of *piensen* is *pilotos.*

GROUP TEN

1. Si el Gobierno quisiera de repente hacerle
   A   B

   cargo de las personas sin ningún tipo de
        C   D

   seguro, costaría demasiado.

2. Los seguros suelen estar básicamente
                 A

   divididos en pólizas individuales y
   B

   familiares, y éstos son caras.
             C   D

3. Casi veinte por ciento más de los gastos
             A

   son dedicados al pago de la burocracia
   B   C

   creada por el actual sistema.
            D

4. Ni habían ningunos programas que
      A   B

   tuvieran mayores influencias en el
      C   D

   desarrollo industrial.

5. Por mucho entusiasmo que pone en su
                     A

   acto, ese actor se encuentra
        B

   definitivamente agotado.
        C   D

6. Sin que debamos lamentarse: todo aquello
               A   B

   tuvo un sentido y lo absurdo sería querer
                     C   D

   mantenerlo.

7. Aunque resulte impolítico recordarlo, ese
         A   B

   señor y esa señora eran entonces los

   símbolos y como tal, detestados.
            C   D

8. Para quienes busquen la tranquilidad, se
        A   B

   sugiere Tavira y Colina por su ubicación en
      C   D

   la costa del sur.

9. El hecho de ser situada a tres kilómetros
           A   B

   del mar han apartado a Tavira de otras
            C   D

   aldeas.

10. Faro, cuyas murallas no sirvieron para
        A   B

    detenerse las sucesivas invasiones, cuenta
      C   D

    con varios canales.

11. A la buena comida casera se une unos
                   A   B

    precios bastante moderados, unos 1.500
          C

    por persona.
    D

12. Allí se encuentra Faro, situada cerca del
                     A

    puente sobre el Guadiana el que han
            B   C

    cofinanciada España y Portugal.
       D

Answers and Answer Explanations for Group Ten

1. (B) *hacerse.* The reflexive pronoun is needed in the context of this sentence where the action of the government reflects back upon itself. The government will take it upon itself to take charge of people. *De* is correct because the meaning of the expression is *of. Ningún* is also correct because it is preceded by *sin.* The negative indefinite adjective is also shortened before masculine singular nouns, such as *tipo. Quisiera* is correct because this is an *if-then* statement, as indicated by the conditional tense in the last clause.

2. (C) *éstas.* The noun that this demonstrative pronoun replaces is *pólizas,* which is feminine plural. The verb *estar* is correct here because it describes a state of being. *Caras* describes *pólizas.*

3. (B) *están.* Not all examples of *ser* plus a past participle and followed by *por* are examples of the passive voice. The prepositional phrase introduced by *por* does not refer to the action of dedicating the expenditures to the payment by the bureaucracy. Rather, it refers to a resultant action. An example of the difference between *ser* and *estar* would be found in the sentence *La puerta estaba abierta.* (*The door was open.*) In this case the verb describes a resultant state of being of the door. As the result of what someone did, the door was left open. Compare this implied meaning of *estar* with the true passive voice: *La puerta fue abierta* (*The door was opened*). The last example uses the verb *ser* and the past participle. Implicit in the meaning in Spanish is that someone opened the door, that there was an agent. Notice that in English the word in the true passive is *opened,* a verbal form. With the verb *estar,* the meaning is *open,* indicating an adjectival form, describing the state of being of the door. *Por* is correct because it is appropriate in the expression *percent. El* is correct because *sistema* is masculine. *Dedicados* is a past participle that describes *gastos,* so it is correct.

4. (A) *había.* This third person form of *haber* that means *there was* is invariably in the third person singular, in spite of the fact that it is followed by a plural noun. Remember that *programas* is also masculine, so *ningunos* is correct. Also, *tuvieran* is correct since it occurs in an adjective clause that refers to a nonexistent antecedent. *Mayores* is the plural form of this comparative adjective that means *greater.*

5. (A) *ponga.* The subjunctive is used in the adjective clause *por mucho...que* because the antecedent is indefinite. *Ese* is the correct demonstrative adjective. *Definitivamente* is the correct form for an adverb, describing *se encuentra.* And *agotado* describes *ese actor.*

6. (A) *lamentarnos.* The subject of the verb *debamos* is *nosotros* so the reflexive pronoun after *lamentar* needs to be the first person plural also. *Aquello* is correct because it refers to an indefinite antecedent, the whole idea of how ridiculous everything was. *Sería* is correct in the sequence of tenses, since *tuvo* precedes *sería. Querer* is correct because it serves as the object of the verb *sería.* Remember that *sin que* always takes the subjunctive in the past and present tenses.

7. (C) *tales.* This adjective refers to *símbolos,* and should be plural. It cannot agree in gender, but should agree in number with the noun that it describes. *Resulte* is correct, although *aunque* can take either the indicative or the subjunctive. In the sense of this sentence, the subjunctive is appropriate. *Recordarlo* is correct since the infinitive is the object of the verb, and the neuter pronoun refers to the idea of remembering. *Detestados* is correct because mixed gender groups are always described using masculine plural adjectives.

8. (C) *sugieren.* The third person plural form is used because the subject is *Tavira* and *Colina. Quienes* is correct because the pronoun refers to people. The present subjunctive, *busquen,* is correct because *quienes* is an indefinite antecedent. *Por* is correct because the preposition expresses for what reason these two villages are known.

9. (A) *estar.* The use of the verb *estar* is correct in this case because it indicates physical location. *Aldeas* is a feminine noun, so *otras* must end with -*as.*

10. (C) *detener.* This verb should not be reflexive in this case. When the reflexive pronoun is used, the meaning is *to stop (oneself),* which is not the meaning of the verb in the context of this sentence. *Cuyas* describes *murallas,* not *Faro,* so it is correct. *Para* indicates purpose, *in order to,* so it is correct. *Faro* is the subject of *cuenta,* which is correct.

11. (B) *unen.* The subject of this verb is *precios* so the verb must be in the third person plural. *Se* is correct because it indicates the impersonal reflexive pronoun that substitutes for the passive voice construction. *Bastante* is an adverb, which means that it will not agree in gender or number with anything. Remember that adverbs can modify adjectives, which means that sometimes an adverb (with invariable endings) will modify a word that can have variable endings. *Por* is used to express the meaning of *each,* or *apiece.*

12. (D) *cofinanciado.* The subject of *han* is *España* and *Portugal,* but *han* is a helping verb that takes a past participle to form the perfect tenses. When the past participle follows the verb *haber* the ending is always -*o.* *El* is correct because it refers to *el río Guadiana.* *Situada* refers to the *aldea* of Faro.

GROUP ELEVEN

1. Una comarca española y otra <u>francés</u>,
   A
   <u>separadas</u> <u>por</u> la frontera <u>van</u> a ser
   B   C   D
   escenario de los juegos.

2. Que el artista <u>diera</u> o no su vida <u>por</u> el arte
              A   B
   es <u>algo</u> que necesita demostración más
     C
   <u>pleno</u>.
    D

3. Cree que <u>el</u> arte <u>ha</u> de reproducir seres de
          A   B
   una naturaleza donde <u>sople</u> el viento y
                C
   <u>reine</u> el frío y el calor.
    D

4. Su temperamento no <u>deja</u> lugar a dudas y
               A
   corrobora <u>cuán</u> cierto es su carácter, <u>tanta</u>
         B   C
   en su arte <u>como</u> en la guerra.
         D

5. <u>Tal</u> documento dijo que no sólo el trabajo
    A
   noble, <u>pero</u> <u>hasta</u> la mínima expresión
        B   C
   <u>brota</u> <u>de</u> lo nativo.
    D

6. Tomó asiento <u>ante</u> una mesa y estiró <u>las</u>
             A   B
   piernas <u>por</u> ayudar la circulación,
         C
   <u>entorpecida</u> por la inactividad.
       D

7. Se <u>lo</u> manifestó, <u>estando</u> en la cárcel, a un
     A   B
   amigo, —Yo quiero hacer <u>mías</u> <u>tantos</u>
                   C   D
   temas como puedo.

8. <u>Siendo</u> hijo de una <u>gran</u> figura le abre a
    A   B
   uno puertas, pero lo que sí depende <u>de</u>
                          C
   uno es que no se las <u>cierren</u>.
               D

9. <u>Desde</u> hace muchos años <u>pronunciaba</u>
   A   B

   conferencias, <u>pero</u> acaba <u>de</u> clausurar el
                         C   D

   curso del Ateneo.

10. Todos los quehaceres no <u>le impidió</u> que
                            A   B

   <u>visitara</u> a su mamá, ya vieja <u>pero</u> vivaz.
   C   D

11. <u>Poca dada</u> a hablar de su vida personal,
     A   B

   ella dice, siempre que el tema <u>sale</u>, —<u>Soy</u>
                                 C   D

   feliz.

12. De <u>lo que</u> procura no <u>mencionar</u> es de su
      A   B

   primer esposo, con <u>que</u> acabó <u>separándose</u>.
                     C   D

Answers and Answer Explanations for Group Eleven

1. (A) *francesa.* This adjective refers to *una comarca,* so it needs to be feminine. *Separadas* refers to the two *comarcas,* indicated by the use of the two adjectives of nationality, *española y francesa. Por* means *by* in the context of this sentence. The subject of *van* is the two villages.

2. (D) *plena.* This adjective describes *demostración,* which is feminine. *Diera* is correct because the clause presents a hypothetical, or nonexistent, situation. The subjunctive is used in such cases. The meaning is *would give. Por* is correct because its meaning in the context of this sentence is *in exchange for. Algo* is the appropriate indefinite pronoun to mean *something.*

3. (D) *reinen.* The subject of the verb is *el frío y el calor,* which means that the verb should be third person plural. *Arte* takes a masculine article because the word begins with a stressed *a. Ha de* is a proper impersonal expression of obligation. *Sople* is correct because the present subjunctive is indicated by the indefinite antecedent; such a nature may or may not exist.

4. (C) *tanto.* This word is not followed by an adjective or a noun in this clause, so it should be invariable, *tanto. Deja* is used correctly because it occurs in the main clause and the subject is *temperamento. Cuán* is a correct shortened form of *cuánto* or *cuánta. Como* is the other part of the expression *tanto ... como.*

5. (B) *sino.* The conjunction *sino* is indicated here because two opposites are contrasted in this sentence. *De* is the proper preposition to use following *brotar,* and shows origin. *Tal* is an adjective that describes *documento,* which is singular. *Hasta* means *even, up to, until,* in the context of this sentence, and is correctly used.

6. (C) *para.* The meaning of the preposition in this case is *in order to,* which means that *por* is not correct. *Ante* is correct because it is a preposition meaning *before* in the context of this sentence. Remember that the possessive adjective *sus* would not be used to indicate *his* and that the definite article *las* is correct before *piernas. Entorpecida* is correct because it refers to *circulación.*

7. (C) *míos.* This possessive pronoun refers to *temas,* which is masculine plural. *Lo* is correct; it refers to an indefinite antecedent or an abstraction. *Estando* is a correct use of a present participle to describe in what manner the subject was acting. *Tantos* is correct because it refers to *temas.*

8. (A) *ser.* The infinitive is used as a noun in this context, although you will notice that in English the present participle *being* is normally used. Remember that in Spanish the present participle is not used in place of a noun. Also remember that the present participle, when it appears at

the beginning of a sentence is usually translated *by* + (present participle). *By asking...* is an example of the meaning of the present participle used to express cause, means or manner, without any introductory word. *Grande* is shortened before masculine and feminine singular nouns. Also, remember that *depender* is followed by the preposition *de*. The present subjunctive of *cerrar* is used because it is used after *depender de*.

9. (B) *pronunció*. The use of the preterit *pronunció*, with the present tense of the verb *haber*, indicates time *ago* in the context given here. *De* is correct because after the verb *acabar*, the meaning of the expression is *to have just*. This expression indicates that the past action is completed in the verb *pronunciar*.

10. (B) *impidieron*. The subject of the verb is *los quehaceres*, not *le*. The subjunctive is used in the dependent clause in the verb *visitara* because the verb in the main clause expresses a command, request, or desire. *Pero* is correct because *vieja* and *vivaz* are not contrasting characteristics.

11. (A) *Poco*. This word is an adverb, used in this sentence to modify an adjective. Adverbs do not agree with any referents or antecedents. *Dada* is correct because it refers to the subject, *ella*. The indicative is used in this case after *siempre que* because the sentence states a fact or given truth. Remember that the subjunctive is used to communicate uncertainty, doubt, or conjecture about what the speaker knows actually happened. *Ser* is an appropriate verb with *feliz*, since it describes an inherent characteristic.

12. (C) *quien*. The relative pronoun refers to a person, so *que* is not used. *Lo que* is an indefinite relative pronoun, which is appropriate in the context of this sentence since the referent is not specified. *Mencionar* is used as the object of the verb *procura*, and the infinitive is the correct part of speech to use. *Separándose* is used to describe the action of the verb *acabó*. The reflexive pronoun on the end is appropriate because the action refers back upon the subject.

GROUP TWELVE

1. Si <u>percibiríamos</u> toda la comunicación
       A
   constante <u>del</u> mundo, <u>nos</u>
         B   C
   <u>enloqueciéramos</u>.
       D

2. Yo <u>oía</u> perfectamente a esa señora, no
    A
   porque <u>fuese</u> su voz <u>aguda</u> y potente, <u>pero</u>
        B   C   D
   porque era suave.

3. No <u>hubiera</u> sido correcto que en un diálogo
      A
   dama-caballero, ella se <u>pusiera</u> a tocar con
                    B
   <u>sus</u> manos <u>los</u> del caballero.
    C   D

4. A mi edad yo no me imaginaba <u>como</u>
                      A
   <u>podía</u> <u>ser</u> una mujer abandonada <u>por</u> su
    B C   D
   esposo.

5. En suma, para <u>mi</u>, la mujer era <u>algo</u>
         A   B
   <u>misterioso</u>, con un ruido personal, como <u>el</u>
    C   D
   de caracolas marítimas.

6. El actual Panteón de los Reyes es el <u>tercer</u>
                         A
   de <u>los</u> que sucesivamente se <u>fueron</u>
       B   C
   <u>construyendo</u> en Segovia.
     D

7. Más tarde cuando <u>le</u> <u>terminó</u> la basílica, <u>el</u>
   A   B   C

   mismo rey ordenó que se <u>traslade</u> el
                           D

   panteón a otra bóveda.

8. El panteón es <u>de</u> planta octagonal, y <u>se</u>
   A   B

   accede a <u>ella</u> a través de una escalera que
   C

   <u>parte</u> de la antesacristía.
   D

9. <u>Numerosas</u> turistas preguntan a <u>los</u> guías si
   A   B

   estos dos espacios serán ocupados <u>un</u> día
   C

   <u>por</u> los Reyes actuales.
   D

10. El rey fue un <u>gran</u> español, enamorado <u>de</u>
    A   B

    su patria, <u>que</u> hizo mucho <u>por</u> la paz del
    C   D

    país.

11. Ella no puede evitar <u>el</u> ser <u>reconocido</u> en
    A   B

    plena calle, y ser saludada por una señora

    que <u>se</u> interesó <u>por</u> su vida.
    C   D

12. Yo aspiro que mis hijos <u>hablen</u> <u>buen</u> de su
    A   B

    padre y se sientan <u>orgullosos</u> de <u>él</u>.
    C   D

Answers and Answer Explanations for Group Twelve

1. (A) *percibiéramos.* The subjunctive should be used in the *si* clause of *if-then* statements. Remember that the *-iera* form of the past subjunctive may be used in place of the conditional, but the conditional cannot be used in the *si* clause. *Del* is the correct word to use since it is the combination of *de* and *el.* *Enloquecer* is used reflexively in this sentence to give the meaning of *to go crazy.* Remember that the reflexive is used to mean *to go* or *to become* when used with some verbs, such as *enriquecerse, envejecerse,* or *entristecerse.*

2. (D) *sino.* Since the meaning of this conjunction is *but rather, pero* is not used. The imperfect tense is appropriate in the context of this sentence because it describes the action. The time frame in which the action takes place is indefinite. The past subjunctive is appropriate in the verb *fuese,* because it indicates something that is contrary to fact, something that was not the case in this situation. *Voz* is feminine so *aguda* is the correct gender and number for this adjective.

3. (D) *las.* The gender of *manos* is feminine, even though the noun ends in *-o,* so the article indicating possession must be *las.* Although the sentence is not an *if-then* statement, the meaning of the sentence deals with a hypothetical situation: *It would not have been correct if she had played the man's part.* The past subjunctive is appropriate in this context, both for *hubiera* and for *pusiera* because the speaker is dealing with a hypothetical situation. *Sus manos* is used in this case to differentiate *her* hands from *his.* Although normally the possessive adjective is not used to modify parts of the body, in some cases it is necessary to avoid confusion.

4. (A) *cómo.* The interrogative is used in this context to pose the implicit question *What would it have been like. Ser* is correct because the passive voice is used, as indicated by *por* and the agent, *esposo.* The imperfect is used to describe the action, not narrate it. The action takes place in an unspecified time.

5. (A) *mí.* The object of the preposition pronoun must have a written accent to differentiate it from the possessive adjective, *mi. Algo* is the appropriate indefinite pronoun meaning *something. Misterioso* is the correct gender and number to agree with *algo. El* refers to *ruido*, so it is the correct gender and number.

6. (A) *tercero.* This ordinal number is not shortened unless it comes directly in front of a noun. *Los* refers to *panteón. Los que* is a relative pronoun that refers to the plural noun *panteones. Fueron* is the correct person and number for this impersonal construction that is used in place of the true passive voice. *Construyendo* is the present participle that is used as an adverb. The verb *fueron* is the verb *ir* instead of *ser.* Remember that for the progressive forms, the verb *estar* is used with the present participle, not the verb *ser.*

7. (D) *trasladara.* The past subjunctive needs to be used because of the preterit in the main clause, *ordenó. Le* is correct because it refers to *el rey*, for whom the basilica was being built. *El* is the proper gender and number definite article for *rey.* The preterit is used for *terminó* to indicate action that was completed at a specified time in the past.

8. (C) *él.* This pronoun refers to *el panteón*, which is masculine. The referent is normally the noun that the prepositional phrase describes, not the noun in the modifying prepositional phrase. In other words, the reference is to *panteón*, not *planta* in the phrase *de planta octagonal. Se* is used in the impersonal, passive structure, meaning *one accesses*, or *it is accessed. Parte* is the present indicative, which is used here to state a simple fact: the stairs go off from the sacristy to the *panteón.*

9. (A) *Numerosos.* The masculine plural adjective is used because *turistas* is invariable in its ending. For mixed gender groups, the masculine form is normally used. One assumes that all tourists ask, not just female tourists. Remember that nouns that end with *-ista* are masculine, so the *-a* on the end is not an indicator of gender. The words *día* and *guías* are also masculine, even though they end in *-ía. Por* means *by* which is the appropriate preposition in this true passive voice construction.

10. (C) *el cual.* The masculine relative pronoun is used here to indicate which of the previous nouns is the antecedent of the pronoun. Since *patria* is feminine, using *el cual* designates the antecedent. Remember that *grande* is shortened before singular nouns. *Por* is used to mean *for the sake of* or *on behalf of.* The use of *de* is correct after *enamorar.* In the passive voice, the preposition *de* can be used in place of *por* if the agent is a person or people. Learn to look for the verb *ser*, a past participle, *por* or *de,* and an agent in order to recognize the passive voice.

11. (B) *reconocida.* The past participle, used here as an adjective, refers to *ella*, which is feminine. *El* is used before the infinitive when the infinitive is used as a noun, as is the case here. *El ser* is the object of the verb *evitar. Interesarse por* is an expression meaning *to be interested in.*

12. (B) *bien.* An adverb is necessary here to describe the action of the verb *hablen. Buen* is an adjective and cannot describe a verb. *Bien* is an adverb and is correct. The present subjunctive is used in *hablen* and *sientan* because the verb occurs in a dependent noun clause when the verb in the main clause, *aspiro*, expresses a wish. *Orgullosos* refers to *mis hijos,* and *él* refers to *su padre.*

CHAPTER 6 Reading Strategies

The following section contains suggestions for how to read quickly and efficiently. The material is divided into different areas of comprehension. The reading passages on the exam can be very difficult if you do not read very much. The difficulties you may encounter are discussed in the following order:

1. Understanding unfamiliar vocabulary.
2. Getting the main idea.
3. Reading for details
   a) setting; b) time; c) characters or things; d) plot.
4. Interpretation
   a) comparisons and contrasts; b) analyzing parallel structures;
   c) tone or attitude; d) intended reader.

These discussions contain sample passages and describe how to approach the task. After each sample there is a discussion of which answers are correct or incorrect. The logic of the answer is also explained. Pay close attention to the logic so you can understand where your errors were in thinking if you chose incorrectly. After the sample selections and questions and answers, there are five sets of selections. In the reading comprehension part of the exam some questions deal with the general theme of the selection and with information about what happens in it. Then there are questions about meanings that can be inferred or deduced by understanding some of the nuances of meaning of phrases, expressions, grammar, or cultural material contained in the selection. Other questions ask what specific phrases, structures, or words mean, where could a sentence or phrase be added to the text, or how to make a prediction based on what is stated in the text. In all, there are about 35 to 40 questions. Remember that this part of Section I accounts for 30 percent of the final score.

Suggestions for Reading

You can learn to read with greater comprehension by keeping the following strategies in mind:

1. Scan the whole passage to get a general idea about the content and style.
2. Reread the passage to focus on details.
3. Identify the main focus or idea of the passage. Look for the repetition of subjects or objects of verbs. Or look for words that are topically related.
4. Identify possible sources of the passage, whether it came from fiction, instructions for how to use something, a newspaper or magazine report, or some other source.
5. Note translations of words if there is any vocabulary footnoted.
6. Identify the characters in the selection.
7. Identify the time frame of the selection, when it takes place, how long the action lasts, and when it ends.
8. Identify what action takes place.
9. Identify why the action takes place.
10. Identify similes, metaphors, analogies, symbols, and/or allusions.

11. Note word selection of nouns, adjectives, and adverbs as well as syntax to determine the tone and mood of the selection.

12. Make inferences about what the selection communicates based on an understanding of the logic of the selection.

13. Visualize the passage while reading if it deals with description, a narration of action, or any instructional type of information.

Dealing with Vocabulary in Reading Comprehension

The meaning of unfamiliar vocabulary can frequently be determined from the context. In selecting answers with words you do not know, be wary of answers containing words that appear similar or are repeated exactly from the text. Use a process of elimination to select correct answers. At times questions may deal with lexical aspects of the passage, a word that may be uncommon or a *modismo* that is somewhat unusual. In these cases, if the word or expression is unknown, there are strategies for determining meaning. The most important clue can usually be found in information communicated in surrounding words, or, in other words, the context of the item. If the word is a noun modified by an adjective, base your interpretation on the meaning of the adjective if it is known. If the word is an adjective, consider the meaning of the noun and the context of the noun. If the word is a verb, find the subject of that verb and then the subject and/or object of the preceding and succeeding verbs, then make an educated guess about the meaning. Also consider the tense and mood of the conjugated verbs. There should be some logical continuity in the action accomplished or described.

In the following passages:

1. Read the selection.
2. Study the question.
3. Refer back to the passage.
4. Answer the question.

READING SELECTIONS AND EXPLANATIONS

Dealing with Unfamiliar Vocabulary

SELECTION ONE

    El dibujante Mingote ha presentado docenas de veces el tipo humano del oficinista público, que no siente ninguna afinidad o relación de simpatía con quien aguarda minuto tras minuto. Como en muchos sitios no
Línea hay servicio de información ocurre que, tras una cola de media hora, al
(5) que espera se le dice que le falta tal o cual sello en su instancia, sello que tiene que ir a buscar y perder el turno a no ser que el ordenanza—véase Intermediarios—se lo facilite mediante una propina. Estoy seguro de que si se les propusiera a muchas oficinas del Estado...

1. En la línea 5, ¿a qué tipo de sello se refiere?
   (A) una estampilla para poner en un sobre
   (B) una señal impresa para un documento oficial
   (C) una especie de anillo para marcar cera
   (D) un mueble para sentarse

The correct answer is **B** since people may have to go to various places to obtain the proper one, "*...sello que tiene que ir a buscar y perder el turno a no ser que el ordenanza ... se lo facilite...*". While there are also lines to purchase stamps at the post office, usually there is no need to go anywhere else to obtain what is needed to mail a letter. The type of *sello* mentioned in the above passage refers to an authorization or a permit bestowed by an official (*oficinista público* and *el ordenanza*), someone amenable to receiving a tip for a favor done. Obviously, *sello* is not to be confused with *silla* (a type of *mueble para sentarse*), even though the two words share common consonants.

SELECTION TWO

Desperté, cubierto de sudor. Del piso de ladrillos rojos, recién regado, subía un vapor caliente. Una mariposa de alas grisáceas revoloteaba encandilada alrededor del foco amarillento. Salté de la hamaca y

Línea descalzo atravesé el cuarto, cuidando de no pisar algún alacrán salido de

(5) su escondrijo a tomar el fresco. Me acerqué al ventanillo y aspiré el aire del campo. Se oía la respiración de la noche, enorme, femenina. Regresé al centro de la habitación, vacié el agua de la jarra en la palangana de peltre y humedecí la toalla. Me froté el torso y las piernas con el trapo empapado, me sequé un poco y, tras de cerciorarme que ningún bicho

(10) estaba escondido entre los pliegues de mi ropa, me vestí y calcé. Bajé saltando la escalera pintada de verde. En la puerta del mesón tropecé con el dueño, sujeto tuerto y reticente. Sentado en una sillita de tule, fumaba con el ojo entrecerrado.

—¿Onde va, señor?

(15) —A dar una vuelta. Hace mucho calor.

—Hum, todo está ya cerrado. Y no hay alumbrado aquí. Más le valiera quedarse.

Alcé los hombros, musité "ahora vuelvo" y me metí en lo oscuro. Al principio no veía nada. Caminé a tientas por la calle empedrada.

(20) Encendí un cigarrillo. De pronto salió la luna de una nube negra, iluminando un muro blanco, desmoronado a trechos.

1. La expresión "Caminé a tientas..." en la línea 19 significa que el narrador
   (A) irá de compras.
   (B) intenta andar por las calles.
   (C) se pierde.
   (D) anda cuidadosamente.

The correct answer is **D** because in the sentence immediately before, the narrator states that he cannot see anything, "*Al principio no veía nada.*" The darkness makes it difficult to see until the moon comes out to light up the scene. The word *tienda,* implied in **A** is a distractor; it makes no sense in the context of the passage; it is nighttime and no stores would be open. Choice **B** is also incorrect because the narrator does not simply attempt to take a walk; he in fact does so, albeit carefully. *Intentar* is a false cognate; it does not necessarily mean *to intend.* Rather, it means *to attempt.* Be careful not to translate words literally. Choice **C** is incorrect; nowhere in the surrounding context is there any suggestions that he gets lost.

SELECTION THREE

Ahora, por fin, se había apaciguado. Estaba allí arrinconado al pie del horcón. Había venido su hijo Justino y su hijo Justino se había ido y había vuelto y ahora otra vez venía.

Línea   Lo echó encima del burro. Lo apretó bien apretado al aparejo para que
(5)   no se fuese a caer por el camino. Le metió su cabeza dentro de un costal para que no diera mala impresión. Y luego le hizo pelos al burro y se fueron, arrebatados, de prisa, para llegar a Palo de Venado todavía con tiempo para arreglar el velorio del difunto.

—Tu nuera y los nietos te extrañarán—iba diciéndole—. Te mirarán a
(10)   la cara y creerán que no eres tú. Se les afigurará que te ha comido el coyote, cuando te vean con esa cara tan llena de boquetes por tanto tiro de gracia como te dieron.

1. En la línea 6, ca qué se refiere "...para que no diera mala impresión" en el contexto del pasaje?
   (A) Significa que cuántos lo vieran se asustarían.
   (B) Indica que el hijo se avergüenza de su papá.
   (C) Quiere decir que tiene algo de malo.
   (D) Significa que el papá no había sido hombre muy culto.

The correct answer is **A** because the narrative has just stated that the man's head was covered by a sack. The words *creerían que no eres tú* and *esa cara tan llena...por tanto tiro de gracia como te dieron* indicate that the face was very disfigured. The other alternatives are incorrect because of various distractors: in **B** the "*mala impresión*" does not mean that his son is ashamed of the way his father looks; in **C** "*mala impresión*" does not mean that the man is ill; and in **D** the level of education does not create the "*mala impresión.*" The use of *para que* denotes that he does indeed look very bad, and that the purpose of the sack over his head is to conceal his face from everyone.

SELECTION FOUR

El magistrado Miguel Angel del Arco, del juzgado de instrucción número 6 de Granada decretó el viernes la prisión incondicional del médico granadino Juan Valdés y la libertad provisional bajo fianza de
Línea   doscientas cincuenta mil pesetas para el escritor José Heredia Maya, por
(5)   su presunta implicación en relación con un robo de objetos de arte ocurrido entre el uno y el tres de mayo pasado, en el Carmen de los Mínimos de Granada, de propiedad municipal.

Este robo ha dado pie ya a varias decisiones políticas—en cuanto evidencia negligencia en la custodia de bienes públicos—, entre ellas
(10)   la personación del PP en el sumario y la petición de dimisión de tres concejales socialistas pedida por el grupo municipal del Partido Popular cuyas investigaciones han permitido demostrar que se han detectado hasta ahora cuatro intentos de robo y tres advertencias del jefe de patrimonio municipal al concejal de cultura advirtiendo sobre
(15)   la necesidad de trasladar los objetos del Carmen o dotar al mismo de vigilancia.

1. La línea 15, "...o dotar al mismo de vigilancia." tiene que ver con
   (A) los planes de los concejales municipales.
   (B) regalos para aumentar la colección de objetos de arte.
   (C) ofertas de auxilio financiero para cuidar el patrimonio municipal.
   (D) consejos del jefe que se subvencione la colección para protegerla.

The correct answer is **D**. This alternative paraphrases the words of the text; *subvencionar* means *to underwrite* and *dotar* means *to provide funds*. If you do not recognize *subvención* or *dotar*, the meaning can be deduced from the previous clause: *la necesidad de trasladar...o.* Look for *lado* in *trasladar* and the prefix *tras-* to arrive at the meaning of *to move*. Then, if the objects are not going to be moved, *or* indicates that they will stay where they are and need to be guarded. *Vigilar* sounds like *vigil*, implying watching over something. The *jefe* only offers advice, not funds for protecting the collection, which makes choice **C** incorrect. Choice **A** is incorrect because although the councilmen are worried about the thefts, the text does not mention that they are actually concerned about taking steps to provide protection. Choice **B** is incorrect because the advice is to improve protection, not increase the size of the collection. The keys word to recognize in the surrounding text are *advertir* and the noun, *advertencia*.

Identifying the Theme or Main Idea

1. The theme sometimes is not mentioned at the beginning of the passage.
2. Look for the relationship between words, nouns, and verbs especially, to indicate the theme of a passage.
3. Do not be misled by isolated nouns or names.
4. Do not be misled by false cognates.

When you scan a passage, you should make a mental note of those words that you recognize and begin to think about what they all have in common. Pay particular attention to nouns and verbs. Do not worry about words that you do not recognize. Later you can determine which of the words are really important from among those that you do not know. In the following four short selections, read them for the general idea. The question that follows each one would be a possible multiple-choice question concerning identification of the main idea or theme of the passage. The selection will be presented again with the pertinent vocabulary underlined so that you can more easily identify the underlying connection between the words.

Questions About Theme or Main Idea

SELECTION ONE

El dibujante Mingote ha presentado docenas de veces el tipo humano del oficinista público, que no siente ninguna afinidad o relación de simpatía con quien aguarda minuto tras minuto. Como en muchos sitios no
Línea hay servicio de información ocurre que, tras una cola de media hora, al
(5) que espera se le dice que le falta tal o cual sello en su instancia, sello que tiene que ir a buscar y perder el turno a no ser que el ordenanza—véase Intermediarios—se lo facilite mediante una propina. Estoy seguro de que si se les propusiera a muchas oficinas del Estado...

1. El tema de esta selección es
   (A) oficinas en lugares públicas.
   (B) comprando estampillas al correo.
   (C) discusión de dibujos de Mingote.
   (D) maneras de tratar con una burocracia.

The correct answer is **D**, because none of the other alternatives apply to the passage as a whole even though they include words that might indicate a topic dealing with a drawing, a line, a turn, and a stamp. Look again at the passage with key words underlined, then look to see where there is a word that stands out in the group of related words. Notice where the key word occurs in the paragraph.

El <u>dibujante</u> Mingote ha presentado docenas de veces <u>el tipo humano</u> del <u>oficinista</u> pública, que no siente <u>ninguna afinidad</u> o <u>relación de sim-</u><u>patía</u> con quien aguarda minuto tras minuto. Como en muchos sitios no
Línea hay <u>servicio de información</u> ocurre que, tras <u>una cola</u> de media hora, al
(5)   que espera se le dice que le falta tal o cual <u>sello</u> en su <u>instancia</u>, <u>sello</u> que tiene que ir a buscar y perder <u>el turno</u> a no ser que el <u>ordenanza</u>— véase Intermediarios—se lo facilite mediante <u>una propina</u>. Estoy seguro de que si se les propusiera a <u>muchas oficinas del Estado</u>...

From the words, *tipo humano*, *servicio*, *cola*, *sello*, and *turno*, the theme of some kind of public office is apparent. But none of the alternatives other than **D** deal with the meanings implied by *propina*. Dealing with a bureaucracy with a *propina*, however, can include meanings of all the other underlined nouns. Simply because the noun *sello* is repeated does not mean that it is the main topic.

SELECTION TWO

Desperté, cubierto de sudor. Del piso de ladrillos rojos, recién regado, subía un vapor caliente. Una mariposa de alas grisáceas revoloteaba encandilada alrededor del foco amarillento. Salté de la hamaca y
Línea descalzo atravesé el cuarto, cuidando de no pisar algún alacrán salido de
(5)   su escondrijo a tomar el fresco. Me acerqué al ventanillo y aspiré el aire del campo. Se oía la respiración de la noche, enorme, femenina. Regresé al centro de la habitación, vacié el agua de la jarra en la palangana de peltre y humedecí la toalla. Me froté el torso y las piernas con el trapo empapado, me sequé un poco y, tras de cerciorarme que ningún bicho
(10)   estaba escondido entre los pliegues de mi ropa, me vestí y calcé. Bajé saltando la escalera pintada de verde. En la puerta del mesón tropecé con el dueño, sujeto tuerto y reticente. Sentado en una sillita de tule, fumaba con el ojo entrecerrado.
        —¿Onde va, señor?
(15)   —A dar una vuelta. Hace mucho calor.
        —Hum, todo está ya cerrado. Y no hay alumbrado aquí. Más le valiera quedarse.
        Alcé los hombros, musité "ahora vuelvo" y me metí en lo oscuro. Al principio no veía nada. Caminé a tientas por la calle empedrada. Encendí
(20)   un cigarrillo. De pronto salió la luna de una nube negra, iluminando un muro blanco, desmoronado a trechos.

1. Esta selección trata de
   (A) la vida nocturna de un campesino.
   (B) la incomodidad de una noche calurosa a un viajero.
   (C) actividades nocturnas de los insectos.
   (D) preparaciones matutinas de un forastero.

The correct answer is **B**. Although the scene takes place in a rural setting, the lodging lacks many modern amenities (such as running water), and there are many references to insects, none of these answers takes into account the fact that the narrator of the selection is a traveler, except for choice **B**. The fact that the narrator is a traveler is never explicitly stated. Also, do not be misled by the word *mariposa* and the list of activities of getting up, washing up, and dressing, all of which are usually associated with daylight activity. A focused first reading and attention to certain words that denote certain kinds of activity will reveal the narrator's point of view in the list of activities.

<u>Desperté</u>, cubierto de sudor. Del piso de ladrillos rojos, recién regado, subía un vapor caliente. Una mariposa de alas grisáceas revoloteaba encandilada alrededor del <u>foco</u> amarillento. <u>Salté de la hamaca</u> y
Línea descalzo <u>atravesé</u> el cuarto, <u>cuidando</u> de no pisar algún alacrán salido de
(5) su escondrijo a tomar el fresco. Me acerqué <u>al ventanillo</u> y <u>aspiré el aire del campo</u>. Se oía la respiración de <u>la noche</u>, enorme, femenina. <u>Regresé</u> al centro de la habitación, <u>vacié</u> el agua de <u>la jarra</u> en la <u>palangana</u> de peltre y <u>humedecí la toalla</u>. Me froté el torso y las piernas con el <u>trapo empapado</u>, me sequé un poco y, tras de <u>cerciorarme</u> que ningún bicho
(10) estaba escondido entre los pliegues de mi ropa, <u>me vestí y calcé</u>. Bajé saltando la escalera pintada de verde. En la puerta del mesón <u>tropecé con el dueño</u>, sujeto tuerto y reticente. <u>Sentado</u> en una sillita de tule, fumaba con el ojo entrecerrado. Con voz ronca me preguntó:
    —<u>¿Onde va, señor?</u>
(15)   —<u>A dar una vuelta</u>. Hace mucho calor.
    —Hum, <u>todo ya está cerrado</u>. Y no hay alumbrado aquí. <u>Más le valiera quedarse</u>.
    <u>Alcé</u> los hombros, musité "<u>ahora vuelvo</u>" y <u>me metí</u> en lo oscuro. Al principio <u>no veía nada</u>. <u>Caminé a tientas</u> por la calle empedrada. <u>Encendí</u>
(20) un cigarrillo. De pronto <u>salió la luna</u> de una nube negra, <u>iluminando</u> un <u>muro blanco</u>, desmoronado a trechos.

The question that the *dueño* asks indicates that the two characters are not acquainted, and the advice that the *dueño* gives the narrator indicates that the former is local and the latter is a stranger to the location. Although choice **D** mentions a *forastero*, the activities listed would normally occur in the morning so the words referring to nighttime, darkness, and the light bulb preclude **D** as an answer. All of the actions taken by the narrator do, however, pertain to what a person would do to cool off on a hot night: going to the window, washing up at a washbasin, going outside.

SELECTION THREE

Ahora, por fin, se había apaciguado. Estaba allí arrinconado al pie del horcón. Había venido su hijo Justino y su hijo Justino se había ido y había vuelto y ahora otra vez venía.

Línea   Lo echó encima del burro. Lo apretó bien apretado al aparejo para que
(5)   no se fuese a caer por el camino. Le metió su cabeza dentro de un costal para que no diera mala impresión. Y luego le hizo pelos al burro y se fueron, arrebatados, de prisa, para llegar a Palo de Venado todavía con tiempo para arreglar el velorio del difunto.

    —Tu nuera y los nietos te extrañarán—iba diciéndole—. Te mirarán a
(10)   la cara y creerán que no eres tú. Se les afigurará que te ha comido el coyote, cuando te vean con esa cara tan llena de boquetes por tanto tiro de gracia como te dieron.

1. El acontecimiento en que enfoca este trozo es
   (A) la visita de un pariente.
   (B) un viaje fúnebre.
   (C) la bienvenida para un visitante.
   (D) una plática entre padre e hijo.

The correct answer is **B** because the whole passage deals with the death of Justino's father. The word *fúnebre* is closely associated with the meanings of the words *velorio* and *difunto* since they all relate to death. Also, although many types of relatives are mentioned, Justino talks about how the dead man will be received, and the burro is mentioned many times, the common denominator is the fact that the man was executed and Justino is taking his body home for a proper burial. Look again at the passage with some of the key words underlined to see how the association is made between all of them to indicate the main idea of the passage.

Ahora, por fin, se había <u>apaciguado</u>. Estaba allí <u>arrinconado</u> al <u>pie del horcón</u>. Había venido su hijo Justino y su hijo Justino se había ido y había vuelto y ahora otra vez venía.

Línea   Lo echó <u>encima del burro</u>. Lo <u>apretó</u> bien <u>apretado al aparejo</u> para que
(5)   no se fuese a <u>caer por el camino</u>. <u>Le metió su cabeza dentro del costal</u> para que no diera <u>mala impresión</u>. Y luego le hizo pelos al burro y se fueron, <u>arrebatados</u>, <u>de prisa</u>, para llegar a Palo de Venado todavía con tiempo para arreglar <u>el velorio del difunto.</u>

    —Tu nuera y los nietos <u>te extrañarán</u>—iba diciéndole—. Te mirarán a la
(10)   cara y creerán que <u>no eres tú</u>. Se les afigurará que <u>te ha comido el coyote</u>, cuando te vean con <u>esa cara tan llena de boquetes</u> por tanto <u>tiro de gracia</u> como <u>te dieron.</u>

In the first paragraph, *apaciguado*, *arinconado*, and *al pie del horcón* all indicate a body at the foot of a stake. In the second paragraph, the underlined words all describe what Justino does with the body and ends with the key words, *velorio del difunto*. The last paragraph describes what his family will think has happened to him, and ends with words that refer back to the first paragraph and the images of the execution: "*esa cara tan llena de boquetes*" and "*tiro de gracia*." Do not be misled by the direct discourse; Junstino speaks to his dead father. Remember that it is not necessary to know the precise mean-

ing of every word; among these underlined words the common denominator is
the fact that Justino's father was executed, brutally.

SELECTION FOUR

El magistrado Miguel Angel del Arco, del juzgado de instrucción
número 6 de Granada decretó el viernes la prisión incondicional del
médico granadino Juan Valdés y la libertad provisional bajo fianza de
Línea doscientas cincuenta mil pesetas para el escritor José Heredia Maya, por
(5) su presunta implicación en relación con un robo de objetos de arte ocurrido entre el uno y el tres de mayo pasado, en el Carmen de los Mínimos de Granada, de propiedad municipal.

Este robo ha dado pie ya a varias decisiones políticas—en cuanto evidencia negligencia en la custodia de bienes públicos—, entre ellas la
(10) personación del PP en el sumario y la petición de dimisión de tres concejales socialistas pedida por el grupo municipal del Partido Popular
cuyas investigaciones han permitido demostrar que se han detectado
hasta ahora cuatro intentos de robo y tres advertencias del jefe de patrimonio municipal al concejal de cultura advirtiendo sobre la necesidad
(15) de trasladar los objetos del Carmen o dotar al mismo de vigilancia.

1. ¿Cuál es el tema de este pasaje?
   (A) el latrocinio de bienes públicos.
   (B) la mala fortuna de un médico.
   (C) la política del gobierno municipal.
   (D) el sistema de investigación policíaca.

The correct answer is **A** because *latrocinio* is a synonym for *robo*, which is
the focus of the selection. Notice the word *ladrón* embedded in *latrocinio*, with
the letter *d* changed to a *t*. Although the case of Juan Valdés and José Heredia
Maya is the subject of the first paragraph, they are examples of a larger problem
that is addressed in the second paragraph, thereby obviating choice **B**. Political
parties are mentioned in the second paragraph, as are investigations. But these
two answers are not comprehensive enough to include the topic of robberies
and protection of an art collection. Look again at the passage with underlined
words to see the association and relationships between ideas.

El magistrado Miguel Angel del Arco, del juzgado de instrucción
número 6 de Granada decretó el viernes la prisión incondicional del
médico granadino Juan Valdés y la libertad provisional bajo fianza de
Línea doscientos cincuenta mil pesetas para el escritor José Heredia Maya, por
(5) su presunta implicación en relación con un robo de objetos de arte ocurrido entre el uno y el tres de mayo pasado, en el Carmen de los Mínimos de Granada, de propiedad municipal.

Este robo ha dado pie ya a varias decisiones políticas—en cuanto evidencia negligencia en la custodia de bienes públicos—, entre ellas la
(10) personación del PP en el sumario y la petición de dimisión de tres concejales socialistas pedida por el grupo municipal del Partido Popular
cuyas investigaciones han permitido demostrar que se han detectado
hasta ahora cuatro intentos de robo y tres advertencias del jefe de patrimonio municipal al concejal de cultura advirtiendo sobre la necesidad
(15) de trasladar los objetos del Carmen o dotar al mismo de vigilancia.

The underlined words show that even though the paragraph names the persons involved in the theft, the topic that is being discussed is the fate of municipal property, as indicated by the last two words in the first paragraph. The following paragraph picks up the topic and generalizes from the specific case and shows how that case is indicative of a larger problem that involves some council members of the Partido Popular. Beyond the political repercussions of the thefts, is the whole problem of how to protect the municipal patrimony from further theft, like the kind mentioned in the first paragraph. In this example, the repetition of the words *robo, bienes públicos, intentos de robo,* and *trasladar los objetos* ties all the other aspects of the passage together thematically.

Reading for Details

After the main idea or theme of the passage has been identified, there are a variety of questions that are asked about specific information contained in the texts. These details can relate to questions of setting or origin (where), time (when), character, definition or identification (who or what), purpose and reason (why), or manner (how). Many times these questions can be easily recognized by focusing on a particular word or phrase, but the answer will most often be a rephrasing of a word or string of words in the text. In the following passages, read the passage and answer the question, then look at the subsequent discussion that shows how to find the information asked.

Questions About Setting and/or Origin

SELECTION ONE

Nada podía andar peor, pero al menos ya no estábamos en la maldita lancha, entre vómitos y golpes de mar y pedazos de galleta mojada, entre ametralladoras y babas, hechos un asco, consolándonos cuando
Línea podíamos con el poco tabaco que se conservaba seco porque Luis (que
(5) no se llamaba Luis, pero habíamos jurado no acordarnos de nuestros nombres hasta que llegara el día) había tenido la buena idea de meterlo en una caja de lata que abríamos con más cuidado que si estuviera llena de escorpiones. Pero qué tabaco ni tragos de ron en esa condenada lancha, bamboleándose cinco días como una tortuga borracha, haciéndole
(10) frente a un norte que la cacheteaba sin lástima, y ola va y ola viene, los baldes despellejándonos las manos, yo con un asma del demonio y medio mundo enfermo, doblándose para vomitar como si se fueran a partir por la mitad. Hasta Luis, la segunda noche, una bilis verde que le sacó las ganas de reírse, entre eso y el norte que no nos dejaba ver el faro de Cabo Cruz, un desastre que nadie se había imaginado.

1. El narrador de este episodio cuenta la ocasión en que se encontró con un grupo
   (A) pasando mal rato en un crucero.
   (B) perdido en alta mar.
   (C) de marineros en una batalla naval.
   (D) de pescadores mareados en una excursión.

The correct answer is **B**. All these alternatives refer to people at sea, as indicated by *lancha, golpes de mar, bamboleándose, un norte que la cacheteaba, ola va y ola viene,* and *faro de Cabo Cruz.* The references to being seasick, indicated by the words *entre vómitos,* y *doblándose para vomitar como si se fueran a partir por la mitad,* would apply to part of the answers of **A** and **D**, but not all of the information in those alternatives is correct. The *lancha* is not the kind of vessel in which one takes a *crucero*, a *cruise*. Also there is no mention of *pescadores*. These characters are not well provisioned for going fishing; their equipment is *tabaco, galletas, ron*, and *ametralladoras*. Fishermen might take the first three items, but not the last. The weapons, *ametralladoras*, might indicate alternative **C**, but there is no mention of any other boats, so this is not the best answer. The fact that the group is lost at sea is implicit in *ya no estábamos en la maldita lancha*, the fact that they had few provisions, and finally, *el norte no nos dejaba ver el faro de Cabo Cruz, un desastre que nadie se había imaginado*. The fact that they inadvertently drift out to sea indicates that they are not engaged in battle, and that they are lost.

SELECTION TWO

Rafael Frühbeck de Burgos fue nombrado ayer director general de Música de la *Deutscheoper* de Berlín. El director español, que también es el titular de la Orquesta Sinfónica de Viena, reúne así dos puestos

Línea musicales de gran relevancia en Europa. Frühbeck permanecerá cinco

(5) años al frente de la ópera de Berlín y estrenará su cargo al próximo 28 de agosto con *La Bohème*. En el otoño dirigirá *Don Carlos, Los Maestros Cantores de Nuremberg,* y *Carmen*.

1. Según este párrafo, Rafael Frühbeck tiene origen
   (A) austríaco.
   (B) alemán.
   (C) burgalés.
   (D) berlinés.

The correct answer is **C**. Looking back in the passage there are a number of proper nouns and adjectives of nationality that provide information. The text states that Rafael Frühbeck is a director, and the next sentence states that the director is Spanish. The word *burgalés* is the only adjective that pertains to Spain. Questions of this sort at times require some knowledge of geography, especially knowing in which countries certain cities are found, as well as in which part of a country a particular city can be found. Burgos is a well known city in Spain, but recognition of the adjective that designates origin may be required. Be careful to understand what information is needed to complete the question or sentence correctly. In this case, the question asks, "What is Rafael's origin?"

SELECTION THREE

Se me durmió la pierna derecha y la froté con el tobillo izquierdo. La abuela me pasó el misal y me miró con dureza. Incliné la cabeza sobre el libro y cerré los ojos. Tenía hambre. Con las prisas no tuve tiempo de

Línea desayunar. Me dije que, cuando creciera, haría como tía Emilia, que

(5) fumaba lentamente, sentada en la cama, hasta las doce del mediodía, mirando las fotografías y los titulares de los periódicos. Todas las voces se levantaron. El sol reverberaba en los cristales de las vidrieras. Sobre el paladar negro de la nave estaba el sol, y nosotros, pensé, como Jonás, dentro de la ballena, con sus enormes costillas. Imaginé la quemazón

(10) verde de la cúpula, como un gran *puzzle* de oro y arco iris:

—...Te Marty-rum candi-da-tus Laudat ex-er-ci-tus...

1. Esta escena tiene lugar en
   (A) una alcoba.
   (B) un barco.
   (C) una iglesia.
   (D) en una biblioteca.

The correct answer is **C**. The Biblical reference to Jonah, taken in conjunction with some other words, all indicate a church instead of the other places. The word *nave* in this case refers to an architectural feature of the sanctuary instead of a ship, which means that choice **B** is incorrect. There are various references to activities that take place in a house, but it is never actually stated that the characters are in a house.

Questions About Time One of the more difficult aspects of reading is determining the temporal aspect of the passage. There are various aspects of time in a written text: actual time (the moment in which a situation or action takes place in the text), elapsed time (how much time passes between the beginning until the end of some situation or action), historical time (when something happened in the past from the perspective of the actual time in the passage), or time as an abstraction or dimension of reality. In addition to deciding how time is viewed in the passage, be aware that frequently numerical quantities will be expressed in various ways, such as expressing the quantity of "half a dozen" as "six." For practice, read the following passages and identify the aspects of time represented in the selection.

PASSAGE ONE

Según un artículo en *ABC* del 31 de mayo de 1992, la vida, en todas sus formas, ha estado desarrollándose en la tierra durante cuatro mil millones de años de evolución y hace sólo unos cuarenta y cinco millo-
Línea nes de años comenzaron a asentarse casi todas las especies de la actuali-
(5) dad. Hoy la actividad humana está acelerando mil veces el ritmo natural de extinción de la diversidad biológica, ya que las especies no pueden asimilar el cambio producido en el ecosistema. Unas 40.000 especies, en general, desaparecen cada año. Con ello se disminuye nuestra capacidad de supervivencia en el planeta, a pesar de que el homo sapiens sólo
(10) exista desde hace alrededor de medio millón de años. Impedir que la biodiversidad crezca es el precio de mantener un sistema productivo.

De seguir el ritmo actual, una de cada cuatro especies, tanto de flora como de fauna, sobre todo continentales, corre peligro de extinción en los próximos veinte años. Cerca de 5.000 especies animales y 20.000
(15) plantas conocidas podrían extinguirse en los próximos años y un millón, en total, para el próximo siglo (entre el 15 y 20 por 100 de todas las especies vivientes para el año 2000). Ninguna zona de la tierra está a salvo. Ya en el siglo XVII se extinguía un mamífero cada cinco años. En los últimos cuatrocientos años desaparecieron unas 400 especies. Durante la
(20) última parte de este siglo se ha extinguido una especie cada dos años.

1. Según este trozo, ¿cuántos años habría el ser humano habitado en la tierra?
   (A) unos cuatro mil millones de años.
   (B) unos cuarenta y cinco millones de años.
   (C) unos quinientos mil años.
   (D) un millón de años.

2. Según este trozo, es posible que desaparezca del 15 hasta el 20 por ciento de las especies dentro de
   (A) los próximos 100 años.
   (B) la próxima década.
   (C) los próximos cinco años.
   (D) los próximos dos años.

3. Según este pasaje
   (A) tenemos bastante tiempo para resolver los problemas de la extinción de las especies.
   (B) el tiempo pasa más rápido ahora que antes en cuanto al desarrollo y evolución de las especies.
   (C) las formas de vida de flora y fauna se desarrollan a un ritmo desigual al del ser humano.
   (D) el ritmo natural de extinción actual está acelerándose más rápido que nunca.

The correct answer for Question 1 is **C**. The question asks essentially when *homo sapiens* first appeared and how much time has elapsed since then. Since the precise date for the appearance of *homo sapiens* is unknown, the temporal point of reference is the present and time is measured from the present back into the past. In the article the figure of half a million years appears, hence five hundred thousand is the correct answer. The number of years is expressed in a different way in the answer than in the passage (five hundred thousand instead of half a million). Make sure that the subject is understood even when it is rephrased ("*ser humano*" instead of "*homo sapiens*").

The correct answer for Question 2 is **B**. This question asks about elapsed time—how much time will pass from the time that the article is written until the end of this century. Since the article is dated 1992, the elapsed time will amount to less than a decade. To answer the question look back in the passage for the statement that address this specific topic, then figure how much time has elapsed, or will go by from the date of publication until the year 2000.

The correct answer for Question 3 is **D** because the rate of extinction is the purpose of mentioning of all the facts and figures given in the second paragraph. Choice **A** is incorrect because the article states that the human species is adversely impacting other forms of life on earth. Choice **B** is incorrect because time in and of itself does not move, slowly or quickly. This question really deals with the rate at which events transpire, rates that are relative in that the rate of evolution or extinction is not the same for all forms of life. Choice **C** is incorrect because it refers only to the rate of development, which is not the focus of the article.

Questions About Character, Object Definition, or Identification

One of the problems to be encountered in short passages for reading comprehension is identifying who is speaking, or about whom or what the narrator is speaking, or to whom or what something is done. This information is usually found in the placement of nouns and in gender and/or number of pronouns in indirect discourse. However, frequently in direct discourse (dialogue), often the speaker of a line of dialogue is not explicitly stated. In the following selection identify who the speakers are and what they are.

PASSAGE ONE

Cuando vio el carro perdiéndose por la carretera bajó a la cocina. El viejo dormitaba junto al fuego. Le contempló, y se dijo: "Si tuviera valor le mataría". Allí estaban las tenazas de hierro, a su alcance. Pero no lo

Línea haría. Sabía que no podía hacerlo. "Soy cobarde. Soy una gran cobarde y
(5) tengo amor a la vida". Esto la perdía: "este amor a la vida...".

—Viejo—exclamó. Aunque habló en voz queda, el vagabundo abrió uno de sus ojillos maliciosos. "No dormía. Es un viejo zorro".

—Ven conmigo—le dijo—. Te he de hablar.

El viejo la siguió hasta el pozo. Allí Mariana se volvió a mirarle.

(10) —Puedes hacer lo que quieras, perro. Puedes decirlo todo a mi marido, si quieres. Pero tú te marchas. Te vas de esta casa, en seguida...

El viejo calló unos segundos. Luego, sonrió.

—¿Cuándo vuelve el señor posadero?

1. En esta selección, Mariana es
   (A) una gran cobarde.
   (B) la esposa del posadero.
   (C) buena amiga del vagabundo.
   (D) la cocinera de la posada.

2. La persona con quien habla Mariana es
   (A) un huésped mal acogido.
   (B) un viejo zorro.
   (C) un forastero perezoso.
   (D) el señor posadero.

The correct answer for Question 1 is **B**. In the selection, Mariana says the old man can tell her husband. The old man asks when her husband will return. "*El viejo calló unos segundos*" indicates that he says the subsequent line. From the sequence the correlation between *marido* and *el señor posadero* can be made. Choice **A** is incorrect because Mariana is not really a coward; she does work up the nerve to tell the old man to leave. Although she does state, *Soy una gran cobarde...*, the question refers to the whole passage. Taken in its entirety, Choice **A** is incorrect. That she does not kill him does not make her a coward. She is not his friend if she is requiring him to leave, and she is not the cook, making Choices **B** and **D** incorrect, also.

The correct answer to Question 2 is **A**. Although she calls him a *zorro*, it is a figure of speech. He is a stranger, but there is no evidence in this selection that he is lazy. He is not the innkeeper because he is asking when the innkeeper is going to return. In the last two lines of dialogue, the speaker is indicated by placement of nouns, *el viejo* and Mariana, immediately before the spoken lines. The old man is a stranger, and he does sit around the house, but this is not the best answer because the characteristic that makes him an unwelcome guest is not his sloth, but his malevolence. She thinks that he knows something about her that she does not want her husband to know. Neither is he the husband of Mariana, indicating that the last alternative is incorrect.

PASSAGE TWO

Sin apenas tiempo para disfrutar de su viaje de novios, Carlos Sainz ha vuelto a tomar el volante de su Toyota Celica GT4 para afrontar una nueva prueba del Campeonato del Mundo de Rallys.

Línea
(5)

En efecto, en la mañana del 12 de mayo Sainz y su mujer empezaron su viaje a las islas Bermudas, que duró muy poco. Después de una semana de descanso, ya estaba el piloto madrileño en Grecia junto con su copiloto Luis Moya, realizando el recorrido de entrenamiento de la 34 edición del Acrópolis, una carrera que se destaca entre las más duras del campeonato, pero que para Carlos Sainz tiene un significado muy espe-

(10) cial, ya que allí consiguió su primera victoria en una prueba del Mundial, concretamente hace ahora dos años.

1. Quién dirigirá el equipo en la competencia en Grecia será
   (A) la señora Sainz.
   (B) Luis Moya.
   (C) Carlos Sainz.
   (D) un entrenador griego.

2. La competencia a la cual se refiere en el pasaje es
   (A) una carrera de caballos en Grecia.
   (B) una carrera aérea entre pilotos de aviones.
   (C) un partido de campeonato de la Copa Mundial.
   (D) una carrera de coches deportivos.

The correct answer for Question 1 is **C**. Carlos, as the subject of the phrase, "*ha vuelto a tomar el volante*," is identified as the driver, or *piloto madrileño*, about which the passage speaks. Luis Moya and la señora Sainz are secondary figures in the passage; one is the co-driver and the other Carlos' wife, making Choices **A** and **B** incorrect. There is no Greek trainer, meaning that Choice **D** is incorrect also.

The correct answer for Question 2 is **D**. *Toyota Celica GT4* and *Rallys* both refer to car racing, to which Sainz has returned. Choices **A**, **B**, and **C** are based on distracting factors. *Piloto* is the subject of the verb in "*estaba el piloto madrileño en Grecia*," but nowhere in the passage is any association made with anything other than cars. The word *Mundial* is also a distractor in Choice **D** since there is possible confusion between the world championship race and the World Cup in soccer competition. However, the word *Copa* never appears, nor are there any references to soccer.

Questions About Purpose and Reason

Determining motivation (why something happens, or why someone does a particular thing, or for what reasons things will happen), requires careful reading to understand the initial situation and the development of action or thought throughout the passage. By understanding the sequence of events and changes in the nature of events, the logic of the passage can be seen. In passages that narrate an event, pay close attention to the actions and their results. The questions about purpose or reason will require the reader to determine which actions or events in the series reveal the appropriate response to the question. For example: *The man worked hard all day. He went home, ate dinner, he relaxed after dinner, then went to bed early.* Question: *Why did the man go to bed early?* Answer: *He went to bed early because he was tired*. The answer explains why (the reason). In Spanish this information answers the question asked by the interrogative pronoun *¿por qué?* If, in English, the question asks *Why did the man go to bed early?* an answer could be *He went to bed early (in order) to get some rest for the next day*. This answer tells for what purpose the man went to bed early. In Spanish this is the answer to a question using the interrogative pronoun *¿para qué?* At times purpose is indicated by the use of the subjunctive after adverbial conjunctions of purpose or concession (such as *para que, a fin de que, con tal (de) que, a no ser que, a menos que, en caso (de) que*, for example). In the following passages look for the logic of the passages that reveals reason or purpose. A change in direction of events, which means there is a reason and purpose for the change.

PASSAGE ONE

Pero Marini siguió pensando en la isla, mirándola cuando se acordaba o había una ventanilla cerca, casi siempre encogiéndose de hombros al final. Nada de eso tenía sentido, volar tres veces por semana a mediodía
Línea sobre Xiros era tan irreal como soñar tres veces por semana que volaba a
(5) mediodía sobre Xiros. Todo estaba falseado en la visión inútil y recurrente; salvo, quizá, el deseo de repetirla, la consulta al reloj pulsera antes de mediodía, el breve, punzante contacto con la deslumbradora franja blanca al borde de un azul casi negro, y las casas donde los pescadores alzarían apenas los ojos para seguir el paso de esa otra irrealidad.
(10) Ocho o nueve semanas después, cuando le propusieron la línea de Nueva York con todas sus ventajas, Marini se dijo que era la oportunidad de acabar con esa manía inocente y fastidiosa. Tenía en el bolsillo el libro donde un vago geógrafo de nombre levantino daba sobre Xiros más detalles que los habituales en las guías. Contestó negativamente, oyén-
(15) dose como desde lejos, y después de sortear la sorpresa escandalizada de un jefe y dos secretarias se fue a comer a la cantina de la compañía donde lo esperaba Carla.

1. ¿Por qué no quiso Marini aceptar la oferta de la compañía para cambiar su ruta aérea?
   (A) Quería sorprender a su jefe.
   (B) Le gustaban tanto los pasajeros en su ruta oriental.
   (C) Le fascinaba tanto la geografía de su línea acostumbrada.
   (D) Se sentía incapaz de separarse de su sueño.

The correct answer is **D** because none of the other answers are inclusive enough. The passage refers to his *manía*, but it has a dual aspect: 1) the sight of the island, and, 2) the routine of looking at his watch to see that they fly over Xiros at noon. He calls his habit "innocent and tiresome," but all of the preceding paragraph indicates that his *manía* is more like an obsession that is neither "innocent" nor "tiresome" to him. At the end of the passage Marini is given the option of changing routes, and considers it, but decides not to, even to his own surprise. The sequence of events in the beginning all reveal his anticipation and fascination with the sight of the island at the same time every flight, even to the extent that he carries a book about it in his pocket.

PASSAGE TWO

Hace poco tiempo, Filiberto murió ahogado en Acapulco. Sucedió en Semana Santa. Aunque despedido de su empleo en la Secretaría, Filiberto no pudo resistir la tentación burocrática de ir, como todos los años, *Línea* a la pensión alemana, comer el *choucrout* endulzado por el sudor de la *(5)* cocina tropical, bailar el sábado de gloria en La Quebrada, y sentirse "gente conocida" en el obscuro anonimato vespertino de la playa de Hornos. Claro, sabíamos que en su juventud había nadado bien, pero ahora, a los cuarenta, y tan desmejorado como se le veía, ¡intentar salvar, y a medianoche, un trecho tan largo! Frau Müller no permitió que se *(10)* velara—cliente tan antiguo—en la pensión; por el contrario, esa noche organizó un baile en la terracita sofocada, mientras Filiberto esperaba, muy pálido en su caja, a que saliera el camión matutino de la terminal, y pasó acompañado de huacales y fardos la primera noche de su nueva vida. Cuando llegué, temprano, a vigilar el embarque del féretro, Fili-*(15)* berto estaba bajo un túmulo de cocos; el chófer dijo que lo acomodáramos rápidamente en el toldo y lo cubriéramos de lonas, para que no se espantaran los pasajeros, y a ver si no le habíamos echado la sal al viaje.

1. ¿Cuál era el propósito del baile en la terracita de la pensión de Frau Müller?
   (A) Lo organizó para que todos felicitaran a Filiberto por su nuevo empleo.
   (B) No quería que supieran sus otros clientes que Filiberto había muerto.
   (C) Lo organizó para que Filiberto se sintiera mejor.
   (D) Frau Müller lo hizo a fin de que los clientes de la pensión lo velaran.

The correct answer is **B** because Filiberto is dead, awaiting transport in his *caja*. His *nueva vida* is a euphemism for his next life (after death), and *pálido* refers to the appearance of his body. The passage also states that Frau Müller prohibited the wake and Filiberto was removed from the "*pensión*" as soon as possible, to be packed off on a truck beneath other freight so that no one would see him. At the beginning of the passage is a description of Filiberto's visit to the *pensión* before his death, all of which is narrated in the indicative. The phrase "*...Filiberto esperaba, muy pálido en su caja, a que saliera el camión matutino de la terminal...*" indicates that the purpose for Filiberto's wait was to be transported in a box back to his former residence. Other verbs in the subjunctive at the end of the passage also indicate that people would be frightened upon seeing a body riding along with them ("*...cubriéramos de lonas, para que no se espantaran los pasajeros...*"), indicating that he is dead.

Questions of Interpretation

There are several facets to the process of making inferences in order to interpret the meaning of a passage and to draw conclusions about it. Some of the strategies are comparing and contrasting events or ideas expressed in the selection, identifying the tone of the passage as well as what type of prose it is (parody, allegory, satire, humorous writing, expository prose, etc.), determining the intended reader of the passage and what purpose the piece serves (essay to persuade, instructional material, narrative to entertain the reader, or inform the reader). This stage of the process of reading usually comes after questions about specific information in the passage have been answered. How the reader responds to the selection is always relevant to the process of interpretation. One should be careful not to read too much into what a passage says, but how the reader responds to or what he thinks about what the author has said is relevant.

Comparing and Contrasting Ideas

Meanings can be communicated through comparisons and contrasts, both of which can be stated in two ways: explicitly, or implicitly (figuratively). Explicit language means that the object or action named by a word or words has no meaning other than the stated one. The words "mean" precisely what they say. In some types of passages this type of language predominates, such as in instructions for how to use equipment. Figurative language, on the other hand, conveys meaning on a number of levels, depending on the number of figurative meanings that can be attributed to the object or action named. Figurative meanings are based on associations or analogies. In interpretation of figurative language, a common knowledge about the named objects or actions is essential. In terms of interpretation of reading selections for the AP Spanish Language Exam, a broad knowledge about Spanish culture is indispensable. Read the following passages to see if the difference between explicit and figurative language is apparent.

PASSAGE ONE

El Servicio de Patrullaje—otro de los deberes que son de competencia de la Prefectura—tiene por finalidad guardar las costas argentinas en ejercicio de su soberanía. La institución lo ejercita con naves adaptadas a
Línea los requerimientos del medio en que debe actuar, y cumpliendo las
(5) siguientes funciones: intervenir en el ejercicio de la Policía de Seguridad de la Navegación; constatar el cumplimiento de los convenios internacionales de la navegación en aguas jurisdiccionales; prestar auxilio en los casos de inundaciones, incendios u otros siniestros, producidos en aguas jurisdiccionales; intervenir en la vigilancia para el cumplimiento
(10) de las leyes y reglamentos nacionales referentes a caza y pesca marítima; prestar asistencia y salvamento a las vidas y bienes, en aguas nacionales o mar libre; además de lo específicamente determinado y de otras funciones que se le puedan asignar circunstancialmente—campañas hidrográficas, escoltas a regatas fluviales y oceánicas, participación en activi-
(15) dades náutico-deportivas, etcétera, funciones que contribuyen a la capacitación del personal superior, subalterno y del cuerpo de cadetes, en las actividades marineras.

1. Todas las palabras referentes al agua en este pasaje
   (A) representan todas las esferas de la vida humana tanto como las regiones del mar.
   (B) muestran una correspondencia entre las responsabilidades del Servicio de Patrullaje y diferentes etapas de la vida de la nación.
   (C) describen todas las responsabilidades del Servicio de Patrullaje.
   (D) indican las aguas incluidas en la jurisdicción del Servicio de Patrullaje.

The correct answer is **D**, because although the passage deals with the responsibilities of the Coast Guard, the question asks about the meaning of the word *waters*. No other figurative meaning of *mar* is apparent in the context of this passage. This is a listing of what the duties are and where the Coast Guard has authority.

PASSAGE TWO

Dos veranos más tarde volví a las montañas. Un día, pasando por el cementerio—era ya tarde y se anunciaba la noche en el cielo: el sol, como una bola roja, caía a lo lejos, hacia la carrera terrible y sosegada de
Línea la llanura—, vi algo extraño. De la tierra grasienta y pedregosa, entre las
(5) cruces caídas, nacía un árbol grande y hermoso, con las hojas anchas de oro: encendido y brillante todo él, cegador. Algo me vino a la memoria, como un sueño, y pensé: "Es un árbol de oro". Busqué al pie del árbol, y no tardé en dar con una crucecilla de hierro negro, mohosa por la lluvia. Mientras la enderezaba, leí: IVO MÁRQUEZ, DIEZ AÑOS DE EDAD.
(10) Y no daba tristeza alguna, sino, tal vez, una extraña y muy grande alegría.

1. ¿Qué significa el árbol de oro?
   (A) lo bueno que es la muerte.
   (B) la tristeza de la muerte.
   (C) la hermosura de la naturaleza.
   (D) lo precioso que es la vida.

The correct answer is **D**. This narrator has stumbled across a graveyard where she sees a tree, illuminated by a setting sun so that it appears to be golden. The tree stands in sharp contrast with the colorless surrounding countryside. When she reads the headstone beneath the tree she discovers the name of someone she used to know. The sight causes her to reflect on the nature of life. The "golden" tree brings into focus for her a renewed appreciation for life and she feels satisfied and comforted by the chance encounter with a memory from the past.

Parallel Structures

Explicit meanings are evident in statements in passages that use parallel structures to compare or contrast things, events, or concepts. Parallel statements repeat information in identical words or in rephrased expressions. Contrasts are stated using antithetical statements (one in which one statement is the opposite of the other). Antithetical statements are sometimes preceded by conjunctions such as *pero, sino, sino que, al otro lado, sin embargo, no obstante, mas*, or *en cambio*. But when meanings are stated figuratively, they can be communicated through the use of figures of speech such as simile, metaphor, metonymy, paradox, personification, synecdoche, oxymoron, or hyperbole. Figurative meanings derive from analogous or associative meanings that sometimes presuppose a common cultural knowledge, and thus can be difficult to interpret without some knowledge of the cultural context of the language. Studying the figures of speech is a primary means of interpretation, however. In the following passages look for comparisons and contrasts in parallel structures.

PASSAGE ONE

    Abrigo la profunda creencia de que si todos dijésemos siempre y en
cada caso là verdad, la desnuda verdad, al principio amenazaría hacerse
inhabitable la Tierra, pero acabaríamos pronto por entendernos como

Línea hoy no nos entendemos. Si todos, pudiendo asomarnos al brocal de las

(5)   conciencias ajenas, nos viéramos desnudas las almas, nuestras rencillas
y reconcomios todos fundiríanse en una inmensa piedad mutua.
    Veríamos las negruras del que tenemos por santo, pero también las blan-
curas de aquel a quien estimamos un malvado.

1. Decir la verdad es
   (A) revelar todos nuestros secretos.
   (B) reconocer todas las faltas de nuestros enemigos.
   (C) sentirse más piadoso.
   (D) pensar que todos nuestros vecinos son santos.

2. La frase, "acabaríamos pronto por entendernos como hoy no nos enten-
demos" significa que
   (A) todos reconocerán a sus enemigos o amigos.
   (B) no hablamos ni escuchamos a nuestros prójimos.
   (C) la Tierra es un infierno.
   (D) la Tierra será un paraíso.

   The correct answer to Question 1 is **C**. From studying the structures of the
sentences in the passage, parallel structures are apparent: "*dijésemos siempre
... la verdad*" and "*nos viéramos desnudas las almas...*" Since this is an *if-then*
statement, all the verb forms in the conditional tense depend on the existence
or truth of the *if* portion of the statement. Further, since the verbs "*dijésemos*"
and "*nos viéramos*" are the only two verbs in the past subjunctive of an *if-then*
structure, the concepts they state are analogous in the context of this passage.
This correlation of grammatical structure is a primary indicator of the correct
answer, given also the fact that the whole passage focuses on what would happen if the truth were always told. All of the other alternative answers are *then*
portions of the *if-then* structure and present hypothetical results or conse-
quences of the hypothetical action proposed in the *if* portion of the statement.
The rest of the answer depends upon understanding the figurative meaning of
the expression "*desnudas las almas.*" The phrase, "*fundiríanse en una
inmensa piedad mutua*" does correlate in meaning and structure to the compound portion of the *then* statement: "*amenazaría hacerse inhabitable la
Tierra pero acabaríamos pronto por entendernos....*"

   The correct answer for Question 2 is **B**. There are two parts that are antithetical in this phrase in question: "*entendernos*" and "*no nos entendemos.*"
Choice **B** is the only combination of contrasting ideas. The conditional in
acabaría indicates the hypothetical nature of understanding. Not speaking or
talking are actual realities that lead to a lack of understanding, making the
understanding hypothetical. The last two choices generalize too much about
what the writer says. Always be carefully to study alternatives that include
words like *siempre* or *todo el tiempo* because many times they are too general
to be true. They only offer a metaphorical interpretation of a single portion of
the *then* portions of the *if-then* statements in the passage.

PASSAGE TWO

—¡Díles que no me maten, Justino! Anda, vete a decirles eso. Que por caridad. Así díles. Díles que lo hagan por caridad.

—No puedo. Hay allí un sargento que no quiere oír hablar nada de ti.

Línea
(5)
—Haz que te oiga. Date tus mañas y díle que para sustos ya ha estado bueno. Díle que lo haga por caridad de Dios.

—No se trata de sustos. Parece que te van a matar de a de veras. Y yo ya no quiero volver allá.

—Anda otra vez. Solamente otra vez, a ver qué consigues.

—No. No tengo ganas de ir. Según eso, yo soy tu hijo. Y, si voy mucho
(10) con ellos, acabarán por saber quién soy y les dará por afusilarme a mí también. Es mejor dejar las cosas de este tamaño.

1. ¿Cuál era la actitud del padre de Justino?
   (A) resignado
   (B) impávido
   (C) desesperado
   (D) asustado

2. ¿Cómo caracterizaría el tipo de hijo que parece ser Justino?
   (A) egoísta
   (B) cruel
   (C) cariñoso
   (D) temeroso

The answer for Question 1 is **C**. The lines by these two speakers, Justino and his father, alternate between commands and refusals. Justino's father's every line is a command for his son to go ask, tell, or beg for his life. Justino's every line communicates his desire to not become involved. Through the repetition of the command, "*Díles,*" the father communicates his desperation, not resignation, fear, or intrepid behavior. The repetitious structure in this case shows the degree or intensity of the man's feeling for life. His son's repeated denial to grant his father's wish shows an equal fear of dying, or at least as strong a desire to remain among the living.

The correct answer for Question 2 is **D**. Justino's fear for his own life overwhelms any familial love that he may have felt for his father. His constant denial and proffered "reasons" are not convincing; they sound like excuses, except that there is a grain of truth to the gravity of the situation as he sees it. The sergeant is intransigent: "*no quiere oír hablar nada de ti.*" Finally at the end he confesses that he does not want to press too much because the sergeant apparently does not realize yet that Justino is the man's son, and Justino does not want the sergeant to know. Although Justino may also be self-centered and cruel, his primary reaction is fear, which is indicated by the constant repetition of his denial and after each denial an explanation of his position in the matter.

Determining Tone or Attitude

One of the more difficult aspects of reading is determining the tone of the passage. The tone or attitude of the passage refers to the author's relationship to his material or to his reader, or both. By changing voice or manner a writer can create a particular tone in a work. Sometimes the attitude of the writer is revealed in figures of speech, such as hyperbole (exaggeration), various types of images (simile, metaphor, or metonym), humor (puns), or other devices such as personification. In the following passages, notice the choice of words and how they are used in order to create a particular tone. This tone or attitude at times can indicate what type of writing the passage presents.

PASSAGE ONE

El primordial objeto de la vida, para muchos millones de norteamericanos, está en "divertirse" o "troncharse de risa". "Divertirse" no es ningún asunto complicado. El cine constituye la mayor de las

Línea diversiones. Bailar, jugar a los naipes, patinar o besar y abrazar en un
(5) coche a un muchacha en cualquier momento es divertirse. Mirar los grabados en una revista y beber jugo de naranja es también una gran diversión. A los norteamericanos les satisface todo y gozan de todo. Encontrarse en la calle a Peter Lorre es un gran entretenimiento; platicar con una hórrida jamona en un fonducho de mala muerte es magnífico;
(10) presenciar un buen accidente automovilístico en la calle es demasiado maravilloso para describirlo con palabras.

1. Ante el espectáculo de los norteamericanos tratando de divertirse en todo momento, este narrador se muestra
   (A) aburrido.
   (B) entretenido.
   (C) no afectado.
   (D) escéptico.

The correct answer is **B**. This narrator show a certain detached amusement for the phenomenon he is describing, as is shown in the words he chooses to name his topic: "*El primordial objeto de la vida....*" Among the basic human drives, entertainment does not usually rank along with self-preservation. The overstatement (hyperbole), indicates immediately that this narrator is somewhat detached; he is not commenting on what entertainment means to him, but what it means to the people he is observing. He then enumerates things that North Americans find entertaining, a list that culminates with the sight of an automobile accident. Any spectacle is entertaining. His expression, "*una hórrida jamona en un fonducho de mala muerte,*" also communicates his detachment and amusement through word selection and overstatement. Choice **C** is a possible answer, but not the best answer. One does not get the impression from this passage that the writer is entirely indifferent to the subject matter; if he found it entertaining enough to write about, he is not totally indifferent.

PASSAGE TWO

Todas las personas interesadas en que el camello pase por el ojo de la aguja, deben inscribir su nombre en la lista de patrocinadores del experimento Niklaus.

Línea Desprendido de un grupo de sabios mortíferos, de esos que manipulan
(5) el uranio, el cobalto y el hidrógeno, Arpad Niklaus deriva sus investigaciones actuales a un fin caritativo y radicalmente humanitario: la salvación del alma de los ricos.

Propone un plan científico para desintegrar un camello y hacerlo que pase en chorro de electrones por el ojo de una aguja. Un aparato receptor
(10) (muy semejante en principio a la pantalla de televisión) organizará los electrones en átomos, los átomos en moléculas y las moléculas en células,

reconstruyendo inmediatamente el camello según su esquema primitivo. Niklaus ya logró cambiar de sitio, sin tocarla, una gota de agua pesada. También ha podido evaluar, hasta donde lo permite la discreción de la

(15)   materia, la energía cuántica que dispara una pezuña de camello. Nos parece inútil abrumar aquí al lector con esa cifra astronómica.

1. ¿Por qué parece que este escritor no toma en serio el experimento del científico Arpad Niklaus?
   (A) Porque cita la manera exacta de proceder con el experimento.
   (B) (Líneas 1–2) Porque usa el subjuntivo en la frase, "en que el camello pase por el ojo de la aguja,..."
   (C) (Líneas 6–7) Porque se burla del propósito del experimento, "la salvación del alma de los ricos".
   (D) (Líneas 16–17) Por el comentario editorial al final, "Nos parece inútil abrumar aquí al lector con cifras..."

The correct answer is **D** because all the other responses are encompassed by the word, *abrumar*. Choice **A** is incorrect because all of the details of the experiment serve mostly to illustrate the incredulity of the writer. In Choices **B** and **C**, the responses refer to specific places in the text where the writer shows his disbelief, but tone or attitude is revealed in the passage as a whole. Both alternatives also state the same concept. In the Biblical reference, the camel passing through the eye of the needle and the salvation of the rich man's soul are synonymous events. *Cifra astronómica* reflects incredulity because of the number of atoms involved and the amount of energy required to transport the camel. The Spanish words make no comment about metaphorical meaning. The Biblical reference is a point of departure for the idea of the selection.

Determining the Intended Reader

The reading passages that appear on the AP Spanish Language Exam represent a wide variety of sources. Most often the intended reader can be determined by the content of the passage. Many passages are narratives told in the third person, and the intended reader is anyone who is interested enough to pick up the literature to read it. In other cases, the writer addresses the reader directly, and from the context provided within the passage, the reader can identify himself. In other cases, the passage may be an essay that tries to convince a specific kind of reader to take a certain position. In the following passage, the content and the language show that this piece is directed toward a certain type of reader.

PASSAGE ONE

Quien desee comer una manzana y tenga ante si un manzano de su propiedad, cargado de manzanas maduras al alcance de la mano, no tiene problema alguno para hacerse con ellas. Coge una manzana y, con

Línea ello, ha conseguido lo que pretendía. Los problemas comienzan cuando

(5)   las manzanas cuelgan tan altas que resulta difícil alcanzarlas. El objetivo, cogerlas, no cabe lograrlo sin dificultades. Se tropieza con un óbice en el logro de nuestro objetivo. ¿Cómo se podrá comportar uno ante esta nueva situación?

Se puede renunciar a las manzanas, si la necesidad de comerlas no es

(10) muy acuciante o si se sabe por experiencia que no se halla preparado para tal situación, es decir, si no se siente uno con fuerzas suficientes para coger una manzana de un árbol elevado.

Pero también cabe la posibilidad de que comience uno a intentar conseguir su objetivo, o dicho de otro modo, de que trate de buscar, sin plan

(15) previo alguno, los medios y métodos apropiados para lograrlo. Intenta uno sacudir violentamente al árbol de un lado para otro y se da cuenta de que su tronco resulta demasiado grueso para poderlo mover. Arroja piedras a las manzanas y comprueba que para esto le falta la práctica requerida. Echa mano de un palo y trata de alcanzar con él las man-

(20) zanas, pero el palo resulta demasiado corto.

Muchos intentos, muchos fracasos. Tal vez—tras largo esfuerzo—un éxito fortuito.

Pero también se puede proceder de la siguiente manera: se sienta uno y reflexiona sobre la situación.

1. ¿A quién parece estar dirigido este pasaje?
   - (A) un campesino hambriento
   - (B) un chico pequeño
   - (C) una persona perezosa
   - (D) una persona pragmática

The correct answer is **D** because the object of this passage is to interest the reader in learning how to solve everyday problems. This writer appeals to the reader's reason by presenting a concrete example of a problem, then offering a variety of solutions, none of which is the most efficient manner of solving the problem. This writer is addressing a reader who wants to learn how to think logically when confronted by problems, not act impulsively. A pragmatic person is one who will analyze the situation, then take the most appropriate action, which in this case is to sit and contemplate the situation.

CHAPTER 6: Answer Sheets for Practice Reading Comprehension Passages

Primer Grupo, Selección Uno
1. Ⓐ Ⓑ Ⓒ Ⓓ
2. Ⓐ Ⓑ Ⓒ Ⓓ
3. Ⓐ Ⓑ Ⓒ Ⓓ
4. Ⓐ Ⓑ Ⓒ Ⓓ
5. Ⓐ Ⓑ Ⓒ Ⓓ
6. Ⓐ Ⓑ Ⓒ Ⓓ
7. Ⓐ Ⓑ Ⓒ Ⓓ

Primer Grupo, Selección Dos
1. Ⓐ Ⓑ Ⓒ Ⓓ
2. Ⓐ Ⓑ Ⓒ Ⓓ
3. Ⓐ Ⓑ Ⓒ Ⓓ
4. Ⓐ Ⓑ Ⓒ Ⓓ
5. Ⓐ Ⓑ Ⓒ Ⓓ
6. Ⓐ Ⓑ Ⓒ Ⓓ
7. Ⓐ Ⓑ Ⓒ Ⓓ
8. Ⓐ Ⓑ Ⓒ Ⓓ

Primer Grupo, Selección Tres
1. Ⓐ Ⓑ Ⓒ Ⓓ
2. Ⓐ Ⓑ Ⓒ Ⓓ
3. Ⓐ Ⓑ Ⓒ Ⓓ
4. Ⓐ Ⓑ Ⓒ Ⓓ
5. Ⓐ Ⓑ Ⓒ Ⓓ
6. Ⓐ Ⓑ Ⓒ Ⓓ
7. Ⓐ Ⓑ Ⓒ Ⓓ

Primer Grupo, Selección Cuatro
1. Ⓐ Ⓑ Ⓒ Ⓓ
2. Ⓐ Ⓑ Ⓒ Ⓓ
3. Ⓐ Ⓑ Ⓒ Ⓓ
4. Ⓐ Ⓑ Ⓒ Ⓓ
5. Ⓐ Ⓑ Ⓒ Ⓓ
6. Ⓐ Ⓑ Ⓒ Ⓓ

Segundo Grupo, Selección Uno
1. Ⓐ Ⓑ Ⓒ Ⓓ
2. Ⓐ Ⓑ Ⓒ Ⓓ
3. Ⓐ Ⓑ Ⓒ Ⓓ
4. Ⓐ Ⓑ Ⓒ Ⓓ
5. Ⓐ Ⓑ Ⓒ Ⓓ
6. Ⓐ Ⓑ Ⓒ Ⓓ
7. Ⓐ Ⓑ Ⓒ Ⓓ
8. Ⓐ Ⓑ Ⓒ Ⓓ

Segundo Grupo, Selección Dos
1. Ⓐ Ⓑ Ⓒ Ⓓ
2. Ⓐ Ⓑ Ⓒ Ⓓ
3. Ⓐ Ⓑ Ⓒ Ⓓ
4. Ⓐ Ⓑ Ⓒ Ⓓ
5. Ⓐ Ⓑ Ⓒ Ⓓ
6. Ⓐ Ⓑ Ⓒ Ⓓ
7. Ⓐ Ⓑ Ⓒ Ⓓ
8. Ⓐ Ⓑ Ⓒ Ⓓ

Segundo Grupo, Selección Tres
1. Ⓐ Ⓑ Ⓒ Ⓓ
2. Ⓐ Ⓑ Ⓒ Ⓓ
3. Ⓐ Ⓑ Ⓒ Ⓓ
4. Ⓐ Ⓑ Ⓒ Ⓓ
5. Ⓐ Ⓑ Ⓒ Ⓓ
6. Ⓐ Ⓑ Ⓒ Ⓓ
7. Ⓐ Ⓑ Ⓒ Ⓓ
8. Ⓐ Ⓑ Ⓒ Ⓓ

Segundo Grupo, Selección Cuatro
1. Ⓐ Ⓑ Ⓒ Ⓓ
2. Ⓐ Ⓑ Ⓒ Ⓓ
3. Ⓐ Ⓑ Ⓒ Ⓓ
4. Ⓐ Ⓑ Ⓒ Ⓓ
5. Ⓐ Ⓑ Ⓒ Ⓓ
6. Ⓐ Ⓑ Ⓒ Ⓓ
7. Ⓐ Ⓑ Ⓒ Ⓓ

Tercer Grupo, Selección Uno
1. Ⓐ Ⓑ Ⓒ Ⓓ
2. Ⓐ Ⓑ Ⓒ Ⓓ
3. Ⓐ Ⓑ Ⓒ Ⓓ
4. Ⓐ Ⓑ Ⓒ Ⓓ
5. Ⓐ Ⓑ Ⓒ Ⓓ
6. Ⓐ Ⓑ Ⓒ Ⓓ
7. Ⓐ Ⓑ Ⓒ Ⓓ
8. Ⓐ Ⓑ Ⓒ Ⓓ

Tercer Grupo, Selección Dos
1. Ⓐ Ⓑ Ⓒ Ⓓ
2. Ⓐ Ⓑ Ⓒ Ⓓ
3. Ⓐ Ⓑ Ⓒ Ⓓ
4. Ⓐ Ⓑ Ⓒ Ⓓ
5. Ⓐ Ⓑ Ⓒ Ⓓ

Tercer Grupo, Selección Tres

1. Ⓐ Ⓑ Ⓒ Ⓓ
2. Ⓐ Ⓑ Ⓒ Ⓓ
3. Ⓐ Ⓑ Ⓒ Ⓓ
4. Ⓐ Ⓑ Ⓒ Ⓓ

Tercer Grupo, Selección Cuatro

1. Ⓐ Ⓑ Ⓒ Ⓓ
2. Ⓐ Ⓑ Ⓒ Ⓓ
3. Ⓐ Ⓑ Ⓒ Ⓓ
4. Ⓐ Ⓑ Ⓒ Ⓓ
5. Ⓐ Ⓑ Ⓒ Ⓓ
6. Ⓐ Ⓑ Ⓒ Ⓓ
7. Ⓐ Ⓑ Ⓒ Ⓓ

Cuarto Grupo, Selección Uno

1. Ⓐ Ⓑ Ⓒ Ⓓ
2. Ⓐ Ⓑ Ⓒ Ⓓ
3. Ⓐ Ⓑ Ⓒ Ⓓ
4. Ⓐ Ⓑ Ⓒ Ⓓ
5. Ⓐ Ⓑ Ⓒ Ⓓ
6. Ⓐ Ⓑ Ⓒ Ⓓ
7. Ⓐ Ⓑ Ⓒ Ⓓ

Cuarto Grupo, Selección Dos

1. Ⓐ Ⓑ Ⓒ Ⓓ
2. Ⓐ Ⓑ Ⓒ Ⓓ
3. Ⓐ Ⓑ Ⓒ Ⓓ
4. Ⓐ Ⓑ Ⓒ Ⓓ
5. Ⓐ Ⓑ Ⓒ Ⓓ
6. Ⓐ Ⓑ Ⓒ Ⓓ

Cuarto Grupo, Selección Tres

1. Ⓐ Ⓑ Ⓒ Ⓓ
2. Ⓐ Ⓑ Ⓒ Ⓓ
3. Ⓐ Ⓑ Ⓒ Ⓓ
4. Ⓐ Ⓑ Ⓒ Ⓓ
5. Ⓐ Ⓑ Ⓒ Ⓓ
6. Ⓐ Ⓑ Ⓒ Ⓓ
7. Ⓐ Ⓑ Ⓒ Ⓓ
8. Ⓐ Ⓑ Ⓒ Ⓓ

Cuarto Grupo, Selección Cuatro

1. Ⓐ Ⓑ Ⓒ Ⓓ
2. Ⓐ Ⓑ Ⓒ Ⓓ
3. Ⓐ Ⓑ Ⓒ Ⓓ
4. Ⓐ Ⓑ Ⓒ Ⓓ
5. Ⓐ Ⓑ Ⓒ Ⓓ
6. Ⓐ Ⓑ Ⓒ Ⓓ
7. Ⓐ Ⓑ Ⓒ Ⓓ
8. Ⓐ Ⓑ Ⓒ Ⓓ

Quinto Grupo, Selección Uno

1. Ⓐ Ⓑ Ⓒ Ⓓ
2. Ⓐ Ⓑ Ⓒ Ⓓ
3. Ⓐ Ⓑ Ⓒ Ⓓ
4. Ⓐ Ⓑ Ⓒ Ⓓ
5. Ⓐ Ⓑ Ⓒ Ⓓ
6. Ⓐ Ⓑ Ⓒ Ⓓ

Quinto Grupo, Selección Dos

1. Ⓐ Ⓑ Ⓒ Ⓓ
2. Ⓐ Ⓑ Ⓒ Ⓓ
3. Ⓐ Ⓑ Ⓒ Ⓓ
4. Ⓐ Ⓑ Ⓒ Ⓓ
5. Ⓐ Ⓑ Ⓒ Ⓓ
6. Ⓐ Ⓑ Ⓒ Ⓓ
7. Ⓐ Ⓑ Ⓒ Ⓓ
8. Ⓐ Ⓑ Ⓒ Ⓓ

Quinto Grupo, Selección Tres

1. Ⓐ Ⓑ Ⓒ Ⓓ
2. Ⓐ Ⓑ Ⓒ Ⓓ
3. Ⓐ Ⓑ Ⓒ Ⓓ
4. Ⓐ Ⓑ Ⓒ Ⓓ
5. Ⓐ Ⓑ Ⓒ Ⓓ
6. Ⓐ Ⓑ Ⓒ Ⓓ

Quinto Grupo, Selección Cuatro

1. Ⓐ Ⓑ Ⓒ Ⓓ
2. Ⓐ Ⓑ Ⓒ Ⓓ
3. Ⓐ Ⓑ Ⓒ Ⓓ
4. Ⓐ Ⓑ Ⓒ Ⓓ
5. Ⓐ Ⓑ Ⓒ Ⓓ
6. Ⓐ Ⓑ Ⓒ Ⓓ

PRACTICE READING COMPREHENSION PASSAGES
(Section I, Part B)

To briefly review the steps for reading:

1. Scan the passage to get the general idea.
2. Reread more carefully to:
   a) identify key vocabulary words,
   b) identify the characters,
   c) identify the setting,
   d) understand what has happened.
3. Evaluate the information you have gotten from the passage to:
   a) determine the tone and mood of the piece,
   b) determine the intended reader,
   c) draw conclusions about the message of the piece.
4. Read the multiple-choice alternatives and select the best one.

If you are unsure of the answer after reading the choices, ask yourself what kind of information the questions ask. Review the passage, then try the question again.

Remember that if you do not recognize a word, you should still be able to figure out what is going on in the passage. Reading does not mean translating, so do not try to translate every word to answer the questions.

The answer sheets are on pages 197 and 198, and the answers are given on page 229.

PRIMER GRUPO, SELECCIÓN UNO

A las cuatro merendamos juntos, pan y pasas, sentados en el sofá, y cuando nos levantamos, no sé por qué, mi padre no quiso que limpiara el espaldar que el albañilito había manchado de blanco con su chaqueta;
Línea me detuvo la mano y lo limpió después sin que lo viéramos. Jugando, al
(5) albañilito se le cayó un botón de la cazadora, y mi madre se le cosió; él se puso encarnado, y la veía coser; muy admirado y confuso, no atreviéndose ni a respirar. Después le enseñé el álbum de caricaturas, y él, sin darse cuenta, imitaba los gestos de aquellas caras, tan bien, que hasta mi padre se reía. Estaba tan contento cuando se fue, que se olvidó de
(10) ponerse al andrajoso sombrero, y al llegar a la puerta de la escalera, para manifestarme su gratitud, me hacía otra vez la gracia de poner el *hocico de liebre*.

—¿Sabes, hijo mío, por qué no quise que limpiara el sofá? Porque limpiarle mientras tu compañero lo veía era casi hacerle una reconven-
(15) ción por haberlo ensuciado. Y esto no estaba bien: en primer lugar, porque no lo había hecho de intento, y en segundo lugar, porque le había manchado con ropa de su padre, que se la había enyesado trabajando; y lo que se mancha trabajando no ensucia; es polvo, cal, barniz, todo lo que quieras, pero no suciedad. El trabajo no ensucia. No digas nunca de
(20) un obrero que sale de su trabajo: "Va sucio". Debes decir: "Tiene en su ropa las señales, las huellas del trabajo". Recuérdalo. Quiero mucho al albañilito: primero, porque es compañero tuyo, y además, porque es hijo de un obrero. —*Tu padre*.

1. ¿De qué trata esta selección?
   (A) De la conducta apropiada de un anfitrión.
   (B) De los modos de mantenerse limpio en casa.
   (C) De la conducta apropiada de un huésped.
   (D) De los modos de disciplinar a un hijo.

2. Al levantarse del sofá, ¿qué le molestaba al hijo?
   (A) Que la ropa del visitante estaba sucia.
   (B) Que se vieron algunas huellas del trabajo en el sofá.
   (C) Que en la chaqueta del albañilito faltaba un botón.
   (D) Que la chaqueta mostraba señales del trabajo.

3. ¿Cómo se sentía el albañilito cuando observó a la mamá reparando la ropa?
   (A) Estaba muy triste.
   (B) Se avergonzó.
   (C) Se enojó.
   (D) Se arrepintió.

4. ¿En la línea 18, qué quiere decir, *lo que se mancha trabajando no ensucia*?
   (A) Indica que no puede ensuciarse trabajando.
   (B) Significa que el padre no vio que la chaqueta estaba sucia.
   (C) Significa que trabajar no es una desgracia.
   (D) Quiere decir que el padre se sentía superior a los obreros.

5. ¿Por qué no quería el papá que su hijo limpiara el sofá de inmediato?
   (A) No quería que el albañilito viera a su hijo trabajando.
   (B) Quería que la madre lo hiciera.
   (C) Quería que el albañilito viera lo que había hecho.
   (D) No quería parecer descortés al invitado.

6. ¿Qué determina la diferencia entre el hijo y el albañilito?
   (A) Los aspectos socio-económicos de los dos.
   (B) El nivel de formación educativa de los dos.
   (C) Las características personales de los dos.
   (D) La edad de los dos.

7. ¿Cómo es la relación entre el papá y el hijo?
   (A) Parece que el padre es muy exigente.
   (B) Parece que los dos gozan de relaciones muy estrechas.
   (C) Parece que el chico no le hace mucho caso al padre.
   (D) El chico parece ser muy mimado por su padre.

PRIMER GRUPO, SELECCIÓN DOS

Borja se quedó quieto, con los hombros un poco encogidos. Retrocedió tanto que salió fuera del porche, y la lluvia le caía por la frente y la mejillas, de forma que éste nunca podría comprender. (Yo sí, pobre

Línea   amigo mío, yo sí te entendía y sentía piedad.) Intentó sonreír, pero sus

(5)   labios temblaban, y se cobijó de nuevo en el porche, humillado como jamás le viera nadie. Juan Antonio y los del administrador parecía que nos miraban, a Manuel y a mí, con envidia. Y me dije: "¿Cómo es posible

que todos estemos enamorados de él?" Y odié la guitarra de Sanamo, que nos envenenó. Cada vez que Manuel y yo queríamos separar nuestras

(10) manos, Jorge ponía la suya encima y lo impedía.

Borja se sentó, con los codos sobre las rodillas y la cara entre las manos. No sabíamos si lloraba o reía, o simplemente si le dolía la cabeza de tanto como bebió.

Se oía la música de la guitarra de Sanamo, y la lluvia, acabándose.

(15) Todo brillaba muy pálidamente en temblorosas gotas: los racimos verdes, azul y oro, las hojas del magnolio, los cerezos, las rosas de octubre.

Entonces Jorge dijo:

—¿Sabéis, muchachos? No creáis que al morir recordaréis hazañas, ni

(20) sucesos importantes que os hayan ocurrido. No creáis que recordaréis grandes aventuras, ni siquiera momentos felices que aún podáis vivir. Sólo cosas como ésta: una tarde así, unas copas de vino, esas rosas cubiertas de agua. ¿No lo crees, Matia?

Yo no le dije nada.

1. ¿Qué tiempo hace?
   (A) Es octubre.
   (B) Es la temporada lluviosa.
   (C) Está despejado.
   (D) Es de verano.

2. ¿Dónde estarán los chicos?
   (A) Estarán en un restaurante elegante.
   (B) Estarán en un parque en al campo.
   (C) Estarán en la casa de un viejo amigo.
   (D) Estarán en una pensión para viejos.

3. ¿Por qué están los chicos allí?
   (A) Manuel y la narradora buscan la bendición de Jorge.
   (B) Quieren que Sanamo les entretenga con su música.
   (C) Ellos parecen haber buscado refugio de la lluvia.
   (D) Todos los chicos buscan la amistad de Jorge.

4. ¿Por qué está tan triste Borja?
   (A) Cree que Jorge le ha rechazado.
   (B) A los otros chicos no les gusta.
   (C) No le gusta la música de Sanamo.
   (D) Está triste porque bebió demasiado vino.

5. En líneas 7–8, qué significa la pregunta *¿Cómo es posible que todos estemos enamorados de él?*
   (A) Quiere decir que la narradora admira mucho a Jorge.
   (B) La narradora no sabe qué pensar de este hombre.
   (C) Parece que ella preferiría estar en otro lugar.
   (D) Le molesta un poco toda la atención que recibió Borja.

6. ¿Qué revela del carácter de Jorge lo que éste dice al fin de la selección?
   (A) Es muy orgulloso.
   (B) Es sentimental.
   (C) Es muy tacaño.
   (D) Es muy travieso.

7. ¿Cómo se describirían las relaciones entre Manuel y los otros chicos?
   (A) Manuel es distinto entre todos los chicos.
   (B) Le tienen celos porque es el favorito de Jorge.
   (C) Lo admiran por ser buen amigo de Borja.
   (D) A todos los chicos les gusta.

8. ¿Quién narra estos recuerdos?
   (A) Borja.
   (B) Manuel.
   (C) Jorge.
   (D) Matia.

PRIMER GRUPO, SELECCIÓN TRES

En verano se ven menos horas de televisión, según los estudios de audiencia. Los días son más largos. Los espectadores encuentran elementos sustituidores de ocio fuera de su hogar habitual. La publicidad *Línea* floja y disminuye la presión competitiva. Este año, sin embargo, y a (5) excepción de Atena 3, que apenas modificará su programación, la lucha por ganar más cuota de pantalla no baja la guardia. La más agresiva es Tele 5, que prepara las maletas para situarse en las playas. En la de Marbella ya ha contratado a su alcalde para que haga de presentador.

Para los jóvenes, Tele 5 ha preparado una versión reducida de *La* (10) *quinta marcha*, que se emitirá al mediodía desde distintos emplazamientos turísticos y playeros. En esta misma línea de seguimiento a la audiencia consumidora de discos y refrescos, se mueve *Hablando se entiende la basca*, una versión del programa de Coll que se realizará en el mismo escenario de *Hablando se entiende la gente*, el teatro de la (15) ONCE de Madrid. Chavales entre 10 y 17 años ofrecerán diariamente su espectáculo conducido por unos de los presentadores de *La quinta marcha*.

1. ¿Qué tendencias se han notado entre los televidentes españoles?
   (A) Durante el invierno miran menos porque están tan ocupados.
   (B) Durante el verano miran menos porque prefieren disfrutar del tiempo fuera de casa.
   (C) No hay diferencia entre el número de horas que miran en verano e invierno.
   (D) Depende más de la edad del televidente cuánto miran en el verano.

2. ¿Cómo han respondido los productores de programación a la situación?
   - (A) Hay gran cooperación entre todos los canales para atraer más televidentes.
   - (B) Todos los canales recurren a medidas muy agresivas para atraer al televidente.
   - (C) Los programas se han hecho más al tanto para todos los televidentes.
   - (D) Todas las estaciones menos Tele 5 están esforzándose para atraer televidentes.

3. ¿Qué actitud reflejan las estaciones?
   - (A) Reflejan cierta desesperación para aumentar el número de espectadores.
   - (B) Reflejan una nueva actitud agresiva para promover los negocios.
   - (C) Reflejan cierta resignación a las vacilaciones de cada estación y temporada.
   - (D) Reflejan indiferencia para las modalidades de los jóvenes modernos.

4. ¿A qué tipo de televidente está dirigido el programa *La quinta marcha*?
   - (A) Es para los turistas en Madrid.
   - (B) Es para turistas en las playas.
   - (C) Es de más interés para los jóvenes.
   - (D) Está dirigido a gente profesional.

5. ¿Cómo se propone atraer más televidentes entre el público?
   - (A) Un canal va a contratar a más jóvenes.
   - (B) Un canal va a contratar a unos turistas en Marbella.
   - (C) Unos van a olvidarse de todas las viejas estrellas de la televisión.
   - (D) Unos van a ofrecer programas de viajes a Marbella.

6. ¿Qué tipo de programa es *Hablando se entiende la gente*?
   - (A) Es teatro en la pantalla pequeña.
   - (B) Es un programa de viajes para turistas.
   - (C) Es un programa con algo para los jóvenes.
   - (D) Es un programa para ciegos en la televisión.

7. ¿De dónde procede este trozo?
   - (A) Es un folleto del Consejo de Turismo sobre la televisión.
   - (B) Es un guión para los televidentes.
   - (C) Es de una revista que trata las novedades en la televisión.
   - (D) Es de una obra literaria tratando la vida moderna.

PRIMER GRUPO, SELECCIÓN CUATRO

Para los que todavía se quedaban fuera se han multiplicado los artículos de los espontáneos, las "Cartas al Director" y, sobre todo, siguen vigentes las "pintadas". Esas pintadas que permitían el anonimato y que eran lógicas, en cierto modo, cuando sus autores no tenían otro medio de hacer oír su voz desde la clandestinidad a que el Régimen los tenía condenados, siguen ahora cuando la voz y la letra son libres, porque siempre queda gente que tiene que estrujar y luego manipular las opiniones de otros para impulsar sus propias ideas sobre el aborto o del precio del pan, de Gibraltar o del País Vasco.

Línea

(5)

(10)   Y las manifestaciones callejeras se suceden. Pueden hacerse para la defensa del medio ambiente o contra un alcalde superviviente de la dictadura, a favor de los obreros panaderos o del Polisario, pero a juzgar por las fotografías o televidiarios, lo más importante para los participantes es estar allí, ser vistos y oídos. Cada vez que una cámara de cine o

(15)   fotografía les enfoca miran fijos, sonríen, levantan los brazos; en las fotos de periódicos, los de delante aparecen satisfechos y orgullosos; los de detrás, se asoman por entre las cabezas entre los afortunados para "estar" a su vez común en esas fotografías de grupos infantiles.

1. ¿Qué aspecto de la vida comenta este trozo?
   (A) Unas libertades civiles que permiten manifestaciones.
   (B) Nuevas libertades para expresión pública.
   (C) Los cambios entre la gente en la vida pública.
   (D) Los abusos de la libertad de expresión pública.

2. ¿Qué son *Cartas al Director*?
   (A) Manifestaciones para funcionarios.
   (B) Artículos de espectadores a directores del cine.
   (C) Declaraciones de gente en contra del Régimen.
   (D) Comunicaciones dirigidas a la redacción de un periódico.

3. En las líneas 5–6, ¿a quiénes se refieren las palabras *desde la clandestinidad a que el Régimen los tenía condenados*?
   (A) Se refieren a personas que pintaron en vez de escribir para expresar sus ideas.
   (B) Se refieren a gente que antes tenía que pagar al diario para que publicara sus opiniones.
   (C) Se refieren a personas que querían efectuar cambios sociales fuera del sistema.
   (D) Se refieren a personas prohibidas por el estado de hacer cualquier tipo de declaración antigubernamental.

4. ¿Por qué se suceden las manifestaciones callejeras, según este autor?
   (A) A esa gente sólo le interesa ser vista.
   (B) Esa gente celebra sus nuevas libertades.
   (C) Protestan la censura del gobierno.
   (D) Quieren efectuar grandes cambios sociales.

5. ¿Cómo reaccionan esas personas al ver una cámara?
   (A) Tratan de ocultar los rostros.
   (B) Se enorgullecen de su supuesta importancia.
   (C) Tienen miedo de ser reconocidos por el Régimen.
   (D) Se enfadan porque sacan fotografías de ellas.

6. ¿Cuál es la actitud de ese autor?
   (A) Le tiene mucha simpatía a esa gente.
   (B) Comprende bien sus sentimientos y sus frustraciones.
   (C) Muestra una actitud de admiración a esa gente.
   (D) Menosprecia a esa gente.

SEGUNDO GRUPO, SELECCIÓN UNO

Por eso Scherer dice que "la patria y un sentido elemental y primitivo de la hombría llegaron a ser para el joven Siqueiros dos conceptos difíciles de disociar", y alude que la patria era, para el pintor, "el sol y el

Línea machismo".

(5)   Una anécdota del Siqueiros adolescente puede ilustrar este punto. Hacia el año 1911, cuando se hablaba en México de la reforma agraria, un día en que estaban reunidos con el padre del futuro pintor, en casa de éste, varios hacendados de Morelos y de Guanajuato, llegó el joven. Uno de los reunidos, don Jesús Covarrubias, le dijo: "¿Con qué tú, David, eres

(10)   de los que dicen que lo tuyo es mío y lo mío es mío?" El joven—tenía apenas catorce años—sólo replicó con una especie de gruñido y miró a su padre, quien dirigióle una mirada de reprobación. Después—cuenta el pintor—que los circunstantes empezaron a hacerle insinuaciones vagas, bromas y preguntas que ellos mismos contestaban como si las respuestas

(15)   fueran del interpelado. Este, pasado un rato, dijo con energía: "Yo lo único que sé es que todos los hacendados son una bola de ladrones." Su padre, como es natural, le echó del comedor, donde se hallaban. El salió lentamente, "en deliberada actitud de desafío." Miró con insolencia a uno por uno de los reunidos y se detuvo frente a su padre. "No creo—

(20)   declaró muchos años después—haberlo visto con odio, pero sentí como si en la hondura verde de mis ojos se formara algo así como una mancha turbia." Por fin, salió del comedor, y destrozó muebles y objetos de tres habitaciones. En seguida abandonó la casa paterna, a la que ya no volvió nunca.

(25)   David Siqueiros y Diego Rivera sentían la necesidad de "expresarse con voces genuinas." Los dos se preguntaban cómo podría ser el futuro programa de revolución pictórica de México. Sus ideas partían de la base de la falta de mercado para la pintura en su país. De ahí el que pensaran que el género primordial de actividad tendría que ser el muralismo.

1. ¿Quién fue David Siqueiros?
   (A) Fue crítico de arte mexicano.
   (B) Fue hacendado rico.
   (C) Fue líder para la reforma agraria.
   (D) Fue muralista.

2. ¿En qué sentido era la patria *sol y el machismo* para Siqueiros?
   (A) La patria encarnaba toda la fuerza vital del mexicano.
   (B) La belleza natural del paisaje mexicano inspiraba tanto al artista como al campesino.
   (C) El trabajo de los mexicanos era seguir la lucha para la reforma agraria contra los ricos.
   (D) La patria pertenecía a los hombres mexicanos.

3. ¿Quiénes visitaban en casa de su padre un día?
   (A) Los amigos del joven David Siqueiros.
   (B) Unos ricos.
   (C) Unos pintores famosos.
   (D) Unos campesinos.

4. ¿Qué insinuó José Covarrubias en lo que le dijo a David Siqueiros?
   (A) Que sabía que David pertenecía a un grupo promoviendo un nuevo estilo de arte.
   (B) Que sabía que David quería que los ricos repartieran sus terrenos a los pobres.
   (C) Que sabía que los jóvenes siempre se rebelaban contra la autoridad.
   (D) Que David Siqueiros era ambicioso y avaro porque quería el dinero que tenía.

5. ¿Por qué se enojó su padre con el joven?
   (A) El joven acusó a uno de sus amigos de haberle robado algo.
   (B) El joven había pintado mal las casas de los hacendados ricos.
   (C) La injuria de su hijo le dio vergüenza.
   (D) El hijo desafió a su padre en la presencia de los invitados.

6. ¿De qué se dio cuenta el joven durante esa cena?
   (A) Su padre tenía buen sentido de humor.
   (B) Supo que los ricos eran sarcásticos.
   (C) Supo que su padre no lo quería.
   (D) Los valores de su padre no eran los suyos.

7. ¿Con quién compartió el joven pintor sus ideas?
   (A) Con Diego Rivera.
   (B) Con sus padres.
   (C) Con los hacendados.
   (D) Con Jesús Covarrubias.

8. ¿Cómo se relacionan el movimiento artístico del muralismo y el de la reforma agraria?
   (A) Los dos se basan en un mercado libre.
   (B) Los dos se basan en el concepto de que la voz popular sólo se expresaba por el arte.
   (C) Los dos se basan en una rebelión contra una aristocracia que oprimió a los pobres.
   (D) Los dos expresan la creencia de que la única actividad auténtica es la pintura.

SEGUNDO GRUPO, SELECCIÓN DOS

La tradicional rosca de Reyes es el centro de atención de la fiesta de cada 6 de enero por ser una de las tradiciones más antiguas de la iglesia católica que permite la convivencia familiar y recuerda la llegada de los
Línea Tres Reyes Magos.
(5)   Esta tradición llegó a México proveniente de España en los primeros años del Virreinato y formó parte de las festividades de año nuevo para recordar la llegada a Jerusalén de los tres Reyes Magos que desde Oriente llevaron regalos al niño Jesús.

Desde entonces, cada 6 de enero las familias mexicanas se reúnen para
(10) partir la tradicional rosca de Reyes—un bizcocho fino—de forma alveolar que contiene en promedio tres figuras de plástico en forma de niño y que simbolizan al hijo de Dios.

Según la religión católica, quien encuentre la figura deberá vestir y presentar al niño Dios en la iglesia durante la fiesta del Día de la Cande-
(15) laria el 2 de febrero para celebrar los 40 días de su nacimiento.

Desde la Edad Media las familias españolas acostumbraban servir una merienda en la cual se partía la rosca de Reyes. Algunas fuentes históricas aseguran que se trata de una costumbre romana que tomó la iglesia católica y la unió a la Navidad.

(20) Antiguamente la rosca y el chocolate—con el que se suele acompañar—se preparaban en casa, pero en la actualidad se pueden conseguir en cualquier panadería o tienda comercial para celebrar el 6 de enero en compañía de familiares y amigos.

La rosca es un bizcocho muy fino elaborado cuidadosamente con
(25) harina, azúcar, mantequilla y huevos, pasta finamente preparada la cual se agrega a un molde y se adorna con trozos de fruta seca y azúcar glacé, distribuida al gusto.

La festividad continúa hasta el Día de la Candelaria, cuando nuevamente se reúne la familia para celebrar la presentación del niño Dios en
(30) la iglesia y comer los tradicionales tamales verdes, rojos y de dulce acompañados con atole de maíz.

La celebración ha perdurado durante generaciones gracias a la tradición familiar y a los comerciantes, que aprovechan la ocasión para incrementar sus ganancias mediante la venta de roscas de todos tamaños y
(35) precios, que varían entre cinco y quince dólares cada una.

1. ¿Qué es una rosca de Reyes?
   (A) Es una estatua pequeña del niño Jesús que se presenta a la iglesia el 6 de enero.
   (B) Es un tipo de torta con pequeñas figuras escondidas adentro.
   (C) Es un tipo de regalo traído por los Reyes Magos.
   (D) Es una fiesta que tiene la familia durante el mes de enero.

2. ¿Cuándo se celebra esta antigua tradición navideña?
   (A) El veinticinco de diciembre.
   (B) El seis de enero.
   (C) El dos de febrero.
   (D) Cuarenta días después del dos de febrero.

3. ¿En qué consiste la costumbre?
   (A) Los miembros de la familia se visten en trajes romanos para ir a la iglesia.
   (B) Todos compran regalos para presentar al niño Jesús el Día de la Candelaria.
   (C) Todos van a una panadería para comprar una rosca para la fiesta en casa.
   (D) Se celebra el Día de los Reyes Magos visitando a la iglesia y con comida especial.

4. ¿Qué tiene que hacer el que encuentra la figura del niño?
   - (A) Tiene que vestirse en traje romano para ir a la iglesia.
   - (B) Tiene que preparar la fiesta para el Día de la Candelaria.
   - (C) Tiene que llevarla a Jerusalén.
   - (D) Tiene que presentarse en la iglesia con la figura.

5. ¿De dónde procede la tradición mexicana de la rosca?
   - (A) Tiene raíces durante la época colonial de México.
   - (B) Empezó con el Nacimiento.
   - (C) Tiene raíces en las costumbres de la iglesia católica medieval.
   - (D) Los romanos empezaron la costumbre con una fiesta pagana.

6. ¿Qué quieren los comerciantes?
   - (A) Quieren que todos pasen mucho tiempo en las iglesias.
   - (B) Quieren que todos regalen muchos juguetes a los niños.
   - (C) Quieren que todos aprovechen de la oportunidad de descansar en casa.
   - (D) Quieren que todos coman mucho y compren mucho.

7. ¿Qué cambio se ha notado en la celebración de la rosca de Reyes?
   - (A) Ahora es más difícil reunir a toda la familia.
   - (B) Antes siempre se preparaba la rosca en casa.
   - (C) Ahora se celebra el 2 de febrero en vez del 6 de enero.
   - (D) Antes los comerciantes vendieron roscas más finas.

8. ¿Qué permite esta costumbre?
   - (A) Permite que toda la familia se reúna para ayudar a los comerciantes.
   - (B) Permite que los comerciantes disfruten de un descanso de sus negocios.
   - (C) Permite que la iglesia estreche las relaciones con la comunidad comercial.
   - (D) Permite que los niños se sientan parte de la comunidad religiosa.

SEGUNDO GRUPO, SELECCIÓN TRES

Entonces comenzaron entre ellas una de esas conversaciones en que a mí, aunque esté presente, no me dan intervención, porque van a decir cosas que saben que yo no he de admitirles.

Línea   —Y no parece que tenga veintiséis años.

(5)   —Desde luego que no. Por lo menos tiene veintiocho.

  —No ha hablado en ningún momento.

  —¡Nos miraba, y en qué forma!

  —Parecía asustada.

  —No, asustada no. Sorprendida, estupefacta.

(10)   —Y mucha desenvoltura no aparenta tener.

  —Les digo que es una santita que nunca salió de su casa. Por eso ahora anda así.

  —Y se vino vestida bien modestamente.

  —Tenía una media corrida.

(15)   —Y los zapatos llenos de polvo.

—Oigan, ¿no será sorda? ¿No será que no oye lo que se le dice y por eso nos miraba así?

—Pero no, si cuando yo le pregunté...

—Pues algo raro hay en ella. Todavía no sé lo que es, pero ya lo sabré.
(20) Déjenme estudiarla.

Y yo me acordé de aquellas manchas rojas en el antebrazo de Rosaura ¡y sentí una indignación!

—¡Vean qué tres serpientes he traído yo al mundo!—exclamé, mirándolas con furia—. La señorita Eufrasia, al lado de ustedes, es Santa
(25) Eufrasia. No quería decirles nada, pero veo que es necesario. La pelea de Rosaura con el padre fue como para llamar a la policía. Tiene los brazos llenos de cardenales.

Me miraron, horrorizadas.

1. ¿Quién narra lo que pasa en este trozo?
   (A) La señorita Eufrasia.
   (B) Una de las chicas.
   (C) La mamá de las chicas.
   (D) Una chica huérfana.

2. ¿De qué hablan?
   (A) Hablan de una joven que está visitando a la familia.
   (B) Hablan de una chica que es compañera de clase en la escuela.
   (C) Hablan de una santa que visitaba la casa.
   (D) Hablan de una joven pobre que visitaron en su casa.

3. ¿Por qué no quiere intervenir la narradora?
   (A) Tiene miedo de que revelara algo inoportuno.
   (B) Le da vergüenza que las chicas sean tan crueles.
   (C) Le ha prometido a la chica no decirles nada.
   (D) No quiere intervenir en asuntos ajenos.

4. ¿Con qué intenciones hablan las tres chicas?
   (A) Hablan para conocer mejor a la chica.
   (B) Hablan para adivinar la identidad de la chica.
   (C) Están chismeando.
   (D) Les interesa ayudarle.

5. ¿En las líneas 24–25, qué quiere decir la frase *La señorita Eufrasia, al lado de ustedes, es Santa Eufrasia*?
   (A) Indica que las chicas son tan buenas como si fueran santas.
   (B) Quiere decir que a la narradora le parece que las tres chicas son muy crueles.
   (C) Significa que la narradora cree que una persona cualquiera puede ser santa.
   (D) Indica que la narradora no cree que la señorita Eufrasia sea santa.

6. ¿Qué quiere la narradora que hagan las tres chicas?
   (A) Quiere que ellas se callen.
   (B) Quiere que ellas sean más piadosas
   (C) Quiere que las chicas la conozcan mejor.
   (D) Quiere que las tres le muestren más respeto.

7. ¿Por qué se quedan horrorizadas las tres chicas?
   (A) No pueden creer que les hable la narradora con tanta franqueza.
   (B) Les ofende que haya intervenido la narradora en sus conversaciones.
   (C) Dudan que la narradora les haya dicho la verdad.
   (D) Les escandalizan los hechos del caso que acaba de decirles la narradora.

8. ¿Qué puede ser el pensamiento central de este trozo?
   (A) A las mujeres les gusta chismear todo el tiempo.
   (B) Los pobres no tienen ningunos derechos.
   (C) No se debe juzgar sin saber todos los datos del caso.
   (D) La intolerancia tiene raíces en la falta de comunicación.

SEGUNDO GRUPO, SELECCIÓN CUATRO

La Oficina de Tierras del Estado está conduciendo un programa en la parte baja de la Laguna Madre para determinar si proyectos privados y estructuras localizadas en los terrenos costeros estatales, están adecuada-
Línea mente permitidos.

(5) "Hemos concedido un período de gracia para permitir que toda persona que esté usando los terrenos costeros públicos para cualquier propósito particular, tal como desembarcadero, puedan obtener un permiso sin tener que pagar multa", señaló el Delegado de Tierras.

El programa de condescendencia exige la inspección de propiedades
(10) en Laguna Alta, Laguna Vista y La Gran Isla, para verificar que los propietarios acaten las respectivas leyes. Las propiedades del estado no pueden ser utilizadas para ningún propósito sin el debido permiso escrito por parte de la Oficina y el pago correspondiente.

Cada propietario de terreno comercial o residencial, debe recibir una
(15) carta de notificación sobre la inspección a realizarse. Después de la inspección, los propietarios recibirán una carta de la Oficina de Tierras del Estado informando sobre el estado de su propiedad, notificándole que todo está en orden, o que es necesario algún cambio.

Las personas que están utilizando propiedades del estado sin la
(20) debida autorización, tendrán hasta el 1° de junio para solicitar un plazo sin tener que pagar multas, o bien para notificar a la oficina de tierras la fecha en que se corregirá dicha situación.

1. ¿De dónde procederá este trozo?
   (A) Manual para burócratas.
   (B) Un anuncio público distribuido por el gobierno.
   (C) Artículo de una revista.
   (D) Un texto de leyes sobre propiedades públicas.

2. ¿De qué ubicación geográfica será?
   (A) De una localidad urbana.
   (B) De una localidad agraria.
   (C) De una localidad del litoral.
   (D) De una localidad montañosa.

3. ¿A quiénes está dirigido?
   (A) Está dirigido a comerciantes de terrenos costeros.
   (B) Está dirigido a los que usan los embarcaderos estatales.
   (C) Está dirigido a todas las personas que viven cerca de las Lagunas.
   (D) Está dirigido a la Oficina de Tierras del Estado.

4. ¿A qué ley se refiere este trozo?
   (A) La que otorga permiso para utilizar los terrenos públicos.
   (B) La que reglamenta la industria pesquera.
   (C) La que permite la investigación de utilización de terrenos públicos.
   (D) La que trata el establecimiento de viviendas en terrenos públicos.

5. ¿Qué problema revela?
   (A) Unas personas usan terrenos públicos ilegalmente.
   (B) Unas personas no están pagando los debidos impuestos en sus terrenos.
   (C) Unas personas no tienen autorización de usar los embarcaderos públicos.
   (D) Unas personas ignoran las leyes.

6. A causa del problema, ¿qué hará el Estado?
   (A) El Estado encarcelará a los que no cooperan.
   (B) El Estado perdonará a todos los que no se conforman.
   (C) El Estado prohibirá a los que no tienen permiso que utilicen los terrenos públicos.
   (D) El Estado instituirá un programa de condescendencia.

7. Quién use propiedad del Estados, deberá
   (A) Recibir una carta de notificación y luego ser informado del estado de la propiedad.
   (B) Pedir un plazo sin multa alguna o proveer una solución.
   (C) Pagar la multa y efectuar la solución de inmediato.
   (D) Esperar hasta el 1º de junio y luego solicitar la autorización.

TERCER GRUPO, SELECCIÓN UNO

Patrocinado por el Instituto de Cultura e invitado por el Instituto Guatemalteco, vengo a pasar un mes en Guatemala. A mi regreso, todos, amigos, parientes, colegas y hasta simples conocidos, me han asediado con su curiosidad por este país, del que por desgracia tan poco se conoce en Europa. Un mes, por modo cierto, es muy poco tiempo para llegar al conocimiento de cualquier cosa importante y desde luego mucho menos para captar las esencias tan complejas y los matices tan variopintos de un país como Guatemala.

Línea

(5)

En todos los medios sociales en los que me he desenvuelto, la cortesía
(10)   natural y algo más importante y sincero, como es la cordialidad, son la
regla. En cada momento de mi vida allí, he tenido la sensación
entrañable de encontrarme en mi propio país y también de que "el solo
hecho de ser español" ya era algo importante en Guatemala. Esto no
implica, ni mucho menos, en el nativo o residente, servilismo ni ausen-
(15)   cia de un lógico y acertado orgullo nacional, sino que si los "peninsu-
lares" nos colocamos en la natural posición de hermanos, ellos como
hermanos nos acogen.

Lo que no aceptan, y hacen muy bien, es la actitud más o menos
veladamente "paternalista" y protectora, que el desconocimiento de la
(20)   realidad hace adoptar a muchos de los que intentan "españolear" en
América. Creo sinceramente que la única razón de los alientos que los
guatemaltecos han prodigado a mis modestas actuaciones públicas se ha
debido a mi sentir, sinceramente expresado, de que tanto más tenía yo
que aprender de ellos, como ellos de mí.

(25)   El intelectual guatemalteco es curioso de todos los saberes, hábil con-
versador, que sabe escuchar y decir—cada cosa a su tiempo—y de una
cultura extensa e intensa, sin el mal de la pedantería. Como uno de los
más gratos recuerdos de esta mi entrañable Guatemala, tengo el del
"redescubrimiento" del apacible coloquio—hoy casi olvidado entre
(30)   nosotros—con el designio más de aprender que de enseñar, el sentido de
la mutua comprensión y la tolerancia liberal que preside toda mente
selecta.

1. ¿Quién es el autor de este trozo?
   (A) Es guatemalteco que actualmente vive en España.
   (B) Es turista casual en Guatemala.
   (C) Es embajador cultural español en Guatemala.
   (D) Es un peninsular invitado por una organización guatemalteca.

2. Al pasar un mes en Guatemala este señor
   (A) ha intentado "españolizar" a los indígenas.
   (B) ha investigado las actitudes de los guatemaltecos hacia los españoles.
   (C) ha dictado algunas conferencias de cuando en cuando.
   (D) ha visitado con los intelectuales entre los guatemaltecos.

3. ¿Qué actitud mostraba este autor?
   (A) Se sentía muy superior por ser español entre guatemaltecos.
   (B) Se sentía bien acogido.
   (C) Se sentía muy humillado porque los guatemaltecos eran tan
       inteligentes.
   (D) Se sentía muy dispuesto a regresar a su país cuanto antes.

4. ¿Qué característica de los guatemaltecos le impresionó más?
   (A) La envidia que le tenían porque era europeo.
   (B) Lo pedante que eran los guatemaltecos intelectuales.
   (C) Su gran curiosidad intelectual en cuanto a todo el mundo.
   (D) Su soberbia que no les permitió admitir la superioridad española.

5. ¿Qué crítica implícita hay en lo que dice este autor?
   (A) Critica a sus propios compatriotas.
   (B) Critica a los europeos con negocios en Guatemala.
   (C) Critica a los guatemaltecos por ser tan serviles.
   (D) Critica la pereza guatemalteca.

6. ¿Qué revela la actitud de los guatemaltecos en cuanto a las relaciones con los españoles?
   (A) Los guatemaltecos siempre han entendido mejor a los españoles que al revés.
   (B) Los guatemaltecos siempre han entendido peor a los españoles que al revés.
   (C) Las dos nacionalidades siempre se han tratado como iguales.
   (D) Nunca se han entendido bien.

7. ¿Qué sugiere que se aprenda de los guatemaltecos?
   (A) Sugiere que se aprenda a apreciar el arte de no hacer nada.
   (B) Sugiere que todo el mundo imite la sinceridad de los guatemaltecos.
   (C) Sugiere que todos viajen a Guatemala para experimentar esta cultura.
   (D) Sugiere que todos los intelectuales sean más pedantes, tal como los guatemaltecos.

8. ¿Cómo sería posible caracterizar a este escritor?
   (A) Es un hombre muy sincero pero ingenuo.
   (B) Es un hombre muy intelectual.
   (C) Es un hombre intenso.
   (D) Es un hombre discreto.

TERCER GRUPO, SELECCIÓN DOS

Emitido por: AERONAVES NACIONALES:

Boleto de pasaje y del talón de equipaje

Aviso sobre limitaciones de responsabilidades sobre equipajes:

Línea
(5)
Las limitaciones de responsabilidad del transportista sobre el equipaje facturado, serán de aproximadamente (U.S.) $9.07 por libra y sobre el equipaje no facturado serán de (U.S.) $400.00 por pasajero.

Noticia importante

BIENVENIDOS A BORDO

Estimado Pasajero:

(10)
Para mayor comodidad y seguridad, si Ud. interrumpe su viaje por más de 48 horas le solicitamos que reconfirme su intención de usar la continuidad o el retorno de su viaje. Para tal efecto le rogamos que informe a nuestras oficinas en el lugar donde Ud. intenta reanudar su viaje con 48 horas de anticipación a la hora de salida de su vuelo. La no-

(15)
reconfirmación de su salida podría traer como consecuencia la cancelación de su reserva. Esperamos su colaboración para seguir brindándole nuestro tradicional servicio.

CUPÓN DE REEMBOLSO

El reembolso solo se hará al pasajero, a menos que se indique otra per-

(20)
sona en la parte inferior de esta casilla, caso en el cual, solo podrá hacerse a la persona designada y no al pasajero, siempre y cuando entregue este cupón, los cupones que no hayan sido usados y el talón de exceso

de equipaje. El presente reembolso está sujeto a las tarifas, normas y regulaciones del transportador, así como a las leyes y demás disposi-

(25) ciones gubernamentales.

1. Este trozo parece ser
   (A) De un folleto de una línea aérea.
   (B) De un contrato entre un pasajero y una línea aérea.
   (C) El documento de embarque que se le entrega para poder embarcar.
   (D) De un anuncio para Aeronaves Nacionales.

2. Si Ud. tiene reservas para un vuelo de vuelta el doce de diciembre, a las catorce horas ¿para cuándo tendrá Ud. que reconfirmar su vuelo?
   (A) El 9 de diciembre, a las siete de la mañana.
   (B) El 10 de diciembre, a las dos de la tarde.
   (C) El 11 de diciembre, a las cuatro de la tarde.
   (D) El 12 de diciembre, a la una de la tarde.

3. Se necesita un *talón de equipaje* para
   (A) Probar responsabilidad financiera de la línea aérea.
   (B) Poder llevar el equipaje de mano en la cabina.
   (C) Declarar el valor y peso del equipaje.
   (D) Reclamar el equipage al aduanero.

4. ¿Qué propósito tiene el cupón de reembolso?
   (A) Para que otra persona pueda usar el boleto que no se ha usado.
   (B) Para que la línea aérea pague al pasajero por usar los servicios de ésta.
   (C) Para que el gobierno le pague la parte que no se ha usado.
   (D) Para que la línea aérea pague la parte que no se ha usado.

5. Las palabras *nuestro tradicional servicio* indica
   (A) Que la línea esta muy orgullosa de su servicio.
   (B) Que es una vieja línea tradicional.
   (C) Que es una línea establecida y reconocida.
   (D) Que su servicio es igual al de cualquier otra línea.

TERCER GRUPO, SELECCIÓN TRES

Muy señor nuestro:

En relación a su carta enviada el 2 de febrero donde se expresa su interés en recibir información de la Región de Castilla y León les comu-

Línea nico que el Gobierno de la Región presta su total apoyo y colaboración

(5) para que se efectúen inversiones en la Comunidad Autónoma de Castilla y León.

Para que puedan llegar a tener un primer conocimiento de nuestra región les envió un folleto informativo en inglés, así como indicaciones sobre las posibles líneas de ayuda de las que se puedan beneficiar.

(10) Al margen de estas medidas de apoyo, le informo que se dan en nuestra Región circunstancias muy favorables para la adquisición de suelo industrial, disponible en Polígonos Industriales ya equipados. La mayoría de éstos se pueden obtener con ventajas adicionales en función de la demanda de la empresa. Por otro lado, hemos de informarle del hecho

(15) de que muchos ayuntamientos ceden parte de sus terrenos industriales a

título gratuito o por un precio simbólico para la instalación de nuevas industrias en los mismos.

También estimamos de gran interés para los posibles inversores en la Región de Castilla y León (España-Europa) la existencia de una amplia
(20) gama de incentivos que premian la creación de empleo, así como la existencia de una sociedad de capital-riesgo (INCRIS, S.A.) cuyo objeto es la promoción o fomento de sociedades no financieras mediante la participación temporal en su capital y la prestación a las sociedades participadas de servicios de asesoramiento, asistencia técnica y otros complemen-
(25) tarios, teniendo como recursos propios iniciales, 1.000 millones de pesetas.

Estamos a su entera disposición para cualquier ampliación de información que aquí se cita, así como sería un placer para nosotros, que se desplazaran a conocer personalmente esta Región y sus instituciones.
(30) Atentamente,
El Director General de Economía

1. ¿De quién es esta carta?
   (A) Del contador de una empresa grande.
   (B) De un representante gubernamental.
   (C) De un agente de bienes raíces.
   (D) De un banco que está solicitando clientes.

2. ¿Cuál es el propósito de la carta?
   (A) Solicitar préstamos y dinero para el desarrollo regional.
   (B) Atraer industrias a la región.
   (C) Ofrecer ayuda financiera para los naturales de la región.
   (D) Crear sociedades en la región para apoyar el desarrollo económico.

3. ¿Qué se ofrece hacer en la carta?
   (A) Se ofrece negociar con los ayuntamientos locales.
   (B) Se ofrece invertir el dinero de los extranjeros que vienen a la región.
   (C) Se ofrece enviar solicitudes a los posibles clientes de empresas en la región.
   (D) Se ofrece establecer sociedades para ayudar y apoyar las industrias.

4. Parece que esta región
   (A) Goza de muchas condiciones favorables para la industria.
   (B) Tiene mucho territorio subdesarrollado.
   (C) Tiene mucha experiencia en invertir dinero.
   (D) Se encuentra bien desarrollada económicamente.

TERCER GRUPO, SELECCIÓN CUATRO

Verdad es que el llamado realismo, cosa puramente externa, aparencial, cortical y anecdótica, se refiere al arte literario y no al poético o creativo. En una creación la realidad es una realidad íntima, creativa y de
Línea voluntad. Un poeta no saca sus criaturas por los modos del llamado rea-
(5) lismo. Las figuras de los realistas suelen ser maniquíes vestidos.

¿Cuál es la realidad íntima, la realidad real, la realidad eterna, la realidad poética o creativa de un hombre? Sea hombre de carne y hueso o sea de los que llamamos ficción, que es igual. Porque Don Quijote es tan real

como Cervantes; Hamlet o Macbeth tanto como Shakespeare. ¿Qué es lo
(10)   más íntimo, lo más creativo, lo más real de un hombre? Nos dice Oliver
Wendell Holmes que cuando conversan dos, Juan y Tomás, hay seis en
conversación. Los tres Juanes son: 1) El Juan real; conocido sólo para su
Hacedor, 2) El Juan ideal de Juan; nunca el real, y a menudo muy desemejante de él, y 3) El Juan ideal de Tomás; nunca el Juan real ni el Juan
(15)   de Juan, sino a menudo muy desemejante de ambos. Es igual para
Tomás. Los tres Tomases son: 1) El Tomás real, 2) El Tomás ideal de
Tomás, y 3) El Tomás ideal de Juan.

Es decir, el que uno es, el que se cree ser y el que le cree otro. Y Oliver
Wendell Holmes pasa a disertar sobre el valor de cada uno de ellos.
(20)   Pero yo tengo que tomarlo por otro camino que el intelectualista yanqui Wendell Holmes. Y digo que, además del que uno es para Dios—si
para Dios es uno alguien—y del que es para los otros y del que se cree
ser, hay el que quisiera ser. Y que éste, el que uno quiere ser, es en él, en
su seno, el creador, y es el real de verdad.

1. ¿En qué se interesa más este autor?
   (A) Una definición de la realidad.
   (B) Lo que piensan los intelectuales ingleses.
   (C) La multiplicidad de facetas de una personalidad.
   (D) Una definición de una obra de arte.

2. ¿Cómo puede Don Quijote ser tan real como Cervantes?
   (A) Si ni hubiera vivido el autor, no hubiera sido personaje ficticio.
   (B) Si el autor no hubiera pensado en su creación, no hubiera sido
        famoso.
   (C) Los dos nunca existieron de veras porque no hay prueba tangible de
        sus vidas.
   (D) Los dos trascienden la vida corporal del autor.

3. Según el autor de la selección, ¿cuántas personalidades hay en una con-
   versación entre dos?
   (A) Hay tres.
   (B) Hay cuatro.
   (C) Hay seis.
   (D) Hay ocho.

4. En la línea 5, cuando el autor afirma que *las figuras de los realistas suelen
   ser maniquíes vestidos,* lo dice porque
   (A) Los maniquíes vestidos generalmente se ven muy realistas.
   (B) Sólo los idealistas son capaces de comprender la realidad.
   (C) Estas figuras son verdaderas sólo en su aspecto externo.
   (D) La realidad es limitada, igual que un maniquí vestido de persona.

5. ¿Qué quiere añadir este escritor a la teoría del escritor yanqui?
   (A) Además de estas personalidades diferentes, hay dos más en cada persona.
   (B) Cree que lo que una persona quiere ser tiene tanta realidad como las otras.
   (C) Propone una personalidad divina más allá de la que uno quiere ser.
   (D) Advierte que nunca se sabe con quién habla una persona.

6. ¿En qué consiste la realidad de un hombre para este escritor?
   (A) Opina que la realidad, a menos que sea creativa, es superficial.
   (B) Dice que la realidad existe sólo cuando tiene forma palpable.
   (C) Piensa que la llamada realidad es pura inspiración creativa.
   (D) Dice que hay muchas realidades externas, no solamente una.

7. ¿Cómo se caracteriza este autor?
   (A) Es un autor muy inseguro de quién es.
   (B) Es un autor que sabe bien quién es.
   (C) Es un autor que quiere argüir con sus lectores.
   (D) Es un autor que conoce bien al ser humano.

CUARTO GRUPO, SELECCIÓN UNO

Entre los jóvenes de clase media, y a veces de clase obrera que con grandes sacrificios llegan a los estudios superiores, tiene lugar, por otra parte, la transformación cultural más interesante de la década. Quizás la historia cultural del México independiente pueda dividirse en tres etapas. La primera, hasta finales de la dictadura de Díaz, muestra una marcada tendencia—que las grandes excepciones, de Fernández de Lizardi a Posadas, no alcanzan a suprimir—a los que Antonio Caso llamó "la imitación extralógica": una cultura importada, como las mansardas que en las casas de la Colonia Juárez esperaban inútilmente la ventisca invernal. Pero a fines del Porfiriato, las novelas de Rabasa y Frías, la poesía de Othón, los grabados de Posada anunciaban un descubrimiento: el de México por sí mismo. La Revolución, en esencia un paso del no ser, o del ser enajenado, al ser para sí, fue el acto mismo de ese descubrimiento—los actos coinciden con las palabras y la apariencia con el rostro: la máscara cae y todos los colores, voces y cuerpos de México brillan con su existencia real. Un país dividido en compartimientos estancos entra en contacto con sí mismo. Las formidables cabalgatas de la División del Norte y del Cuerpo del Noroeste por todo el territorio de la república son un abrazo y un reconocimiento: los mexicanos saben por primera vez cómo hablan, cómo cantan, cómo ríen, cómo aman, cómo beben, cómo comen, cómo injurian y cómo mueren los mexicanos.

Del choque revolucionario surgió una doble tendencia cultural, positiva en cuanto permitió a los mexicanos descubrirse a sí mismos, y negativa en cuanto llegó a un extremo chauvinista, tipificado popularmente en la frase "Como México no hay dos" que sólo acentúa nuestra forzosa relación bilateral con los Estados Unidos. Curiosa y suicida coincidencia de cierta izquierda y de la derecha cierta: la xenofobia, la afirmación de la singularidad mexicana, la invención estimágtica de "ideas exóticas" para denigrar, sencillamente, las ideas que no se comprenden o se juzgan peligrosas para la ortodoxia de los unos o las ganancias de los otros.

Línea

(5)

(10)

(15)

(20)

(25)

(30)

1. ¿Cómo se diferencian los jóvenes modernos de los de la época del Porfiriato?
   (A) Creen que saben más.
   (B) No tienen identidad auténtica.
   (C) Son más artísticos.
   (D) Disfrutan de más oportunidades.

2. ¿Qué pasó en la primera etapa de la gran transformación mexicana?
   (A) Estalló la rebelión contra la dictadura de Porfirio Díaz.
   (B) Los mexicanos imitaron a las modas ajenas.
   (C) El pueblo se escondió tras máscaras regionales.
   (D) El país se dividió en varios departamentos.

3. ¿Cómo empezaron algunos a mostrar su independencia?
   (A) Unos artistas iniciaron unas nuevas tendencias artísticas.
   (B) La División del Norte se encontró con el Cuerpo del Noroeste.
   (C) Mexicanos de todas partes se juntaron en contra de Porfirio Díaz.
   (D) Unos mexicanos empezaron a pensar de una manera no muy lógica.

4. ¿Qué es lo que se veía al caer la máscara?
   (A) Se veía muchos colores brillantes.
   (B) Descubrieron que eran xenofóbicos.
   (C) Reconocieron sus diferencias regionales.
   (D) Se enteraron de cómo eran sus compatriotas.

5. ¿Qué aspecto positivo tiene la doble tendencia cultural mexicana?
   (A) Los mexicanos reconocieron sus semejanzas.
   (B) Supieron que tenían que juntarse para luchar contra los Estados Unidos.
   (C) Descubrieron el valor de la cultura autóctona.
   (D) Descubrieron que a todos les gustaron los colores vivos.

6. ¿En la línea 25, qué quiere decir la frase *Como México no hay dos*?
   (A) Hay sólo una raza mexicana.
   (B) No se puede permitir influencias extranjeras en México.
   (C) No hay diferencias políticas entre los mexicanos.
   (D) Todas las regiones de México gozan de oportunidades iguales.

7. Últimamente ¿en qué consiste la transformación discutida en esta selección?
   (A) El fomento de revolución artística.
   (B) La creación de regiones únicas.
   (C) Un proceso de autoidentificación mexicana.
   (D) El reconocimiento de la superioridad cultural mexicana.

CUARTO GRUPO, SELECCIÓN DOS

Comunicarse en este país es un laberinto. Cada organismo tiene su propia red de transmisión, sin control alguno, dentro de un espectro donde las interferencias, escuchas y *pinchazos* están a la orden del día.
Línea El gobierno quiere poner orden en todo este caos y prepara un ley de
(5) ordenación de las comunicaciones, que se remitirá a las Cortes el próximo verano. Ahora policía, ambulancias, bomberos, radioaficionados,

teléfonos sin hilos, etcétera, forman toda una tela de araña donde unos atrapan las conversaciones de los otros, y viceversa. Todo un galimatías. La futura ley de las comunicaciones promoverá una *autopista* donde

(10) cada servicio público tendrá su carril para circular sin peligro de choque (interferencias) con el que camina al lado. Los servicios privados se podrán enganchar a esa autopista (red digital de servicios integrados). Todos pagarán el peaje (utilización de la red) a Telefónica.

La creación de la red digital de servicios integrados de banda ancha—

(15) la autopista—se contempla en el horizonte de aquí a veinticinco años. Para entonces, todos los servicios públicos que hoy tienen su propia red de transmisión pasarán por esa red única, evitándose así la duplicidad de costos y el caos circulatorio de las ondas en el espacio.

La red integrada hará que los actuales servicios domésticos de teleco-

(20) municaciones (teléfono, TV, radio y transmisión de datos) vayan por un solo conducto. En un futuro próximo se integrarán los llamados nuevos servicios telemáticos, como el videotex, teletex, facsímil, datáfono, telealarmas, videoconferencia, videocompra y correo electrónico, además de la televisión por cable y/o satélite y las redes públicas de

(25) transmisión de datos. Es decir, voz, imagen y datos.

Para unificar todo este galimatías en una sola red se invertirán, a precios actuales, más de cuatro *billones* de pesetas en los próximos veinte años. La fibra óptica—la tecnología del futuro en materia de telecomunicaciones—será el soporte por el que se transmita todo ese conjunto de

(30) informaciones.

Vocabulario:
galimatías = gibberish, nonsense

1. ¿Cuál es el tema de esta selección?
   (A) Las novedades en la telecomunicación.
   (B) Los problemas insolubles de la comunicación.
   (C) Las aportaciones de la nueva tecnología a la telecomunicación.
   (D) Mejoramientos en servicios públicos de telecomunicaciones.

2. La *autopista* se refiere en este caso
   (A) A los caminos por donde circulan carros con teléfonos portátiles.
   (B) A las ondas en el espacio.
   (C) A los carriles para las ondas en el espacio.
   (D) A un solo conducto para todo tipo de telecomunicación.

3. ¿Cuál problema hay actualmente con la telecomunicación?
   (A) Las llamadas se pierden.
   (B) No se puede transmitir datos.
   (C) La variedad de modos de transmisión es problemática.
   (D) Nadie quiere pagar el peaje a la Telefónica.

4. ¿Quién pagará para desarrollar todas las posibilidades de la fibra óptica?
   (A) La Telefónica tendrá que invertir para realizar todas las posibilidades.
   (B) El gobierno tiene toda la responsabilidad de desarrollarlas.
   (C) Los negocios que utilizan la tecnología tendrán que pagarla.
   (D) Los conductores de carros en la *autopista* tendrán que pagar el peaje.

5. Este escritor anticipa
   (A) Que toda la tecnología futura aumentará los problemas.
   (B) Que la tecnología que ha creado el problema también facilitará la resolución.
   (C) Que habrá más y más choques en la *autopista.*
   (D) Que habrá muchas redes en el futuro.

6. ¿Qué se evitaría si se pudiera inaugurar una red integrada?
   (A) De realizarse esa solución, no se tendría que pagar doble por los servicios.
   (B) Si hubiera una red integrada, todos los servicios públicos tendrían su propia onda.
   (C) Se evitaría tantos hilos por todas partes.
   (D) Si se realizara esta *autopista*, el gobierno no tendría que controlarla.

CUARTO GRUPO, SELECCIÓN TRES

Desde el 27 de mayo se hicieron a la mar, desde Guayaquil, las tres balsas que forman la nueva expedición del valeroso santanderino Vital Alsar.

Línea   En 1966 intentó Alsar este mismo recorrido Guayaquil-Australia, pero
(5)   lo hizo con menor preparación, y a los 143 días de navegación se le hundió la balsa. Lejos de desanimarse, lo que hizo inmediatamente fue comenzar a preparar otra expedición, esta vez más cuidada, y acompañándose de un grupo de marinos tan arriesgados como él.

Vital Alsar tiene en la actualidad cuarenta años. Su vida se la cambió
(10)   la lectura del libro de Thor Heyerdhal sobre la *Kon Tiki.* Ha pasado años trabajando y ahorrando para esa gran aventura, que deberá llevarlo, en unas balsas construidas con material vegetal, desde Guayaquil hasta Mooloolaba, junto a Brisbane, en Australia. Las tres balsas que forman la expedición que se encuentra en estos momentos rumbo a Australia, lle-
(15)   van los nombres del punto de partida, del de llegada, y de Aztlan, que es el sitio mexicano donde se reunieron los expedicionarios para dirigirse a Guayaquil.

Dadas las nacionalidades de los componentes, Vital Alsar no ha querido que ninguna de las balsas lleve bandera de un país determinado,
(20)   sino que las ha adornado con banderas blancas como símbolo de fraternidad internacional.

La expedición está calculada para una duración de cinco a seis meses. Se confía mucho en que esta vez las balsas resistirán, porque se ha seguido al pie de la letra la tradición de los indios ecuatorianos según la
(25)   cual la madera tiene que ser de árbol hembra y cortada durante luna llena. La explicación científica de este hecho que los indios efectuaban empíricamente es que durante la luna llena el árbol acumula mayor cantidad de savia, y ésta impide luego la saturación por agua. Los troncos de estas balsas fueron cortados y arrojados al río que los llevó, por más de
(30)   ochenta millas, hasta Guayaquil donde se comenzó la construcción.

1. ¿Qué tipo de aventura planeaba Vital Alsar?
   (A) Pensaba emprender un viaje imposible.
   (B) Pensaba recrear la trayectoria de un viaje épico.
   (C) Pensaba navegar desde Australia hasta Ecuador.
   (D) Pensaba explorar las selvas en busca de balsas.

2. ¿Qué es la balsa?
   (A) Es una especie de árbol cuya madera resiste bien el agua.
   (B) Es un tipo de nave para cruzar el océano.
   (C) Es un tipo de planta de cuyas hojas se construyen barcos.
   (D) Es un tipo de expedición.

3. ¿Por que fracasó la primera expedición?
   (A) Las primeras balsas no pudieron resistir el agua.
   (B) Alsar no leyó con cuidado el libro de Thor Heyerdhal.
   (C) La primera tripulación consistiá en marineros cobardes.
   (D) Alsar ignoró la tradición de los indios ecuatorianos.

4. ¿Cómo se llaman las tres balsas?
   (A) Guayaquil, Mooloolaba, y Aztlan.
   (B) Guayaquil, Brisbane, y Mooloolaba.
   (C) Mooloolaba, Brisbane, y Aztlan.
   (D) Mooloolaba, Australia, y Guayaquil.

5. ¿Por qué no llevará la expedición una bandera?
   (A) La tripulación no pudo ponerse de acuerdo de cuál usar.
   (B) Alsar no quiere agraviar a nadie.
   (C) Así se celebran las diferencias.
   (D) No hay una bandera internacional.

6. Según la sabiduría popular, ¿qué tipo de madera es necesario usar?
   (A) Es necesario que se corte un árbol de una región fluvial.
   (B) Es preciso que sea un árbol empapado de agua.
   (C) Sólo los árboles que hayan acumulado mucha savia sirven.
   (D) Es mejor que sea madera seleccionada por una expedición científica.

7. ¿Con qué cuenta Alsar para realizar esta expedición?
   (A) La sabiduría popular de los indígenas.
   (B) La precisión científica para construir bien las balsas.
   (C) Buen tiempo y una luna llena.
   (D) Tradición y preparación cautelosas.

8. ¿Cómo es Vital Alsar?
   (A) Es necio.
   (B) Es ingenuo.
   (C) Es atrevido.
   (D) Es introvertido.

CUARTO GRUPO, SELECCIÓN CUATRO

Ir a matar al príncipe de Orange. Ir a matar y cobrar luego los veinticinco mil escudos que ofreció Felipe II por su cabeza. Ir a pie, solo, sin
recursos, sin pistola, sin cuchillo, creando el género de los asesinos que

Línea piden a su víctima el dinero que hace falta para comprar el arma del
(5) crimen, tal fue la hazaña de Baltasar Gérard, un joven carpintero de
Dole.

A través de una penosa persecución por los Países Bajos, muerto de
hambre y de fatiga, padeciendo incontables demoras entre los ejércitos
españoles y flamencos, logró abrirse paso hasta su víctima. En dudas,
(10) rodeos y retrocesos invirtió tres años y tuvo que soportar la vejación de
que Gaspar Añastro le tomara la delantera.

El portugués Garpar Añastro, comerciante en paños, no carecía de
imaginación, sobre todo ante un señuelo de veinticinco mil escudos.
Hombre precavido, eligió cuidadosamente el procedimiento y la fecha
(15) del crimen. Pero a última hora decidió poner un intermediario entre su
cerebro y el arma: Juan Jáuregui la empuñaría por él.

Juan Jáuregui jovenzuelo de veinte años, era tímido de por sí. Pero
Añastro logró templar su alma hasta el heroísmo, mediante un sistema
de sutiles coacciones cuya secreta clave se nos escapa. Tal vez lo abrumó
(20) con lecturas heroicas; tal vez lo proveyó de talismanes; tal vez lo llevó
metódicamente hacia un consciente suicidio.

Lo único que sabemos con certeza es que el día señalado por su patrón
(18 de marzo de 1582), y durante los festivales celebrados en Amberes
para honrar al duque de Anjou en su cumpleaños, Jáuregui salió al paso
(25) de la comitiva y disparó sobre Guillermo de Orange a quemarropa. Pero
el muy imbécil había cargado el cañón de la pistola hasta la punta. El
arma estalló en su mano como una granada. Una esquirla de metal
traspasó la mejilla del príncipe. Jáuregui cayó al suelo, entre el séquito,
acribillado por violentas espadas.

1. ¿Dónde tiene lugar esta narrativa?
   (A) En Portugal.
   (B) En el sur de España.
   (C) En el norte de Europa.
   (D) En Granada.

2. El primer asesino en acercarse a la víctima fue
   (A) Guillermo de Orange.
   (B) Baltasar Gérard.
   (C) Gaspar Añastro.
   (D) Juan Jáuregui.

3. Garpar Añastro quería que
   (A) Baltasar Gérard matara a Guillermo de Orange.
   (B) Juan Jáuregui matara a Galtasar Gérard.
   (C) Juan Jáuregui matara a Guillermo de Orange.
   (D) Baltasar Gérard matara a Juan Jáuregui.

4. ¿Por qué querían los asesinos matar a su víctima?
   (A) Los portugueses odiaban a los flamencos.
   (B) Baltasar Gérard necesitaba dinero para comprar madera.
   (C) Querían ganar una recompensa.
   (D) Juan Jáurigui era imbécil.

5. ¿Cómo ayudó Gaspar Añastro a Juan Jáuregui a superar su timidez?
   (A) Le ofreció veinticinco mil escudos.
   (B) Le entrenó con mitos y leyendas de guerra.
   (C) Le convenció de la verdad de la tarea.
   (D) Le prometió festejarlo al realizar el proyecto.

6. ¿Quién murió a fin de cuentas?
   (A) El duque de Anjou.
   (B) Guillermo de Orange.
   (C) Gaspar Añastro.
   (D) Juan Jáuregui.

7. ¿Cómo murió?
   (A) Lo acuchillaron.
   (B) Lo fusilaron.
   (C) Murió de hambre.
   (D) Se suicidó.

8. ¿Cómo era Juan Jáuregui?
   (A) Era heroico.
   (B) Era intrépido.
   (C) Era inteligente.
   (D) Era necio.

QUINTO GRUPO, SELECCIÓN UNO

En el trayecto que se me había encomendado recorrer, hay un puente, en el que a intervalo de un minuto, debían circular por una vía única dos trenes: el que yo manejaba y un tren de mercancías. Sabiendo el

Línea peligro de estos cruces, se me habían hecho mil recomendaciones,
(5) inútiles, por otra parte, pues es de suponer la atención que pondría yo en las señales luminosas.

Al acercarnos al puente en cuestión, divisé claramente la luz verde, que me daba libre paso, y respirando aliviado, aumenté un poco la velocidad de nuestra marcha, no mucho sin embargo, dado que había

(10) que cruzar un puente y podría resultar peligroso.

Segundos después se sintió una sacudida intensísima y se oyó un ruido horrible: los dos trenes chocaron, se incendiaron y se desmenuzaron. Hubo cientos de muertos y miles de heridos. Por una rara casualidad yo quedé ileso. ¡Ojalá hubiera muerto!

(15) Nunca podré olvidar un espectáculo tan espantoso. Como siempre sucede en las catástrofes, la sensación de espanto no es simultánea con el choque; sólo al cabo de algunos minutos, cuando vi las llamas de los coches que ardían, cuando distinguí las dos locomotoras semi-erguidas como dos hombres que luchan por derribarse, cuando oí los lamentos de

(20)   los heridos y vi las ambulancias que acudían a levantar las víctimas, sólo
entonces me di cuenta de lo que acababa de suceder.

1. ¿Qué se narra en este trozo?
   (A) Un encuentro entre amigos.
   (B) Un desastre natural.
   (C) Una colisión.
   (D) La circulación de trenes.

2. ¿Qué es el narrador?
   (A) Un bombero.
   (B) Un pasajero.
   (C) Un espectador.
   (D) Un conductor.

3. Según lo que dice, este narrador
   (A) No llevaba mucho tiempo en su empleo.
   (B) Es aficionado a los trenes.
   (C) Tenía mucha experiencia manejando trenes.
   (D) No conocía bien el territorio que atravesaba.

4. ¿Cuál fue la causa del acontecimiento?
   (A) El narrador se durmió mientras trabajaba.
   (B) El narrador no hizo caso de un semáforo.
   (C) El otro conductor se equivocó.
   (D) El narrador iba en exceso de la velocidad.

5. ¿Qué significan las palabras *¡Ojalá hubiera muerto!* en la línea 14?
   (A) El narrador estaba mal herido.
   (B) El narrador se sentía responsable.
   (C) No sintió que tantos inocentes murieran.
   (D) Se sentía culpable por escapar daño.

6. ¿Cómo reaccionó el narrador a lo que pasó?
   (A) Se quedó atónito.
   (B) Fue traumatizado.
   (C) Estaba asustado.
   (D) Estaba tranquilo.

QUINTO GRUPO, SELECCIÓN DOS

Cuando vi a Dora por tercera vez en brazos de un amigo diferente no
esperé más. Y tomé una decisión: no la volvería a ver en mi vida.

Dicen que el mejor remedio para estas cosas es viajar; hasta tal punto
Línea debe ser cierto que tuve una vez una novia que, después de haberme
(5) hecho sufrir como inocente en el infierno me recomendó ella misma el
cambio de lugar. Cosa que me inspiró el doble temor de que esa mujer
me estaba tomando por imbécil y tenía comisión por envío de clientes a
un balneario.

Como estábamos en pleno febrero bien podía elegir Mar del Plata, "la
(10) aristocrática playa". La vida agitada y tonta del balneario me haría olvidar.

Reuní unos pesos, unas camisas y saqué un boleto "fin de semana".
Subí al vagón, no sin pensar un poco, involuntariamente, en la posible
aventura de viaje.

Es realmente asombroso, pero es el caso que los "magazines" ilustra-
(15) dos y las escritoras americanas tienen una pasión morbosa por ese tema:
Irremediablemente, sube al tren "momentos antes de la salida" (¡qué gracia! bueno fuera "momentos después de la salida"), el joven escritor, elegante, atlético y famoso. La casualidad quiere que la bella y misteriosa
viajera lea en ese mismo instante su última novela. (Un detalle siempre
(20) es "su última novela"; podría suceder, tratándose de un escritor prolífico
y famoso, que la hermosa joven leyese la penúltima o la antepenúltima.
Pero según parece hay un consorcio de escritores de esta categoría y
nadie puede introducir innovaciones al estilo de la sociedad que es
intangible). Una conversación se entabla pronto, sobre todo cuando los
(25) dos interlocutores son jóvenes.

1. ¿Qué le aconsejó una vez una mujer a este narrador?
   (A) Que se fuera de vacaciones.
   (B) Que hablara con un escritor de "magazines".
   (C) Que llevara a unos clientes a un balneario.
   (D) Que tuviera una aventura.

2. ¿Por qué decidió visitar Mar del Plata?
   (A) Porque todos los aristócratas iban allí en el invierno.
   (B) Porque habría mucha actividad vacía para pasar el tiempo.
   (C) Porque todos los escritores estarían allí.
   (D) Porque podría leer muchos libros.

3. ¿Qué desea olvidar este narrador?
   (A) Una novela que leyó.
   (B) Un negocio fracasado.
   (C) Una relación amorosa.
   (D) Una joven que leyó su novela.

4. ¿En qué tema tienen las escritoras americanas *una pasión morbosa*?
   (A) Los amores fracasados.
   (B) La posibilidad de aventuras inesperadas.
   (C) Conversaciones casuales en trenes.
   (D) Viajes ferrocarrileros con autores famosos.

5. ¿Qué hizo al subir al vagón?
   (A) Entabló una conversación con un escritor.
   (B) Observó el encuentro de dos otros pasajeros.
   (C) Empezó a leer una novela a una joven.
   (D) Imaginó una aventura entre dos personas.

6. ¿Qué parece opinar el narrador del joven escritor?
   (A) Admira su atleticismo.
   (B) Envidia su popularidad.
   (C) Se enoja que tenga tanto éxito.
   (D) Lo odia porque es famoso.

7. En la línea 21, ¿cuál es el tono de las palabras *que la hermosa joven leyese la penúltima o antepenúltima*?
   (A) Sarcástico.
   (B) Irónico.
   (C) Trágico.
   (D) Chismoso.

8. ¿Cuál es la actitud del narrador en este trozo?
   (A) Está deprimido.
   (B) Parece muy desilusionado.
   (C) Está muy enamorado.
   (D) Tiene buen sentido de humor.

QUINTO GRUPO, SELECCIÓN TRES

Complemento indispensable del estudio de las enfermedades simuladas es el de la *simulación de la salud*, por sujetos verdaderamente enfermos, o sea la disimulación de la enfermedad. Su objetivo se comprende fácilmente: cuando el estar enfermo determina una situación de inferioridad en la lucha por la vida, el sujeto recurre a la simulación de la salud.

En la vida ordinaria es frecuentísimo. Las reglas de la más simple urbanidad la imponen en el trato de gentes; pocas personas habrá que nunca hayan disimulado una dolencia de poca monta, para recibir con la sonrisa en los labios a un amigo o amiga estimada. Se asiste a tertulias disimulando una cefalalgia, a un banquete disimulando una dispepsia o una colitis, a una cita amorosa disimulando una cistitis. Muchos lectores habrán disimulado en su juventud alguna enfermedad que reputaban vergonzosa, hasta que la intensidad de los síntomas los obligó a denunciarse al médico y a su propia familia.

Disimulan sus enfermedades cuantos están obligados a probar que gozan de perfecta salud para ser admitidos en un establecimiento o corporación, o para aspirar a ciertos empleos; nunca faltarán médicos complacientes que se hagan cómplices activos de estas disimulaciones, expidiendo certificados falsos. Entre esas disimulaciones de la salud existe un grupo especial que recientemente ha alcanzado extraordinaria importancia en medicina forense. El desarrollo de las instituciones de seguros sobre la vida ha producido formas especiales de simulación para explotarla fraudulentamente. Sujetos poco escrupulosos aseguran en su favor la vida de parientes enfermos; rara manifestación de la lucha por la existencia, cuyo estudio agregaría un capítulo interesante a la psicopatología de los parásitos sociales.

Línea (5) (10) (15) (20) (25)

1. ¿Cuál es el tema de esta selección?
   (A) Maneras de disimular.
   (B) Razonamientos para fingir.
   (C) Un análisis psicológico de los embusteros.
   (D) Consecuencias de la urbanización.

2. ¿Con qué motivo disimulan enfermedades algunas personas?
   (A) Quieren provocar la simpatía de sus amigos.
   (B) Quieren revelar la negligencia de los médicos.
   (C) Son mentirosas patológicas.
   (D) Creen que la cortesía requiere que finjan sus enfermedades.

3. ¿Cómo juzgaría este autor la disimulación de enfermedades?
   (A) Cree que es de poca consecuencia.
   (B) Cree que es imperdonable.
   (C) Cree que depende de la situación y edad de la persona.
   (D) Cree que la disimulación consta una decepción criminal.

4. En cambio, la disimulación de salud a veces
   (A) Se debe a complejos de martirio.
   (B) Se exige para superar las contrariedades de la vida.
   (C) Se debe a la avaricia de algunos médicos.
   (D) Se debe a la necesidad de mantener las apariencias.

5. ¿Cuál ha sido el resultado del establecimiento de instituciones de seguros?
   (A) Ahora no se recurre a la disimulación para conseguir lo que quieren.
   (B) Se ha prolongado la vida a causa de mejor atención a la salud.
   (C) Hay más enfermos ahora que antes.
   (D) Se ha aumentado el fraude.

6. Un ejemplo de *los parásitos sociales* (línea 27) sería
   (A) Médicos poco escrupulosos.
   (B) Personas que se enferman para allegar fondos propios.
   (C) Las instituciones de seguros.
   (D) Parientes de enfermos que suscriben pólizas a su propio beneficio.

QUINTO GRUPO, SELECCIÓN CUATRO

No conozco otro deporte que nos pueda librar tan completamente de
la pesadilla de la vida. ¡Cuánta renovación espiritual debo a las montañas! Hay que levantarse de vez en cuando también corporalmente por

Línea encima de las masas humanas y de sus ciudades estrechas. El deporte
(5) alpinista somete todas las fuerzas del cuerpo a un solo fin. La subida
requiere una adaptación constante de todas las fibras orgánicas a las dificultades de la subida. Los pulmones se extienden, la sangre se renueva y
la vida celular de todo el organismo se hace más intensa. A medida que
alcanzamos mayor altura nuestro esfuerzo crece y pronto estamos
(10) ansiosos de llegar a nuestro fin. La vista se expande libremente y nuevos
paisajes jamás contemplados aparecen poco a poco. En fin, llegamos a la
cima, y un panorama sublime se extiende a nuestros pies. No se puede
imaginar una vida más libre, más concentrada, más sana y más feliz que
una caminata de dos o tres semanas por los cerros nevados de los Alpes
(15) de un refugio al otro, llevando consigo en la mochila todo lo poco que el
hombre precisa. Significa una renovación completa de todo el organismo. Mi mejor deseo es poder continuar esta clase de deportes hasta la
edad más avanzada que pueda alcanzar. Me causa una satisfacción singular encontrar aquí a los bordes del Nahuel Huapi, el primer refugio en

(20) tierra argentina. Ojalá que sea el principio de un movimiento deportivo andino para toda la juventud de hoy, para que aprenda a conocer todas las bellezas de su gran país. En estas bellezas íntimamente sentidas radica el amor intenso por la tierra natal. No se puede imaginar a algún artista nacional que no esté penetrado en todo su ser por las bellezas

(25) propias de las diferentes provincias del suelo de la patria. El gran valor educativo del deporte andino está en el hecho de que requiere un esfuerzo concentrado de toda la personalidad. Sólo un esfuerzo máximo nos llena con el sentimiento de la superioridad ganada y nos revela la belleza sublime de la montaña alta.

1. ¿Por qué alaba tanto al alpinismo este narrador?
   (A) Tiene atractivos casi místicos.
   (B) Se pierde cuidado.
   (C) Se puede sentirse superior a las masas.
   (D) Se puede dormir mejor después de practicarlo.

2. Este deporte requiere que
   (A) Una persona viaje a Europa para subir montañas.
   (B) Una persona dedique la vida al deporte.
   (C) Una persona enfoque en el momento presente.
   (D) Una persona ame su país.

3. ¿Qué recomienda este narrador a los jóvenes?
   (A) Que estudien la biología antes de participar.
   (B) Que experimenten las inconveniencias de la vida sencilla.
   (C) Que aprendan a apreciar la naturaleza.
   (D) Que se hagan artistas para sentir más intensamente la belleza.

4. ¿Cuál ha sido la experiencia personal del narrador?
   (A) El deporte le ha proporcionado nuevas vistas hermosas.
   (B) A causa del deporte se siente más joven que nunca.
   (C) Debido al esfuerzo físico ha gozado de una renovación total.
   (D) Ha aprendido a apreciar las montañas andinas más que las europeas.

5. Sobre todo, ¿qué aprenderá la juventud al participar en este deporte?
   (A) Aprenderán a subir montañas.
   (B) Extrañarán las montañas mientras vivan entre las masas.
   (C) Entrañarán toda la belleza natural del país.
   (D) Aprenderán que son superiores a otros seres humanos.

6. ¿Cuál parece ser la ocasión de esta declaración?
   (A) La dedicación de una reserva andina.
   (B) La dedicación de una estación veraniega.
   (C) La dedicación de un negocio alpinista.
   (D) La dedicación de una montaña andina.

Answers for Reading Comprehension

Primer Grupo, Selección Uno
1. A 2. B 3. B 4. C
5. D 6. A 7. B

Primer Grupo, Selección Dos
1. B 2. C 3. A 4. A
5. B 6. B 7. A 8. D

Primer Grupo, Selección Tres
1. B 2. C 3. B 4. B
5. A 6. C 7. C

Primer Grupo, Selección Cuatro
1. D 2. D 3. D 4. A
5. B 6. D

Segundo Grupo, Selección Uno
1. D 2. A 3. B 4. B
5. C 6. D 7. A 8. C

Segundo Grupo, Selección Dos
1. B 2. B 3. D 4. D
5. C 6. D 7. B 8. D

Segundo Grupo, Selección Tres
1. C 2. A 3. A 4. C
5. B 6. B 7. D 8. C

Segundo Grupo, Selección Cuatro
1. B 2. C 3. C 4. A
5. A 6. D 7. B

Tercer Grupo, Selección Uno
1. D 2. C 3. B 4. C
5. A 6. A 7. B 8. D

Tercer Grupo, Selección Dos
1. B 2. B 3. A 4. D
5. A

Tercer Grupo, Selección Tres
1. B 2. B 3. D 4. A

Tercer Grupo, Selección Cuatro
1. C 2. D 3. D 4. C
5. C 6. A 7. D

Cuarto Grupo, Selección Uno
1. D 2. A 3. A 4. D
5. C 6. B 7. C

Cuarto Grupo, Selección Dos
1. C 2. D 3. C 4. C
5. B 6. A

Cuarto Grupo, Selección Tres
1. B 2. A 3. A 4. A
5. D 6. C 7. D 8. C

Cuarto Grupo, Selección Cuatro
1. C 2. D 3. C 4. C
5. B 6. D 7. A 8. D

Quinto Grupo, Selección Uno
1. C 2. D 3. A 4. C
5. C 6. B

Quinto Grupo, Selección Dos
1. A 2. B 3. C 4. B
5. D 6. B 7. A 8. B

Quinto Grupo, Selección Tres
1. B 2. A 3. C 4. B
5. D 6. D

Quinto Grupo, Selección Cuatro
1. A 2. C 3. C 4. C
5. C 6. A

PART FOUR WRITING SKILLS

GENERAL CONSIDERATIONS (Section II, Part A)

Description of the Exam

This section consists of four free response tasks in which you will demonstrate your ability to use the written language. The four tasks are (1) paragraph completion with root words, (2) paragraph completion without root words, (3) informal writing, and (4) formal writing. Paragraph completion with root words takes 7 minutes and counts 2.5 percent of the total score. Paragraph completion without root words takes 8 minutes and counts another 2.5 percent. Informal writing takes 10 minutes and counts 5 percent. Formal writing takes 55 minutes and counts 20 percent. The combined writing part counts 30 percent of the final score. While the first two tasks (paragraph completion with and without root words) of the exam have remained virtually unchanged during many years, the informal and formal writing tasks have undergone significant changes lately by the addition of print and audio source materials that accompany the questions for the topic of every essay.

Knowing the way the tasks are organized can help you organize the writing of the essay. There is a general progression in the nature of the tasks. At the beginning (paragraph completion with root words), all the cues are presented to you. Next (paragraph completion without root words), the task is similar, except that there are no words provided to indicate what is needed to complete the meaning of the passage. For informal writing you have only a short writing sample, such as a memo or an e-mail, which you must develop. Finally there is formal writing, with no prescribed length, where you simply show how well you can write an essay.

There are two aspects of language that you show in your writing. The first is your vocabulary—words, phrases, and expressions—as well as grammar and syntax. The other aspect is the content of your writing. In the exam there are source materials that are provided with the prompts that define the topic. The exam will test your ability to understand the language used in the source materials, both printed and audio, and your ability to express in writing your thoughts and reactions to the question posed in the prompt. The essay is expository or persuasive, meaning that you are to refer to information contained in the source materials and incorporate it into your response to a question related to the source material.

Scoring

The first two tasks of the free response exercises are graded as correct or incorrect. For the informal and formal writing tasks, the grading is holistic: No points are deducted for incorrect grammar or words that do not mean what you think they mean. The grader forms an overall impression of your ability based on how the sample measures up against the rubrics for writing. Both language and content are important in your response. Your language should be clear, free of grammatical errors that would confuse your reader or of words that do not say exactly what you want them to say. Content includes not only your own ideas and thoughts, but how well you have incorporated pertinent information from the print and audio sources provided.

Using This Book

There are five sets of exercises in this chapter that are designed to help you focus on the most common grammatical problems: (1) Paragraph completion with root words with one-word answers, (2) paragraph completion with root words with two-word answers, (3) paragraph completion without root words,

(4) informal writing, and (5) formal writing. In previous chapters you have done multiple choice exercises to review vocabulary and grammar. In this chapter you are to produce correct words and grammar without seeing any suggestions like those found in multiple choice options. You will see that there is a difference between recognizing a correctly conjugated verb, for example, and knowing how to conjugate it without seeing any model. This chapter provides lots of practice in this respect.

The paragraph completions in this book are not exactly the same as the paragraph completions that appear on the exam, because the material in this book is designed to help you review the grammar and vocabulary you need for the actual exam. The paragraph completion with root words has been divided into two parts, one with one-word answers and another with two-word answers, to help you familiarize with the kind of sentence structures in which you would use two-word answers. For the informal and formal writing sections, the writing practice in this book more closely resembles the format and topics you may see on the exam. In practicing with these exercises, you are encouraged to pre-think the writing tasks. That way, during the actual exam you will be better prepared to answer without spending too much time searching for the right words. Pay particular attention to register (use of second-person *tú* or *vosotros* and third-person *usted* or *ustedes*).

The formal writing task practice in this chapter offers you some samples based on printed and audio sources. You are to incorporate specific details from both in your response. There will be suggestions on how to organize your thoughts for the formal essay. Remember that all writers have personal styles and that you should develop your own. Also remember that there are some aspects of good writing that are common to all styles. The following pages have some exercises to help you review the grammar you need to know, take notes on the source materials provided, organize your ideas, and write a strong essay. There are some suggestions to help you develop certain aspects of writing, such as description, narrative, analysis, and opinion. Vocabulary is provided to help you organize your thoughts in a logical manner, so that your essay is richer and clearer.

Preparing for the Exam

For paragraph completion with root words, there are 33 selections with groups of about 10 items in each selection. For paragraph completion without root words, there are 20 samples, along with answers and explanations to help you figure out how to do the task. All these exercises focus on the kind of grammatical structures you need to include in your writing samples on the last two tasks of the exam. Before you begin this chapter, you should review vocabulary from other sections, as well as the grammar synopsis in the appendix of this book. Explanations for the answers follow each practice set. Instead of focusing only on getting the right answer, concentrate on the grammatical rule that the item reviews. Try to correct any misconceptions about how to say something coherently and intelligibly in Spanish, so that when the moment comes to write your last two responses, you will show excellent command of grammar and vocabulary.

The topics that are listed in the book are not necessarily the topics that will appear on the exam, but they are designed to help you think about broad issues and formulate some opinions. The process that you develop for discussing the topics will be useful to you in writing an essay on the exam because you will not have to waste time trying to decide how to say what you want to say.

CHAPTER 7

Free-Response Tasks
(Section II, Part A)

TASK 1: PARAGRAPH COMPLETION WITH ROOT WORDS—LONG PASSAGES

In paragraph completion exercises, root words are prompts telling you which words you must use to complete the selection in a logical and grammatical way. The word is written under the blank lines to the right of the paragraph. The root words are different parts of speech, such as infinitives, adjectives, or pronouns, to test a variety of grammar points that include verb conjugation, adjective noun agreement, definite and indefinite articles, adjective constructions of equality or inequality, and superlative constructions. For example, if you see an infinitive for the root word, you must determine in what conjugated form this infinitive needs to go in the blank.

If you have to conjugate the verb, then you need to determine the subject, the mood (indicative or subjunctive), and the correct tense (present, preterit, imperfect, and so on). No credit is given if you omit accent marks (á, é, í, ó, ú) or other diacritical marks, such as the tilde (ñ) or the dieresis (ü). If an accent is written where it does not belong, the whole word is also incorrect. You may need to use more than one word (in compound tenses, for example). Even if there is no change, you need to write the word on the line in the blank provided. At times there may be more than one correct answer. If so, you will receive credit for any of the possibilities.

On the following pages are exercises to give you practice for this part of the exam. Here is how to do this section:

1. Scan the whole passage.
2. If the word is a verb, find the subject and notice the tenses of other verbs in the paragraph.
3. If the word is an adjective, locate the noun to which it refers and decide the gender and number of that noun.
4. If the construction is a comparison, make sure to use the correct form of *tan, tanto, tantos, tanta,* or *tantas,* according to the part of speech it precedes.
5. Review other points of grammar in the back of this book if you are unsure about any other structures.

Directions: On the numbered line corresponding to a numbered blank in the selection, write the correct form of the word needed to complete the passage logically and grammatically. All spelling and all diacritical marks must be correct. You may use more than one word. You must write the answer on the line after the number, even if you do not change the root word in any way. You have 7 minutes to read and write your responses.

EXERCISES AND ANSWERS

GROUP ONE

El caso es que la princesa, bella,

brillante y sonriente no es feliz. En verdad,

tiene que esforzarse para parecer tan son-

riente. Y ahora tiene que soportar que

___(1)___ sus tristezas ___(2)___ que la

___(3)___ a desear la paz. Es mucha carga

___(4)___ responsabilidad, y los discursos

de bienvenida, y toda la agenda que le deja

poco tiempo para vivir. Pero siempre se

comporta como si no ___(5)___ nada. A

veces, viéndola tratar de aparecer elegante

y ___(6)___ , se pregunta si tendría ___(7)___

rasgo de acidez ___(8)___ . Hay que

preguntarse si, por toda la riqueza que

___(9)___ como princesa, de veras ___(10)___

la pena.

1. _____
   (publicar)

2. _____
   (profundo)

3. _____
   (llevar)

4. _____
   (tanto)

5. _____
   (pasar)

6. _____
   (sencillo)

7. _____
   (alguno)

8. _____
   (disimulado)

9. _____
   (tener)

10. _____
    (valer)

Answers and Answer Explanations for Group One

1. *publiquen* *Publicar* is an orthographic verb. The subjunctive is used because this is a dependent noun clause after a verb of volition.
2. *profundas* This adjective modifies *tristezas*, a feminine plural noun.
3. *llevan* The subject is *tristezas*. This verb occurs in an adjective clause with a known antecedent, so the indicative is correct.
4. *tanta* This comparative structure requires that the adjective agree in gender and number with the noun, *responsabilidad*. All words that end in *-dad* are feminine.
5. *pasara* The past subjunctive must always be used after *como si*. The subject of *pasara* is *ella*, the same subject as for *se comporta*.
6. *sencilla* The adjective agrees with *ella*. The referent is given in the direct object pronoun at the end of the verb form: *viéndola*.
7. *algún* This adjective is apocopated, and an accent is written over the *u* in the last syllable. No credit is given if the accent is not written on the vowel.

8. *disimulado*   This adjective modifies *rasgo*, not *acidez*, so the masculine singular form is used.

9. *tenga*   The subjunctive is used because this is a dependent adjective clause and the antecedent, *riqueza,* is indefinite. In the adjective clauses look for the construction *por* + (adjective) + *que...* to indicate to you to use the subjunctive.

10. *vale*   The present indicative is used because the present subjunctive is not frequently used after *si*.

GROUP TWO

Me estuve muy quieta, ____(1)____ en la

cama, mirando recelosa alrededor,

asombrada del retorcido mechón de mi

propio cabello que resaltaba oscuramente

contra mi hombro. Habituándome a la

penumbra, ____(2)____ , uno a uno, los

desconchados de la pared, las grandes

enzarzadas de la cama, como serpientes,

dragones o misteriosas figuras que apenas

me atrevía a mirar. Incliné el cuerpo

cuanto ____(3)____ hacia la mesilla, para

coger el vaso de agua ____(4)____ ,

y entonces, en el vértice de la pared,

descubrí una hilera de hormigas que

____(5)____ por el muro. Solté el vaso que se

____(6)____ al caer, y me ____(7)____ de nuevo

entre las sábanas, tapándome la cabeza. No

me decidía a sacar ni ____(8)____ mano, y

así estuve mucho rato, ____(9)____ los

labios. Hice recorrer mi imaginación como

por ____(10)____ bosque y jardín

desconocidos hasta tranquilizarme.

1. _____ (sentado)
2. _____ (localizar)
3. _____ (poder)
4. _____ (tibio)
5. _____ (trepar)
6. _____ (romper)
7. _____ (hundir)
8. _____ (uno)
9. _____ (morderse)
10. _____ (alguno)

Answers and Answer Explanations for Group Two

1. *sentada*   This past participle functions as an adjective and the antecedent is feminine, indicated by the ending of the previous adjective: *quieta*.
2. *localicé*   *Localizar* is an orthographic verb. The preterit indicative is used because the action occurred in a defined point of time in the past. If no accent is used, no credit is given, since the verb without the accent would be a present subjunctive form.
3. *pude*   The preterit indicative is used here because the action takes place in a defined point in time in the past. The meaning of the preterit of *poder* is *managed,* or *was able to.*
4. *tibia*   This adjective modifies *agua*, which is a feminine noun, even though in the singular form a masculine article, *el*, is used.
5. *trepaban*   The imperfect indicative is used here to describe an action. The narrator is telling what the ants *were doing*, in which case the imperfect is indicated.
6. *rompió*   The preterit indicative is used because the action occurred at a specific point of time in the past. The action is narrated, not described.
7. *hundí*   The preterit indicative is used because the action takes place at a specific point in time in the past. The action is narrated.
8. *una*   *Mano* is a feminine noun, requiring the feminine form of the indefinite article, *una*.
9. *mordiéndome*   The present participle is used as an adverb, showing the attitude or how the narrator was huddled under the sheets on the bed. Remember to use the first person singular reflexive pronoun to agree with the subject of the verb *estuve*.
10. *algún*   The indefinite adjective *alguno* is shortened before masculine singular nouns, such as *bosque*. Notice that there is an accent written on the final syllable. *Algunos* is correct if the adjective refers to *jardines* and *bosques*.

GROUP THREE

Su agradable y delicado perfume,

____(1)____ a una eficacia indiscutible

____(2)____ inigualable, han sido, sin lugar a

dudas, las claves del éxito de este producto

y el motivo de que millones de personas

____(3)____ tanto tiempo ____(4)____ en este

producto, que lejos de ser una moda o un

invento es EL DESODORANTE. Toda una

línea de higiene personal ha sido ____(5)____

1. _____
   (unido)

2. _____
   (y)

3. _____
   (llevar)

4. _____
   (confiar)

5. _____
   (crear)

al amparo de la imagen de marca más

fuerte en el mundo. La ____(6)____ fidelidad

de marca de que goza este producto, lo ha

situado en un privilegiado ____(7)____

puesto que siempre ha intentado____(8)____

alcanzado por las restantes marcas de la

competencia. Desde su creación, hace ya

más de 50 años, este producto ____(9)____

liderando el mercado nacional. ____(10)____

Ud. en nuestro producto.

6. _____
   (grande)

7. _____
   (primero)

8. _____
   (ser)

9. _____
   (venir)

10. _____
   (confiar)

Answers and Answer Explanations for Group Three

1. *unido*   The adjective agrees with the noun *perfume,* not with the noun's adjectives: *agradable* and *delicado.* The following sentence makes clear that the qualities of the perfume, combined with the effectiveness of the product are the keys to the success of the product.

2. *e*   The conjunction *y* changes because the initial letter of the following word is *i, inigualable.*

3. *lleven*   The present subjunctive is used because in the adverbial clause motivation, or purpose, is expressed.

4. *confiando*   The present participle is used as an adverb to describe how people are using so much time.

5. *creada*   The feminine form of the past participle is used because it is the object of *ser.* It agrees with the subject of *ha sido,* which is *línea.*

6. *gran*   The adjective, *grande,* is apocopated before singular nouns, such as *fidelidad.* Use the apocopated (shortened), form with both masculine and feminine singular nouns.

7. *primer*   The adjective, *primero,* is apocopated before masculine singular nouns, such as *puesto.*

8. *ser*   The infinitive is used because it is the object of the verb: *ha intentado.*

9. *viene*   The present indicative is used because the verb occurs in the main clause with an expression of time.

10. *Confíe*   The command form is indicated by the placement of *Ud.* after the verb. Notice the accent written on the *i.*

GROUP FOUR

Al sol, ya se sabe, hay que ___(1)___ con

las espaldas bien ___(2)___. ___(3)___

imprudencia nos está ___(4)___ , pues este

astro, que ___(5)___ una memoria de

elefante, puede ___(6)___ factura cuando

menos nos lo esperamos. Sirve que

nosotros lo ___(7)___ en cuenta al comprar

un bronceador. Vale que ___(8)___ uno

que nos ___(9)___ seguridad total de los

efectos de los rayos ultravioleta. Ahora

___(10)___ del sol veranal traspasa

cuestiones estéticas.

1. _____
   (acercarse)

2. _____
   (cubierto)

3. _____
   (ninguno)

4. _____
   (permitido)

5. _____
   (poseer)

6. _____
   (pasarse)

7. _____
   (tener)

8. _____
   (buscar)

9. _____
   (ofrecer)

10. _____
    (protegerse)

Answers and Answer Explanations for Group Four

1. *acercarse*   Although the verb is preceded by *que*, in this case it forms part of the expression *hay que*, which requires the infinitive.
2. *cubiertas*   The past participle is used as an adjective and refers to the noun, *espaldas*.
3. *Ninguna*   The negative indefinite adjective refers to a feminine noun, *imprudencia*. The feminine form of this adjective is never shortened.
4. *permitida*   The past participle is used as an adjective and refers to the subject of the verb *está*, which is *imprudencia*.
5. *posee*   The present indicative is used because it occurs in an adjective clause referring to a definite antecedent, *astro*, which in turn is another name for *el sol*.
6. *pasarnos*   The infinitive is used because it is the object of the verb *puede*. The first person plural indirect object pronoun is used because the first person plural subject is indicated in the following verb: *esperamos*.
7. *tengamos*   The present subjunctive is used because it occurs in a dependent noun clause after an impersonal expression: *sirve que*.
8. *busquemos*   The present subjunctive is used because it occurs in a dependent noun clause after an impersonal expression: *Vale que*. Notice

that not all impersonal expressions begin with the verb *ser*. If you can determine that the subject of the verb is *it* and it has no specific antecedent, you can always recognize when to use the subjunctive after an impersonal expression.

9. *ofrezca*   The present subjunctive is used because it occurs in a dependent adjective clause in which the antecedent is indefinite, *uno*, which in turn refers to *un bronceador*.

10. *protegernos*   The infinitive is used because it is the subject of the verb *traspasa*. The first person plural object pronoun is used because *our* reactions to the power of the sun's rays has been the topic of the passage.

GROUP FIVE

Estas Olimpiadas prepárate a ganar.

____(1)____ dos códigos de barras de

____(2)____ producto que tú ____(3)____ a

Marca X al Apartado 999, 38565 Madrid, y

un fantástico Lulu de Oro puede ser tuyo.

O bien ____(4)____ millón de pesetas. Los

sorteos se ____(5)____ ante notario el treinta

de junio, el treinta de julio y el ____(6)____

de septiembre del año próximo. ¡Anímate!

Tienes mucho que ganar. Y ____(7)____ que

____(8)____ más cartas ____(9)____, más fácil

será ganar. No ____(10)____ escapar tu Lulu.

Es una ocasión de oro.

1. _____
   (Enviar)

2. _____
   (cualquiera)

3. _____
   (querer)

4. _____
   (uno)

5. _____
   (celebrar)

6. _____
   (primero)

7. _____
   (recordar)

8. _____
   (cuánto)

9. _____
   (mandar)

10. _____
    (dejar)

Answers and Answer Explanations for Group Five

1. *Envía*   The affirmative familiar singular command form of the verb is indicated by the use of the second person singular command in the first sentence, *prepárate*. Do not be confused because the object in the sentence comes first. This stylistic device, inverting the word order of the sentence, simply emphasizes the noun, *Olimpíadas*.

2. *cualquier*   This indefinite adjective is apocopated before nouns of both genders.

3. *quieras* The present subjunctive is used because the verb occurs in a dependent adjective clause after an indefinite antecedent: *un producto*.

4. *un* The apocopated form of *uno* is required before the number *millión*. Notice that *millón* takes the preposition *de* when it is followed by a noun.

5. *celebrarán* This verb is the *se* substitute for the passive voice. *Los sorteos* is plural, so the verb is in the third person plural.

6. *primero* The ordinal number for the first day of the month is not apocopated.

7. *recuerda* The affirmative familiar singular command form is required because the context of the verb in the selection and the meaning of the word indicate an instruction to the reader.

8. *cuántas* The interrogative form agrees with *cartas*.

9. *mandes* The present subjunctive is used because it occurs in an adjective clause referring to *cuántas cartas*, an indefinite antecedent.

10. *dejes* The verb is a negative familiar singular command, which is indicated by the context of the verb.

GROUP SIX

El Real Decreto dice: *El producto*

cosmético indicará la fórmula cualitativa y

cuantitativa de las substancias ___(1)___

presencia ___(2)___ *en la denominación*

del producto o en su publicidad. ___(3)___

quiere decir que todos los productos en

cuya confección ___(4)___ materias activas

naturales provenientes de plantas deben

especificar claramente el porcentaje de

materia activa en sus etiquetas, estuches y

publicidad. Consecuente con esto, y con

___(5)___ más de 75 años ___(6)___ con

1. _____
(cuyo)

2. _____
(anunciarse)

3. _____
(Este)

4. _____
(intervenir)

5. _____
(nuestro)

6. _____
(trabajar)

extractos naturales de plantas, le

informamos que nuestros productos tienen

un porcentaje exacto porque en nuestra

opinión, ___(7)___ porcentajes son los

necesarios para que ___(8)___ materias

activas ___(9)___ el beneficio natural

esperado de la planta. ___(10)___ la forma

de averiguar la materia activa que cada

producto contiene, usted debe decidir lo

que más le conviene.

7. _____
   (ese)

8. _____
   (dicho)

9. _____
   (realizar)

10. _____
    (conocer)

Answers and Answer Explanations for Group Six

1. *cuya*   This possessive agrees with *presencia*, not *sustancias*.
2. *se anuncie*   The present subjunctive is used because it occurs in an adjective clause referring to the indefinite antecedent *presencia*.
3. *Esto*   The neuter demonstrative pronoun is used here because *This* refers to the whole idea expressed in the previous sentence.
4. *intervengan*   The present subjunctive is used because the verb occurs in a dependent adjective clause with an indefinite antecedent *confección*. The subject is *materias*.
5. *nuestros*   This possessive modifies *años* so it is masculine plural.
6. *trabajando*   This present participle tells how an action was done.
7. *esos*   The masculine plural form of the demonstrative adjective is used because it modifies *porcentajes*.
8. *dichas*   The feminine form of the past participle is used because it functions as an adjective modifying the word *materias*.
9. *realicen*   The present subjunctive is used because it occurs in a dependent adverbial clause after *para que*.
10. *Conociendo*   The present participle functions as an absolute. An absolute construction means that the present participle refers to the whole sentence that follows it.

GROUP SEVEN

La Ley Civil ___(1)___ ayuda en

___(2)___ modo a que las parejas ___(3)___

se lo ___(4)___ un poco más antes de

presentar la demanda de divorcio: el

matrimonio entra de nuevo en vigor si los

separados vuelven a convivir. Si a pesar de

todo el divorcio se presenta como la

opción más ___(5)___, hay que ___(6)___

que ___(7)___ un año desde que se firmó la

solicitud de separación. No es necesario

que se haya ___(8)___ sentencia. También

se puede acceder al divorcio sin una

separación previa, aunque ___(9)___

transcurrir dos años y ___(10)___ las causas

debidamente.

1. _____ (español)

2. _____ (cierto)

3. _____ (separado)

4. _____ (pensar)

5. _____ (aconsejable)

6. _____ (esperar)

7. _____ (transcurrir)

8. _____ (dictado)

9. _____ (deber)

10. _____ (acreditar)

Answers and Answer Explanations for Group Seven

1. *española* This adjective modifies *ley*, which is a feminine singular noun. The form, *español*, is the masculine singular form of the adjective of nationality, and thus does not change, but the feminine form adds an *a*.

2. *cierto* This adjective modifies *modo*, which is a masculine singular noun; therefore, there is no change in the form.

3. *separadas* This adjective modifies *parejas*, which is feminine plural. The adjective must also be feminine plural.

4. *piensen* This verb occurs in an adverbial clause introduced by the conjunction, *a que*, which indicates purpose or cause. The subjunctive is always used after this adverbial conjunction.

5. *aconsejable* Adjectives that end in *-ble* do not change the ending to make them agree in gender. But if the noun had been plural, the ending on this adjective would have been made plural by adding *-s*.

6. *esperar* Even though this verb comes after *que*, in this case it is part of a modismo. *Hay que* is always followed by the infinitive form of the verb and expresses impersonal obligation.

7. *transcurra* The present subjunctive is used because *hay que esperar* is considered an impersonal expression. *Transcurra* occurs in a dependent noun clause, introduced by *que* after an impersonal expression in the main clause.

8. *dictado*   The past participle in this case functions verbally. The invariable form of the past participle is always used after *haber*; therefore, the ending is *-o*.

9. *deben*   The conjunction *aunque* can take either the indicative or the subjunctive, depending on the degree of uncertainty about the veracity of the statement. In this case the context makes it rather plain that according to the spirit of the law governing divorce, couples ought to wait two years before filing. When no uncertainty is implied, the indicative is used.

10. *acreditar*   The infinitive is used because the verb functions as the object of another verb. *Deben* in this case functions as a modal verb, which means that another verb is needed to complete the meaning of *deber*. The verb *transcurrir* is also used as an object of the modal verb, and the conjunction *y* indicates that the two verbs form a compound object.

GROUP EIGHT

Por fin, a ____(1)____ dos días de

navegación, el buque ____(2)____ en la

enseñada de Labadee, ____(3)____ isla

arrendada por los armadores para diversión

de su clientela que, ____(4)____ de una

moneda especialmente ____(5)____ para el

crucero, podía comprar caracolas marinas y

corales ____(6)____ de Taiwan, sin ____(7)____

las botellas de *Coca-cola*. Un grupo de

tambores y bidones musicales recibía en

fila a ____(8)____ turistas. Luego de una

sesión intensa de sol, la misma charanga

caribeña les ____(9)____ después de horas en

idéntica formación, aunque ____(10)____ la

voluntad.

1. _____
   (el)

2. _____
   (fondear)

3. _____
   (diminuto)

4. _____
   (provisto)

5. _____
   (acuñado)

6. _____
   (traído)

7. _____
   (olvidar)

8. _____
   (el)

9. _____
   (despedir)

10. _____
    (pedir)

Answers and Answer Explanations for Group Eight

1. *los* This definite article modifies *días*, which is a masculine plural noun. Even though *día* ends in *a*, it is masculine.

2. *fondeó* The preterit indicative is used because the action is completed in the past. It is the beginning of the narrative on what happened when the cruise ship arrived at the port of call. Even if you do not know what the verb means, the use of the preterit is obvious from the words *por fin* and *dos días*.

3. *diminuta* This adjective modifies *isla*, which is feminine singular; therefore *diminuta* is used in the feminine singular form.

4. *provista* This adjective refers back to *clientela*, which is a feminine singular noun.

5. *acuñada* This adjective modifies *moneda*, which is feminine singular. Even if the meaning of *acuñada* is unknown, knowing that *moneda* is feminine singular provides enough information to arrive at the correct answer.

6. *traídos* This past participle used as an adjective refers to both *caracolas* and to *corales*. Since one of the nouns is feminine and the other masculine, the masculine plural form of the adjective is used.

7. *olvidar* This verb occurs after a preposition, in which case the infinitive form of the verb is always used.

8. *los* The noun *turistas* is one of those nouns that ends with an invariable form, *-ista, -istas*. The rule for mixed gender groups means that the masculine plural article should be used with *turistas*.

9. *despedía* This verb is frequently a reflexive verb. In this case, however, the subject is *charanga*, a third person singular subject, and the object pronoun, *les*, is a third person plural pronoun. The imperfect is used because the action is described and there is no reference to the beginning and/or the end of the action stated in the passage.

10. *pidiendo* The present participle occurs as an adverb describing manner in an explanatory clause, introduced by *aunque*. The conjunction *aunque* can also be followed by a conjugated verb. In this sentence, the present participle is used to avoid repetition of sentence structure. The implied meaning of the present participle in this case is *pedía*.

GROUP NINE

Se había producido una estampida entre

los burlangas, y cada ___(1)___ de ellos

encontró refugio en los rincones más

insospechados mientras los ___(2)___ iban

___(3)___ el garrito patas arriba con su

furor ___(4)___ de manifestarse ante

Luisito, el Nabo, que estaba ___(5)___

detrás de una cortina. Parecía que lo

1. _____
   (uno)

2. _____
   (jabalí)

3. _____
   (poner)

4. _____
   (tratar)

5. _____
   (esconder)

____(6)____ reconocido por el olfato, y hacia

él se ____(7)____ ambas fieras a un tiempo,

pero el joven atracador vestido de

esmoquin tuvo los reflejos a punto para

sacar la recortada del armario, y sin

pensarlo nada ____(8)____ un par de

disparos que fueron suficientes. En medio

de un charco de sangre quedaron

____(9)____ dos hombres desconocidos que

habían ____(10)____ los icarios transformados

en cerdos por la dama Georgina.

6. _____
   (haber)

7. _____
   (abatir)

8. _____
   (soltar)

9. _____
   (tumbado)

10. _____
    (ser)

Answers and Answer Explanations for Group Nine

1. *uno*   The noun *burlangas* is masculine, as is indicated by the definite article, *los*. *Uno* refers to *burlanga*. The verb *encontró* is singular, which indicates that *uno* must be third person singular.
2. *jabalíes*   The plural of words that end with a stressed -í is formed by adding -es. The written accent is retained.
3. *poniendo*   The present participle (*gerundio* in Spanish) is used as an adverb in order to describe how they went. After verbs of motion and perception the present participle is frequently used adverbially.
4. *tratando*   The present participle is used here to describe further how they went, even though no conjunction is used to indicate that the structure is compound.
5. *escondido*   The past participle is used as an adjective, that is masculine singular in this case because it refers to Luisito, el Nabo.
6. *habían*   The subject of this verb is *los jabalíes*, who are pursuing Luisito, el Nabo. The imperfect form of the verb is used (the pluperfect is indicated by the past participle *reconocido*) because the action is described, not narrated.
7. *abatieron*   The verb is used in the preterit in this case because it narrates, or retells, the action when the wild boars finally located their quarry.
8. *soltó*   The subject of the verb is the young hunter, *el joven atracador*, who had the presence of mind, *tuvo los reflejos*, to shoot at the *jabalíes*. The preterit is used because the action is begun and completed at a definite moment in time in the past.
9. *tumbados*   The past participle in this case refers back to the *jabalíes*, as is indicated by the use of the third person plural of the verb *quedaron*. The past participle is masculine because *jabalíes* is a masculine plural noun.
10. *sido*   The pluperfect is used because the time frame indicated is prior to a point of time in the past, when they had been shot by the young hunter. *Sido* is the past participle that must follow the helping verb *haber*.

GROUP TEN

Del mismo modo, hoy nos ____(1)____ por

el abandono de las relaciones ____(2)____. El

tocadiscos, la radio, la televisión y el vídeo

han ido ____(3)____ a las gentes en sus casas

y ____(4)____ el ocio en onanismo. Las

computadoras y el fax pueden lograr que

las personas ni siquiera se ____(5)____ que

juntar para el trabajo. Cada vez se vive más

en la soledad, en la unidad aislada, en el

individuo. Hoy todo ____(6)____ nos parece

terrible, pero quizás dentro de un par de

siglos los humanos ____(7)____ hacia atrás y

se pregunten: "Y esos bárbaros del siglo

XX, ¿cómo ____(8)____ vivir así de

____(9)____, así de mezclados? ¿Cómo

podían necesitar el contacto sucio y

ancestral de los amigos? ¿Cómo se las

arreglaban para trabajar en ____(10)____ caos

invasor de una oficina?"

1. _____
(doler)

2. _____
(interpersonal)

3. _____
(encerrar)

4. _____
(convertir)

5. _____
(tener)

6. _____
(este)

7. _____
(mirar)

8. _____
(poder)

9. _____
(promiscuo)

10. _____
(el)

Answers and Answer Explanations for Group Ten

1. *dolemos*   The verb is used in the first person plural in this case because it is reflexive. Frequently the indirect object pronoun is used with *doler* and the subject of the verb is whatever it is that causes the hurt. But in this instance the reflexive is indicated because *doler* is followed by the prepositional phrase, *por el abandono...* Farther down in the passage, the subject, *we*, is indicated again in the phrase, *Todo esto nos parece....* This is an example of a passage that needs to be read in its entirety before the fill-ins are begun; otherwise, subtleties such as the subject, or the narrative voice in this passage, would be missed.

2. *interpersonales* The adjectives that end with -*l* can only agree in number with the nouns they modify, not gender. The adjective modifies *relaciones*, not *abandono*.

3. *encerrando* The present participle is used to describe the action of the verb, which is a verb of motion, *han ido*.

4. *convirtiendo* This present participle, like *encerrando*, describes the action of the verb, which is indicated by the conjunction *y*. *Convertir* is a Class II stem changing verb, which accounts for the change of the *e* to *i* in the stem of the present participle.

5. *tengan* The expression *pueden lograr* indicated volition (request, will, permission) in the main clause, so the subjunctive is needed in the dependent clause.

6. *esto* The neuter form of the demonstrative pronoun is used because it refers to the preceding concept, not to any noun in particular. In the last portion of the passage, the speaker tries to put the current perception of isolation in perspective by asking rhetorically if what we consider modern will not appear as strange to people of the next century.

7. *miren* The present subjunctive is used after *quizás* to express conjecture. *Quizás* indicates the uncertainty of the speaker. Also, *pregunten* is in the subjunctive, indicating probability.

8. *podrían* The conditional is used to express probability or conjecture in the past. From the perspective of the future, the people who ask the question could not know how or why present day people do and think the way they do, a perspective communicated by the conditional tense.

9. *promiscuos* The adjective is plural because it refers to *esos bárbaros*.

10. *el* *Caos* is a masculine singular noun.

GROUP ELEVEN

Por descuido o porque uno se pone a

hacer otra cosa cuando se está trabajando

con el ordenador, a veces la pantalla se

queda ___(1)___ durante mucho tiempo

con un texto o ___(2)___ imagen visible.

No se estropea la unidad central del

ordenador ni se pierden datos, pero el

monitor tal vez ___(3)___ daños por el

efecto ___(4)___

1. _____
   (encendido)

2. _____
   (uno)

3. _____
   (sufrir)

4. _____
   (denominado)

pantalla quemada, que además puede

producir problemas en la vista. Para

evitarlo existen programas de protección

que eliminan la imagen del monitor al

cabo de unos minutos de permanecer

____(5)____. Después para regresar a la tarea

interrumpida, basta con ____(6)____ una

tecla. En el interior de la pantalla hay

partículas de fósforo que brillan cuando

son ____(7)____ por un haz de electrones,

pero después de un bombardeo prolongado

en el mismo punto el fósforo se desgasta y

queda un brillo fantasma. Este efecto hace

que se ____(8)____, por ejemplo, líneas de

texto ____(9)____ cuando el monitor está

____(10)____ .

5. _____
(inalterado)

6. _____
(pulsar)

7. _____
(activado)

8. _____
(ver)

9. _____
(fijo)

10. _____
(apagado)

Answers and Answer Explanations for Group Eleven

1. *encendida*   The past participle refers to *pantalla*, which is feminine singular. The verb *quedar* is used to mean *to be* in this instance, making the past participle function as an adjective.
2. *una*   The noun *imagen* is feminine.
3. *sufra*   The present subjunctive is used in this instance after *tal vez* to indicate conjecture or the probability that the computer screen could suffer from a problem called *burned screen*.
4. *denominado*   The adjective refers to *efecto* not *pantalla*, so it is masculine singular.
5. *inalterada*   The adjective refers to *la imagen*, and thus is feminine singular form.
6. *pulsar*   The infinitive is used because it follows a preposition.
7. *activadas*   The feminine plural form is used because it refers to *partículas*. When the noun is followed by a prepositional phrase that describes the noun, such as *de fósforos*, be sure to correctly identify the referent of the adjective.
8. *vean*   The present subjunctive is used because it occurs in a dependent noun clause, following the verb *hace*, which indicates volition. The plural is used because the *se* substitute for the passive voice is used and the subject is *líneas*.

9. *fijas*   The adjective refers to *líneas*, not to *texto*, which is contained in a prepositional phrase describing *líneas*. The noun is a feminine plural form.

10. **apagado**   The noun that this adjective modifies is *monitor*, which means that this past participle used as an adjective must be a masculine singular form.

GROUP TWELVE

El azar me había ___(1)___ en cierto

banquete junto a un hombre amable y

jovial, con patillas, ojos astutos, nariz

___(2)___ y una corbata que ___(3)___ tres

vueltas alrededor de su largo cuello antes

de anudarse.

—¡Mozo! ¡___(4)___ aquí, amigo! Va

usted a traerme ___(5)___ una cerveza, y

que no ___(6)___ de la casa Bornoil, ¿eh?

No se había servido todavía la sopa y

___(7)___ caballero ___(8)___ ya ___(9)___

ruido como si se ___(10)___ en el postre.

1. _____ (poner)
2. _____ (puntiagudo)
3. _____ (dar)
4. _____ (venir)
5. _____ (correr)
6. _____ (ser)
7. _____ (este)
8. _____ (hacer)
9. _____ (tanto)
10. _____ (estar)

Answers and Answer Explanations for Group Twelve

1. *puesto*   This word is the irregular past participle of *poner*, which is required because it follows the auxiliary verb *haber*.

2. *puntiaguda*   The noun that this adjective modifies, *nariz*, is feminine singular; thus the correct form ends in *-a*.

3. *daba*   The third person singular is required because the subject of the verb is *corbata*. The imperfect is used because the sentence describes the man's attire.

4. *Venga*   The polite singular command, Ud., is required in this instance. The direct address of *Mozo* indicates that the relationship between the two is formal, even though the speaker also uses the word *amigo*. In addition, in the following sentence, *usted* is used to indicate the third person singular.

5. *corriendo*   The present participle is used to show in what manner the *mozo* is to bring the beer, indicating an adverb.

6. *sea* The present subjunctive is required because the beer has not been brought yet. The verb occurs in a dependent noun clause. The main clause is omitted, but *que* before the verb means that the following clause is dependent. *Quiero* or some other verb of wishing or wanting is understood in this kind of a sentence.

7. *este* The demonstrative adjective modifies *caballero*, a masculine singular noun. The correct masculine singular form is *este*.

8. *hacía* The imperfect is used because the period of time to which the speaker refers is indefinite.

9. *tanto* The noun *ruido* is masculine singular, which requires that *tanto* agree in gender and number with the noun. Only when *tanto* is followed by an adjective or adverb is it shortened.

10. *estuviese, estuviera* Either form of the past subjunctive is always required after *como si.*

GROUP THIRTEEN

Había ___(1)___ decir, por ejemplo, que

una de las habitaciones principales de la

casa de don Carlos había sido ___(2)___

por él en ___(3)___ especie de museo en el

que se conservaban, ___(4)___, siempre

escrupulosamente cuidadas y limpias, las

pertenencias de Estela. Pues bien, su

sucesora sería la más celosa guardiana de

la veneración que a ese, no, museo no,

altar, se le debía. Hasta que el mismo

Carlos le ___(5)___ que no ___(6)___ y

ella, por obediencia, fuera ___(7)___ que

crecieran las telarañas y se extendiera el

moho y se ___(8)___ los hongos. Pues

nadie volvería a acordarse de aquel cuarto

cerrado ___(9)___ tantos otros abiertos y

que ___(10)___ atención y cuidado.

1. _____
   (oír)

2. _____
   (convertido)

3. _____
   (uno)

4. _____
   (intacto)

5. _____
   (rogar)

6. _____
   (exagerar)

7. _____
   (dejar)

8. _____
   (multiplicar)

9. _____
   (haber)

10. _____
    (requerir)

Answers and Answer Explanations for Group Thirteen

1. *oído*   The past participle is required after the verb *haber*. The important thing to remember about verbs like *oír* is that there is an accent written on the past participle. Other past participles like *oído* are *leído, creído,* and *traído.*

2. *convertida*   This past participle functions as an adjective and refers back to *una* of the *habitaciones* earlier in the sentence. This sentence is a good example of the true passive voice in Spanish. You can identify it by the verb *ser, había sido,* the past participle, *convertida,* the preposition indicating the agent, *por,* and the agent *él.*

3. *una*   The noun *especie* is feminine singular, which requires the feminine singular indefinite article, *una.*

4. *intactas*   This adjective refers to *las habitaciones.* The fact that it is plural is indicated by the *se* substitute for the passive voice that immediately precedes the adjective, *se conservaban.* In addition, all the other adjectives in the series are feminine plural.

5. *rogara, rogase*   The past subjunctive is indicated by *hasta que.* Even though this passage is told in the past tense, from the perspective in time of the speaker, Carlos has not said anything yet; therefore, that event is considered future (an unaccomplished happening), and is rendered in the subjunctive. Additionally, in a parallel structure the following portion of the compound clause shows the past subjunctive *-y ella, por obediencia, fuera... que crecieran las telerañas.*

6. *exagerase, exagerara*   The imperfect subjunctive is used in a dependent noun clause after a verb of volition. Don Carlos begs Estela not to exaggerate. Additional cues are found in the parallel structures in which the past subjunctive, *crecieran telerañas,* is also used in a dependent noun clause.

7. *dejando*   The present participle is used after the verb *ir.* It describes the action of the verb by showing the manner in which the action is accomplished. Do not confuse the verbs *ir* and *ser* in this kind of question. *Por* in this sentence does not indicate the passive voice. Nor would a past participle for *dejar,* modifying *ella* make sense in this context, either.

8. *multiplicaran, multiplicasen*   This verb is part of a series of verbs in the past subjunctive: *crecieran* and *extendiera.* They all occur as dependent clauses following a verb of volition, *dejar.* This verb is plural because this is the *se* substitute for the passive voice. The verb must be either singular or plural depending on the number of the noun that is the subject. *Hongos* is the plural subject; therefore, *multiplicaran* must also be plural.

9. *habiendo*   The present participle is used because the function of the verb in this clause is to describe the action of the verb: *volvería a acordarse. Habiendo* means *there being....*

10. *requerían*   The imperfect is used in this instance because the action of the verb is not carried out at a specific moment in time in the past. The plural form of the verb is used because the subject of the verb is the nominalized adjective *otros,* which refers to *cuartos.*

GROUP FOURTEEN

No puedo explicarte la alegría que

___(1)___ al ___(2)___ tu cariñosa carta. La

noticia que me das de tu próximo

matrimonio con Juan Alonzo conmocionó

a ___(3)___ la familia. Todos me encargan

que los ___(4)___ muy sinceramente. Yo

___(5)___ que vengas pronto por la capital

para hacer las compras de tu ajuar.

Además, por supuesto te ___(6)___ el mes

entrante cuando ___(7)___, aunque bien yo

___(8)___ que en esta materia no necesitas

ayuda ___(9)___ pues tienes un gusto y

elegancia ___(10)___.

1. _____
   (experimentar)

2. _____
   (recibir)

3. _____
   (todo)

4. _____
   (felicitar)

5. _____
   (confiar)

6. _____
   (acompañar)

7. _____
   (venir)

8. _____
   (saber)

9. _____
   (alguno)

10. _____
    (exquisito)

Answers and Answer Explanations for Group Fourteen

1. *experimenté* The first person preterit is used because the time to which the speaker refers is a specific moment in the past, the moment when the speaker opened the letter. The first person is indicated by the subject of the first verb, *puedo*.

2. *recibir* The infinitive is used in this instance as a noun, even though in English the translation would call for a present participle used as a noun. *Al* is always followed by an infinitive verb form.

3. *toda* The adjective modifies *la familia*, a feminine singular noun. Family is a collective noun; even though it refers to a group of people, the singular is required because the noun itself is singular.

4. *felicite* The present subjunctive is used in this instance because it occurs in a dependent noun clause, after the verb *encargar*, which indicates volition. The subject of *felicite*, *yo*, is indicated by *me*, the object pronoun in front of *encargan*. The direct object pronoun *los* refers to the persons to whom the narrator is talking, *tú*, and her fiance. Remember that in Spanish America the third person plural is used in place of the second person plural forms. But in Spain, the second person plural, *vosotros*, is commonly used.

5. *confío*   This verb in the present tense carries a written accent on the stem of the verb in those persons and number where the stress should fall on the stem, in the first, second, third singular, and third persons plural.

6. *acompañaré*   The future indicative is used because the action has not yet taken place (indicated by the words *el mes entrante*), and the verb occurs in the main clause.

7. *vengas*   *Cuando* is an adverbial conjunction of time. The present subjunctive is used since the action has not happened.

8. *sé*   The first person singular of *saber* is irregular. Be sure to write the accent on the verb form to distinguish it from a pronoun.

9. *alguna*   This indefinite adjective, which usually precedes the noun, is feminine singular because it refers to *ayuda*. Where it is placed in regard to the noun does not change the rule for making adjectives agree in gender and number with the nouns they modify, except for apocopated masculine forms. Notice that *alguna* comes after the noun and that the verb is negated. This is an idiomatic use of *alguna*, instead of using *ninguna* before the noun. The word order is important.

10. *exquisitos*   The plural form of the adjective is used because it refers to both *gusto* and *elegancia*. In cases where one noun is masculine and one is feminine, the masculine plural form of the adjective is used.

GROUP FIFTEEN

En respuesta a ____(1)____ crisis,

recomiendo que ____(2)____ nosotros un

programa masivo de construcciones de

prisiones. Un ____(3)____ paso importante

sería convertir ____(4)____ de las cárceles de

mínima y mediana seguridad ____(5)____ ,

en prisiones de ____(6)____ seguridad para

acomodar a criminales ____(7)____. Creo

firmemente que el único impedimento al

crimen es el castigo garantizado. No

veremos una reducción en el crimen hasta

que ____(8)____ a implementar ____(9)____

sistema de castigo que ____(10)____ ambos

adecuado y cierto.

1. _____
   (este)

2. _____
   (comenzar)

3. _____
   (primero)

4. _____
   (alguno)

5. _____
   (existente)

6. _____
   (máximo)

7. _____
   (violento)

8. _____
   (empezar)

9. _____
   (uno)

10. _____
    (ser)

Answers and Answer Explanations for Group Fifteen

1. *esta*   The noun that this demonstrative adjective modifies, *crisis*, is feminine singular.

2. *comencemos*   The present subjunctive is used because the verb occurs in a dependent noun clause after a verb of volition: *recomendar*. That the first person plural is the subject is indicated by the subject pronoun that follows the verb. Usually the subject pronoun precedes the verb, but not always.

3. *primer*   The adjective is apocopated (the *-o* is dropped before masculine singular nouns) because the noun it modifies is *paso*.

4. *algunas*   The feminine plural form of the indefinite adjective is used here as a pronoun, *some of the prisons*, because the referent is *cárceles*, a feminine plural noun. Grammatically, a singular indefinite pronoun is possible, but it is not logical in this case since the speaker is talking about some of the prisons, not just one.

5. *existentes*   The adjective is plural because it refers to *cárceles*, not to *seguridad*.

6. *máxima*   This adjective modifies *seguridad*, which, like all nouns that end with *-dad*, is feminine.

7. *violentos*   This adjective modifies a masculine plural noun, *criminales*, so it must end with *-os*.

8. *empecemos*   This verb follows an adverbial conjunction of time, *hasta*. Since the verb in the main clause is in the future tense, *veremos*, the action in the dependent clause has not happened yet, and is expressed using the present subjunctive. The subject, the first person plural, is the same as the other verb meaning *to begin*, *comencemos*, at the beginning of the passage.

9. *un*   The noun that this indefinite adjective modifies is masculine singular, even though it ends with *-a*. *Uno* is always apocopated before masculine singular nouns.

10. *sea*   The present subjunctive is used in this instance because it occurs in a dependent adjective clause that refers to an indefinite, or nonexistent antecedent, *sistema*.

GROUP SIXTEEN

Hoy en día hay ___(1)___ temas en los

Estados Unidos que ___(2)___ más

pasiones irracionales que el bilingüismo.

En los últimos seis años, 17 estados

___(3)___ pasado resoluciones ___(4)___

del inglés la lengua oficial. Los partidarios

del movimiento *Lengua pura*, ___(5)___

1. _____
   (poco)

2. _____
   (provocar)

3. _____
   (haber)

4. _____
   (hacer)

5. _____
   (llamado)

alegan que éste está ___(6)___ . ___(7)___

por una organización ___(8)___ en

Washington que ha reclamado en varias

ocasiones entre 250.000 y 3.000.000

miembros que pagan cuotas, este

movimiento tiene una filosofía muy

simple: el inglés es, y debe permanecer

para siempre, la única lengua de los

Estados Unidos. En tal clima tan ___(9)___

es útil hacer una distinción entre la

educación bilingüe y el bilingüismo. Esta

distinción no es ___(10)___ con frecuencia

por los partidarios del *Lengua pura*.

6. _____
   (crecer)

7. _____
   (Dirigido)

8. _____
   (basado)

9. _____
   (caldeado)

10. _____
    (hecho)

Answers and Answer Explanations for Group Sixteen

1. *pocos* The noun that this adjective modifies, *temas*, is a masculine plural form. Review nouns that end in *-a* if you missed this item.

2. *provoquen* This verb occurs in a dependent adjective clause. It describes *pocos temas*, which is an indefinite antecedent. The subjunctive is used in such a case, and the present tense is used because other verbs in the passage are present tense.

3. *han* The present perfect tense is used here because the time frame that is indicated is the immediate past. The selection of present perfect indicates continual action up to the present.

4. *haciendo* The present participle is used here adverbially; it describes the action of the verb, *han pasado*.

5. *llamado* The past participle functions as an adjective that modifies *movimiento*, not *partidarios*, since it is the movement that is called *Lengua pura*.

6. *creciendo* The present participle functions as a verbal after the verb *estar*, indicating the present progressive form of the verb.

7. *Dirigido* The past participle functions as an adjective, describing *movimiento*.

8. *basada* This adjective describes *organización*, a feminine noun. All nouns that end with *-ción* are feminine.

9. *caldeado* This adjective modifies *clima*, a masculine singular noun. *Caldo* means *stew* or *soup*, therefore as an adjective it would mean *soupy*, implying that the climate for bilingual education in the United States is heated and muddled.

10. *hecha* The past participle of *hacer* here refers to the *distinción*. This is an example of the true passive voice in Spanish with the construction of *to be* + *past participle* + *by* + *agent*.

GROUP SEVENTEEN

El momento actual es el más importante

y más crucial que jamás ha ____(1)____ la

humanidad. De la sabiduría colectiva que

nosotros ____(2)____ durante los próximos

____(3)____ años depende el que la

humanidad sea ____(4)____ a un desastre sin

paralelo o que ____(5)____ un ____(6)____

nivel de dicha, seguridad, bienestar e

inteligencia. No sé qué es lo que ____(7)____

la humanidad. Hay graves motivos para

temer, pero ____(8)____ bastantes

posibilidades de una buena solución, que

hacen que las esperanzas no ____(9)____

irracionales. Y debemos actuar sobre

____(10)____ esperanzas.

1. _____
   (enfrentar)

2. _____
   (demostrar)

3. _____
   (veinte)

4. _____
   (lanzado)

5. _____
   (alcanzar)

6. _____
   (nuevo)

7. _____
   (escoger)

8. _____
   (existir)

9. _____
   (resultar)

10. _____
    (tal)

Answers and Answer Explanations for Group Seventeen

1. *enfrentado* This is the past participle of the verb needed in the perfect tense. The present perfect is used to indicate the immediate past. The present moment is the most crucial that the world *has* ever *seen,* with the idea of continuous time up to the present being underscored by the use of the word *jamás.*

2. *demostremos* Since the existence of collective wisdom is questionable from the perspective of the speaker in this passage, the present subjunctive is used. The rest of the passage indicates that the speaker views the present moment as a turning point with equal chance for great progress or total annihilation of the human race.

3. *veinte* Cardinal numbers such as *veinte* do not agree in gender or number with the nouns they modify, except for *uno* when it modifies a noun.

4. *lanzada* This past participle, used as an adjective, describes *la humanidad*. Following the verb *ser* the past participles agree in gender and number with the nouns to which they refer.

5. *alcance* The present subjunctive is used because it occurs in a dependent noun clause after the verb *depender*. This verb parallels *sea* in the previous clause, indicated by the conjunction *o. La humanidad* is the subject.

6. *nuevo* This adjective modifies *nivel*, which is masculine singular.
7. *escogerá* The future indicative is indicated by the context of the sentence and the passage. Unlike *no creer*, *no saber* does not indicate the subjunctive. *Lo que* is the subject of the verb.
8. *existen* The present indicative is used because it occurs in a main clause. Even though the verb *temer* occurs in the previous clause, the clause containing *existir* is introduced by *pero*, meaning that it is an independent clause.
9. *resulten* The present subjunctive is used in a dependent noun clause after a verb of volition: *hacen*.
10. *tales* This word is an adjective that occurs in many idiomatic expression. When used to modify a noun, it can only agree in number, since it ends with a consonant.

GROUP EIGHTEEN

____(1)____ en términos abstractos no es,

por supuesto, la única forma de alcanzar la

generalidad ética; también se la puede

lograr, y quizás mejor, si se ___(2)___

emociones generalizadas. Pero para la

mayoría de la gente ____(3)____ es difícil. Si

se siente hambre, se ___(4)___ grandes

esfuerzos, en caso necesario, para

conseguir alimentos; si los que tienen

hambre son los hijos ____(5)____ , puede que

se ___(6)___ una urgencia aun mayor. Si

un amigo está ___(7)___ de hambre, con

seguridad se esforzará uno para aliviar su

desgracia. Pero si se entera uno que

millones de personas en todo el mundo se

___(8)___ en peligro de muerte por

desnutrición, el problema es tan ___(9)___

1. _____
   (pensar)

2. _____
   (sentir)

3. _____
   (éste)

4. _____
   (hacer)

5. _____
   (suyo)

6. _____
   (sentir)

7. _____
   (morirse)

8. _____
   (encontrar)

9. _____
   (vasto)

y tan distante que, a menos que se

10. _____

(tener)

_____(10)_____ alguna responsabilidad oficial,

se olvidará muy pronto del problema.

Answers and Answer Explanations for Group Eighteen

1. *Pensar*   The verb functions as the subject of the verb *es*, in which case the infinitive must be used. Contrast this with the English, where the gerund is normally used.

2. *siente*   After the conjunction *si*, the indicative is normally used in the present tense. Although the subjunctive is used to express uncertainty, in Spanish the present subjunctive is usually not used after *si*. Notice all the other constructions in the passage where the present indicative is used, also.

3. *esto*   The antecedent for this demonstrative pronoun is the whole preceding thought, in which case the neuter pronoun is appropriate.

4. *harán*   The future indicative is used in the *se* substitute for the passive voice. The use of the present indicative in the *si* clause means that either the present or the future tenses will be used in the next clause. The future is more appropriate here because the speaker is talking about hypothetical situations, not something that is about to happen in the near future.

5. *suyos*   This possessive adjective agrees with the noun it modifies, *hijos*, not with the possessor, the parents of the children.

6. *sienta*   The present subjunctive is used in a dependent noun clause after an impersonal expression: *puede ser*.

7. *muriéndose*   The present participle is used as a verbal after the verb *estar* to form the present progressive. The pronoun is added to the end of present participles, and an accent is written over the first syllable of the participial ending because the pronoun adds a syllable to the word. Notice the stem change from an *-o* to a *-u*, because this verb is a Class II stem changing verb.

8. *encuentran*   The present indicative is used here because the verb occurs in an adjective clause. In the context of the passage the present is appropriate here instead of the future because the speaker is talking about present-day conditions, not hypothetical situations.

9. *vasto*   The adjective modifies *problema*, which is masculine singular. The gender of the noun is given in the article that precedes the noun. If the noun is unfamiliar, learn to look for other indicators of the gender and do not simply look to see if the ending is an *-o* or an *-a*. See the Appendix for a listing of common nouns that are of the opposite gender than that indicated by the ending.

10. *tenga*   The present subjunctive is used here because the verb occurs in a dependent adverbial clause, following the conjunction *a menos que*, which indicates concession or condition.

GROUP NINETEEN

Sigue ___(1)___. Ha sucedido un

accidente desagradable, esta mañana al

salir de la escuela. Un tropel de

muchachos, apenas ___(2)___ a la plaza, se

pusieron a hacer bolas con ___(3)___ nieve

que hace las bolas pesadas como piedras.

Mucha gente ___(4)___ por la acera. Un

señor gritó: —¡Alto, chicos!— Y

precisamente en aquel momento se

___(5)___ un grito agudo en la otra parte

de la calle, se vio un viejo que ___(6)___

perdido su sombrero y andaba vacilando,

___(7)___ la cara con las manos, y a su

lado un niño que ___(8)___ —¡Socorro,

socorro!— En seguida ___(9)___ gente de

todas partes. Le habían dado una bola en

un ojo. Todos los muchachos corrieron a la

desbandada, ___(10)___ como saetas.

1. _____
(nevar)
2. _____
(llegar)
3. _____
(aquel)
4. _____
(pasar)
5. _____
(oír)
6. _____
(haber)
7. _____
(cubrirse)
8. _____
(gritar)
9. _____
(acudir)
10. _____
(huir)

Answers and Answer Explanations for Group Nineteen

1. *nevando*   After the verb *seguir* the present participle is commonly used to elaborate on the action of the verb, to tell what kept on happening.
2. *llegaron*   The adverb, *apenas*, meaning *scarcely*, indicates a specific moment when the action took place. Thus the preterit is appropriately used to narrate the event. The use of the preterit in the next clause, *se pusieron*, also indicates narration.
3. *aquella*   The noun that the demonstrative adjective modifies, *nieve*, is feminine singular.
4. *pasaba*   The imperfect is used to describe background action. While the boys made snowballs, people *were going by*. When no beginning or ending to the action is indicated, then the imperfect is used. Notice that *gente* takes the singular ending.
5. *oyó*   The preterit is used in this *se* substitute for the passive voice, because the action, a pained shout, occurred at a specific moment in time in the past, indicated by *aquel momento*.

6. *había*   The pluperfect is the appropriate tense because the action took place prior to the event in the past to which the speaker refers. Before the man began walking about erratically, he had lost his hat, but the moment at which it happened is not the actual time frame of the narrative.

7. *cubriéndose*   The present participle describes the action of the old man, indicated in the verb *andaba vacilando*. The present participle *vacilando* functions as an adverb, because verbs of motion or perception are often followed by the present participle functioning as an adverb. Remember that when a pronoun is added to the end of the present participle, an accent is written on the first syllable of the participial ending.

8. *gritaba*   The imperfect tense is used here because the action is described, not narrated. The child did not shout—*Socorro*—once and stop; he *was shouting*. The period of time that he continued to shout is indefinite.

9. *acudió*   The preterit is used to indicate that at a specific moment in the past the action occurred. *En seguida* frequently indicates the use of the preterit, because a specific moment in time is mentioned. *Gente*, the subject, follows the verb.

10. *huyendo*   The present participle is used to describe the action of the boys who ran away from the scene. Notice the *i* of the ending changes to *y* between two vowels. If you missed this spelling change you may need to review conjugation of verbs ending in *-uir*. (But do not confuse *-uir* endings with *-guir* endings.)

GROUP TWENTY

Ayer tarde ____(1)____ a la escuela de

niñas que está al lado de la ____(2)____ para darle el

cuento del muchacho paduano a la maestra Silvia,

que lo ____(3)____ leer. ¡____(4)____ muchachas hay

allí! Cuando llegué, ____(5)____ a salir, ____(6)____

muy contentas por las vacaciones de Todos Santos

y Difuntos, y ¡qué cosa tan ____(7)____ presencié

allí! Frente a la puerta de la escuela en la otra

acera, estaba con un codo apoyado en la pared y

con la frente ____(8)____ en la mano, un

deshollinador muy pequeño, de cara

1. _____
(ir)

2. _____
(nuestro)

3. _____
(querer)

4. _____
(setecientos)

5. _____
(empezar)

6. _____
(todo)

7. _____
(conmovedor)

8. _____
(apoyado)

completamente negra, con su saco y su   9. _____

                                                        (haber)

raspador, que lloraba por ___(9)___

                                                      10. _____

perdido por un agujero en el bolsillo roto   (limpiar)

los seis reales que había ganado ___(10)___

chimeneas.

Answers and Answer Explanations for Group Twenty	1. *fui* The preterit indicative is used because the point in time is specific, *ayer*. The first person is indicated later in the passage in the verb *llegué* and *presencié*.

1. *fui* The preterit indicative is used because the point in time is specific, *ayer*. The first person is indicated later in the passage in the verb *llegué* and *presencié*.

2. *nuestra* The feminine singular possessive pronoun is used because the referent is *escuela*.

3. *quería* The imperfect is used to mean *wanted*. Remember that the meaning of the verb *querer* is different in the preterit.

4. *Setecientas* The number *cientos* agrees with the noun that it precedes.

5. *empezaban* In the past tense *empezar* usually is used in the preterit. Since it refers to a specific moment when something happened, the action has a definite beginning. In the context of this passage, however, the speaker is describing a scene and the students *were beginning* to leave. The imperfect is the appropriate past tense. *Contentas* indicates a plural subject.

6. *todas* The referent for this nominalized adjective is *muchachas*, so the form of the adjective needs to be feminine plural.

7. *conmovedora* This adjective modifies *cosa*, which is feminine singular.

8. *apoyada* The adjective modifies *frente*, whose gender is indicated by the article in front of the noun. Do not be misled because the word appears earlier modifying a masculine singular noun, *codo*.

9. *haber* The perfect tense is indicated because the action took place at a time prior to the moment when the speaker saw the boy. The infinitive form of *haber* is indicated by the preposition *por*.

10. *limpiando* The present participle further describes how the boy earns his living. It is used as an adverb.

TASK 2: PARAGRAPH COMPLETION WITH ROOT WORDS—SHORT PASSAGES

The free response part is like the previous one, except that the word that is omitted is always a verb form. You are to conjugate the verb in parentheses next to the line that corresponds to the blank in the sentence and write the correct form on the appropriate line. Unlike the previous exercise, however, at times there will be more than one word necessary to complete the meaning of the sentence. In other words, you sometimes need to use a compound verb form. On the exam you will have about seven or eight minutes to complete this part.

Look at the example to make sure you understand the directions.

In the following sentences, one verb has been omitted. Using the infinitive in the corresponding item number, write the correct form of the verb in the appropriate blank.

1. Los niños cantaban cuando yo _____   1. _____(entré)_____
   en la sala de clase.   (entrar)

2. Si yo hubiera estado allí, no lo _____   2. ___(habría creído)___
   tampoco.   (creer)

The exercises on the following pages are like the free-response fill-ins on the exam. After completing a set of ten you will find the answers and a brief explanation of the grammar. Check to see what kinds of verb forms you missed and review the guidelines for conjugating verbs, for uses of the preterit and imperfect, and for the indicative and subjunctive that are found in the Appendix.

You should plan to spend approximately ten minutes on each set.

EXERCISES AND ANSWERS

GROUP ONE

1. Nos pidió que no le _____ fotos,   1. _____
   pero sí permitió grabar la conversación.   (tomar)

2. El señor Higgins _____ que los
   chicos llevasen su tesoro al señor   2. _____
   Gómez inmediatamente.   (proponer)

3. Es una oportunidad de la cual se debe
   _____ si sería posible.   3. _____
                                                    (aprovechar)

4. Cuando haya demostrado que sirve
   perfectamente para lo segundo,   4. _____
   _____ mi vida en el primer terreno.   (enfocar)

5. Las ciudades necesitan fábricas y colegios que _____ la educación básica.

5. _____
   (proveer)

6. Pero si las predicciones del gobierno resultan acertadas, esos empleos industriales _____ cada vez más escasos.

6. _____
   (ser)

7. Rogamos que sus esfuerzos _____ al bienestar de la comunidad.

7. _____
   (contribuir)

8. El curandero llevaba tres décadas ejerciendo su terapia con gran éxito cuando yo lo _____.

8. _____
   (conocer)

9. El mes pasado yo también critiqué a los que trataron de derrumbar el gobierno, hasta que _____ que sólo querían justicia.

9. _____
   (saber)

10. Soy un trabajador infatigable, y mientras Dios me _____ salud seguiré al pie del cañón.

10. _____
    (dar)

Answers and Answer Explanations for Group One

1. *tomáramos*   The imperfect subjunctive is used in the dependent clause after *pedir*. The subject is indicated by the indirect object pronoun *nos*. The tense is indicated by the use of the preterite in the verb *pedir*.

2. *propuso*   The preterit is used here because it is an action that occurred in a definite moment in time in the past. The verb occurs in the main clause, so the indicative mood is used.

3. *aprovechar*   The infinitive is used because it functions as the object of the verb *deber*.

4. *enfocaré (enfoco)*   The future or present indicative is used because it occurs in the main clause with an adverbial conjunction of time. When *cuando* is followed by the subjunctive, the verb in the main clause should be in the present or future indicative, or a command form.

5. *proveen*   In this adjective clause the indicative is used to state a fact, or a generally accepted belief.

6. *serán*   Even though this is an *if-then* type of statement, the verb in the *if* clause is in the present tense, which indicates that the future tense is appropriate in the *then* portion of the statement. The action has not happened yet.

7. *contribuyan, contribuyeran*   The present subjunctive is used because the verb occurs in a dependent noun clause after a verb of volition: *rogamos*. Since the first person plural of the verb *rogar* is the same for the present or preterit tense, either the present or past subjunctive is correct.

8. *conocí*   The sense of the verb in this sentence is "when I *met* him." The preterit of *conocer* has this meaning.

9. *supe*   The sense of the verb in this sentence is "until I *found out* that they wanted only justice." The preterit of *saber* has this meaning.

10. *dé*   The conjunction *mientras* in this case means *as long as*. The speaker communicates that he does not have any insight into God's timetable, so he uses the subjunctive. Expressions concerning God's will or petitions to God usually take the subjunctive in any case. Other examples of such expressions would be: *¡Qué Dios te bendiga! ¡Qué Dios le ampare! ¡Qué te vayas con Dios!*

GROUP TWO

1. Los juegos ofrecen tipos de ejercicios para cualquier función de la inteligencia con el fin de que _____ su capacidad.

1. _____
   (aumentar)

2. Este libro yo _____ a escribirlo hace muchos años, cuando vivía con mis abuelos.

2. _____
   (empezar)

3. Lo maravilloso del regalo es que al abrir el tapón de la botella, se _____ el perfume de las rosas, su esencia guardada en vidrio.

3. _____
   (oler)

4. En ningún momento por toda la vida _____ ella de haber tomado la decisión de casarse con él.

4. _____
   (arrepentirse)

5. Don Fermín llamó a todos los chicos, —¡ _____ acá, muchachos! Os regalaré unos caramelos si venís pronto.

5. _____
   (venir)

6. El director del banco exige que el cliente _____ los préstamos lo más pronto posible.

6. _____
   (pagar)

7. Lo más lamentable del empleo es el ruido de las familias de los reos que reclaman que nosotros no los _____ por ser parientes.

7. _____
   (castigar)

8. Después de caerme en el charco y _____ hasta los huesos, me puse de pie y me fui corriendo.

8. _____
   (empaparse)

9. Estoy segura que mis hermanos _____ el mismo pavor que yo al ver al director a la puerta.

9. _____
   (sentir)

10. No _____ forma de convencerla en   10. _____
ese momento de que eran otra cosa: de que   (haber)
eran algo así como el espíritu del mal.

Answers and Answer Explanations for Group Two

1. *aumente*   The present subjunctive is used in an adverbial clause after a conjunction of proviso, or condition.
2. *empecé*   The sentence contains an expression of time that in English refers to time *ago*, time past. The preterit is required in this type of construction with the present tense verb, *hace,* to indicate the concept of *ago*, a word that is not translated literally into Spanish.
3. *huele*   This verb is used in the present indicative in a main clause.
4. *se arrepintió* This verb is used in the preterit indicative because it occurs in the main clause and refers to completed past time.
5. *venid*   The second person affirmative command is indicated by the indirect object pronoun and in the verb in the following sentence, *venís.*
6. *pague*   The present subjunctive is used in a dependent noun clause in this sentence after *exigir*, a verb of volition.
7. *castiguemos*   The present subjunctive is used in the dependent noun clause after a verb of volition, *reclamar.*
8. *empaparme*   The infinitive is used as the object of a preposition in a compound construction. The pronoun on *empapar* should be the first person singular to agree with the subject of the conjugated verb.
9. *sintieron*   The indicative is used in this dependent noun clause because it follows an expression of certainty. *Mis hermanos* is the subject.
10. *hubo*   The preterit of *haber* is used since the moment in time is definite past.

GROUP THREE

1. Es decir, venderse siempre sale caro,   1. _____
no importa que _____ por dinero u   (ser)
otra cosa.

2. Es lo que dice a todos: —No _____   2. _____
porque sois sucios.   (tocar)

3. Para que haya guerra tiene que   3. _____
_____ dos bandos que luchen y   (haber)
ahora en realidad no los hay.

4. Las grandes ciudades no van a resolver   4. _____
sus problemas hasta que nosotros   (crear)
_____ nuevos empleos.

5. Sus padres le prohibieron que el   5. _____
enfermo _____ con nosotros.   (jugar)

6. Me acerqué sigilosamente, _____   6. _____
contra la pared hasta llegar a la puerta.   (pegarse)

7. Luego, al mediodía, entraron en la
tienda y _____ aceite.

7. _____

(pedir)

8. El chico entró pero no _____ que
yo le viera.

8. _____

(querer)

9. El pequeño implora al pastor que le
_____ una flauta de la caña que le
presenta.

9. _____

(fabricar)

10. Cuando tiene una cicatriz es preciso
que no la _____ para evitar más
inflamación del tejido.

10. _____

(rascar)

Answers and Answer
Explanations for
Group Three

1. *sea*   The present subjunctive is used in the dependent noun clause after
an impersonal expression in this sentence.

2. *toquéis*   The second person plural negative command is indicated by
the next verb in the sentence, *sois*.

3. *haber*   The infinitive is used because it is the object of the expression
tener que.

4. *creemos*   This verb form is the first person plural present subjunctive of
the verb *creer*. *Crear* occurs here in an adverbial clause introduced by a
conjunction of time. Within the time frame of the sentence, the action of
the dependent clause has not happened, so the subjunctive is used.

5. *juegue*   The present subjunctive is used because it occurs in a dependent noun clause after a verb of volition, *prohibir*. The third person singular subject is indicated by the indirect object pronoun *le*, and the possessive adjective *sus*.

6. *pegándome*   The present participle is used because the verb in this
clause describes the action of the verb in the main clause: *me acerqué*.
The first person singular reflexive pronoun is used because the subject
of the first verb is first person singular.

7. *pidieron*   The third person plural preterit is used because the action is
completed in the past as part of a series of actions.

8. *quería*   The imperfect is indicated by the past subjunctive of the verb in
the dependent noun clause. If the meaning of the context is that the boy
refused to let anyone see him, then the preterit *(quiso)* can be used.

9. *fabrique*   The present subjunctive is used in the dependent noun clause
after a verb of volition. The third person singular is indicated by *al pastor*.

10. *rasque*   The present subjunctive is used in the dependent noun clause
after an impersonal expression (other than *cierto, seguro,* etc.).

GROUP FOUR

1. Iba asimilando cuanto veía con una condición de pintor como quizás no _____ otro en la historia de la pintura.

   1. _____
      (haber)

2. Hemos querido que cada sala _____ una obra maestra colgada en alguna pared.

   2. _____
      (tener)

3. Nosotros pedimos que los cuadros que no _____ de aquí se exhibiesen aquí el año próximo.

   3. _____
      (ser)

4. Si hubiéramos de asegurar los propios cuadros del Prado, la cifra _____ enormemente.

   4. _____
      (subir)

5. Sería una pena que no hubiera ningún ciudadano español que se lo _____.

   5. _____
      (ganar)

6. Entonces la gente viene a ver al cuadro para que se _____ la novela en su imaginación al verlo.

   6. _____
      (reconstruir)

7. No creo que se _____ medidas excepcionales para alcanzar esa meta.

   7. _____
      (necesitar)

8. Todos los jueves se _____ para discutir el idioma español.

   8. _____
      (reunir)

9. Esa gigante obra seguramente _____ la labor habitual de los académicos.

   9. _____
      (constituir)

10. _____ de tonterías y empecemos a aceptar que no queremos tocar algo concreto.

    10. _____
        (dejarse)

Answers and Answer Explanations for Group Four

1. *hubiera, hubiese*   The past subjunctive is used here after *quizás* to indicate probability or uncertainty on the part of the speaker.
2. *tenga*   The present subjunctive is used in the dependent noun clause after an expression of desiring, *hemos querido*, showing volition.
3. *eran*   The indicative is used because it occurs in an adjective clause and the referent is known. The imperfect is used because the time frame of the sentence is the past, but no specific moment is designated in the sentence.

4. *subiría*   The conditional is used in this *if-then* statement because the past subjunctive occurs in the *if* portion of the statement. *Subiera* would also be a correct answer.

5. *ganara, ganase*   The past subjunctive is used because the verb occurs in an adjective clause. The referent is an indefinite or nonexistent person: *no ... ningún ciudadano español.*

6. *reconstruya*   The present subjunctive is used because the verb occurs in a dependent adverbial clause after a conjunction showing purpose, *para que.*

7. *necesiten*   The present subjunctive is used because the verb occurs in a dependent noun clause after an expression of doubt in the main clause, *no creer.*

8. *reúnen*   The indicative is used because the verb occurs in the main clause of the sentence. The accent is added to place the appropriate stress on the stem of the verb, not the ending. Other correct answers are: *reunieron, reunían, reunirán.*

9. *constituye*   The present indicative is used in the main clause of the sentence.

10. *Dejémonos*   The first person plural, indirect command is indicated by the use of the same verbal form in the second verb in the sentence. This is a compound subject.

GROUP FIVE

1. Quizás no _____ exactamente como nos los muestran, pero queremos creer en ellos.

1. _____
   (ser)

2. Les caerán múltiples ofertas que seleccionarán si no _____ tomar decisiones erróneas.

2. _____
   (querer)

3. Tiene que aguantar que todos le _____ con su padre.

3. _____
   (comparar)

4. Me dijo que en caso de no _____ torero, hubiera querido ser veterinario.

4. _____
   (ser)

5. Ahora estoy muy contento de que yo me _____ comprar lo que me dé la gana.

5. _____
   (poder)

6. Estuvo veinte años _____ a los Estados Unidos antes de vender su primera casa.

6. _____
   (ir)

7. Ella siguió la vocación de maestra que es lo que quería hacer desde _____ muchos años.

7. _____
   (hacer)

8. Mi madre quería que yo _____ a coser, como había enseñado a sus otras hijas.

8. _____
   (aprender)

9. Tendrán que esforzarse mucho para que _____ todas las pinturas a Madrid.

9. _____
(llegar)

10. Eso es lo que _____ esta exposición de otras.

10. _____
(distinguir)

Answers and Answer Explanations for Group Five

1. *sean*   The present subjunctive is indicated here by the use of *quizás*, and the information contained in the second clause of the sentence. The number (plural) is indicated by the ending of *muestran* and *ellos*.

2. *quieren*   The third person plural is used because in this *if-then* statement, the tense of the verb in the *then* portion of the sentence is future. The present subjunctive is not usually used after *si*.

3. *comparen*   The present subjunctive is used because the verb occurs in a dependent noun clause after a verb in the main clause that expresses obligation: *tiene que aguantar*.

4. *ser*   The infinitive is used because it is the object of the preposition *de*.

5. *pueda*   The present subjunctive is used in the dependent noun clause after a verb expressing emotion: *estoy muy contento*.

6. *yendo*   The present participle is used as an adverb because it describes the action of the main verb, *estuvo*.

7. *hacía*   The imperfect is used because this is an expression of time using *hacer*. Since the other verbs in the sentence are in the past, the imperfect is used to indicate a period of time in the past without regard to beginning or end.

8. *aprendiera*   The past subjunctive is used in the dependent noun clause after a verb expressing a wish: *quería*.

9. *lleguen*   The present subjunctive is indicated in the adverbial clause by the conjunction that expresses purpose: *para que*.

10. *distingue*   The present indicative is used in this noun clause because the sentence simply states a fact. The verb in the main clause is not the kind that would require the subjunctive.

GROUP SIX

1. Nos gusta que usted nos _____ un poco este concepto tan novedoso.

1. _____
(explicar)

2. Aunque _____ mañana, tendré que ir al partido de mi niño.

2. _____
(llover)

3. ¿Hay alguien que _____ qué deseará hacer él cuando tenga diecisiete años?

3. _____
(saber)

4. A mí no me extraña que _____ más población en el sur de la Florida.

4. _____
(haber)

5. Su consejero le sugirió que _____ más en la Bolsa esta semana.

5. _____
(invertir)

6. Nosotros _____ que todos tuvieran   6. _____
   la misma actitud hacia la   (querer)
   modernización de la economía.

7. —¡Oiga usted! Es que yo creo que   7. _____
   _____ más.—exclamó el   (merecer)
   pordiosero indignado.

8. Yo no _____ de haber cometido el   8. _____
   desliz de haberlo dicho así en esos   (deber)
   términos.

9. Por consiguiente, hasta que _____   9. _____
   el resultado final, tampoco podemos   (saber)
   imaginar que todo está bien.

10. Imagínate que estamos en un duelo y   10. _____
    ya _____ por qué no lo hago ahora.   (ver)

Answers and Answer Explanations for Group Six

1. *haya explicado* The present perfect subjunctive is used in the dependent noun clause after a verb that expresses emotion in the main clause: *nos gusta*. Other correct answers are *explique, explicara, explicase,* or *hubiera explicado.*

2. *llueva* The conjunction *aunque* can take either the indicative or the subjunctive. In this sentence, the context indicates that the speaker does not know if it will rain or not. Whether it does or not, the speaker will go to the ball game.

3. *sepa* The present subjunctive is used in the dependent adjective clause since the speaker expresses uncertainty about what the referent knows.

4. *haya* The present subjunctive is used in the dependent noun clause after a verb in the main clause that expresses emotion: *me extraña.*

5. *invirtiera* The past subjunctive is used in the dependent noun clause after a verb in the main clause that expresses a request, or volition: *sugirió.*

6. *querríamos* The conditional indicative is indicated by the use of the past subjunctive in the dependent noun clause. Although the conditional is the best choice, other correct verb forms would be *queremos* or *queríamos*, depending on the context for this sentence.

7. *merezco* The present indicative is used because it occurs after an expression of certainty in the verb in the main clause, *creo.*

8. *debería* The conditional is indicated by the context of the sentence. The speaker simply states a fact. No hypothetical situations or statements contrary to fact are expressed in this sentence. *Debía* would also be a correct form.

9. *sepamos* The present subjunctive is used because it occurs in a dependent adverb clause after a conjunction indicating time that has not yet happened. The first person plural subject is indicated by the use of the same subject in the next clause.

10. *verás* The future indicative is used because the action expressed has not happened and the verb occurs in a main clause. The subject, *tú*, is also the subject of the first verb.

GROUP SEVEN

1. Tuvieron que esperar hasta el siglo XIX para que la gente de la región les _____ el secreto de su ubicación.

    1. _____
    (revelar)

2. Quiero que _____ ustedes a un establecimiento donde les espera un aroma extraordinario.

    2. _____
    (acercarse)

3. Hace un momento le _____ la misma cosa a otra persona que me lo preguntó.

    3. _____
    (decir)

4. ¡Qué casualidad que el libro _____ coincidido con el éxito colosal de tu padre!

    4. _____
    (haber)

5. Yo tenía que seguir la tradición a pesar de que _____ parecer un poco absurdo.

    5. _____
    (poder)

6. Mi padre estaba convencido de que yo _____ genio.

    6. _____
    (ser)

7. Espero que los lectores, como mínimo, _____ la mitad de lo que me he reído yo.

    7. _____
    (reírse)

8. Mi papá quería que yo trabajara en el almacén, pero no _____ hacerlo porque tenía otros planes.

    8. _____
    (querer)

9. Si tuviera mala suerte, el chico _____ equivocado, como le había sucedido antes.

    9. _____
    (estar)

10. Nosotros _____ que ustedes conocieran a otra persona que se llamaba Miguel.

    10. _____
    (querer)

Answers and Answer Explanations for Group Seven

1. *revelara*   The past subjunctive is used in the dependent adverbial clause after a conjunction expressing purpose: *para que*. The past tense is indicated by the preterit in the main clause.
2. *se acerquen*   The present subjunctive is used in the dependent noun clause after a verb expressing a wish (volition) in the main clause.
3. *dije*   The preterit is used in this sentence because the verb *preguntó* indicates elapsed time: *a momento ago*. The subject is given in the indirect object pronoun before *preguntó*.

4. *haya*   The present subjunctive is used to express conjecture and is indicated by the use of *¡Qué!* at the beginning of the sentence. Since no other tense is used in the sentence, another possible answer would be *hubiera* or *hubiese*.

5. *pueda*   The present subjunctive is used in the dependent adverbial clause to express conjecture by the speaker. After the conjunction *a pesar de que,* the indicative or the subjunctive can be used, but in this context the speaker seems unsure about how the tradition may seem.

6. *era*   The imperfect indicative is used in the dependent noun clause because the verb in the main clause expresses certainty.

7. *se rían*   The present subjunctive is used in the dependent noun clause because the verb in the main clause expresses a wish, or hope: *espero que.*

8. *quise*   The preterit is indicated by the context in the sentence. The meaning in the preterit, negative form, is *to refuse,* which is indicated when the speaker says that he had other plans than what his father wished.

9. *estaría*   This is an *if-then* statement with the past subjunctive in the *if* portion of the sentence. Another acceptable form would be *estuviera* since the past subjunctive can be used in place of the conditional. (Remember that only the *-iera* form of the past subjunctive can be used as the substitute.)

10. *quisiéramos*   The past subjunctive is used to express a request politely. This is called a softened statement, since a direct command would be rude in such a circumstance. Another verb form that is acceptable is the conditional, *querríamos.*

GROUP EIGHT

1. Es una meta por la que lucho diariamente y por la cual seguiré mejorando mi juego y _____ cada día.

   1. _____
   (esforzarse)

2. Galerías Preciados fue el primer gran almacén que _____ en España nuevas técnicas de ventas.

   2. _____
   (introducir)

3. No hay manera de moverlos del frente de la televisión y por mucho que usted _____, no le prestan atención.

   3. _____
   (hacer)

4. En realidad ese programa es bastante divertido, pero yo prefiero que ellos me _____ a pasear.

   4. _____
   (sacar)

5. Las bacterias marinas luminiscentes, en presencia de compuestos tóxicos, _____ apagando progresivamente.

   5. _____
   (irse)

6. Es que su capacidad de adaptación al medio les permite vivir en cualquier lugar donde _____ comida disponible.

   6. _____
        (haber)

7. Pronto, a menos que se _____ de inmediato, el mal será irreversible para las generaciones del futuro.

   7. _____
        (actuar)

8. Es muy probable que de los distritos auríferos los españoles _____ la mayor parte del oro que se comerció allí.

   8. _____
        (extraer)

9. En algunos lugares se excavaban pozos de 18 metros de profundidad, apenas suficientemente anchos para que _____ un hombre.

   9. _____
        (caber)

10. Los europeos no _____ de la existencia de esas ruinas incaicas hasta el año 1911 de nuestra era.

   10. _____
        (saber)

Answers and Answer Explanations for Group Eight

1. *esforzándome*   The present participle is used following the verbs *seguir* and *continuar* to indicate continued action. Notice that an accent is written on the first syllable of the present participle ending when a pronoun is added to the end.

2. *introdujo*   The preterit is used because in the sentence there is a specific time when the action began, a given time the new sales techniques were introduced.

3. *haga*   The present subjunctive is used in the adjective clause because it refers to an indefinite antecedent. The construction *por* + an adjective + a verb always takes the subjunctive because the antecedent is *however*, or *no matter*.

4. *saquen*   The present subjunctive is used in the dependent noun clause after a verb of volition: *prefiero*.

5. *se van*   The present indicative is used in main clauses. Since there are no other indications of time, any third person plural form in an indicative tense could be used.

6. *haya*   The present subjunctive is used after *donde* since the antecedent, *cualquier lugar*, is indefinite. This is an adjective clause.

7. *actúe*   The present subjunctive is used in the dependent adverbial clause after the conjunction of concession: *a menos que*. The present is necessary because of the future tense in the main clause. Notice the accent mark over the *u*.

8. *extrajeran, extrajesen*   The past subjunctive is used in the dependent noun clause after the impersonal expression in the main clause. Even though the tense of the verb in the impersonal expression is in the present, the selection of the past subjunctive is indicated by the use of the preterit in the last verb in the sentence: *se comerció*.

9. *cupiera, cupiese* The past subjunctive is used in the dependent adverbial clause after the conjunction of purpose. The past tense is indicated because of the use of the imperfect in the verb in the main clause.

10. *supieron* The preterit indicative is used in the main clause because the sense of the sentence is that the Europeans *found out* or *discovered* something. Since there was a beginning to when they knew, the preterit is used.

GROUP NINE

1. Se pondrán de relieve toda clase de condiciones que, si usted las _____, verá que encierran oportunidades.

1. _____ (analizar)

2. Luisa le tapó la boca, susurrando, —_____ quieto, o vas a revelar nuestro escondite.

2. _____ (Estarse)

3. —Ten cuidado, chico, para que no _____ en el musgo de los adoquines.

3. _____ (deslizar)

4. El coordinador manifestó que _____ que la gente sufriera una epidemia de cólera.

4. _____ (temer)

5. Al ver los ojos sonrientes de sus amigos, Pedro _____ y todos corrieron a abrazarse.

5. _____ (sonreír)

6. Los campesinos no quieren que los burócratas lejanos les _____ más impuestos imprevistos.

6. _____ (exigir)

7. Me alegro tanto de que _____ que no te diré nada, aunque bien lo mereces.

7. _____ (volver)

8. Esa noche los chicos _____ pensando en todos los regalos que iban a recibir.

8. _____ (dormirse)

9. El policía no dejó que nosotros _____ una plática con ella sobre el accidente.

9. _____ (mantener)

10. No _____ Ud. la calle sin mirar el tráfico calle arriba y calle abajo.

10. _____ (cruzar)

Answers and Answer Explanations for Group Nine

1. *analiza*   The present indicative is used in this sentence after the conjunction *si* because the future is used in the *then* portion of the *if-then* statement.

2. *Estate*   This form is the second person singular affirmative command form (tú). The person and number of the command is indicated by the following verb, *vas*. Notice that the accent is dropped from *está*.

3. *deslices*   The present subjunctive is used in the dependent adverb clause after the conjunction *para que*, which indicates purpose. The second person singular is indicated by the use of the familiar singular command at the beginning of the sentence.

4. *temía*   The imperfect indicative is used in this dependent clause because the verb in the main clause is not one that would require the use of the subjunctive (a verb of volition, emotion, doubt, denial, or an impersonal expression). The imperfect is also indicated by the use of the past subjunctive in the dependent noun clause that follows.

5. *sonrió*   The preterit indicative is indicated by the context of the sentence. The action occurs in a specified moment in the past.

6. *exijan*   The present subjunctive is used in the dependent noun clause after a verb expressing a wish in the main clause: *no quieren*.

7. *hayas vuelto*   The present subjunctive is used in the dependent noun clause after a verb expressing emotion: *me alegro*. The present perfect subjunctive is the best choice for this sentence completion. Another correct form would be *vuelvas*.

8. *se durmieron*   The indicative is used because this main clause states a fact. The preterit is used because *Esa noche* defines the time frame of the action.

9. *mantuviéramos, mantuviésemos*   The past subjunctive is indicated by the use of the preterit in the verb of volition in the main clause.

10. *cruce*   The present subjunctive form of the verb is used because this is a third person singular command form, *usted*.

GROUP TEN

1. Nunca creí que _____ tanta gente a una fiesta de ese tipo.

    1. _____ (venir)

2. Le _____ mucho la ayuda que me ofreció anoche con el proyecto.

    2. _____ (agradecer)

3. Querido, por favor, no _____ nosotros más de quién tiene la culpa de esta disputa.

    3. _____ (reñir)

4. Raquel empezó a correr por las calles, _____ a Jaime, quien había perdido su perro.

    4. _____ (seguir)

5. Tome Ud. el momento y _____ peso con este régimen tan sencillo.

    5. _____ (reducir)

6. A medida que _____ los minutos, la situación se ponía más y más grave.

    6. _____ (transcurrir)

7. Espero que esto no _____ que Uds. van a eliminar esta sección de ocio en forma permanente.

7. _____
   (significar)

8. Pensamos que todos los artefactos deben estar en un lugar donde _____ ser estudiados.

8. _____
   (poder)

9. Dentro de los próximos años seguramente nosotros _____ más avances tecnológicos.

9. _____
   (ver)

10. Señor, me _____ ayudarlo, pero en este momento me encuentro en condiciones lamentables también.

10. _____
    (gustar)

Answers and Answer Explanations for Group Ten

1. *viniera, viniese* The past subjunctive is used in this sentence because *nunca* negates the verb *creer*. After the negative of *creer* the subjunctive is used in the dependent noun clause. The past tense is used because *creí* is in the preterit.

2. *agradezco* The first person indicative is used because *me* before *ofreció* indicates the subject of the first verb. Another correct answer could be *agradecí*, since the speaker could have thanked his benefactor in the past.

3. *riñamos* This is the first person plural indirect command, that is usually translated *Let's not....*

4. *siguiendo* The present participle is used as an adverb because it describes the action of the verb: *empezó a correr*.

5. *reduzca* The polite command is indicated by the first verb in the sentence, *Tome*. Remember that verbs that end in *-ucir* add a *z* before the *c* in the first person singular present indicative and in the present subjunctive.

6. *transcurrían* The imperfect is used here to emphasize that time is passing without reference to when the action began or ended. The imperfect in the other verb forms in this sentence also indicate the imperfect in the first verb.

7. *signifique* The present subjunctive is used after *espero* in the dependent noun clause. Since *espero* is in the present, the present subjunctive is used.

8. *puedan* The present subjunctive is used in this dependent adjective clause because the referent is indefinite. The speaker hopes that such a place exists where the artifacts can be displayed, but offers no indication that he knows such a place exists.

9. *veremos* The future is used to indicate something will happen, but has not yet transpired. The present should not be used in place of the future in this case because the frame of reference is not the immediate future.

10. *gustaría* The conditional is used to indicate a provisional situation.

GROUP ELEVEN

1. Me gustaría comunicarme con alguna
   persona que quizás me _____ cómo
   se hace este proyecto.

   1. _____
      (decir)

2. A pesar de que _____ el Río
   Grande para los estadounidenses, lleva
   nombre *Río Bravo* para los mexicanos.

   2. _____
      (ser)

3. Después de la tormenta de anoche, nos
   sorprende de que _____ bien
   despejado hoy.

   3. _____
      (amanecer)

4. En esa isla la vida sigue _____ en
   torno al mar.

   4. _____
      (girar)

5. Cuando abrí la puerta tuve un gran
   susto; el fantasma me _____ el ojo.

   5. _____
      (guiñar)

6. Hechas las oraciones finales de la
   misa, los feligreses _____ de
   alegría.

   6. _____
      (sollozar)

7. Nos inquieta la posibilidad de que los
   extranjeros _____ balnearios, en
   vez de lugareños.

   7. _____
      (establecer)

8. Se abrió la puerta en la oscuridad y de
   repente yo _____ el paso pesado
   del intruso avanzar hacia el despacho.

   8. _____
      (oír)

9. Hace un rato yo _____ la
   invitación pero ahora no la encuentro.

   9. _____
      (ver)

10. El viejo volvió sobre sus pasos y
    desapareció de vista, _____ a cada
    uno de su mala suerte.

    10. _____
        (gruñir)

**Answers and Answer
Explanations for
Group Eleven**

1. *diga* The present subjunctive is used in this sentence to express uncertainty or conjecture on the part of the speaker. After *quizás* the subjunctive may or may not be used, depending on the degree of doubt implied.
   The rest of this sentence makes clear that this speaker is very uncertain
   about the situation.

2. *es* The indicative is used because this is a statement of fact. The verb
   occurs in the main clause.

3. *amanezca* The third person singular present subjunctive of the verb is
   used in the dependent noun clause after a verb of emotion, *nos sorprende*.

4. *girando* After the verb *seguir* the present participle is used.

5. *guiñó* This verb is different in the way that it is conjugated. Notice that in the third person singular, the *i* in the verb ending is omitted in the preterit. This only happens with *-ir* endings after *ñ* in the third person singular and plural.

6. *sollozaron* The preterit is used because there is a beginning of the action. The action is narrated instead of described.

7. *establezcan* The present subjunctive is used in the dependent noun clause after a verb in the main clause that expresses an emotion: *nos inquieta*.

8. *oí* The preterit of *oír* is used in this clause because it is introduced by *de repente*, which indicates a specific moment when the action began.

9. *vi Hace*, followed by the time expression, *un rato*, followed by the preterit indicates elapsed time that is translated as *ago* in English. The present tense of *encontrar* is dictated by *ahora*.

10. *gruñendo* The present participle is used as an adverb here to describe the action of the verb, *desapareció*. Notice that after *ñ*, the *i* in the present participle ending is dropped.

GROUP TWELVE

1. ¡Qué _____ yo cantar como ella! Esa cantante tiene la voz de un ruiseñor.

1. _____
   (saber)

2. La verdad es que lo robasteis. No me _____ que no.

2. _____
   (decir)

3. Todos contribuyen a que la pobre _____ sus sueños.

3. _____
   (realizar)

4. La obra de tejar los finos textiles requiere que el tejedor _____ la más estricta atención.

4. _____
   (prestar)

5. La nota dijo al viejecito que les _____ noticias de sus intenciones.

5. _____
   (dar)

6. Pronto venía una noticia _____ que asistiera a la conferencia el próximo día.

6. _____
   (requerir)

7. —¡_____, señor! No aguanto más sus disparates. ¡Que se calle de una vez para siempre!

7. _____
   (oír)

8. _____ unos años que la conocía cuando por primera vez ella ganó el premio.

8. _____
   (hacer)

9. El ladrón cautelosamente _____ la
llave en la cerradura, abrió la puerta y
entró.

9. _____
(introducir)

10. _____ eso, el cliente embravecido
asaltó al propietario de la taberna.

10. _____
(decir)

Answers and Answer Explanations for Group Twelve

1. *supiera*, *supiese*   The past subjunctive is used here to express a wish for something that is contrary to fact. This speaker does not sing like a nightingale, but wishes she did.

2. *digáis*   The second person plural command is indicated by the ending of the verb in the previous sentence, *robasteis*. Remember that the second person plural command is the same form as the second person plural present subjunctive.

3. *realice*   In this adverb clause, *a que* indicates purpose, requiring the subjunctive in the dependent clause. Since the tense in the main clause is present, the present subjunctive is used.

4. *preste*   The present subjunctive is used in the dependent noun clause after the verb *requerir*, which indicates a request or requirement.

5. *diera*, *diese*   The past subjunctive is used after *dijo* in this sentence where the verb indicates a request or command. *Viejecito* is the subject of the verb in the dependent clause. If the verb *decir* does not mean that a request or implicit command is intended, the indicative is used.

6. *requiriendo*   The present participle is used here to describe the action of the verb, *venía*. Notice that this verb has a stem change.

7. *Oiga*   This is a formal command. The information provided in subsequent sentences clarifies that the first sentence is a command.

8. *Hacía*   The imperfect in this sentence indicates indefinite time in the past when the action occurred. The information in this clause is background information that sets the stage for the narration of the second verb, *(ella) ganó el premio*.

9. *introdujo*   The preterit is used because the action is narrated. The action is a series of events that happened at a certain moment in the past. Notice that verbs that end with *-ducir* have an irregular stem in the preterit that contains *j*.

10. *Habiendo dicho*   The present perfect form is used here to indicate an action that took place immediately prior to the action narrated in the second verb. Another correct answer is *Diciendo*.

GROUP THIRTEEN

1. En un abrir y cerrar de ojos el peatón
desafortunado _____ equilibrio al
borde de la calle y se cayó.

1. _____
(perder)

2. Espero que todos los invitados
_____ en esa sala para la
presentación de regalos.

2. _____
(caber)

3. A medida que fabricó la cesta, observé
la manera del tejedor diestro cuando
_____ los ramales.

3. _____
(interponer)

4. Puede llegar el día en que si queremos
   ver una langosta en nuestro plato
   _____ que pintarla.

4. _____
   (tener)

5. Apenas _____ el pordiosero a la
   puerta, la posadera se la cerró de
   golpe.

5. _____
   (llegar)

6. Los patrones no quieren que los
   inversionistas _____ todos sus
   fondos en planes frívolos.

6. _____
   (arriesgar)

7. El hijo continúa la tradición. Es lo que
   _____ su distinguido padre
   difunto.

7. _____
   (querer)

8. —_____ pobres— dijo el joven,
   refiriéndose a la paja —No teníamos
   oro ni plata para usar.

8. _____
   (ser)

9. Su padre le enseñó a tejer _____
   veinticinco años.

9. _____
   (hacer)

10. No es extraño que toda la familia
    _____ a reunir las materiales.

10. _____
    (dedicarse)

Answers and Answer Explanations for Group Thirteen

1. *perdió* The preterit is used to narrate this action that took place in a specific moment in the past. Remember to write the accent over the *o* of the ending in the third person singular -*er* and -*ir* ending in the preterit.

2. *quepan* The present subjunctive is used after *esperar* in the dependent noun clause. Notice that the form for the verb *caber* is irregular in the present subjunctive because the first person singular present indicative is irregular. Only the first person singular is irregular in the present indicative. You might want to review the conjugation of *caber* in the Appendix of this book.

3. *interpuso* The preterit is used here because this is a definite moment in the past when the action occurred. The speaker was observing a weaver who made a hat.

4. *tendremos* The future is used to indicate time that is to come. The present is probably not the best choice in this sentence because the speaker is not necessarily talking about the immediate future, but *some day* in the future.

5. *llegó* The preterit in this case also refers to an action that was completed in the past. There was a beginning and end to the action.

6. *arriesguen* The present subjunctive is used after *querer*. Notice that there is a spelling change in this verb form because it ends with -*gar*.

7. *quisiera, quisiese, querría* This adjective clause refers to *lo que* which is an indefinite relative pronoun. The subjunctive expresses the speaker's uncertainty about what the deceased father would want. The conditional would express conjecture. The pluperfect subjunctive or

conditional perfect are also possibilities that move the time frame farther back to a time prior to when the father died. These possibilities are: *hubiera querido, hubiese querido,* or *habría querido.*

8. *Éramos*   The imperfect describes the state of being of the speaker and his family. That the subject is plural is indicated by the verb in the next sentence.

9. *hace*   The present tense of *hacer* plus the preterit indicate that the event happened twenty years *ago.*

10. *se dedique*   After the impersonal expression *No es extraño,* the present subjunctive is used. Notice the spelling change because the infinitive ends with *-car.* Also notice that the noun *familia* is a singular noun requiring a singular verb ending.

TASK 3: PARAGRAPH COMPLETION WITHOUT ROOT WORDS

In the following selections there is one word that is missing. In many instances it is a pronoun, a preposition, a single verb or adjective, or a definite or indefinite article. You are to insert the one word that makes logical and grammatical sense in the context of the selection. Before doing this section, it would be a good idea to review verbs that require specific prepositions after them, such as *consistir en*, and to check the difference between *por* and *para*. Be sure to check your answers after each set so that you do not reinforce mistakes you may be making.

Directions: First read through the selection. Then write a word on the numbered line that corresponds to the numbered blank in the text. Write only ONE word that completes the meaning of the selection. No credit will be given for words that are not spelled correctly or words that lack correct accent marks. You have 8 minutes to complete this part of the exam.

EXERCISES AND ANSWERS

GROUP 1
Que se queja del tiempo

Recientemente llegó a España una ola de

frío, causando ___(1)___ todos los que

estaban hartos ___(2)___ calor una oportu-

nidad de recoger los esquís y dirigirse a las

montañas más cercanas. ___(3)___ cambio,

para los acostumbrados ___(4)___ clima

tropical, ___(5)___ molestaba la necesidad

de arriesgar sus vidas en las carreteras

cubiertas de nieve y bloqueadas con los

choques que siempre resultaban.

1. _____

2. _____

3. _____

4. _____

5. _____

GROUP 2
El consumo electrónico en la Feria en Las Vegas

Lo que vale para Estados Unidos vale para

el resto de los países desarrollados. Parece

que ___(1)___ una necesidad imperiosa

por cambiarse de teléfono móvil, ___(2)___

de tener varias consolas electrónicas en la

habitación. ___(3)___ la Organización, la

saturación del mercado es ___(4)___ que

no se contempla en ambientes ___(5)___

eufóricos como la gran Feria Anual del

Consumo Electrónico de Las Vegas,

donde acudieron empresas o visitantes

de 110 países.

1. _____

2. _____

3. _____

4. _____

5. _____

GROUP 3
La salsa es dinámica. Una entrevista.
(*Richie Ray y Bobby Cruz hablan con* Semana, *1/15/06*)

La vieja reguetona no es _____(1)_____ tema de

reguetón _____(2)_____ una fusión. De hecho

es bueno recordar que la salsa _____(3)_____

llama así porque es una mezcla de estilos

que de por sí no _____(4)_____ gustaba a los

puristas de los años 60. La salsa es eso.

Mezclas, cruce de influencias, experi-

mentación, riesgo, es algo dinámico. No

se puede estancar _____(5)_____ limitar.

1. _____

2. _____

3. _____

4. _____

5. _____

GROUP 4
Una obra de arte natural: la yema de huevo
(*CocinaonTerra.com*)

Hay quien opina que el huevo, sobre todo

el de gallina, se divide en tres partes:

_____(1)_____ protectoras, la cáscara y la clara,

y una deliciosa, la yema; _____(2)_____ hecho,

el genio de todos los cocineros que en el

mundo _____(3)_____ sido no ha bastado

_____(4)_____ conseguir una "salsa" _____(5)_____

la yema de huevo.

1. _____

2. _____

3. _____

4. _____

5. _____

GROUP 5
Inmigrantes han comenzado a dar a Texas una nueva identidad
(*Terra.com*)

"Vamos rumbo a un nuevo Texas", aseguró   1. _____

el ex secretario ____(1)____ vivienda de   2. _____

Estados Unidos, Henry Cisneros, ____(2)____   3. _____

hablar sobre el cambio demográfico   4. _____

____(3)____ experimenta la entidad   5. _____

____(4)____ una reciente entrevista. Las

consecuencias de este cambio ____(5)____

observarán en el terreno social, político

y económico.

GROUP 6
Detrás de la taza de café
(© Copyright Terra Networks, S. A.)

Al alzar una taza de café colombiano y   1. _____

llevárselo ____(1)____ la boca, usted   2. _____

cumplirá ____(2)____ la última etapa, y   3. _____

la definitiva, de un proceso que pudo   4. _____

____(3)____ empezado cuatro años ____(4)____   5. _____

cuando una semilla fue sembrada en

las montañas cafeteras de Colombia.

La historia se inicia en el vivero, donde

cerca de 1 millón ____(5)____ personas

siembran café.

GROUP 7
Con sabor a Cuba...
(*Terra.com*)

Descubre las recetas de un menú cubano.

Empieza _____(1)_____ un mojito como aperi-

tivo y continúa con uno de los ocho platos

fuertes que escogimos. Luego, _____(2)_____

quieres preparar una cena realmente típica,

deberás seguir con el postre. Tenemos flan,

arroz con leche _____(3)_____ vasos de

guayaba con queso. Suaves y exquisitos,

estos postres se repiten en _____(4)_____ toda

América Latina, pero de país _____(5)_____

país el sabor cambia y se convierte

en único.

1. _____

2. _____

3. _____

4. _____

5. _____

GROUP 8
El Callejón del Beso

Dice la leyenda que las parejas que pasen

_____(1)_____ el Callejón y no se den un beso

en el tercer escalón, tendrán siete años de

mala suerte; y _____(2)_____ el contrario, si

se besan con amor disfrutarán de 15 años

de buena fortuna. Pero _____(3)_____ es una

leyenda. _____(4)_____ todos modos los

poblanos gozarán de buena suerte si

vienen muchos turistas _____(5)_____ haber

oído de la leyenda.

1. _____

2. _____

3. _____

4. _____

5. _____

GROUP 9
El juego de pelota en el mundo hispano

La historia del juego de pelota en el mundo

hispano se remonta a la época precolom-

bina, sin los aspectos casi religiosos que

_____(1)_____ caracterizan actualmente. En el

Popol Vuh se cuenta el conflicto _____(2)_____

los dioses del infierno y del cielo, en

_____(3)_____ cual triunfaron los dioses

benévolos. _____(4)_____ no se lo asocia

actualmente con ritos religiosos, ha

llegado a ser casi una religión por el gran

entusiasmo que muestran los aficionados

en el estadio _____(5)_____ días de partido.

1. _____

2. _____

3. _____

4. _____

5. _____

GROUP 10
Ciudad de México
(*Terra.com*)

Pocas ciudades en el mundo tienen

_____(1)_____ atractivos culturales como

Ciudad de México. Su historia comenzó a

escribirse en tiempos del siglo XIV, cuando

los aztecas _____(2)_____ fundaron en el lugar

donde apareció un águila parada _____(3)_____

un nopal devorando una serpiente. Allí,

edificaron una ciudad grandiosa, con

templos y palacios, que deslumbró a los

españoles que la conquistaron. Años

1. _____

2. _____

3. _____

después, es ___(4)___ de los primeros   4. _____

destinos turísticos y la ciudad más poblada   5. _____

___(5)___ mundo.

GROUP 11
Secretos del mar. Por Tito Rodríguez, Director del Instituto
Argentino de Buceo

___(1)___ menudo se comete el error de   1. _____

creer que el instinto y el aprendizaje se   2. _____

oponen entre ___(2)___ . Mientras que el   3. _____

instinto es el conocimiento heredado, el   4. _____

aprendizaje se adquiere ___(3)___ del   5. _____

nacimiento. Una ventaja del aprendizaje

___(4)___ el instinto es que el compor-

tamiento ___(5)___ puede modificar rápi-

damente, dando respuesta inmediata a

situaciones cambiantes.

GROUP 12
El mejor oficio del mundo. Por Gabriel García Márquez
(*Etcétera*, enero 2006)

La grabadora oye ___(1)___ no escucha,   1. _____

repite—como un loro digital—pero no   2. _____

piensa, es fiel pero no tiene corazón, y a   3. _____

fin ___(2)___ cuentas su versión literal no   4. _____

será tan confiable como ___(3)___ de quien   5. _____

___(4)___ atención a las palabras vivas del

interlocutor, ___(5)___ valora con su

inteligencia y las califica con su moral.

GROUP 13
La Florida busca fuentes de energía alternativas. Por David Royse
(*AP*, 12 de enero 2006)

Pero en varias ocasiones recientemente, ha   1. _____

hablado de una forma ___(1)___ más   2. _____

inusual de producir energía: la quema de   3. _____

bagazo, la parte que queda de la caña de   4. _____

azúcar ___(2)___ se le ha extraído el   5. _____

azúcar. En varios lugares alrededor

___(3)___ mundo, el bagazo se quema para

alimentar las mismas plantas de proce-

samiento. No ___(4)___, en algunos casos,

no hay suficiente bagazo como para vender

a una compañía ___(5)___ su uso público.

GROUP 14
En familia, ¿cómo le podemos enseñar a los niños a ahorrar?
(*Terra.com*, 15 de enero 2006)

___(1)___ planeta se mueve a base de   1. _____

bienes materiales, siendo ___(2)___ de los   2. _____

más importantes y codiciados el dinero.   3. _____

Todos necesitamos y deseamos cosas que   4. _____

tienen un precio en metálico. Los niños no   5. _____

están exentos de esto y ___(3)___ lo tanto

parece ser una buena idea ___(4)___ de

enseñar el valor del dinero y del ahorro

___(5)___ que son pequeños.

GROUP 15
Viaje desde Ecuador a las prodigiosas islas Galápagos.
Por Andrés Fernández Rubio
(*Terra.com*)

Las dos hembras de lobo marino asoman   1. _____

____(1)____ repente dentro ____(2)____ agua,   2. _____

sin hacerse notar, demostrando sus dotes   3. _____

de nadadoras consumadas. Aman el juego,   4. _____

giran y ____(3)____ vueltas en alegres contor-   5. _____

siones. Una de ellas se lanza de frente

____(4)____ un torpedo y se detiene a unos

centímetros del cristal de las gafas del

buceador, mira al intruso con curiosidad y

en una pirueta se desvía y pasa a su lado

____(5)____ rozarlo.

GROUP 16
La Fundación Santa Teresa

La Fundación Santa Teresa, localizada en   1. _____

el Departamento de Guanajuato, ____(1)____   2. _____

misión es otorgar becas y créditos educa-   3. _____

tivos a ____(2)____ que ____(3)____ necesiten,   4. _____

contribuye en ____(4)____ medida a la for-   5. _____

mación de líderes capacitados a desarrollar

económica y socialmente en la vida

comunitaria del Estado. Con tal que el

solicitante merezca la oportunidad,

nada ____(5)____ faltará para realizar el

sueño educativo.

GROUP 17
Coordinación del Programa de desarrollo humano. Oportunidades
(Dirección General Adjunta de Comunicación y Difusión, México, D. F.
Gob.mx, 15 de enero 2006)

El Índice de Desarrollo Humano es un   1. _____

instrumento universal desarrollado   2. _____

___(1)___ la Organización de las Naciones   3. _____

Unidas ___(2)___ la medición del nivel de   4. _____

bienestar, situación de vida y salud, y el   5. _____

acceso a la educación de la población. El

IDH ___(3)___ compuesto de tres variables:

la esperanza de vida al nacer; el logro

educativo, medido ___(4)___ la alfabeti-

zación de adultos y la tasa combinada de

matriculación ___(5)___ los diversos nive-

les escolares, y el Producto Interno Bruto

real per capita.

GROUP 18
¿Mi trabajo o mi bebé? Cómo conciliar la vida familiar con el trabajo
(Organización para la Cooperación y Desarrollo Económicos,
Fondo de Cultura Económico. *Gob.mx*, 15 de enero 2006)

En ___(1)___ obra se abordan los desafíos   1. _____

que enfrentan las parejas jóvenes para   2. _____

equilibrar las carencias de trabajo   3. _____

___(2)___ las necesidades familiares, y las

implicaciones que sobre ___(3)___ tienen

las tendencias sociales y el mercado labo-

ral. Cada uno de los países que aquí se

analizan enfrenta retos demográficos,   4. _____

sociales y culturales diversos y es   5. _____

____(4)____ como se destacan las posibili-

dades con que cuenta toda sociedad para

resolver ____(5)____ problemas.

GROUP 19
Bienvenido a la UMED. Por Ing. J. Fausto Gutiérrez Aragón
(*UMEX.edu.mx*, 15 de enero 2006)

Reciba un cordial saludo y sea bienvenido   1. _____

a nuestra sociedad de aprendizaje, la   2. _____

Universidad Mexicana de Educación a   3. _____

Distancia, la cual me honra ____(1)____ ser 4. _____

su Rector. El esfuerzo ____(2)____ interés   5. _____

de la UMED son atender las necesidades

educativas de todo estudiante, articulando

los elementos necesarios ____(3)____

facilitarle el acceso a la información

indispensable ____(4)____ que con su propio

empeño y actitud positiva enfrente el reto

de estudiar mediante ____(5)____ sistema

que le consumiría más tiempo y mayor

esfuerzo como estudiante independiente.

GROUP 20
Semáforo de alerta volcánica ¿Qué hacer cuando el semáforo está en rojo, si la instrucción es evacuar?
(*Gob.mx*)

Conserva la calma, reúne ___(1)___ tu

familia, pónles una identificación, cuida

que puertas y ventanas queden cerradas y

coloca una sábana o tela blanca ___(2)___

la calle para comprobar que se trata de un

domicilio evacuado. ___(3)___ inmediata-

mente a los centros de reunión. Lleva sólo

___(4)___ indispensable. Al llegar al refu-

gio temporal regístrate y ubícate en el sitio

que se ___(5)___ indique.

1. _____

2. _____

3. _____

4. _____

5. _____

Answers

Group 1

1. *a* After the word *causado*, *por* is used to express the reason why something is done. However, in this sentence, *todos* refers to people and functions as the object of the verb *causando*. When a person or something is personified, use the personal *a*.
2. *del* After the expression *estar harto*, the preposition *de* is used. Remember that *de* is always combined with the masculine article *el*, making the contraction *del*.
3. *En* *En* is part of the expression *en cambio*. Many such expressions must simply be memorized. If you missed this item, begin a list of the expressions you need to learn.
4. *al* The correct preposition to use after *acostumbrar* is *a*. Just as the article *el* is combined with the preposition *de*, *a* is combined with *el* to make *al*. Remember that many words that end with *ama, ema, ima, oma* end with the letter *a*, but the nouns are really masculine.
5. *les* The only word that makes logical sense in the context is a pronoun. To find the correct number and person, you need to refer to the subject of the expession *están hartos de*, and determine that it is third person plural. The verb *molestar,* like *gustar* and many others, requires the indirect object pronoun. The subject of the verb *molestar* is *necesidad.*

Group 2

1. *hay* If you look at this sentence, you will see that there is no verb in the main clause. In some such cases a verb will be needed to complete the sentence. The only verb that makes sense is one meaning "there is."

2. *o, y* The selection talks about the necessity of changing cell phones or having electronic equipment at home. Either conjunction would work in either case.

3. *Según* The word that logically completes the sentence here is the word meaning "according to," which is *según*. Although *dice* would make sense, syntactically it does not make sense when the phrase begins the sentence because in declarative sentences, especially in formal writing, the subject comes before the verb.

4. *algo, la* An indefinite pronoun meaning "something" works best in this sentence. The relative pronoun *la (que)* could also be used, meaning "that which."

5. *tan* In the adjective structure of *tanto ... como, tan* is shortened to *tan* before adverbs and adjectives. It remains *tanto* in front of nouns.

Group 3

1. *un, el* The correct gender of *tema* is masculine. Use either a definite or indefinite article.

2. *sino* Even if you do not know the word *reguetón*, notice that it describes *tema*. The selection goes on to talk about how *salsa* is different because it is a mixture, *mezcla*, of styles. The information in that next sentence should tell you to use the conjunction *sino* to indicate something contrary to the noun that precedes it. Make sure you scan the whole selection to look for the whole context. You do not use *que* after *sino* because no verb follows the conjunction.

3. *se* The reflexive pronoun *se* represents the noun *salsa*. Thus, *se llama así* becomes "(it) calls itself this way."

4. *les* The only pronoun possible is *les* because it refers to *los puristas*. Remember that the subject of the verb *gustar* is the object in English. "It is pleasing to the purists" is the literal translation of the structure in English.

5. *ni* Use the negative conjunction here to mean "or." When the verb is negated with "No" or a negative adjective, pronoun, or adverb, use a negative after the verb. *Ni* is the negative of *o*.

Group 4

1. *dos* You need a number here to complete the meaning. The number "three" is mentioned. Although there are three nouns that follow, the word *protectoras* describes *la cáscara y la clara* and the adjective *deliciosa* describes *la yema*.

2. *de* This is an expression that is worth remembering. *De hecho* means "in fact."

3. *han* The subject of the verb is *cocineros*, not *mundo*. Do not be mislead by whether nouns right before or after the blank are singular or plural. Always look for the subject of the verb.

4. *para* The preposition *para* expresses purpose, which is the meaning in this context. It means "in order to." Remember that the infinitive follows a preposition. The pronouns are always attached to the ends of infinitives and never come before it, so you can easily eliminate that option.

5. *como* This is difficult, because you have to understand the rest of the sentence. Implicit is the meaning that nothing has served like an egg to make a sauce. The key words are the basic sentence, *el genio ... no ha bastado ... como la yema*.

Group 5

1. *de*   The preposition *de* connects the nouns *ex secretario* and *vivienda*. Remember that a noun cannot modify another noun in Spanish, so they are connected with the preposition *de*. *Vivienda* may resemble the present participle *viviendo*, but the last letter *a* tells you that the word is a noun.

2. *al*   The only word that makes sense here is one that means "upon"—in Spanish, *al*. Before the infinitive, you could also use the article *el* to make the infinitive function as a noun, but *hablar* in this case is not the subject of the verb in the main clause.

3. *que*   The most common way to connect clauses is *que*, which is the only word that would connect the two clauses in the sentence.

4. *en*   The preposition *en* indicates the occasion when Mr. Cisneros talked about the new Texas.

5. *se*   This is the *se* substitute for the passive voice. No agent is stated. The direct object pronoun is not used here unless there is *se* already in front of the blank.

Group 6

1. *a*   The preposition *a* indicates movement in some direction, toward some place, in this case the mouth. Use the preposition *a* after verbs of motion or to indicate direction.

2. *con*   The preposition that follows *cumplir* is *con*. When you learn the infinitive, learn the preposition that commonly follows it and you will not have any problems with this type of question.

3. *haber*   The word can be a verb form, either conjugated, or a participle, or infinitive. In this case, the infinitive follows *poder*, and the verb *haber* comes before past participles, like *empezado*. Relying on the Spanish rules for which parts of speech to use with *poder* and past participles is more reliable for getting a right answer than spending time translating the phrase.

4. *atrás*   Make sure you know all the adverbs for location, not just the most common ones. *Atrás* means "back" in the sense of "past" or "in the past." The context compares the final product of the coffee plant, the cup of coffee, with the seeds that were planted.

5. *de*   After the number *millón*, the preposition *de* is used to mean "a million people."

Group 7

1. *con*   The verb *empezar* is followed by the preposition *a* when it is followed by another infinitive. In this sentence, it is followed by a noun, so use *con*, meaning "begin with."

2. *si*   Look at the whole sentence to see what goes in the blank. The sentence is an "if-then" sentence, and the clue is in *Luego, ... deberás seguir con*. The personal pronoun *tú* does not really make sense in this sentence when the second clause is added.

3. *o, y*   Either conjunction will work in this case, although it makes more sense to use *o* because the whole selection talks about making selections from the menu, instead of simply listing them. You are being given directions to make a selection.

4. *casi*   The word *toda* eliminates all other options. Nothing else will work between *el* and *toda* except *casi*, meaning "almost."

5. *en* The phrases "from ... to" in Spanish is *de ... en.* The word *cambia* implies a series of countries. Do not try to translate literally or the phrase will not make sense.

Group 8

1. *por* The preposition *por* in this sentence means "along" or "through," which is a common use with *pasar,* followed by the noun for some kind of way or road.

2. *por* The preposition *por* in this sentence is used in an expression that is a way of saying "on the other hand." If you do not know this phrase, put it on your list of phrases to learn and use.

3. *sólo* Although the other phrase that would work is *no más,* the directions call for one word. Make sure to learn synonyms. There are always multiple ways of saying something.

4. *de* The preposition *de* is part of the idiom *de todos modos.* Here you have no other choice but to memorize it.

5. *por* In this case *por* expresses manner or means. Tourists "having heard" about the story is the meaning.

Group 9

1. *lo* The pronoun refers to the *juego de pelota* in the first sentence. It is a direct object pronoun. The pronoun does not refer to *aspectos casi peligrosos.* Remember that *actualmente* means "presently." It is a false cognate.

2. *entre* The context talks about a conflict, then mentions two types of gods, good and evil. The only word that works in this case is *entre,* meaning "between."

3. *el* The word *el* goes with *cual* making a relative pronoun that refers to *conflicto.* The article that goes with *cual* has to be the same gender and number as the noun to which it refers.

4. *Aunque* You need to understand the whole sentence in order to see that the word here is "although." The two clauses are contradictory, with the clause *no se lo asocia,* followed by the clause *ha llegado a ser.* The only word that makes sense is *aunque.* There are other phrases that would fit, but none would consist of one word.

5. *los* Remember that *día* is a masculine noun. With days of the week, *los* means "on."

Group 10

1. *tantos* Although *atractivos* has the ending of some adjectives, in this sentence it is a noun. The word *como* later on in the sentence means that the only word that fits in this sentence is *tantos.*

2. *la* The direct object pronoun refers to *Ciudad de México,* which is the name of the city (*la ciudad*), so it is the word that grammatically and logically fits the sentence. When you see a blank in front of a conjugated verb, you should always think of pronouns and negatives as possible answers.

3. *sobre* If you know the ancient story of the eagle that landed atop a nopal to indicate the chosen land for the last tribe to migrate to the Central Valley of Mexico, then this answer is easy. *Sobre* means "on top of" and is the best answer here. The preposition *en* could also be used.

4. *uno* The preposition *de (los primeros)* after the blank reduces the possible answers to one, *uno.* It is not shortened to *un* because it does not come immediately in front of a masculine singular noun.

5. *del* This is a superlative construction. Remember that if you translate literally, you will use the wrong preposition in Spanish. To express superlatives in Spanish use *de*, and *de* followed by *el* is always *del*, meaning "in the world."

Group 11

1. *A* This is part of an expression meaning "often." There are others that also mean the same thing, such as *muchas veces* and *frecuentemente*, which is a cognate. It is always helpful to learn expressions that are not cognates.

2. *sí* Although *entre* is often followed by a pronoun, in the context of this paragraph the correct word is *sí*, meaning "between the two of them," or "themselves."

3. *después* The learning that the article discusses happens after birth, so *después* is the only word that works.

4. *sobre* A common meaning for *sobre* is "about," which is what it means in this sentence. The preposition *de* does not work, because the article *el* would be combined with the preposition to form *del*.

5. *se* This is another example of the *se* substitute for the passive voice. It often comes before the verb *poder*, especially when the expression means "it can be said...."

Group 12

1. *pero* The conjunction *pero* is used to introduce other clauses in this group, and makes sense in this case. The verb *oye* communicates a different activity than *escucha*.

2. *de* *A fin de cuentas* is an expression meaning "in the end," or "in the final analysis."

3. *la* This word relates to *su versión*, referring to the tape recorder's version that is compared with "that of," *la de*, the person who pays attention to live words.

4. *pone* *Poner atención* is an expression for "to pay attention." Make sure not to try to translate literally. The verb tense is the present indicative because there is no structure that would indicate the subjunctive.

5. *las* This word is the direct object of *valora* and refers to *palabras*. You can find a parallel structure in the following clause, *las califica con su moral*.

Group 13

1. *todavía* The only word that makes sense here is "yet," or "still." The word *aún* can also be used, but if it is, it should have a written accent. Without the accent, *aun* has the meaning of "until" or "even," as in "even though."

2. *cuando* This adverb is indicated by the verb *queda* and *extraído*.

3. *del* The word *alrededor* is followed by *de*, and in this case is combined with *el* to make *del*.

4. *obstante* This is an expression that must be memorized. It means the same thing as *sin embargo*, which means "nevertheless."

5. *para* "For the benefit of" is the meaning of *para* in this case. It indicates purpose.

Group 14

1. *Nuestro*   Remember that *planeta* is masculine, in spite of ending with the letter *a*. Other correct answers are *Un*, or *El*, or *Este*.
2. *uno*   This word refers to *bienes*, which is a masculine plural noun. You can tell gender by the article *los*, which follows in the comparison stated.
3. *por*   *Por lo tanto* is an expression using *por* that has to be memorized. It means "therefore."
4. *la*   *La* is here an article substituting for the noun *idea*.
5. *desde*   In the context of the selection, "since" childhood is the meaning of the phrase. Remember that there is more than one meaning for most words. *Desde* also means "from."

Group 15

1. *de*   *De repente* is an expression meaning "suddenly." *De* is the only word that makes the expression complete.
2. *del*   *De* most often follows *dentro*. Although *agua* is a feminine noun, in the singular form it begins with a stressed *a*, so it takes a masculine singular article. The article is used here to designate the water in a particular place. Thus, the preposition *de* is combined with the article *el* and we get the contraction *del*.
3. *dan*   *Dar vueltas* is another expression for "turning around," and it is a good expression to remember. Use the same verbal tense as the preceding verb, *giran*.
4. *como*   Here *como* is used to indicate a simile, "like a torpedo," to describe the actions of the animals.
5. *sin, para*   "Without" or "in order to" are the two words that would make sense in this context. A preposition is necessary before the infinitive.

Group 16

1. *cuya*   "Whose" is the word that makes the most sense logically and grammatically. Remember that *cuya* is feminine here, because it always has the same gender and number (singular or plural) as the noun it precedes. The definite article *la* would not make sense in the whole sentence.
2. *los*   This word is part of a relative pronoun that is the subject of *necesiten*. There is no antecedent to indicate gender, so use the masculine form. Another correct word could be *cuántos*.
3. *los*   The word is a direct object here, referring to *becas y créditos*. No other single pronoun by itself would make sense.
4. *gran*   The expression *en gran medida* is common. Remember that *grande* is shortened before singular nouns of either gender.
5. *le*   Before verbs like *faltar, gustar, importar, molestar,* and others, use an indirect object pronoun.

Group 17

1. *por*   The passive voice is used in this sentence, with *ser* followed by a past participle, followed by *por* and then the agent of the action.
2. *para*   *Para* indicates purpose in the sentence "in order to" make a measurement of standard of living.
3. *está*   The verb *estar* is required in the sentence because of the past participle *compuesto*, which is used as an adjective. The verb describes the condition or state of being of the *Índice de Desarrollo Humano*.
4. *por*   The sentence requires *por* because the measurement is made "by means of" adult literacy.
5. *en*   The meaning here is the combined rate of enrollment "in" diverse school levels or grades, not "by." Therefore, *de* is not a good choice. In

the context of the selection, the focus is on the population "in" school and adult literacy, not the process of enrolling students in school.

Group 18

1. *esta*   *Esta* is the best word, although *la* would also be grammatically and logically correct.
2. *con*   The word *equilibrar las carencias de trabajo* followed by *necesidades familiares* makes *con* the most logical word to put in the blank. A preposition is the only word that makes grammatical sense.
3. *ellas*   The pronoun refers to *las parejas jóvenes* and must agree in gender and number.
4. *así*   This word functions as the object of *es*, and makes sense in the sentence because it talks about the analysis of the working situations that will reveal possibilities for resolving problems.
5. *sus, los*   Either word would serve to make sense of the sentence. Remember that *problema* is masculine.

Group 19

1. *por*   *Por* in the sentence indicates manner, mode, or means, and means "by means of." The speaker is honored "by" being the Director of the University.
2. *e*   The only word that works in the sentence is "and." For the University, both effort and interest are involved in attending to the students' needs. When the conjunction *y* comes before a word beginning with the letter *i*, the *y* changes to *e*.
3. *para*   The meaning is "in order to" facilitate the access to necessary information. *Para* expresses purpose.
4. *para*   The only option that works in the sentence is *para* because you will find the subjunctive later on in the sentence (the verb *enfrente*). Unless you recognize the word *enfrente* as a verb, you will probably fail to find the right word. After *que*, however, you need a verb. *El reto* is the object of a verb and will make no sense in the sentence if it does not function as such.
5. *un*   Remember that *sistema* is masculine. The indefinite article *un* is the best word, although *el* would not be incorrect. It would not make much sense logically, however. The difference is "the challenge of studying by means of a system that will consume..." and "the challenge of studying by means of the system that...."

Group 20

1. *a*   The personal *a* is necessary in this blank because the object of the verb is the family.
2. *hacia*   The word "toward" is the most logical in the sentence. The instructions call for putting a white cloth or sheet facing the street, so that authorities will know that the house has been evacuated. The word *en* does not work, because it makes no sense to put a sign in the street.
3. *Ve*   Your should have noticed that all the commands are familiar (*tú* commands). The logical choice of a word is the command for "go." Other verbs of motion could be used, such as *sal, corre,* or *huye,* but *ve* is the most logical because it indicates an ordered evacuation. The preposition *a* after *inmediatamente* tells you that a verb of motion is needed.
4. *lo*   The neuter article is the only choice for this blank. It means "the indispensable things."

5. *te*   The indirect object pronoun is used here with the *se* substitute for the passive in the phrase "the site that may be indicated to you." Because all of the verbs are directed to you, *tú*, there is no other choice.

TASK 4: INFORMAL WRITING

Suggestions   This section consists of a prompt with information about the kind of message you are to write. You will have 10 minutes to complete this section. Make sure that you use as much good language as possible. You should also incorporate all of the appropriate greetings and closings, organize your note, memo, or letter so that it mirrors a natural communication. Be sure to use the appropriate register. If it is a message to someone you would address as Mr., Mrs., or some other title, don't forget to use *Ud.* or *Uds.* If it is someone you would call by the first name, use *tú, Uds.,* or *vosotros.*

In order to finish in the allotted time, think through what you are going to say before beginning to write. Do not simply write one sentence for each of the suggested prompts. Elaborate on your ideas. You may write more than one paragraph.

Some critical points of grammar that you should incorporate are correct verb forms when you conjugate them, correct adjective and noun agreement, and correct uses of the subjunctive. When you are asked to imagine your response to something like *su reacción a...* or *sus deseos para...*, you should consider them natural opportunities to show your command of grammar.

Just for quick review before doing this section, remember the common structures that require the use of the subjunctive, and study the following structures you could use in your writing sample.

In noun clauses when there is a change of subject, use the subjunctive after the following verbs when the verbs express will, emotion, or doubt, or after an impersonal expression:

> *alegrarse de que*
> *tener miedo que*
> *temer que*
> *dudar que*
> *molestarle (a uno) que*
> *frustrarle (a uno) que*
> *sorprenderle (a uno)*
> *esperar que*
> *querer que*
> *desear que*
> *hacerle (a uno) que*
> *emocionarle (a uno)*
> *sentir que*
> *arrepentirse que*
> *darle (a uno) lástima*

You should also be careful to use correctly the prepositions *por* or *para*, and to watch for infinitives that take prepositions that are not literal translations, for example, *depender de*. In addition, this would be a good scenario to use exclamations such as *¡Qué lástima que no estuvieras con nosotros!* or others like it. These expressions are common in informal writing and very appropriate in this part of the exam. You can also use some of the situations described in the oral practice section of this book by making them written instead of oral. For example, you can imagine any situation in your family, school, community, or country, in which you have felt happy, sad, surprised, afraid, or doubtful. You can try to remember any time when you had to write a message of some sort, and imagine other situations similar to the ones in the practice exercises.

Samples of Informal Writing

The samples that follow should give you some idea of what is expected on this part of the free-response informal writing part. Remember that when the directions say to comment on *sus reacciones* or *sus esperanzas*, you can use a variety of phrases, not just the words *alegrarse, esperar,* or *desear.*

After each sample there is a commentary about the errors found in the sample. The errors are indicated in boldface type so that you will know that the language is incorrect.

> Directions: Below you will see instructions for a writing sample that responds to the topic described. Be sure to include the information mentioned in your response. You will have 10 minutes to write your message in your test booklet.

Habrá un estudiante de intercambio que vendrá a pasar un semestre con Ud. en su casa y escuela. Al recibir las noticias, escríbale una carta para presentársele y darle la bienvenida. Incluya Ud. los siguientes puntos:

- saludos apropiados y presentación
- su reacción a las noticias de su visita
- sus esperanzas para el semestre
- avísele Ud. que le escribirá más tarde

Sample One

Hola, Miguel,

   Yo llamo Paco y **yo gusto** ver **a Ud.** cuando **viene** para **atender** a **nos** escuela. **Yo gusto** también que **voy** a vivir en mi casa. Mi casa es tu casa. Mi familia es **simpático**. Espero que **Ud.** gusta **ser** en mi casa. Nosotros vamos a **tener un buen tiempo**. Escribo **a Ud.** más tarde. Digo **a Ud. que** necesita llevar pasar el semestre aquí. La vida es muy **differente** aquí.

Su amigo,
Paco

Rating: Low
Commentary
   This sample rates a very low score because it contains numerous conspicuous examples of bad grammar and shows very little sensitivity. If the student is the same age, *tú* should have been used. The sample contains literal translations from English to Spanish, such as the frequent use of *a Ud.* instead of the correct indirect pronoun *le, tener un buen tiempo* instead of *disfrutar del tiempo juntos, divertirse,* or *pasar un buen rato.* The writer also uses *atender* instead of *asistir a.* The verb *gustar* is consistently misused. The writer should

have written *me gusta* or *me gustará* in the first usage, and *me gusta* in the second. The subjunctive should have been used in the third example of the verb *gustar* in the structure *espero que le guste a Ud.* There are never any double letters *f* in Spanish. The possessive adjective for "our" is *nuestra* to agree with *escuela.* Also, *ser* should have been *estar. Simpático* needs to be *simpática* to agree with *familia.* There are other errors also, such as omitted prepositions and accents. Overall, this sample shows that the writer has a limited capability to communicate in writing in Spanish.

Sample Two

Miguel,

Soy Paco y será un placer tenerte en casa con nosotros el año que viene. Sé que te gustará estar aquí con nosotros. Estoy seguro que estarás confortable en nuestra casa porque es muy grande. Nuestra escuela es muy grande pero estoy seguro de que no habrá problema para ti porque todos los muchachos son muy simpáticos y los profesores, aunque son duros, son muy buenos. Espero que puedas disfrutar del tiempo con nosotros el semestre que viene. Te escribiré más tarde con sugerencias para lo que necesites llevar. Estoy seguro que será divertido.

Paco

Rating: Medium
Commentary

This sample includes neither an appropriate greeting nor a closing, indicating that the writer is not familiar with how one should begin or end a personal letter. The informal address, *tú*, is used correctly. The sample does contain correct grammar and a variety of verb tenses, but mostly relies on the prompts for what to say. The vocabulary does seem somewhat limited. *Confortable*, for example, is an Anglicism, and *cómodo* would be a better word to use. *Duro* is also a literal translation and can mean that the teachers assign hard work. However, it would be much better to know words like *exigentes, aplicados,* or *compasivos* to be a little more descriptive of what the teachers are like. The writer has correctly used the subjunctive and correctly conjugated irregular verbs in the future. Overall, this sample shows that the writer can coherently express himself in Spanish, but it is not an outstanding sample of writing.

Sample Three

Hola, Miguel,

Me llamo Paco y ¡cuánto me alegra oír que vengas para estudiar en nuestro colegio el semestre que viene! Tu visita nos ofrecerá una gran oportunidad de compartir nuestras culturas, para ti, para enseñarme un poco de cómo es la vida en tu país. Y para mí, será una oportunidad de probarme como un hermano, porque soy el único hijo de mis padres.

Puedo vernos ahora cuando vayamos a los partidos de fútbol. Será muy diferente aquí, porque el fútbol es del estilo americano en vez del latino. Ya verás, de todos modos, que los aficionados son locos, no importa cuál sea el estilo. Cuando vengas podremos ir a muchas fiestas, conocer a muchas chicas, y hablar de mi asunto favorito, la música. Espero que te guste la música popular también.

Ya tengo tarea para mañana, pues, no puedo escribirte muy detalladamente en este momento. Te escribiré más tarde para avisarte qué traer. Te sugeriré que lleves muchos pantalones cortos, por ejemplo, porque no somos nada de formales aquí. Te veo pronto.

Tu amigo,
Paco

Rating: High
Commentary

This sample demonstrates that the writer is aware of the appropriate greetings and closings, as well as register. He is also aware of some cultural differences that might strike the exchange student as different, but he puts a positive spin on the difference. Fans are fans, according to the writer. The letter has a nice flow that communicates the writer's pleasure and some of the things he anticipates doing with the visitor. The grammar, including verbs and structures, is correct for the most part, and the vocabulary is appropriate.

When you practice on the following exercises, keep in mind:

- Your message should have a natural flow to it.
- Show a range of verb tenses.
- Make good use of the subjunctive.
- Use good vocabulary, with a variety of words.
- Do not repeat yourself.
- Avoid overuse of common adjectives such as *bueno, malo, interesante, impresionante,* or others like them.
- Use appropriate greetings and closings when necessary.
- Use the appropriate register.
- Use correct syntax.
- Avoid Anglicisms.
- Do not insert any English into the writing sample.

EXERCISES

Practice Exercises   For practice, write your own responses to the following prompts.

> Directions: Below you will see instructions for a writing sample that responds to the topic described. Be sure to include the information mentioned in your response. You will have 10 minutes to write your message in your test booklet.

1. Para su cumpleaños recibió un regalo de sus abuelos. Escríbales una carta agradeciéndoles por el regalo. En la carta mencione lo siguiente:

- lo que recibió
- cuánto le gustó
- planes para usar el regalo
- sus esperanzas de verlos pronto

2. Ud. es secretario o secretaria de su club de español. Ud. tiene que colaborar con un club de español de otra escuela para una fiesta. Ha recibido un correo electrónico de la secretaria del otro club, pidiéndole información sobre sus planes para invitar a los estudiantes de su escuela a la fiesta. En su correo electrónico a su amiga, incluya:

- su reacción a los planes para la fiesta
- su reacción al propósito de la fiesta
- qué propone hacer en la fiesta
- sus deseos para los invitados

3. Ud. está de vacaciones en España durante el verano y está escribiendo a su mejor amigo o amiga desde un ciber-café. En el mensaje electrónico, dígale lo siguiente:

- dónde está
- un suceso muy impresionante
- su reacción al acontecimiento
- sus esperanzas para el resto del viaje

4. Imagine haber recibido permiso de sus padres para invitar a un amigo o a una amiga para acompañarle en un viaje durante el descanso de primavera. Incluya Ud. lo siguiente:

- invítelo a acompañarle en un viaje
- comuníquele su entusiasmo
- sugiera planes para las actividades durante la semana
- sugiera cómo preparar para el viaje

5. Ud. está estudiando en Guatemala durante el verano. Escriba una tarjeta postal a su profesor de español comunicándole lo siguiente:

- cómo son las clases
- cómo le va hasta ese momento
- sus expectativas de las clases
- sus preocupaciones

6. Un estudiante de intercambio que regresó a su país de origen le ha escrito invitándole a visitarlo durante el descanso de primavera. Desafortunadamente, no le será possible hacerlo. Escríbale una carta incluyendo lo siguiente:

- déle las gracias
- explíquele por qué no puede venir
- comuníquele sus deseos

7. Debe anotar los acontecimientos de cada día de la semana y los viernes presentarlos en su clase de español. Escriba lo que diría después de una semana en que hubo mucho trabajo que le pareció muy difícil.

- describa la mayor dificultad que tuvo
- describa sus sentimientos
- describa sus temores

8. Ud. está solicitando empleo en una compañía durante el verano y tiene que escribir una carta al gerente pidiéndole una entrevista. Con la carta le ha mandado también un resumen de su historia de empleo. Incluya lo siguiente:

   • su presentación al gerente
   • sus motivos
   • solicitud para una entrevista
   • esperanzas respecto al trabajo

9. Después de una entrevista con el gerente de una compañía en la que solicitó práctica como interno durante el verano, escríbale una carta dándole las gracias por la entrevista. Incluya lo siguiente:

   • las gracias por la entrevista
   • su impresión de la compañía
   • su reacción a la entrevista
   • sus esperanzas para el futuro

10. Ud. está de viaje en otro país con un grupo de estudiantes. Una noche dejó algo de valor en un hotel. Al llegar al próximo hotel se da cuenta de la pérdida. Escriba un mensaje a sus padres y explíqueles lo qué pasó, incluyendo lo siguiente:

   • qué dejó y dónde
   • su reacción
   • su solución para recuperar lo perdido
   • sus esperanzas para el resto del viaje

11. Ud. tiene un amigo que desempeñó un papel importante en un drama en la escuela el fin de semana pasado. Ud. le manda un correo electrónico en el cual describe su reacción al drama, incluyendo:

   • su entusiasmo por su actuación
   • el punto culminante de la obra
   • la reacción del resto del público
   • sus recomendaciones para el futuro de su amigo actor

12. Ud. planeó una fiesta de despedida para un amigo o amiga que se mudaba a otra ciudad, pero otro compañero no pudo venir. Escríbale una carta en la que le cuenta algo de la fiesta.

   • qué pasó en la fiesta
   • la reacción que el amigo o la amiga había tenido
   • la reacción de los que vinieron
   • sus sentimientos al ver que el amigo o la amiga se iba

13. Un primo o una prima acaba de recibir un premio por haber ganado una competencia de debate. Escríbale un mensaje electrónico comentando su éxito.

   • incluya comentarios sobre la competencia
   • su reacción a las noticias
   • el significado del premio
   • predicción del futuro

14. Ud. acaba de participar en un proyecto para renovar la casa de una familia humilde. Después de terminar el proyecto, escriba una carta a un pariente favorito diciéndole lo que hizo.

- haga una descripción breve del proyecto
- su contribución
- sus sentimientos
- sus esperanzas para la familia

15. Ud. escribe algo en su diario personal todas las noches. Después de un día en que recibió algunas noticias estupendas, escriba lo que escribiría en el diario esa noche. Incluya lo siguiente:

- qué es lo estupendo que pasó
- sus sentimientos
- el significado del suceso

TASK 5: FORMAL WRITING

Suggestions

This part of the exam requires that you understand written and spoken Spanish in order to gather information to include in your formal essay. The essay is to be expository or persuasive. That means that you will be asked to explain something or to try to persuade a reader to accept your opinion about something. The main focus in the essay should be topic development, organization of ideas, and language use, with equal importance given to each aspect.

For the formal writing task you will have one to four different sources of information that you are to incorporate into your essay. Some sources will be printed, and you will have 7 minutes to read that material. You will also hear audio sources, and you should take notes while you listen so that you can incorporate that information into your essay as well. You must refer to all of the sources in your essay, not just the one you understood the best. In the process you must be able to understand, analyze, critique, and synthesize the source materials in order to incorporate them successfully into your essay.

A knowledge of historical and cultural aspects of life in the Spanish-speaking world is very important in this section. The more you know about the topics, the easier it will be for you to compare and contrast the information in the source material.

Preparing Yourself

- Make sure you can understand spoken Spanish of the sort you would hear on broadcast interviews or in film dialogue.
- Practice taking notes on audio sources before the exam, so you can take good notes on exam day.
- Practice writing well-organized essays.
- Review grammar and vocabulary you may find in the source materials.

Writing the Essay

- Make sure you refer to all the source material.
- Organize your ideas before you begin writing.
- Avoid simply listing what was communicated in each source and relating it to the question in separate paragraphs.

- In the introduction to your essay, state what you are going to explain or indicate your position regarding the question.
- In the paragraphs in which you develop your ideas, have one topic sentence for each paragraph.
- In each paragraph support your ideas with information from the sources.
- In your conclusion, do not simply repeat your introduction. Instead, combine your arguments in a coherent paragraph.
- Do not bother erasing or using correction fluid to delete words you want to change. Simply cross them out.
- Use good grammar and vocabulary. Your writing sample should be free of glaring grammatical or syntactic mistakes.
- Remember that accents and spelling count.
- If you have time, proofread your essay.

How to Do the Samples

In the following pages you will find three sample questions of the type you will see on the exam. For the expository essay, you will explain something in answer to the question in the prompt. For example, if you are to write about the importance of music as an expression of national identity, you could use the following outline:

- Introduction—state the topic, music as an expression of national identity, and narrow the topic to a specific range of thoughts, especially those suggested in the source information.
- First paragraph—music as an expression of cultural differences.
- Second paragraph—music as an expression of cultural similarities.
- Third paragraph—ways that music transcends national boundaries.
- Conclusion—the importance of music as a universal language.

In the persuasive essay you must persuade the reader to accept your point of view. Below is a suggested format for a persuasive essay.

- Introduction—state the topic you are going to discuss and give some idea of the direction of your argument.
- First paragraph—analyze one aspect of the topic.
- Second paragraph—analyze another aspect of the topic.
- Conclusion—based on what you have said in the essay, give your opinion in answer to the original question.

Each paragraph in the body of your essay should have one main idea. The topic sentence can come anywhere in the paragraph; it may be the first sentence in the paragraph, or it could be the last one. Each paragraph should contain at least three sentences. There is no correct or magical number of paragraphs, so you may have three or more. You should avoid writing only one long paragraph because usually the ideas will be poorly developed and poorly organized. Two-paragraph essays also lack a middle in which you can develop your ideas. Three paragraphs should be a minimum.

Scoring the Samples

The grader will be looking for three things, (1) organization of ideas, (2) incorporation of information from the source material, and (3) language used to express the ideas. The sample can show low, medium, or high ability. Each level has the following general characteristics.

Low: This essay is either one long paragraph, or it has an introduction followed by a repetition of the same idea, albeit rephrased, in the rest of the essay. Generalizations may predominate, with no references to specific information contained in the source materials. There are numerous errors in grammar, syntax, and vocabulary. The writer's capability to read, comprehend oral Spanish, and write Spanish is greatly limited. There may be structures that are grammatically correct, but they do not contribute to the development of an idea in the essay. The essay may even be comprehensible in Spanish, but does not rise to the level of an adequate expository or persuasive essay.

Medium: The essay shows general competence. It makes references to most of the source materials, but not all of them. There are grammatical errors in the structures used, but the errors are random. There may be mistakes in using accents and other diacritical marks. The vocabulary is adequate, but an English mode of thinking and phrasing sentences may be apparent. The essay may lack a conclusion, or the conclusion may be only a repetition of the introduction. The writer may have also simply listed what the sources said, instead of integrating the information into his or her thoughts and processing it to answer the essay's question. The overall impression after reading the essay is that it is not as developed as it could have been, and the grammar is good, but not great.

High: The essay is comprehensive in its development and in its expression. Synthesis and analysis outweigh summaries of information contained in the source materials. The essay shows excellent command of all of the conventions of written Spanish, grammar and syntax are correct, the vocabulary includes a broad range of words and expressions, and orthography and spelling are correct, although there may be occasional errors. The errors that do occur do not interfere with the communication of ideas. Ideas are logically organized. The essay has a clear introduction, good development of ideas throughout, and a strong conclusion. There is an ease of language that is apparent. The writer uses the appropriate register in his or her comments about the sources and offers different perspectives.

Keep these rubrics in mind as you practice the sample essays in this book.

The Practice Exercises There are four topics for practice on the following pages. For additional topics, keep in mind that they will probably deal with anything related to cultural topics such as music or literature, current events such as immigration, social trends such as the growing diversity of the population in the United States, famous Spanish-speaking people, the positive contributions of Hispanics to United States culture, the influence of Hispanics in United States history, tourism, or anything about the natural world such as the environment in Spanish-speaking countries. Keep in mind the striking similarities in different countries of issues like immigration. You can easily find material to read on the Internet. Also, you can find audio sources from radio stations on the web, as well as streaming television programming. Movies either in Spanish or dubbed are also good sources for practice in listening.

Keep the following strategies in mind:

- Do not spend time trying to translate every word in the print material.
- Do not worry if you cannot understand every word of the audio source.
- Each source will provide a unique perspective or point of view.
- Try to get the main idea about each source.
- In your essay compare and contrast the ideas you find in the sources.
- If you have any personal knowledge or experience about the topic, include it.
- In your introduction and conclusion it is good to include your own thoughts.
- Be sure to write a good introduction and a strong conclusion.

For the first sample, do not worry about how much time it takes you to write the essay. Each time you do an essay, try to take less time. For the final practice essay, time yourself to make sure you do not take too much time in going over sources and organizing ideas.

EXERCISES

Question One

> Directions: You will now read a question that is based on information contained in Sources 1–4. The sources are both print and audio. First, read the print material. Next, you will hear the audio material. You should take notes on the spaces provided in the test booklet while you listen. Spend about 7 minutes reading and 3 listening. Take about 5 minutes to plan. Then you will have 40 minutes to write your essay.
>
> In your essay you should make reference to specific information from all of the source materials. Do not simply summarize what is contained in them. Incorporate them into your essay. Use appropriate grammar and vocabulary.

¿Cree Ud. que el ecoturismo realmente ofrece la mejor oportunidad para el desarrollo sustentable?

Source One
El ecoturismo. Ciudad Virtual de Antropología y Arqueología
(*http://www.naya.org.ar/turismo/congreso/ponencias/elias_alcocer.htm*)

La industria turística aprovecha este fenómeno y lo comercializa, procurando de alguna forma proveer servicios para los turistas. En el caso de México, la publicidad de las zonas turísticas comenzó concretamente en el año de 1961 con la creación del Consejo Nacional de Turismo. Los atractivos naturales, la tradición histórica y cultural, y su ubicación geográfica hacen que México cuente con un gran potencial; sin embargo, el turismo exige el desarrollo de vías de acceso a las zonas de atracción turística y de facilidades que permitan la permanencia de más días del visitante en el lugar.

La construcción de infraestructura para tal fin, inevitablemente transforma el aspecto físico del lugar, y si no es debidamente planificado puede llegar a afectar la calidad del medio ambiente natural, y hasta podría deteriorar la calidad de vida de los mismos habitantes.

Se planteaba básicamente como la actividad que iba a solucionar los problemas de la zona, pero desafortunadamente en la actualidad se nota que quizás los que menos se han beneficiado son los ciudadanos comunes.

La industria turística está presente principalmente en aquellos lugares en donde existen playas, zonas arqueológicas, lugares de belleza escénica o de importancia religiosa, y es ahí en donde se ha estado estimulando un desarrollo económico, ya que se generan empleos relacionados con los servicios prestados a los turistas. En varias de las regiones turísticas del país también se ha propiciado la generación de empleos relacionados con el abastecimientos de servicios básicos que incluyen alcantarillado, pavimentación, drenaje, construcción de letrinas o fosas sépticas, suministro de energía eléctrica para servicios, agua potable, plantas de tratamiento de aguas, vías de acceso y medios de comunicación tales como teléfono, correos, etc. Otro rubro sería el de la construcción de carreteras, aeropuertos, vías férreas, puertos marítimos. También está la construcción de hoteles de todo tipo, instalaciones y accesorios, prestación de servicios turísticos de carácter hotelero, restaurantero, agencias de viajes, guías de turistas, comercios especializados y transportación turística. Otras de las fuentes de empleo residen en las actividades agropecuarias, industrias proveedoras de aparatos electrónicos, línea blanca, utensilios de cocina, cristalería, comestibles y textiles, entre otros.

Pero lo que casi nunca sale en las estadísticas o en los informes de resultados, es realmente el estado en que las personas tienen que sobrevivir al trabajar en los lugares turísticos. Aunque reciben salarios engañosamente altos, éstos se les van en los servicios caros, sufren condiciones a veces infrahumanas de vida, una alta concentración de problemas sociales, incluyendo el alcoholismo, drogadicción, vandalismo, prostitución, desintegración familiar, y en el caso de las etnias, la pérdida de su integridad como grupo cultural. El ambiente natural también puede sufrir efectos tales como la contaminación o la sobre-explotación de sus recursos.

Source Two
Principios, ventajas y potencialidades del ecoturismo
(*www.ciberamerica.org/Ciberamerica/Castellano/Areas/turismo/ecoturismo*)

En este momento la aportación económica del ecoturismo es de suma importancia, sobre todo por parte de las autoridades, y en algunos países ya es parte de un turismo que ha llegado a ser el principal proveedor de divisas derivadas del uso de la tierra. Dos ejemplos de buenas prácticas a la hora de distribuir los ingresos de esta actividad son los de Costa Rica y Belice, lo que indujo a numerosos gobiernos o entidades privadas a enviar misiones a estos países, con el propósito de aprovechar la experiencia acumulada.

En este sentido, lo más apropiado es un turismo cuidadosamente regulado, practicado por personas genuinamente interesadas en la naturaleza, dispuestas a causar el menor disturbio posible y respetuosas de las costumbres locales. Una técnica para reducir tal impacto es la "zonificación" de áreas protegidas, delimitando las áreas más frágiles con acceso restringido mientras que en otras áreas se permita sólo la visita manteniéndose en el sendero todo el tiempo.

Las áreas protegidas tienen una importante función. En efecto, el uso por parte de ecoturistas supone la generación de beneficios, tanto tangibles (empleos locales, por ejemplo) como otros (biodiversidad, protección de aguas y suelos). El ecoturismo en muchas instancias ha favorecido la conservación de la naturaleza. Tales argumentos se aplican también a la conservación de los parques marinos y su influencia beneficiosa sobre la productividad para la pesca en áreas cercanas o a veces situadas a considerable distancia. Hay que evitar que ambos sectores, la pesca y la llegada de ecoturistas compitan. Las zonas protegidas de arrecifes de coral han evitado su posible destrucción y permitido la recuperación de la pesca, especialmente de alevines en estas áreas, además de proveer nuevos empleos. Un proceso similar se ha llevado a cabo en humedales y otros entornos.

Por otro lado, el fomento del ecoturismo favorece la conservación de la biodiversidad.

Source Three

Buscarán solucionar conflicto por venta de artesanías en Chichén Itzá

(Comisión Nacional para el Desarrollo de los Pueblos Indígenas
cdi.gob.mx/index.php?id_seccion=1302)

La Comisión de Asuntos Indígenas de la Cámara de Diputados servirá de enlace para buscar una solución al conflicto entre el INAH y vendedores de artesanías que ocupan las inmediaciones de la zona arqueológica de Chichén Itzá. En entrevista, el presidente de esa Comisión, Javier Manzano Salazar explicó que lo mejor para las partes es buscar puntos de acuerdo que permitan descartar el uso de la fuerza pública para resolver ese problema. El Instituto Nacional de Antropología e Historia (INAH) interpuso una serie de demandas contra los vendedores ante las constantes quejas de acoso a los turistas que visitan esa zona arqueológica.

CD 2 TRACK 15

Source Four *(Listen to the recording first. Read the text below only after completing your essay, to verify that you heard all the information correctly.)*

Entrevista a dos personas sobre el medio ambiente en las Islas Galápagos

(Narrador) Hoy tenemos el placer de acoger al señor Benavides y al señor Domínguez. El señor Domínguez es Presidente de Los Pescadores Artesanales de Puerto Aurora. El señor Benavides es Director de la Fundación de Conservación de las Islas Galápagos en Ecuador. Bienvenidos, señores. Estamos para hablar unos momentos de los efectos de la Ley de Régimen Especial para la Conservación y Desarrollo Sustentable de la Provincia de Galápagos, ambos para el Parque y para el pueblo que vive cerca de él.

(Sr. Benavides) Le agradezco mucho la oportunidad de hablar un poco de la actualidad del Parque Galápagos porque hoy como antes, se ve amenazado por actividades humanas en varios sectores. Como se sabe, la Ley Especial de Galápagos que el Congreso Nacional promulgó en 1999 tenía por objetivo garantizar la conservación del ecosistema. Hasta el año 1971 no se veían fauna ni flora exóticas allí, ni había tanta presura de la actividad humana en el campo y los pueblos.

(Sr. Domínguez) También para nosotros no encontramos ningunos problemas. Pudimos mantener a nuestras familias con la pesca, pero actualmente es bien difícil.

(Narrador) ¿A qué se atribuye la dificultad, Sr. Domínguez?

(Sr. Domínguez) Parece que hoy, con la escasez de pez, casi no se puede mantener a la familia. Nosotros también nos encontramos en conflicto con pescaderos industriales y los pescadores atraídos para la pesca deportiva. También parece que las aguas están llenas de barcos privados de turistas. Esto no cuenta los barcos grandes con ejércitos de turistas que vienen para pasar el día.

(Sr. Benavides) Para nosotros dentro del Parque, se ven los efectos que han causado esas invasiones, ambas de pescadores y turistas. Los pescadores reclaman sus antiguos derechos, pero el hecho es que hay más demanda que surtido. Nosotros propusimos cuotas en las toneladas de peces de varias especies para aliviar la situación, pero...

(Sr. Domínguez) El hecho es que nosotros los pescadores artesanales tenemos el derecho de pescar en estas aguas porque llevamos siglos de hacerlo. Los otros no deben tener los mismos derechos.

(Sr. Benavides) No sólo es cuestión de derechos. El problema es que actualmente los pueblos cerca del Parque introducen flora y fauna y microorganismos al Parque que antes no se veían. Pero allí están. La ley nos obliga proteger el Parque como patrimonio de la nación. También vemos el deterioro del campo a causa de la agricultura y todo el desarrollo para el ecoturismo.

(Narrador) Los turistas sí llevan desarrollo económico, pero nos queda ver si ese desarrollo puede reemplazar los antiguos modos de sostenerse. Actualmente hay una gran cantidad de yates pequeños, barcos de carga, y cruceros internacionales que navegan por las islas, dejando residuos a menudo.

(Sr. Domínguez) Los recursos están allí. Para los turistas, la naturaleza, para los pueblos en las islas, las huertas, para nosotros, los peces, de todo tipo, tiburón, calamar, pulpo, pepino de mar, atún, canchalagua, de todo. Las actividades pesqueras en la provincia marina son nuestro patrimonio.

(Sr. Benavides) De acuerdo, pero al agotar los recursos, no tendremos nada. No hay alternativa más que el desarrollo sustentable.

(Narrador) Entonces todavía le queda al gobierno regular los permisos de pesca artesanal, así como los del turismo y la actividad agrícola.

Question Two

> Directions: You will now read a question that is based on information contained in Sources 1–4. The sources are both print and audio. First, read the print material. Next, you will hear the audio material. You should take notes on the spaces provided in the test booklet while you listen. Take about 7 minutes to read and 3 to listen to the audio. Take about 5 minutes to plan. Then you will have 40 minutes to write your essay.
>
> In your essay you should make reference to specific information from all of source materials. Do not simply summarize what is contained in them. Incorporate them into your essay. Use appropriate grammar and vocabulary.

¿Cuál sería la dieta más nutritiva para los jóvenes?

Source One
La dieta ideal, ¿existe?

(*www.sabormediterraneo.com/salud/nutricion1.htm*)

Todos sabemos que existen multitud de dietas: para el tratamiento y prevención de enfermedades, dietas adaptadas a las distintas etapas de la vida, para perder esos kilos que nos sobran...

Cualquier dieta (sea la que sea) para ser considerada de muy adecuada tiene que cumplir con un doble requisito:

1) asegurarse que la persona obtiene las calorías suficientes para mantener un peso corporal constante dentro de los límites considerados normales para esa persona.
2) que en la dieta estén representados alimentos de los distintos grupos: lácteos y huevos; carnes, pescados, aves y caza; grasas y aceites; cereales y leguminosas; verduras y frutas, en las proporciones adecuadas para que la persona pueda obtener todos los nutrientes que a diario el organismo necesita.

Source Two
Hasta qué punto conviene ser vegetariano. La Opinión Digital

(*www.laopinion.com/salud/salud_nutrition.html*)

Realmente, la carne, como cualquier otro alimento excepto la leche materna para su descendiente en el primer período de la vida de los mamíferos, no es indispensable para la nutrición del hombre, pero es un valioso componente de gran riqueza nutritiva en las dietas de muchas personas que gozan de buena salud y no ejerce en los sujetos normales los efectos nocivos que el vegetarianismo le atribuye. Existe la creencia popular de que la alimentación vegetariana es más saludable que una que incluya carne u otros productos derivados de animales.

Lo cierto es que todo tipo de alimentación cuenta con beneficios nutritivos y puede también presentar aspectos problemáticos.

La selección de alimentos que escoge la persona es el factor que determina si una alimentación es saludable o no. Si se elige una alimentación vegetariana, es importante asegurarse de ingerir cantidades suficientes de vitamina B_{12} y calcio, especialmente durante la adolescencia.

Una alimentación vegetariana bien planeada tiende a incluir niveles menores de grasa saturada y colesterol, así como niveles más altos de fibra y elementos nutrientes derivados de las plantas que una alimentación no vegetariana.

Especialistas en nutrición del programa de Extensión Cooperativa de la Universidad de California citan diversas investigaciones que indican que una alimentación con tales características puede reducir el riesgo de desarrollar diabetes, presión arterial alta, problemas del corazón y obesidad.

Sin embargo, los beneficios mencionados pueden obtenerse también con una alimentación que incluya productos animales. Con una planificación cuidadosa y el consumo de carnes magras y productos animales con poca grasa, así como frutas y verduras, se puede llevar una alimentación con poca grasa saturada y colesterol y rica en fibra y nutrientes derivados de plantas.

Además, el consumo de productos animales facilita obtener las cantidades recomendables de calcio, zinc, hierro y vitamina B_{12}.

Source Three
Dietas de moda. Crítica a las promesas milagrosas

(*www.enplenitud.com/nota.asp?articuloID=23*)

La estética ha dejado de ser monopolio de las mujeres. Los hombres también quieren lucir bien y no dudan en consultar para obtener un mejor estado físico. Las dietas de moda circulan con soluciones mágicas que dicen resolver el problema a la brevedad, descuidando el hecho que en muchos casos se trata de una enfermedad, la obesidad, y por lo tanto debe ser tratada con seriedad. La salud no tiene precio y tampoco es un acto de magia.

A lo largo del tiempo, los modelos van cambiando y, lo que era ideal en el Renacimiento, está lejos de ser aceptado socialmente en este siglo. Hombres y mujeres no dudan a la hora de optar por productos light y largas horas de gimnasio.

Una amplia información es la que circula sobre cómo liberarse de la pesadilla de la gordura. En general, son recetas mágicas que prometen resultados increíbles en muy corto tiempo; pero luego de varios intentos y sin conseguir el tan ansiado logro, los "dietantes" pierden las esperanzas, hasta que aparece una nueva alternativa milagrosa.

El charlatanerismo prolifera cada vez más, basándose en dietas absurdas y promesas de curación definitiva.

Es un negocio, y se basa en la falta de lectura crítica y en la credulidad popular, pero lo que ofrece es tentador y quién no intentó alguna vez las famosas dietas de la Luna, la Sopa, la Fuerza Aérea, la Disociada, etcétera.

CD 2 TRACK 16

Source Four *(Listen to the recording first. Read the text below only after completing your essay, to verify that you heard all the information correctly.)*

El vegetarianismo y la dieta vegetariana

(*www.terra.es/alimentacion/articulo/html/ali121.htm*)

Recomendaciones de los teóricos del vegetarianismo

- Consumir pan integral o arroz moreno en lugar de pan blanco y arroz refinado.
- Dar una gran importancia a los frutos secos como fuente de proteína dentro de una comida.

- Favorecer el consumo de legumbres y pastas elaboradas con harina integral.
- Dentro de los productos lácteos consumir yogurt natural descremado.
- En la dieta vegetariana estricta se incluye la leche de soja en polvo.
- La única comida en la que debe aparecer regularmente una pequeña cantidad de azúcar o miel es el desayuno, ya que el organismo no puede digerirlo a otra hora.

Razones para excluir la carne

Algunas de las razones que aducen los vegetarianos para excluir la carne como producto destinado a la nutrición del ser humano son las siguientes:

- Ni la contextura física ni la dentadura del hombre corresponde a la de un animal carnívoro.
- Nuestros jugos digestivos carecen de la acidez necesaria para digerir la carne y es sólo por el hábito que el estómago se adapta a esa función. Incluso aseguran que un hombre que no haya ingerido nunca carne al hacerlo por primera vez, experimenta una especie de intoxicación semejante a la alcohólica.
- La descomposición de toda sustancia animal produce toxinas mucho más peligrosas que las procedentes de la descomposición vegetal.

Question Three

> Directions: You will now read a question that is based in information contained in Sources 1–3. The sources are both print and audio. First, read the print material. Next, you will hear the audio material. You should take notes on the spaces provided in the test booklet while you listen. Take about 7 minutes to read and 3 minutes to listen to the audio. Take about 5 minues to plan. Then you will have 40 minutes to write your essay.
>
> In your essay you should make reference to specific information from all of the source materials. Do not simply summarize what is contained in them. Incorporate them into your essay. Use appropriate grammar and vocabulary.

Se dice que los autores representan su época. ¿Cómo se diferencian los autores de habla española de hoy de los de la generación anterior?

Source One
El fin de la sospecha. La literatura española de los últimos años demuestra un empuje esperanzador.

(*Tendencias del arte*, 17 de enero 2006. *www.tendencias21.net/El-fin-de-la-sospecha_a493.html*)

Jóvenes de los noventa: magníficos narradores

Estos escritores comparten el tiempo de sus publicaciones con jóvenes creadores que comienzan a publicar después de los fastos del 92. En esta época se genera una eclosión de magníficos narradores, de excelentes escritores con una formación universal, lectores en varios idiomas, filólogos en su mayoría, cultos y cultivados, sin anclajes ideológicos ni sociales que no sean dar cuenta del mundo en el que viven a través de la literatura, escritores, en fin, muy literarios pero, a la par, profunda y sabiamente humanos.

La penúltima generación de narradores es la que en esta década de los noventa y principios del siglo XXI están dando unos frutos más que granados, lo que hace augurar un panorama prometedor a la narrativa hispana.

Creo que la característica común de tan variada y excelente pléyade de narradores es su afán por colocar el punto de mira de sus referentes en escritores hispanos de otra tradición, más fantástica o cervantina, o bien por ampliar el marco de influencias a otras literaturas (Nabokov, Pynchon, Calvino, Celine) y hacia otras soluciones narrativas.

Todos estos autores dan muestras suficientes del empuje con que la narrativa española de los últimos años manifiesta una saludable capacidad de integración y mutua influencia entre las distintas generaciones que conviven, un ojo avizor a lo que se hace en otros países y lenguas, y una definitiva pérdida de complejos, que se suma a una decidida apuesta por la posmodernidad en su alto sentido, no en el feble y débil. Son autores que resistirían sin lugar a dudas una crítica que analice tanto los contextos como el valor intrínseco de lo literario, una crítica enmarcada en la antes mencionada "Teoría Literaria Integral."

Source Two
Enfoque—Escritores latinos optan por el realismo no mágico
(*Rueters on terra.com.co/cultura/literatura/03-12-2005/nota264506.html*)

El autor colombiano Jorge Franco no es un realista mágico. Es sólo un realista. En su novela "Rosario Tijeras" escribe sobre un cadáver que se va de fiesta y una heroína criminal que besa a sus víctimas antes de volarles los sesos.

Se podría decir que los escritores colombianos, quienes están abandonando el estilo más famoso de la literatura latinoamericana, ya no necesitan del realismo mágico.

Luego de 41 años de guerra civil y los excesos del narcotráfico, la plena realidad cotidiana ya es lo suficientemente difícil de creer.

Pero la persistente hambre de lectores en Europa y Estados Unidos por obras latinoamericanas llenas de narrativas sobre curas levitantes y bebés con colas, molesta a la nueva generación de novelistas urbanos.

Un ejemplo es Efraim Medina, autor colombiano de una obra decididamente sin realismo mágico. Medina dice que su compatriota Gabriel García Márquez, ganador del premio Nobel de Literatura y cuya obra "Cien años de soledad" llevó al realismo mágico a ser conocido en todo el mundo, debería de "hacerle un favor a Colombia y donarse a un museo."

La respuesta del escritor Franco a una pregunta sobre el realismo mágico es más templada que la de Medina.

"A mí no me afectó para nada esa sombra de García Márquez", dijo a Reuters el autor, un hombre de contextura delgada y de voz suave, en el apartamento de su madre en Bogotá.

Agregó que García Márquez, de 78 años, ha sido muy bueno con él y que Medina siempre está en busca de peleas.

Pero el escritor admite su frustración y la de muchos otros novelistas latinoamericanos de su generación.

"Reconozco que cuando estamos buscando traducciones en otros idiomas, sobre todo en el primer mundo, todavía como que siente uno que quieren más realismo mágico (…) las abuelas volando y todas esas cosas raras, las mariposas amarillas."

El realismo mágico surgió en un período en que América Latina se modernizaba rápidamente. El nacionalismo y el pensamiento izquierdista le dieron nueva importancia a las tradiciones rurales que durante mucho tiempo fueron marginalizadas por una oligarquía europeizada.

Realismo urbano

Pero América Latina está cambiando y su literatura lo refleja.

"Yo siento que con el crecimiento de nuestras ciudades, Bogotá, Buenos Aires, Ciudad de México, son ciudades que tienen situaciones muy similares a muchas ciudades europeas, en su problemática, sus cuestiones sociales", dijo Franco.

"Entonces y finalmente estas ciudades son lo que nos están nutriendo a nosotros con toda la información para escribir", agregó. "Hay un lenguaje más cercano a esas ciudades pero que no tiene nada que ver con el asunto del realismo mágico", explica el autor.

Franco obtuvo éxito a pesar de su comienzo tardío en la escritura. De joven quería hacer películas, pero luego se percató de su aptitud por la ficción cuando seguía escribiendo guiones imposibles de convertir en películas durante una breve estadía en una academia de cinematografía en Londres.

"Fue un descubrimiento encontrar que a través de la palabra escrita también podía contar historias y, por suerte, creo que tenía lo único que se necesita para ser escritor y eso es ser buen lector", concluyó Franco.

CD 3 TRACK 1

Source Three *(listen to the recording first. Read the text below only after completing your essay, to verify that you heard all the information correctly)*

Los jóvenes escritores de ahora son menos comprometidos. Por Itzíar de Francisco, Josefina Aldecoa.

(14 de enero 2006. *www.elcultural.es/HTML/20060112/Letras/LETRAS16282.asp*)

P: Y a los jóvenes escritores españoles ¿los ve comprometidos con nuestro tiempo como ustedes lo fueron con el suyo?

R: Las circunstancias del país han cambiado profundamente. Quizás hoy no sea tan grande el compromiso social e histórico de los jóvenes escritores. La literatura ha cambiado en todos los sentidos. Cada escritor se expresa de acuerdo con la visión del mundo que le rodea y de su propia concepción de lo que quiere transmitir.

P: ¿Cómo recuerda la España con la que se encontró al volver de Londres?

R: Era regresar al mundo que había dejado. Sólo fueron unos meses de ausencia y aquí todo seguía igual políticamente.

P: ¿Qué aprendió de Martín Gaite y de Sánchez Ferlosio?

R: Yo creo que ninguno aprendía del amigo o del compañero cercano. Todos los jóvenes escritores teníamos puntos de coincidencia en la visión del mundo pero cada uno la expresábamos a nuestra manera en cuanto a la técnica y la utilización del idioma.

P: Su formación está impregnada del espíritu de la Institución Libre de Enseñanza. En estos días en los que se ha hablado tanto y se sigue hablando de reformas educativas, ¿cree que se debería recuperar ese espíritu?

R: Rotundamente sí. En lo fundamental, en el proyecto educativo serio, amplio, ambicioso, sí.

P: Lo más duro de dirigir un colegio es...

R: Tratar de hacerlo bien a cada momento.

P: ¿Qué libro deben haber leído todos sus alumnos?

R: Hay muchos. Cada uno comienza su afición a la lectura en busca de afinidades o respuestas a sus preguntas.

P: ¿Qué reformas educativas le gustaría que se llevasen a cabo?

R: Yo soy partidaria de una educación liberal, crítica, europeísta.

P: Un consejo para un joven escritor....

R: Ser fiel a sí mismo.

P: Y otro para un joven maestro...

R: Ser consciente de que en sus manos está el futuro del alumno.

P: ¿Le queda pendiente alguna asignatura con la escritura? ¿Más poesía?

R: Como casi todos los jóvenes escritores yo empecé escribiendo poesía. Creo que era la forma más espontánea de expresar lo que me pasaba por dentro. Pero encontré en la prosa mi propia forma de expresión. Creo que fue la Pardo Bazán quien dijo que "para ser una prosista hay que ser antes un mal versificador."

Question Four

> You will now read a question that is based in information contained in Sources 1–4. The sources are both print and audio. First, read the print material. Next, you will hear the audio material. You should take notes on the spaces provided in the test booklet while you listen. Take about 7 minutes to read and 3 minutes to listen to the audio. Take about 5 minutes to plan. Then you will have 40 minutes to write your essay.
>
> In your essay you should make reference to specific information from all of the source materials. Do not simply summarize what is contained in them. Incorporate them into your essay. Use appropriate grammar and vocabulary.

¿Cómo muestra la cocina española su universalidad?

Source One
La gastronomía española
(*www.spaindreams.com/cas/gastro.htm*)

Uno de los mayores atractivos de España es sin duda el de su cocina, que es una de las mejores del mundo por la calidad y variedad de sus productos. No puede hablarse con rigor de una cocina nacional, sino de múltiples cocinas regionales influidas en cada caso por la climatología y las formas de vida autóctonas.

La cocina española se distingue por utilizar tradicionalmente en la preparación de los alimentos el aceite de oliva como grasa vegetal y la manteca de cerdo como grasa animal, así como la gran variedad de frutas y verduras que aportó la cultura árabe a la mesa y otros elementos como la patata y el tomate llegados de América.

Por otra parte, el gran desarrollo de la cocina española en los últimos lustros se debe también a la aparición de grandes profesionales que han sabido reinterpretar los platos y recetas tradicionales en consonancia con el tiempo actual, dotando a la gastronomía española de una nueva dimensión en presencia y sabores.

Source Two
Gastronomía Peruana. Historia de la cocina peruana
(*www.gastronomiaperu.com/index.php*)

La cocina peruana es considerada como una de las más variadas y ricas del mundo. Gracias a la herencia pre incaica, incaica y a la inmigración española, africana, chino-cantonesa, japonesa e italiana principalmente hasta el siglo XIX, reúne, mezcla y acriolla una gastronomía y exquisitos sabores de cuatro continentes, ofreciendo una variedad inigualable e impresionante de platos típicos de arte culinario peruano en constante evolución, imposible de enumerarlos en su totalidad. Basta mencionar que sólo en la costa peruana, hay más de dos mil sopas diferentes.

Es de conocimiento en todo el mundo que la cocina peruana ha encontrado ya un espacio dentro de las más reconocidas del mundo. Recientemente ha sido publicado en inglés, en el sitio web de Epicurious, un importante artículo sobre las bondades y la importancia de nuestra cocina. Reproducimos parte de la publicación: "Como dicen, todo lo antiguo se ha convertido en nuevo." Y en el caso del Perú, cuando decimos "viejo" nos referimos a antiguo. Uno de los ejemplos de cómo nuestros chefs están mirando hacia las raíces andinas, es el uso novedoso que se le da a la quinua, un grano que se remonta a los incas, con un ligero sabor a nuez y 3000 años de antigüedad, bien llamada "comida maravillosa", baja en carbohidratos y rica en proteínas.

Cualquier persona que haga turismo en el Perú, es inmediatamente conquistada por la riqueza culinaria local, y si es una gourmet, siempre buscará la excusa para regresar y deleitarse con algún sabor nuevo para su exigente paladar.

La cocina tradicional peruana es una fusión de la manera de cocinar de los españoles con la de los nativos peruanos. Productos básicos como la papa, maíz, maní, ají, y pescados y mariscos de nuestro mar, se remontan hasta el imperio incaico, que floreció en los Andes por miles de años. Cuando los conquistadores españoles llegaron en el siglo 16, trajeron con ellos los postres de estilo europeo y otros ingredientes como el pollo, la carne de res y frutas cítricas. Más adelante llegaron los inmigrantes africanos, italianos, chinos y japoneses que ayudaron a crear una sabrosa comida que hasta la fecha se come en los hogares y restaurantes peruanos.

Source Three
Las tapas. El noble arte del tapeo
(*www.accua.com/gastro/conten/GAS587.asp*)

Desde su nacimiento, a mediados del siglo XIX en Andalucía, el tapeo no sólo se ha convertido en todo un arte sino que se ha extendido a lo largo y ancho de la península y se ha convertido en una de nuestras costumbres gastronómicas más apreciadas.

Hace 150 años, las tapas de aquella época poco o nada tenían que ver con lo que hoy se ha dado en llamar "cocina en miniatura." En aquel entonces, no eran más que unas pequeñas rodajas de embutido cuya función principal era la de "tapar" la copa de vino o cerveza para evitar que cayeran moscas y otros "intrusos" no deseados en la bebida. Pero, en la mayoría de los casos, para lo que servían era para "tapar" el agujero del estómago que dejaba el vinito de antes de la comida.

Las tapas han ido evolucionando con el paso del tiempo. De las simples rodajas de embutido y las aceitunas, hemos pasado a poder elegir entre varias tapas en los bares y, lo que es más importante, a ver cómo se abren, día sí y día también, locales especializados en tan diminuto plato.

El ir de tapas ha dejado de ser una especie de aperitivo (palabra que viene del latín "aperire", que significa abrir) de la comida para convertirse en un buen sustituto del almuerzo y la cena. Ir de tapas es un verdadero acto social. No en vano, significa compartir un espacio abierto con otras personas a las que quizá no se conoce, pero de una forma mucho más informal que, pongamos por caso, un cóctel.

CD 3 TRACK 2

Source Four *(Listen to the recording first. Read the text below only after completing your essay, to verify that you heard all the information correctly.)*

Entrevista entre un turista de la ruta gastronómica española y Ramón Inique, natural de Barcelona

(Turista) Ya están cambiando las costumbres en cuanto a la comida, ¿verdad?

(Ramón) Sin duda. La facilidad de conseguir comestibles de todas partes del mundo remite a la integración de sabores desconocidos anteriormente en la gastronomía nacional.

(Turista) ¿Pero no es que le faltaban a los cocineros productos locales y especialidades de renombre?

(Ramón) Claro que no. ¿Quién no ha oído de las famosas tapas de Barcelona? Hoy se encuentran en plenitud de libros de recetas. Hasta en Nueva York es de moda ir de tapas y probarse lo mejor del orgullo de la cocina española. Pero también se puede encontrarlas en Londres, en París, en Tokio, pues... por todo el mundo.

(Turista) Sí, los he visto en las librerías. Pero de las que me he probado, no tienen el mismo sabor que una tapa aquí. Puede ser que haya otro aspecto que no se puede exportar.

(Ramón) Seguramente el ambiente en el que se saborea la delicia influye en cómo se la percibe. No se puede por completo imitar el aire, ni los sonidos, ni la lengua que se oye al disfrutarlas en otro lugar. También se prohíbe la exportación de algunos de los ingredientes. El jamón serrano, por ejemplo, no se permite exportar a todos los lugares done se querría tenerlo. Aun cuando se puede, la frescura se pierde en el transporte. Los ingredientes más frescos siempre resultan en los sabores más deseados.

(Turista) Me ha convencido. Probaré las tapas mientras esté aquí. Pero cuando vuelva a casa, por cierto intentaré reproducir algunas de ellas. Aunque no goce de los mismos sabores, experimentaré el placer de evocar las fantásticas memorias del viaje. Podré imaginarme que estoy de vuelta. También compraré unos de estos libros de recetas para preparar tapas. Quizás trataré de inventar mis propias recetas para tapas americanas al estilo español.

AFTER YOU FINISH WRITING

- **Proofread what you have written.** Many students have learned to include formulaic examples of the use of the subjunctive, but then make simple errors such as using incorrect verb forms, or using adjectives and nouns that do not agree in gender and number. These basic errors do not create a good impression.
- **When you reread what you have written, check your grammar.** Use the following items as a checklist and practice checking these points of grammar.
  - Identify the gender of nouns.
  - Identify the person and number of the subject to make sure that the verb ending agrees.
  - Make sure that the sequence of tenses is correct, i.e., that if you begin in the present tense, that you do not randomly switch from present to past and then to any other tense unless it is appropriate.
  - Check to see that the spellings of stem changes, orthographic changes, and irregular verb forms are correct.
  - Make sure that you have not used English words unless there are no Spanish equivalents; for example, "Super Bowl," if you are talking about professional sports.
  - Make sure that you have used accents and other diacritical and punctuation marks correctly.
- **The secret to good proofreading to correct mistakes is knowing the questions to ask. Refresh your memory about the mistakes you are most likely to make and look for them when you proofread.** For example, you could ask, "What is the gender of this noun?" or "What is the correct ending for preterite verb forms?" or "Is this an irregular verb?" You may even want to make a short checklist of your weak points when you proofread.

USEFUL VOCABULARY

By using a few words and expressions from the following glossary of terms, your essay should have a clearer organization and sound more complete. Select a few words or transitional phrases from the following list. You can use them to talk about any topic and you should practice using them so you will remember them easily on the exam.

Expressions for Introductions

al principio	at the beginning
ya	already
todavía	still
a partir de	from the time that...
conviene	it is fitting, suitable, convenient
es necesario, preciso, interesante, etc.	it is necessary, interesting, etc. (or use another tense of *ser*)
con respecto a	with respect to
en cuanto a	with regard to
en lo tocante a	with regard to
tratar con	to deal with, to have to do with
tiene que ver con	to have to do with
a continuación	below, following

Defining Concepts

ejemplificar	to serve as an example
consistir en	to consist of (notice the difference in prepositions)
constar de	to consist of, to be composed of
caracterizarse por	to be characterized by
significar	to signify
querer decir	to mean
servir para	to serve to
sugerir (ie, i)	to suggest

Developing and Relating Ideas

de hecho	in fact
del punto de vista...	from the point of view of...
de la perspectiva de...	from the perspective of
de verdad, de veras	really
en conexión	in connection
en realidad	really
a lo mejor	perhaps, maybe
mejor dicho	more exactly, rather

Making Comparisons

no obstante	nevertheless
sin embargo	nevertheless
en cambio	on the other hand
al contrario	on the contrary
tanto mejor	so much the better
por la mayor parte	for the most part, mostly
según	according to

Showing Logic or Reasoning

a cause de	because of
por consiguiente	therefore
por eso	for that reason
bien pensado	well thought-out
como consecuencia	as a consequence
por lo tanto	for that reason, therefore

Drawing Conclusions

en breve	in short
al fin y al cabo	in the final analysis
al final	finally
por fin	finally
por último	lastly
después de todo	after all
de lo anterior... se ve que...	from the above...one sees that...
en todo	all in all
en conclusión	in conclusion
en resumen	in conclusion

PART FIVE   SPEAKING SKILLS

INTRODUCTION TO SPEAKING SKILLS

The speaking part of the AP Spanish Language Examination is completely revised for 2007. Like the writing part of the exam, the speaking part incorporates new skill areas. There are now two parts: informal speaking and a formal oral presentation. Both tasks together take about 20 minutes, and count 20 percent of the score on the exam.

Informal Speaking

In informal speaking you have a simulated conversation in which a recorded part is played for you and you answer it by recording your response. You will have time to review the script for the conversation before beginning. The script will give you directions about what to say. During the course of the conversation, you will have five or six 20-second opportunities to speak. This is not as hard as it sounds. It is a good opportunity for you to use expressions, exclamations, and conversational strategies to speak in a natural way

Formal Oral Presentation

The formal oral presentation also features reading and listening comprehension. You will have five minutes to read a short selection. Then you will listen to an audio selection. As you listen you should take notes so that you can make reference to details from the selection in your presentation. After the audio is played you will have two minutes to prepare a response to a question related to the print and audio selections. After the two minutes you will have another two minutes to record your response.

The formal oral presentation may consist of making comparisons, contrasts, explanations of something, or any other topic about which you can talk for two minutes. Formal implies an academic setting, so the language to be used in this part of the exam corresponds to the fifth or sixth semester of college work. You may also be asked to narrate something that you read or heard about in the source materials. You need to be able to synthesize the information, not simply lift phrases from the source materials, and incorporate it into your speech sample. The audio source may be from any kind of broadcast source.

Suggestions

In many ways this part of the exam may seem more difficult than the previous format, because it does require attention to source materials that you need to incorporate into your responses. In your responses you will be required to draw upon your knowledge of the Spanish-speaking world. The more you know about Spanish history, people, places, and culture, the easier it will be for you to understand the source materials, and the easier it will be for you to formulate your responses. Make every effort to read and listen to as much Spanish as you can in preparation for taking the exam. There is no single text or course that will really prepare you for the exam. You have to make the effort to learn as much as you can. The listening practice will also improve your own pronunciation, if you try to reproduce the good pronunciation you hear.

In preparation for the simulated conversation, you need to make sure you have an adequate vocabulary. The following chapters in this book are designed to help you review vocabulary you may want to use. In addition, there are a number of expressions that are useful to remember. After the sections on grouped vocabulary, there are oral practices. Some of them involve imagining a conversation with someone about a given topic. It is very useful to imagine conversations, even if you have the opportunity to talk to Spanish-speaking persons often. Imagining conversations allows you to cover topics that you would not ordinarily discuss with other people. You want to pre-think as many topics as you can so that you have the words you need to do your best.

In preparation for the formal oral presentation, it is also useful to do the additional practices after each group of words to further commit the vocabulary to memory. There are additional multiple choice exercises to practice vocabulary. For words you do not know and consistently miss, make a list of them to use in extra practice. Focus special attention on verbs. You can work your way around nouns you do not know, but verbs are harder to get around. Make sure you have a good dictionary, and use it often.

Scoring the Informal Oral Presentation (Simulated Conversation) Samples

Low: Samples that scored low were very limited in content. The speaker seemed to be confused about what to say regarding the given scripted prompts that were required in the five or six places to record. Sometimes pronunciation was poor and confusing to the listener. The comments were not appropriate for the recorded prompts that were played. The response recorded was not really related to what was said on the recording. There were frequent and long pauses and hesitations. Frequent grammatical and syntactical errors hindered intelligibility. The vocabulary was very limited. The speaker was definitely lacking enough knowledge of Spanish to be adequately understood.

Medium: Although the responses followed the script adequately, they were minimal. Vocabulary was somewhat limited, and grammatical structures sometimes interfered with comprehension. When additional information was appropriate, the speaker faltered because of inability to elaborate. The speaker often used sentence fragments or a short phrase to maintain the conversation. The sample showed generally good pronunciation and fluency, but pauses were frequent. Although there were some places where the speaker did not respond appropriately to the scripted prompts, his or her conversation was generally understandable. The speaker did communicate thoughts and ideas, although they were not well developed.

High: The speaker responded appropriately to the prompts in the script and could easily carry on a conversation by using appropriate grammar, vocabulary, and syntax. Pronunciation, fluency, and intonation were excellent. The student clearly had a superior command of the Spanish language. There may have been some minor errors, but overall intelligibility was high. The sustained level of speaking ability was excellent throughout the conversation.

Scoring the Formal Oral Presentation (Integrated Skills)

Low: The response was limited in content, because it did not contain information from the two source materials. The response was minimally related to the question asked. At times the presentation lacked organization. Delivery of the response was halting and contained pauses while the speaker tried to figure out what to say, perhaps because the speaker was trying to translate from English to Spanish during the delivery or because the speaker wanted to use a particular word and could not remember the vocabulary. At that point the speaker stopped instead of using other words to rephrase the idea. There were grammatical and syntactic errors caused by interference from English. The speaker had problems with pronunciation and intonation, and often the pronunciation was so unclear that the listener did not understand what the speaker was trying to say. The response demonstrated that the speaker had limited ability to express himself in Spanish.

Medium: Responses in this category addressed the question and established a relationship with the topic. However, sometimes the responses did not make reference to both source materials. The responses were choppy and incomplete. Delivery was halting in places. The speaker relied on phrases lifted from the source materials instead of using original language. The grammatical and syntactical structures were coherent, but there were consistent errors that revealed incomplete knowledge of the language. There was good self-correction, however. Although there were some problems with pronunciation, the speaker was understandable. Basic ability to communicate in a formal presentation was present.

High: The responses showed that the speaker had excellent pronunciation and the delivery flowed naturally. The speaker demonstrated good command of language as evidenced by word selection, grammar, and syntax. The speaker responded appropriately to the question with a well-organized and articulated speech sample. Although there were some pauses, they did not indicate heavy dependence on English to communicate the ideas. Although there were some minor errors, they were random and did not indicate lapses in knowledge. Overall, the speaker sustained a high level of speaking ability.

Early Steps

Before practicing with the speaking exercises at the end of the vocabulary sections of this chapter, it would be a good idea to listen to any kind of spoken Spanish to get accustomed to listening to audio source materials. Good sources for listening include television, radio, films, Internet audio sources, and songs.

On the speaking part of the exam:

- Do not use English in your responses unless there is no Spanish equivalent for the word you want to use.
- Do not use inappropriate language, such as curse words.
- Do not leave long pauses in your response.

Remember the following points:

- Say something in the spaces provided in the scripted conversation.
- Incorporate as much grammar and variety of vocabulary as you can in the response.
- Use the time before recording to think of Spanish vocabulary to use.
- Use the time before you record to organize your thoughts.
- Remember that the whole speaking part only takes about 20 minutes. If you are anxious, it will not last long.

- The speaking part does not count as much as the reading and writing parts of the exam.
- All speakers will find the task of incorporating the source materials more difficult than simply telling a story.
- Self-correction is good.
- You know more Spanish than you think, and if you can relax, you will remember more of it.

In each chapter there are specific suggestions for practice. The *Práctica Oral* after each set of grouped vocabulary is especially useful for helping to learn new words. After the thematic vocabulary with personal questions, there are scripted conversations for you to practice simulated conversations.

CHAPTER 8 General Considerations for the Oral Examination

The following section contains word lists of vocabulary that would be useful on the examination. The words are not exactly grouped thematically, because it is difficult to remember a specific word from a whole list of vocabulary words. Instead, words that you ought to know for the listening, reading, writing, and speaking parts of the test are used in context. Included are some exercises to help you practice them. Vocabulary is never tested in this format on the exam, but this is vocabulary of the level you will find on the exam. The list is not comprehensive, but should give you an idea of the level of vocabulary you need to know. The words on the lists are generally grouped by part of speech. Remember that on the exam you will not see any prompts to help you remember vocabulary, so the more you practice using appropriate words, the more likely you are to remember them. Use the following steps to make the best use of this section.

1. Study the words on the list at the beginning of each unit. To study the words you should
   - study groups of five words at a time,
   - cover the English with a paper or card and quiz yourself to see if you remember what the word means,
   - mark the words you do not remember within three seconds,
   - go on to another five words,
   - and, finally, go back over the whole list, focusing especially on the marked words.

After learning the words from Spanish to English, cover the Spanish and learn them from English to Spanish.

2. As you review or learn a vocabulary word, use it in a simple sentence.
3. Think of related forms of the word. Sometimes there will be a related word in parentheses to help you learn to recognize the same words in different parts of speech.
4. Think of contexts in which you would expect to use the word.
5. Draw the word in your mind and repeat the word in Spanish as you picture it.
6. Draw a picture on paper representing the word and repeat it in Spanish as you do the drawing. The picture does not have to be realistic, just something to help you remember what the word looks like in Spanish.
7. Think of other words with similar meanings, or words that you can associate with the one you are studying.
8. Finally, do the exercises that follow the lists. Remember that even though there is only one most appropriate word for each blank, seeing the other words and recalling their meaning as you do the exercises will help you to learn them.

There will be some words you may have to look up in the glossary at the end of this book, or in a dictionary. When doing the practice questions, be sure to look up words you want to use to express yourself. All the questions deal with topics you may hear on the exam, so practicing now is important. Be thorough in doing your practice exercises so that you will use as many words as possible. Remember to use complete sentences. Verbs are especially important. A command of verb tenses demonstrates competence, and the expressions, or *modismos*, make your language more fluent. In forming your responses to questions and situations, draw on your personal experience, but feel free to be a little creative. The evaluator does not know you and is only looking for a speech sample that will show how well you can speak Spanish. The more you elaborate using good vocabulary and structures, the more language you will use, and the higher your score will be.

VOCABULARY LISTS, ORAL PRACTICE, AND SITUATIONS

CARACTERÍSTICAS PERSONALES

bizco	= *cross-eyed, blinking*
calvo	= *bald, hairless*
cicatriz	= *scar*
cojo	= *lame, one-legged* (cojear = *to limp*)
discapacitado	= *handicapped*
manco	= *one-armed*
minusválido	= *handicapped*
sordo	= *deaf*
tuerto	= *one-eyed*
zurdo	= *left-handed*
cobarde	= *coward*
necio	= *fool*
soltero	= *bachelor*
viudo	= *widower*
apenas	= *scarcely, hardly*
por supuesto	= *of course*
por ejemplo	= *for example*
en realidad	= *really*
aguantar	= *to tolerate, to stand (someone)*
compartir	= *to share*
comportarse	= *to behave*
depender de	= *to depend on (notice the preposition after the verb)*
distraer	= *to distract*
guardar	= *to maintain, to keep*
heredar	= *to inherit*

mezclar	= *to mix* (la mezcla = *the mixture*)
molestar	= *to bother* (la molestia = *the bother*)
resultar	= *to end up, to result in* (el resultado = *result*)
soler (ue)	= *to be accustomed to, to be in the habit of*
soportar	= *to tolerate, to stand (someone)*
agotado	= *worn out, very tired* (agotar = *to wring out, to wear out*)
ajeno	= *foreign, distant*
alegre	= *happy, joyful, delighted*
amargo	= *bitter*
angustiado	= *anxious* (la angustia = *anxiety, worry*)
aplicado	= *diligent, hard-working* (aplicar = *to apply oneself*)
avariento	= *miserly* (el avaro = *miser*)
bondadoso	= *gracious, generous*
celoso	= *jealous*
codiciado	= *envy* (codiciar = *to covet*)
confiado	= *confident, trusty* (confiar = *to confide, to trust*)
confuso	= *confused* (confundir = *to confuse*)
desafortunado	= *unfortunate*
descuidado	= *sloppy, unkempt*
dichoso	= *happy, blissful*
dotado	= *talented, gifted* (dotar = *to endow with, to provide with*)
ensimismado	= *self-absorbed, egocentric, turned toward the inside*
fiel	= *loyal, faithful*
furtivo	= *sneaky, stealthy*
gracioso	= *funny, amusing, charming*
incansable	= *tireless*
indeleble	= *indelible, permanent*
indiscreto	= *indiscreet, unwise*
ingenuo	= *naïve, ingenuous*
inocuo	= *innocuous, harmless*
inquieto	= *worried, nervous, anxious* (inquetar = *to unsettle, to disquiet*)
manso	= *gentle, kind*
mezquino	= *mean, stingy, petty*
nocivo	= *noxious, harmful*
orgulloso	= *proud*
ostentoso	= *ostentatious, overdone style*
perezoso	= *lazy* (la pereza = *laziness*)
rendido	= *worn out, done in, very tired* (rendir = *to subdue, to yield*)
ruidoso	= *noisy*
sobresaliente	= *outstanding* (sobresalir = *to stand out*)
solo	= *lone, alone*
sospechoso	= *suspicious* (sospechar = *to suspect*)
tacaño	= *stingy*
terco	= *stubborn, obstinate*
tranquilo	= *calm* (tranquilizar = *to calm*)
vano	= *vain, self-aware*
zurdo	= *left-handed*

EJERCICIO A

Empareje cada palabra en la Columna A con la definición en la Columna B, escribiendo la letra de la mejor selección.

Columna A

___ 1. gracioso
___ 2. mezquino
___ 3. furtivo
___ 4. codiciado
___ 5. sospechoso
___ 6. tacaño
___ 7. fiel
___ 8. alegre
___ 9. amargo
___ 10. orgulloso
___ 11. celoso
___ 12. manso
___ 13. minusválido
___ 14. terco
___ 15. aplicada
___ 16. soportar
___ 17. heredar
___ 18. comportarse
___ 19. soler
___ 20. compartir
___ 21. por supuesto
___ 22. por ejemplo
___ 23. apenas

Columna B

a. un sabor desagradable
b. característica de una persona que no deja a un amigo en peligro
c. feliz
d. expresión para indicar algo obvio, o evidente
e. envidioso
f. sentimiento que se tiene al alcanzar una meta
g. diligente
h. encantador
i. de manera secreta, sin que nadie lo vea
j. una ilustración de lo que se quiere decir
k. suave, de manera sutil
l. discapacitado
m. actitud que no quiere admitir un error
n. un momento o algo que acaba de ocurrir, o casi no ocurre
o. desconfiado
p. recibir de sus antepasados
q. acostumbrarse
r. dividir entre varias personas
s. manera de actuar
t. que no es generoso
u. aguantar
v. malo, sin caridad ni piedad, malévolo
w. deseado

EJERCICIO B

Escoja la mejor palabra para cumplir el sentido de la oración.

El estudiante más popular de la escuela es la persona que es muy _(1)_ por sus amigos, la que nunca revela un secreto. También, sería una persona _(2)_, porque siempre es bueno poder contar con ella en caso de emergencia. Los cínicos, con su actitud _(3)_ envenenan una relación con palabras y acciones detestables, y es mejor evitarlos por completo. Nadie _(4)_ a ese tipo sarcástico tampoco. En cuanto a los otros, _(5)_ es el que tenga un amigo _(6)_, porque se divierte mucho con ese tipo de amigo. Se dice que los más creativos son los _(7)_, pero no hay prueba, aunque hay estudios que indican que el hemisferio izquierdo del cerebro domina el pensamiento de ese tipo. A veces, los _(8)_ son los más _(9)_ porque han experimentado discriminación en su vida y se identifican con otros _(10)_.

___ 1. a) sensato	b) confiada	c) mezquino	d) terco
___ 2. a) ostentosa	b) descuidada	c) fiel	d) nociva
___ 3. a) ruidosa	b) amarga	c) angustiada	d) alegre
___ 4. a) hereda	b) comparte	c) mezcla	d) aguanta
___ 5. a) dotado	b) dichoso	c) manso	d) minusválido
___ 6. a) tacaño	b) gracioso	c) celoso	d) inocuo
___ 7. a) zurdos	b) cojos	c) mansos	d) rendidos
___ 8. a) discapacitados	b) calvos	c) sospechosos	d) cobardes
___ 9. a) aplicados	b) sensatos	c) perezosos	d) sordos
___ 10. a) ingenuos	b) vanos	c) solteros	d) desafortunados

RESPUESTAS

Ejercicio A

1. h	2. v	3. i	4. w	5. o
6. t	7. b	8. c	9. a	10. f
11. e	12. k	13. l	14. m	15. g
16. u	17. p	18. s	19. q	20. r
21. d	22. j	23. n		

Ejercicio B

1. b—confiada	6. b—gracioso
2. c—fiel	7. a—zurdos
3. b—amarga	8. a—discapacitados
4. d—aguanta	9. b—sensatos
5. b—dichoso	10. d—desafortunados

EJERCICIO C: PRÁCTICA DE LECTURA
Lea la selección para practicar el reconocimiento del vocabulario. Luego utilice las palabras en la Práctica Oral y las Situaciones.

Soy una hija entre dos otros, un hermano mayor y una hermana menor. Los tres **compartimos** muchas características personales, pero diferimos en cuanto a otros aspectos. **Por ejemplo**, soy morena, pero mi hermana menor es rubia, y mi hermano, **calvo**. Gracias a Dios, no **heredé** esa característica. **Por supuesto**, prefiero pensar que soy **confiada, bondadosa, mansa, aplicada, tranquila, incansable, alegre, fiel, encantadora** y **dichosa**. Es posible **heredar** esas características de los padres y esos adjetivos describen los míos perfectamente. Pero, **en realidad**, no hay nadie que sea ejemplo de tantas características tan **codiciadas**. Todo el mundo sufre en un momento u otro de debilidades personales, las cuales se ven manifestadas cuando tratamos con otra gente. **Por ejemplo**, cuando alguien nos **molesta**, **solemos** responder de manera **abrupta**, mostrando que somos **furtivos, tacaños, vanos, necios, distraídos, mezquinos, indiscretos, ostentosos, descuidados** o **tercos**. Hay ciertas características que se esperan de ciertas personas a veces. Muchas veces los ladrones suelen ser **furtivos** y **mezquinos**, pero no son **descuidados**. Los que son **ostentosos** con lo que roban muchas veces no **gozan de** su libertad mucho tiempo. Los **avaros** son **tacaños**, o sea, poco **generosos**. Prefieren guardar todo para sí mismo. Así **resulta** muchas veces que son muy **ensimismados**, también.

Muchas veces las características personales corresponden a condiciones físicas, como con la gente **coja, manca, sorda, ciega, tuerta**, o un **soltero** o un **viudo**, cuya relación interpersonal a veces **depende de** las percepciones o las limitaciones impuestas por su **discapacidad** o **minusvalía**. A veces el aspecto sugiere la historia de una persona, como una **cicatriz** que indica algún encuentro o accidente **desafortunado** en el pasado. Es difícil **soportar** o **aguantar** las actitudes de superioridad de los más **dotados** cuando no tienen la menor simpatía por prójimos que no **comparten** sus talentos. Pero otras personas tienen características **inocuas,** porque **apenas** se notan. Siempre es mejor no **guardar sentimientos** de **amargura, celos** ni **rencor**, porque esas emociones **nocivas** resultan en la infelicidad. **En realidad**, estas características se **mezclan** en cada persona, porque no hay nadie que sea un ser humano perfecto.

Preguntas sobre la lectura

1. ¿Cómo es la narradora?
2. Compare la narradora con sus hermanos.
3. ¿Qué características personales se hereden de los padres que son buenas?
4. ¿Qué características personales no son tan buenas?
5. ¿Qué características se asocian con los ladrones?
6. ¿Cómo son los minusválidos? ¿Se heredan sus características físicas?
7. ¿Cómo es la gente muy dotada?
8. En realidad, ¿cómo es la persona típica?

EJERCICIO D: PRÁCTICA ORAL
Conteste las preguntas usando el vocabulario de esta unidad.

1. Descríbase: cómo es usted, cuáles son las características más sobresalientes de su personalidad.
2. Describa cómo querría ser si pudiera ser diferente.
3. Describa las características personales de su mejor amigo, y cuáles con las características que aprecia usted en un amigo perfecto.
4. Describa a una persona minusválida y cómo influyen sus limitaciones en cómo es.
5. ¿Cree que las características personales se aprenden o se heredan? Explique y dé ejemplos.
6. ¿Qué características heredó de su padre? ¿De su madre?
7. ¿Comparte algunas características personales con sus hermanos, si los tiene?
8. Describa a su mejor amigo.
9. Describa a una persona que no le cae bien.
10. Describa las características personales de una persona a quien usted admira.

EJERCICIO E: SITUACIONES
Discuta las situaciones usando el vocabulario de esta unidad.

1. Para una solicitud de la universidad, usted debe describirse. Escriba un ensayo en el cual se describe.

2. En una composición para una clase tiene que escribir un ensayo sobre la persona más interesante que jamás haya conocido. Descríbala en detalle, cómo es y a qué atribuye usted sus características personales. En otras palabras, explique por qué es como es en su opinión.

3. Una noche usted presenció el robo de una tienda y es el único testigo del crimen. Tiene que describir a la policía a la persona que vio, incluso todos sus atributos físicos y su actitud.

4. En su trabajo como aduanero en un aeropuerto, usted ve a todo el mundo que pasa por la aduana. Describa las características de una persona sospechosa.

5. Un filósofo español propuso que dentro de cada uno de nosotros está la persona que quisiéramos ser. Describa su ser ideal, cómo sería éste si fuera perfecto.

LA FAMILIA

los antepasados	= *ancestors*
la ascendencia	= *origin, line of ancestors*
los bisabuelos	= *great grandparents*
la costumbre	= *custom* (acostumbrarse = *to get used to, to become accustomed*)
la familia extensa	= *extended family*
la genealogista	= *genealogist*
la hazaña	= *deed, exploit, adventure*
el hogar	= *home, hearth*
la madrastra/el padrastro	= *stepmother/stepfather*
la madurez	= *maturity* (madurar = *to mature*)
el mecedor	= *rocking chair* (mecer = *to rock*)
el nene	= *baby*
la niñez	= *childhood*
la nuera/el yerno	= *daughter-in-law/son-in-law*
el orgullo	= *pride*
los padres	= *parents (mother and father together)*
los parientes	= *relatives*
el relato	= *story*
los suegros	= *in-laws (mother- and father-in-law)*
los tatarabuelos	= *great, great grandparents*
la vejez	= *old age* (envejecerse = *to grow old*)
acabar de	= *to have just (done something)*
apreciar	= *to appreciate* (el aprecio = *appreciation*)
aprovechar	= *to benefit from*
conmemorar	= *to commemorate* (la conmemoración = *memorial*)
consistir en	= *to consist of (Notice the preposition after the verb.)*
crecer	= *to grow*
criar	= *to raise*
ejercer	= *to exert influence* (ejercicio = *exercise*)
entretener	= *to entertain, to amuse* (el entretenimiento = *entertainment*)

estrechar las relaciones	= *to get closer, to bring closer* (estrecho = *close*)
hacer el papel	= *to play a role*
llevarse bien	= *to get along with each other*
realizar	= *to fulfill, to realize (in the sense of fulfill)*
regalar	= *to give a gift* (el regalo = *the gift*)
reunir	= *to get together, to unite* (la reunión = *the meeting*)
vincular	= *to tie together* (el vínculo = *the tie, link*)
a medida que	= *as (time going by), during the time that*
a menudo	= *often, frequently*
en adelante	= *forward, ahead*
predilecto	= *favorite*

EJERCICIO A
Empareje cada palabra en la Columna A con la definición en la Columna B, escribiendo la letra de la mejor selección.

Columna A

___ 1. madurez
___ 2. crecer
___ 3. hogar
___ 4. a menudo
___ 5. aprovechar
___ 6. predilecto
___ 7. vincular
___ 8. nuera
___ 9. conmemorar
___ 10. parientes
___ 11. ascendencia
___ 12. orgullo
___ 13. vejez
___ 14. suegros
___ 15. mecedor

Columna B

a. ligar, juntar con lazos figurativamente
b. estar satisfecho por haber hecho algo bueno
c. miembros de la familia extensa
d. la sabiduría acumulada por vivir muchos años
e. los últimos años de la vida
f. mueble usado por las madres para tranquilizar a los nenes
g. ponerse más viejo, envejecerse
h. los padres de la esposa o del marido
i. muchas veces
j. sacar beneficio de algo
k. favorito
l. la esposa del hijo de la familia
m. de origen
n. el lugar donde se reúne la familia, donde está el corazón
o. honrar a alguien, o recordar algo bueno que ocurrió

EJERCICIO B
Escoja la mejor palabra para cumplir el sentido de la oración.

La mayoría de los estadounidenses son de _(1)_ europea o africana, aunque hay más y más asiáticos ahora. En el _(2)_, cada familia conmemora su propia herencia cultural cuando observan _(3)_ y tradiciones que pertenecen a su país de origen. En la _(4)_, los parientes ejercen mucha influencia porque comparten las responsabilidades de _(5)_ a los jóvenes. Estos _(6)_ familiares proveen un sentido de continuidad generacional en la que cada individuo _(7)_ la sabiduría de los otros del grupo. Promociona el _(8)_ personal, y _(9)_ crecen los niños, se acercan cada vez más a los papeles que ejemplifican sus propios padres. Así aprenden a vivir tranquilos con los cuñados y los (10).

En la última reunión de mi familia, mi abuelo, quien es el (11) de la familia, nos contó algunas de las historias más interesantes de los (12) más distinguidos. Nos entretenía con (13) de viajes largos, y dificultades y obstáculos que nos parecían casi insuperables ahora. Sin electricidad, televisión, computadoras, ni coches, la vida era más sencilla y la familia más unida. Entre mis (14) , había uno que vino a esta tierra en búsqueda de oportunidad hace más de cien años, y la encontró cuando conoció a su esposa futura y se casó con ella. Nadie tenía tiempo para sentarse en un (15) al jubilarse, porque la vida era bien dura.

1. a) vejez	b) historia	c) ascendencia	d) madurez
2. a) lugar	b) hogar	c) orgullo	d) papel
3. a) costumbres	b) abuelas	c) parientes	d) suegras
4. a) costumbre	b) madurez	c) genealogista	d) familia extensa
5. a) ejercer	b) estrechar	c) realizar	d) criar
6. a) parientes	b) suegros	c) vínculos	d) orgullosos
7. a) aprecia	b) aprovecha	c) realiza	d) ejerce
8. a) relato	b) sentimiento	c) orgullo	d) bienestar
9. a) en adelante	b) a medida que	c) a menudo	d) apenas
10. a) relatos	b) hogares	c) suegros	d) sueños
11. a) antepasado	b) mecedor	c) genealogista	d) nene
12. a) antepasados	b) nenes	c) mecedores	d) hogares
13. a) costumbres	b) relatos	c) mecedores	d) vínculos
14. a) suegros	b) cuñados	c) tatarabuelos	d) padrastros
15. a) vínculo	b) mecedor	c) hogar	d) papel

RESPUESTAS

Ejercicio A

1. d	2. g	3. n	4. i	5. j
6. k	7. a	8. l	9. o	10. c
11. m	12. b	13. e	14. h.	15. f

Ejercicio B

1. c—ascendencia	9. b—a medida que
2. b—hogar	10. c—suegros
3. a—costumbres	11. c—genealogista
4. d—familia extensa	12. a—antepasados
5. d—criar	13. b—relatos
6. c—vínculos	14. c—tatarabuelos
7. b—aprovecha	15. b—mecedor
8. c—orgullo	

EJERCICIO C: PRÁCTICA DE LECTURA
Lea la selección para practicar el reconocimiento del vocabulario. Luego utilice las palabras en la Práctica Oral y las Situaciones.

Muchas personas hoy en día se interesan en la historia familiar, enfocando en las **hazañas** de los miembros ilustres, o **conmemorando** la bondad de una **tatarabuela** o el genio de otros **antepasados**. La familia es la unidad social más importante en una cultura, porque dentro de la familia se **realizan** las tradiciones y los valores de una cultura. La familia **consiste en** varios miembros, incluyendo **abuelos, cuñados, madrastras, hermanastros, suegros,** y **los nenes,** en los cuales se ve una visión del pasado y el futuro. En el **hogar,** los jóvenes aprenden los **comportamientos** apropiados y los valores de la sociedad. El **orgullo** de la familia es importante para que cada individuo tenga un sentimiento de seguridad que refuerce la confianza personal.

A menudo la familia se **reúne** para celebrar un suceso importante en la vida de un miembro, como su cumpleaños, o un día feriado religioso. **Regalan** regalos al honrado para marcar un paso **adelante** hacia su **madurez. A medida que crecen** los jóvenes, aprenden a **apreciar** a los adultos de la familia. Las reuniones sirven para fortalecer los **vínculos** familiares entre los miembros de la familia para que cada uno **realice** su potencial. Cuando todos **comparten** sus experiencias, los jóvenes **aprovechan los recuerdos** de los viejos, y los viejos **gozan de** la vitalidad de los jóvenes. También es importante que los jóvenes sepan que los **ancianos** no están resignados al **mecedor.** Por supuesto, no todos **se llevan bien** todo el tiempo, pero si una persona se **reúne** con su familia, facilita la oportunidad para **estrechar las relaciones.**

Preguntas sobre la lectura
1. ¿En qué consiste una unidad familiar?
2. ¿Para qué sirve la familia?
3. ¿Por qué es importante estar orgulloso de su familia?
4. ¿Qué hace una familia al reunirse?
5. ¿Qué aprenden los jóvenes al asistir a las reuniones familiares?
6. ¿Cómo aprovechan los ancianos la reunión?
7. ¿Cómo se estrechan las relaciones en una familia?

EJERCICIO D: PRÁCTICA ORAL
Conteste las preguntas usando el vocabulario de esta unidad.

1. Describa a su familia, indicando las relaciones entre todos sus miembros.
2. Narre la historia de uno de sus antepasados.
3. Explique las ventajas y desventajas de ser el único hijo de la familia.
4. Describa cómo cambia la familia a medida que crecen los hijos.
5. Describa a su pariente predilecto.
6. Describa los papeles tradicionales de los hombres y las mujeres en la familia.
7. Describa cómo y por qué están cambiando los papeles tradicionales en la familia.

8. Enumere los deberes de los hijos en una familia.

9. ¿Cuáles son las responsabilidades de los padres en una familia?

10. ¿Qué le dicen sus padres de su propia niñez? ¿Cómo difiere ésta de la suya?

11. ¿Le gustaría haber vivido en la época cuando eran jóvenes sus padres?

12. ¿Cómo se resuelven los conflictos de los familiares que no se llevan bien en su familia?

EJERCICIO E: SITUACIONES
Discuta las situaciones usando el vocabulario de esta unidad.

1. Está encargado de reunir a su familia extensa. Proponga un plan para juntar a toda la familia, y actividades para cada generación.

2. Para una historia de su familia, describa algunas tradiciones que celebran ustedes durante los días feriados, ya sean religiosos o patrióticos.

3. Para escribir una composición sobre la diferencia entre su vida y la de sus padres a su edad, compare su vida durante su niñez y la de sus padres a su edad.

RECUERDOS DEL PASADO

las afueras	= *out of doors*
la alfombra	= *carpet, rug*
la almohada	= *pillow* (almohada de plumas = *feather pillow*)
la aspiradora	= *vacuum cleaner* (aspirar = *to inhale, to aspire*)
las avispas	= *wasps*
la cadena	= *chain* (encadenar = *to chain up*)
las cenizas	= *ashes*
la colcha	= *bedspread, counterpane (of a bed)*
el colchón	= *mattress*
las cortinas	= *curtains*
el desván	= *attic*
las escaleras	= *stairs*
el eslabón	= *link (of chain)* (eslabonar = *to link, to join*)
el estante	= *bookcase, shelves*
los estornudos	= *sneezes* (estornudar = *to sneeze*)
el grifo	= *faucet, tap*
las herramientas	= *tools (for making repairs)*
las hormigas	= *ants*
el hueco	= *hole*
la llave	= *key, faucet*
la limpieza	= *cleanliness* (limpiar = *to clean*)
la mosca	= *housefly, fly*
la nube	= *cloud*
los quehaceres	= *chores*
los pedazos	= *pieces*
los peldaños	= *steps (of stairs)*

las persianas	= *blinds (at a window)*
el polvo	= *dust*
el sillón	= *armchair*
el sartén	= *frying pan*
el sótano	= *basement*
el techo	= *roof*
las tijeras	= *scissors*
el umbral	= *threshold (of a doorway)*
atender	= *to attend (to), to take care of (not to attend a school)*
arreglar	= *to fix, to arrange, to repair*
bordar	= *to embroider*
brotar	= *to surge forth, to come up, to spring up*
callar	= *to become quiet, to stop talking*
colocar	= *to place, to put, to locate*
coser	= *to sew*
crujir	= *to creak, to make a rustling sound*
diseñar	= *to design*
encerrar	= *to encircle, to enclose*
enchufar	= *to plug in (an electrical appliance)*
envolver	= *to wrap up, to wrap around*
fregar	= *to scrub*
gotear	= *to drip* (la gota = *drop*)
latir	= *to beat (like a heart)* (el latido = *beat*)
mantener	= *to maintain* (el mantenimiento = *maintenance*)
medir	= *to measure* (la medida = *the measure*)
mudarse	= *to move (from one house, or place, to another)*
permanecer	= *to remain*
rodear	= *to surround* (el rodeo = *round up, rodeo*)
surtir	= *to sprout, to spurt, to gush* (el surtido = *the supply*)
ubicar	= *to locate* (la ubicación = *the placement, the location*)
a tientas	= *to grope in the dark*
cabalmente	= *exactly, completely, entirely*
cautelosamente	= *cautiously, warily*
concienzudamente	= *conscientiously, with care*
en puntillas	= *on tiptoes*
paulatinamente	= *slowly, little by little, gradually*

EJERCICIO A

Empareje cada palabra en la Columna A con la definición en la Columna B, escribiendo la letra de la mejor selección.

Columna A

___ 1. umbral
___ 2. polvo
___ 3. enchufar
___ 4. diseñar
___ 5. escaleras
___ 6. almohadas
___ 7. persianas
___ 8. sótano
___ 9. hormigas
___ 10. ubicar
___ 11. arreglar
___ 12. medir
___ 13. coser
___ 14. brotar
___ 15. crujir
___ 16. envolver
___ 17. paulatinamente
___ 18. cauteloso
___ 19. techo
___ 20. estornudos

Columna B

a. surtir
b. lo que se hace con papel para preparar un regalo
c. insectos que se ven a menudo en busca de azúcar
d. usar una aguja para bordar diseños en tela, o hacer ropa
e. hacer un ruido
f. usar una regla para tomar el tamaño de algo
g. la parte de una casa por donde se entra
h. reparar
i. con cuidado
j. lo que se hace para dar electricidad a un aparato
k. materia que se encuentra si no se limpia a menudo
l. muchos peldaños forman esto
m. poco a poco
n. la parte más baja de una casa
o. dibujar, o formar un plan artístico o arquitectónico
p. pequeños colchones que se usan en una cama o en un sofá
q. localizar
r. reacción producida en alguien con alergias
s. la parte más alta de una casa y que la protege del tiempo
t. algo para una ventana, que se abre y se cierra

EJERCICIO B

Escoja la mejor palabra para cumplir el sentido de la oración.

Cuando visité a mis abuelos la última vez, mi abuelita estaba sentada en su (1) , (2) algo para su nieta Eva. Mientras lo hacía, el mueble (3) ligeramente y la abuelita murmuraba en voz baja. Al verme, me sonrió dulcemente, dirigiéndome una palabra acogedora e invitándome a acercarme. A la izquierda, entre los libros de un (4) , un gato nos miraba (5) , porque tenía miedo de los visitantes a la casa. Yo no la visitaba a menudo porque vivíamos lejos. El gato (6) estiró una pata, después otra, y bostezó.

Mi abuela se levantó y me abrazó. Después de la cena, después de lavar los platos, (7) el sartén y limpiar el mostrador de la cocina, nosotras subimos las (8) al (9) donde guardaba grandes misterios. Entre otras cosas, bajo una (10) de (11) , había un gran baúl. La (12) del baúl tenía una cerradura que mi abuela abrió con una (13) . La (14) en el suelo, entre los restos de (15) y (16) muertas del calor del (17) por encima de nuestras cabezas. Entre (18) , ella sacó unos pendientes de oro que guardaba dentro del baúl. Me los regaló para que los tuviera para mi fiesta de quinceañera el próximo mes.

Mientras tanto, mi abuelo cuidaba el jardín para quitar la mala hierba que __(19)__ por entre las flores y vegetales. Después, __(20)__ las __(21)__ del baño porque siempre __(22)__ bien la casa. De vez en cuando lo oía __(23)__ sus __(24)__ eléctricas para reparar lo que estaba roto, como una silla sin respaldo firme. Siempre me encantaba visitar a mis abuelos. Mientras los acompañaba por allí y por allá, compartíamos tanto historias como __(25)__ cotidianos y siempre quedaba con recuerdos familiares hermosos.

___ 1. a) alfombra	b) mecedor	c) persiana	d) estante
___ 2. a) cosiendo	b) rodeando	c) ubicando	d) brotando
___ 3. a) surtía	b) se mudaba	c) conseguía	d) crujía
___ 4. a) eslabón	b) hueco	c) estante	d) polvo
___ 5. a) cautelosamente	b) a tientas	c) cabalmente	d) en puntillas
___ 6. a) sumamente	b) paulatinamente	c) roncamente	d) a tientas
___ 7. a) enchufar	b) fregar	c) encerrar	d) latir
___ 8. a) cadenas	b) almohadas	c) escaleras	d) herramientas
___ 9. a) sótano	b) desván	c) techo	d) estante
___ 10. a) nube	b) cama	c) mosca	d) llave
___ 11. a) tijeras	b) polvo	c) cortinas	d) persianas
___ 12. a) cadena	b) llave	c) limpieza	d) herramienta
___ 13. a) colcha	b) escalera	c) llave	d) hormiga
___ 14. a) encerró	b) colocó	c) enchufó	d) alquiló
___ 15. a) pedazos	b) sillones	c) moscas	d) frutas
___ 16. a) quehaceres	b) persianas	c) avispas	d) huecos
___ 17. a) peldaño	b) techo	c) estante	d) colchón
___ 18. a) pedazos	b) eslabones	c) polvos	d) estornudos
___ 19. a) rodeaba	b) callaba	c) ensuciaba	d) brotaba
___ 20. a) se fijó	b) arregló	c) partió	d) ubicó
___ 21. a) avispas	b) cenizas	c) llaves	d) cortinas
___ 22. a) conseguía	b) permanecía	c) alquilaba	d) mantenía
___ 23. a) enchufar	b) diseñar	c) envolver	d) medir
___ 24. a) tijeras	b) huecos	c) quehaceres	d) herramientas
___ 25. a) quehaceres	b) sillones	c) estornudos	d) peldaños

RESPUESTAS

Ejercicio A

1. g	2. k	3. j	4. o	5. l
6. p	7. t	8. n	9. c	10. q
11. h	12. f	13. d	14. a	15. e
16. b	17. m	18. i	19. s	20. r

Ejercicio B

1. b—mecedor
2. a—cosiendo
3. d—crujía
4. c—estante
5. a—cautelosamente
6. b—paulatinamente
7. b—fregar
8. c—escaleras
9. b—desván
10. a—nube
11. b—polvo
12. a—cadena
13. c—llave

14. b—colocó
15. c—moscas
16. c—avispas
17. b—techo
18. d—estornudos
19. d—brotaba
20. b—arregló
21. c—llaves
22. d—mantenía
23. a—enchufar
24. d—herramientas
25. a—quehaceres

EJERCICIO C: PRÁCTICA DE LECTURA

Lea la selección para practicar el reconocimiento del vocabulario. Luego utilice las palabras en la Práctica Oral y las Situaciones.

Al recordar las casas de la niñez, todo depende de la perspectiva de la persona. Bien recuerdo escenas dentro de la casa de mis abuelos y en las **afueras,** por ejemplo, los álamos y otros árboles altos que la **rodeaban**. La casa de mis abuelos adonde mis abuelos **se mudaron** al **jubilarse** estaba **ubicada** cerca de un río. Recuerdo que los **peldaños** de la **escalera** al entrar en la casa me parecían tan altos que me costaba mucho trabajo subirla. Al pasar por el **umbral** se sentía la tranquilidad y se olía el pan dulce que procedía de la cocina. En la sala de estar, poco usada, había un **estante** con muchos libros **envueltos** en **polvo** por falta de un lector frecuente. No es que mi abuela no se preocupaba de la **limpieza** (recuerdo que me **tapaba** los oídos cuando **enchufaba** la **aspiradora**), sino que le faltaba el tiempo de **atender** a todos los **quehaceres domésticos** y no se sentaba a menudo en la sala formal. En sus ratos libres, **solía medir** un **pedazo** de tela para hacer **colchas** para las camas de los nietos o **bordaba** toallas o vestidos o blusas para las nietas. Todavía tengo una que me hizo. En las blusas, mi abuela **diseñaba** jardines florales que parecían **surtir** del fondo verde. Qué bonito tener un jardín del que **brotan** flores todo el año.

De noche, recuerdo la alcoba, el **colchón** viejo y las **persianas** cerradas que ocultaban la luz del sol al amanecer. Pero al cerrarlas, se levantaba una **nube** de **polvo** que producía grandes **estornudos**, como si un volcán hubiera arrojado **cenizas** en el aire del cuarto. Mi abuela, un poco ciega, no **se fijaba** en el polvo por no poder verlo. Las **cortinas** gruesas **encerraban** toda la ventana en la habitación de modo que no se veía la oscuridad de la noche del campo. Cuando llovía, las **gotas** producían un **ruido** tremendo en el **techo** metálico, que me parecía el sonido de muchos tambores. El sonido **latía** suavemente al principio, luego, **a medida** que caía con más fuerza la lluvia, parecía el chorro de un río que caía sobre el **techo** de la casa. Entonces, retrocedía **paulatinamente** el mugir de la tempestad; parecían pasos lentos de una bestia saliendo **cautelosamente** hasta cesar.

Recuerdo a mi abuelo. Pasaba el tiempo **arreglando** los aparatos de la casa. Lo recuerdo con sus **herramientas, reparando** las **llaves** que **goteaban** en el baño, o el **lavaplatos** para que mi abuelita no tuviese que **fregar** las cacerolas y ollas a mano. O bien se ocupaba de **callar** el **crujido** del **mecedor** de mi abuelita cuando ella **cosía** de noche delante del fuego. Por lo general, **mantenía** todo bien arreglado para que pudieran **permanecer** en su propio hogar el mayor tiempo posible.

Preguntas sobre la lectura
1. ¿Dónde vivían los abuelos de la narradora?
2. ¿Por qué era tan agradable entrar en la casa?
3. ¿Qué hacía la abuela en casa?
4. ¿En qué se fijaba al acostarse de noche en la alcoba?
5. Describa la alcoba.
6. ¿Qué solía hacer el abuelo?

EJERCICIO D: PRÁCTICA ORAL
Conteste las preguntas usando el vocabulario de esta unidad.

1. Describa una visita a la casa de sus abuelos cuando era niño. ¿Cómo era la casa? ¿Cómo eran los abuelos en la perspectiva de un niño?
2. Describa una tradición que tenía su familia al visitar a los abuelos.
3. Describa la casa en que vivía cuando era niño. ¿Tenía desván? ¿Qué se pone en un desván?
4. Describa las ventajas de tener un sótano en una casa. ¿Qué tendría usted en el sótano, si lo tuviera?
5. Describa su propia casa.
6. Cuando sus parientes visitan a su familia, ¿se quedan en su casa? ¿Qué cambios hacen usted y su familia para acomodar a los visitantes?
7. Describa el cuarto favorito en su casa. ¿Por qué le gusta más que otros?
8. ¿En qué se diferencia una casa en la que viven unos ancianos o personas minusválidos de una casa de familia con adolescentes? ¿Por qué hay esas diferencias?
9. Describa cómo se limpia una càsa.
10. ¿Por qué es importante limpiar su cuarto de vez en cuando?
11. ¿Por qué a muchos jóvenes no les gusta mantener su habitación en orden?
12. ¿Qué preparativos se necesita hacer para la visita de parientes en su casa?

EJERCICIO E: SITUACIONES
Discuta las situaciones usando el vocabulario de esta unidad.

1. Unos tíos de otra ciudad vienen a visitar a su familia. Pero ustedes no tienen una alcoba para acomodarlos. Usted necesita dormir con su hermano o hermana mientras ellos están en su casa. Discuta los planes para compartir el cuarto por una semana.
2. Durante sus vacaciones de primavera, usted participará en un proyecto para arreglar las casa de unos ancianos que viven en el campo. Describa lo que haría para ayudarlos a mantener su casa y campo.
3. Usted tiene una empresa de limpieza para arreglar los desvanes y los sótanos de gente que se muda. Describa cómo sería un día típico en ese trabajo.

LA ESCUELA

el ademán	= *expression, look, gesture*
el ala (f)	= *wing*
la asignatura	= *subject (in a class)*
el aula (f)	= *classroom*
la beca	= *scholarship*
la cárcel	= *jail, jail cell*
el celular	= *cell phone*
el chiste	= *joke*
la conferencia	= *lecture*
la enseñanza	= *teaching*
el gesto	= *gesture*
el grito	= *shout, cry (to shout)* (gritar = *to shout*)
el cable	= *wire*
la índole	= *nature*
la jaula	= *cage*
la lectura	= *reading*
el logro	= *achievement* (lograr = *to achieve*)
la materia	= *subject*
la mochila	= *backpack*
el móvil	= *cell phone*
el prójimo	= *fellow man, neighbor*
el sendero	= *path*
la sonrisa	= *smile* (sonreír = *to smile*)
el toque	= *touch, tap* (tocar = *to touch, to tap, to play music*)
el truco	= *trick*
la Red	= *Internet, the Web*
aburrirse	= *to get bored*
alcanzar	= *to reach, to achieve*
adelantar	= *to get ahead*
aprobar	= *to pass (a course in school)*
aprovecharse	= *to take advantage of* (provecho = *benefit*)
asistir a	= *to attend (school or a class)*
atraer	= *to attract*
atribuir	= *to attribute to*
borrar	= *to erase*
carecer	= *to lack*
constar de	= *to consist of (Notice the preposition.)*
depender de	= *to depend on (Notice the preposition.)*
desplegar	= *to spread out, to fan out*
dictar	= *to give (a lecture* = dictar una conferencia)
fracasar	= *to fail (anything except a subject in school)* (el fracaso = *failure*)
empujar	= *to push on, to push out*
encarcelar	= *to put in jail*
entregar	= *to turn over to, to turn in*
ingresar	= *to enter (a school, a program)*
matricular	= *to matriculate, to register in a school* (la matrícula = *enrollment*)
parecer	= *to seem*

preocuparse	= *to worry* (la preocupación = *worry, care*)
proporcionar	= *to furnish, to provide*
realizar	= *to fulfill, to realize (in the sense of to fulfill)*
rechazar	= *to reject* (el rechazo = *rejection*)
soportar	= *to tolerate, to stand*
superar	= *to overcome*
suspender	= *to fail a course, a class*

no caber duda	= *without a doubt*
de repente	= *suddenly*
llevar a cabo	= *to carry out*
tener éxito	= *to be successful*

desdeñoso	= *disdainful* (desdeñar = *to disdain*)
despojado	= *deprived of* (despojar = *to deprive of rights*)
desprovisto	= *lacking* (desproveer = *to deprive of provisions*)
eficaz	= *efficient*
imprescindible	= *essential, indispensable*
incorpóreo	= *disembodied*

EJERCICIO A

Empareje cada palabra en la Columna A con la definición en la Columna B, escribiendo la letra de la mejor selección.

Columna A

___ 1. el ala
___ 2. borrar
___ 3. la sonrisa
___ 4. el truco
___ 5. realizar
___ 6. la Red
___ 7. no caber duda
___ 8. proporcionar
___ 9. desprovisto
___ 10. el sendero
___ 11. desplegar
___ 12. la asignatura
___ 13. imprescindible
___ 14. fracasar
___ 15. eficaz
___ 16. el cable
___ 17. empujar
___ 18. constar de
___ 19. carecer
___ 20. desdeñoso

Columna B

a. llevar a cabo
b. hilo metálico que conduce electricidad
c. abrir para revelarse, como un abanico
d. vía para caminantes
e. con seguridad, sin sospecha
f. actitud de desprecio
g. parte que usa un pájaro para volar
h. estado de no tener nada
i. no tener éxito
j. necesario
k. consistir en
l. sistema electrónico para compartir información
m. proveer
n. serie de clases
o. acción ingeniosa para obtener algo
p. faltar
q. una expresión de placer o alegría
r. mover con fuerza
s. de manera hábil
t. quitar de la superficie

EJERCICIO B
Escoja la mejor palabra para cumplir el sentido de la oración.

Nunca olvidaré el (1) que me hizo mi compañero de clase cuando estaba en la escuela secundaria. Un día sonó mi (2) en una (3) de clase, la clase de historia, mi (4) menos favorita. Me avergoncé tanto que no sabía qué hacer. Como sabe todo el mundo, no se permiten los (5) durante las clases, pero se me olvidó apagar el mío en mi (6) al entrar en la escuela. El profesor estaba dictando una (7) (8), y toda la clase miró por todas partes para averiguar de dónde procedía el sonido. El profesor dejó de hablar y (9) me miró. No hice ningún (10) ni (11) para no llamar la atención, puse la mirada más inocente posible. Pero (12) de dónde venía el sonido.

Y en ese momento, mi compañero me miró e hizo un gesto de hablar por teléfono. El profesor lo notó. Me levanté, y con una (13) tonta, traté de fingir una actitud inocente, sin éxito. Al principio, el profesor me miró de manera (14), porque, por supuesto, el sonido distraía a toda la clase. Tenía miedo de no (15) la clase porque sabía que el profesor no soportaba a nadie que llevara esos aparatos a la clase. Veía desaparecer todos mis planes de conseguir una (16) y (17) en una universidad.

En fin, me lo quitó. El (18) de la (19) a veces nos (20) oportunidades de aprender lecciones que no están en los libros. Esa experiencia no (21) de importancia, porque cuando se lo (22) al profesor, me dijo que para (23) en la escuela es necesario recordar las reglas. No me trató con desdén, ni se enfadó conmigo. El (24) de mi compañero me aportó la oportunidad de conocer mejor a mi profesor de historia, que no era tan duro conmigo como había pensado. Supongo que todo (25) la actitud.

___ 1. a) gesto	b) truco	c) ala	d) grito
___ 2. a) cédula	b) toque	c) logro	d) móvil
___ 3. a) sala	b) lectura	c) materia	d) mochila
___ 4. a) conferencia	b) asignatura	c) índole	d) aula
___ 5. a) logros	b) ademanes	c) celulares	d) prójimos
___ 6. a) gesto	b) jaula	c) aula	d) mochila
___ 7. a) lectura	b) conferencia	c) Red	d) beca
___ 8. a) desdeñosa	b) desprovista	c) eficaz	d) aburrida
___ 9. a) de repente	b) imprescindible	c) incorpóreo	d) eficaz
___ 10. a) hilo	b) gesto	c) logro	d) sendero
___ 11. a) toque	b) ademán	c) además	d) prójimo
___ 12. a) llevaba a cabo	b) tenía éxito	c) dependía	d) no cabía duda
___ 13. a) Red	b) enseñanza	c) sonrisa	d) constaba de
___ 14. a) imprescindible	b) sospechosa	c) desprovista	d) índole
___ 15. a) aprobar	b) atraer	c) rechazar	d) fracasar
___ 16. a) Red	b) beca	c) asignatura	d) materia
___ 17. a) desplegarme	b) empujarme	c) realizarme	d) matricularme
___ 18. a) logro	b) sendero	c) móvil	d) ademán
___ 19. a) sonrisa	b) conferencia	c) enseñanza	d) lectura
___ 20. a) parece	b) proporciona	c) soporta	d) suspende
___ 21. a) carecía	b) superaba	c) asistía	d) dictaba
___ 22. a) desplegué	b) realicé	c) suspendí	d) entregué
___ 23. a) adelantar	b) borrar	c) carecer	d) desplegar
___ 24. a) gesto	b) chiste	c) toque	d) cable
___ 25. a) alcanza	b) lleva a cabo	c) carece	d) depende de

RESPUESTAS

Ejercicio A

1. g	2. t	3. q	4. o	5. a
6. l	7. e	8. m	9. h	10. d
11. c	12. n	13. j	14. i	15. s
16. b	17. r	18. k	19. p	20. f

Ejercicio B

1. b—truco	14. b—sospechosa
2. d—móvil	15. a—aprobar
3. a—sala	16. b—beca
4. b—asignatura	17. d—matricularme
5. c—celulares	18. b—sendero
6. d—mochila	19. c—enseñanza
7. b—conferencia	20. b—proporciona
8. d—aburrida	21. a—carecía
9. a—de repente	22. d—entregué
10. b—gesto	23. a—adelantar
11. b—ademán	24. b—chiste
12. d—no cabía duda	25. d—depende de
13. c—sonrisa	

EJERCICIO C: PRÁCTICA DE LECTURA

Lea la selección para practicar el reconocimiento del vocabulario. Luego utilice las palabras en la Práctica Oral y las Situaciones.

No existe la escuela perfecta para todo el mundo. Para algunos alumnos el **chiste** de **colocar** la "j" delante de la palabra "**aula**" significa lo que es estar en la escuela todo el día—**encarcelarse** en una **jaula**. **No cabe duda** que a muchos les cuesta mucho trabajo **soportar** todas las clases y el estrés que sufren durante los años de la **escuela secundaria**. Pero para otros estudiantes, el **sendero** de la **enseñanza** les **proporciona** entrada a un mundo entero de oportunidades después de la adolescencia. Para estos, la escuela es una aventura, por la cual se extienden los horizontes y **despliegan** las **alas** mentales.

Pocos alumnos se encuentran hoy en día en **salas de clase** en las que sólo se sientan para oír a un profesor que les **dicta una conferencia**. **No cabe duda** de que a muchos les cuesta mucho trabajo **aguantar** las clases tradicionales, de **tomar apuntes**, repasos, exámenes y **pruebas**. **Se aburren** fácilmente, y no **disimulan** una actitud **desdeñosa** hacia los que **soportan** la **enseñanza** tradicional. Los estudiantes **obligados** a sentarse en una **sala** se sienten **despojados** de su libertad. En contraste, los proyectos **llevados a cabo** en **conjunto** ahora **parecen** ser la metodología más **corriente**.

No obstante, hay muchos que se benefician con los métodos tradicionales y **alcanzan** grandes **logros**. **Aprueban** sus exámenes, **salen bien** en sus **asignaturas**, **enfocan** bien sus **materias** y reciben **becas** al graduarse para **matricularse** en las mejores universidades. **Aprovechan** sus oportunidades y cultivan maneras útiles de estudiar y aprender de otros. **Se destacan** por poder organizar todo **eficazmente**.

Se puede atribuir esas diferencias a la tecnología y la **índole** de los estudiantes contemporáneos. Las computadoras **portátiles (celulares** o **móviles)** y la comunicación instantánea facilitan la distribución de información de manera rápida, lo cual tiene grandes consecuencias para los sistemas educativos. Al **entrar en la Red**, parece que se encuentra todo sin necesidad de salir de la casa o el cuarto. Y, en cierto modo, **tienen razón** esos alumnos modernos. Mas necesitan **acordarse de** que esa experiencia **carece** de contacto humano diario. El contacto **llevado a cabo** sin **cable** resulta en contacto virtual con una voz **incorpórea**, deshumanizada. Se pierde el calor de una **sonrisa** o la mirada directa del **prójimo** que comunica con un **ademán**, o un **gesto**, un **suspiro**, un **grito**. La educación que **consta de** la comunicación impersonal, **desprovista** del contacto humano, es una educación parcial.

Otros estudiantes optan por caminos diferentes. Se educan en casa o **ingresan** en programas especiales. Les atraen a muchos los programas de intercambio para aprender del mundo **más allá** de su propio barrio. Les **bastan** una **mochila**, un pasaporte y unos boletos. **Borran** de la memoria cualquier pensamiento de salas de clase, **empujan** las puertas y **se entregan** al mundo para aprender de él. No **rechazan** ninguna oportunidad de explorar el mundo y a veces **superan** grandes obstáculos para **realizar** su sueño de una educación práctica.

No importa la escuela a que asista un estudiante, lo **imprescindible** es actuar con el deseo de aprender. El mundo del mañana será muy diferente al de hoy. La educación debe servirle al estudiante que quiere **adelantar**. Las escuelas modernas son muy diferentes de las del pasado y el **truco** será encontrar alguna manera de aprender sin perder contacto con lo más importante, el **toque** individual y humano.

Preguntas sobre la lectura

1. Cuente el chiste de la sala de clase.
2. ¿Por qué sienten algunos alumnos que la escuela es una jaula?
3. ¿Cómo es una clase con enseñanza tradicional?
4. Describa la carrera de un estudiante típico.
5. ¿Cuál es la meta de muchos estudiantes en la escuela secundaria?
6. ¿Cómo ha cambiado la experiencia educativa para los estudiantes contemporáneos?
7. ¿Cuáles son los beneficios de la tecnología para los estudiantes?
8. ¿De qué carece la educación en una sala de clase virtual?
9. ¿Qué otra manera hay para aprender del mundo además de sentarse en una sala de clase?
10. ¿Cuál será el truco de aprender en el futuro?

EJERCICIO D: PRÁCTICA ORAL

Conteste las preguntas usando el vocabulario de esta unidad.

1. Cuente un acontecimiento interesante que le ocurrió una vez en la escuela.
2. ¿Qué estilo de enseñanza prefieren los profesores en su escuela? ¿Dictan conferencias o hacen discursos?
3. ¿Qué manera de aprender prefiere usted: conferencias, lecturas por parte propia, o seminarios? Explique por qué.
4. ¿Cómo eran sus amigos en la escuela? ¿Le hacían trucos de vez en cuando? Describa uno.
5. ¿Qué significa el ademán de levantar los hombros? ¿Tienen usted y sus amigos ciertos ademanes favoritos? Descríbalos.
6. ¿Qué obstáculos ha superado para graduarse de la escuela secundaria?
7. ¿Qué se aprende al superase obstáculos que no se aprende de otra manera?
8. ¿Qué oportunidades le proporciona una educación universitaria?
9. ¿Cómo sería su vida si no tuviera que asistir a la escuela?
10. ¿Cómo aprende usted mejor? Describa cómo estudiar para la clase de historia, por ejemplo.
11. ¿Qué metas académicas ha alcanzado este año en la escuela?
12. ¿Qué sueños espera realizar en el futuro?
13. ¿Cómo ha cambiado la tecnología la manera de aprender en su escuela?
14. Proponga un plan para aprender fuera de la escuela.
15. ¿Qué ventajas tienen los estudiantes internos en colegios que no tienen muchos estudiantes que regresan a casa cada tarde?

EJERCICIO E: SITUACIONES

Discuta las situaciones usando el vocabulario de esta unidad.

1. Sus hijos han regresado a casa un día quejándose de que las clases son aburridas. ¿Cómo respondería a sus quejas?
2. En la universidad el próximo año, usted tendrá la oportunidad de estudiar en otro país. Explique cómo sería el programa ideal para estudiar en el extranjero.
3. Todos los estudiantes en la universidad el próximo año tendrán computadoras portátiles o aparatos digitales personales. Explique el protocolo para usarlos en las clases. Además, explique las ventajas y desventajas de tenerlos por todas partes.
4. Su consejero universitario le ha llamado a su oficina para hablarle de sus dificultades académicas. Explíquele cuáles son y proponga un plan para resolverlas.
5. Como parte de un conjunto de estudiantes que deben aconsejar a la escuela secundaria sobre las maneras de mejorar la enseñanza, desarrolle un plan para realizar esos mejoramientos.

EL FÚTBOL Y EL BÉISBOL

el aficionado	= *a fan* (*of a sport*)
el árbitro	= *referee*
el codo	= *elbow*
la competencia	= *match, competition*
la gallardía	= *gracefulness*
el hastío	= *disgust*
el hombro	= *shoulder*
la jugada	= *a play in a game* (jugar = *to play a game*)
la manga	= *sleeve*
el ocaso	= *late afternoon*
el palo	= *bat, pole, stick*
las pestañas	= *eyelashes* (pestañear = *to blink, to wink*)
el portero	= *goalie (in soccer), doorman*
el silbato	= *whistle (instrument)* (silbar = *to whistle*)
la sombra	= *shadow*
el sudor	= *sweat* (sudar = *to sweat*)
cabalmente	= *exactly, perfectly*
detenidamente	= *thoroughly, carefully* (detener = *to stop*)
súbitamente	= *suddenly*
a fondo	= *in depth, perfectly, thoroughly*
a la vez	= *at the same time*
ni siquiera	= *not even*
agachar	= *to stoop down, to bow down*
agarrar	= *to grab, to grasp at*
alabar	= *to praise* (la alabanza = *praise*)
aletear	= *to flap (wings)*
dar con	= *to go up against, to strike against*
derretir	= *to melt*
derrotar	= *to defeat* (la derrota = *defeat*)
elogiar	= *to praise, to extol* (el elogio = *eulogy, praise*)
emocionarse	= *to get excited* (la emoción = *emotion, feeling*)
empatar	= *to tie (score in a game)*
enfocar	= *to focus on* (el enfoque = *focus*)
enloquecer	= *to go crazy* (loco = *crazy, mad*)
entablar	= *to initiate, to begin (a negotiation)* (la tabla = *board, game board*)
entrenar	= *to train* (entrenador = *coach, trainer*)
estallar	= *to break out* (el estallido = *crash, snap, report, as of a firearm*)
fijarse	= *to notice, to note* (fijo = *fixed, firm, settled, permanent*)
hinchar	= *to swell*
incorporarse	= *to gather together, to get up*
marcar un gol	= *to score a goal, to make a point (in a game)*
patear	= *to kick, to stomp* (la pata = *foot of an animal*)
rasguñar	= *to scratch* (el rasguño = *scratch*)
socorrer	= *to help* (el socorro = *help*)
sonar	= *to sound (to blow a whistle)* (el sonido = *sound, noise*)
tenderse	= *to stretch out (on one's back)*

EJERCICIO A
Empareje cada palabra en la Columna A con la definición en la Columna B, escribiendo la letra de la mejor selección.

Columna A

___ 1. sonar
___ 2. aletear
___ 3. árbitro
___ 4. silbato
___ 5. derretir
___ 6. súbitamente
___ 7. a fondo
___ 8. elogiar
___ 9. empatar
___ 10. enfocar
___ 11. hinchar
___ 12. pestañas
___ 13. sudar
___ 14. agacharse
___ 15. portero
___ 16. sombra
___ 17. cabalmente
___ 18. emocionarse
___ 19. tenderse
___ 20. agarrar
___ 21. hombro
___ 22. alzar
___ 23. manga
___ 24. derrota
___ 25. fijarse

Columna B

a. profundamente
b. perder de manera lastimosa
c. perfectamente
d. acción que hace un pájaro para volar
e. ponerse boca arriba o abajo en el suelo o en la playa
f. la parte del cuerpo de donde viene el brazo
g. lo que hace el cuerpo al hacer ejercicio cuando hace calor
h. partes del cuerpo que rodean los ojos
i. inclinarse
j. hacer un ruido
k. levantar
l. una parte de una camisa o un abrigo
m. tomar en la mano
n. notar, poner atención en algo
o. transformar en un líquido
p. hombre que toma decisiones en una competencia
q. terminar un partido con el mismo número de goles
r. cuando una parte del cuerpo se hace más grande
s. algo producido al ocultar la luz del sol o un globo
t. un jugador que protege el gol
u. estar agitado, tener sentimientos fuertes
v. de repente
w. aparato o sonido para llamar la atención
x. alabar
y. concentrar

EJERCICIO B
Escoja la mejor palabra para cumplir el sentido de la oración.

Hacía mucho calor ese día cuando los dos equipos se encontraron en el campo al atardecer. En el ocaso las __(1)__ oscurecían la verde hierba. Los dos equipos no perdieron tiempo en entrar en la lucha, ninguno de los jugadores ni siquiera pensaba en sus preocupaciones del día pasado. Todos __(2)__ en el partido, el mundo y la vida reducidos a un rectángulo verde, un mantel desplegado para el juego. Cuando el primer jugador __(3)__ la pelota, __(4)__ la batalla. Pronto todo el campo se volvió un remolino de polvo, piernas, brazos, manos, cabezas, gritos y movimientos frenéticos. Los jugadores ya no __(5)__ más que en la __(6)__ y el calor. El sudor __(7)__ por las pestañas, los cuellos y las frentes indicaba una lucha feroz. Unos __(8)__ las mangas de otros jugadores para impedir su carrera por la pelota, los codos __(9)__ en el aire húmedo. __(10)__, un jugador se cayó al suelo, gritando "¡ (11) !", y, agarrando el tobillo, (12) en la hierba y el polvo en medio del campo. Después de un momento, (13) lentamente, mientras sus compañeros corrieron para ayudarle. Cojeando, alcanzó la línea que marcaba el límite del juego. Más tarde, los aficionados (14) cada vez que marcó un gol un equipo o el otro. Después de cada gol, el portero (15) para recoger la pelota y lanzarla al aire otra vez. Los (16) sonaban los (17) para detener el partido de vez en cuando.

Cuando sonó el último silbato, un equipo había conquistado al otro, y todos los jugadores del equipo vencedor (18) al entrenador en los hombros para llevarlo del campo. Nadie había querido que (19) los dos equipos, porque todos querían llevar el trofeo a casa, (20) la (21) de los compañeros valientes. No satisface nada como un gol marcado (22) . Los que perdieron salieron murmurando su (23) , unos pobres con los tobillos (24) , los cuerpos cubiertos de rasguños, como si hubieran dado con gatos fieros. Después de toda competencia, los aficionados entablan una crítica, comentando (25) todos los juegos para alabar a sus jugadores predilectos. O, si pierden, lloran la (26) .

___ 1. a) pastillas   b) gallardías   c) sombras   d) mangas
___ 2. a) derritieron   b) derrotaron   c) agarraron   d) enfocaron
___ 3. a) pateó   b) empató   c) se tendió   d) rasgó
___ 4. a) sudó   b) estalló   c) aleteó   d) alabó
___ 5. a) entablaban   b) se fijaban   c) empataban   d) rasgaban
___ 6. a) competencia   b) conferencia   c) sombra   d) manga
___ 7. a) derrotabo   b) caía   c) demoraba   d) sudaba
___ 8. a) agarraban   b) agachaban   c) pateaban   d) derrotaban
___ 9. a) alabando   b) elogiando   c) aleteando   d) pateando
___ 10. a) Cabalmente   b) Detenidamente   c) Súbitamente   d) Lentamente
___ 11. a) Socorro   b) Hola   c) Ojo   d) A fondo
___ 12. a) se fijó   b) se tendió   c) estalló   d) rasgó
___ 13. a) hinchó   b) alabó   c) enfocó   d) se incorporó
___ 14. a) se fijaban   b) estallaban   c) se enloquecieron   d) elogiaron
___ 15. a) se pateó   b) se agachó   c) derritió   d) hinchó
___ 16. a) codos   b) hombros   c) árbitros   d) silbatos
___ 17. a) silbatos   b) hastíos   c) ocasos   d) porteros
___ 18. a) entrenaron   b) enfocaron   c) alzaron   d) se incorporaron
___ 19. a) emparejaran   b) socorrieran   c) alzaran   d) empataran
___ 20. a) fijándose   b) tendiéndose   c) incorporando   d) elogiando
___ 21. a) gallardía   b) sombra   c) competencia   d) manga
___ 22. a) detenidamente   b) sumamente   c) cabalmente   d) súbitamente
___ 23. a) socorro   b) portero   c) hastío   d) ocaso
___ 24. a) derretidos   b) sudados   c) derrotados   d) hinchados
___ 25. a) sumamente   b) súbitamente   c) ni siquiera   d) detenidamente
___ 26. a) gallardía   b) derrota   c) sombra   d) manga

RESPUESTAS
Ejercicio A

1. j	2. d	3. p	4. w	5. o
6. v	7. a	8. x	9. q	10. y
11. r	12. h	13. g	14. i	15. t
16. s	17. c	18. u	19. e	20. m
21. f	22. k	23. l	24. b	25. n

Ejercicio B

1. c—sombras	14. c—se enloquecieron
2. d—enfocaron	15. b—se agachó
3. a—pateó	16. c—árbitros
4. b—estalló	17. a—silbatos
5. b—se fijaban	18. c—alzaron
6. a—competencia	19. d—empataran
7. b—derretido	20. d—elogiando
8. a—agarraban	21. a—gallardía
9. c—aleteando	22. c—cabalmente
10. c—Súbitamente	23. c—hastío
11. a—Socorro	24. d—hinchados
12. b—se tendió	25. d—detenidamente
13. d—se incorporó	26. b—derrota

EJERCICIO C: PRÁCTICA DE LECTURA
Lea la selección para practicar el reconocimiento del vocabulario. Luego utilice las palabras en la Práctica Oral y las Situaciones.

Para muchos hispanos, pocos temas **alzan** más el interés que los deportes, especialmente el fútbol y el béisbol. No se necesitan más que un **palo** y una pelota, unos amigos, un campo abierto y un poco de sol para **disfrutar** de una tarde divertida. Luego, cuando los **aficionados** se reúnen para **elogiar** a sus **equipos** favoritos, se creería que sus héroes **deportistas** eran sus mejores amigos. Recuerdan cada **jugada** de cada **competencia**, los **goles** marcados, la velocidad con que corrían, los **daños** que sufrieron, las veces que el **portero se agachó** para **recoger** la **pelota**, las veces que un jugador **rasguñó** por casualidad a otro, cada vez que un jugador **rompió** el uniforme de otro al **agarrarle** la **manga**, cada vez que un jugador se enojó cuando perdió una oportunidad para **marcar un gol**, cada vez que la **competencia** terminó **empatada**, cada vez que sufrió una **derrota imprevista** o cada vez que un jugador **pateó** la pelota y **marcó un gol**. Y cuando la **gallardía** de unos **da con** el **disgusto** de los **derrotados**, **estallan** las luchas entre los **aficionados**.

En comparación con los **aficionados** del fútbol, los interesados en el béisbol se comportan con mayor **decoro**, correspondiente al modo más **apaciguado** de este juego. La **competencia** del **juego** dura menos tiempo que un partido de fútbol. Hay menos jugadores corriendo **a la vez** en el campo en el béisbol. La acción del **partido se desarrolla** más lentamente, lo cual no quiere decir que el **juego carezca** de emoción. Todos los **espectadores** se levantan cuando un jugador pega la pelota con tanta fuerza que la **lanza** fuera del parque. Todos **gri-**

tan cuando un **árbitro** no parece ver de la misma manera que los **aficionados**. El béisbol **goza de** más popularidad en unos países que en otros, pero el fútbol se juega por todas partes del mundo hispano. **Sin embargo**, no cabe duda de que cuando **suena el silbato** para comenzar el **partido**, todos **se emocionan** por ver el espectáculo. No importa el calor, el **sudor**, las preocupaciones **cotidianas**, todos **enfocan** la acción del momento. Cuando alguien **marca un gol**, todos los **espectadores se incorporan** como si todos fueran uno.

Preguntas sobre la lectura

1. ¿Por qué son tan populares el fútbol y el béisbol entre los hispanos del mundo?
2. ¿Qué recuerdan los aficionados al hablar de sus equipos favoritos?
3. Describa la acción de un partido de fútbol.
4. ¿Qué hace el portero?
5. Describa la gallardía de los vencedores en un partido.
6. ¿Por qué estallan luchas entre los aficionados a veces?
7. ¿En qué se diferencia el béisbol del fútbol?
8. Describa el juego de béisbol.
9. ¿Para qué sirve el árbitro en un partido?
10. ¿Con qué se empieza y se termina un partido de fútbol?
11. ¿Cómo reaccionan los aficionados cuando su jugador favorito marca un gol?

EJERCICIO D: PRÁCTICA ORAL
Conteste las preguntas usando el vocabulario de esta unidad.

1. Explique la importancia de los deportes para los aficionados.
2. Describa cómo se juega el fútbol.
3. Cuente lo que pasó en el último partido que vio. ¿Quiénes jugaron? ¿Quiénes ganaron? ¿Cómo jugaron los equipos?
4. ¿Cuál deporte es más peligroso, el fútbol o el béisbol? ¿Por qué?
5. ¿Por qué es más popular el fútbol entre los hispanos que el fútbol norteamericano?
6. ¿Quiénes son los mejores jugadores de béisbol?
7. ¿A qué se debe el éxito de un buen equipo?
8. ¿Cómo se debe celebrar el triunfo de un partido?
9. ¿Por qué sueñan muchos muchachos con jugar como profesionales en un deporte?
10. ¿Cuáles son las características de un buen árbitro?
11. ¿Cuáles son las características de un jugador excelente?
12. Describa su deporte favorito.
13. ¿Por qué es importante hacer ejercicio todos los días?
14. ¿Cree que los jugadores profesionales ganan demasiado dinero? Explique su respuesta.
15. ¿Qué beneficios se obtienen de un equipo profesional en su comunidad?
16. ¿Cree que los deportistas son héroes? Explique por qué.

EJERCICIO E: SITUACIONES
Discuta las situaciones usando el vocabulario de esta unidad.

1. Su familia quiere ir a un partido de béisbol. Describa los preparativos.
2. Usted es árbitro en una competencia entre dos equipos escolares. No se llevan bien las dos escuelas, y usted necesita mantener la paz cuando un grupo de aficionados se entusiasma demasiado. Explique lo que les diría para apaciguarlos.
3. Usted es periodista para el diario de su escuela y tiene que escribir un resumen de un partido de fútbol para el campeonato regional. Describa el triunfo de un equipo.
4. Usted y sus amigos se reúnen para ver la Copa Mundial y comentan el juego de su equipo favorito. Describa los comentarios que harían sobre sus jugadores favoritos.
5. Usted es el entrenador de un equipo escolar y debe prepararlo para un partido muy importante, un campeonato. Hay un trofeo muy grande que quieren ganar. Explique lo que les diría a sus jugadores para motivarlos.

LA VIDA PASTORIL

el álamo	= *poplar tree*
el caracol	= *snail* (caracolear = *to wheel around, to move slowly*)
la cosecha	= *harvest* (cosechar = *to harvest*)
el cubo	= *pail, bucket*
la escarcha	= *frost*
los escombros	= *rubbish*
el espantapájaros	= *scarecrow*
la higuera	= *fig tree*
la huerta	= *vegetable garden*
el huerto	= *orchard*
el ladrillo	= *brick*
el ladrón	= *thief*
el medio ambiente	= *environment*
la muñeca/el muñeco	= *doll*
la muralla	= *wall*
el muro	= *wall*
la nuez (las nueces)	= *nut*
el olmo	= *elm tree*
la orilla	= *bank of a river, or a body of water*
el pozo	= *water well*
la renta	= *income*
el roble	= *oak tree*
el sauce llorón	= *willow tree*
la semilla	= *seed* (sembrar = *to sow seeds, to plant*)
la sequía	= *drought* (secar = *to dry*)
el tamaño	= *size*
el tronco	= *tree trunk*

ancho	= *wide*
cálido	= *hot*
cuesta arriba	= *uphill*
destartalada	= *run down, jumbled*
estancado	= *stagnant* (estancar = *to stagnate, to stand still*)
flojo	= *limp, loose, weak, floppy*
lozano	= *spirited, luxuriant, fresh, brisk*
recto	= *straight*
mediante	= *through, with the help of*
amontonar	= *to pile up* (el montón = *heap, a large pile*)
aportar	= *to cause, to bring, to contribute*
atender	= *to attend to, to pay attention to*
atreverse	= *to dare*
complacer	= *to please*
cultivar	= *to cultivate, to grow*
derribar	= *to throw down, to knock down*
derrumbar	= *to fall down*
descolgar	= *to take down* (colgar = *to hang up*)
divisar	= *to perceive indistinctly, to see at a distance*
enlatar	= *to preserve in cans or jars* (la lata = *can*)
enrojecer	= *to turn red* (rojo = *red*)
entretanto	= *meanwhile*
espantar	= *to scare* (el espanto = *the fright, scare*)
florecer	= *to flower* (la flor = *flower*)
helar	= *to freeze* (el helado = *ice cream, adj. = frozen*)
hundir	= *to submerge* (hondo = *deep, profound*)
hurtar	= *to steal, to rob*
jubilarse	= *to retire from a job*
largarse	= *to go or to move away* (largo = *long*)
picotear	= *to peck*
regar (ie)	= *to water, to irrigate*
reembolsar	= *to repay*
rendir	= *to yield, to give up, to render*
renunciar	= *to give up, to resign*
resucitar	= *to revive*
retirar	= *to withdraw*
sacudir	= *to shake, to jolt*
sembrar	= *to plant seeds*
tiritar	= *to shiver*
veranear	= *to spend the summer*

EJERCICIO A
Empareje cada palabra en la Columna A con la definición en la Columna B, escribiendo la letra de la mejor selección.

Columna A

___ 1. aportar
___ 2. muro
___ 3. cuesta arriba
___ 4. sembrar
___ 5. hurtar
___ 6. pozo
___ 7. jubilar
___ 8. huerta
___ 9. regar
___ 10. lozano
___ 11. cubo
___ 12. florecer
___ 13. derribar
___ 14. escombro
___ 15. destartalado
___ 16. enlatar
___ 17. espantar
___ 18. recto
___ 19. divisar
___ 20. largarse
___ 21. higuera
___ 22. muñeco
___ 23. caracol
___ 24. sequía
___ 25. escarcha

Columna B

a. ver a lo lejos
b. falta de agua
c. un animalito con sólo un pie
d. poner agua para plantas
e. proporcionar, proveer
f. conservar en latas o vasijas
g. empujar o pegar para derrumbar
h. asustar
i. un obstáculo artificial que rodea una finca o un pasto
j. una fila o línea que sigue sin doblar
k. deteriorado, desordenado
l. irse
m. agua helada producida cuando hace mucho frío
n. vivo, fresco
o. lo que hacen las plantas antes de producir frutas
p. juguete para los niños
q. lo que se hace en un jardín para tener plantas
r. lugar donde se encuentra agua
s. recipiente para llevar agua
t. una especie de jardín para vegetales
u. dejar de trabajar
v. tomar algo sin permiso
w. subir una colina
x. un árbol con una pequeña fruta redonda
y. los restos de algo

EJERCICIO B
Escoja la mejor palabra para cumplir el sentido de la oración.

Pocas personas (1) para trabajar más. Pero después de pasar la vida encarceladas en un cubículo de una oficina, muchas personas disfrutan de la vida al aire libre, cuidando su jardín. No hay nada que tranquilice más que la vista de una (2) en pleno (3) , y la promesa de todo tipo de frutas y verduras frescas. Uno se (4) fácilmente del aire (5) de un edificio para respirar libremente. Recuerdo la huerta de mi abuelo con quien (6) cada año. En camino (7) por (8) la casa a lo lejos. Siempre sabíamos que al pasar la casa (9) de su vecino más cercano, estábamos por llegar. El (10) hecho de piedras marcaba los límites de su finca, y pronto veíamos los (11) rojos de su casa con la (12) al lado de la entrada.

La última vez que lo visité, había una (13) dura. Todas las mañanas ese año, salíamos de la casa bien temprano por la puerta anterior, y prosiguiendo (14) , llegábamos a las filas (15) del (16) . Mientras mi abuelo (17) las plantas, yo buscaba _(18)_ entre los troncos de los árboles. Como había poca lluvia ese año, casi no los encontraba. A veces le ayudaba a llevar agua en un _(19)_ metálico del _(20)_ en medio del huerto. Ese año mi abuelo _(21)_ maíz, pero lo perdió a causa del frío una noche. ¡Qué triste fue despertar esa mañana y percibir _(22)_ por todo el campo! Pero lo sembró otra vez, y ya estaba bastante bien crecido. Puso un _(23)_ para guardar la _(24)_. Con la sequía, los pájaros _(25)_ a picotear los granos más que nunca por falta de alimento. Habrían _(26)_ la mayor parte de la cosecha si mi abuelo no hubiera tenido cuidado. Tenía los brazos tan _(27)_ que las mangas de la camisa parecían alas. El sombrero en la cabeza parecía de _(28)_, y le cubría el rostro como si fuera un _(29)_ ocultando su cara con el ala _(30)_ del sombrero. Cuando había buena cosecha, mi abuela _(31)_ el producto del trabajo de mi abuelo y tenían comida para los días fríos del invierno. ¡Qué gusto disfrutar del sabor de frutas frescas en esos días tan _(32)_!

___	1. a) se retiran	b) jubilan	c) siembran	d) derriban
___	2. a) higuera	b) sequía	c) muralla	d) huerta
___	3. a) escombro	b) cubo	c) florecimiento	d) campo
___	4. a) larga	b) ancha	c) ansia	d) suda
___	5. a) lozano	b) estancado	c) cercano	d) recto
___	6. a) veraneábamos	b) saboreábamos	c) espantábamos	d) regábamos
___	7. a) derribábamos	b) hurtábamos	c) divisábamos	d) ansiábamos
___	8. a) escurrir	b) divisar	c) sembrar	d) jubilar
___	9. a) lozano	b) destartalada	c) cálida	d) floja
___	10. a) muro	b) tamaño	c) cubo	d) espantapájaros
___	11. a) escombros	b) ladrillos	c) robles	d) troncos
___	12. a) sequía	b) ladrillo	c) cosecha	d) higuera
___	13. a) higuera	b) sequía	c) muñeca	d) semilla
___	14. a) cuesta arriba	b) destartalado	c) lozanos	d) flojos
___	15. a) cálidas	b) estancadas	c) rectas	d) sequías
___	16. a) huerto	b) ladrón	c) caracol	d) muro
___	17. a) hurtaba	b) regaba	c) regateaba	d) arriesgaba
___	18. a) caracoles	b) escarchas	c) olmos	d) espantapájaros
___	19. a) muro	b) nuez	c) cubo	d) huerto
___	20. a) pozo	b) ladrón	c) escombro	d) muro
___	21. a) enlató	b) sembró	c) derrumbó	d) floreció
___	22. a) escarcha	b) sequía	c) muñeca	d) muralla
___	23. a) olmo	b) pozo	c) roble	d) espantapájaros
___	24. a) cosecha	b) escarcha	c) muralla	d) sequía
___	25. a) regaban	b) derribaban	c) divisaban	d) se atrevían
___	26. a) hurtado	b) sembrado	c) enlatado	d) regado
___	27. a) inocuos	b) cálidos	c) flojos	d) perezosos
___	28. a) escarcha	b) muñeca	c) semilla	d) muralla
___	29. a) ladrón	b) cubo	c) espantapájaros	d) pozo
___	30. a) ancha	b) lozana	c) cálida	d) nociva
___	31. a) hurtaba	b) enlataba	c) se atrevía	d) derrumbaba
___	32. a) rectos	b) recios	c) cálidos	d) anchos

RESPUESTAS

Ejercicio A

1. e	2. i	3. w	4. q	5. v
6. r	7. u	8. t	9. d	10. n
11. s	12. o	13. g	14. y	15. k
16. f	17. h	18. j	19. a	20. l
21. x	22. p	23. c	24. b	25. m

Ejercicio B

1. b—jubilan	17. b—regaba
2. d—huerta	18. a—caracoles
3. c—florecimiento	19. c—cubo
4. a—larga	20. a—pozo
5. b—estancado	21. b—sembró
6. a—veraneábamos	22. a—escarcha
7. d—ansiábamos	23. d—espantapájaros
8. b—divisar	24. a—cosecha
9. b—destartalada	25. d—se atrevían
10. a—muro	26. a—hurtado
11. b —ladrillos	27. c—flojos
12. d—higuera	28. b—muñeca
13. b—sequía	29. a—ladrón
14. a—cuesta arriba	30. a—ancha
15. c—rectas	31. b—enlataba
16. a—huerto	32. c—cálidos

EJERCICIO C: PRÁCTICA DE LECTURA

Lea la selección para practicar el reconocimiento del vocabulario. Luego utilice las palabras en la Práctica Oral y las Situaciones.

El cultivo de las **cosechas** de los alimentos que compramos en los supermercados **pertenecen** por lo general a las grandes **empresas** agrícolas, mas en los países menos **desarrollados** todavía hay muchas personas que **dependen de** la **cosecha** para **sobrevivir de** día **en** día y **de** año **en** año. Los hombres **descuelgan** los abrigos por la mañana y salen al campo para **sembrar** la tierra. Hay tantos tipos y tamaños de agricultura como en cualquier otra industria, de las parcelas de frijoles y maíz más humildes, hasta las plantaciones de árboles para la producción de **madera** y goma, y plantaciones de flores para exportar al mercado desde un continente a otro por avión. Mientras unos **campesinos** se esfuerzan para sacar la vida de la tierra, otros dueños de plantaciones **contratan** a muchos para **cultivar** sus campos e **invierten** miles de dólares en la producción de comestibles para el mercado mundial. Lo que no se vende de inmediato se **enlata** para vender más tarde. Los que viven en los centros urbanos muchas veces **atienden** sus **huertas** y jardines para gozar del sabor de verduras frescas y para el **bienestar** mental. **Hundiendo** las **semillas** en la tierra, uno se siente **vinculado** con ella, con **raíces** como los plantas mismas.

A causa de la gran destrucción del **medio ambiente** en muchos lugares, **ligado** con el tema de la agricultura está el del medio ambiente. Sobre todo se ve el problema de la **escasez** del agua. Cuando hay una **sequía,** todos sufren por igual. La gente que ha cortado los bosques para **leña** o para **pastos** para **ganado anhela** las **sombras** de los **álamos** y los **robles.** Todavía hay **sauces llorones** a las **orillas** de los **riachuelos**, pero estos árboles no cuentan con un bosque digno del nombre. A consecuencia, la piel se **enrojece** fácilmente con **quemaduras** por falta de **sombra. Perforando pozos** por todas partes, a veces se encuentra agua. Pero los grandes proyectos de construcción de acueductos para **regar** los campos áridos resultan a veces en más **pérdida** de agua, y la **pérdida** de capital **gastado** en el proyecto. La tierra **quemada** y **rendida** no **aporta** grandes **cosechas. Entretanto**, el desierto sigue **avanzando** por muchas partes del mundo. **Mediante** un **compromiso** entre los que **cultivan** la tierra y los que quieren conservarla, será posible **compartir** el planeta para todos.

Preguntas sobre la lectura

1. ¿Cómo se diferencia la agricultura en los países desarrollados y los menos desarrollados?
2. ¿Qué hace la gente de las ciudades para tener vegetales y flores frescos?
3. ¿Qué relación se establece entre hombre y tierra al sembrarla?
4. ¿Cómo están ligadas la agricultura y la ecología?
5. Describa lo que significa una sequía en un país.
6. ¿Cómo se puede resolver el problema de la falta de agua en una región?
7. ¿Cuál será el propósito de la cooperación entre los campesinos y los que quieren conservar el medio ambiente?

EJERCICIO D: PRÁCTICA ORAL
Conteste las preguntas usando el vocabulario de esta unidad.

1. Describa el lugar en que usted vive. ¿Es campo abierto o está en la ciudad?
2. ¿Cuál es el valor de tener una huerta?
3. Describa las ventajas de vivir en el campo.
4. ¿Cuáles serían las desventajas de vivir en el campo?
5. ¿Por qué creen muchos muchachos que es muy aburrido vivir en el campo?
6. ¿Cómo ha cambiado el cultivo de alimentos hoy en día?
7. ¿Conoce a alguien que viva en el campo? Compare su vida con la de él.
8. ¿Le gusta acampar de vez en cuando? Describa la experiencia.
9. ¿Cree que faltará la tierra para cultivar un día?
10. ¿Cómo es posible que sea más barato importar flores a los Estados Unidos de Centroamérica para vender en los supermercados que crecerlas en los Estados Unidos?

EJERCICIO E: SITUACIONES
Discuta las situaciones usando el vocabulario de esta unidad.

1. Tiene que arreglar una excursión de una clase de una escuela primaria a una finca. Explíqueles qué van a ver y la importancia del lugar.

2. Usted es el gerente de un supermercado en una ciudad. Hay un grupo de campesinos que tienen huertas de alimentos orgánicos (crecidos sin insecticidas) y quieren venderlos en su tienda. Elabore una conversación con el grupo y explique los beneficios del negocio.

3. Usted es guía en una finca histórica, en la que se presenta la vida de los antepasados que colonizaron el campo. Todo el trabajo se hace aquí de manera tradicional, usando herramientas antiguas. Explique a un grupo de muchachos cómo se hacía el trabajo en la época de antaño.

4. Usted es un activista del movimiento contra la globalización. Prepare un reportaje contra la globalización de las empresas agrícolas.

LOS VIAJES

la arruga	= *wrinkle* (arrugar = *to wrinkle up*)
el atavío	= *attire, dress*
el balneario	= *resort, spa*
la brisa	= *breeze*
el chubasco	= *rain shower*
los clavos	= *nails* (clavar = *to nail*)
el cohete	= *rocket*
el delantal	= *apron*
el desahogo	= *ease, relief from pain* (desahogarse = *to alleviate, to relieve*)
el desamparado	= *homeless person*
el embotellamiento	= *traffic jam*
el estacionamiento	= *parking lot, place* (estacionar = *to park a vehicle*)
el farol	= *streetlight, lamp*
el forastero	= *stranger*
los fuegos artificiales	= *fireworks*
las gafas	= *sunglasses*
la inundación	= *flood* (inundar = *to flood*)
la limosna	= *alms, charity*
el lodo	= *mud*
el lujo	= *luxury*
la madrugada	= *dawn, early rising* (madrugar = *to get up early in the morning*)
el martillo	= *hammer*
el mendigo	= *beggar*
el muelle	= *dock, pier*
el murmullo	= *murmur* (murmurar = *to murmur*)
el neumático	= *tire of a car*
el ocaso	= *sunset*
la ola	= *wave (in the ocean)*
la orilla	= *border, strip of land, like a beach*
el parador	= *inn, resting place* (parar = *to stop*)
el peatón	= *pedestrian*
el pinchazo	= *blowout (of a tire)*
el recuerdo	= *memory, souvenir* (recordar = *to remember*)

el relámpago	= *lightning* (relampaguear = *to lighten, to flash, to sparkle*)
el remolcador	= *tow truck, tug* (remolcar = *to tow*)
el semáforo	= *traffic light*
el serrucho	= *handsaw*
el suspiro	= *sigh* (suspirar = *to sigh*)
el susurro	= *whisper* (susurrar = *to whisper, to murmur, to rustle*)
la tabla	= *board (for a game, or surfing)*
la temporada	= *season*
el toldo	= *awning, tent, tarpaulin*
el trueno	= *thunder* (tronar = *to thunder*)
la tubería	= *plumbing, tubing*
descalzo	= *shoeless, barefooted* (calzar = *to shoe*)
desinflado	= *flat, deflated* (desinflar = *to deflate*)
despejado	= *clear* (despejar = *to clear, to become bright*)
mentiroso	= *liar* (mentir = *to lie*)
perspicaz	= *astute, wise*
albergar	= *to lodge* (el albergue = *lodging*)
alquilar	= *to rent* (el alquiler = *rent*)
anhelar	= *to long for* (el anhelo = *longing, strong desire*)
arrancar	= *to start (a car), to yank out, to pull out*
arrimarse	= *to come close to, to approach*
asomarse	= *to appear, as in a window*
circular	= *to go around, to move around*
demorar	= *to delay* (la demora = *delay*)
detenerse	= *to stop*
erigir	= *to erect, to put up*
escampar	= *to clear off*
embotellamiento	= *traffic jam*
frenar	= *to brake* (el freno = *brake of a car*)
olfatear	= *to smell* (el olfato = *the sense of smell*)
parar	= *to stop*
pronosticar	= *to predict, to foretell* (el pronóstico = *prediction*)
remar	= *to row (a boat)* (el remo = *oar for a rowboat*)
saltar	= *to jump* (el salto = *leap, jump*)
secuestrar	= *to kidnap* (el secuestro = *kidnapping*)
velar	= *to sail* (la vela = *sail, candle*)
zarpar	= *to sail*
a causa de	= *because of*
a pesar de que	= *in spite of*
a propósito	= *on purpose, by the way*
al menos	= *unless*
con tal que	= *unless*
de un sentido	= *one-way (street)*
para que	= *in order to*

EJERCICIO A

Empareje cada palabra en la Columna A con la definición en la Columna B, escribiendo la letra de la mejor selección.

Columna A · *Columna B*

___ 1. demorar

___ 2. descalzo

___ 3. a propósito

___ 4. madrugada

___ 5. relámpago

___ 6. zarpar

___ 7. gafas

___ 8. ombligo

___ 9. martillo

___ 10. arrimar

___ 11. freno

___ 12. perspicaz

___ 13. forastero

___ 14. desahogo

___ 15. toldo

___ 16. pinchazo

___ 17. remar

___ 18. inundación

___ 19. temporada

___ 20. pronosticar

___ 21. asomarse

___ 22. embotellamiento

___ 23. mendigo

___ 24. farol

___ 25. a causa de

a. lo que se usa para parar un automóvil

b. sagaz, astuto

c. tardar en llegar

d. sin zapatos

e. herramienta para ensartar clavos

f. acercarse a algo, colocar cerca de algo

g. un neumático desinflado

h. un extranjero

i. mover por el agua usando remos

j. velar

k. cuando el agua cubre la tierra o la superficie de algún lugar

l. la luz repentina de una tormenta, seguida por el sonido del trueno

m. expresión para explicar por qué ocurre algo

n. aparecer en una apertura, como una ventana

o. para expresar un objetivo

p. parte del cuerpo donde entró el cordón umbilical

q. parte del año para una actividad

r. una luz para alumbrar una calle de noche

s. alivio de algo

t. una persona que pide limosnas o piedad de otra gente

u. una carpa, especie de protección del sol y el tiempo

v. gran conjunto de automóviles que impide el movimiento

w. predecir algo, como el tiempo

x. objeto que se usa para proteger los ojos de la luz del sol

y. parte del día muy temprano por la mañana

EJERCICIO B

Escoja la mejor palabra para cumplir el sentido de la oración.

Durante las vacaciones del verano pasado, participé en un viaje de servicio a un país en el extranjero. Mientras mis mejores amigos se fueron rumbo a un hotel de (1) en la Florida, preparados para (2) tendidos al sol en las playas en desahogo completo, yo buscaba (3) en una iglesia en una comunidad pequeña, armado con un (4), (5), y un (6), preparado para construir una casa en la comunidad. Mis amigos pasaron su tiempo en el mar, en barcos (7), o (8) en lagos cerca del hotel. Nada les ocurrió aparte de uno que se cayó al agua cuando (9) del barco al (10) al (11) durante un chubasco y se deslizó en la superficie mojada. Miraban (12) la televisión para ver lo que diría el meteorólogo al (13) el tiempo. Afortunadamente, estaba (14) la mayoría del tiempo. De vez en cuando sufrieron por un __(15)__ __(16)__ todos los otros visitantes a la playa, pero lo pasaron bien por la mayor parte.

Para mi grupo, llovía a cántaros cuando llegamos. El avión, procedente de otro lugar, demoró varias horas para salir por problemas mecánicos. Pronto __(17)__ el cielo de todas las nubes, dejándonos con __(18)__ por todas partes. __(19)__ un __(20)__ para protegernos (en la __(21)__ lluviosa nunca se sabía cuándo empezaría a llover), e iniciamos el trabajo. __(22)__ tuviéramos bastante tiempo para concluir la obra, nos levantábamos bien temprano por la __(23)__ y no nos deteníamos hasta después del __(24)__ . Para llegar al sitio, manejábamos un coche destartalado, con frenos de calidad dudosa. Todas las tardes a las cuatro en punto, casi se podía __(25)__ la lluvia y la tormenta siempre nos advertía de su llegada con un __(26)__ y __(27)__ , y repentinamente, se oía el rumor de gotas dando contra la vegetación hasta llover como si alguien hubiera destapado la __(28)__ celestial. Por supuesto, todos nos mojábamos, y al regresar al santuario, nos quitábamos los zapatos e íbamos __(29)__ mientras se secaban los zapatos. De noche, por la luz del __(30)__ en la esquina, charlábamos del día. Trabajábamos todos los días __(31)__ que lloviera todo el día, en cuyo caso jugábamos con los chicos del pueblo o tocábamos guitarras y cantábamos.

Cuando regresamos a casa, comparamos las vacaciones entre los amigos. Los de la playa regresaron quejándose de los __(32)__ pidiendo limosnas en las calles, de los __(33)__ con quienes bebían en los clubes nocturnos, y todo tipo de cosas sin importancia. Mientras tanto, yo me acordaba de las sonrisas de mis amigos nuevos, sus padres __(34)__ y del bien que habíamos hecho __(35)__ toda la lluvia. Me sentía muy agradecida por la experiencia y __(36)__ pasar más tardes compartiendo el trabajo y la satisfacción con otros. Especialmente recordé la feria con que terminamos nuestra estancia allí, los __(37)__ y los __(38)__ y la música tan viva de la fiesta. No me quejo de nada.

___ 1.	a) lujo	b) semáforo	c) serrucho	d) lodo
___ 2.	a) remar	b) pararse	c) broncearse	d) anhelar
___ 3.	a) gafas	b) albergue	c) clavos	d) atavíos
___ 4.	a) pinchazo	b) peatón	c) deshabitados	d) martillo
___ 5.	a) remolca-dores	b) clavos	c) trueno	d) relámpago
___ 6.	a) tubería	b) parador	c) toldo	d) serrucho
___ 7.	a) veleros	b) desinflados	c) descalzos	d) mentirosos
___ 8.	a) bronceando	b) erigiendo	c) saltando	d) remando
___ 9.	a) se asomó	b) saltó	c) albergó	d) olfateó
___ 10.	a) arrancar	b) pronosticar	c) arrimarse	d) anhelar
___ 11.	a) peatón	b) serrucho	c) muelle	d) embotel-lamiento
___ 12.	a) a causa de	b) a pesar de	c) para que	d) a propósito
___ 13.	a) pronosticar	b) velar	c) anhelar	d) olfatear
___ 14.	a) descalzo	b) despejado	c) desinflado	d) perspicaz
___ 15.	a) lodo	b) semáforo	c) ocaso	d) embotel-lamiento
___ 16.	a) a propósito	b) a causa de	c) para que	d) a menos que
___ 17.	a) escampó	b) se asomó	c) demoró	d) saltó
___ 18.	a) lujo	b) martillo	c) lodo	d) serrucho
___ 19.	a) Nos paramos	b) Erigimos	c) Saltamos	d) Demoramos
___ 20.	a) peatón	b) serrucho	c) toldo	d) semáforo

___ 21.	a) temporada	b) arruga	c) madrugada	d) gafa
___ 22.	a) A causa de	b) A menos que	c) A propósito	d) Para que
___ 23.	a) madrugada	b) temporada	c) muralla	d) inundación
___ 24.	a) martillo	b) toldo	c) ocaso	d) mendigos
___ 25.	a) saltar	b) olfatear	c) erigir	d) broncear
___ 26.	a) relámpago	b) albergue	c) farol	d) forastero
___ 27.	a) parador	b) poniente	c) trueno	d) lujo
___ 28.	a) gafa	b) tubería	c) madrugada	d) arruga
___ 29.	a) mendigos	b) desinflados	c) mentirosos	d) descalzos
___ 30.	a) semáforo	b) farol	c) pinchazo	d) peatón
___ 31.	a) a menos	b) por lo menos	c) no menos	d) a causa de
___ 32.	a) desinflados	b) lujosos	c) perspicaces	d) desamparados
___ 33.	a) despojados	b) mentirosos	c) despejados	d) escampados
___ 34.	a) mentirosos	b) lujosos	c) perspicaces	d) desplegados
___ 35.	a) a causa de	b) a pesar de	c) a propósito	d) a menos que
___ 36.	a) anhelaba	b) arrimaba	c) se asomaba	d) albergaba
___ 37.	a) inundaciones	b) fuegos artificiales	c) gafas	d) madrugadas
___ 38.	a) cohetes	b) ombligos	c) remolcadores	d) desahogos

RESPUESTAS

Ejercicio A

1. c	2. d	3. o	4. y	5. l
6. j	7. x	8. p	9. e	10. f
11. a	12. b	13. h	14. s	15. u
16. g	17. i	18. k	19. q	20. w
21. n	22. v	23. t	24. r	25. m

Ejercicio B

1. a—lujo	20. c—toldo
2. c—broncearse	21. a—temporada
3. b—albergue	22. d—Para que
4. d—martillo	23. a—madrugada
5. b—clavos	24. c—ocaso
6. d—serrucho	25. b—olfatear
7. a—veleros	26. a—relámpago
8. d—remando	27. c—trueno
9. b—saltó	28. b—tubería
10. c—arrimarse	29. d—descalzos
11. c—muelle	30. b—farol
12. d—a propósito	31. a—a menos
13. a—pronosticar	32. d—desamparados
14. b—despejado	33. b—mentirosos
15. d—embotellamiento	34. c—perspicaces
16. b—a causa de	35. b—a pesar de
17. a—escampó	36. a—anhelaba
18. c—lodo	37. b—fuegos artificiales
19. b—Erigimos	38. a—cohetes

EJERCICIO C: PRÁCTICA DE LECTURA
Lea la selección para practicar el reconocimiento del vocabulario. Luego utilice las palabras en la Práctica Oral y las Situaciones.

Abundan los **embotellamientos** en cualquier lugar donde haya mucho tráfico y poco terreno, como en los **balnearios** y en los grandes centros urbanos. Los **semáforos** que aseguran el flujo del tráfico, a menudo lo impiden cuando cambian de color para permitir a los **peatones** cruzar las calles o para dejar a otros coches entrar en la calle. Por supuesto, en las calles estrechas un coche **estropeado** en medio del camino puede resultar en mucha **congestión** por todas partes. Y cuando llega el **remolcador** para quitar el vehículo del camino, a veces no cabe en la calle. Un **pinchazo** en un lugar **inoportuno**, un **semáforo** que no **funciona** bien, los **forasteros** perdidos que buscan **estacionamiento**, la multitud de turistas buscando **recuerdos** en las tiendas, todo contribuye a la congestión urbana, aun en los **balnearios** más remotos y lujosos. Aunque muchas veces se encuentran calles de **un sentido** para facilitar la **circulación** de vehículos, difícilmente se puede disfrutar del **desahogo** veraniego cuando hay que preocuparse con el tráfico todo el tiempo.

No obstante, siempre hay necesidad de descansar, de ir de vacaciones. Las mujeres **anhelan** el momento cuando pueden **colgar el delantal** y subir al coche para ir de vacaciones, no importa adonde. Al **tendernos** en la arena caliente de la playa, escuchando el **murmullo** de las **olas** en la **orilla**, el **susurro** de las hojas de las palmas y el **suspiro** de las **brisas**, perdemos nuestras preocupaciones. Para los hombres, las vacaciones ofrecen la oportunidad de **relajarse** con los amigos, nadar en las **olas**, **bucear** o **montar tablas** en las **olas**. Eso sí, no olvidemos que la luz fuerte del sol produce **daños** en la piel, como **quemaduras y arrugas** más tarde en la vida. Todas las actividades al aire libre estimulan la buena salud. Y las vacaciones nos **proporcionan** tiempo para pensar un poco y **recuperar** las fuerzas.

Preguntas sobre la lectura
1. ¿Para qué sirven los semáforos?
2. ¿Cuáles son las causas de los embotellamientos y la congestión urbana?
3. ¿A quién se llama para quitar un coche estropeado de una calle?
4. ¿Por qué se va de vacaciones?
5. ¿Cómo se pasa el tiempo en la playa?
6. ¿Qué actividades hay para hacer en la playa?
7. ¿Qué peligros hay al quedarse demasiado tiempo al sol del mediodía?

EJERCICIO D: PRÁCTICA ORAL
Conteste las preguntas usando el vocabulario de esta unidad.

1. ¿A dónde le gusta ir de vacaciones?
2. ¿Qué actividades le gusta hacer en la playa?
3. ¿Cuán distintos son los balnearios en las montañas de los de la costa?
4. ¿Por qué es importante descansar?
5. ¿Dónde pasó sus últimas vacaciones? ¿Qué hizo?
6. ¿Con quién le gusta ir de vacaciones?
7. ¿Haría un joven las mismas actividades con la familia que con sus mejores amigos en las vacaciones? Explique su respuesta.

8. ¿Cuáles son los beneficios de los viajes de servicio?

9. ¿Hizo alguna vez un viaje de servicio comunitario a una comunidad en el extranjero? Descríbalo.

10. ¿Quiénes se benefician más de los viajes de servicio comunitario, los que dan o los que reciben? Explique.

11. ¿Preferiría ir de vacaciones para visitar los museos de Europa, o para velar en el Mar Caribe? Explique su selección.

12. ¿Por qué no piensan los jóvenes en los peligros de nadar en el océano?

13. A pesar de todas las advertencias, ¿por qué entran algunas personas al océano cuando hay peligro de corrientes fuertes?

14. ¿Le gustaría ser salvavidas en la playa o en una piscina durante el verano? ¿Por qué?

15. ¿Qué tipos de recuerdos le gusta tener de sus vacaciones? ¿Qué suele coleccionar como recuerdo? ¿Por qué?

EJERCICIO E: SITUACIONES
Discuta las situaciones usando el vocabulario de esta unidad.

1. Usted está encargado de arreglar las vacaciones para su familia este año. Describa los preparativos que haría.

2. Usted es dueño de un balneario en las montañas. Prepare un anuncio para atraer clientes a su lugar. Haga lo mismo para un balneario cerca de una playa.

3. Su familia va de vacaciones en la costa de la Florida y le dice que puede invitar a un amigo. Invítelo y dígale qué tiene planeado hacer durante las vacaciones.

4. Al regresar a la escuela, la profesora de la clase de español le pide hacer un reportaje sobre sus vacaciones del verano. Reporte lo que hizo durante el verano pasado.

LOS NEGOCIOS

el alambre	= *wire for fences*
el almacén	= *warehouse, storehouse*
la bancarrota	= *bankruptcy*
el bolsillo	= *pocket*
la caja	= *box*
la cartera	= *wallet, pocketbook*
el combustible	= *fuel*
el comerciante	= *merchant*
el comestible	= *food*
la compra	= *the purchase*
el costal	= *sack, gunny sack, for carrying grain, for example*
la cuenta	= *account (bank account), bill for services or merchandise*
el dependiente	= *clerk*
la deuda	= *debt (deber = to owe, to have to, + inf.)*
el dueño	= *owner*
la empresa	= *company*

el escaparate	= *window, store window case*
la fábrica	= *factory (*fabricar = *to manufacture)*
los fondos	= *funds*
las fresas	= *strawberries*
la ganancia	= *earnings*
el guacamayo	= *macaw*
la huelga	= *strike by employees or workers*
el impuesto	= *tax (*imponer = *to impose)*
la lechuga	= *lettuce*
el lobo	= *wolf*
el loro	= *parrot*
la manifestación	= *demonstration, by workers or people (*manifestar = *to show)*
el mono	= *monkey*
el patrón	= *boss, chief*
el peso	= *the weight (*pesar = *to weigh)*
la procedencia	= *of origin (*proceder = *to come from)*
el propietario	= *owner*
el presupuesto	= *budget*
el recibo	= *receipt for a purchase (*recibir = *to receive)*
el rollo	= *rolls (such as of currency, wire, or film)*
el sueldo	= *salary*
la tarjeta de crédito	= *credit card*
el trámite	= *transaction*
la venta	= *sale (*vender = *to sell)*
la vitrina	= *window glass*
avisar	= *to advise, to warn*
arriesgar	= *to risk (*el riesgo = *risk)*
confeccionar	= *to make, to produce*
darse cuenta	= *to realize, to become aware of, to learn*
enfermarse	= *to get sick (*enfermedad = *sickness)*
esconder	= *to hide (*el escondite = *hiding place)*
escurrirse	= *to slip away, to slide, to sneak off*
invertir	= *to invest money (*inversión = *investment)*
realizar	= *to fulfill, to realize in the sense of "to complete"*
rebajar	= *to lower prices (*la rebaja = *the reduction, rebate, discount)*
reemplazar	= *to replace*
regatear	= *to bargain over prices*
saborear	= *to taste, to savor (*el sabor = *taste, flavor)*
sobrar	= *to be left over, to have left over*
surtir	= *to supply (*el surtido = *supply)*
a la vez	= *at the same time*
al contado	= *in cash, form of payment*
al extranjero	= *abroad, in a foreign country*
al fin y al cabo	= *in the end, finally*
debido a	= *owing to*
de hecho	= *in fact*
de venta	= *for sale*

de vez en cuando	= *from time to time*
en efectivo	= *in cash, form of payment*
quizás, quizá	= *perhaps*
tal vez	= *perhaps*
todavía	= *still*

EJERCICIO A

Empareje cada palabra en la Columna A con la definición en la Columna B, escribiendo la letra de la mejor selección.

Columna A

___ 1. escaparate
___ 2. sabor
___ 3. fresa
___ 4. dueño
___ 5. costal
___ 6. caja
___ 7. quizás
___ 8. de venta
___ 9. riesgo
___ 10. huelga
___ 11. empresa
___ 12. deuda
___ 13. a propósito
___ 14. regatear
___ 15. guacamayo
___ 16. fábrica
___ 17. surgir
___ 18. presupuesto
___ 19. ajeno
___ 20. alambre

Columna B

a. una bolsa grande para llevar cosas como arroz
b. extranjero
c. anuncio del deseo de recibir pago por algo
d. lo que se debe a otra persona
e. acción hecha por obreros contra una empresa
f. cable para construir una cerca, un gallinero o un cerco para animales
g. lugar para ver desde la calle lo que se vende en una tienda
h. dinero disponible para algo
i. discutir el precio de mercancía
j. lugar para confeccionar productos
k. un pájaro tropical de colores azul, rojo, amarillo y verde
l. propietario
m. gusto al poner algo en la boca
n. objeto, generalmente cúbico, en el que se ponen cosas
o. compañía
p. una acción con cierto peligro
q. una fruta roja del verano
r. brotar
s. tal vez
t. con intención

EJERCICIO B

Escoja la mejor palabra para cumplir el sentido de la oración.

Cuando pasé por el _(1)_ de mi tienda favorita de animales domésticos, al otro lado de la _(2)_ vi el _(3)_ más precioso que jamás había visto en la vida. Me miró de una manera tan _(4)_ que no pude resistir la _(5)_ y entré en la tienda. Al hablar con el _(6)_, _(7)_ de que ese animal podría ser mío por $100 porque estaba _(8)_ ese día. _(9)_ un poco porque vi que tenía muchas ganas de vendérmelo. Concluimos la _(10)_ y me dio un _(11)_. _(12)_, _(13)_ la falta de _(14)_ de animales exóticos el propietario estaba pensando declararse en _(15)_. _(16)_ lagartos en la tienda, pero se vendían fácilmente los pájaros tropicales, como los _(17)_ y los _(18)_. Me dijo que no sabía por qué tanta gente quería comprar los pájaros exóticos, porque su cuidado exigía mucho espacio. Era necesario tener una jaula grande de __(19)__ , como un __(20)__ , para guardarlos. Le pagué al __(21)__ cien dólares __(22)__ , me lo puse en un costal, y salí de la tienda muy satisfecha con la __(23)__ . Me aseguró que si no me gustara, o si se __(24)__ el animal, me lo __(25)__ . El lagarto no dijo nada mientras lo llevaba a casa.

Cuando llegué a casa lo puse en su nuevo hogar en el sótano, con unos papeles, una __(26)__ de un árbol, y alimentación y agua. Por supuesto, se __(27)__ por debajo del papel para __(28)__ de inmediato, __(29)__ porque no le gustó toda la luz que le caía donde lo tenía colocado. __(30)__ salía para beber un poco de agua. El próximo día salí otra vez para comprar una __(31)__ más grande. No le compraba __(32)__ especiales, le ofrecía lechuga y otras verduras. Cuando salía para comer, __(33)__ las hojas un poco, pero nunca comió mucho. Pronto vi que no tendría que __(34)__ nada de mi __(35)__ en darle de comer. Todavía no me decía nada, ni para quejarse, ni para alabarme por haberlo comprado.

Al fin y al cabo, lo devolví a la tienda porque nunca me respondió cuando le dirigí la palabra. Ahora sé por qué había tantos lagartos de venta. Los lagartos no hablan mucho.

___ 1. a) costal	b) fondo	c) trámite	d) escaparate
___ 2. a) vitrina	b) huelga	c) venta	d) manifestación
___ 3. a) hilo	b) alambre	c) lagarto	d) costal
___ 4. a) lastimosa	b) cotidiana	c) liviana	d) nociva
___ 5. a) gallardía	b) tentación	c) caja	d) deuda
___ 6. a) presupuesto	b) lobo	c) propietario	d) sueldo
___ 7. a) realicé	b) escurrí	c) eché la culpa	d) me di cuenta
___ 8. a) de hecho	b) de venta	c) debido a	d) en efectivo
___ 9. a) Regateamos	b) Regalamos	c) Escondimos	d) Surtimos
___ 10. a) venta	b) deuda	c) bancarrota	d) caja
___ 11. a) presupuesto	b) propietario	c) dueño	d) recibo
___ 12. a) De venta	b) De hecho	c) Al contado	d) En efectivo
___ 13. a) debido a	b) de venta	c) al contado	d) en el extranjero
___ 14. a) presupuesto	b) dueño	c) impuesto	d) surtido
___ 15. a) procedencia	b) bancarrota	c) fábrica	d) ganancia
___ 16. a) Regateaban	b) Surtían	c) Sobraban	d) Invertían
___ 17. a) dueños	b) rollos	c) guacamayos	d) fondos
___ 18. a) loros	b) lobos	c) propietarios	d) impuestos
___ 19. a) escaparate	b) fondo	c) alambre	d) impuesto
___ 20. a) fresa	b) deuda	c) fábrica	d) gallinero
___ 21. a) impuesto	b) fondo	c) dependiente	d) sueldo
___ 22. a) de hecho	b) en efectivo	c) a la vez	d) debido a
___ 23. a) compra	b) fresa	c) huelga	d) manifestación
___ 24. a) regateara	b) realizara	c) se enfermara	d) sobrara
___ 25. a) advertiría	b) reemplazaría	c) invertiría	d) arriesgaría
___ 26. a) fresa	b) lechuga	c) rama	d) procedencia
___ 27. a) regateó	b) invirtió	c) estalló	d) escurrió
___ 28. a) surtir	b) sobrar	c) saborear	d) esconderse
___ 29. a) en efectivo	b) quizás	c) aunque	d) todavía
___ 30. a) Debido a	b) De vez en cuando	c) Al contado	d) En el extranjero
___ 31. a) caja	b) lechuga	c) vitrina	d) procedencia

___ 32. a) comestibles   b) huelgas   c) fábricas   d) cajas
___ 33. a) sobraba   b) saboreaba   c) regateaba   d) surgía
___ 34. a) invertir   b) escurrir   c) esconder   d) arriesgar
___ 35. a) dueño   b) propietario   c) presupuesto   d) alambre

RESPUESTAS

Ejercicio A

1. g	2. m	3. q	4. l	5. a
6. n	7. s	8. c	9. p	10. e
11. o	12. d	13. t	14. i	15. k
16. j	17. r	18. h	19. b	20. f

Ejercicio B

1. d—escaparate
2. a—vitrina
3. c—lagarto
4. a—lastimosa
5. b—tentación
6. c—propietario
7. d—me di cuenta
8. b—de venta
9. a—Regateamos
10. a—venta
11. d—recibo
12. b—De hecho
13. a—debido a
14. d—surtido
15. b—bancarrota
16. c—Sobraban
17. c—guacamayos
18. a—loros
19. c— alambre
20. d—gallinero
21. c—dependiente
22. b—en efectivo
23. a—compra
24. c—enfermara
25. b—reemplazaría
26. c—rama
27. d—escurrió
28. d—esconderse
29. b—quizás
30. b—De vez en cuando
31. a—caja
32. a—comestibles
33. b—saboreaba
34. d—arriesgar
35. c—presupuesto

EJERCICIO C: PRÁCTICA DE LECTURA
Lea la selección para practicar el reconocimiento del vocabulario. Luego utilice las palabras en la Práctica Oral y las Situaciones.

El tema de la globalización de los **negocios** llama la atención en las tiendas y los mercados, donde se ve **mercancía** producida en el **extranjero** que se vende por menos de lo que nos cuesta producirla en los Estados Unidos. Pero la economía de veras es muy **compleja**, como se ve si se siguen las **huellas** de un producto de la **fábrica** al mercado. Casi todos los productos tienen una historia internacional. Los productos para el mercado doméstico en su **mayoría proceden** de otros países en desarrollo, los zapatos llegan de China, Brasil o Italia. Los **aparatos** electrónicos **provienen** de **empresas** asiáticas o coreanas, o quizás de un país escandinavo. Algunos automóviles se producen en el sur de los Estados Unidos, pero otros vienen de Asia. **De hecho**, un coche contiene partes **fabricadas** en todas partes del mundo.

No sólo la **mercancía** nos llega de países **extranjeros**, sino también algo tan **cotidiano** como la comida. Las frutas frescas nos **ofrecen** un **sabor** delicioso del sol y la tierra de donde vienen: las uvas chilenas, las **fresas** mexicanas, las naranjas brasileñas, todas nos **avisan** de su **procedencia**. Como se sabe, el petróleo viene de los países árabes o de Rusia. El café nos llega en **costales** de los países latinoamericanos. En otros **negocios**, las **imágenes radiográficas** de los médicos se leen en India, y muchas de las llamadas telefónicas que hacemos para hacer reservaciones con las líneas aéreas o pedir **mercancía** de un catálogo pasan por el aire a otros países.

Ha **cambiado** también el **modo** de pagar la **mercancía**, que ahora se hace por **tarjeta de crédito** o una transacción electrónica **bancaria**. Es posible **invertir fondos**, pagar las **cuentas**, **ahorrar** dinero y realizar cualquier **trámite** sin **tocar** un **billete**. El **sueldo** se paga electrónicamente en muchos lugares. El dinero **en efectivo** está desapareciendo en muchos lugares porque casi nunca se paga **al contado**. A veces, **debido al peso** del peso, se requieren **costales** para llevar la **pesada moneda** de países que sufren de inflación. Y los **rollos** de **billetes** ya no **caben** dentro de un **bolsillo** o una **cartera** normal. Los **billetes** que sí se usan **surgen** de **cajeras automáticas**, y casi nunca se ve a un **banquero** humano a menos que se tenga necesidad de **pedir** un **préstamo** del banco o de **arreglar** algo **tocante** a una **cuenta**.

Poco a poco, el **mercado virtual** está **reemplazando** el **mercado** regular. Pero en otros lugares se encuentran los mercados al **aire libre**, donde se puede todavía **regatear** con los vendedores. Especialmente en los fines de semana, se ven **mercados** o **ventas** de garaje. Sin importar el **tamaño** de la **venta**, el cliente en esos lugares busca **rebajas** y a menudo las encuentra. En cualquier plaza en un país de habla española se ve mucha libertad de comercio. La **ganancia** del comerciante en ese tipo de lugar es pura **ganancia**. Muchas veces ni se pagan los **impuestos de venta**.

Preguntas sobre la lectura

1. ¿De dónde proceden muchos productos de venta en los Estados Unidos?
2. ¿Qué tipo de trabajo se hace en otros países?
3. ¿En qué es diferente la manera de pagar las cuentas hoy en día?
4. ¿Por qué no se lleva mucha moneda en efectivo en los países con mucha inflación?
5. ¿En qué se diferencia la venta de mercancía en un mercado al aire libre de la de un almacén?
6. Describa el mercado virtual.

EJERCICIO D: PRÁCTICA ORAL
Conteste las preguntas usando el vocabulario de esta unidad.

1. Si pudiera establecer su propio negocio, ¿qué tipo tendría? Explique su selección.
2. Describa al empleado ideal.
3. Describa al propietario ideal.
4. ¿Tuvo alguna vez un empleo? Descríbalo.
5. ¿Cuáles son los negocios más importantes para una comunidad?
6. ¿Qué negocios producen la ganancia más grande?

7. ¿Qué problemas tienen los negocios que dependen de productos de otros países?

8. ¿Cree que es buena la globalización del comercio moderno? Explique su respuesta.

9. ¿Cuáles son las ventajas de tener su propio negocio? ¿Las desventajas?

10. En su comunidad, ¿hay muchos productos de otros países? Descríbalos.

EJERCICIO E: SITUACIONES
Discuta las situaciones usando el vocabulario de esta unidad.

1. Usted acaba de comprar una tienda de música. Desarrolle un plan para promocionarla.

2. Usted es propietario de una tienda y tiene una entrevista con un joven que quiere conseguir un puesto en su tienda. Elabore la conversación con él, describiéndole todo que quiere que haga.

3. Usted acaba de conseguir un trabajo de media jornada porque todavía tiene que estudiar para graduarse de la escuela. El patrón quiere que usted trabaje más de lo planeado, o de lo contrario arriesga perder el trabajo. Explíquele por qué no puede hacerlo y convénzalo que lo deje seguir trabajando.

4. Usted desea invertir su sueldo para ahorrar dinero para su educación universitaria. Desarrolle un plan para invertirlo. ¿En qué tipos de empresas invertiría su dinero? ¿Por qué?

5. El próximo año usted vivirá en un apartamento en la universidad. Explique los gastos de su presupuesto y cómo manejará su dinero.

EL TRABAJO Y LAS CARRERAS

el abogado	= *lawyer*
la alfarería	= *pottery, pottery making*
el anuncio	= *advertisement* (anunciar = *to announce, to advertise*)
el basurero	= *trashman* (la basura = *trash, garbage*)
el bombero	= *fireman*
la carrera	= *career, a race (of cars or horses)*
el consultorio	= *doctor's office*
la contabilidad	= *accounting* (contar = *to count, to relate a story*)
el deber	= *duty*
el derecho	= *law, right*
el empleo	= *job, work* (emplear = *to hire, to employ, to use*)
el encargado	= *in charge of, responsible for* (encargar = *to put in the care of*)
el entrevistador	= *interviewer*
la facultad	= *a school in a university, like a department*
la formación	= *preparation, background, training* (formar = *to form*)
el gerente	= *manager*
la incertidumbre	= *uncertainty* (cierto = *certain, sure*)
la informática	= *data processing*
la jornada	= *day's work*

la pereza	= *laziness, sloth* (perezoso = *lazy*)
la pesadilla	= *nightmare*
la promoción	= *advertising*
la prueba	= *test, proof* (probar = *to prove, to test, to try*)
el puesto	= *position, stall (for selling goods)*
el remordimiento	= *remorse, regret* (remorder = *to cause remorse*)
el reto	= *challenge, threat, menace*
el sacerdote	= *priest*
el solicitante	= *applicant* (solicitar = *to solicit, to ask for*)
el tripulante	= *crewmember* (la tripulación = *the crew of a plane or ship*)
la uña	= *fingernail*
la zozobra	= *anxiety*
analfabeto	= *illiterate, uneducated*
atónito	= *astonished, amazed*
capaz	= *capable* (la capacidad = *capacity*)
diestro	= *skillful, handy, clever* (adiestrar = *to train, to teach*)
desafortunadamente	= *unfortunately*
eclesiástica	= *relating to the church*
hábil	= *talented*
incómodo	= *uncomfortable*
ingenioso	= *ingenious, clever*
insólito	= *unusual, unaccustomed*
riguroso	= *demanding, rigorous* (el rigor = *rigor, difficulty*)
sólido	= *solid, massive, firm*
afrontar	= *to face, to confront*
arrojar	= *to throw*
aconsejar	= *to advise* (el consejero = *adviser, counselor*)
adelantarse	= *to get ahead* (delante de = *in front of*)
anunciar	= *to announce, to advertise* (el anuncio = *ad, announcement*)
conformar	= *to conform*
conseguir	= *to get*
contratar	= *to hire* (el contrato = *contract*)
cumplir	= *to fulfill*
desafiar	= *to challenge* (el desafío = *challenge, dare*)
despedir	= *to fire from a job, to let go (from a job)*
destrozar	= *to shatter*
ejecutar	= *to accomplish, to do a job*
ejercer	= *to perform, to exert, to practice* (el ejercico = *exercise, practice*)
entrevistar	= *to interview* (la entrevista = *interview*)
equivocarse	= *to be mistaken* (la equivocación = *mistake*)
esforzarse	= *to strive, to try* (el esfuerzo = *effort, strong attempt*)
experimentar	= *to experience*
hacerse	= *to become*

indagar	= *to investigate* (la indagación = *investigation*)
involucrar	= *to involve*
naufragar	= *to shipwreck* (el náufrago = *shipwrecked person*)
obtener	= *to get*
otorgar	= *to grant, to authorize, to consent to, to agree to*
precipitar	= *to hurry, to hasten, to rush*
promocionar	= *to promote*
reclamar	= *to demand (one's rights, for example)*
reclutar	= *to recruit*
roer	= *to gnaw, to bite*
solicitar	= *to apply for, to solicit* (el solicitante = *applicant*)
sujetar	= *to subdue*
verter	= *to spill, to shed, to empty*
vigilar	= *to watch over, to keep vigil*

EJERCICIO A

Empareje cada palabra en la Columna A con la definición en la Columna B, escribiendo la letra de la mejor selección.

Columna A

___ 1. naufragar
___ 2. precipitar
___ 3. conformar
___ 4. reclamar
___ 5. contabilidad
___ 6. insólito
___ 7. pereza
___ 8. vigilar
___ 9. zozobra
___ 10. promoción
___ 11. tripulante
___ 12. verter
___ 13. arrojar
___ 14. conseguir
___ 15. promocionar
___ 16. diestro
___ 17. reto
___ 18. analfabeto
___ 19. sigiloso
___ 20. despedir
___ 21. indagar
___ 22. reclutar
___ 23. puesto
___ 24. encargado
___ 25. pesadilla

Columna B

a. un sueño malo
b. tirar, lanzar, echar
c. ansiedad
d. obtener
e. estimular interés en comprar
f. una persona que trabaja en un barco o un avión
g. amenaza
h. algo para generar entusiasmo
i. sin saber leer ni escribir
j. lo que pasa cuando un barco se pierde en una tempestad
k. muy capaz
l. silencioso
m. sin ánimo, sin ganas de trabajar
n. decir a un empleado que ya no trabaja en la empresa
o. investigar
p. tener la responsabilidad por algo
q. derramar
r. observar algo o a alguien
s. raro, diferente, anormal
t. un empleo, una posición
u. profesión financiera
v. concordar o estar de acuerdo
w. exigir, los derechos, por ejemplo
x. reunir personas para algo
y. apurar

EJERCICIO B
Escoja la mejor palabra para cumplir el sentido de la oración.

La primera vez que (1) un (2) después de graduarme, me sorprendió lo difícil que era. Al principio sólo sabía que no quería (3) secretaria, enfermera en un (4), ni profesora de niños de un jardín de infantes. Pero tampoco tenía la (5) para hacerme profesional como doctora, abogada, ni (6), ni contadora, ni nada. Primero (7) la (8) de las empresas que anunciaban puestos vacantes, sin encontrar nada que me gustara. Entonces me (9) con una gran multitud de empresas, donde los (10) me (11) con cuidado, y la (12) de las entrevistas casi me (13). Siempre salía (14) las (15), aunque sabía que era tan (16) como cualquier otro. Por fin, (17) un (18) de recepcionista en un hospital; era trabajo de (19) completa por unos seis meses. Después, tuve que volver a iniciar la búsqueda. Por fin encontré una posición de secretaria en una iglesia, oficio que no (20) con mucha destreza. El (21) era muy amable, pero ese trabajo de índole eclesiástica tampoco me sirvió para encontrar el sendero a una (22). Fue un trabajo sin oportunidad para (23). Gracias a Dios, no me (24) por todos los errores que hice porque no sabía ni taquigrafiar. De veras, fue un (25) producir una página sin (26) varias veces. Por supuesto, pronto (27) a ese puesto también. Se dice que al cerrar una puerta, ya se abre otra, y así fue.

Llegué a la universidad lista para entrenarme para una carrera legítima, como (28), medicina, (29), contabilidad, cualquier profesión que me (30) una vida (31). Una vez en la universidad en la (32) de Lenguas Extranjeras, me (33) para enseñar unas clases y vi que me fascinaba el proceso de aprendizaje de los estudiantes. Pronto me (34) por la senda para conseguir un título, mientras seguía enseñando todo el tiempo. La carrera me había encontrado y me hice profesora a pesar de no quererlo cuando era niña. Nunca he sentido ningún (35) por haber tomado esa decisión. La enseñanza es una carrera (36), valiosa y segura. También, siempre le satisface al profesor ver en los estudiantes la chispa de entendimiento cuando de repente comprenden algo. Ahora (37) sobre distintas carreras a mis estudiantes. La búsqueda de la carrera perfecta es rigurosa pero no tiene que ser una (38).

___ 1. a) recluté b) aconsejé c) destrocé d) solicité

___ 2. a) puesto b) desafío c) reto d) consultorio

___ 3. a) hacerme b) ejecutar c) experimentar d) renunciar

___ 4. a) interlocutor b) reto c) consultorio d) encargado

___ 5. a) pereza b) informática c) contabilidad d) formación

___ 6. a) consultorio b) bombero c) derecho d) gerente

___ 7. a) indagué b) afronté c) desafié d) entrevisté

___ 8. a) zozobra b) pereza c) promoción d) pesadilla

___ 9. a) recluté b) otorgué c) entrevisté d) me esforcé

___ 10. a) entrevista-
         dores b) entrevistas c) consultorios d) retos

___ 11. a) naufragaron b) vigilaron c) renunciaron d) despidieron

___ 12. a) zozobra b) pereza c) uña d) amenaza

___ 13. a) reclamó b) destrozó c) reclutó d) experimentó

___ 14. a) solicitando b) promocio-
         nando c) royendo d) vertiendo

___ 15. a) alfarerías b) uvas c) pesadillas d) uñas

___ 16. a) hábil b) insólito c) analfabeta d) atónita

___ 17. a) conseguí	b) naufragué	c) precipité	d) otorgué
___ 18. a) desafío	b) empleo	c) consultorio	d) tripulante
___ 19. a) jornada	b) propaganda	c) pesadilla	d) contabilidad
___ 20. a) solicité	b) conseguí	c) entrevisté	d) ejecuté
___ 21. a) bombero	b) sacerdote	c) reto	d) basurero
___ 22. a) informática	b) carrera	c) cartera	d) contabilidad
___ 23. a) esforzarme	b) solicitar	c) precipitar	d) adelantarme
___ 24. a) despidió	b) reclutó	c) precipitó	d) royó
___ 25. a) bombero	b) derecho	c) desafío	d) remordimiento
___ 26. a) equivocarme	b) indagar	c) involucrar	d) verter
___ 27. a) renuncié	b) despedí	c) roí	d) involucré
___ 28. a) sacerdote	b) derecho	c) empleo	d) puesto
___ 29. a) carrera	b) informática	c) pereza	d) jornada
___ 30. a) indagara	b) reclutara	c) involucrara	d) otorgara
___ 31. a) sigilosa	b) atónita	c) insólita	d) cómoda
___ 32. a) alfarería	b) pesadilla	c) Facultad	d) formación
___ 33. a) reclutaron	b) vigilaron	c) precipitaron	d) vertieron
___ 34. a) otorgué	b) indagué	c) precipité	d) vigilé
___ 35. a) reto	b) remordimiento	c) bombero	d) puesto
___ 36. a) capaz	b) incómoda	c) atónita	d) sólida
___ 37. a) precipito	b) aconsejo	c) involucro	d) vigilo
___ 38. a) jornada	b) zozobra	c) pesadilla	d) uña

RESPUESTAS

Ejercicio A

1. j	2. y	3. v	4. w	5. u
6. s	7. m	8. r	9. c	10. h
11. f	12. q	13. b	14. d	15. e
16. k	17. g	18. i	19. l	20. n
21. o	22. x	23. t	24. p	25. a

Ejercicio B

1. d—solicité	20. d—ejecuté
2. a—puesto	21. b—sacerdote
3. a—hacerme	22. b—carrera
4. c—consultorio	23. d—adelantarme
5. d—formación	24. a—despidió
6. b—bombero	25. c—desafío
7. a—indagué	26. a—equivocarme
8. c—promoción	27. a—renuncié
9. c—entrevisté	28. b—derecho
10. a—entrevistadores	29. b—informática
11. b—vigilaron	30. d—otorgara
12. a—zozobra	31. d—cómoda
13. b—destrozó	32. c—Facultad
14. c—royendo	33. a—reclutaron
15. d—uñas	34. c—precipité
16. a—hábil	35. b—remordimiento
17. a—conseguí	36. d—sólida
18. b—empleo	37. b—aconsejo
19. a—jornada	38. c—pesadilla

EJERCICIO C: PRÁCTICA DE LECTURA
Lea la selección para practicar el reconocimiento del vocabulario. Luego utilice las palabras en la Práctica Oral y las Situaciones.

Uno de los **derechos** que tiene una persona en la sociedad capitalista es el de seguir cualquier **carrera** que le guste. La selección de una carrera a veces **depende de** los intereses de la persona y otras veces corresponde a las **habilidades** de la persona. La persona **capaz por lo general** trabajará con una variedad de **empresas** durante su vida. Se puede empezar con una **formación** fuerte, **conseguir** un título y luego estudiar medicina, **derecho**, **ingeniería** u otro campo de especialización en la universidad. La persona **analfabeta** no tendrá las mismas oportunidades, pero sí puede establecer su propia **empresa**. Tendría que **indagar** las posibilidades, **solicitar** un préstamo del banco o un amigo, crear **promoción** para **promocionar** su negocio y manejar bien sus **recursos**. Por otra parte, las grandes **empresas reclutan** trabajadores entre los graduados de las universidades todos los años. Si una persona se dedica al arte, es un poco más difícil establecerse. La **zozobra** que resulta de la **incertidumbre** de encontrar trabajo que pague bastante a veces procede de falta de planeamiento. Si va a pasarse la vida trabajando, vale que la pase en un negocio **involucrado** en lo que más le interese.

La **entrevista** muchas veces produce gran ansiedad porque el solicitante joven no se da cuenta de sus derechos. Hay ciertos temas que no se deben preguntar. En la **entrevista** no debe figurar la religión, la edad, el sexo, la **raza**, ni la política del solicitante. Pero en realidad, **desafortunadamente** hay discriminación. Y a veces el **entrevistador** sabe que hay muchos **solicitantes** y no tiene que **contratar** a una persona que no le guste por cualquier razón.

Para que funcione una sociedad, se necesitan diversos tipos de trabajadores. Hay un **empleo** para cada uno, y bastará con **cumplir** con el **deber** para que todo salga bien y todos gocen de la buena vida. O por lo menos, esto es lo que nos dice la teoría. La **prueba** se presenta cuando el joven **afronta** la vida con todas las posibilidades **desplegadas** para escoger la **carrera** más apropiada. Si usted no sabe lo que quiere hacer, vale **probar** una variedad de asignaturas en la universidad, participar en una variedad de actividades en la comunidad, o **experimentar** el mundo de los negocios trabajando a **jornada incompleta**. Vale tener presente, también, que siempre puede cambiar de camino y seguir otra **carrera** después de **emprender** una, **con tal que** tenga los **recursos** financieros para hacerlo. A veces se **empeña** el **porvenir** al **perseguirse** un sueño. Pero más vale **esforzarse** por **realizar** el sueño que vivir con el **remordimiento** de un sueño **incumplido**. Así, al fin de su vida, no llorará por las oportunidades perdidas.

Preguntas sobre la lectura
1. ¿De qué depende la selección de una carrera?
2. ¿Qué preparativos se hacen para prepararse para una carrera?
3. ¿Qué posibilidades tienen los que no tienen una buena educación?
4. ¿Cuáles son las necesidades de una sociedad?
5. ¿Cuándo se da cuenta un joven de qué quiere hacer para ganarse la vida?
6. ¿Cómo puede aprender de las posibilidades disponibles si no sabe lo que desea hacer?
7. ¿De qué depende la posibilidad de cambiar de idea en cuanto a una carrera?
8. ¿Por qué vale la pena seguir los sueños en la vida?

EJERCICIO D: PRÁCTICA ORAL
Conteste las preguntas usando el vocabulario de esta unidad.

1. ¿Qué piensa hacer para ganarse la vida?
2. ¿Qué le gustaría hacer, si pudiera hacerse un profesional?
3. ¿Cuáles son las ventajas de hacerse profesional?
4. ¿Cómo puede contentarse con un trabajo manual?
5. ¿Qué le aconsejan sus padres o profesores que haga?
6. ¿Es más importante ganar mucho dinero o estar contento en la vida? Explique su respuesta.
7. ¿Ha participado en una entrevista una vez para un empleo? Describa su experiencia.
8. ¿Por qué se ponen tan nerviosos muchos solicitantes al entrevistarse para un empleo?
9. ¿Cree que lo que aprende en la escuela le servirá para una carrera?
10. ¿Qué se necesita aprender para tener éxito en un empleo?

EJERCICIO E: SITUACIONES
Discuta las situaciones usando el vocabulario de esta unidad.

1. Usted está encargado de contratar a un dependiente para la tienda de música. Discuta cómo sería una entrevista con un joven que solicita el empleo.
2. Usted no sabe qué carrera seguir. Imagínese una conversación con un consejero o sus padres para ayudarle a tomar una decisión. Discuta sus intereses y posibilidades.
3. Usted quiere tener un trabajo durante el verano para ver cómo sería trabajar todos los días. Imagínese el tipo de trabajo que querría hacer y la entrevista para conseguirlo.
4. Un día en su escuela hay un anuncio de una feria para promocionar varios programas preparatorios para ciertas carreras como medicina, ingeniería, derecho, informática, contabilidad y ventas para grandes empresas. Describa las oportunidades potenciales de esos trabajos.

PRACTICE FOR CONVERSATION

I. Autobiografía (Ud. y su familia)

Vocabulario

SUSTANTIVOS

el acontecimiento	event	*la habilidad*	talent
los adolescentes	teens	*la identidad*	identity
la característica	characteristic	*la independencia*	independence
el desarrollo	development	*la niñez*	childhood
la edad	age	*el suceso*	event

VERBOS

asemejar	to resemble	*parecer*	to seem
establecer	to settle, establish		

ADJETIVOS

aplicado	industrious	*modesto*	modest
extrovertido	outgoing	*perezoso*	lazy
hablador	talkative	*simpático*	kind
introvertido	introspective	*tímido*	timid

Conteste Ud. a las preguntas en español en oraciones completas:
(Answer the following questions in Spanish in complete sentences for the practice of using correct verb forms.)

Autobiografía del individuo

1. Describa Ud. a sí mismo o sí misma, sus aspectos físicos y de carácter. ¿Cómo es Ud.?
2. ¿Qué talentos o habilidades especiales tiene Ud.?
3. ¿Goza Ud. de buena salud? ¿A qué atribuye Ud. su buena o mala salud?
4. ¿Qué habilidades especiales tiene Ud.?
5. ¿De qué se alegra Ud. más?
6. ¿De qué tiene Ud. más miedo?
7. ¿De qué se arrepiente Ud. más en su vida?
8. ¿Diría Ud. que es una persona religiosa? Explique.
9. Describa Ud. el acontecimiento del cual Ud. se siente más orgulloso y por qué.
10. ¿Qué piensa que dirían sus amigos de Ud.?
11. Si tuviera que escoger una palabra para describirse a sí mismo (misma), ¿cuál sería? ¿Por qué?
12. ¿A quién admira Ud. más? ¿Por qué?
13. ¿Qué le gusta hacer en su tiempo libre?
14. ¿A qué o a quién atribuye Ud. sus buenas características personales?
15. Si Ud. pudiera cambiar un aspecto de su personalidad, ¿cuál sería? ¿Por qué?
16. Si pudiera ser otra persona, ¿quién sería? ¿Por qué?

17. Si fuera millonario o millonaria, ¿cómo gastaría su dinero? Explique Ud. por qué lo gastaría de tal manera.

Su niñez

18. Cuándo era niño, o niña, ¿cómo era? ¿extrovertido, -a?, ¿introvertido, -a? ¿tímido, -a? ¿aventurero, -a? ¿curioso, -a? ¿perezoso, -a? ¿aplicado, -a? ¿simpático, -a? ¿guapo, -a? ¿dormilón, -a? ¿trabajador, -a? etc. Dé Ud. un ejemplo de esta característica.
19. ¿Ha cambiado su personalidad mucho? ¿Cómo?
20. ¿Cuál fue el acontecimiento más importante para Ud. cuando era niño o niña?
21. ¿Cuál fue el suceso más emocionante para Ud. cuando era niño o niña?
22. ¿Dónde vivían Ud. y su familia cuando era niño?
23. De todos los lugares en que Ud. haya vivido, ¿cuál le gustó más? ¿Por qué?
24. ¿Cree Ud. que el lugar en el cual Ud. creció influyó mucho en su desarrollo psicológico? Explique.
25. ¿Adónde ha viajado Ud.? ¿Qué lugar le interesó más?
26. ¿Adónde le gustaría poder viajar si pudiera viajar a cualquier lugar? ¿Por qué?
27. ¿Ha visto Ud. muchos cambios en su vida? ¿Cuáles?
28. ¿Hubo una experiencia que haya influido más que otra en su vida? Descríbala.

Sus hermanos o hermanas

29. ¿Tiene Ud. hermanos? ¿Se lleva Ud. bien con ellos? Describa Ud. en detalle, con ejemplos, cómo se lleva con ellos y por qué.
30. ¿Cuáles son algunas de las ventajas y desventajas de tener hermanos?
31. ¿Le gustaría o no ser el único hijo o la única hija de la familia?
32. ¿Cree Ud. que hay una diferencia entre lo que se espera del primer nacido de la familia y del último?
33. ¿Hay mucha diferencia entre las personalidades de los hermanos de una familia? ¿Por qué?
34. ¿Cuáles son algunas de las razones por las cuales riñen los niños de una familia?
35. ¿Cuáles son las ventajas de tener muchos familiares? ¿las desventajas?

Sus padres

36. ¿Se lleva Ud. bien con sus padres? Describa en detalle, con ejemplos, cómo son sus relaciones con sus padres.
37. ¿A quién se parece Ud. en su familia? ¿A su papá o a su mamá? ¿Cómo? ¿En qué aspectos se parece Ud. a sus padres?
38. ¿Por qué es tan difícil establecer su propia identidad para los jóvenes? Explique con ejemplos de su propia vida.
39. ¿Cómo deben los padres castigar a los hijos que les desobedecen? Dé Ud. un ejemplo.
40. ¿Por qué es difícil a veces para los padres saber a quién creer y qué pensar de lo que les dicen sus hijos?
41. ¿Qué lecciones ha Ud. aprendido de sus padres?
42. ¿Qué responsabilidades deben los chicos tener en la casa? Explique Ud. usando su propia familia como un ejemplo.
43. ¿Qué contribución pueden los chicos hacer en una familia? Explique Ud. usando su propia familia como un ejemplo.

44. ¿Siempre les dice Ud. la verdad a sus padres? ¿Por qué, ya sea sí o no?
45. ¿Es difícil para Ud. a veces admitir culpabilidad de algo o piensa Ud. que siempre tiene razón?

Tradiciones familiares

46. ¿Qué tradiciones tiene su familia?
47. ¿Cómo celebran Uds. los cumpleaños de los miembros de la familia?
48. ¿Cuál es el cumpleaños más importante para Ud. y por qué?
49. ¿Cómo celebran Ud. y su familia los días feriados como el Día de la Independencia?
50. ¿Tiene Vd. parientes que viven cerca de o en la misma ciudad? ¿Le gustaría más si vivieran cerca o lejos? ¿Por qué?

Su futuro

51. ¿Dónde querrá vivir en el futuro? ¿Cerca de su familia o no? ¿Por qué?
52. Explique cómo podría cambiar sus relaciones con sus padres en el futuro.
53. ¿Querrá casarse algún día? ¿Por qué?
54. ¿Cómo será su esposo o esposa?
54. ¿Cómo espera Ud. desarrollar sus talentos o habilidades?
55. ¿Piensa que su personalidad cambiará o no? Explique.

II. La escuela

Vocabulario

SUSTANTIVOS

el aula	classroom	*la matrícula*	registration
el bachillerato	high school diploma	*la mayoría*	the majority
		el nivel	the level
la beca	scholarship	*las notas,*	
la carrera	career	*las calificaciones*	grades
la cifra	number	*el papel*	role
el comité	committee	*el pensamiento*	thought
la comprensión	comprehension	*el período*	period
la conferencia	lecture	*la presión*	pressure
el conocimiento	knowledge	*la primaria*	elementary school
el curso	course (of study)		
el derecho	right	*el privilegio*	privilege
la desventaja	disadvantage	*el procedimiento*	procedure
el director	principal	*la prueba*	test
la disciplina	discipline	*el puntaje*	score
la enseñanza	the teaching	*el requisito*	requirement
la especialización	major	*la sabiduría*	wisdom
el estrés	stress	*la secundaria*	high school
la facultad	faculty	*el sistema*	system
la habilidad	skill, talent	*la tarea*	work
el horario	schedule	*tiempo completo*	full time
la lectura	reading	*el título*	diploma
la licenciatura	university degree	*la ventaja*	advantage, benefit
la materia,	subject		
la asignatura			

VERBOS

aburrirse	to get bored	entrenarse	to train
acostumbrarse	to get used to	escoger	to choose
aprender	to learn	experimentar	to experience
aprobar	to pass	gozar de	to enjoy
aprovecharse	to take advantage of	graduarse	to graduate
		imponer	to impose
asistir a	to attend	influir	to influence
comportarse	to behave	ingresar	to enroll
conseguir	to get	intentar	to try, attempt
consistir en	to consist of	matricular	to register
dedicarse	to dedicate oneself	quejarse	to complain
		realizar	to fulfill
discutir	to discuss	repasar	to review
distraer	to distract	salir bien	to do well
educar	to educate	solicitar	to apply
enseñar	to teach, show	suspender,	to fail
entender	to understand	reprobar	

MODISMOS

dictar (una clase)	to give (a class) (una conferencia = a lecture)	presentarse a presentarse al examen	to apply for to take an exam
estar cansado	to be tired	prestar atención	to pay attention
estudiar mucho	to study hard	sacar (buenas)	to get (good)
ganarse la vida	to earn a living	notas	grades (malas
hacer una pregunta	to ask a question		notas = bad
interesarse por	to be interested in		grades)
		tener éxito	to be successful
llamar la atención	to call one's attention to	tomar apuntes	to take notes

ADJETIVOS

aburrido	boring	extracurricular	extracurricular
agotado	worn out	infatigable	untiring
alternativo	alternative	llamativo	eye-catching
analfabeto	illiterate	ocioso	lazy, slothful
anticuado	ancient, old	optativo	elective
antipático	mean	perezoso	lazy
aplicado, trabajador	hard working	predilecto	favorite
cotidiano	daily	satisfecho	satisfied
divertido	fun	simpático	nice
emocionante	exciting	social	social
estudiantil	student	torpe	dense
estupendo	great	tranquilo	quiet
exigente	demanding		

Los edificios

1. ¿Son nuevos o viejos los edificios de su escuela? Descríbalos.
2. ¿Es muy importante tener edificios muy modernos o no? ¿Por qué?
3. Dé Ud instrucciones para llegar a su casa de su escuela.
4. Dé Ud. instrucciones a sus padres para llegar al aula en que se reúne su primera clase del día.
5. Si uno se enferma en la escuela, ¿adónde se va para recibir atención?
6. Describa Ud. la cafetería de su escuela. ¿Es adecuada o no?
7. Frecuentemente se dice que la comida en las cafeterías de las escuelas no es buena. ¿Por qué no les gusta a muchos estudiantes comer en las cafeterías?
8. ¿Qué recomienda Ud. para mejorar la oferta de comida en la cafetería?
9. ¿Cómo es su escuela? ¿Grande? ¿Pequeña? ¿Cuántos estudiantes tiene, aproximadamente? ¿Cuántos profesores? Describa Ud. su escuela en detalle.
10. ¿Cuáles son algunas ventajas de las escuelas grandes? ¿Desventajas?
11. ¿Cuáles son las ventajas de escuelas pequeñas? ¿Desventajas?
12. ¿Qué tipo de ambiente tiene una escuela con edificios viejos?
13. Si fuera Ud. arquitecto encargado de diseñar un escuela nueva, ¿cómo mejoraría Ud. el planeamiento de los edificios?
14. Si Ud. entrara en una escuela con dibujos por todas las paredes y suelos sucios, ¿qué pensaría del lugar?

Las escuelas nuevas y las viejas

15. ¿Cómo son diferentes las escuelas modernas de las de sus padres?
16. ¿Cree Ud. que las escuelas modernas son mejores que las de sus padres?
17. ¿Qué necesitaban estudiar sus padres para conseguir trabajo después de la escuela?
18. ¿Cómo ha cambiado la materia que se enseña en la escuelas modernas?
19. ¿Cuál debe ser el papel de los padres en las escuelas superiores?
20. ¿Qué conflictos hay a veces en las escuelas entre los intereses de los padres y la comunidad?
21. Hay una tendencia en ciertas comunidades de permitir que las compañías privadas manejen los negocios de las escuelas públicas. ¿Qué opina Ud. de dejar a una compañía privada que maneje una escuela?

Tipos de escuelas

22. ¿Cree Ud. que es buena idea tener escuelas distintas para los muchachos y las muchachas? ¿Por qué?
23. ¿Cuáles son las diferencias entre las escuelas públicas y las privadas?
24. ¿Cuáles son las ventajas y desventajas de las escuelas públicas?
25. ¿Cree Ud. que es mejor tener mucha diversidad de estudiantes en una escuela o es mejor un grupo más homogéneo?
26. ¿Qué se puede hacer para asegurar la diversidad de estudiantes en su escuela?
27. Si pudiera escoger a cualquier escuela a que asistir, ¿a cuál escogería? ¿Por qué?

Las clases

28. ¿Cómo son sus clases? ¿Cuántos estudiantes hay en ellas?
29. ¿Por qué se aburren muchos estudiantes en sus clases?
30. ¿Goza Ud. de mucho éxito académico en sus estudios?
31. ¿Cuál es la clase más difícil para Ud.? ¿Por qué?
32. ¿Cuál es la clase más fácil?
33. ¿Por qué son más fáciles algunas clases que otras?
34. ¿Qué puede Ud. hacer para mejorar sus notas en la escuela?
35. ¿Tienen los estudiantes de su escuela que hacer muchas tareas por la noche?
36. ¿Cuánto tiempo deben los estudiantes dedicar a los estudios cada noche?
37. Describa Ud. la mejor manera de estudiar para un examen importante.
38. ¿Qué significan las notas que los estudiantes reciben en su escuela?
39. Si un estudiante está suspendiendo una clase, ¿cree Ud. que los padres deben poder exigirle enfocar más en los estudios y quitarle algunos privilegios?
40. Cree Ud. que se debe aprobar a los estudiantes que no sepan la materia en los cursos? ¿Por qué sí o no?
41. Si Ud. fuera director de una escuela y se le presentara un padre que quería que su hijo aprobara un curso sin haber hecho nada, ¿qué haría Ud.?
42. Si Ud. fuera profesor o profesora de una clase de matemáticas y un estudiante estuviese suspendiendo el curso, ¿qué le aconsejaría?
43. Comente Ud. sobre la presión para sacar buenas notas en su escuela.
44. ¿Por qué es más difícil aprender en algunas clases y no en otras?
45. ¿Qué les distrae más a los estudiantes en una clase?
46. ¿Cuáles son las ventajas de tener un código de vestimenta en la escuela?
47. ¿Por qué es importante aprender y saber leer aun cuando todo el mundo aprende tanto de las imágenes visuales ahora?
48. ¿Cree Ud. que las escuelas deben ofrecer cursos tratando problemas sociales, como el SIDA, el abuso de las drogas, etc.? Explique.
49. En muchas escuelas secundarias, menos muchachas que muchachos siguen estudios de matemáticas y ciencias. ¿Por qué?
50. ¿Cree Ud. que los muchachos reciben más atención del profesor o profesora que las muchachas? Explique por qué cree Ud. que sí o que no.
51. ¿Quiénes deben determinar los temas a estudiarse de las escuelas, los estudiantes, los padres, los profesores, o un comité comunal de educación? ¿Por qué?
52. ¿De qué se quejan más los estudiantes de su escuela?

Actividades extracurriculares

53. ¿En qué actividades extracurriculares participa Ud.?
54. ¿Son muy importantes los deportes en su escuela?
55. ¿Son demasiado importantes los deportes en su escuela? ¿Por qué piensa Ud. que sí o que no?
56. ¿Hay un programa de bellas artes en su escuela?
57. Describa Ud. la actividad extracurricular más importante de su escuela.
58. ¿Tiene su escuela muchos bailes? Descríbalos.
59. ¿Tienen un trabajo muchos de los estudiantes después de las clases?
60. ¿Qué se aprende en las actividades extracurriculares que no se aprende en las clases?

Escuela primaria

61. ¿Recuerda Ud. el día en que ingresó en la escuela primaria? Cuente lo que recuerda.
62. ¿Tiene Ud. buenas memorias del primer año de la escuela primaria? Descríbalo.
63. ¿Cómo fue la profesora del primer año?
64. ¿Quién era su mejor amigo de la escuela primaria?
65. ¿Cuál era su materia favorita en la escuela primaria? ¿Por qué?
66. ¿Cree Ud. que podría ser un maestro o maestra tan bueno como su maestra o maestro favorito?

La universidad

67. ¿Por qué quieren tantos estudiantes asistir a la universidad ahora?
68. ¿Cómo tiene que prepararse para poder matricularse en la universidad?
69. ¿Por qué es tan difícil conseguir una beca para la universidad para muchos estudiantes?
70. ¿Qué cualidades buscan las universidades en los solicitantes de becas?
71. ¿Por qué cree Ud. que la educación universitaria cuesta tanto hoy día?
72. ¿Cuál debe ser el papel de los deportes en la universidad?
73. ¿Qué es lo que le influiría más en la selección de una universidad?
74. ¿Cree Ud. que ha recibido buena preparación para los estudios universitarios? Explique.
75. Si pudiera escoger a cualquier universidad para matricularse, ¿cuál sería? ¿Por qué?
76. ¿Cree Ud. que la educación universitaria vale todo lo que cuesta hoy día? ¿Por qué?
77. ¿Defiende Ud. la libertad académica en las universidades? ¿Debe una persona tener el derecho de decir lo que se le antoje?

La tecnología y la educación

78. ¿Cuál ha sido el efecto de la tecnología en la educación?
79. ¿Cómo será la escuela del año 2010?
80. ¿Cuáles son algunas de las ventajas de usar computadoras en las aulas de las escuelas?
81. ¿Cree Ud. que se puede sustituir las computadoras por los profesores en las salas de clase? ¿Cómo?
82. ¿Cómo ha cambiado el propósito de las escuelas hoy día?
83. Describa Ud. su escuela ideal.
84. Si los estudiantes del futuro pudieran sentarse en casa y estudiar sus lecciones por medio de la tecnología moderna, con teléfono y televisión, ¿qué necesidad habría para las escuelas tal como las conocemos hoy?
85. Se dice que en el futuro no se necesitaría saber nada, sino tan sólo saber cómo y dónde buscar lo que se necesita. ¿Qué opina Ud.?
86. ¿Cuál ha sido el efecto de la televisión en la enseñanza y las maneras en que aprenden los chicos?

La facultad y administración

87. ¿Quién es su profesor predilecto? ¿Por qué?
88. Describa Ud. el mejor profesor o la mejor profesora de su carrera estudiantil.
89. ¿Qué características tienen los profesores buenos?

90. ¿Por qué hay más mujeres que enseñan que hombres?

91. ¿Le gustaría ser director de una escuela secundaria? Explique cómo podría ser buen director.

92. ¿Cuánto tiempo hace que Ud. se encontró con un profesor que no le gustó? ¿Qué hizo Ud. para resolver su problema?

93. Muchas veces en las escuelas grandes los directores parecen no enterarse bien de los asuntos cotidianos de la escuela. ¿Qué resultados tiene esta situación?

La enseñanza

94. Para poder gozar de mucho éxito en la vida ¿se necesita más una educación buena o la experiencia práctica? ¿Por qué?

95. ¿Por qué cree Ud. que la buena educación es importante?

96. ¿Cuál debe ser el propósito de las escuelas? ¿Deben tratar de enseñar valores?

97. ¿Cree Ud. que la libertad académica le da al estudiante o profesor el derecho de decir cualquier cosa?

98. ¿Se debe enseñar ideas y conceptos controvertibles en las escuelas?

99. Actualmente a muchas escuelas les faltan los fondos para desarrollar un programa adecuado y así preparar a sus estudiantes para el futuro. ¿Qué deberían esas escuelas poder hacer para mejorar sus programas y para atraer mejores profesores?

Los compañeros de clase

100. Describa Ud. a sus mejores amigos en la escuela.

101. ¿Cuál es la ventaja de tener amigos que no asisten a la misma escuela que Ud.?

102. ¿Asiste Ud. a muchas actividades de escuela con sus amigos? ¿Cuáles?

103. ¿Qué características determinan quiénes serán los estudiantes más populares en su escuela?

104. Describa Ud. el gobierno estudiantil en su escuela.

105. ¿Cree Ud. que es más importante ser inteligente o popular?

106. ¿Sería fácil o difícil acostumbrarse a las rutinas de su escuela para un nuevo estudiante? ¿Por qué?

107. Cuando por primera vez llega un nuevo estudiante a una nueva escuela, ¿qué le aconsejaría para hacer nuevas amistades?

108. ¿Cuál ha sido la experiencia más inolvidable que le haya sucedido en la escuela?

109. Ud. tiene la oportunidad de regresar a una reunión de graduados de su escuela secundaria. ¿A quién o qué le gustaría ver más? ¿Por qué?

La disciplina en las escuelas

110. ¿Por qué se rebelan tanto muchos estudiantes contra los dictámenes de la vieja generación?

111. ¿Hay problemas en su escuela con la disciplina? ¿Cómo sería posible mantener buena disciplina en la escuela sin violar los derechos personales de los estudiantes?

112. ¿Cómo se debe castigar a los estudiantes que desobedecen la autoridad de los profesores y a los directores de la escuela?

113. ¿Qué derechos deben los estudiantes tener en una escuela?

III. El ocio

SUSTANTIVOS

las amistades	friendships	*la función*	show
la atracción	attraction	*el lujo*	the luxury
la aventura	adventure	*el ocio*	leisure
la banda	band	*la orquesta*	orchestra
la ciencia ficción	science fiction	*el pasatiempo*	pastime
el cine	the movies	*la película*	a film
la competencia	contest, match	*la revista*	magazine
el concierto	concert	*la sinfonía*	symphony
la entrada	ticket	*el teatro*	theater
el entretenimiento	entertainment	*el video*	video
el espectáculo	show	*el videocasete*	videocassette
la estrella	star	*la videograbadora*	video camera

VERBOS

aplaudir	to clap, to applaud	*estrenar*	to show
		fatigarse	to wear out
descansar	to rest	*gozar de*	to enjoy
distraerse	to amuse oneself	*oír*	to hear
divertirse	to have a good time	*regocijar*	to delight
		reírse	to laugh
entretener	to entertain	*relajarse*	to relax
escuchar	to listen to	*tocar*	to play music

ADJETIVOS

aburrido	boring	*lento*	slow
atrevido	daring	*maravilloso*	marvelous
cómico	funny	*pavoroso*	frightening
diverso	diverse	*relajado*	relaxed
divertido	fun, amusing	*sorprendente*	surprising
emocionante	moving	*soso*	dull
estelar	stellar	*vivaz*	lively
juvenil	juvenile		

En general

1. ¿Qué hace Ud. para relajarse?
2. ¿Por qué es tan importante el ocio para mucha gente hoy?
3. ¿Qué tipo de entretenimiento le gusta más? ¿Por qué?
4. Si tuviera un día libre inesperado de la escuela, ¿qué haría Ud.?
5. ¿Cree Ud. que para divertirse es necesario gastar mucho dinero?
6. Describa Ud. una actividad que a Ud. le gusta hacer que no cuesta mucho dinero.
7. ¿Cuál ha sido la experiencia más divertida para Ud.?
8. ¿Cuál es la diferencia entre los entretenimientos de los niños pequeños y los adolescentes?
8. ¿Cómo era diferente el ocio para sus padres o abuelos? ¿Por qué?

9. ¿Cómo cambia la manera de divertirse a medida que crece un joven?
10. Para relajarse durante las vacaciones, ¿qué hace Ud.?
11. ¿Qué tipo de actividad le gusta hacer fuera de la casa?
12. ¿Cuáles son algunas de las actividades o deportes populares en la playa?
13. ¿Cuáles son algunas de las maneras de disfrutar de las vacaciones en las montañas?
14. ¿Cómo ha cambiado la tecnología la manera en que uno se divierte hoy en día?
15. Como resultado de los avances de la tecnología muchas de las actividades son actividades solitarias. ¿Qué se pierde con este tipo de actividad? ¿Es bueno o malo?
16. Los pasatiempos solitarios resultan en cierto ensimismamiento de la persona que participa en ellos. ¿Es buena o mala esta tendencia a la soledad?
17. ¿Cuál sería la actividad más divertida que Ud. podría imaginar?
18. Si sus padres no estuvieran en casa, ¿sería buena idea tener una fiesta sin que estuvieran ellos? ¿Por qué?
19. Muchos muchachos pasan mucho tiempo hablando por teléfono para relajarse. ¿Qué discuten?
20. ¿Cree Ud. que hay una diferencia entre lo que discuten las muchachas de lo que discuten los muchachos? ¿Cuál?

Las lecturas

21. ¿Prefiere Ud. leer periódicos o revistas o mirar programas de televisión para entretenerse?
22. ¿Lee Ud. revistas de vez en cuando? ¿Qué tipo lee?
23. ¿Cree Ud. que si las revistas fueran emitidas por medios electrónicos, más gente las leería?
24. ¿Hay un protocolo que determina quién llama a quién cuando un muchacho quiere salir con una muchacha? ¿Debe una muchacha llamar a un muchacho?
25. ¿Cómo han cambiado las normas sociales para los jóvenes de hoy?
26. ¿Cuánto tiempo pasa Ud. hablando por teléfono con sus amigos?
27. Cuando una pareja sale para cenar en un restaurante elegante, ¿quién debe pagar la cuenta?

La música

28. Hay muchos tipos de conciertos: conciertos de cantantes, de grupos de rock, de orquestas filarmónicas. ¿Qué tipo le gusta? Explique.
29. ¿Qué valor tienen las lecciones de música para los jóvenes? ¿Cómo puede ser pasatiempo la música?
30. ¿Cuáles son algunos de los instrumentos de una orquesta sinfónica?
31. Describa Ud. la diferencia entre la música clásica y la música popular, de rock u otro tipo.

Las películas

32. ¿Cree Ud. que se debe tener censura de películas para los jóvenes?
33. ¿Cuál fue la película más emocionante que Ud. haya visto? Descríbala.

34. Se dice que a los jóvenes les gustan las películas de acción, aventura, o ciencia ficción más que otro tipo. ¿Cree Ud. que hay una diferencia entre el tipo de película que atrae a los varones y el que atrae a las muchachas? Explique.

35. ¿Quiénes son sus actores y actrices favoritos? ¿En qué películas se destacaron?

36. ¿Qué tipo de película prefiere Ud.? ¿Por qué?

37. Si Ud. fuera director de películas, ¿a qué actor o actriz le gustaría contratar?

38. ¿Qué tipo de película le gustaría rodar si pudiera hacer cualquier tipo? ¿Por qué?

39. ¿Lee Ud. muchas revistas o mira muchos programas que enfocan en las vidas de las estrellas del cine?

40. ¿Por qué les atraen tanto a tantas personas todos los detalles de las vidas privadas de las estrellas?

41. ¿Por qué cree Ud. que las estrellas de la pantalla son tan admiradas por las jóvenes?

42. ¿Cree Ud. que los actores y las actrices son admirados por las mismas razones? Comente por qué.

43. ¿Cómo son diferentes las películas modernas de las de hace treinta o cuarenta años atrás?

44. Si fuera actor o actriz, ¿habrá unos tipos de escenas que no haría? ¿Cuáles y por qué?

Televisión

45. Se dice que muchos programas noticieros se parecen más a programas de entretenimiento que de noticias. ¿Está Ud. de acuerdo o no? ¿Por qué?

46. ¿Qué revelan los programas de televisión de los valores de la sociedad?

47. Muchos critican que hoy hay menos diferencia entre la realidad y la fantasía en la televisión. ¿Qué opina Ud.? ¿Por qué?

48. Al mirar programas de otras culturas se nota que hay una diferencia entre el contenido y el estilo de presentar la materia visualmente. ¿Por qué?

49. ¿Qué pasará al cine como negocio cuando se pueda mirar todas las películas en la televisión en su propia casa?

50. ¿Por qué son tan divertidos los vídeos para los jóvenes hoy?

51. ¿Qué atracción tienen los programas de MTV?

52. ¿Qué se aprende mirando la televisión?

53. ¿Qué tipos de habilidades se desarrollan mirando la televisión?

54. ¿Cree Ud. que es posible utilizar la televisión mejor para educar a la población? ¿Cómo?

55. Se dice que el tipo de programa que ve un joven influye mucho sobre su personalidad. ¿Está Ud. de acuerdo o no? ¿Por qué?

56. Muchos jóvenes no miran mucho la televisión hoy en día. ¿Qué hacen en vez de mirarla?

57. ¿Cuál es la diferencia entre ver la televisión y pasar horas en la red, mirando la pantalla de su computadora?

IV. Las amistades

SUSTANTIVOS

la amistad	friendship	*la confianza*	trust

VERBOS

aconsejar	to advise	*desear*	to desire, to wish
aguantar	to tolerate	*envidiar*	to envy
apoyar	to support	*extrañar*	to miss
codiciar	to covet	*llevarse (bien)*	to get along with
comportarse	to behave	*mentir*	to lie
confiar, contar con	to trust, count on	*odiar*	to hate
crecer	to grow	*preocuparse*	to worry
cuidarse de	to take care of		

MODISMOS

contar con	to count on	*tener celos*	to be jealous
echar de menos	to miss		

ADJETIVOS

afectuoso	affectionate	*manso*	gentle
bello	beautiful	*mayor*	older
cariñoso	caring	*mejor*	best
codicioso	jealous	*menor*	younger
comprensivo	understanding	*mezquino*	mean
confiable	trustworthy	*mutuo*	mutual
egoísta	self-centered	*peor*	worst
feo	ugly	*sensato*	reasonable
fiel	loyal	*simpático*	nice
íntimo	intimate, close	*sincero*	sincere
lisonjero	flattering	*vivaz*	vivacious

Sus amigos

1. Describa Ud. a su mejor amigo. ¿Cómo es?
2. ¿Qué características se destacan en un amigo bueno?
3. ¿Cree Ud. que a menudo se buscan características diferentes en las amigas que en los amigos? ¿Por qué?
4. Cuándo Ud. y su mejor amigo no están de acuerdo, ¿cómo resuelven sus problemas?
5. ¿Cuál sería la única cosa que haría su mejor amigo que Ud. no perdonaría?
6. Si pensara Ud. que su mejor amigo le mintió, ¿cómo reaccionaría?
7. Si su mejor amigo le pidiera revelar un secreto que otra persona le había dicho, ¿se lo revelaría? ¿Por qué?
8. Si su mejor amigo le pide hacer algo que no quiere hacer, ¿qué hará?
9. ¿Dónde se reúne con sus amigos? ¿Por qué han Uds. escogido ese lugar?
10. ¿Le gusta a Ud. que vengan sus amigos a su casa, o prefiere Ud. visitarlos en sus casas? ¿Por qué?
11. ¿Cómo se puede mantener la amistad con alguien si a los padres de Ud. él o ella no les gusta?

Las amistades

12. ¿Cuáles son los beneficios de tener muchos amigos?
13. ¿Es necesario tener muchos amigos para estar contento?
14. ¿Cuánto influye la ropa en las primeras impresiones?
15. ¿Por qué tienen algunas personas celos de sus amigos?
16. ¿Cómo trata Ud. a una persona a quién no puede aguantar?
17. Muchas veces entre los adolescentes hay una tendencia de buscar amistades sólo de entre los contemporáneos. ¿Qué ventajas hay de tener amigos de otras generaciones y de otras escuelas?
18. Muchas veces se ve que las personas que son buenos amigos cuando son jóvenes no lo son al llegar a su adolescencia. ¿Por qué cree Ud. que es normal cambiar los amigos al entrar en una nueva etapa de la vida?
19. Si Ud. fuera consejero o consejera de adolescentes, ¿qué consejos le daría a un joven que no tiene muchos amigos para que pueda encontrar a algún amigo nuevo?
20. ¿Cómo se puede mantener una amistad a larga distancia?

V. El trabajo

SUSTANTIVOS

la carrera	career	*la huelga*	strike
el comerciante	businessman	*el jefe*	boss
el dueño,		*el juez*	judge
el propietario	owner	*el líder*	leader
el empleo,		*la manifestación*	demonstration
el trabajo	work	*el negocio*	business
la entrevista	interview	*el obrero*	worker
la fábrica	factory	*el sindicato*	union
la ficha	token	*la solicitud*	application
el formulario	form	*el sueldo*	pay
el gerente	manager	*el taller*	shop

Profesiones y Vocaciones

el abogado	lawyer	*el ingeniero*	engineer
el alcalde	mayor	*el marinero*	sailor
el atleta	athlete	*el mecánico*	mechanic
el basurero	garbageman	*el médico, doctor*	doctor
el bombero	firefighter	*el ministro*	minister
el campesino	farmer	*la niñera*	baby sitter
el carnicero	butcher	*el obrero*	worker
el carpintero	carpenter	*el panadero*	baker
el comerciante	merchant	*el párroco*	priest
el concejal	council member	*el periodista*	newspaperman
la criada	maid	*el piloto*	pilot
el director	director	*el plomero*	plumber
la enfermera	nurse	*el policía*	policeman
el fotógrafo	photographer	*el redactor*	editor
el funcionario	civil servant	*el reportero*	reporter

el sacerdote	priest	*el soldado*	soldier
la secretaria	secretary	*el trapero*	rag picker

VERBOS

aprovecharse	to take advantage of	*llenar*	to fill
		lograr	to achieve
avanzar	to advance	*negociar*	to negotiate
conseguir	to get	*obtener*	to obtain
contratar	to hire	*rechazar*	to reject
despedir	to fire	*rellenar*	to fill out
entrevistar	to interview	*trabajar*	to work

MODISMOS

ganarse la vida   earn a living

Para conseguir un trabajo

1. ¿Cómo puede una agencia de trabajos ayudar en la búsqueda de empleo?
2. ¿Dónde se puede encontrar noticias de puestos vacantes?
3. ¿Qué tipo de datos se preguntan en formularios de solicitud?
4. ¿Ha sido Ud. entrevistado alguna vez para una posición? Describa Ud. la experiencia.
5. ¿Tiene Ud. un trabajo después de las clases? Si lo tiene, descríbalo.
6. ¿Es difícil para los jóvenes conseguir trabajo? ¿Por qué?
7. ¿Qué se necesita saber para poder avanzar en el empleo?
8. ¿Cómo influye un empleo después de las clases sobre los estudios en la escuela?

Trabajos para el futuro

9. ¿Cree Ud. que una educación debe solamente prepararle para conseguir un empleo después de graduarse?
10. ¿Cuán diferentes serán los trabajos del futuro de los de hoy?
11. ¿Cree Ud. que será posible hacer todo el trabajo en computadoras en la casa en el futuro?

La entrevista

12. ¿Qué sería lo más difícil de pedir al solicitarse una posición con una compañía?
13. En una entrevista para un empleo, ¿cómo se puede preparar para tener éxito?
14. En una entrevista ¿cómo respondería si se le preguntara algo sobre un tema que por razones religiosas o personales Ud. no puede responder?
15. ¿Cómo se debe vestirse para entrevistarse?
16. Si fuera Ud. director de una empresa, ¿contrataría Ud. a una persona que no se presentara bien?

Las carreras

17. ¿Qué quería Ud. ser cuando era pequeño? ¿Por qué?
18. ¿Por qué les impresionan tanto a los niños pequeños los oficios de bombero, policía o cartero?
19. ¿Cuál es la diferencia entre una carrera y un empleo cualquiera?

20. ¿Qué carrera quiere Ud. seguir? ¿Por qué?
21. ¿Cuál debe ser la base para escoger una carrera?
22. ¿Qué carreras serán más necesarias en el futuro?
23. Si el único empleo posible fuera con una compañía el responsable de gran abuso del medio ambiente, ¿trabajaría para ella?
24. ¿Cómo se diferencian los trabajos actuales de los de hace cincuenta años?
25. ¿Cuáles son las responsabilidades de una empresa para con sus empleados? ¿Viceversa?
26. ¿Qué papel tienen los sindicatos en las industrias modernas?
27. Si trabajara con una compañía cuyos empleados se declararon en huelga, ¿les daría su apoyo o no? ¿Por qué?
28. ¿Cómo sería su jefe o gerente idóneo?
29. Si Ud. estuviera encargado de la supervisión de una oficina, ¿qué tipo de jefe sería? ¿Sería comprensivo? ¿Sería exigente?
30. Si tuviera un empleado que no hacía el trabajo bien, ¿qué haría Ud. para resolver el problema?
31. Si Ud. fuera el gerente de una empresa, ¿cómo sería su empleado ideal?
32. ¿Hay algún tipo de trabajo que rechazaría si necesitara trabajo? ¿Cuál? ¿Por qué?
33. ¿Debe el gobierno garantizar empleo para todos? Comente Ud.

VI. La Salud

SUSTANTIVOS

el aliento	breath	*la fiebre*	fever
el antibiótico	antibiotics	*la frente*	forehead
la aspirina	aspirin	*la garganta*	throat
el bigote	beard	*los hombros*	shoulders
la boca	mouth	*el hospital*	hospital
el brazo	arm	*la inyección*	injection, shot
el cabello	hair (head)	*la lengua*	tongue
la cabeza	head	*la mano*	hand
las caderas	hips	*la medicina*	medicine
el cáncer	cancer	*el médico, el doctor*	doctor
la cara, el rostro	face	*la mejilla*	cheek
el catarro	cold	*la muñeca*	wrist
las cejas	eyebrows	*las nalgas*	hips
el cinturón	waist	*la nariz*	nose
la columna vertebral	spine	*los oídos*	ears (inner)
el cuello	neck	*los ojos*	eyes
el cuerpo	body	*las orejas*	ears
la cura	cure	*los párpados*	eyelashes
el curandero	healer	*las pastillas,*	pills
los dedos	fingers, toes	*las píldoras*	pills
los dientes	teeth	*el pecho*	chest, breast
el dolor	pain	*el pie*	foot
la enfermedad	illness	*la pierna*	leg
la espalda	back	*el pelo*	hair (body)

la receta	prescription	*el talón*	heel
el régimen, la dieta	diet	*la temperatura*	temperature
el remedio	remedy	*el tobillo*	ankle
el resfriado	cold	*el torso*	torso
la rodilla	knees	*el yeso*	plaster cast
la salud	health		

VERBOS

atender	to attend	*mantenerse*	to keep in
auscultar	to listen to (heart)	*mejorarse*	to get better
bostezar	to yawn	*morir*	to die
cuidar	to care for	*operar*	to operate
doler	to ache, hurt	*padecer*	to suffer
ejercer	to exercise	*ponerse*	to become
empeorar	to get worse	*recuperar*	to recuperate
enfermarse	to get sick	*respirar*	to breathe
estornudar	to sneeze	*romper*	to break
fallecer	to die	*sentirse*	to feel
fracturar	to break	*sufrir*	to suffer
lastimarse	to get hurt	*toser*	to cough

ADJETIVOS

consciente	conscious	*peligroso*	dangerous
eficaz	effective	*roto*	broken
grave	serious	*sano*	healthy
manso	gentle		

MODISMOS

guardar cama	to stay in bed

La buena salud

1. ¿Cómo se mantiene de buena salud?
2. ¿Se preocupan mucho los jóvenes hoy de la salud o no? Explique.
3. ¿Es buena idea hacer ejercicio para mantener la buena salud? ¿Por qué? ¿Qué tipo de ejercicios es mejor? ¿Qué le recomendaría a un amigo que haga para mantenerse en buena salud?
4. Se ha dicho que muchos jóvenes no se ejercitan bastante. ¿Qué condiciones o situaciones contribuyen a la falta de ejercicio entre los adolescentes?
5. Si tuviera una invitación para participar en un juego deportivo o pasar dos horas en una actividad pasiva, como leer un libro, mirar la televisión o hablar en el teléfono, ¿cuál haría? ¿Por que?
6. ¿Quiénes se preocupan más de su salud?
7. ¿Qué peligros hay para las muchachas que quieren parecerse a modelos de moda que se ven en revistas para las jóvenes de hoy?
8. ¿Qué se debe enseñar de la salud en los cursos de salud en las escuelas?
9. ¿Dónde se aprende lo que se necesita saber para mantenerse de buena salud?

10. ¿En qué consiste una comida saludable?
11. ¿Cuáles son las influencias de la dieta en la salud?
12. ¿Por qué es muy difícil cambiar los gustos de los jóvenes en cuanto a la comida?
13. ¿Por qué les gusta a tantos jóvenes comer mucho azúcar?
14. ¿Por qué no es bueno comer mucho azúcar?
15. ¿Por qué no comen bien muchos jóvenes?
16. ¿Cuáles con algunos de los cambios que se ven en las costumbres de las familias en cuanto a las comidas?
17. ¿Cree Ud. que la comida que se compra en los supermercados es saludable? Explique.
18. ¿Hay prácticas poco higiénicas en la producción de comida? Comente.
19. ¿Es buena la comida que tienen en la cafetería de su escuela? ¿Por qué sí o no?
20. ¿Le gusta probar platos nuevos? ¿Cómo reacciona, Ud. a la comida exótica?
21. ¿En qué restaurante le gusta comer más? ¿Por qué?
22. ¿Qué tipo de comida no le gusta a Ud.? ¿Por qué?
23. ¿Cree Ud. que los padres deben obligar a los niños a comer comida que no les gusta, como zanahorias?
24. ¿Le gusta cocinar? ¿Qué platos son sus especialidades?
25. ¿Quién debe tener la responsabilidad de comprar y preparar la comida en una casa? ¿Por qué?
26. ¿Cuánta relación hay entre la salud y la personalidad de una persona?
27. ¿Cuánto influyen las actitudes hacia la vida en la salud? ¿Por qué? ¿Puede dar un ejemplo?
28. ¿Qué relación hay entre la salud física y mental?

Las enfermedades
29. Cuando Ud. no se siente bien, ¿qué hace?
30. Cuando Ud. tiene un catarro, ¿qué puede hacer para curarlo?
31. ¿Qué le gusta o no le gusta de esperar en el consultorio del médico?
32. ¿Es el médico que tiene Ud. ahora el mismo que tenía cuando era niño o niña?
33. ¿Le gustaba visitar al médico cuando era niño o niña? ¿Por qué?
34. ¿Cuándo visitó Ud. al médico la última vez? ¿Por qué? Describa Ud. la visita.
35. ¿Por qué es buena idea hacer caso de lo que le dice un médico cuando no se siente bien?
36. ¿Por qué cuesta tanto hoy día recibir buena atención médica?

En el hospital
37. ¿Una vez tuvo que ir al hospital? ¿Por qué?
38. ¿Cómo son las enfermeras en el hospital?
39. Si se le rompiera la pierna, ¿qué haría?
40. ¿Le gusta visitar a los amigos cuando están en el hospital? ¿Por qué?
41. ¿Qué le llevaría Ud. a un amigo en el hospital para animarlo?

VII. La casa

SUSTANTIVOS

la acera	sidewalk	la hierba	grass
la alcoba	bedroom	la madera	wood
la arquitectura	architecture	la mecedora	rocking chair
el azulejo	tile	los muebles	furniture
el baño	bathroom	la pared	wall
el barrio	neighborhood	el patio	patio
la buhardilla	attic	la reja	grating
la butaca	easy chair	la sala	living room
la casa	house	el sótano	basement
el cemento	cement	el suelo	floor
el césped	lawn	el techo	roof
la choza	hut	la vecindad	area
la cocina	kitchen	el vecindario	neighborhood
el despacho	office	el vecino	neighbor
el desván	attic	la ventana	window
el diván	sofa	la verja	grill
el domicilio	residence	el vestíbulo	foyer
el dormitorio	bedroom	el vidrio	glass (window)
el edificio	building	la vivienda	housing
el estante	bookcase	el zaguán	entry

VERBOS

construir	to construct	hervir	to boil
destruir	to destroy	lavar	to wash
fregar	to scrub	limpiar	to clean
freír	to fry	regar	to water

ADJETIVOS

arquitectónico	architectural	impresionante	impressive
elegante	elegant		

Su casa

1. ¿De qué estilo es la arquitectura de su casa?
2. ¿Cuál es su habitación favorita en casa? ¿Por qué?
3. ¿Cuánto tiempo hace que vive Ud. en su casa? ¿Cómo ha cambiado la casa durante ese tiempo?
4. ¿Comparte Ud. un dormitorio con un hermano o hermana? ¿Qué problemas habría entre hermanos que comparten un dormitorio?
5. ¿Tiene su casa un sótano? Descríbalo.
6. ¿Tiene su casa una buhardilla? ¿Qué hay en la buhardilla?
7. Cuándo era niño, ¿dónde jugaba más en su casa?
8. Cuando Ud. era niño, ¿había algunas habitaciones prohibidas? ¿Por qué?
9. A muchos adolescentes no les gusta pasar mucho tiempo en casa. ¿Dónde pasaría Ud. el tiempo en vez de su casa?

10. ¿Le gusta a Ud. el barrio en que vive? ¿Por qué? Si quisiera vivir en otro barrio, ¿dónde le gustaría vivir?
11. Si pudiera cambiar algún aspecto de su casa, ¿cuál sería?
12. ¿Cómo sería su casa ideal? Descríbala en detalle.

La vivienda

13. ¿Por qué necesitan unas personas una casa de un solo piso?
14. Describa Ud. cómo ha adornado las paredes de su casa.
15. En su barrio o vecindario, ¿son iguales arquitectónicamente todas las casas, o son diferentes? ¿Cómo?
16. ¿Cómo son semejantes o diferentes las casas de su barrio?
17. ¿Cuáles son las ventajas de una casa en la ciudad en vez del campo?
18. ¿Cuáles son algunas de las desventajas de vivir en la ciudad? ¿Cuáles son las ventajas de vivir en el campo?
19. ¿Cuáles son las desventajas de vivir en el campo?
20. ¿Qué problemas hay con ser dueño de su propia casa?
21. ¿Por qué cuesta mucho mantener una casa?
22. ¿Cuáles son algunas de las ventajas de alquilar una casa en vez de ser propietario?

La arquitectura

23. ¿Qué revelan las preferencias artísticas y la arquitectura en cuanto a la personalidad de una familia?
24. ¿Cómo influyen los colores de las paredes en las actitudes o las emociones de los habitantes de la casa?
25. ¿Por qué hay tanta diferencia entre la arquitectura de las casas de varias regiones del país?
26. ¿Cómo son diferentes los estilos arquitectónicos de las casas en otros países?
27. ¿Qué determina el material de que se construye una casa?
28. ¿Cuáles son algunos de los mejoramientos de las casas modernas?
29. Si Ud. fuera arquitecto, ¿en qué parte de la casa pondría Ud. el garaje? ¿En frente? ¿Detrás? ¿Al lado? ¿Por qué?
30. ¿Qué tipos de aparatos se necesitan en una cocina para preparar la comida?
31. En muchas casas la cocina es la habitación más usada por la familia. ¿Por qué?
32. ¿Cómo se diferencian las cocinas de las casas modernas de las viejas?
33. ¿Cómo se diferencian las casas viejas de las casas modernas? ¿Qué cuarto ha cambiado más?
34. ¿Para qué sirve un garaje además de guardar un coche o varios coches?
35. ¿Cómo se diferencian las casas de vacaciones de las casas en que se vive todo el año?

Responsabilidades caseras

36. ¿Cuáles son algunos de los aparatos que se usan para limpiar en la casa?
37. ¿De dónde vendrá todo el polvo en una casa?
38. ¿Por qué se debe limpiar la casa frecuentemente?
39. Si Ud. tuviera una persona para limpiar la casa, ¿cómo le explicaría el uso de la aspiradora o el lavaplatos?

40. ¿Tiene Ud. que cortar la hierba? ¿Deben los padres pagar a los jóvenes que hacen tal tipo de trabajo para la familia?
41. ¿Qué problemas presenta una casa en un lugar con mucha hierba y césped?
42. ¿Deben los padres pagar a sus hijos por ayudar con las tareas domésticas?
43. ¿Qué responsabilidades deben tener los chicos en casa? ¿Por qué?

VIII. Las relaciones

SUSTANTIVOS

el parentesco	lineage	*el vínculo*	tie
los parientes	relatives		

VERBOS

aguantar	to tolerate	*envidiar*	to envy
aislar	to isolate	*influir*	to influence
amparar	to help	*mantener*	to maintain
apoyar	to support	*ofender*	to offend
atrever	to dare	*querer*	to love, to wish
confiar	to confide	*reaccionar*	to react
confiar en	to trust	*relacionar*	to relate
enajenar	to alienate	*socorrer*	to help

ADJETIVOS

amistoso	friendly	*cariñoso*	loving

MODISMOS

contar con	to count on	*estrechar las relaciones*	to become closer

Relaciones entre miembros de la familia

1. ¿En quién puede Ud. confiar más, un miembro de su familia o un amigo?
2. ¿Cómo se diferencian las relaciones entre amigos y miembros de una familia?
3. ¿Qué les aconsejaría a unos hermanos que se riñen todo el tiempo?
4. ¿Por qué hay adolescentes aislados de sus padres?
5. ¿Por qué tienen algunos adolescentes problemas de comunicación con sus padres?
6. ¿Cómo cambia la relación con los padres si falta el padre o la madre en la familia?
7. Actualmente muchas familias son más pequeñas que antes. ¿Cómo han cambiado las relaciones familiares entre las familias más pequeñas?
8. ¿Por qué es difícil mantener las buenas relaciones con parientes que viven lejos?
9. ¿Cree Ud. que es natural que las relaciones con algunos parientes son mejores que con otros? ¿Por qué?
10. ¿Cómo se pueden estrechar las relaciones entre su familia y sus parientes que viven lejos?

Relaciones entre amigos

11. Describa el comportamiento apropiado para mostrar respeto a un amigo.
12. ¿Cree Ud. que es fácil o difícil hacerse amigo de una persona muy diferente que Ud.? ¿Por qué?
13. ¿Cree Ud. que es inevitable que algunas personas no puedan portarse bien con otras? ¿Por qué?

Relaciones entre miembros de una comunidad

14. ¿Dónde aprende uno a relacionarse bien con otras personas?
15. ¿Por qué hay tantos problemas en las escuelas entre los distintos grupos étnicos?
16. ¿Qué recomendaría Ud. para mejorar las relaciones entre las razas en las escuelas secundarias de este país?
17. Ud. quiere ser elegido presidente de los estudiantes de su escuela y tiene que dirigirles la palabra en una asamblea. ¿Qué les sugeriría a los estudiantes que hicieran para mejorar las relaciones entre los estudiantes de su escuela?
18. Muchas personas dicen que el énfasis en clubes exclusivos para grupos étnicos subraya las diferencias entre ellos en vez de estimular la cooperación mutua. ¿Qué opina Ud.? ¿Está Ud. de acuerdo? Explique.
19. ¿Cree Ud. que es posible llevarse bien con todo el mundo o no? ¿Por qué?

IX. La ropa

SUSTANTIVOS

la blusa	blouse	*la moda*	fashion
el bolsillo	pocket	*los pantalones*	pants
la bufanda	scarf	*los pantalones cortos*	shorts
los calcetines	socks	*el pañuelo*	handkerchief
la camisa	shirt	*el rebozo*	shawl
la camiseta, el jersey	t-shirt	*la ropa*	clothes
la chaqueta	jacket	*el saco*	blazer
el cinturón	belt	*el sombrero*	hat
el estilo	style	*el traje*	suit, dress
la falda	skirt	*el vestido*	suit
la gorra	cap	*los zapatos*	shoes
la manga	sleeve		

VERBOS

probarse	to try on	*vestirse*	to dress

MODISMOS

estar de moda	to be in style	*ir de compras*	to go shopping

Lo que lleva usted

1. ¿Qué tipo de ropa lleva en sus momentos de ocio?
2. ¿Qué tipo de ropa es apropiado para asistir a una ocasión formal? Descríbala Ud.
3. ¿Qué tipo de ropa llevaría para unas vacaciones en la playa? ¿En las montañas y esquiando?
4. Describa Ud. la ropa que lleva a la escuela durante el año escolar.
5. ¿Cree Ud. que los chicos deben usar uniformes en la escuela o no? ¿Por qué?
6. ¿Cuáles son algunas de las ventajas de tener un uniforme para la escuela?
7. ¿Qué llevaría Ud. a la escuela si pudiera llevar cualquier ropa que quisiese?
8. ¿Quién decide qué ropa debe comprar Ud. para la escuela? ¿Por qué?
9. ¿Por qué le gusta o no ir a comprar la ropa con su mamá?
10. ¿Quién debe lavar y planchar su ropa? ¿Por qué?
11. ¿Cómo debe procederse con ropa que ha dejado de usarse?
12. Cuando Ud. crece un poco, y la ropa ya no le cabe bien, ¿qué hace con ella?
12. ¿Le gusta a Ud. llevar colores vivos o no? ¿Por qué?
14. ¿Está muy de moda la ropa que lleva Ud.?

El estilo y la moda

15. ¿Cuál es la diferencia entre el estilo y la moda en cuanto a la ropa?
16. ¿Por qué cree Ud. que se cambian los estilos tanto?
17. ¿Cuál es la relación entre las estaciones y la ropa que se lleva en ellas? Descríbala.
18. Describa Ud. la diferencia entre la ropa que llevaban sus padres cuando eran jóvenes y la que Ud. lleva actualmente.
19. Se dice que es más aceptable vestirse de manera casual actualmente que hace diez o quince años. ¿Cree Ud. que sea así? ¿Por qué?
20. ¿Cree Ud. que la ropa que cuesta más es mejor que la que cuesta menos? ¿Por qué?
21. ¿Cree Ud. que se debe juzgar a otros en base de la ropa que llevan?
22. ¿Qué revela la ropa de la personalidad de la persona que la lleva?
23. ¿Qué se observa del vestido típico de los hombres de negocios? Describa Ud. la ropa de un hombre de negocios.
24. Se dice que las chicas se preocupan más de la ropa que los chicos. ¿Qué opina Ud.? Dé ejemplos para apoyar su opinión.
25. Si una amiga llevara un vestido que no le cae bien, ¿se lo diría o no? ¿Por qué?

X. La comunidad

SUSTANTIVOS

el aeropuerto	airport	*el estadio*	stadium
el alcalde	mayor	*el ferrocarril*	railroad
la aldea	village	*el gobierno*	government
el almacén	store, grocery store	*la iglesia*	church
		la manzana	city block
el apartado postal	P. O. box	*la cuadra*	block
el autopista	highway	*el mercado*	market
el ayuntamiento	town council	*la parada*	bus stop
el banco	bench, bank	*el parque*	park
el buzón	mailbox	*la plaza*	plaza (public
la caja	box		square)
la calle	street	*el pueblo*	town, people
la carretera	highway	*el restaurante*	restaurant
la casa de correo	post office	*el supermercado*	supermarket
el centro	downtown	*el taller*	shop
la elección	election	*la tienda*	store
la escuela	school	*el vecindario,*	
la estación	station	*el barrio*	neighborhood

VERBOS

gobernar	to govern	*votar*	vote
ubicar	to situate, to locate		

Su comunidad

1. ¿Le gusta el lugar donde vive o no? ¿Por qué?
2. ¿Cómo es la ciudad en que vive Ud.? Descríbala.
3. ¿Cuánto tiempo le cuesta ir al almacén más cercano de su casa?
4. ¿Cuál es el parque más bonito de su comunidad?
5. ¿Viene el correo a su casa o tiene un apartado postal?
6. ¿Hay muchos restaurantes elegantes en su pueblo? Describa Ud. el más elegante.
7. ¿Hay muchas iglesias en su comunidad?
8. ¿Es grande el centro en su pueblo o ciudad?
9. ¿Hay una estación del ferrocarril o un aeropuerto en su comunidad? ¿Es grande o pequeño? Descríbalo.
10. ¿Qué tipos de transporte urbano tiene su comunidad? ¿Autobuses? ¿Trenes? ¿Un metro? ¿Cuáles son las ventajas de usarlos?
11. ¿Qué parte de la comunidad es su favorita? ¿Por qué?
12. ¿Tiene su comunidad muchas actividades para los jóvenes durante los veranos? ¿Cuáles son?
13. Generalmente, ¿dónde se reúnen los jóvenes en su comunidad?
14. ¿Dónde está el cine en su comunidad, en el centro o los suburbios?
15. ¿Hay algunas tradiciones especiales en su comunidad? Descríbalas Ud.
16. ¿Qué aspecto de la vida en su comunidad le gusta más?
17. ¿Hay mucha diversidad en su comunidad? ¿Es bueno tener mucha diversidad? ¿Por qué?

18. ¿Es el clima un aspecto de su comunidad que le gusta o no? ¿Por qué?

19. Si Ud. pudiera vivir en otro lugar, ¿dónde querría vivir? ¿Por qué?

20. ¿Qué le molesta más de la vida en su comunidad?

21. ¿Qué problemas hay en su comunidad? ¿Hay lugares deshabitados? ¿Hay mucho desempleo? ¿Hay muchos problemas con contaminación del aire y agua? ¿Hay mucho tráfico?

22. ¿A qué se deben estos problemas?

23. ¿Hay fábricas en su comunidad?

24. ¿Qué efecto tienen las fábricas sobre el medio ambiente de la comunidad?

25. Si una familia se mudara a su comunidad, ¿en qué barrio le recomendaría establecerse? ¿Por qué?

26. Describa el alojamiento que recomendaría a unos turistas llegados a la comunidad y por qué se los recomendaría.

27. Describa Ud. las atracciones más interesantes en su comunidad para algunos visitantes.

28. Describa Ud. las festividades del último día feriado que celebró su comunidad.

29. Cuente Ud. un acontecimiento de la historia de su comunidad que le interesaría a un visitante.

30. Si Ud. saliera de su comunidad y volviera después de cincuenta años, ¿piensa Ud. que habría cambiado? ¿Cómo?

El gobierno local

31. ¿Quién es el alcalde de su comunidad?

32. ¿Es buen alcalde o no? ¿Por qué?

33. ¿Quién es la persona más importante en su comunidad? ¿Por qué es la más importante?

34. ¿Tiene su comunidad un ayuntamiento? ¿Son elegidos los concejales?

35. ¿Qué les recomendaría a los oficiales de su comunidad para mejorar la vida allí?

36. ¿Qué cambiaría de su comunidad, si pudiera?

37. ¿Qué ventajas tienen las ciudades grandes? ¿Qué desventajas?

38. ¿Por qué les gusta a muchas personas vivir en pueblos pequeños?

39. ¿Qué diferencias hay entre las ciudades de las diferentes regiones de los Estados Unidos?

40. Describa Ud. una ciudad grande.

41. ¿Por qué le gustaría o no vivir en una ciudad grande?

CHAPTER 9 Practice for the Oral Examination
(Section II, Part B)

INFORMAL SPEAKING (SIMULATED CONVERSATION)

Description

The objective of the informal speaking part is to provide a sample of speech in a simulated conversation. The prompt for this part consists of a script with directions about the kind of information you are to contribute to the conversation. There will be a sentence that will give you the context and the topic of the conversation. You will have 30 seconds to read the script provided for the conversation. After 30 seconds, the entire conversation will be played so you can hear the other speaker's lines of dialogue. After listening to the whole conversation from beginning to end, you will have one minute to think through what to say. The lines you are to speak as well as those of the other speaker are clearly marked. After one minute, the conversation will be played again and you will record your part of the conversation in the spaces provided on the recording. You will have 20 seconds to respond. There will be five or six spaces for you to speak. At times you may be asked to initiate the conversation, or you may have to respond to something the other speaker says.

Suggestions

Clearly, there is a wide range of expressions that would be appropriate in each conversation. The conversation cannot be so specific that there is only one correct response or answer to a question. If will be helpful to know a range of expressions that are common in conversations at different points of the talk. For example, if you are asked to give a greeting, you should have a number of them. Pick an expression that would correspond to the context. If you are to talk to a close friend, you would use *tú* in addressing him or her. If it is morning, your would say *Buenos días*, instead of *Buenas noches*. If you are to close the conversation, you can close with any number of expressions, from *Hasta luego* to a more formal kind of closing for a more formal conversation, such as *Gracias por los consejos*, or *Le agradezco mucho por su ayuda*. There will be times for you to express reactions, issue an invitation, make a suggestion, ask a question for additional information or for clarification, or make an observation about a familiar topic. Some of the expressions are short and could be used at the beginning of your response while you formulate what you are going to say. Expressions such as *¡Qué va!, ¡Ni idea!, ¡Qué lata!, ¡Qué idea!, ¡No me digas!, ¡Ni modo!, A ver, bueno pues,* are all exclamations that continue a conversation and fulfill the requirements of the conversation, while at the same time they give you time to think.

In addition to vocabulary, be sure to make a mental note of the grammar you may want to use in the conversation. There may be natural opportunities to use the subjunctive, for example. When you are asked to give a reaction, you can use the subjunctive in the case following a verb of emotion, doubt, or an impersonal expression. When you are asked to make a recommendation, you can use the subjunctive after a verb of volition, such as *querer, recomendar, aconsejar, sugerir,* or *mandar, exigir, requerir,* or the most common one, *pedir.* The grammar you use in the informal speaking part is similar to the kind you would use in the informal writing part of the exam. You might want to quickly review some of the suggestions for grammar from page 503.

In a normal conversation, some hesitation is acceptable, but long pauses while you translate from English to Spanish are going to be obvious. To maintain a natural flow to the conversation, think ahead. When you see that a reaction is called for in the script, you can make a mental note of words to expect to either hear or use. Remember that writing out words or sentences takes time. If you start writing down things to say, you will lose too much of the 30 seconds allotted. When you look at the script before listening to the conversation, make a quick mental note of:

- where the conversation takes place
- with whom you are speaking
- what the main topic is, and
- what kind of information you need to supply in the conversation.

Standard informal and formal greetings should be so familiar to you that you do not need to spend time thinking about them. If you know how to begin and end the conversation, you can focus on the middle part when you review the script before recording your responses. The rest of the topic will be about something every teenager might have in common, so you can anticipate the topics in part, if you think through your own life experiences.

Strategies for completing the informal speaking part of the exam should include the following points:

- Read the script carefully
- Make an immediate note of the context to determine time and place
- Decide immediately whether to use *tú, Ud.,* or *Uds.*
- Look to see what the topic is
- Think of verbs you will need to use in Spanish
- Jot down verbs you associate with specific reactions mentioned in the script
- Do not try writing out sentences
- Do not fixate on a particular vocabulary word you may want to use
- If you cannot think of one way to say something, rephrase using words you do know
- Correct yourself if you realize that you have made a mistake
- Relax.

Script Sample   Below is a sample of a script similar to the sort you will see on the informal speaking part, and of the steps you will follow to do this part.

1. You have 30 seconds to review the following instructions.

Directions: Below is a simulated conversation. You will have 30 seconds to read the script, which contains instructions about what to say. The conversation will then be played so you can hear it. After hearing the conversation, you will have one minute to reread the script. At the end of one minute, the conversation will be played again. The second time it is played, you will have 20 seconds to record your part of the script in the appropriate spots in the dialogue.

Imagine que un amigo le dejó un mensaje telefónico en su ausencia, pidiéndole llamarlo por teléfono.

(a) Usted lo llama.
(b) Usted escucha la voz de su amigo y habla con él.

Paco:	(El teléfono suena. Paco contesta.)
Ud.:	Saludos.
	Explique la razón por la llamada.
Paco:	Le explica por qué dejó el mensaje.
Ud.:	Reaccione a su idea.
Paco:	Continuación de la conversación.
Ud.:	Otra vez, reaccione.
	Hágale una pregunta.
Paco:	Contesta a la pregunta. Hace su propia pregunta.
Ud.:	Conteste a la pregunta de Paco.
Paco:	Se pone de acuerdo.
Ud.:	Finalice los planes.
	Despedida.
Paco:	Se despide y cuelga el teléfono.

CD 3 TRACK 3   2. After 30 seconds you would listen to the whole conversation, without your part. You will not see the following script, just the part above, but as you follow the script, note the information contained in the other speaker's part, in this case, Paco's part.

(El teléfono suena.)

Paco: **Hola.**

Ud.:   Saludos.
          Explique la razón por la llamada.

Paco: **Ah, sí, gracias por llamarme. Querría invitarte a acompañarme a la escuela este fin de semana. Hay un drama buenísimo que se da, se llama *Sueño*.**

Ud.:	Reaccione a su idea.
Paco:	**Me dijeron que nuestro compañero de clase es fantástico en el drama.**
	Interpreta el papel de un rey. Como recuerdas, leímos una parte de este drama en la obra _La vida es sueño_ en la clase de español hace un mes. Me gustaron esos versos de "¿Qué es la vida? Una ilusión," ... etcétera.
Ud.:	Otra vez, reaccione. Hágale una pregunta.
Paco:	**Sí. Los otros de la clase ya han ido y dicen que les gustó ¿Te gustará ir conmigo? Te invito.**
Ud.:	Conteste a la pregunta de Paco.
Paco:	**¡Estupendo! Te encontraré enfrente del teatro a las siete.**
Ud.:	Finalice los planes. Despedida.
Paco:	**De acuerdo, amigo. Nos vemos. (Paco cuelga el teléfono.)**

3. You will now have one minute to review the topic and figure out what you could say in response to what Paco has said. You will have 20 seconds each time it is your turn.

4. The conversation is played again. This time you record your responses in the appropriate places.

5. The recording is finished. You will check to see that your voice was recorded.

Now study the model and do the practices, so that when you get to the exam the task will be familiar to you. You can easily imagine your own sample conversations with a little practice. The more you practice, the more comfortable and relaxed you will be and the better your speech sample will be.

Practice Exercises

CD 3 TRACK 4

Practice Conversation One

Ud. está de viaje. Se encuentra en una ciudad desconocida y se ha perdido en el centro, no muy lejos de su hotel. Tiene que preguntar a alguien cómo se llega al hotel. Ud. entra en una tienda para preguntar a un dependiente cómo llegar allá.

(a) Ud. entra en la tienda y se acerca al mostrador.

(b) El dependiente le saluda.

Dependiente:	(Saludos apropiados.)
Ud.:	(Responde apropiadamente.)
	(Le hace una pregunta.)
Dependiente:	(Contesta a la pregunta.)
	(Le hace una pregunta.)
Ud.:	(Responde que no tiene la dirección.)
Dependiente:	(Le pide otros nombres.)
Ud.:	(Le nombra otro lugar.)
Dependiente:	(Responde con otra pregunta.)
Ud.:	(Le da otro detalle descriptivo.)
	(Le pide la dirección.)
Dependiente:	(Le dice que lo reconoce.)
	(Le instruye cómo llegar.)
Ud.:	(Reacción apropiada.)
	(Se despide del dependiente.)
Dependiente:	(Se despide.)

CD 3 TRACK 5

Practice Conversation Two

Durante su último año de escuela superior, Ud. ha visitado una universidad en la cual quiere matricularse y donde habla con el guía estudiantil que le acompaña en su visita. Ud. y el guía hablan.

(a) El guía lo encuentra frente al centro estudiantil de la universidad.

(b) Ud. se acerca, le llama la atención con cortesía, se presenta, e inicia la conversación. Empiece ahora.

Ud.:	(Se presenta al guía.)
Guía:	(Le responde.)
	(Le hace una pregunta.)
Ud.:	(Le contesta.)
Guía:	(Responde con entusiasmo.)
	(Le invita a seguirle mientras habla.)
Ud.:	(Le hace una pregunta.)
Guía:	(Le responde con un hecho interesante.)
Ud.:	(Reacciona.)
	(Hace una observación.)
Guía:	(Añade algo a la historia.)
Ud.:	(Ofrece una conclusión.)

Practice Conversation Three

Ud. es un estudiante nuevo en una escuela. Su familia acaba de mudarse a esta nueva ciudad y Ud. tiene que cultivar un nuevo grupo de amigos en la escuela.

(a) Es el primer día de clases y se sienta cerca de una chica.
(b) Ella inicia la conversación.

Chica:	(Saluda.)
	(Le hace una pregunta.)
Ud.:	(Responde.)
Chica:	(Le hace una pregunta.)
Ud.:	(Contesta la pregunta.)
	(Le hace una pregunta.)
Chica:	(Contesta a su pregunta.)
	(Ofrece datos personales.)
	(Le hace otra pregunta.)
Ud.:	(Le responde con información personal.)
Chica:	(La invita.)
Ud.:	(Responde a la invitación.)
Chica:	(Le informa de los detalles.)
	(Le hace una pregunta.)
Ud.:	(Le informa que desea ir con ellos en el futuro, pero el viernes que viene no podrá.)
Chica:	(Termina la conversación.)

Practice Conversation Four

Este verano Ud. necesita encontrar empleo para ahorrar dinero para la universidad. Tiene una entrevista con la gerenta de una compañía donde quiere obtener empleo. Imagine la conversación entre Ud. y la gerenta.

(a) Ud. entra en la oficina de recursos humanos para hablar con la gerenta de la compañía.
(b) Ud. solicita empleo en la oficina.

Gerenta:	(Le saluda.)
Ud.:	(Responde apropiadamente.)
Gerenta:	(Le hace una pregunta.)
Ud.:	(Le explica sus razones.)
Gerenta:	(Reacciona de buena manera.)
	(Le hace otra pregunta.)
Ud.:	(Le cuenta algo que ha hecho.)
	(Le expresa sus esperanzas.)
	(Le hace una pregunta.)
Gerenta:	(Le contesta.)
	(Le ofrece un puesto.)
Ud.:	(Acepta la oferta.)
Gerenta:	(Le responde.)
Ud.:	(Le da las gracias.)
	(Se despide de ella.)

CD 3 TRACK 8

Practice Conversation Five

Para la próxima edición del periódico de su revista estudiantil Ud. necesita entrevistar al director de la cafetería de su escuela porque los alumnos acaban de hacer una encuesta sobre la comida en la cafetería y la falta de comida nutritiva en el menú.

(a) Ud. se encuentra con el director en su oficina, ubicada cerca de la cafetería.

(b) Él la saluda y empieza la conversación.

Director:	(La saluda.)
Ud.:	(Le responde apropiadamente.)
Director:	(Comentario sobre sus relaciones con los estudiantes.)
	(Le hace una pregunta.)
Ud.:	(Explica el propósito de la visita.)
	(Le hace una pregunta.)
Director:	(Contesta a la pregunta.)
Ud.:	(Le cuenta los resultados de la encuesta.)
	(Le hace otra pregunta.)
Director:	(Le hace una pregunta de respuesta.)
Ud.:	(En su respuesta comunica los deseos de los estudiantes.)
Director:	(Propone una idea.)
Ud.:	(Reacciona a la idea.)
Director:	(Responde con sus deseos.)
Ud.:	(Se despide de él.)

CD 3 TRACK 9

Practice Conversation Six

Ud. llama por teléfono a un amigo para pedirle consejo sobre un proyecto que ambos necesitan llevar a cabo para una clase de ciencias. Tienen que arreglar los planes para terminar con el proyecto.

(a) Ambos tienen que preparar una presentación oral y decidir quién hará qué parte del proyecto.

(b) Su amigo, Diego, sabe más que Ud. del tema. Conversan por teléfono. Él habla primero.

(Suena el teléfono.)

Diego:	(Saludos.)
Ud.:	(Saludos.)
	(Le explica el tipo de ayuda que Ud. necesita.)
Diego:	(Responde.)
Ud.:	(Acepta su oferta.)
	(Propone algo que puede hacer.)
Diego:	(Está de acuerdo.)
	(Hace una pregunta.)
Ud.:	(Expresa su inquietud con las matemáticas.)
	(Responde con una sugerencia.)
Diego:	(Sugiere un plan de acción.)
Ud.:	(Se pone de acuerdo.)

	(Le hace una pregunta.)
Diego:	(Concluye los planes.)
Ud.:	(Responde.)
	(Se despide de él.)
Diego:	(Se despide.)

CD 3 TRACK 10

Practice Conversation Seven

Imagine que está en el norte, en febrero, y necesita una blusa de cierto estilo para un papel en un drama en la escuela. Ud. va a comprarla. Entra en una tienda y habla con una dependienta sobre lo que necesita.

(a) En la tienda la dependienta se le acerca y la saluda.
(b) Ud. le comunica lo que necesita. Ella es muy simpática.

Dependienta:	(Se dirige a Ud.)
Ud.:	(Responde apropiadamente.)
	(Le explica lo que necesita.)
Dependienta:	(Comenta sobre su pedido.)
	(Comenta sobre la mercancía.)
	(Ofrece mostrársela.)
Ud.:	(Le agradece.)
	(Le dice lo que busca en particular.)
Dependienta:	(Le sugiere algo.)
	(Le hace una pregunta.)
Ud.:	(Contesta la pregunta.)
	(Expresa una preferencia.)
	(Le hace otra pregunta.)
Dependienta:	(Contesta.)
	(Expresa una opinión.)
Ud.:	(Responde.)
Dependienta:	(Concluye el trato.)
Ud.:	(Expresa gratitud.)
Dependienta:	(Le responde.)
	(La invita a volver.)

CD 3 TRACK 11

Practice Conversation Eight

Imagine Ud. que trabaja en un restaurante. Un día un cliente entra para almorzar. Parece que es la primera vez que esta persona ha venido al restaurante.

(a) El cliente que entra es un hombre vestido de manera informal. Parece muy simpático.
(b) Ud. es el mesero que debe servirle. Ud. inicia la conversación cuando el cliente se sienta.

Ud.:	(Se dirige apropiadamente al cliente.)
	(Le hace una pregunta.)
Cliente:	(Responde.)
	(Pide más información.)
Ud.:	(Responde.)

	(Le hace otra pregunta.)
Cliente:	(Le pide información.)
Ud.:	(Nombra unos platos.)
Cliente:	(Le pide una sugerencia.)
Ud.:	(Sugiere uno de los platos que nombró recién.)
Cliente:	(Acepta su sugerencia.)
	(Le hace una pregunta.)
Ud.:	(Le nombra la selección.)
Cliente:	(Completa su selección.)
Ud.:	(Termina la conversación.)

CD 3 TRACK 12

Practice Conversation Nine

Un día Ud. se despierta con síntomas tan malos que no puede asistir a sus clases. Tiene que llamar a la enfermera de la oficina médica de su doctor para pedir una cita.

(a) Ud. se ha enfermado. Tiene síntomas de gripe. Llama a la oficina de su doctor.

(b) La enfermera contesta. Ella empieza a hablar cuando suena el teléfono.

(Suena el teléfono.)

Enfermera:	(Saludo apropiado.)
Ud.:	(Responde apropiadamente.)
	(Explica el motivo de su llamada.)
Enfermera:	(Le hace una pregunta.)
Ud.:	(Explica sus síntomas.)
Enfermera:	(Le hace otras preguntas.)
Ud.:	(Contesta.)
	(Hace una pregunta.)
Enfermera:	(Comenta sobre su estado.)
	(Hace una pregunta.)
Ud.:	(Explica que sí, pero con una condición.)
Enfermera:	(Responde.)
Ud.:	(Responde apropiadamente.)
	(Se despide.)
Enfermera:	(Se despide.)

CD 3 TRACK 13

Practice Conversation Ten

Después de un partido de fútbol especialmente emocionante, Ud. y un amigo están en un restaurante, charlando del partido. Maldonado, un jugador del equipo opuesto, recibió un trofeo por ser el jugador más valioso del partido. Uds. discuten tal selección.

(a) Ambos hablan sobre la selección de Maldonado. Ud. cree que mereció haber sido seleccionado.

(b) Su amigo, Juan, piensa que no lo mereció.

Juan:	(Expresa una opinión.)
Ud.:	(Expresa una opinión contraria.)
Juan:	(Reacciona.)
Ud.:	(Defiende su opinión.)
Juan.:	(Pide justificación.)
Ud.:	(Explica su razonamiento.)
Juan:	(Reacciona.)
Ud.:	(Consuela a su amigo.)
	(Hace una pregunta.)
Juan:	(Acepta por fin.)
	(Hace una pregunta.)
Ud.:	(Expresa su opinión sobre el resultado del partido.)
Juan:	(Conluye el tema.)

SCRIPTS OF THE PRACTICE CONVERSATIONS

Practice Conversation One

(a) Ud. entra en la tienda y se acerca al mostrador.

(b) El dependiente le saluda.

Dependiente:	Buenas tardes, señor. ¿En qué puedo servirle?
Ud.:	(Responde apropiadamente.)
	(Le hace una pregunta.)
Dependiente:	Bueno, no estoy seguro. Me parece familiar pero en este momento no lo recuerdo exactamente. ¿Tiene Ud. la dirección?
Ud.:	(Responde que no tiene la dirección.)
Dependiente:	A ver, ¿por casualidad está cerca de un lugar bien conocido? Quizás si supiera yo otro negocio o restaurante cerca, podría reconocerlo.
Ud.:	(Le nombra otro lugar.)
Dependiente:	Tampoco reconozco ese lugar. Puede ser que sea tan nuevo que no lo conozco. Pues, ¿recuerda Ud. otro detalle, como el color del edificio, algo en las ventanas de enfrente, unas escaleras, algo distinto?
Ud.:	(Le da otro detalle descriptivo.)
	(Le pide la dirección.)
Dependiente:	Ah, sí. ¡Ese hotel! Es pequeño, pero muy bueno. Está a una distancia de dos cuadras. Doble Ud. aquí a la izquierda, siga recto hasta llegar a la próxima esquina. Está en esa bocacalle.
Ud.:	(Reacción apropiada.)
	(Se despide del dependiente.)
Dependiente:	No hay de qué.

Practice Conversation Two

(a) El guía lo encuentra frente al centro estudiantil de la universidad.

(b) Ud. se acerca, le llama la atención con cortesía, se presenta, e inicia la conversación. Empiece ahora.

Ud.:	(Se presenta al guía.)
Guía:	Mucho gusto, Ramón. Bienvenido a nuestra universidad. Estaba esperándote. Bueno, todos los estudiantes tienen interés en ver los dormitorios, los gimnasios, la biblioteca y la cafetería. Podríamos terminar con la cafetería y tomar un café. Dime, ¿qué deseas visitar primero?
Ud.:	(Le contesta.)
Guía:	Veo que has oído mucho sobre el programa de ciencias. Ese programa es muy bueno. Mira, ¿por qué no empezamos a caminar a la facultad de ciencias mientras te doy algunos datos sobre el programa que quizás no conozcas?
Ud.:	(Le hace una pregunta.)
Guía:	Sí, ese profesor es muy famoso, pero también muy excéntrico. Un día los estudiantes desenchufaron su computadora antes de que él entrara. Al ver que la computadora no funcionaba, el profesor se puso un gorro extraño y pretendió ser un mago. Como es un genio, ¡hizo todos los cálculos en su cabeza!
Ud.:	(Reacciona.)
	(Hace una observación.)
Guía:	Después de lucirse ante los estudiantes, el profesor les dijo que todos podían ser magos como él y lo único que necesitaban era estudiar más. Y les dio diez problemas de cálculo adicionales que debieron resolver.
Ud.:	(Ofrece una conclusión.)

Practice Conversation Three

(a) Es el primer día de clases y se sienta cerca de una chica.

(b) Ella inicia la conversación.

Chica:	Hola. Creo que no te conozco. ¿Eres estudiante nueva aquí?
Ud.:	(Responde.)
Chica:	¿De dónde viniste, Raquel?
Ud.:	(Contesta la pregunta.)
	(Le hace una pregunta.)
Chica:	Sólo llevo dos años aquí, pero los alumnos son muy comprensivos. Me hicieron sentirme muy cómoda inmediatamente. Pero tienes que aprovechar toda oportunidad para conocerlos. Si tienes algunos intereses especiales, puedes encontrar fácilmente a otros alumnos con intereses iguales ya que hay muchos clubes. ¿Qué te gusta hacer en tu tiempo libre?
Ud.:	(Le responde con información personal.)
Chica:	¡Ni me digas! También me encanta el boliche. Siempre hay mucho tiempo para charlar con los amigos mientras se juega. Mira, tenemos un equipo de boliche en la escuela. ¿Por qué no vienes con nosotros este viernes?

Ud.:	(Responde a la invitación.)
Chica:	Nos reunimos a las siete aquí en el estacionamiento para ir todos juntos. ¿Puedes?
Ud.:	(Le informa que desea ir con ellos en el futuro, pero el viernes que viene no podrá.)
Chica:	Pues, habrá otra oportunidad en el futuro. Bueno, ya ha entrado la profesora. No le gusta cuando hablamos después de empezar la clase.

Practice Conversation Four

(a) Ud. entra en la oficina de recursos humanos para hablar con la gerenta de la compañía.

(b) Ud. solicita empleo en la oficina.

Gerenta:	Muy buenos días, Sr. Díaz. ¿Cómo está Ud.?
Ud.:	(Responde apropiadamente.)
Gerenta:	Le agradezco por venir a hablar con nosotros. Tenemos un grupo de empleados muy dedicados en esta oficina y estamos muy orgullosos del trabajo que hacemos. Nuestro trabajo es un poco especializado, pero sí tenemos algunos puestos de internado para verano para estudiantes especiales. ¿Con qué motivo quiere Ud. trabajar para una compañía de telecomunicaciones?
Ud.:	(Le explica sus razones.)
Gerenta:	Um, muy interesante. Su interés en los aspectos técnicos es muy importante. Pero, ¿tiene Ud. alguna experiencia con la aplicación de esa tecnología que le interesa al trabajo que hacemos nosotros?
Ud.:	(Le cuenta algo que ha hecho.) (Le expresa sus esperanzas.) (Le hace una pregunta.)
Gerenta:	Por supuesto que siempre es mejor tener experiencia antes de tener un puesto de responsabilidad, pero sé que eso es muy difícil para los jóvenes cuando están empezando sus carreras. Le podemos ofrecer un puesto en la oficina si quiere empezar la semana que viene.
Ud.:	(Acepta la oferta.)
Gerenta:	Excelente. Estoy segura que esta experiencia nos beneficiará a los dos. No olvide llamarme si tiene otra pregunta.
Ud.:	(Le da las gracias.) (Se despide de ella.)

Practice Conversation Five

(a) Ud. se encuentra con el director en su oficina, ubicada cerca de la cafetería.

(b) Él la saluda y empieza la conversación.

Director:	Buenos días, Margarita. ¿Qué tal?
Ud.:	(Le responde apropiadamente.)
Director:	Me alegro. Uds. no me visitan mucho. ¿A qué debo el placer de tu visita hoy?

Ud.:	(Explica el propósito de la visita.)
	(Le hace una pregunta.)
Director:	Había oído que Uds. estaban haciendo esa encuesta. Me interesa saber qué opinan los estudiantes del menú. Sabes que es un negocio muy delicado equilibrar el dinero que recibimos de los alumnos con los gastos por la comida y el mantenimiento del local.
Ud.:	(Le cuenta los resultados de la encuesta.)
	(Le hace otra pregunta.)
Director:	¿Qué proponen los estudiantes que ofrezcamos en el menú?
Ud.:	(En su respuesta comunica los deseos de los estudiantes)
Director:	Siempre queremos satisfacer los deseos de los estudiantes. A ver si podemos formar un comité estudiantil para oír sus consejos.
Ud.:	(Reacciona a la idea.)
Director:	Entonces podemos dirigirnos al problema juntos para ofrecer algo que sea más saludable y algo con lo que no perdamos dinero. Muchas gracias por haber venido para hablar conmigo. Esperaré tu llamada para reunirnos otra vez.
Ud.:	(Se despide de él.)

Practice Conversation Six

(a) Ambos tienen que preparar una presentación oral y decidir quién hará qué parte del proyecto.

(b) Su amigo, Diego, sabe más que Ud. del tema. Conversan por teléfono. Él habla primero.

(Suena el teléfono.)	
Diego:	Hola, habla Diego.
Ud.:	(Saludos.)
	(Le explica el tipo de ayuda que Ud. necesita.)
Diego:	Oye, no hay problema. Está bien si esto es lo que quieres hacer. Yo puedo hacer todos los cálculos de los problemas que tenemos que resolver si esto es un problema para ti.
Ud.:	(Acepta su oferta.)
	(Propone algo que puede hacer.)
Diego:	Perfecto. Esto será más fácil para mí también. Como sabes, no me gusta hablar frente a la clase. Siempre me pone muy nervioso. ¿Cuándo quieres que te dé la materia?
Ud.:	(Expresa su inquietud con las matemáticas.)
	(Responde con una sugerencia.)
Diego:	Entonces sería buena idea juntarnos para que te explique las respuestas. ¿Por qué no nos encontramos en el Waffle House esta noche para hablar?
Ud.:	(Se pone de acuerdo.)
	(Le hace una pregunta.)
Diego:	Digamos a las diez. Esto me dará tiempo para terminar con toda la tarea.
Ud.:	(Responde.)
	(Se despide de él.)
Diego:	Hasta luego.

Practice Conversation Seven

(a) En la tienda la dependienta se le acerca y la saluda.

(b) Ud. le comunica lo que necesita. Ella es muy simpática.

Dependienta:	Buenos días, señorita. ¿En qué puedo servirle hoy?
Ud.:	(Responde apropiadamente.)
	(Le explica lo que necesita.)
Dependienta:	Como ve Ud., no tenemos mucha ropa de ese tipo este mes. Cuando hace mucho frío generalmente tenemos más para la nieve que para el sol. Pero sí tengo algunos artículos en espera de las necesidades de viajeros que van a Florida. Déjeme mostrárselos.
Ud.:	(Le agradece.)
	(Le dice lo que busca en particular.)
Dependienta:	Tenemos unas blusas preciosas en colores muy bonitos que le harán juego con el color del pelo. ¿Cuál es su talla?
Ud.:	(Contesta la pregunta.)
	(Expresa una preferencia.)
	(Le hace otra pregunta.)
Dependienta:	Sí. Por supuesto. Tenemos la amarilla en un tamaño grande, si la quiere. El color amarillo le cae muy bien. ¿Quiere probársela?
Ud.:	(Responde.)
Dependienta:	Ha hecho una selección muy buena. Estoy segura de que estará muy satisfecha.
Ud.:	(Expresa gratitud.)
Dependienta:	El placer es mío. Vuelva Ud. cuando necesite otra ropa de verano. Adiós.

Practice Conversation Eight

(a) Un cliente que entra es un hombre vestido de manera informal. Parece muy simpático.

(b) Ud. es el mesero que debe servirle. Ud. inicia la conversación cuando el cliente se sienta.

Ud.:	(Se dirige apropiadamente al cliente.)
	(Le hace una pregunta.)
Cliente:	Buenas tardes. Sí, querría un vaso de agua, por favor. Me podría dar el menú?
Ud.:	(Responde.)
	(Le hace otra pregunta.)
Cliente:	Creo que estoy listo para pedir algo. Pero querría saber si Uds. tienen una especialidad de casa.
Ud.	(Nombra unos platos.)
Cliente:	Todo me parece bueno. ¿Tiene Ud. alguna sugerencia para ayudarme a decidir?
Ud.:	(Sugiere un plato de los que nombró recién.)
Cliente:	Sí, creo que hoy tengo hambre para pollo asado. ¿Y los vegetales del día?
Ud.:	(Le nombra la selección.)

| Cliente: | Bueno, tomaré los tomates y los pepinos. Gracias. |
| Ud.: | (Termina la conversación.) |

Practice Conversation Nine

(a) Ud. se ha enfermado. Tiene síntomas de gripe. Llama a la oficina de su doctor.

(b) La enfermera contesta. Ella empieza a hablar cuando suena el teléfono.

(Suena el teléfono.)

Enfermera:	Buenos días. La oficina del doctor González.
Ud.:	(Responde apropiadamente.)
	(Explica el motivo de su llamada.)
Enfermera:	¿Cuáles son los síntomas que tiene Ud.?
Ud.:	(Explica sus síntomas.)
Enfermera:	Ya oigo que no se siente bien. ¿Qué temperatura tiene Ud.? ¿Qué toma para la tos?
Ud.:	(Contesta.)
	(Hace una pregunta.)
Enfermera:	Bueno, una temperatura tan alta casi siempre indica una infección. Puede ser que el doctor querrá verlo. Parece que hay posibilidad de que se mejore más rápido si lo ve pronto. Otro paciente canceló para las dos. ¿Puede venir a esa hora?
Ud.:	(Explica que sí, pero con una condición.)
Enfermera:	Dejémoslo para las dos, y si no puede, avíseme.
Ud.:	(Responde apropiadamente.)
	(Se despide.)
Enfermera:	Esperamos verlo esta tarde.

Practice Conversation Ten

(a) Ambos hablan sobre la selección de Maldonado. Ud. cree que mereció haber sido seleccionado.

(b) Su amigo, Juan, piensa que no lo mereció.

Juan:	No puedo creer que le dieron el trofeo del jugador más importante del partido a Maldonado. Nosotros casi lo vencímos.
Ud.:	(Expresa una opinión contraria.)
Juan:	¡Ni modo! ¿En qué piensas? No jugó limpio. Los árbitros no vieron la mitad de lo que hacía él.
Ud.:	(Defiende su opinión.)
Juan.:	¿Dices que lo único que cuenta es ganar? ¿No crees que hay otras cosas quizás más importantes?
Ud.:	(Explica su razonamiento.)
Juan:	Bueno, no estoy convencido. Maldonado tuvo suerte esta vez. Y no se debe confundir la suerte con el talento.
Ud.:	(Consuela a su amigo.)
	(Hace una pregunta.)
Juan:	Quizás tengas razón. Puede ser que en un día cualquiera, cada cual puede ganar. Si nosotros hubiéramos tenido una jugada más, quizás hubiéramos podido ganar. ¿No lo crees?
Ud.:	(Expresa su opinión sobre el resultado del partido.)

Juan: Bueno, habrá otro día. Y un día alguien lo vencerá. Y lo tendrá bien merecido. Todavía me molesta que recibiera el trofeo.

FORMAL ORAL PRESENTATION

Description

The objective of the formal oral presentation is to evaluate how well you can integrate various skill areas. It consists of a question that has two prompts from the source material. One of the prompts is written, and you will have five minutes to read it. The second prompt is an audio selection that will be played for you. You should take notes as you listen, so that you can refer to specifics found in the audio source (which will only be played once). After you have read and listened to the source material, you will have two minutes to consider the way you want to answer the question. After two minutes have passed, you will begin to record your response. At the end of two minutes you will be told to stop.

The question will deal with the sort of speech sample you would provide in an academic setting, or in a formal presentation to a group of people. It will require you to tell about something that has happened, to present an opinion to persuade someone of your opinion, to present information about a topic, or to make some other kind of comment about the topic of the question.

Recommendations

Cultural topics are considerations in preparing the questions and in the intended responses. You need to pull knowledge from a wide variety of sources, including the information from both source materials, your own experience, and what you know or have learned so far about the topic. You may be expected to comment and make predictions about what is going to happen in certain instances.

The written text could come from a literary selection, or newspapers, or any other source of written language. The audio will come from any kind of broadcast source. You should be familiar with those sources from your preparation in other chapters of this book.

Both content and language count in the evaluation of this skill area. You need to be able to synthesize what you hear. Do not simply repeat words you hear in the sources. You also need to be able to retell what has happened in some cases, or describe what is going to happen. You may have to summarize arguments about a topic, or defend or agree with a point of view. Your speech sample needs to show the best vocabulary and grammar you have at your command.

Scoring of the speech sample takes into consideration the following points:

- pronunciation
- fluency
- vocabulary
- syntax
- grammar
- organization
- inclusion of source material

Scoring Speech Samples

When the speech sample is rated, you should think about the rubrics for three general categories of performance.

Low: The response at this level has limited content. It may omit points from either or both of the source materials provided. It may not even be connected to the question that is asked. The delivery of the presentation is fragmented, marked by frequent pauses or moments when the student seems to be at a loss for a particular word. The response may contain words that are lifted from the printed text or spoken on the audio source, with little original language used at an appropriate level. The speaker may resort to English words, or invent words in Spanish based on English vocabulary. The Spanish may show great influence from English structures. The pronunciation may be so poor that it is difficult to recognize the Spanish words that the speaker is trying to say. Overall, the response in this category demonstrates that the speaker communicates in Spanish with significant difficulty.

Medium: This response does deal with the topic of the question. It may contain a very complete reference to either the print or the audio source. The response shows some organization and development of thought. The basic structures are correct and the vocabulary is appropriate. There is good self-correction. The student shows comprehension of the source materials, and some familiarity with the topic, at least enough to respond to the question appropriately. Pronunciation and intonation are good and do not interfere with comprehension. There are still linguistic lapses in expression. The sample may begin well but be weaker at the end, or it may not have a conclusion. Overall, the sample at this level is good.

High: The sample in this category clearly shows strong competence and proficiency in the use of Spanish. The sample answers the question, taking into account information from both source materials. The information is rephrased to fit into what the speaker wishes to say. There is a natural transition from one sentence to another, and the language shows creative ability with the words used. The speaker refers to the source materials, but at the same time is able to articulate original ideas about the topic. There may be some minor lapses in grammar or vocabulary and some pauses, but none that interrupts the flow of the sample. The speaker at this level clearly has a strong command of the language.

Suggestions

When you prepare to take this part of the exam, keep in mind the context. Some of the practices at the end of the grouped vocabulary chapter would be a good place to review some contexts. Remember that cultural material is always a component of these questions. Any way that you can relate the vocabulary to what you know about the Spanish-speaking world will be helpful in thinking about possible topics. Some suggestions for preparing for the formal oral presentation include:

- Read the question carefully.
- Take notes on the audio selection.
- Use the two minutes you have to think about what you want to say.
- Do not write out sentences to read. You will not have enough time to write out two minutes worth of presentation, and the ending will be weak.
- Write down infinitives you may want to use.
- Begin with a topic sentence; an idea you will develop in your two minutes.
- Think about how you want to close your presentation.
- Practice speaking about anything for two minutes, so you know how long two minutes are.
- Use complete sentences in your presentation.
- Do not merely quote the sources, use your own words.
- Do not try to translate literally what you want to say from English to Spanish.
- Practice often.
- Relax.

Sample Question

Now try some of the exercises in this book. Below is a sample of a typical question. For each practice, read the passage, then list to the audio selection. Use your own paper to take notes. Refer to the transcripts when necessary.

Directions: Below you will see a question with two accompanying sources of information. You have 5 minutes to read the printed text. After 5 minutes, you will hear a recording. You should take notes in the space provided. After the recording has been played, you will have 2 minutes to plan your response to the questions. After 2 minutes, you will be instructed to begin your recording. At the end of 2 minutes you will be told to stop recording. This will be the end of the language examination.

Imagine Ud. que debe comentar en una clase sus opiniones sobre la pregunta que viene a continuación. En sus comentarios debe incluir información proveniente de los dos materiales suplementarios.

¿Cómo ha cambiado el estatus de la mujer en la sociedad?

Formal Oral Presentation Source One

Sor Juana Inés de la Cruz. Mujer Moderna en el Siglo XVIII

De niña gozó de todo un mundo de letras, debido a su estancia con su abuelo materno, quien le abrió las puertas de la literatura. A la edad de nueve años, la joven Juana de Asbaje y Ramírez de Santillana, su nombre completo, ya había aprendido el latín, a causa de toda la literatura a su alcance. Su nombre recorrió todo la región, hasta llegar a oídos del Virrey de Nueva España. La invitó a la corte, y allí permaneció como dama de honor para la Virreina la Marquesa. Parece que pasó varios años disfrutando de una vida que correspondía al nivel social al que se había levantado. Pero por ser hija natural, la oportunidad de casarse le resultó remota.

Después de dos años, la joven tan encantadora y lista renunció los placeres de la corte y se dedicó a la iglesia, entrando en el convento de San Jerónimo donde cumplió el término de sus años en este mundo. Una vez internada en el convento, se dedicó a las letras, amontonando una impresionante biblioteca de unos 4.000 libros, una cantidad asombrosa en aquel entonces. Floreció intelectualmente y concentró los esfuerzos en estudiar todo un rango de asuntos, de la teología, la pintura, la ciencia, y, sobre todo, las letras. A medida que pasaban los años, su renombre aumentaba a la vez, hasta que se dio con un padre celoso de su potencia e influencia. La buena monja se empeñaba en reclamar su fidelidad a la voluntad de Dios en cuánto investigaba. Sus razonamientos no persuadieron a los obstinados clérigos. Resignada, Sor Juana no quiso continuar su carrera literaria. Se sometió, rindiendo sus pertenencias a los pobres. Murió poco después, una de las estrellas de la literatura colonial de México, sin que lo quisieran sus detractores. Unas de sus palabras más famosas se encuentran en los famosos versos de una redondilla.

> Hombres necios que acusáis
> a la mujer sin razón,
> sin ver que sois la ocasión
> de lo mismo que culpáis;
> . . .
>
> Bien con muchas armas fundo
> que lidia vuestra arrogancia,
> pues en promesa e instancia
> juntáis diablo, carne y mundo.

Formal Oral Presentation Source Two (Audio)

CD 3 TRACK 14   Listen to the CD. A script of the recording is on page 430.

EXERCISES

Practice Exercise One

Question: ¿Qué características contribuyen al llamado *color local* de un lugar?

Source One
La Boca

(*Alojargentina.com*)

En un barrio típico de inmigrantes de los más distintos orígenes, entre los que se destacan griegos, yugoslavos, turcos e italianos, sobre todo genoveses. La calle Caminito, de apenas 100 metros de longitud, es peatonal. Es una calle tan pequeña como particular. En ella no hay puertas. Algunas ventanas, algún balcón lleno de plantas y de ropas colgadas a secar. Sus paredes pintadas de diferentes colores recuerdan a Venecia. En ellas hay todo tipo de murales, cerámicas y distintos adornos. Al principio era simplemente un ramal del ferrocarril, llena de tierra, yuyales y piedras. Al lugar se lo llamaba "la curva", la que luego se convirtió en "un caminito" que acortaba distancias. Ese fue el famoso "caminito" por el que transitaba a diario Juan de Dios Filiberto, quien luego escribió el tango que lleva su nombre. La iniciativa de ponerle ese nombre a la calle surgió nada menos que de su amigo Benito Quinquela Martín. Hoy es una calle turística, no sólo visitada por los extranjeros, sino por argentinos de todo el país, orgullosos de ese lugar tan pintoresco. El Club Atlético Boca Juniors, ubicado en Brandsen 805, es uno de los clubes de fútbol más importantes del país y fue fundado por cinco jóvenes habitantes del barrio de la Boca en 1905. El nombre de la institución fue tomado directamente del barrio, pero se le agregó la palabra "Juniors" que le daba a la denominación algo más de prestigio, contrastando con la fama de "barrio difícil" que se había ganado la Boca por aquel entonces. Su estadio de fútbol tiene capacidad para 50.000 espectadores y en su barrio social y deportivo se practican otras disciplinas deportivas.

Formal Oral Presentation Source Two (Audio)

CD 3 TRACK 15

Listen to the CD. A script of the recording is on page 431.

Practice Exercise Two

Question: ¿Cómo se establece la relación entre forma y función en la arquitectura para la época contemporánea?

Source One
Fundamentos para la formación socio-humanista del arquitecto.
Por Elio Pérez Ramírez
(*reduc.cmw.edu.cu*)

La arquitectura es un satisfacer de necesidades humanas y manifestación de la cultura en un momento histórico concreto. Podemos considerar y proponemos como arquitectura socialmente adecuada o apropiada aquella que armonice los aspectos mediados por los principios del desarrollo sustentable.

En la producción teórica sobre arquitectura y diseño hay conocimientos relativamente recientes que resultan de interés, siendo éstos el diseño ambiental y el ambiente humano. El segundo expresa que el ambiente en que existimos es una resultante dada por la interacción dialéctica de un medio físico y un medio socio-cultural. El diseño ambiental será por tanto la acción del proyecto integral sobre todos los componentes del ambiente humano, y de aquí se infiere que la formación socio-humanista del arquitecto puede ser de hecho un factor que coayuda al diseño del ambiente humano.

Por otra parte, en la época contemporánea un fuerte basamento conceptual para la formación socio-humanista tiene que considerar la teoría del Desarrollo Sustentable, o pudiera ser más apropiado la expresión Desarrollo Humano Sustentable, concepción que integra los aspectos incidentes en el desarrollo social teniendo en el centro al ser humano. En el caso de esta carrera, el enfoque en sistema deberá estudiar la relación entre la naturaleza, el ser humano y la arquitectura, de acuerdo a las realidades de hoy. "La relación entre la naturaleza, el ser humano como ser social y la Arquitectura como parte de la sociedad y la cultura, debe convertirse en un sistema integrativo e interactivo, tendiente a lograr la felicidad (el bienestar, la seguridad física y sanitaria, la libertad, democracia, equidad, justicia social y progreso) de todos los seres humanos; en un ambiente interactuante, protegido de cualquier contaminación y con un equilibrado aprovechamiento de los recursos naturales que garantice indefinidamente la vida en el planeta bajo las condiciones antes mencionadas." En resumen, lo humano es una de las dimensiones básicas de la sustentabilidad.

**Formal Oral
Presentation
Source Two (Audio)**

CD 3 TRACK 16   Listen to the CD. A script of the recording is on page 431.

**Practice Exercise
Three**

Question: ¿Hasta qué punto influye la inmigración sobre la identidad nacional de la población en movimiento?

Source One
Ideogramas del encuentro de dos mundos. Por Luis Werner
(© University of Texas, Las Américas. Marzo/abril)

La línea que separa el universo precolombino y la América posterior a la conquista es, en el mejor de los casos, difusa. Constantemente, los historiadores de la época, interesados en el arte, la sociedad y la cultura, buscan límites e interrupciones que indiquen el momento en que se produjo el cambio de lo nativo a lo europeo, el aquí y el allá, lo que estaba antes y lo que vino después. Lo que buscan, en verdad, es una especie de mapa mental, un diagrama de las diferencias entre el Nuevo y el Viejo Mundo y de los caminos e intersecciones que conducen de uno a otro.

En este caso, los mapas no son sólo una metáfora, sino expresiones de espacio, dirección y contigüidades, tan reales como las tierras que procuran representar. Y las representaciones cartográficas coloniales, como las tierras de esa época, son los lugares físicos de encuentro entre colonizadores y colonizados, donde las versiones de la historia y la realidad de unos pueden ser borradas, superpuestas o reemplazadas por las de los otros. ¿Qué mejor, entonces, que estudiar el encuentro colonial analizando los mapas que trazaron juntos?

El 25 de mayo de 1577, el rey Felipe II de España firmó una cédula real que iba adjunta a un cuestionario de cincuenta preguntas. Juan López de Velasco, designado cosmógrafo mayor del Consejo de Indias, fue el encargado de enviar este cuestionario, en el que se pedía un detallado informe sobre todas las comunidades indígenas y españolas bajo el dominio de la corona, con la esperanza de complementar un pormenorizado proyecto cartográfico que se había ordenado para los Países Bajos y España, con elevaciones fijas, coordenadas y distancias lineales exactas.

Formal Oral Presentation Source Two (Audio)

CD 3 TRACK 17

Listen to the CD. A script of the recording is on page 432.

Practice Exercise Four

Question: ¿Qué se expresa en la música popular, o sea, música relacionada con la vida cotidiana, que resulta en una música clásica de su tipo?

**Source One
El corrido**

(InfoMorelos.com)

El corrido es una parte central de la música popular mexicana. Se ha convertido en una de las fuentes más eficientes para la difusión de las historias heroicas o románticas. Estas historias, frecuentemente se ubican en el ambiente de la revolución de 1910; sin embargo, ahora también se abarcan temas como el narcotráfico y la política contemporánea. Los temas más populares y difundidos son el amor engañado, la queja del débil frente al poderoso, el énfasis en actos guerreros, la habilidad especial en el manejo de las armas y el desafío después de haber sufrido alguna injusticia.

En los tiempos de la revolución, los cantantes viajeros recitaban los corridos en las calles o las plazas públicas, para comunicar novedades acerca de los acontecimientos importantes, así como lo habían hecho los trovadores de la Edad Media. La fuerte difusión de los corridos también tiene que ver con la venta de los textos impresos en papel de colores en las ferias y fiestas populares. Estas impresiones frecuentemente estaban ilustradas por el entonces totalmente desconocido artista José Guadalupe Posada.

Estas hojas servían frecuentemente para la difusión de ideas revolucionarias. Eran algo así como celdas de lo subversivo que, normalmente, fueron ignoradas por parte de la censura, ya que estas hojas se consideraban como "asuntos del populacho" sin importancia.

El musicólogo Vicente T. Mendoza opina que el primer corrido fue "Macario Romero", que data del año 1898 y surgió en el estado de Durango. El texto relata un acontecimiento del año 1810.

El corrido es recitado o cantado y tiene parte de sus raíces en la música popular española. La voz principal a veces es apoyada por un refrán cantado por un coro. El acompañamiento consiste principalmente en instrumentos de cuerda, tales como la guitarra, el violín y el guitarrón. A veces también tocan instrumentos de viento, sobre todo trompeta.

Sin embargo, frecuentemente una guitarra basta para cantar los corridos, presentando historias de infidelidad, borracheras, tragedias familiares, atrevidas aventuras y amores a un público que escucha sorprendido, admirado o indignado.

Además existen diferentes concursos para la composición y representación de corridos. Hoy en día, Chabela Vargas, Amparo Ochoa, Cuco Sánchez, Vicente Fernández y otros son los intérpretes más destacados de los corridos tradicionales, mientras que los Tigres del Norte son el representante más conocido del corrido contemporáneo.

Formal Oral Presentation Source Two (Audio)

CD 3 TRACK 18

Listen to the CD. A script of the recording is on page 432.

Practice Exercise Five

Question: ¿Cuál puede ser la importancia de la revolución tecnológica para la gente de Latinoamérica?

Source One
Apocalipsis en los Andes. Por Mary Louise Pratt
(Las Américas. Julio/agosto 1999)

Para los pueblos indígenas y las sociedades tribales de todo el mundo, el fin del milenio actual parece representar efectivamente una especie de encrucijada histórica. Ya no existe un "espacio exterior" ajeno al sistema económico mundial; ya no habrá más primeros contactos o primeros encuentros; terminaron en este siglo. La gente está experimentando un proceso acelerado de penetración, ahora que la globalización ejerce presiones sobre el espacio, la ecología y los recursos con una crueldad y una agresividad cada vez mayores. Muchos pueblos indígenas y sociedades tribales se encuentran hoy día en una situación más vulnerable que hace 25 años.

Al mismo tiempo, en la revolución de las comunicaciones, estos pueblos y sociedades han encontrado nuevas formas de exigir una participación en estos procesos, de hacer valer sus demandas y aspiraciones, de incorporar sus valores y su vision del mundo en el diálogo y las negociaciones y de agruparse para tratar de defender sus intereses comunes. Por ejemplo, la Declaración de Quito de 1991 es uno de los primeros documentos producidos en este siglo por una coalición de pueblos indígenas de todo el continente. Este documento fue el resultado de una convención de dirigentes indígenas que se celebró en el contexto del Quinto Centenario en 1991. A principios de los años noventa se aprobó en Colombia una nueva Constitución en la que por primera vez se reconocían los derechos de los pueblos indígenas y en la que se garantizaba su representación en las cámaras de gobierno. En los debates que se han producido en Canadá con respecto a la soberanía, los derechos de los indígenas han desempeñado un nuevo y crucial papel que ha sido determinante en los resultados, en la medida en que el país acepta el hecho de que no habrá solución legítima a sus problemas constitucionales sin el consentimiento de la numerosa minoría indígena. Del holocausto que sufrió Guatemala en los años ochenta ha surgido una red de intelectuales mayas que persiguen un proyecto cultural y epistemológico de carácter notable y singular. El Tercer Congreso Internacional de Puebos Indígenas, celebrado en 1995, contó con la presencia de delegaciones de Australia, Nueva Zelandia, Escandinavia, Hawaii y las Américas. Bolivia eligió su primer vicepresidente indígena, quién creó espacio para expresiones culturales y políticas muy vigorosas. Y, claro está, por correo electrónico y por fax el Movimiento Zapatista de Chiapas está esparciendo por todo el mundo una crítica muy enérgica y fascinante no sólo del contexto local, sino, en forma más amplia, de todo México y del propio capitalismo mundial.

Formal Oral Presentation Source Two (Audio)

CD 3 TRACK 19

Listen to the CD. A script of the recording is on page 433.

SCRIPTS OF THE FORMAL ORAL PRESENTATIONS

Formal Oral Presentation Source Two (Audio)

CD 3 TRACK 14

Programa *Nuestra América,*
La Habana, 16 de enero 2006

Michelle Bachelet, Nueva Presidenta de Chile

Santiago de Chile, 15 de enero.—Michelle Bachelet ganó hoy las elecciones chilenas tras derrotar al derechista Sebastián Piñera, lo que la convertirá en la primera presidenta de Chile, reportó EFE.

El Ministerio del Interior chileno informó hoy de que, con el 97,71% de los votos escrutados, Bachelet obtuvo el 53,49% frente al 46,50% de Piñera.

El derrotado candidato de la derecha, Sebastián Piñera, reconoció su derrota y felicitó a su rival, a quien deseó "el mayor de los éxitos."

La victoria de Bachelet causó una explosión de alegría en su coalición, en donde el senador democratacristiano Andrés Zaldívar afirmó que la electa Presidenta gobernará para todos los chilenos, "los que votaron por ella y los que no lo hicieron".

Diversas agencias de prensa se referían en la noche de ayer a que casi medio millón de chilenos se lanzaron a las calles para vitorear a Michelle Bachelet, agitando banderas y cantando *Vuelvo,* la canción mítica del grupo local Illapu, que narra la emoción de miles de exiliados durante la dictadura militar, entre ellos la Presidenta electa.

El Gobierno de Bachelet, que tomará posesión de su cargo el 11 de marzo, será el cuarto de la coalición de centroizquierda Concertación por la Democracia desde 1990, destacó EFE.

Desigualdad: Reto para Próximo Presidente
Santiago de Chile, 15 de enero.—El próximo presidente enfrentará el desafío de altos niveles de desigualdad social y desempleo. Organismos oficiales con-

firman que el 20% más acaudalado de los chilenos percibe 15 veces más que el 20 más pobre, y de esa cifra de poderosos, el 1% resulta particularmente concentrador de riquezas.

Chile está ubicado entre los 15 primeros países (de 130) con peor desigualdad de ingresos a nivel mundial y según el Instituto Nacional de Estadísticas, aún 532.607 personas se mantienen analfabetas: 258.262 hombres y 274.345 mujeres. De acuerdo con el último censo, existe un 4,7% de indigentes, es decir 728.063 personas, mientras un 14,08% enfrenta el desamparo no indigente (2.179.653).

CD 3 TRACK 15

Source Two (Audio)
Gime bandoneón tu tango gris. Por Kevin Carrel Footer
(Las Américas. Septiembre/octubre 2003)

El sensual romance entre Buenos Aires y el bandoneón parece salido de un tango: un inmigrante vagabundo de Sajonia, fracasado en su tierra nativa, se traslada a una nueva ciudad, se enamora de una hermosa mujer, pero ella le es infiel. Como en todo tango, él no puede olvidarla. Y así nace el lamento del bandoneón.

Para ser justos en esta historia de amor, ella tampoco lo olvida. Es verdad que si no fuera por Buenos Aires el bandoneón habría sido relegado desde hace mucho tiempo a la lista de oscuras invenciones musicales que han fracasado: un complicado instrumento con extraño sonido no habría sobrevivido mucho tiempo después de su nacimiento en la década de 1840 si no hubiera sido adoptado por Buenos Aires y su nueva música, el tango. Como tantos inmigrantes que dejaron atrás sus vidas para comenzar una nueva en esa tierra lejana, la fusión del bandoneón y la ciudad es tan indeleble que ahora es imposible concebir el bandoneón sin Buenos Aires, o Buenos Aires sin su bandoneón.

CD 3 TRACK 16

Source Two (Audio)
Santuarios insulares de Chiloé. Por Ricardo Carrasco Stuparich
(Las Américas. Mayo/junio 2003)

La isla de Chiloé, un tenaz puesto de avanzada en el confín del continente, es el típico lugar para poner a prueba la intrepidez humana, como de hecho ha sucedido durante siglos. Sus habitantes, los chilotes, resisten el clima lluvioso y tormentoso que envuelve la isla y todo lo que hay en ella en una penetrante soledad. Ante los ojos del que recorre las praderas, lomajes y acantilados de la isla—la más grande de América del Sur después de Tierra del Fuego—hasta sus numerosas iglesias y capillas comienzan a aparecer como faros entre la bruma. No es de sorprender que durante años, innumerables marinos hayan navegado a lo largo de la costa de Chiloé, guiados por los capiteles más altos de algunas de estas iglesias. Pareciera que los hombres de fe siempre han encontrado su camino hacia Chiloé.

En esta isla y el pequeño archipiélago de aproximadamente 200 kilómetros de largo, existen alrededor de ochenta iglesias, la mayoría cobijadas en bahías y ensenadas, como para no perder de vista el encuentro entre la tierra y el mar. Casi todas fueron construidas bajo la dirección de misioneros jesuitas que viajaron y predicaron en la región en los siglos XVII y XVIII, tradición que fue continuada y enriquecida por los franciscanos en el siglo XIX. Recientemente, la

UNESCO declaró Patrimonio de la Humanidad a dieciséis iglesias de Chiloé, señalando que éstas representan un ejemplo único en América Latina de la extraordinaria forma de arquitectura religiosa en madera, una vibrante fusión con materiales y artesanía indígena.

CD 3 TRACK 17

Source Two (Audio)
Identidad social y nacional en América Latina: ¿mito o realidad?
Por Dr. Ángel Rodríguez Kauth

(topis.com.arg)

En todo caso, la identidad de los pueblos iberoamericanos, desde el período en que Iberoamérica estaba habitada por aborígenes hasta la actualidad, solamente tiene como constante una continuidad geográfica, la que vio la luz durante el siglo XIX. Desde que se puso en marcha la gran corriente inmigratoria, proveniente de Europa hacia nuestras costas, hecho que ocurrió desde finales de aquel siglo y hasta aproximadamente 1930, la identidad de nuestros pueblos fue modificándose. Ese movimiento migratorio fue cambiando la identidad—nacional, social y cultural—de cada uno de los pueblos integrados en una Nación/Estado; de tal suerte fue aquel fenómeno, que se ha ido constituyendo una identidad nacional diferente a la existente en la época precolombina y, en estos momentos en que los aluviones inmigratorios se producen dentro del espacio geográfico de toda América—en especial entre países limítrofes—, es posible hablar de una suerte de "latinoamericanización" de nuestros pueblos. Cosa ésta que fundamentalmente está afectando—por ejemplo—a los Estados Unidos de Norteamérica, merced a la "invasión" de hispanohablantes que llegan del resto del continente.

En este lugar no puede dejar de recordarse que América Latina no es un mosaico de culturas ibéricas e indígenas, también en ella han participado activamente las culturas africanas—Brasil, Cuba, Haití, etc.—, las europeas centrales y orientales y, en la actualidad, las corrientes de inmigraciones asiáticas que están dejando marcada su impronta.

Obvio es que todos estos episodios de características migratorias-inmigratorias conllevan en su seno la modificación de las pautas de cualquier metodología con que se pretende estudiar la identidad de tales pueblos.

CD 3 TRACK 18

Source Two (Audio)
Mariachi—Al son de la musa moderna. Por Trudy Balch
(Las Américas. Mayo/junio 1999)

"¿Qué me gusta de la música de mariachi?" Es fácil: "Es lo mejor de México", declara alegremente el hombre de blanco sombrero de vaquero, una de las casi mil personas que esperan el comienzo de un reciente concierto del Mariachi Vargas de Tecalitlán, uno de los grupos más importantes de México. "Levanta el ánimo si estás triste y si estás alegre te hace sentir aun mejor." "Inclusive tomé una pastilla para no emocionarme demasiado", agrega su madre sentada a su lado.

Esta escena, que se multiplica por millones a lo largo de dos siglos o más, da una idea del aprecio que siente la gente por esta música contagiosa que hace vibrar no sólo los corazones de México sino del mundo entero. El Mariachi Vargas había vuelto de Japón poco antes del concierto, que tuvo lugar en Degollado, una población de Jalisco, en el oeste de México. En el último Encuentro

Internacional del Mariachi, festival internacional que se celebra en Guadalajara todos los años en septiembre, una de las bandas que se presentó viajó desde Roma. ¿Su nombre? "Romantitlán", por supuesto.

Aunque los historiadores difieran sobre el origen de la palabra "mariachi", lo que la hace única está fuera de discusión. En primer lugar, los sones: canciones sincopadas y pegadizas cuyos versos de ocho sílabas tratan generalmente de la naturaleza y la cultura local y, desde luego, del amor. Los sones del Mariachi Vargas alternan frecuentemente compases de 6/8 y 3/4, aunque también es común el 6/8. En segundo lugar, los instrumentos: ningún mariachi moderno estaría completo sin varios violines que lleven la melodía y una sección de acompañamiento rítmico formada por guitarra, vihuela (un pequeño instrumento de cinco cuerdas parecido a una guitarra cuya barriga, llamada "joroba" por los mariachis, se asemeja al casco de un bote) y guitarrón (un tipo de vihuela grande de seis cuerdas). Tampoco pueden faltar las trompetas, cuyo sonido metálico aviva la melodía aún más. Aunque no tan común en los grupos modernos, el arpa es también un instrumento tradicional, que sirve doblemente para apoyar el ritmo y para los vivaces solos en los que los dedos parecen bailar.

CD 3 TRACK 19

Source Two (Audio)
Cibercomunidades, medios virtuales, hipertextos, portales y otras promesas de la era digital. Por Dr. José Luis Orihuela

(Encuentro Internacional Comunicación e Integración PUCE, Quito, octubre de 1999. *terra.es*)

El desafío profesional al que nos enfrentamos en el terreno de la comunicación no consiste simpletmente en "adaptarse al cambio", como si de una moda se tratase, ni tampoco se limita a utilizar con naturalidad un nuevo lenguaje. Lo que se plantea como exigencia es mucho más radical y pasa por comprender y controlar las nuevas características de los medios de la comunicación pública. De lo que se trata es de ser protagonistas, no espectadores, de la revolución tecnológica, para poder convertir en realidades las promesas de la era digital.

Señalaré a continuación una serie de convergencias y transiciones que constituyen las notas dominantes del nuevo medio:

- Internet ha provocado la disolución de las fronteras que separaban a los medios en función de su soporte y de los formatos de información.
- El teléfono (es decir las redes de telecomunicaciones) se fusiona con la radio y la televisión y emerge el pointcasting, un sistema de difusión audiovisual a la vez universal y personalizado.
- Finalmente, la comunicación pública y la autoridad editorial se han separado. El papel tradicional de los editores como filtro ... aparece hoy al menos cuestionado y desde luego compartido.

Aquí, la pregunta correcta no es cómo pueden contribuir las nuevas tecnologías de la comunicación al proceso de integración regional y a la preservación de la paz, sino qué tenemos que hacer nosotros para conseguirlo.

El poder, en la era digital, ya no es el control del espacio sino del conocimiento. Las guerras hoy se libran con armas controladas por los mismos ordenadores que se utilizan para hacer *Toy story*, *Titanic* o *La amenaza fantasma*.

Si se trata de hablar de los medios y de la paz, habrá que recordar el carácter instrumental de la tecnología y en consecuencia la urgente necesidad de educar a los usuarios.

Es de vital importancia que nos planteemos la necesidad de extender y democratizar el acceso a Internet en Hispanoamérica, de incorporar nuestros contenidos culturales y nuestra lengua a la Red.

La lengua es uno de los factores estratégicos de mayor importancia en el proyecto de unión entre América Latina y la Red.

Finalmente, los medios masivos de la región pueden impulsar iniciativas conjuntas como el intercambio de profesionales, el desarrollo de programas de prácticas para estudiantes, y la producción en conjunto de materiales (suplementos, programas o servicios de información).

PART SIX APPENDICES

Model Exam Answer Sheet

SECTION I
Part A

1. Ⓐ Ⓑ Ⓒ Ⓓ	9. Ⓐ Ⓑ Ⓒ Ⓓ	17. Ⓐ Ⓑ Ⓒ Ⓓ	25. Ⓐ Ⓑ Ⓒ Ⓓ
2. Ⓐ Ⓑ Ⓒ Ⓓ	10. Ⓐ Ⓑ Ⓒ Ⓓ	18. Ⓐ Ⓑ Ⓒ Ⓓ	26. Ⓐ Ⓑ Ⓒ Ⓓ
3. Ⓐ Ⓑ Ⓒ Ⓓ	11. Ⓐ Ⓑ Ⓒ Ⓓ	19. Ⓐ Ⓑ Ⓒ Ⓓ	27. Ⓐ Ⓑ Ⓒ Ⓓ
4. Ⓐ Ⓑ Ⓒ Ⓓ	12. Ⓐ Ⓑ Ⓒ Ⓓ	20. Ⓐ Ⓑ Ⓒ Ⓓ	28. Ⓐ Ⓑ Ⓒ Ⓓ
5. Ⓐ Ⓑ Ⓒ Ⓓ	13. Ⓐ Ⓑ Ⓒ Ⓓ	21. Ⓐ Ⓑ Ⓒ Ⓓ	29. Ⓐ Ⓑ Ⓒ Ⓓ
6. Ⓐ Ⓑ Ⓒ Ⓓ	14. Ⓐ Ⓑ Ⓒ Ⓓ	22. Ⓐ Ⓑ Ⓒ Ⓓ	30. Ⓐ Ⓑ Ⓒ Ⓓ
7. Ⓐ Ⓑ Ⓒ Ⓓ	15. Ⓐ Ⓑ Ⓒ Ⓓ	23. Ⓐ Ⓑ Ⓒ Ⓓ	
8. Ⓐ Ⓑ Ⓒ Ⓓ	16. Ⓐ Ⓑ Ⓒ Ⓓ	24. Ⓐ Ⓑ Ⓒ Ⓓ	

Part B

31. Ⓐ Ⓑ Ⓒ Ⓓ	37. Ⓐ Ⓑ Ⓒ Ⓓ	43. Ⓐ Ⓑ Ⓒ Ⓓ	49. Ⓐ Ⓑ Ⓒ Ⓓ
32. Ⓐ Ⓑ Ⓒ Ⓓ	38. Ⓐ Ⓑ Ⓒ Ⓓ	44. Ⓐ Ⓑ Ⓒ Ⓓ	50. Ⓐ Ⓑ Ⓒ Ⓓ
33. Ⓐ Ⓑ Ⓒ Ⓓ	39. Ⓐ Ⓑ Ⓒ Ⓓ	45. Ⓐ Ⓑ Ⓒ Ⓓ	51. Ⓐ Ⓑ Ⓒ Ⓓ
34. Ⓐ Ⓑ Ⓒ Ⓓ	40. Ⓐ Ⓑ Ⓒ Ⓓ	46. Ⓐ Ⓑ Ⓒ Ⓓ	52. Ⓐ Ⓑ Ⓒ Ⓓ
35. Ⓐ Ⓑ Ⓒ Ⓓ	41. Ⓐ Ⓑ Ⓒ Ⓓ	47. Ⓐ Ⓑ Ⓒ Ⓓ	53. Ⓐ Ⓑ Ⓒ Ⓓ
36. Ⓐ Ⓑ Ⓒ Ⓓ	42. Ⓐ Ⓑ Ⓒ Ⓓ	48. Ⓐ Ⓑ Ⓒ Ⓓ	54. Ⓐ Ⓑ Ⓒ Ⓓ

Model Exam

SPANISH LANGUAGE

SECTION I - PART A
Listening Comprehension
Time—Approximately 30 minutes

DIALOGUES

Directions: Listen to the following dialogues. After each one, listen to the questions about the dialogue and select the best answer from the choices printed below. Write your answers on the answer sheet on page 435.

Dialogue number 1

CD 3 TRACK 20

1. (A) Quiere acompañarlo a un concierto.
   (B) Quiere ir a un espectáculo con Elena.
   (C) Quiere ir a un partido de fútbol.
   (D) Quiere visitar a su abuelo.

2. (A) No puede esperar hasta que llegue el grupo.
   (B) A él y a su amigo les encanta el grupo.
   (C) A él no le gusta tanto como le gusta a su amiga.
   (D) Los odia tanto que mentirá para escapar de la obligación.

3. (A) Juan aconseja que no le diga la verdad a Elena.
   (B) Juan le recomienda que lleve a su amiga a visitar a su abuela.
   (C) Juan sugiere que Miguel haga las dos actividades.
   (D) Juan sugiere que Miguel le diga a ella que está enfermo.

4. (A) Su amiga es buena amiga de su abuela.
   (B) Elena puede adivinar cuando Miguel le miente.
   (C) Elena es casi un miembro de la familia.
   (D) Miguel nunca le dice nada a su amiga.

5. (A) Juan propone que vayan al partido de fútbol.
   (B) Juan sugiere que le diga que tienen que ir a la biblioteca.
   (C) Juan recomienda que vayan a la biblioteca el domingo.
   (D) Juan recomienda que diga otra mentira a Elena.

6. (A) Miguel decide ir al partido de fútbol.
   (B) Miguel decide asistir al concierto con Elena.
   (C) Miguel decide visitar a su abuela.
   (D) Miguel decide hacer la tarea e ir a la biblioteca.

GO ON TO THE NEXT PAGE

Dialogue number 2

CD 3 TRACK 21

7. (A) Rafael no está bien porque se enfermó antes de un examen.
   (B) Rafael no está bien porque no salió bien en un examen.
   (C) Rafael está deprimido porque tuvo que ir a una fiesta.
   (D) Rafael está deprimido porque pasó mucho tiempo en la biblioteca.

8. (A) Todo sucedió el fin de semana pasada.
   (B) Su desastre ocurrió el día anteayer.
   (C) Pasó ayer.
   (D) Pasó ese mismo día.

9. (A) No estudió porque Ana le invitó a una fiesta.
   (B) No estudió porque algunos amigos le invitaron a jugar.
   (C) No estudió porque quería leer revistas en la biblioteca.
   (D) No estudió porque se aburrió estudiando.

10. (A) Anita festejó a los jugadores de fútbol.
    (B) Anita festejó a su amigo Rafael.
    (C) Anita celebró la visita de un estudiante extranjero.
    (D) Anita invitó a la clase de historia a su casa.

11. (A) Su mamá lo felicitó por su buen éxito.
    (B) Su mamá se alegró de que pudiera jugar con sus amigos.
    (C) Su mamá se enfadó mucho.
    (D) Su mamá lo complació permitiéndole salir ese fin de semana.

12. (A) Una fiesta en casa de Anita.
    (B) Un partido de fútbol.
    (C) La visita de un estudiante de intercambio.
    (D) La visita de Mani, el portero famoso de Los Reyes.

GO ON TO THE NEXT PAGE

NARRATIVES

Directions: Now listen to two short narratives. After each one you will be asked to respond to some questions about the selection you have heard. Select the best answer from among the four choices you are given below. Write your answers on the answer sheet on page 435.

Narrative number 1

CD 3 TRACK 22

13. (A) Algo para comer.
    (B) Un animal doméstico.
    (C) Una maleta llena de ropa.
    (D) Una gallina viva.

14. (A) El tonto interpretó las instrucciones de otra manera.
    (B) El tonto se había comido toda la gallina.
    (C) El tonto estaba dormido en el gallinero.
    (D) El tonto había matado la gallina.

15. (A) El tonto estaba muy orgulloso de su gallinero.
    (B) El tonto quería probar que las gallinas tenían una pata.
    (C) El cura quería ver cómo dormían las gallinas.
    (D) El tonto quería mostrarle al cura donde dormía.

16. (A) El muchacho sabía cuidar bien de la maleta.
    (B) El muchacho sabía que las gallinas tenían una pata.
    (C) El muchacho sabía racionalizar lo que había hecho.
    (D) El muchacho tenía buena imaginación.

Narrative number 2

CD 3 TRACK 23

17. (A) El que habla es profesor de música.
    (B) El que habla es crítico de música clásica.
    (C) El que habla es estudiante de un músico famoso.
    (D) El que habla es músico profesional.

18. (A) Tocaban de manera muy apasionada.
    (B) Tocaban de manera muy restringida.
    (C) Tocaban que si fueran moribundos.
    (D) Tocaban con gran libertad de movimiento.

19. (A) Después de practicar mucho tiempo decidió que no le gustó la vieja manera.
    (B) Decidió seguir las sugerencias de su maestro.
    (C) Siempre practicaba de la manera más natural para sí mismo.
    (D) Nunca tocaba de otra manera.

20. (A) Descubrió una técnica que le permitió mover la mano más.
    (B) Descubrió una técnica con la cual pudo tocar más notas sin mover la mano.
    (C) Supo que tocaba mejor con los brazos pegados a los costados.
    (D) Supo que era posible escandalizar a su profesor de música.

21. (A) Acabó adoptando la forma de su estudiante.
    (B) Acabó despidiéndose de su estudiantes.
    (C) Acabó pretendiendo que la gustaba lo que hizo su estudiante.
    (D) Se escandalizó por lo que hacía su estudiante.

GO ON TO THE NEXT PAGE ▶

LONGER SELECTIONS

Directions: You will now listen to two longer selections, each one about 5 minutes in length. The selection may be a longer narrative, a radio program, an interview, or some other type of material. After you have listened to each narrative, answer the questions below by selecting the best answer from A, B, C, or D. Then mark the answer on the answer sheet (page 435).

Selection number 1

CD 3 TRACK 24

22. ¿Qué suceso cuenta este narrador?
 (A) Narra lo que pasa en un día cualquiera de escuela.
 (B) Narra lo que pasó el día de solicitar entrada en la escuela.
 (C) Narra el día de un examen muy difícil.
 (D) Narra la visita de los padres a la escuela.

23. ¿Cómo se sentían los niños?
 (A) Nerviosos.
 (B) Alegres.
 (C) Deprimidos.
 (D) Seguros de sí mismos.

24. ¿Por qué se preocupaban algunos estudiantes?
 (A) No saben mucho de matemáticas.
 (B) No tuvieron tiempo para hacer el problema.
 (C) Los padres estaban muy preocupados.
 (D) Los estudiantes más listos no querían ayudar a sus compañeros.

25. ¿Cómo era el maestro?
 (A) Parecía un animal.
 (B) Tenía buenos sentimentos.
 (C) Era tiránico y cruel.
 (D) Era tonto.

Selection number 2

CD 3 TRACK 25

26. ¿A quién se dirige este experto del protocolo internacional?
 (A) Se dirige a los presidentes de naciones.
 (B) Se dirige a las señoras que invitan a personas distinguidas a su casa.
 (C) Se dirige a cualquier persona que reciba una invitación al Palacio Real.
 (D) Se dirige tanto a las personas con invitados regulares como los con invitados reales.

27. ¿Cuál es el propósito de tener un protocolo?
 (A) Para que todos los invitados al Palacio Real se comporten cortésmente.
 (B) Para que todos se entiendan cuando hay reuniones en casas privadas.
 (C) Para que cualquier persona se sienta bien cuando acepta invitaciones.
 (D) Para que nadie se sienta olvidado ni infeliz en la cena.

28. ¿Dónde debe sentarse a una pareja o un matrimonio?
 (A) Siempre se coloca al hombre cerca de una señora o señorita guapa.
 (B) Siempre hay que colocar a la señora al lado de otra para que puedan conversar.
 (C) Siempre hay que darles la oportunidad de hablar con otros.
 (D) Siempre es buena idea juntarlos para evitar disputas después de la cena.

GO ON TO THE NEXT PAGE

29. ¿Por qué no se sientan las mujeres en las puntas de la mesa?
    (A) Es más fácil emparejar este sitio, y por eso no se pone a una señora allí.
    (B) Es un sitio muy peligroso, con toda la gente que pasa, por eso no es apropiado.
    (C) Es más fácil entablar conversación con otra persona que esté al lado.
    (D) Es mala suerte colocarlas en ese sitio, por eso no se hace.

30. ¿Qué remedio hay cuando un invitado no puede venir, dejándolo con doce?
    (A) Se puede matar a uno de los invitados.
    (B) Siempre se puede evitar el número trece por nunca invitar a catorce.
    (C) Se puede invitar a otro amigo íntimo al último momento.
    (D) Se puede llamar a uno y cancelar la invitación.

END OF PART A.
YOU MAY CHECK YOUR ANSWERS ON THE QUESTIONS ABOUT THE LONGER SELECTIONS
OR YOU MAY GO ON TO PART B.

PART B
Reading Comprehension
Time—Approximately 40 minutes

Directions: Read the following passages. After each passage there are a number of questions or incomplete statements for you to answer, based on the information provided in the reading selection. Choose the response that best answers the question or completes the sentence.

Selection number 1

Me callé entonces, y durante un tiempo que no pude medir, pero que pudo ser muy largo, no cambiábamos una palabra. Yo
Línea fumaba; él levantaba de rato en rato los ojos
(5) a la pared,—al exterior, a la lluvia, como si esperara oír algo tras aquel sordo tronar que inundaba la selva. Y para mí, ganado por el vaho de excesiva humedad que llegaba de afuera, persistía el enigma de aquella
(10) mirada y de aquella nariz abierta al olor de los árboles mojados.

—¿Usted ha visto un dinosaurio?

Esto acababa de preguntármelo él, sin más ni más.

(15) Lo miré fijamente; él hacía lo mismo conmigo.

—Jamás. ¿Usted lo ha visto?

—Sí.

No se le movía una pestaña mientras me
(20) miraba.

—¿Aquí?

—Aquí. Ya ha muerto ... Anduvimos juntos tres meses.

¡Anduvimos juntos! Me explicaba ahora
(25) bien la luz ultra histórica de sus ojos.

—Era un nothosaurio... Pero yo no fui hasta su horizonte; él bajó hasta nuestra edad... Hace seis meses. Ahora... ahora tengo más dudas que usted sobre todo esto.
(30) Pero cuando lo hallé a la orilla del Paraná, al crepúsculo, no tuve duda alguna de que yo desde ese instante quedaba fuera de las leyes biológicas. Durante tres meses fue mi compañero nocturno. Cuando nuestra fra-
(35) ternidad era más honda, era las noches de lluvia. Cuando la lluvia llegaba por fin y

se desplomaba, nos levantábamos y caminábamos horas y horas y horas sin parar. Mi vida de día proseguía su curso normal
(40) aquí mismo, en esta casa. Vivía maquinalmente de día, y sólo despertaba al anochecer. No sé qué tiempo duró esto. Sólo sé que una noche grité, y no conocí el grito que salía de mi garganta. Y que no tenía
(45) ropa, y sí pelo en todo el cuerpo. En una palabra, había regresado a las eras pasadas por obra y gracia de mi propio deseo. Por eso, lo busqué una noche y cuando lo encontré, el odio de diez millones de años
(50) de vida atemorizada cayó sobre la cabeza del monstruo. Ambos murieron esa noche.

31. ¿Dónde parece haber ocurrido este acontecimiento?
(A) En esa misma casa.
(B) En la selva más remota
(C) Cerca del Paraná.
(D) En las afueras de una ciudad.

32. ¿Qué contó el hombre al narrador?
(A) Contó su regreso a una época prehistórica.
(B) Relató la muerte de dos dinosaurios.
(C) Narró un encuentro con un salvaje.
(D) Contó una extraña amistad con un monstruo prehistórico.

GO ON TO THE NEXT PAGE

33. ¿Cómo cambió la vida del hombre?
    (A) Se volvió loco porque dudaba que pudiera existir un dinosaurio.
    (B) Lentamente se convirtió en contemporáneo del monstruo.
    (C) Se hizo un salvaje porque quería tanto al dinosaurio.
    (D) Poco a poco el hombre perdió contacto con la vida cotidiana.

34. ¿De qué se dio cuenta una noche el hombre?
    (A) Supo que el monstruo iba a devorarlo.
    (B) Reconoció que el monstruo era una alucinación.
    (C) Se dio cuenta de que había contradicho las leyes biológicas.
    (D) Reconoció el salvaje dentro de sí mismo.

35. ¿De qué tenía miedo el hombre?
    (A) Temía perderse por completo en su locura.
    (B) Temía que se matara a sí mismo.
    (C) Temía que el salvaje lo matara.
    (D) Temía que el narrador lo matara.

36. ¿En la línea 51, qué se refiere la palabra *ambos* en la oración: *Ambos murieron esa noche*?
    (A) Se refiere al hombre y al monstruo.
    (B) Se refiere al dinosaurio y al hombre.
    (C) Se refiere al odio y al temor del hombre.
    (D) Se refiere a la causa y al efecto de su trastorno.

37. ¿Qué actitud parece tener el hombre del suceso al contarlo al narrador?
    (A) Lo narró como si fuera la historia más natural del mundo.
    (B) Admitía sus propias dudas con respeto a la veracidad del suceso.
    (C) Admitió que ahora no creía que hubiera pasado como lo recordó.
    (D) No quería admitir la verdad porque revelaría su locura.

38. ¿Cómo se relaciona la lluvia con lo que contaba el hombre?
    (A) La lluvia representa el regreso a la época prehistórica.
    (B) Al llover se borraban las líneas que definen la época prehistórica y la moderna.
    (C) La lluvia es una alusión a los mitos de la creación del universo.
    (D) La lluvia no tiene nada que ver con lo que contaba el hombre.

Selection number 2

¡Esto sí que es una gran venta! Ahora, visitar a familiares y amigos le cuesta hasta un 35 por ciento menos de nuestras tarifas
Línea ya rebajadas. Aeronaves quiere celebrar con
(5) usted su nuevo y cómodo servicio a Mérida, México, y a Tegucigalpa, Honduras, vía Houston, ¡con tarifas super-especiales! Y para celebrar en grande, se han rebajado las tarifas a todas las ciudades que
(10) sirve en Latinoamérica. Pero apúrese, porque debe comprar sus boletos de ida y vuelta, mínimo 7 días antes de viajar, y sólo tiene hasta el 8 de febrero para comprarlos. La nueva y comodísima terminal interna-
(15) cional de Aeronaves en el aeropuerto hace más fácil que nunca viajar a Latinoamérica, incluyendo los trámites de aduana e inmigración. Además, cada vez que viaja con Aeronaves, gana millaje con nuestro pro-
(20) grama Número Uno, una de las maneras más rápidas de ganar viajes gratis. ¡Inscríbase y comience a ganar! Para detalles y reservaciones, llame a su agente de viajes.
    Estas tarifas están basadas en la compra
(25) de boletos de ida y vuelta, los que deben adquirirse no más tarde del 8 de febrero, o sea una semana en adelante. Los boletos deben comprarse un mínimo de 7 días antes de viajar. La máxima estadía es de 60
(30) días y todos los viajes deben terminar el 23 de marzo del año actual, o antes. No se permite viajar del 27 de marzo al 2 de abril. Es mandatorio pasar la noche de un sábado en el viaje. El importe de los boletos no es
(35) reembolsable. Hay un cargo de US$75 si se hacen determinados cambios en las reservaciones. Solicite los detalles. Las tarifas pueden no estar disponibles en todos los vuelos y los asientos son limitados. Ningún
(40) otro descuento es aplicable. El cargo por seguridad de US$10 y el impuesto de embarque de los EEUU de US$6 por persona a Centroamérica, no están incluidos. El cargo por seguridad de US$6 y el
(45) impuesto de embarque de EEUU de US$6 a

GO ON TO THE NEXT PAGE ⟩

México, tampoco están incluidos. Estas
tarifas son para viajes que se originan en
Tejas. El servicio a Guayaquil comenzará el
6 de febrero. Estas tarifas están sujetas a la
(50) aprobación del gobierno y pueden cambiar
sin previo aviso.

39. ¿Qué tipo de materia representa este trozo?
    (A) Es un anuncio de un periódico.
    (B) Es un contrato entre una línea aérea y el
        que compra un boleto.
    (C) Es un aviso de nuevas condiciones en la
        compra de boletos.
    (D) Es de un folleto de turismo de una
        agencia de viajes.

40. ¿Qué oferta se anuncia en esta selección?
    (A) Se anuncian maneras de conseguir viajes
        gratis con su nuevo programa Número
        Uno.
    (B) Se anuncian problemas con los trámites
        de aduana e inmigración.
    (C) Se ofrecen unas reducciones de tarifas.
    (D) Se anuncian las restricciones en viajes
        internacionales.

41. ¿Con qué motivo se promueve esta oferta?
    (A) Se celebran el año de la familia.
    (B) Se celebran es establecimiento del
        programa Número Uno.
    (C) Se celebran su nuevo servicio del nuevo
        aeropuerto.
    (D) Se celebran sus nuevas tarifas rebajadas.

42. Una persona puede aprovechar esta oferta
    con tal que:
    (A) Compre el boleto ocho días en
        anticipación del viaje.
    (B) No compre un boleto sencillo.
    (C) Permanezca la noche de sábado en la
        destinación.
    (D) Todas estas respuestas.

43. Si una persona quiere viajar a Tegucigalpa,
    Honduras, ¿cuánto le costaría extra?
    (A) No le costará extra.
    (B) Le costará $10 más.
    (C) Le costará $16 más.
    (D) Le costará $6 más.

44. Si por alguna razón una persona no puede
    usar el boleto, ¿qué recurso tiene?
    (A) Se puede recibir un reembolso por el
        precio del boleto.
    (B) Con tal que pague cierta cantidad se
        puede cambiarlo.
    (C) Se puede usarlo para recibir un
        descuento en otro boleto.
    (D) El boleto cuenta para millaje en el
        programa Número Uno.

45. ¿En qué consiste el texto del segundo
    párrafo?
    (A) Es una enumeración de destinaciones
        del servicio.
    (B) Contradice lo que ofrecen en el primer
        párrafo.
    (C) Es un anuncio de condiciones y
        limitaciones.
    (D) Rechaza responsabilidad de cumplir
        todos los términos de la oferta.

GO ON TO THE NEXT PAGE ▷

Selection number 3

"Ninguno diga quién es, que sus obras lo dirán." Este proloquio es tan antiguo como cierto; todo el mundo está convencido de

Línea su infalibilidad; y así ¿qué tengo yo que

(5) ponderar mis malos procederes cuando con referirlos se ponderan? Lo que apeteciera, hijos míos, sería que no leyerais mi vida como quien lee una novela, sino que pararais la consideración más allá de la cáscara

(10) de los hechos, advirtiendo los tristes resultados de la holgazanería, inutilidad, inconstancia y demás vicios que me afectaron; haciendo análisis de los extraviados sucesos de mi vida, indagando sus causas,

(15) temiendo sus consecuencias y desechando los errores vulgares que veis adoptados por mí y por otros; empapándoos en las sólidas máximas de la sana y cristiana moral que os presentan a la vista mis reflexiones, y en

(20) una palabra, desearía que penetrarais en todas sus partes la substancia de la obra; que os divirtierais con lo ridículo; que conocierais el error y el abuso para no imitar el uno ni abrazar el otro, y que donde

(25) hallarais algún hecho virtuoso os enamorarais de su dulce fuerza y procuraríais imitarlo. Esto es deciros, hijos míos, que deseara que de la lectura de mi vida sacarais tres frutos, dos principales y uno accesorio:

(30) amor a la virtud, aborrecimiento al vicio y diversión. Ése es mi deseo, y por esto, más que por otra cosa, me tomo la molestia de escribiros mis más escondidos crímenes y defectos; si no lo consiguiera, moriré al

(35) menos con el consuelo de que mis intenciones son laudables. Basta de digresiones, que está el papel caro.

46. ¿A quién o quiénes se dirige este escritor?
(A) Al lector casual.
(B) A sus hijos.
(C) A sus padres.
(D) A sus críticos.

47. ¿Qué ha escrito?
(A) Un papel caro.
(B) Una novela de los hechos malos de su vida.
(C) Un libro sobre proverbios útiles.
(D) Sus reflexiones de su vida.

48. ¿Con qué motivo ha escrito?
(A) Se arrepiente de haber malgastado su vida.
(B) Quiere confesar sus crímenes.
(C) Quiere entretener al lector.
(D) Quiere analizarse.

49. ¿Qué tipo era este escritor?
(A) Parece ser moralista.
(B) Parece ser perezoso.
(C) Parece ser mezquino.
(D) Parece ser agradable.

50. ¿Qué puede el lector sacar de la lectura?
(A) Puede aprender a imitarlo en todas sus obras.
(B) Puede entender que las obras hablan por sí mismas.
(C) Puede aprender a analizar lo que lee.
(D) Puede aprender de las equivocaciones de otros.

51. ¿Qué puede esperar el lector de lo que ha escrito?
(A) Lo que escribe será divertido.
(B) Lo que escribe consistirá en todos sus secretos más íntimos.
(C) Lo que escribe revelará un hombre deprimido.
(D) Escribirá de lo bueno y lo malo de su vida.

52. ¿Qué espera el autor?
(A) Que el lector se entretenga.
(B) Que el lector no lo juzgue.
(C) Que el lector aprenda proverbios.
(D) Que el lector sea mejor que él.

GO ON TO THE NEXT PAGE

53. ¿Cuál es la actitud que demuestra?
    (A) Optimista.
    (B) Pesimista.
    (C) Realista.
    (D) Tiene ilusiones.

54. ¿Qué otro proverbio expresa la misma idea que *Ninguno diga quién es, que sus obras lo dirán*?
    (A) Cada loco con su tema.
    (B) Dime con quién andas, y te diré quién eres.
    (C) Quien se acuesta con perros, se levanta con pulgas.
    (D) El que mucho habla, mucho yerra.

END OF SECTION I

SPANISH LANGUAGE

SECTION II - PART A
Time—Approximately 7 minutes

(On the actual Spanish Language Exam, this free-response section is in a separate sealed booklet.)

Paragraph Completion With Root Words

Directions: Read the following passage, then on the numbered lines to the right, write the form of the word in parentheses needed to complete the passage. More than one word may be necessary to complete the meaning; for example, a compound verb form or a reflexive pronoun may be required. In order to receive any credit, the words must be spelled correctly and the appropriate accent, dieresis, or tilde must be written in the proper places. Be sure to write the word on the proper line, even if no changes are necessary to make it fit grammatically or logically.

Cuentan que un hombre sabio plantó en su jardín un árbol

sabiendo que sólo daría fruta ____(1)____ tres décadas. Este hecho

llegó a oídos del rey, quién le mandó llamar y le dijo, — ____(2)____

muy optimista si esperas vivir hasta que este árbol ____(3)____ fruto.

El sabio le respondió, —Quizás no pueda gozar de este fruto, pero

mis sucesores se beneficiarán como yo me ____(4)____ del trabajo de

mis predecesores.

Pero después de treinta años, el árbol sí ____(5)____ dos frutas.

El sabio fue al palacio del rey para donárselas. El monarca,

agradecido, le recompensó con dos monedas de oro.

Un campesino, enterado de que el rey ____(6)____ al sabio, llenó

una canasta con frutas de su huerta y ____(7)____ en el palacio

____(8)____ la misma recompensa. — ____(9)____ Merced, dijo, —

permitidme donaros estas frutas de mi huerta.

El rey despidió al campesino diciendo—Echad fuera a los

que actúan por imitación sin comprender que sólo se ____(10)____

la originalidad.

1. _____
   (pasado)

2. _____
   (Ser)

3. _____
   (dar)

4. _____
   (beneficiar)

5. _____
   (producir)

6. _____
   (pagar)

7. _____
   (presentarse)

8. _____
   (exigir)

9. _____
   (Vuestra)

10. _____
   (apremiar)

GO ON TO THE NEXT PAGE

Paragraph Completion Without Root Words

Time—Approximately 8 minutes

Directions: In the following selections, first read through each selection. Then write a word on the numbered line that corresponds to the numbered blank in the text. Write only ONE word that completes the meaning of the sentence. No credit will be given for words that are not spelled correctly or words that lack correct accent marks. You have 8 minutes to complete this part of the exam.

Noticia sobre las escuelas en Nuevo México

(*El Vocero Hispano—17 de enero 2006. http://www.elvoceromi.com/news*)

____(1)____ lugar a dudas, la inclemencia de la temporada de

huracanes fue nuevamente la noticia más importante en el

sur de la Florida. No sólo ____(2)____ la cifra récord de 26

tormentas tropicales formadas de junio a noviembre,

____(3)____ por la fuerza y el impacto directo que ____(4)____

de estos fenómenos tuvieron en el sur de los Estados Unidos.

Noticias sobre la longevidad en Cuba

El Vocero Hispano—17 de enero de 2006

Según el galeno, el reto más importante que debe enfrentar la

sociedad cubana en el presente siglo es la longevidad satisfac-

toria y ____(5)____ ello se trabaja en aras de extender la expec-

tativa de vida ____(6)____ nacer a más ____(7)____ 80 años, cifra

que ahora sólo poseen Suecia y Japón.

 Resaltó que en la Isla se trabaja en la reserva de años

de vida ____(8)____ ganar, que en su mayoría está en las

personas mayores de 60 años y precisó que el 60 por ciento

de la esperanza de vida actualmente puede estar en personas

con seis décadas o ____(9)____ . Esta nación insular del Caribe

posee más ____(10)____ dos mil personas que superan la

centuria y más de medio millón que sobrepasan los 80 años.

1. _____

2. _____

3. _____

4. _____

5. _____

6. _____

7. _____

8. _____

9. _____

10. _____

GO ON TO THE NEXT PAGE

Informal Writing

Time—Approximately 10 minutes

Directions: Below you will see instructions for a writing sample that responds to the topic described. Be sure to include the information mentioned in your response. You will have 10 minutes to write your message in your test booklet.

Ud. ha pedido una carta de recomendación a un profesor para enviarla con su solicitud de ingreso a una universidad. Escríbale una carta mencionando los siguientes puntos:

- Salúdelo de manera apropiada.
- Mencione lo que recuerda más de su clase.
- Mencione sus esperanzas para el futuro.
- Despídase apropiadamente.

GO ON TO THE NEXT PAGE

Formal Writing (Integrated Skills)

Time—55 minutes

> Directions: You will now read a question that is based on information contained in Sources 1–4. The sources are both print and audio. First, read the printed material. Next, you will hear the audio material. You should take notes on the spaces provided in the test booklet while you listen. Take about 7 minutes to read and about 3 minutes to listen to the audio. Take 5 minutes to plan. Then, you will have 40 minutes to write your essay.
>
> In your essay you should make reference to specific information from all the source materials. Do not simply summarize what is contained in them. Incorporate them into your essay. Use appropriate grammar and vocabulary.

Los inmigrantes aportan muchos beneficios culturales a los países adonde van. ¿En qué sentido están cambiando las vidas culturales de los anfitriones?

Source One
Movimientos humanos e inmigración

(Fórum, Barcelona 2004. *www.barcelona2004.org/esp/contenidos/dialogos/*)

El Congreso Mundial MHI trata los movimientos humanos y la inmigración desde una triple perspectiva: intercultural, interdisciplinaria e intersectorial.

Los actores de las migraciones se han convertido en los protagonistas de los cambios sociales en este cambio de siglo. Han cambiado los motivos que los mueven de un lugar a otro. Las trayectorias de la migración definen itinerarios nuevos, cambiantes y reversibles, pero sobre todo proyectan la imagen del migrante como una persona que constituye un proyecto personal. La movilidad de las personas genera además redes que tejen las comunidades transnacionales en el mundo, nuevos proyectos vitales e imancipadores (para las mujeres, para los jóvenes, para las comunidades políticas...). Todavía quedan por resolver desplazamientos humanos que son consecuencia de las guerras y las desigualdades. Y al mismo tiempo, es necesario tener muy en cuenta que detrás de cada proyecto migratorio se esconde una gran riqueza humana, social y política.

La inmigración en estados plurinacionales nos obliga a revisar de qué manera se construyen las identidades. Desde el punto de vista de las identidades nacionales que todavía no han encontrado un sitio en un estado, los cambios sociales relativos a la identidad (inmigración, comunidades transnacionales, gestión de corrientes, etc.) fuerzan una nueva definición de los mismos referentes de identidad nacional sin renunciar al anhelo de cohesión social y de creación de vínculos culturales comunitarios.

Source Two
Vale la pena mirar el experimento migratorio de España. Por Marcela Sánchez ·

(*washingtonpost.com,* Jueves, 13 de octubre, 2005)

El gobierno español estima que gracias a la amnistía, trabajadores previamente ilegales aumentarán las contribuciones al fondo de seguridad social este año en un 3 por ciento. Aunque es una cifra todavía modesta, se espera que las contribuciones aumenten. Por otra parte, en balance, los inmigrantes—en su mayoría jóvenes y con pocas personas a su cargo—representan menos demandas al sistema de seguridad pública, según Walter Actis, un especialista en inmigración de la organización de investigación social con sede en Madrid, Colectivo Ioé. Según cifras oficiales, casi un 80 por ciento de los que ya han sido legalizados están entre los 16 y los 39 años de edad.

GO ON TO THE NEXT PAGE

El programa ya está dando un importante vistazo a una fuerza laboral que hasta ahora se había desempeñado lejos del alcance gubernamental. Funcionarios españoles están descubriendo, por ejemplo, que inmigrantes ilegales ganan mejores salarios de lo que pensaban. En vez de contribuir $990 dólares anualmente a la seguridad social, están contribuyendo $1.300 dólares en promedio.

Esto claramente proveerá cierto incentivo para que los trabajadores regresen a sus países de origen, pero no será suficiente si las oportunidades siguen siendo muy inferiores a las de Europa. No hay duda que mejores niveles de vida en América Latina son el camino seguro para reducir el flujo de inmigrantes ilegales y es por eso que algunos consideran la legalización un importante factor de desarrollo.

Una vez que los inmigrantes puedan ir y volver libremente, ganar más, ahorrar más e invertir más, los propios inmigrantes ayudarán a preparar a sus países para su retorno. Enrique Iglesias, secretario general de la Cumbre Iberoamericana y una de las voces mas respetadas acá y en Washington sobre América Latina, dijo en una entrevista que los inmigrantes podrían convertirse en "puentes" para el desarrollo de la región, mucho más allá de lo que ya hacen a través de sus multimillonarias remesas. Pero para que eso suceda, agregó, "no se puede aceptar que los inmigrantes permanezcan fuera del circuito" como ciudadanos de tercera clase.

Source Three
Relacions culturales entre Alemania y la Argentina

(*embajada-alemana.org.ar/culturas/main_becas1.htm*)

La opinión pública de la Argentina se muestra receptiva y con un sentido fraternal frente a Alemania, lo cual también se da a la inversa.

Nuestra cooperación en el ámbito de la política cultural con la Argentina está sustentada en el Convenio Bilateral de Cultura celebrado en 1973. La última reunión (4ta.) de la Comisión Mixta Argentino-Alemana de Cultura se llevó a cabo en Bonn, en abril de 1997.

La actualidad cultural alemana estuvo representada en Buenos Aires durante 1999 y 2000 en máximo nivel por los conciertos de la Orquesta Filarmónica de Berlín dirigida por Claudio Abbado, funciones del Ballet de Hamburgo con John Neumeier y presentaciones de la Big Band de la radio NDR. Todas ellas recibieron la absoluta máxima calificación de los medios locales. Gracias al Instituto Goethe, en particular, también se mostraron facetas del arte alemán y de la cultura alemana contemporáneos así como expresiones artísticas que analizan la historia alemana más moderna y más reciente: "Murx", representada por la *Berliner Volksbühne* con puesta en escena de Christoph Marthaler, la exposición de Baselitz, talleres musicales sobre György Ligeti y sus alumnos, ciclos de conferencias sobre temas de "Identidad", "Tiempo" y "Conceptos modernos de cultura" (Ulrich Beck, Catherine David, Andreas Huyssen, Jürgen Safranski, entre otros).

La representación de la cultura alemana en la Argentina no sólo finalizó a fines de 1999 con una semana de cine en Buenos Aires, donde se exhibieron largometrajes actuales y con la presencia de la realizadora Doris Dörrie, sino que se vio coronada con la visita de Franz Beckenbauer en febrero de 2000 en el marco de una campaña de promoción para la candidatura de Alemania como organizador del Campeonato Mundial de Fútbol de 2006, un hecho destacado de la cooperación deportiva entre ambos países.

A la inversa, en los últimos años se desarrolló en Alemania, particularmente en Berlín, un gran interés no sólo por el tango argentino, sino también por el teatro argentino moderno. Durante 1999 se invitaron a cuatro producciones teatrales de Buenos Aires a participar en el festival *Theater der Welt* en Berlín. Durante el año 2000 fueron tres producciones de la capital argentina que causaron sensación en el teatro Hebbel de Berlín. La estrella argentina del ballet, Julio Bocca, triunfó con su compañía en la EXPO de Hannover y la Orquesta Bandoneón de la ciudad de Tandil, Provincia de Buenos Aires, presentó la clásica cultura argentina del tango en diversas actuaciones en Sajonia.

Source Four (Audio)

CD 3 TRACK 26   Listen to the CD. A script of the recording is on page 460.

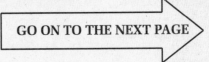

GO ON TO THE NEXT PAGE

Section II—PART B
Time—Approximately 5 minutes

Informal Speaking (Simulated Conversation)

<u>Directions</u>: Below is a simulated conversation. You will have 30 seconds to read the script, which contains instructions about what to say. The conversation will then be played so you can hear it. After hearing the conversation, you will have one minute to reread the script. At the end of one minute, the conversation will be played again. The second time it is played, you will have 20 seconds to record your part of the script in the appropriate spots in the dialogue.

Una amiga le llama y le dice que sus padres acaban de darle permiso para invitar a Ud. para que la acompañe en un viaje a Florida durante las vacaciones escolares de primavera. Discuten los planes.

    (a) Su amiga se llama Eva. Le llama para darle las noticias.
    (b) Ud. colabora en los planes.

     (Suena el teléfono.)
     Eva: (Saludos.)
                   (La da las noticias.)
     Ud.:   (Reacciona.)
                   (Pide detalles.)
     Eva: (Le dice adonde van.)
     Ud.:   (Expresa emoción.)
                   (Hace una pregunta.)
     Eva: (Explica sus esperanzas.)
     Ud.:   (Se pone de acuerdo con ella.)
                   (Agrega un deseo propio.)
     Eva: (Explica por qué no se puede.)
     Ud.:   (Expresa un sentimiento apropiado.)
     Eva: (Ofrece otra actividad alternativa.)
     Ud.:   (La acepta.)
     Eva: (Concluye la conversación, despidiéndose.)
     Ud.   (Se despide.)
                   (Cuelga el teléfono.)

CD 3 TRACK 27   The full script is on page 461.

GO ON TO THE NEXT PAGE

Section II—PART B
Time—Approximately 5 minutes

Formal Oral Presentation

<u>Directions</u>: Below you will see a question with two accompanying sources of information. You have 5 minutes to read the printed text. After 5 minutes, you will hear a recording. You should take notes in the space provided. After the recording has been played, you will have 2 minutes to plan your response to the questions. After 2 minutes, you will be instructed to begin your recording. At the end of 2 minutes you will be told to stop recording. This will be the end of the language examination.

Imagínese que tiene que presentar un reportaje sobre el siguiente tema. En su presentación incluya la información contenida en los dos materiales suplementarios.

Se ha comentado mucho la importancia de conservar las tradiciones folklóricas de la gente. En una presentación de unos dos minutos, diga Ud. por qué es importante saber aún más sobre tradiciones antiguas.

Source One
La destrucción de la agricultura incaica. Por Antonio Elio Brailovsky y Dina Foguelman
(*www.holistica2000.com.ar/ecocolumna226.htm*)

El imperio incaico fue un espectacular ejemplo de eficiencia en el manejo de la tierra y en el respeto al equilibrio ecológico de la región. Ningún sistema posterior consiguió alimentar a tanta población sin degradar los recursos naturales. Los incas basaron su civilización en una relación armónica con su ambiente natural, integrado por los frágiles ecosistemas andinos, y desarrollaron complejos y delicados mecanismos tecnológicos y sociales que les permitieron lograr una sólida base económica sin deterioros ecológicos.

Se pueden ver aún las terrazas de cultivo, construidas como largos y angostos peldaños en los faldeos de las montañas, sostenidos por piedras que retenían la tierra fértil. Las terrazas cumplían la función de distribuir regularmente la humedad. Allí el agua de lluvia iba filtrándose lentamente desde los niveles superiores a los inferiores, utilizándose plenamente la escasa cantidad de líquido disponible. En las áreas más lluviosas y en las de mayor pendiente, las terrazas permitían evitar la erosión, al impedir que el escurrimiento superficial del agua de lluvia arrastrara las partículas del suelo. También facilitaron el aprovechamiento de los diversos pisos ecológicos.

El suelo de las terrazas se mezclaba con guano, el excremento de aves marinas acumulado en las islas y costas. Este recurso era cuidadosamente administrado, porque de él dependía en buena medida la alimentación de la población: para extraerlo, cada aldea tenía asignada una parte de isla o costa, marcada con mojones de piedra que no era permitido alterar. "Había tanta vigilancia en guardar aquellas aves, que al tiempo de la cría a nadie era lícito entrar en las islas, so pena de la vida, porque no las asombrasen y echasen de sus nidos. Tampoco era lícito matarlas en ningún tiempo, so la misma pena", dice el Inca Garcilaso de la Vega.

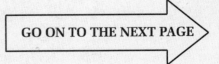
GO ON TO THE NEXT PAGE

Había muy poco suelo que fuera naturalmente apto para el cultivo y había que construirlo metro a metro. Su explotación no hubiera sido posible sin riego, porque la mayor parte de la zona andina es árida o semiárida. Había que ir a buscar el agua a las nacientes de los arroyos y encauzarla mediante una red de canales. Se describen algunos principales, de muchos kilómetros de largo y hasta cuatro metros de diámetro, pero aun para una pequeña superficie aterrazada se consideraba que valía la pena hacer un canal de gran longitud. Para eso, se hacía un surco a lo largo de las montañas y se lo cubría con grandes losas de piedra unidas con tierra para que el ganado no lo destruyese. A veces, al cruzar un valle, era necesario sostener el canal sobre columnas para que el nivel del agua no perdiese altura, construyéndose acueductos similares a los romanos.

Source Two (Audio)

CD 3 TRACK 28   Listen to the CD. A script of the recording is on page 461.

GO ON TO THE NEXT PAGE

MODEL EXAM SCRIPTS

SECTION I, PART A.
LISTENING COMPREHENSION.

CD 3 TRACK 20

DIALOGUE NUMBER ONE

NAR 1: ¡Hola, Juan! Hombre, hace mucho tiempo que no te veo. ¿Qué haces?

NAR 2: ¡Miguel! ¡Hola! Estaba pensando en ti justamente ayer. Vi en la tele que el equipo boliviano vendrá la semana que viene para jugar una exhibición en el estadio. Sé que te interesas mucho en el fútbol. ¿Quieres ir conmigo?

NAR 1: Sí, sí, lo vi también. Me gustaría acompañarte, pero es que prometí a Elena llevarla a un concierto de los Zafios Ingleses que dan un espectáculo ese mismo día. Qué lástima, ¿verdad? Ojalá que pudiera ir al partido porque ese grupo de músicos es malísimo, pero a ella le encanta. ¿Qué puedo hacer?

NAR 2: Pues, déjame pensarlo un poco. Acaso pueda pensar en algo para liberarte. ¿No puedes decirle que tu abuela está enferma y tienes que visitarla esa noche?

NAR 1: Ojalá que fuera tan fácil. No, es que ella está bien enterada de lo que pasa con mi familia. Pues, otra vez, podemos ir a un partido.

NAR 2: No nos rindamos de inmediato, podemos pensar en algo. ¿No tenemos un reportaje para el lunes? Puedes decirle que te hace falta preparar algunas investigaciones en la biblioteca. Así es— tienes que pasar todo el día ese sábado en la biblioteca.

NAR 1: Sé que tienes buenas intenciones, Miguel. Pero es que di la palabra. Ésa con los bolivianos no sería la última oportunidad. Habrá otras. Gracias por tu ayuda. Tal vez la próxima vez.

Preguntas

Número 1. ¿Qué quiere Juan hacer con su amigo?

Número 2. ¿Qué piensa Miguel de los Zafios Ingleses?

Número 3. ¿Qué le recomienda Juan que haga su amigo?

Número 4. ¿Por qué piensa Miguel que no lo creería su amiga?

Número 5. ¿Qué otra idea tiene Juan?

Número 6. ¿Qué decisión toma Miguel al fin de la conversación?

CD 3 TRACK 21

DIALOGUE NUMBER TWO

NAR 1: ¡Hola, Rafael! ¿Qué hay de nuevo?

NAR 2: No mucho. Ando un poco deprimido, de veras.

NAR 1: Pues, ¿por qué? ¿No me dijiste ayer por la mañana que todo te iba bien? Ah, ya recuerdo. También me dijiste que había un examen en la clase de historia el primer período. ¿Verdad? Debe tener algo que ver con ese examen.

NAR 2: Pues, quizás. Pero por la tarde anteayer cuando me senté para estudiar, empecé a pensar en las revistas que había en la biblioteca. Y luego, pensé en las fotos de Mani, el portero del Equipo Real. Y luego, antes de darme cuenta de lo que hacía, salí de la biblioteca. Me encontré con Roberto y algunos de los otros y nos reunimos en el parque para jugar al fútbol.

NAR 1: Bueno, Rafael, todavía tuviste tiempo para estudiar esa noche.

NAR 2: Sí, pero Anita me había invitado a su casa esa noche para un baile con un grupo de sus amigas. Ella quería acoger al estudiante peruano que está en la escuela de intercambio. Fue una fiesta magnífica. No me fue posible salir hasta tarde.

NAR 1: No me digas. La primera clase es de historia y no tuviste tiempo para estudiar.

NAR 2: Ya lo ves. Estoy seguro de que lo suspendí. Y cuando volví a casa ayer, mi mamá me interrogó. Cuando supo lo que me pasó, me regañó. Ahora no puedo salir este fin de semana.

NAR 1: ¡Hombre! Es una lástima porque tenemos esa competencia con Los Reyes de San Miguel Allende este sábado por la tarde.

NAR 2: Sí, pues, no hay remedio. Mi mamá está decidida.

Preguntas

Número 7. ¿Qué le pasa a Rafael?

Número 8. ¿Cuándo sucedió el desastre para Rafael?

Número 9. ¿Por qué no estudió Rafael?

Número 10. ¿A quién festejó Anita en su fiesta?

Número 11. ¿Cómo reaccionó la mamá de Rafael?

Número 12. ¿Qué perderá Rafael ese fin de semana?

CD 3 TRACK 22

SHORT NARRATIVE NUMBER ONE

Un día iba pasando un cura por un pueblo y llegó a una casa donde había un muchacho algo tonto. El cura le dio una maleta, en la cual tenía una gallina cocinada, para que se la cuide.

A la noche, el tonto abrió la maleta y le comió una pata a la gallina. El cura fue después y vio que faltaba una pata; entonces le dijo al muchacho:

—¿Me has comido la pata de la gallina?

—¡No! ¡la gallina tiene una sola pata!

—No puede ser.

—Vamos al gallinero, y va a ver que las gallinas tienen una sola pata.

Llegan al gallinero y las gallinas estaban dormidas, paradas en una pata, y con la otra pata escondida bajo el ala. El cura las vio, y entonces gritó, espantándolas:

—¡Shííúu!

Entonces las gallinas despertaron, se asustaron y soltaron la pata escondida, y el cura dijo:

—¿Has visto que tienen dos patas?

Y el tonto le contestó:

—Si usted le hubiera hecho ¡shíííu! a su gallina, ésta hubiera soltado la pata también.

Preguntas

Número 13. ¿Qué dejó el cura con el muchacho?

Número 14. Cuando el cura volvió, ¿qué descubrió?

Número 15. ¿Por qué le mostró el mozo el gallinero al cura?

Número 16. ¿Por qué no era muy tonto el muchacho?

CD 3 TRACK 23

SHORT NARRATIVE NUMBER TWO

Principalmente creo que he simplificado la técnica del violoncelo, lo he hecho más natural,—dijo Pablo Casals.—He dado mayor libertad a los brazos. Antiguamente los violoncelistas tocaban adoptando una postura muy artificial y completamente agarrados, quedando entumecidos. Tenían la costumbre de mantener los codos pegados a los costados. Yo no podría hacer tal cosa. Nunca me preocupé demasiado de mí mismo. Así, pues, practiqué una natural utilización de los brazos. Y lo mismo con las manos al manejar los dedos. Los violoncelistas acostumbraban a mover continuamente las manos. Yo abrí la mano, dándole más alcance; ahora puedo tocar cuatro notas sin tener que mover la mano mientras que antes sólo podía tocar tres. Mi profesor estaba, desde luego, escandalizado viéndome actuar con tal postura, pues no tenía yo más que trece años cuando ya había empezado a desarrollar mi propia técnica, pero terminó por aceptarla cuando vio los resultados que yo obtenía con ella.

Preguntas

Número 17. ¿Quién habla en esta selección?

Número 18. ¿Cómo tocaban los violoncelistas cuando el narrador empezó su carrera?

Número 19. ¿Cómo hizo su descubrimiento?

Número 20. ¿Qué descubrimiento hizo?

Número 21. A fin de cuentas, ¿cómo reaccionó su profesor?

CD 3 TRACK 24

LONGER SELECTION NUMBER ONE

Estamos aquí ya en los exámenes. Por las calles del rededor de la escuela no se oye hablar de otra cosa a chicos, padres y madres, hasta a las ayas: exámenes, calificaciones, temas, suspensión, mediano, bueno, notable, sobresaliente: todos repiten las mismas palabras. Ayer mañana tocó el examen de Composición, hoy el de Aritmética. Era conmovedor ver a todos los padres conduciendo a sus hijos a la escuela, dándoles los últimos consejos por la calle, y a muchas madres que los llevaba hastan las bancas para mirar si había tinta en el tintero, probar si la pluma escribía bien, y se volvían todavía desde la puerta para decir: —¡Animo! ¡Valor! ¡Cuidado!—Nuestro maestro examinador era Coato, aquel de las barbazas negras que grita como un león, y que jamás castiga. Se veían caras de muchachos blancas como el papel. Cuando el maestro rompió el sobre del oficio del Ayuntamiento mandando el problema que debía servir para tema de examen, no se oía ni una mosca. Dictó el problema en alta voz, mirando ya a uno, ya a otro, con miradas severas: pero se comprendía que si hubiera podido dictar al mismo tiempo la solución para que todos hubiesen sido aprobados, lo habría hecho de buena gana. Después de una hora de trabajo, muchos empezaron a desesperarse, porque el problema era difícil. Uno lloraba. Y muchos no tienen culpa de no saber, ¡pobres chicos! pues no han tenido mucho tiempo para estudiar, y los han descuidado los padres. ¡Pero había una providencia! Había que ver el trabajo que se daba Deroso para ayudar a todos, para hacer pasar de mano en mano una cifra y una operación, sin que lo descubriesen, interesado por unos y por otros, como si fuese nuestro propio maestro. También Garrón, que está fuerte en Aritmética, ayudaba al que podía, hasta Nobis, que, encontrándose apurado, se había vuelto cortés. Estardo estuvo más de una hora inmóvil, sin pestañear, sobre el problema, con los puños en las sienes y los codos en la banca, y después hizo todo en cinco minutos. El maestro daba vueltas por entre los bancos diciendo: —¡Calma! ¡Calma! ¡No hay que precipitarse!—Y cuando veía a alguno descorazonado, para darle ánimo y hacerle reír, abría la boca, imitando al león, como si fuese a tragárselo. Hacia las once, mirando al través de las persianas, vi muchos padres impacientes que se paseaban. Poco antes de las doce llegó mi padre, y alzó los ojos a la ventana donde yo caía; ¡pobre padre mío! A las doce en punto todos habíamos concluido. Era de ver la salida. Todos venían al encsuentro de nosotros, preguntándonos, hojeando los cuadernos, confrontando los trabajos.—¡Cuántas operaciones! ¿Cuál es el total? ¿Y la substracción? ¿Y la respuesta? ¿Y la coma de los decimales?—Mi padre me arrancó de las manos el borrador, miró y dijo:—¡Está bien! —

CD 3 TRACK 25

LONGER SELECTION NUMBER TWO

NAR 1: Tenemos el placer de hablar con José Antonio de Urbina, diplomático profesional y experto en protocolo en la Corte española, quien ha escrito un libro que se titula *El arte de invitar.* Buenos días.

NAR 2: Buenos días. El gusto es mío.

NAR 1: ¿Hay un protocolo español distinto del protocolo austríaco, alemán, belga o inglés? ¿O hay un protocolo internacional?

NAR 2: Hay un protocolo internacional, que es en realidad europeo, ¿verdad? El español, que siempre tuvo gran prestigio, pues, es el mismo. Lo que pasa es que luego en cada país hay matices que son consecuencia de su cultura, de su identidad, etcétera. Pero la esencia es el protocolo europeo.

NAR 1: Este libro, ¿lo ha escrito Ud. para que lo conozcan y se lo sepan de memoria los presidentes de comunidades autónomas, los políticos, o para que nosotros, los ciudadanos de a pie, lo leamos, así, curioseemos en ese gran mundo y sus problemas?

NAR 2: Pues, no. El objetivo es que sea útil para todos, para todos. Curiosamente, cuando estaba escribiendo al principio, pues me di cuenta de que tanto personaje importante—reyes, presidentes— esto le va a asustar al lector de a pie, y por eso ya la segunda mitad la dedico más al lector común. Pero digo lo que es verdad, que, en esencia, el banquete de estos de gala en el Palacio Real y la mesa a la cual, por ejemplo, una señora, unos señores, reúnen unos amigos, en esencia, es lo mismo.

NAR 1: ¿Y cuál es, digamos, la base, la médula de esa esencia, para que aprendamos, por lo menos, lo fundamental?

NAR 2: Pues, la médula es, sencillamente, que la gente esté confortable, que se sienta en su casa. Por supuesto, si hay que comer, que la comida sea buena, ¿verdad? Pero lo esencial es que se encuentren cómodos, porque si no están cómodos, ¿para qué sirve el invitar?

NAR 1: Pero vamos a ver, vamos a ver. Eh, lo de chico, chica, chico, chica, señora, señora... ¿Eso es correcto, no?

NAR 2: Sí, sí, sí, claro.

NAR 1: Eso hay que hacerlo así.

NAR 2: Eso hay que hacerlo.

NAR 1: Parejas o matrimonios juntos, nunca.

NAR 2: Claro, hay que dejarles a los pobres que descansen un poco, y para eso se separan.

NAR 1: ¿Es cierto que hay que hablar en un plato con el de la derecha y en otro con el de la izquierda?

NAR 2: No. Eso depende, porque a lo mejor uno quiere hablar con la de la izquierda, que es una señora, a lo mejor está deseando porque además de que es muy simpática es muy guapa y resulta que ella está hablando con el otro.

NAR 1: Y qué, qué violento, ¿verdad? cuando queda uno descolocado en medio de dos personas que están hablando con otros y no con, con uno. Queda uno solo ahí, es incómodo.

NAR 2: Sí, sí, pasa, pasa. Entonces uno está esperando un poco al quite, es como la caza, ¿verdad? Ya está. Entonces, le dice uno cualquier cosa, entabla conversación, y a veces pasa que uno está demasiado con el de la derecha o la de la izquierda, y entonces es el otro el que se encuentra, ¿eh?

NAR 1: El que se pica.

NAR 2: Sí.

NAR 1: Así que hay que sentarse hombre, mujer, hombre, mujer, nunca las parejas juntas... Eh, dice usted en el libro que las señoras nunca deben estar en las puntas de la mesa.

NAR 2: Claro, es una elemental, diría yo, cortesía hacia la mujer, ¿verdad? Las puntas es un poco el último sitio. No hay que dejar los últimos sitios con señoras.

NAR 1: Sí. En una casa, tal vez esta noche muchos de nuestros oyentes vayan a reunirse con ocho o nueve amigos. Eh, para que se sienten diez personas o doce, ¿hay algún truquillo especial o alguna alerta que quiera usted hacer para que no se caiga en determinado...

NAR 2: Sí, bueno, hay que tener mucho cuidado con el número trece.

NAR 1: Ah, no. ¿Trece, no?

NAR 2: Nunca.

NAR 1: Porque si son trece, ¿qué hacemos? ¿Matamos a uno o invitamos a otro?

NAR 2: Nunca. No, por una razón. La gente es mucho más supersticiosa de lo que creemos. No lo dice, por supuesto.

NAR 1: Ah, ¿pero cuenta a ver si hay trece?

NAR 2: Pero, como el número trece es mala suerte, pues trece nunca. Y entonces, ¿qué haces? Catorce. Pero si se te descuelga un invitado en el último momento quedas en trece. Y claro, pues, ahí está el cuidado. El truco es, le llamas a un íntimo amigo: —*Mira, me pasa esto. ¿Quieres venirte a casa porque es que hemos quedado en trece...?* —Y por supuesto va, claro.

CD 3 TRACK 26

Source Four *(Listen to the recording first. Read the text below only after completing your essay, to verify that you heard all the information correctly)*

El Museo del Barrio celebra 30 años de excelencia promoviendo el arte latino en los Estados Unidos. Por Tania Saiz-Sousa

(*elmuseo.org/30annprs.html*)

Fundado en 1976, El Museo del Barrio ha tenido un gran impacto en la vida cultural de la ciudad de Nueva York, y es ahora una parada principal en la acreditada Milla de los Museos en Manhattan.

"Estamos orgullosos de las raíces puertorriqueñas de El Museo del Barrio, y también hemos extendido nuestra misión para así abarcar a las diversas comunidades latinas que hoy residen en la ciudad de Nueva York", comentó Susana Torruella Leval, directora ejecutiva. "Nuestro trigésimo aniversario marca un momento clave en nuestra historia. Estamos muy entusiasmados con los nuevos diálogos multiculturales y con las oportunidades para preservar y presentar la herencia cultural de los nuevos miembros de nuestra comunidad. También, aumentaremos el ámbito de nuestra colección permanente y exposiciones, y presentaremos nuevos programas educativos para la comunidad, grupos escolares y público asistente a nivel nacional e internacional", agregó Leval.

El aumento considerable en términos de las exposiciones, los programas educativos y número de visitantes—los cuales se han multiplicado en un 500% en los últimos cinco años—preparan a El Museo para los retos del nuevo milenio, y para alcanzar sus planes a corto y largo plazo. Estos planes incluyen la apertura del Teatro Heckscher en el verano del 2000, una joya arquitectónica de los años veinte con murales espectaculares y capacidad para 600 personas, el cual se encuentra localizado en el edificio que ocupa el Museo; la expansión de su tienda de souvenirs Imanosí, en la actualidad un lugar muy importante para impulsar las obras de los artistas latinos a nivel local y nacional; y la creación de ¡Las Américas Cafés!, un lugar de reunión informal donde se servirán cafés, refrescos y bocadillos caribeños y latinoamericanos.

CD 3 TRACK 27

SECTION II, PART B.
INFORMAL SPEAKING SCRIPT

Su amiga le llama y le dice que sus padres acaban de darle permiso para invitar a Ud. para que la acompañe en un viaje a Florida durante las vacaciones escolares de primavera. Discuten los planes.

(a) Su amiga se llama Eva. Le llama para darle las noticias.

(b) Ud. colabora en los planes.

  (Suena el teléfono.)

Eva: Hola, ¿te cuento? ¡Mis papás me dieron permiso para invitarte a acompañarnos a Florida! Iremos cuando lleguen las vacaciones de primavera, ¿qué te parece?

Ud.:   (Reacciona.)
        (Pide detalles.)

Eva: Vamos a ir a Disney World y después seguramente iremos a nadar y a pescar en el océano.

Ud.:   (Expresa emoción.)
        (Hace una pregunta.)

Eva: ¡Ay sí! Espero que nos dejen manejar el coche y así podamos salir con todos los amigos de allá.

Ud.:   (Se pone de acuerdo con ella.)
        (Agrega un deseo propio.)

Eva: No, no creo que podamos andar a caballo, porque el rancho de mi tío está en el norte del estado y eso está muy lejos.

Ud.:   (Expresa un sentimiento apropiado.)

Eva: ¡Pero sí podemos ir a bailar todas las noches! Los papás se acuestan temprano, pero sé que nos permitirán salir hasta las 11.

Ud.:   (La acepta.)

Eva: Bueno, me voy de compras. Qué buenas noticias, ¿no? Adiós, te llamo mañana.

Ud.:   (Se despide.)
        (Cuelga el teléfono.)

Source Two (Audio)

CD 3 TRACK 28

El uso del suelo en América Latina
(*www.eurosur.org/medio_ambiente*)

Análisis más detallados revelan que una tendencia importante de la agricultura latinoamericana ha sido la conversión de cultivos tradicionales como frijol y maíz a "nuevos" cultivos como oleaginosas, en particular soya y sorgo. Se calcula que de la tierra incorporada al cultivo entre 1970 y 1980 cerca de 62% fue para oleaginosas, específicamente soya, y que otro 24% se destinó a trigo, arroz y sorgo. Entre 1978 y 1983 el área destinada al cultivo de soya aumentó en dos millones de hectáreas. El aumento de los cultivos de exportación ha ido asociado con la reducción del uso de la tierra para cultivos tradicionales como el frijol negro en Brasil o el maíz en México.

Se observa también una clara relación entre deforestación y aumento de pastizales para ganadería: entre 1974 y 1983 la producción ganadera en América Latina aumentó 28%. De las tierras de los Andes orientales colombianos incorporadas entre 1960 y 1980 sólo 16% fueron para cultivos, mientras que 54% se dedicaron a la producción ganadera y 31% no fueron utilizadas del todo. Más de la mitad de los nuevos ranchos ganaderos son propiedades de más de 500 hectáreas.

Desde la perspectiva espacial, no cabe duda de que las actividades agropecuarias son las que tienen mayor incidencia sobre el medio ambiente dadas sus extensiones y, por lo tanto, el espacio afectado, la magnitud de las explotaciones y el hecho que América Latina es fundamentalmente una región centrada en la agricultura.

Los impactos que causan las modificaciones del suelo por la intervención humana se han ido magnificando con la creciente mecanización, la aplicación de agroquímicos, en particular fertilizantes sintéticos, plaguicidas, herbicidas y fungicidas, así como el uso de variedades genéticas mejoradas de elevado rendimiento, el aumento del riego, etcétera.

Algunas estimaciones señalan que la superficie cultivable de América Latina podría ampliarse hasta alcanzar entre 27% y 32% del total; sin embargo, esta ampliación de tierras cultivables se haría a costos crecientes. Hay que distinguir entre la incorporación propiamente dicha de nuevas tierras y la recuperación de tierras degradadas. Por ejemplo, se calcula que la incorporación de tierras en áreas desérticas costaría alrededor de 20.000 dólares por hectárea; pero la recuperación de terrazas y bancales abandonados en las zonas andinas altas de Perú y Bolivia sería del orden de los 2.000 dólares por hectárea, y un costo similar tendría la recuperación de tierras salinizadas en las áreas costeras regadas del Perú.

Answers

SECTION I

Part A

1. C	**9.** D	**17.** D	**25.** B
2. C	**10.** C	**18.** B	**26.** D
3. A	**11.** C	**19.** C	**27.** D
4. C	**12.** B	**20.** B	**28.** C
5. D	**13.** A	**21.** A	**29.** C
6. B	**14.** A	**22.** C	**30.** C
7. B	**15.** B	**23.** A	
8. C	**16.** C	**24.** A	

Part B

31. C	**37.** C	**43.** C	**49.** D
32. A	**38.** B	**44.** B	**50.** D
33. D	**39.** A	**45.** C	**51.** D
34. D	**40.** C	**46.** A	**52.** A
35. A	**41.** C	**47.** D	**53.** C
36. D	**42.** D	**48.** A	**54.** B

SECTION II

Paragraph completion with root words

1. *pasadas*
2. *Eres*
3. *dé*
4. *he beneficiado, beneficié*
5. *produjo*
6. *había pagado, pagó*
7. *se presentó*
8. *exigiendo*
9. *Vuestra*
10. *apremia*

Paragraph completion without root words

1. *Sin*
2. *por*
3. *sino*
4. *algunos, unos*
5. *para*
6. *al*
7. *de*
8. *por*
9. *más*
10. *de*

Grammar Review

The following section is a brief review of the most commonly missed points of grammar. The items are divided according to structural function of words. In some of the previous sections you are referred to this section so that you can understand why you have made inappropriate choices in the fill-in-the-blank sections or on the multiple choice section. You need to categorize the kinds of errors you make so that you can learn to recognize the structure. If you do not understand the overall rule, then you will spend time learning specific examples, which may or may not help you on the actual exam.

TONIC STRESS AND WRITTEN ACCENTS

In Spanish the stress (an elevation of the pitch of voice) occurs normally on the second to last syllable of a word when the word ends with any vowel (**a, e, i, o, u**), or the letters **s** or **n**, and no accent is written over the syllable. For words that end with the letters **r, j, l,** or **z**, the stress normally falls on the last syllable. For this reason, all infinitives have a stress on the last syllable. Any deviation from this rule is indicated by writing an accent above the stressed syllable.

When an accent in needed to stress a syllable containing a diphthong (two vowels, a strong and a weak one), or a triphthong (three vowels, one strong and two weak), the accent is written over the strong vowel in the syllable. For example, in the second person plural forms an accent is written over the **á**is and **é**is to indicate the stress on the last syllable of that verb form as in averig**uá**is and entreg**ué**is.

At times the accent is written over a weak vowel to form two syllables out of one. For example: at**aú**d has two syllables because the two vowels are equally emphasized. Normally, in the **au** combination, the sound of the **a** dominates because it is the strong vowel.

Sometimes an accent is written over a vowel to differentiate one part of speech from another. Such is the case with the words **él** (he), and **el** (the), **si** (if), and **sí** (yes), **tú** (you) and **tu** (your), and **mí** (me), and **mi** (my), **dé** (give) and **de** (from), **sé** (be, I know) and **se** (reflexive pronoun). Accents are used to differentiate demonstrative pronouns from demonstrative adjectives, **ése**, ese, etc., as well as interrogative pronouns from relative pronouns, such as **quién** from **quien** and **cuándo** from **cuando**.

NOUNS

Gender of Nouns

Masculine

All nouns are either masculine or feminine, with the gender of the noun usually indicated by the vowel at the end of the word. Generally, nouns that end with **-o** or **-or** are masculine. Frequently on the AP exam you will find the exception to this general rule. You should learn the gender of all nouns when you learn the word. It is helpful to remember that nouns that end with **-ama, ema,** and **-ima** are frequently masculine in spite of the fact that they end with the vowel **-a**. Common nouns that fall into this category are:

el clima	*el planeta*	*el sistema*	*el problema*
el día	*el tema*	*el lema*	*el diploma*
el mapa	*el poema*	*el monarca*	*el Papa*
el cometa	*el idioma*	*el tranvía*	*el albacea*

Usually the names of men, male animals, jobs, and titles concerning men, seas, rivers, mountains, trees, metals, languages, days, months, colors, and infinitives used as nouns are all considered masculine nouns.

Feminine

Most words that end with the vowel **-a** are feminine, along with words that end with **-ción, -dad, -ie, -umbre, -ud,** and **-sión**. For words that end in **-dor**, a masculine ending, an **-a** is added onto the **-dor** ending, thereby making the noun feminine. You should also remember that **mano** is feminine. (*La mano, las manos.*)

Some exceptions to the rule that words that end in **-ud** are feminine are the words:

el ataúd	*el césped*	*el talmud*

There are some nouns that end with the vowel **-a** that are feminine, but require the masculine singular article because the noun begins with a stressed **a** vowel. Some of these nouns are:

el agua	*el alma*	*el ama*	*el ave*
el águila	*el hada*	*el hacha*	*el haba*

When other adjectives modify these nouns, the adjectives take the feminine form:

el *agua* **fría**   **el** *ave* **negra**

In the plural forms, these nouns take feminine articles. For example:

las aguas	*las almas*	*las amas*	*las aves*
las águilas	*las hadas*	*las hachas*	*las habas*

Masculine nouns end with the letters **-o**, **-aje**, or with **-or**, (except for *la sor, la flor, la coliflor,* and *la labor*).

Making Nouns Plural   To make nouns plural: if the noun ends with a vowel you add **-s**. If the noun ends with a consonant (anything other than **-a, -e, -i, -o, -u**) add **-es** to the word. If the noun ends with the letter **z**, it changes to **c** before the **-es** is added to the end.

For example: **la luz, las luces**.

If the noun carries a written accent on the last syllable, remove the written accent since the stress will normally fall on the second to last syllable of any word that ends in the letter **s**.

For example:

la civilización (with a written accent)
las civilizaciones (no written accent)

Some nouns will add a written accent when they become plural forms. For example:

el joven (no written accent)
los jó**v**enes (with a written accent)

With a few nouns the syllable that carries the tonic stress shifts when the noun is made plural, such as: **ré**gimen—regí**menes**, *espé**cimen—especí**menes*, *cará**cter—caract**eres*.

If the written accent occurs on the third to last syllable, do not change it.

Compound nouns that end in a plural form, such as the word *parabrisas*, do not add an **-es** to the end, but the number of the article changes from **el** *parabrisas*, for example, to **los** *parabrisas*. Days of the week that end with **-es** also do not add **-es**, but rather take a plural article, *el jueves, los jueves*.

Nouns that end with an accented vowel also add **-es**. For example *el rubí, los rubíes*.

Remember that if the accent is not written in the correct location, no credit is given for that item in the fill-in-the-blank section of the writing part of the exam.

PRONOUNS

Pronouns are words that function in the place of nouns. There are seven kinds of pronouns. For each person and number they are:

Personal (Subject) Pronouns   These pronouns function as the subject of verbs.

	Singular	Plural
First Person	*yo*	*nosotros, nosotras*
Second Person	*tú*	*vosotros, vosotras*
Third Person	*él*	*ellos*
	ella	*ellas*
	usted	*ustedes*

(*Usted* can be abbreviated: *Ud.* or *Vd.; ustedes* as *Uds.* or *Vds.*)

These pronouns come before the verbs in declarative sentences. They normally come after the verb in questions, but sometimes are used before.

Direct Object Pronouns

These function as the object of the verb and answer the questions *who* or *what*.

	Singular	Plural
First Person	*me*	*nos*
Second Person	*te*	*os*
Third Person	**lo**	**los**
	la	**las**

In Spain the form *le* is used in place of *lo* when the noun the pronoun replaces is masculine.

Indirect Object Pronouns

These function as indirect objects of the verb and answer the questions, *to, for, from, by who* or *whom*.

First Person	*me*	*nos*
Second Person	*te*	*os*
Third Person	*le*	*les*

Reflexive Pronouns

These pronouns show that the action of the verb reflects back on the subject.

First Person	*me*	*nos*
Second Person	*te*	*os*
Third Person	*se*	*se*

Notice in all of the above three types of pronouns, that the first and second forms are the same, only the third person forms are different.

These pronouns are located in the following places:

Before:

1. conjugated verb forms,
2. negative commands.

After and attached to:

1. affirmative commands,
2. present participles (verb forms ending with **-ando** and **-iendo**),
3. infinitives.

When there are two object pronouns, the indirect object pronoun always comes before the direct object pronoun. When a reflexive pronoun and a direct object pronoun are used together, the reflexive object pronoun comes before the direct object pronoun.

When the double object pronouns are both third person (indirect object: *le* or *les*, and the direct object: *lo, la, los, las*), the indirect object is changed to *se*.

When one or two pronouns are added to an affirmative command, an accent is written over the syllable where the stress falls on the verb if the pronouns where not there.

For example:

Lea Ud. el libro. Léalo Ud. (Lea is two syllables, **e** is the stem of the verb.)
Lea Ud. el libro a su hermano. Léaselo Ud.

When one or two pronouns are added to a present participle, an accent is written over the beginning of the present participle ending.
For example:

> *Estoy leyendo el libro. Estoy leyéndolo.*
> *Estoy leyendo el libro a mi hermano. Estoy leyéndoselo.*
> *Imaginaos que estáis vistándonos cuando suena el teléfono.*
> *Estabáis peinándoos cuando llegamos si mal no me acuerdo.*

When two pronouns are added to an infinitive, an accent is written over the infinitive ending.
For example:

> *Voy a leer el libro a mi hermano. Voy a leérselo.*

When one pronoun is added to an infinitive, no accent is written over the infinitive ending because the stress normally falls on the last syllable of infinitives since the words end with the letter **r**.
For example:

> *Voy a leer el libro a mi hermano. Voy a leerlo a mi hermano.*
> *Voy a leer el libro a mi hermano. Voy a leerle el libro.*

Prepositional Pronouns

These pronouns function as the object of a preposition, such as *a, de, en, por, para, sobre, sin,* and *con*. Any preposition, simple or compound, requires the use of these forms.

	Singular	Plural
First Person	*mí*	*nosotros, nosotras*
Second Person	*ti*	*vosotros, vosotras*
Third Person	*él*	*ellos*
	ella	*ellas*
	usted	*ustedes*

In the prepositional pronouns, notice that except for the first and second persons singular, these pronouns are the same forms as for the subject pronouns. In addition to the above forms, with the preposition *con* there is a special form, *conmigo, contigo,* and *consigo*.

Demonstrative Pronouns (this, that, these, those)

These forms are either masculine or feminine, depending on the gender of the nouns to which they refer.

éste	*éstos*	*ése*	*ésos*	*aquél*	*aquéllos*
ésta	*éstas*	*ésa*	*ésas*	*aquélla*	*aquéllas*

When the antecedent (the thing to which these pronouns refer), is a whole idea or phrase, the neuter form can be used:

esto	*eso*	*aquello*

| **Indefinite Pronouns** | These forms have positive and negative forms. |

algo   *nada*
alguien   *nadie*

Relative Pronouns   These pronouns function to introduce dependent clauses.

el que (la que, los que, las que)
el cual (la cual, los cuales, las cuales)
quien quienes

ADJECTIVES

Most of the problems you will find with adjectives are in recognizing the gender of some of the nouns. Usually on the exam there are no clues as to the gender of the nouns; the modifiers are indeterminate because they end in **e**, are possessive adjectives, or there are no modifiers, such as articles. Make sure when you learn nouns that you learn the gender from the beginning so you can avoid problems with agreement of adjective endings and nouns.

All adjectives agree in gender and number with the nouns they modify. This means that if a noun is feminine, singular or plural, the ending of the adjective is feminine, singular or plural.

For example:

La *mujer alt***a** *lleva* **una** *chaqueta negr***a.**
Las *mujeres alt***as** *llevan* **unas** *chaquetas negr***as.**

If the noun is masculine, singular or plural, the endings are masculine, singular or plural.

For example:

El *hombre alt***o** *lleva* **un** *hermos***o** *traje negr***o.**
Los *hombres alt***os** *llevan* **unos** *hermos***os** *trajes negr***os.**

If the adjective ends in an **e**, it cannot agree in gender, only in number.

For example:

El *elefante gigant***e** *es muy inteligent***e.**
Los *elefantes gigant***es** *son muy inteligent***es.**

If an adjective ends with **-or, -ón, -án,** or **-ín,** an **a** is added to form the feminine singular, and **-as** for the feminine plural.

For example:

El *nuev***o** *criado es muy trabajad***or.**
La *nuev***a** *estudiante es muy trabajad***ora.**
Las *nuev***as** *estudiante son muy trabajad***oras.**

Some adjectives are invariable; their endings do not change no matter what the gender of the noun they modify. Some of these are:

maya   azteca   marrón   rosa   alerta   hipócrita

In many cases the **past** participles (forms of the verb ending with **-ado** or **-ido**) can function as adjectives. In these cases, when the past participle always ends with **-o**, simply make the vowel on the end agree in gender and number with the nouns the past participles/adjectives modify. Remember that some past participles are irregular. In some cases there is a different form derived from the verb for the adjective, instead of the past participle. For example, *despertar* has as its past participle, *despertado*. But when used as an adjective, the form is *despierto*. The same is true of the following verbs:

concluir	*concluido*	*concluso*
elegir	*elegido*	*electo*
soltar	*soltado*	*suelto*
sujetar	*sujetado*	*sujeto*
bendecir	*bendecido*	*bendito*
convertir	*convertido*	*converso*
maldecir	*maldecido*	*maldito*

There are a few verbs for which the present participle can be used as an adjective:

hervir	*hirviendo*
arder	*ardiendo*

Position of Adjectives

In general, adjectives that refer to quantity come **in front** of the noun, such as numbers and definite articles.

In general, adjectives that refer to descriptive qualities or characteristics of nouns come **after** the noun.

When there are two or more descriptive adjectives that refer to the same nouns, sometimes one is placed before the nouns; otherwise, they both follow the nouns and are joined by a conjunction, **y**, or are separated by a comma.

There are some adjectives that can come before or after a noun, but whose meaning is determined by where they are placed. The following adjectives are the most common ones of this type:

Adjective	Meaning Before	Meaning After
cierto	some	sure, certain
grande	great, famous	large
mismo	same	only
nuevo	another	modern, just made
solo	only	lone
pobre	unfortunate	destitute, penniless
simple	uncomplicated	silly, stupid
viejo	former	elderly
diferentes	various	not the same
antiguo	former	antique

Some adjectives drop the final **-o** before masculine singular nouns. These adjectives are: **bueno, malo, primero, tercero, veintiuno, uno, alguno,** and

ninguno. The adjectives **alguno** and **ninguno** add a written accent when the final **-o** is dropped: **algún, ningún**.

The adjective **grande** drops the final **-de** before masculine and feminine nouns.

For example:
Una **gran** *dama*   *Un* **gran** *hombre*

The number **ciento** drops the final **-to** before any nouns, masculine or feminine. For example:

cien *años*   **cien** *noches*

The title **santo** drops the final **-to** before all masculine names except those beginning with **Do** or **To**.
For example:

San Amselmo   **Santo Domingo**
San Isidro   **Santo Tomás**

Nominalization of Adjectives	Placing **lo** before an adjective means that it can be used as a noun. For example:

Lo importante (The important thing)
Los rojos (The red ones)

Possessive Adjectives	The possessive adjectives are:

mi, mis	= my	*nuestro, -a* = *nuestros, -as*	our
tu, tus	= your	*vuestro, -a* = *vuestros, -as*	your
su, sus	= his her its your	*su, sus* =	their your

Possessive adjectives agree in gender and number with the objects that are possessed, not with the possessor.
For example:

El chico llevó **sus** *libros.* = The boy took his books.
(**Sus** is plural because **libros** is plural.)

Demonstrative Adjectives	The demonstrative adjectives are:

este = this (masculine)	*estos* = these (masculine)
esta = this (feminine)	*estas* = these (feminine)
esto = this (neuter)	
ese = that (masculine)	
esa = that (feminine)	*esos* = those (masculine)
eso = that (neuter)	*esas* = those (feminine)
aquel = that (masculine)	*aquellos* = those (masculine)
aquella = that (feminine)	*aquellas* = those (feminine)

The significant points of grammar to remember about demonstrative adjectives is the difference between *ese (esos, esa, esas)* and *aquel (aquellos, aquella, aquellas)* is that *ese* refers to objects or persons nearer at hand than *aquel*. This distance can be expressed in temporal or spatial dimensions. For example: *En aquellos días vivía un rey muy poderoso...* meaning *in those long ago times there lived...* (Distance in time is implicit since *aquellos* is used.)

The following suffix can be added to adjectives: *-ísimo*

When the suffix is added to an adjective that ends with **-co**, the spelling is changed to preserve the **k** sound of the **c**.

For example:

poco	*poquísimo*
rico	*riquísimo*

Comparatives of Inequality

To form the comparatives of adjectives and adverbs the following structures are used:

Place **más** or **menos** before the noun, adjective, or adverb; then follow it with **que**.

For example:

*Este estudiante tiene **más** libros **que** el otro.*
*Este estudiante tiene **menos** libros **que** el otro.*
*Este chico es **más** aplicado **que** el otro.*
*Este chico es **menos** aplicado **que** el otro.*
*Este chico trabaja **más** rápidamente **que** el otro.*
*Este chico trabaja **menos** rápidamente **que** el otro.*

The following adjectives have irregular forms in the comparative:

Adjective	Comparative
bueno (good)	**mejor** (better)
malo (bad)	**peor** (worse)
joven (young)	**menor** (younger)
viejo (old)	**mayor** (older)

These comparative forms cannot agree in gender with the nouns they modify, but they can be made plural.

For example:

*Esta máquina es **mejor que** la otra.*
*Estas máquinas son **mejores que** las otras.*
*Esta máquina es **peor que** la otra.*
*Estas máquinas son **peores que** las otras.*
*Esta casa es **mayor que** la otra.* (This house is older than the other one.)
*Estas casas son **mayores que** las otras.* (These houses are older than the other ones.)

The irregular forms for the adjectives **mucho** and **poco** are **más** and **menos.**
For example:

*Hay **mucha** gente en la cafetería.*
*Hay **muchas** personas en la cafetería.* (There are many people in the cafeteria.)

Hay **más** *personas en la cafetería.* (There are more people in the cafetería.)

Hay **poca** *gente en la cafetería.* (There are few people in the cafeteria.)

Hay **pocas** *personas en la cafetería.* (There are few people in the cafetería.)

Mayor in the comparative form means greater and **menor** means lesser: For example:

El asunto de **mayor** *importancia es la cuestión de moralidad.* (The matter of greater importance is the question of morality.)

Es de **menor** *importancia preocuparse de este asunto.* (It is of lesser importance to worry about this matter.)

Comparatives of Equality

The comparatives of equality are formed as follows:

as + adjective or adverb + as

tan + adjective or adverb + **como**

For example:

Este chico es **tan** *alto* **como** *su compañero.* (This boy has as much talent as his friend.)

Este chico corre **tan** *rápido* **como** *su compañero.* (This boy runs as fast as his friend.)

as + the noun + as

tanto (a) + noun + **como**

For example:

Este chico tiene **tanto** *talento* **como** *su compañero.* (This boy has as much talent as his friend.)

Este chico tiene **tanta** *energía* **como** *su compañero.* (This boy has as much energy as his friend.)

Este chico tiene **tantos** *libros* **como** *su compañero.* (This boy has as many books as his friend.)

Este chico tiene **tantos** **como** *su compañero.* (This boy has as many as his friend or This boy has as much as his friend.)

Superlative Constructions

The superlatives of adjectives are formed by placing a definite article (**el, la, los, las**) before the comparative forms.

For example:

Este chico es **el más** *alto* **de** *la clase.* (This boy is the tallest in the class.)

Este chico es **el mejor** *jugador de fútbol* **de** *la clase.* (This boy is the best soccer player in the class.)

Notice that the English word *in* is rendered with **de**.

The expressions for *as soon as possible* are:

cuanto antes

lo más pronto posible

tan pronto como posible

Absolute Superlatives

When no comparison is expressed, the ending **-ísimo** (**-a**, **-os**, **-as**) is added to the adjective.

For example:

> *Tiene* **muchísimos** *problemas.* (He has many, many problems.)
> *Tiene* **muchísima** *tarea.* (He has a lot of work.)

Adjectives ending in a vowel drop the vowel before adding **-ísimo**. Adjectives that end in **-co** change the **co** to **qu**; endings of **-go** change the **g** to **gu**, **z** changes to **c** and **-ble** changes to **-bil**.

For example:

> *Esta película es mal**a**—Esta película es mal**ísima**.*
> *Este hombre es ri**co**—Este hombre es ri**quísimo**.*
> *Este libro es lar**go**—Este libro es lar**guísimo**.*
> *Este chico está feli**z**—Este chico está feli**císimo**.*
> *Este profesor es ama**ble**—Este profesor es ama**bilísimo**.*

When the absolute superlative form is added to an adverb, the form is invariable; it always ends with **-ísimo**.

VERBS

Verbs have four different kinds of forms: (1) the infinitive, (2) the conjugated verb, (3) the past participle, and (4) the present participle.

Infinitives

Infinitives are somewhat different in Spanish than they are in English. In Spanish the function of an infinitive in a sentence can be as the subject of a conjugated verb, the object of a conjugated verb, or the object of a preposition. When the infinitive functions as the subject of a sentence, it is translated into English as a gerund.

For example:

> *El caminar le ayuda mantenerse en forma.* (Walking helps you stay in shape.)
> *Me gusta caminar por el parque.* (I like to walk through the park.)

When the infinitive functions as the object of a verb, it can also be translated as a gerund.

For example:

> *Su padre le dejó salir en seguida.* (His father let him leave immediately.)
> *No pudo soportar más las injurias del gentío en la calle.* (He could not stand the insults of the crowd in the street.)

As the object of a preposition, the translation of the infinitive depends upon the preposition used. The preposition **a** is used after verbs of motion, beginning, inviting, helping, and exhorting.

After the preposition **a** and article **el**, the infinitive indicates that two things are happening simultaneously.

For example:

> *Al divisar la costa por la neblina, lloró por pura alegría.* (Upon seeing the coast through the mist, he cried out of joy.)

In conversational Spanish, the preposition **a**, followed by an infinitive is sometimes used in place of a direct command.
For example:

> *¡A ver!* (Let's just see!)

When the preposition **con** comes before the infinitive, the meaning is one of concession or manner.
For example:

> *Con dedicar más tiempo al trabajo, lo acabarás.* (With a harder effort, you will finish it or If you work a little harder, you will finish it.)

When the infinitive follows the preposition **de**, some kind of condition is indicated.
For example:

> *De haberlo pensado un poco más, no lo habría hecho.* (If he had thought about it a little more, he would not have done it.)

Notice that in this case, the clause introduced by the preposition is part of an if-then statement, and has replaced the clause that normally contains the past subjunctive.
The preposition **por** followed by an infinitive indicates motive for an event or situation.
For example:

> *No le permitieron entrar por no llevar una corbata ni traje formal.*
> (They did not let him in because he was not wearing proper attire.)

The preposition **sin** indicates a negative meaning.
For example:

> *El asunto todavía quedó sin resolver.* (The matter is still unresolved.)

The preposition **para** indicates purpose and means *in order to.*
For example:

> *Lo invitó para hacerle sentirse bien acogido.* (She invited him to make him feel very welcome.)

Conjugated Verb Forms

There are three conjugations: verbs that end with **-ar**, verbs that end with **-er**, and verbs that end with **-ir**. For each conjugation there are different endings indicating tenses and moods. The tenses are:

Indicative	Subjunctive
Present	Present
Present Progressive	Present Progressive
Present Perfect	Present Perfect
Imperfect	Past (Imperfect)

Indicative	Subjunctive
Past Progressive	Past Progressive
Pluperfect	Past Perfect
Preterit	
Pluscuamperfect	
Future	
Future Progressive	
Future Perfect	
Conditional	
Conditional Progressive	
Conditional Perfect	

Within each of these tenses there are four different categories of verbs: (1) regular conjugations, (2) irregular conjugations, (3) stem changing conjugations, and (4) orthographic or spelling change conjugations. To conjugate verbs in all of these categories, take the infinitive ending off of the stem of the verb (the **-ar, -er, -ir** ending) and add the appropriate ending (the ending that agrees with the subject of the verb). For each kind **except** regular verbs, however, there are changes that must be made in the stem of the verb in many verbal tenses. Irregular verbs have forms that do not conform to any regular pattern and these must be memorized. Stem changing verbs can be classified so that the changes are more easily remembered. Orthographic verbs have spelling changes that occur for the letters **c, g,** and **z** when they are followed by certain vowels.

1.   REGULAR VERBS

To conjugate verbs, for the following tenses, take off the infinitive ending, (**-ar, -er,** or **-ir**) and add the following endings:

Simple Indicative Tenses

Present Indicative of **-ar** verbs		Present Indicative of **-er** verbs		Present Indicative of **-ir** verbs	
-o	-amos	-o	-emos	-o	-imos
-as	**-áis**	**-es**	**-éis**	**-es**	**-ís**
-a	-an	**-e**	-en	-e	-en

Preterit Indicative of **-ar** verbs		Preterit Indicative of **-er** verbs		Preterit Indicative of **-ir** verbs	
-é	-amos	**-í**	-imos	**-í**	**-imos**
-aste	-asteis	-iste	-isteis	-iste	-isteis
-ó	-aron	-ió	-ieron	-ió	-ieron

Imperfect Indicative of **-ar** verbs		Imperfect Indicative of **-er** verbs		Imperfect Indicative of **-ir** verbs	
-aba	-ábamos	-ía	-íamos	-ía	-íamos
-abas	-abais	-ías	-íais	-ías	-íais
-aba	-aban	-ía	-ían	-ía	-ían

The following endings are added to the infinitive form of all three conjugations:

Future Indicative	-é	-emos
	-ás	-éis
	-á	-án

Conditional	-ía	-íamos
Indicative	-ías	-íais
	-ía	-ían

(Notice that these endings are the same as endings for the second and third conjugation imperfect endings, except that they are only added to the end of the infinitives.)

Compound Indicative Tenses

To form the compound or perfect tenses, conjugate the verb **haber** in each of the above tenses and follow it with the past participle. The past participle is formed by removing the **-ar, -er,** or **-ir** endings and adding **-ado** for **-ar** verbs and **-ido** for **-er** and **-ir** verbs. The forms for the verb **haber** in each of the above tenses are:

Present Indicative		Imperfect Indicative	
he	*hemos*	*había*	*habíamos*
has	**habeis**	*habías*	*habíais*
ha	*han*	*había*	*habían*

Preterit Indicative		Conditional Indicative	
hube	*hubimos*	*habría*	*habríamos*
hubiste	*hubisteis*	*habrías*	*habríais*
hubo	*hubieron*	*habría*	*habrían*

Future Indicative	
habré	*habremos*
habrás	*habrán*
habrá	*habrán*

There are a number of irregular past participles that are commonly found on the Advanced Placement exam. They are as follows:

abrir	**abierto**	*revolver*	**revuelto**
cubrir	**cubierto**	*deshacer*	**deshecho**
descubrir	**descubierto**	*satisfacer*	**satisfecho**
decir	**dicho**	*bendecir*	**bendicho**
hacer	**hecho**	*maldecir*	**maldicho**
morir	**muerto**	*imponer*	**impuesto**
poner	**puesto**	*oponer*	**opuesto**
romper	**roto**	*suponer*	**supuesto**
soltar	**suelto**	*sobreponer*	**sobrepuesto**
volver	**vuelto**	*componer*	**compuesto**
envolver	**envuelto**	*resolver*	**resuelto**
devolver	**devuelto**		

Simple Subjunctive

Present Subjunctive

To form the present subjunctive, notice that the endings for **-er** and **-ir** verbs are identical.

	-ar			**-er** and **-ir**	
-e		*-emos*		*-a*	*-amos*
-es		*-éis*		*-as*	*-áis*
-e		*-en*		*-a*	*-an*

Past (Imperfect) Subjunctive

There are two sets of endings that can be used interchangeably, although there are some regional preferences for one or the other in some cases in the Spanish-speaking world.

	-ar (Set 1)			**-er** and **-ir (Set 1)**	
-ara		*-áramos*		*-iera*	*-iéramos*
-aras		*-arais*		*-ieras*	*-ierais*
-ara		*-aran*		*-iera*	*-ieran*

	-ar (Set 2)			**-er** and **-ir (Set 2)**	
-ase		*-ásemos*		*-ese*	*-ésemos*
-ases		*-aseis*		*-eses*	*-eseis*
-ase		*-asen*		*-ese*	*esen*

Compound Subjunctive Tenses

To form the present perfect or the pluperfect subjunctive, conjugate the verb **haber** in either the present or the past subjunctive with a past participle (**-ado, -ido**). (See past participles for discussion of irregular past participles.)

haya	*hayamos*	*hubiera o hubiese*	*hubiéramos o hubiésemos*
hayas	*hayais*	*hubieras o hubieses*	*hubieseis o hubieseis*
haya	*hayan*	*hubiera o hubiese*	*hubieran o hubiesen*

2. IRREGULAR VERBS

There are only a dozen or so irregular verbs that you are likely to use on the exam. They are: **caber, dar, decir, estar, hacer, ir, poder, poner, querer, saber, ser, tener, traer, valer, venir, ver.**

CABER

Present Indicative		Present Subjunctive	
quepo	*cabemos*	*quepa*	*quepamos*
cabes	*cabéis*	*quepas*	*quepáis*
cabe	*caben*	*quepa*	*quepan*

Preterite Indicative		Past Subjunctive	
cupe	*cupimos*	*cupiera*	*cupiéramos*
cupiste	*cupisteis*	*cupieras*	*cupierais*
cupo	*cupieron*	*cupiera*	*cupieran*

Imperfect Indicative	
cabía	*cabíamos*
cabías	*cabíais*
cabía	*cabían*

Future Indicative		Conditional Indicative	
cabré	*cabremos*	*cabría*	*cabríamos*
cabrás	*cabréis*	*cabrías*	*cabríais*
cabrá	*cabrán*	*cabría*	*cabrían*

DAR

Present Indicative		Present Subjunctive	
doy	damos	dé	demos
das	dais	des	deis
da	dan	dé	den

Preterite Indicative		Past Subjunctive	
di	dimos	diera	diéramos
diste	disteis	dieras	dierais
dio	dieron	diera	dieran

Imperfect Indicative	
daba	dábamos
dabas	dabais
daba	daban

Future Indicative		Conditional Indicative	
daré	daremos	daría	daríamos
darás	daréis	darías	daríais
dará	darán	daría	darían

DECIR

Present Indicative		Present Subjunctive	
digo	decimos	diga	digamos
dices	decís	digas	digáis
dice	dicen	diga	digan

Preterite Indicative		Past Subjunctive	
dije	dijimos	dijera	dijéramos
dijiste	dijisteis	dijeras	dijerais
dijo	dijeron	dijera	dijeran

(The imperfect indicative is regular.)

Future Indicative		Conditional Indicative	
diré	diremos	diría	diríamos
dirás	diréis	dirías	diríais
dirá	dirán	diría	dirían

ESTAR

(The verb **andar** is conjugated the same as the verb **estar** in the preterite.)

Present Indicative		Present Subjunctive	
estoy	estamos	esté	estemos
estás	estáis	estés	estéis
está	están	esté	estén

Preterite Indicative		Past Subjunctive	
estuve	estuvimos	estuviera	estuviéramos
estuviste	estuvisteis	estuvieras	estuvierais
estuvo	estuvieron	estuviera	estuvieran

Imperfect Indicative

estaba	estábamos
estabas	estabais
estaba	estabam

(The future and conditional forms of this verb are regular.)

HACER

Present Indicative		Present Subjunctive	
hago	hacemos	haga	hagamos
haces	hacéis	hagas	hagáis
hace	hacen	haga	hagan

Preterite Indicative		Past Subjunctive	
hice	hicimos	hiciera	hiciéramos
hiciste	hicisteis	hicieras	hicierais
hizo	hicieron	hiciera	hicieran

(The imperfect forms of this verb are regular.)

Future Indicative		Conditional	
haré	haremos	haría	haríamos
harás	haréis	harías	haríais
hará	harán	haría	harían

IR

Present Indicative		Present Subjunctive	
voy	vamos	vaya	vayamos
vas	vais	vayas	vayáis
va	van	vaya	vayan

Preterite Indicative		Past Subjunctive	
fui	fuimos	fuera	fuéramos
fuiste	fuisteis	fueras	fuerais
fue	fueron	fuera	fueran

Imperfect Indicative

iba	íbamos
ibas	ibais
iba	iban

(The future and conditional forms of this verb are regular.)

OÍR

Present Indicative		Present Subjunctive	
oigo	oímos	oiga	oigamos
oyes	oís	oigas	oigáis
oye	oyen	oiga	oigan

Preterite Indicative		Past Subjunctive	
oí	oímos	oyera	oyéramos
oíste	oísteis	oyeras	oyerais
oyó	oyeron	oyera	oyeran

(Whenever the verb ending contains an unstressed **i** in the ending after a vowel in the stem, as in the third person singular and plural of the second and third conjugation infinitives, **(-ió)**, the **i** is changed to **y**. This happens with the verbs **creer, poseer,** and **leer** in the preterit: **creyó, leyó.** Notice that this will not happen with verbs that end with **-ar** because there is no **i** in the third person singular or plural preterit endings.

(The imperfect, future, and conditional forms of this verb are regular.)

PODER

Present Indicative		Present Subjunctive	
puedo	podemos	pueda	podamos
puedes	podéis	puedas	podáis
puede	pueden	pueda	puedan

Preterite Indicative		Past Subjunctive	
pude	pudimos	pudiera	pudiéramos
pudiste	pudisteis	pudieras	pudierais
pudo	pudieron	pudiera	pudieran

(The imperfect forms for this verb are regular.)

Future		Conditional	
podré	podremos	podría	podríamos
podrás	podréis	podrías	podríais
podrá	podrán	podría	podrían

PONER

Present Indicative		Present Subjunctive	
pongo	ponemos	ponga	pongamos
pones	ponéis	pongas	pongáis
pone	ponen	ponga	pongan

Preterite Indicative		Past Subjunctive	
puse	pusimos	pusiera	pusiéramos
pusiste	pusisteis	pusieras	pusierais
puso	pusieron	pusiera	pusieran

(The imperfect forms of this verb are regular.)

Future		Conditional	
pondré	pondremos	pondría	pondríamos
pondrás	pondréis	pondrías	pondríais
pondrá	pondrán	pondría	pondrían

QUERER

Present Indicative		Present Subjunctive	
quiero	queremos	quiera	queramos
quieres	queréis	quieras	queráis
quiere	quieren	quiera	quieran

Preterite Indicative		Past Subjunctive	
quise	quisimos	quisiera	quisiéramos
quisiste	quisisteis	quisieras	quisierais
quiso	quisieron	quisiera	quisieran

(The imperfect forms of this verb are regular.)

Future Indicative		Conditional Indicative	
querré	querremos	querría	querríamos
querrás	querréis	querrías	querríais
querrá	querrán	querría	querrían

SABER

Present Indicative		Present Subjunctive	
sé	sabemos	sepa	sepamos
sabes	sabéis	sepas	sepáis
sabe	saben	sepa	sepan

Preterite Indicative		Past Subjunctive	
supe	supimos	supiera	supiéramos
supiste	supisteis	supieras	supierais
supo	supieron	supiera	supieran

(The imperfect indicative forms of this verb are regular.)

Future Indicative		Conditional Indicative	
sabré	sabremos	sabría	sabríamos
sabrás	sabréis	sabrías	sabríais
sabrá	sabrán	sabría	sabran

SER

Present Indicative		Present Subjunctive	
soy	somos	sea	seamos
eres	sois	seas	seáis
es	son	sea	sean

Preterite Indicative		Past Subjunctive	
fui	fuimos	fuera	fuéramos
fuiste	fuisteis	fueras	fuerais
fue	fueron	fuera	fueran

Imperfect Indicative	
era	éramos
eras	erais
era	eran

(The future and conditional forms of this verb are regular.)

TENER

Present Indicative		Present Subjunctive	
tengo	tenemos	tenga	tengamos
tienes	tenéis	tengas	tengáis
tiene	tienen	tenga	tengan

Preterite Indicative		Past Subjunctive	
tuve	tuvimos	tuviera	tuviéramos
tuviste	tuvisteis	tuvieras	tuvierais
tuvo	tuvieron	tuviera	tuvieran

(The imperfect forms of this verb are regular.)

Future Indicative		Conditional Subjunctive	
tendré	tendremos	tendría	tendramos
tendrás	tendréis	tendrías	tendríais
tendrá	tendrán	tendría	tendrían

TRAER

Present Indicative		Present Subjunctive	
traigo	traemos	traiga	traigamos
traes	traéis	traigas	traigáis
trae	traen	traiga	traigan

VALER

Present Indicative		Present Subjunctive	
valgo	valemos	valga	valgamos
vales	valéis	valgas	valgáis
vale	valen	valga	valgan

Preterite Indicative		Past Subjunctive	
valí	valimos	valiera	valiéramos
valiste	valisteis	valieras	valierais
valió	valieron	valiera	valieran

(The imperfect forms of this verb are regular.)

Future Indicative		Conditional Indicative	
valdré	valdremos	valdría	valdríamos
valdrás	valdréis	valdrías	valdríais
valdrá	valdrán	valdría	valdría

VENIR

Present Indicative		Present Subjunctive	
vengo	venimos	venga	vengamos
vienes	venís	vengas	vengáis
viene	vienen	venga	vengan

Preterite Indicative		Past Subjunctive	
vine	vinimos	viniera	viniéramos
viniste	vinisteis	vinieras	vinierais
vino	vinieron	viniera	vinieran

(The imperfect forms of this verb are regular.)

Future Indicative		Conditional Indicative	
vendré	vendremos	vendría	vendríamos
vendrás	vendréis	vendrías	vendríais
vendrá	vendrán	vendría	vendrían

VER

Present Indicative		Present Subjunctive	
veo	*vemos*	*vea*	*veamos*
ves	*veis*	*veas*	*veáis*
ve	*ven*	*vea*	*vean*

Preterite Indicative		Past Subjunctive	
vi	*vimos*	*viera*	*viéramos*
viste	*visteis*	*vieras*	*vierais*
vio	*vieron*	*viera*	*vieran*

Imperfect Indicative	
veía	*veíamos*
veías	*veíais*
veía	*veían*

(The future and conditional indicative forms of this verb are regular.)

3. STEM CHANGING VERBS

Verbs whose conjugated forms have a change in the stem (the radical) of the verb can be classified as follows: Class I, Class II, or Class III.

CLASS I

All of the verbs in Class I are **-ar** and **-er** infinitives. These verbs have a change **only** in the **present tense.** The change is from **e** to **ie** and **o** to **ue** in the first, second, and third persons singular and the third person plural. It does not have a change in the first and second person plural because the stress in on the ending of the verb form, not on the stem of the verb. An example of these two changes is:

Present Indicative

pensar (ie)		*volver (ue)*	
pienso	pensamos	**vue**lvo	volvemos
piensas	pensáis	**vue**lves	volvéis
piensa	**pie**nsan	**vue**lve	**vue**lven

In the subjunctive forms, all the stem changes occur exactly as they do in the indicative, in all of the same persons and number:

Present Subjunctive

piense	pensemos	**vue**lva	volvamos
pienses	penséis	**vue**lvas	volváis
piense	**pie**nsen	**vue**lva	**vue**lvan

These verbs are indicated in dictionaries with the letters of the change in parentheses after the infinitive. Other verbs of this Class I change are: *sentarse, empezar, encontrar, contar, costar, despertar, atravesar, recomendar, comenzar, entender, volver, envolver, devolver, revolver, perder, defender, rogar, negar, nevar, oler, soltar, mover, mostrar, demostrar, llover, jugar.*

The verb ***oler*** is irregular in the present because an **h** is added to the beginning of the verb:

Present Indicative		Present Subjunctive	
h**uelo**	*olemos*	h**uela**	*olamos*
h**ueles**	*oléis*	h**uelas**	*oláis*
h**uele**	h**uelen**	h**uela**	h**uelan**

The verb is regular in all other tenses and forms.

CLASS II

These stem changing verbs are all third conjugation verbs (they end with **-ir**). These verbs change **e** to **ie** and **o** to **ue** in the same persons and numbers as the Class I verbs (first, second, third and third persons) in the present tense, but also have a change in the preterit forms. The preterit changes are **e** to **i** and **o** to **u** in the third persons singular and plural.

Present Indicative

sentir (ie,i)		*dormir (ue,u)*	
s**ie**nto	sentimos	d**ue**rmo	dormimos
s**ie**ntes	sentís	d**ue**rmes	dormís
s**ie**nte	s**ie**nten	d**ue**rme	d**ue**rmen

Preterit Indicative

sentir (ie,i)		*dormir (ue,u)*	
sentí	sentimos	dormí	dormimos
sentiste	sentisteis	dormiste	dormisteis
s**i**ntió	s**i**ntieron	d**u**rmió	d**u**rmieron

In the present subjunctive the **e** changes to **ie** in the first, second, and third singular and the third plural forms, and changes from **e** to **i** in the first and second persons plural:

Present Subjunctive

sentir (ie,i)		*dormir (ue,u)*	
s**ie**nta	s**i**ntamos	d**ue**rma	d**u**rmamos
s**ie**ntas	s**i**ntáis	d**ue**rmas	d**u**rmáis
s**ie**nta	s**ie**ntan	d**ue**rma	d**ue**rman

In the preterit forms the change occurs in all forms in the past subjunctive:

sentir (ie,i)		*dormir (ue,u)*	
s**i**ntiera	s**i**ntiéramos	d**u**rmiera	d**u**rmiéramos
s**i**ntieras	s**i**ntierais	d**u**rmieras	d**u**rmierais
s**i**ntiera	s**i**ntieran	d**u**rmiera	d**u**rmieran

Morir is the only other Class II verb in which **o** changes to **ue**. Other verbs that are similar to the above verbs are: *divertirse* and *arrepentir*.

The present participles (**-iendo**) will have the change in the stem of the participle, from **e** to **i** and **o** to **u**. For example: *sintiendo* and *durmiendo*.

CLASS III

These stem changing verbs all end in **-ir** and change **e** to **i** in the first, second, and third persons singular, and third person plural in the present tense. The change in the preterit is from **e** to **i** in the third persons singular and plural. There are no **o** to **ue** changes.

Present Indicative		Present Subjunctive	
pedir (i,i)			
pido	pedimos	pida	pidamos
pides	pedís	pidas	pidáis
pide	piden	pida	pidan

Notice the same stem change occurs in all forms of the present subjunctive.

Preterit Indicative		Past Subjunctive	
pedí	pedimos	pidiera	pidiéramos
pediste	pedisteis	pidieras	pidierais
pidió	pidieron	pidiera	pidieran

The same stem change occurs in all forms of the past subjunctive.

Other verbs that are conjugated like *pedir* are: *elegir, pedir (impedir, despedir), servir, vestir, reñir,* and *reír.*

The verb *reír* has the following changes in accent marks because it is a single syllable stem:

Present Indicative		Present Subjunctive	
río	reímos	ría	riamos
ríes	reís	rías	riáis
ríe	ríen	ría	rían

Preterit Indicative		Past Subjunctive	
reí	reímos	rieran	riéramos
reíste	reísteis	rieras	rierais
rió	rieron	riera	rieran

In the above forms notice that *reír* is a stem changing verb, so the stem contains an **i** in the third person singular and plural, and the accent falls in the normal position for the preterit **-ir** conjugations.

The present participles of Class III verbs will have the stem change of **e** to **i**: *pidiendo, riendo.*

4. ORTHOGRAPHIC VERBS

Verbs that have spelling changes because of the sequence of certain consonants, **c, g,** and **z** when followed by certain vowels, are called orthographic verbs.

The vowels **a** and **o** are hard vowels; **e** and **i** are soft vowels. When the letter **c** is followed by a hard vowel, the sound of **c** is the same as **k** in English. (*Sacar* in Spanish is pronounced as if the **c** were a **k**.) When the **c** is followed by a soft vowel the **c** has an **s** sound. (*Conocer* is pronounced as if the **c** were an **s** in the last syllable.) Therefore, wherever the initial vowel of an ending is the opposite of what is found in the infinitive, there are the following spelling changes:

1. **-car** infinitives. Change the **c** to **qu** when the ending begins with an **e** or an **i**:

Buscar
(preterit indicative, first person singular)

busqué	buscamos
buscaste	buscasteis
buscó	buscaron

(Notice that only the first person singular ending begins with the letter **e**, so it is the only one that changes spelling.)

Buscar
(present subjunctive, all forms)

busque	**busquemos**
busques	**busquéis**
busque	**busquen**

(Notice that all of these endings begin with the letter **e** so there is a change in the spelling. Notice also that there is no accent on the first person singular form.)

Some other common verbs that have this change are: *practicar, explicar, tocar, comunicar, ahorcar, abarcar, embarcar, arrancar, atacar, equivocar, provocar, destacar, marcar, ubicar, evocar, sacar,* and *volcar.*

2. -cer infinitives. Add a **z** before the **c**:

Conocer
(present indicative, first person singular only)

conozco	*conocemos*
conoces	*conocéis*
conoce	*conocen*

(Notice that all the other endings begin with the letter **e**, which is soft, so no other change is needed.)

Conocer
(present subjunctive, all forms)

conozca	*conozcamos*
conozcas	*conozcáis*
conozca	*conozcan*

(Notice that all of the endings in the subjunctive begin with a hard vowel, so all the forms change.)

Some other common verbs that have these changes are: *parecer, perecer, fallecer, crecer, nacer, merecer, establecer, padecer, obscurecer, anochecer, amanecer, acontecer, aborrecer, apetecer, aparecer, complacer, carecer, desaparecer, empobrecer, enriquecer, embrutecer, enrojecer, entristecer, envejecer, florecer, permanecer, pertenecer, torcer,* and *yacer.*

3. -ducir infinitives:
(In the present indicative, add a **z** before the first person singular indicative.)

Traducir
(present indicative, first person singular)

traduzco	*traducimos*
traduces	*traducís*
traduce	*traducen*

(Notice that the first person singular indicative is the only ending that begins with a hard vowel, so it is the only one that adds before **c**.)

Traducir
(present subjunctive, all forms)

traduzca	*traduzcamos*
traduzcas	*traduzcáis*
traduzca	*traduzcan*

(Notice that all the endings begin with the letter **a** so all of the forms add the **z**.) In the preterit change the **c** to **j**:

Traducir
(preterit indicate, all forms)

traduje	*tradujimos*
tradujiste	*tradujisteis*
tradujo	*tradujeron*

Traducir
(past subjunctive, all forms)

tradujera	*tradujéramos*
tradujeras	*tradujerais*
tradujera	*tradujeran*

Some other common verbs that are conjugated like *traducir* are: *producir, conducir, balbucir, lucir, deducir,* and *reducir.*

The letter **g** has two sounds depending on which letter follows it. When **g** is followed by the letter **a, o,** or **u** (as in *pagar*), it has a hard sound like the **g** in the English word *go.*

When the letter **g** is followed by the letter **e** or **i,** then the sound is soft, as in the English word, *general.*

4. -gar infinitives. Add a **u** before the endings with soft vowels:

Pagar
(first person singular in the preterit only)

pagué	*pagamos*
pagaste	*pagasteis*
pagó	*pagaron*

(Notice that the first person is the only ending that begins with the letter **e** in the preterit, so it is the only form that changes in this tense.)

Pagar
(present subjunctive, all forms)

pague	*paguemos*
pagues	*paguéis*
pague	*paguen*

(Notice that all of the present subjunctive endings begin with the letter **e** so all the forms add the **u** before the ending.)

Some other common verbs that are conjugated like *pagar* are: *jugar, llegar, rogar, negar, ahogar, investigar, indagar, obligar, abrigar, castigar, interrogar, embriagar, propagar, entregar, cegar, colgar, desasosegar, entregar, fregar,* and *desplegar.*

5. **-ger** infinitives. Change the **g** to **j** before **a** and **o**:

Escoger

(present indicative, first person singular only)

escojo	escogemos
escoges	escogéis
escoge	escogen

(Notice that the first singular is the only ending that begins with a hard vowel (**a** or **o**) so it is the only form that changes in the indicative.)

Escoger

(present subjunctive, all forms)

escoja	escojamos
escojas	escojáis
escoja	escojan

(Notice that all forms change because the endings all begin with the letter **a**.)

6. **-gir** infinitives. Change the **g** to **j** before **a** and **o**.

Dirigir

(present indicative, first person singular only)

dirijo	dirigimos
diriges	dirigís
dirige	dirigen

(Notice that these forms are the same as for the **-ger** ending infinitives for all the same reasons.)

Dirigir

(present subjunctive, all forms)

dirija	dirijamos
dirijas	dirijáis
dirija	dirijan

(Notice that these forms are the same as for the **-ger** verbs for all the same reasons.)

Some other common verbs that are conjugated like *dirigir* are: *elegir, mugir,* and *exigir.*

7. **-guir** infinitives. Drop the **u** when the ending begins with a hard vowel:

Seguir

(present indicative, first person singular only)

sigo	seguimos
sigues	seguís
sigue	siguen

(Notice that the first person singular is the only ending that begins with a hard vowel, **o**, so it is the only form with a change.)

Seguir
(present subjunctive, all forms)

*si*ga	*si*ga*mos*
*si*ga*s*	*si*gá*is*
*si*ga	*si*ga*n*

(Notice that all of the subjunctive endings begin with the letter **a**, so the **u** is dropped in all six forms.)

8. -zar infinitives. Change the **z** to **c** before endings that begin with soft vowels:

Empezar
(preterit indicative, first person singular only)

empecé	*empezamos*
empezaste	*empezasteis*
empezó	*empezaron*

(Notice that the first person singular is the only ending that begins with a soft vowel, **e**.)

Empezar
(present subjunctive, all forms)

*empie*ce	*empe*cemos
*empie*ces	*empe*céis
*empie*ce	*empie*cen

(Notice that these endings all begin with a soft vowel, **e**, so these forms all change to **c**.)

Some other common verbs that are conjugated like *empezar* are: *analizar, utilizar, comenzar, almorzar, rezar, gozar, avergonzar, cruzar, cazar, destrozar, sollozar, tropezar, esforzar, adelgazar, calzar,* and *reemplazar.*

9. -uir infinitives. Add **y** before the ending when the stem is stressed:

Construir
(present indicative, all forms)

construyo	*construimos*
construyes	*construís*
construye	*construyen*

(Notice that in the first and second persons plural, the first letter of the ending is stressed, so the forms do not add **y**.)

Construir
(present subjunctive, all forms)

construya	*construyamos*
construyas	*construyáis*
construya	*construyan*

(Notice that all forms change because the stem for the subjunctive is the first person singular, present indicative.)

Remember that for **-uir** ending infinitives in the preterit indicative, the unstressed **i** is changed to a **y**:

Construir
(preterit indicative)

construí	*construimos*
construiste	*construisteis*
construyó	*construyeron*

Some other common verbs that are conjugated like *construir* are: *destruir, atribuir, influir, distribuir, sustituir, concluir, disminuir, excluir, fluir,* and *instruir.*

The following verbs have changes in the written diacritical marks because of the phonetics:

10. -uar infinitives. Add written accent marks when conjugated in order to retain the stress on the stem of the verb:

Present Indicative

Graduar
(first, second, and third person singular, and third plural)

gradúo	*graduamos*
gradúas	*graduáis*
gradúa	*gradúan*

(Notice that the stress in the first and second person plural forms is on the first letter of the ending, so the accent mark is omitted.)

Present Subjunctive

Graduar
(first, second, and third person singular, and third plural)

gradúe	*graduemos*
gradúes	*graduéis*
gradúe	*gradúen*

(Notice that these changes are in the same persons and number as the indicative forms.)

11. -guar adds a dieresis over the **u** (**ü**) when the ending begins with an **e**, in order to keep the hard sound of the letter **g** that is found in the infinitive:

Preterit Indicative

Averiguar
(first person singular)

averigüé	*averiguamos*
averiguaste	*averiguasteis*
averiguó	*averiguaron*

(Notice that only the first person singular ending begins with **e**.)

Present Subjunctive

Averiguar

averigüe	*averigüemos*
averigües	*averigüéis*
averigüe	*averigüen*

(Notice that since all of these endings begin with the letter **e**, that the dieresis is written on the letter **u** to preserve the hard sound of the **g**.)

Other verbs like *averiguar* are: *santiguar* and *apaciguar*.

12. -iar infinitives add an accent on the stem.

Present Indicative

Enviar

envío	*enviamos*
envías	*enviáis*
envía	*envían*

(Notice that these changes occur where the stress should fall on the stem, not on the first letter of the ending.)

Present Subjunctive

Enviar

envíe	*enviemos*
envíes	*enviéis*
envíe	*envíen*

(Notice that the accent is written on in the same forms as in the present indicative.)

Use of the Indicative Mood

The indicative mood is used in main clauses, in simple declarative statements, or questions where no doubt, uncertainty, or contrary-to-fact information is expressed. With the indicative mood, the simple present corresponds to several different meanings in English. For example: *hablo* = I **talk**, I **am talking,** I **do talk**, **Do** I **talk**...? and **Am** I **talking**...? In the past there are two simple tenses: the imperfect and the preterit. The imperfect is used to describe background information about an event, to describe an action that was going on at some time in the past without regard for when it began and/or ended, an action that was going on when something else happened, habitual action, repetitive action in the past, and for telling time. The preterit tense is used to stress the fact that an event took place in a finite period of time in the past. An action expressed using the preterit is one that is completed, a definite beginning and/or ending to the action is communicated through the selection of the preterit tense. These actions are said to be narrated instead of described. The preterit is also used to relate events or actions in a series in the past. There are five verbs whose meanings are different in the preterit, based on the meaning implied from the selection of the tense. They are:

Conocer: in the preterit *conocer* means *to meet*.
in the imperfect *conocer* means *knew*.

For example:

> *Yo la conocí en la fiesta.* (I met her at the party.)
> *Yo la conocía antes de la fiesta.* (I knew her before the party.)

Querer: in the affirmative preterit *querer* means *to try*.
> in the negative preterit *querer* means *to refuse*.
> in the imperfect *querer* means *wished* or *wanted*.

For example:

> *Yo quise llamarte anoche.* (I tried to call you last night.)
> *No quise llamarte otra vez.* (I refused to call you again.)
> *Yo quería llamarte anoche.* (I wanted to call you last night.)

Poder: in the preterit *poder* means *managed*, with accomplished action implied.
> in the imperfect *poder* means *could*.

For example:

> *El chico pudo ir a la fiesta.* (The boy managed to go to the party.)
> *El chico podía ir a la fiesta.* (The boy was able to go to the party./
> The boy could go to the party.)

Saber: in the preterit *saber* means *found out*.
> in the imperfect *saber* means *knew*.

For example:

> *Ayer supe la dirección.* (Yesterday I found out the address./
> Yesterday I discovered the address.)
> *Ayer sabía la dirección.* (Yesterday I knew the address.)

Tener: in the preterit *tener* means *received*.
> in the imperfect *tener* means *had*.

For example:

> *Ayer tuve una carta.* (Yesterday a received a letter.)
> *Ayer tenía una carta.* (Yesterday I had a letter.)

The future is used to express actions that have not yet taken place. This tense is also used to express conjecture (the probability or supposition) that something will happen. This meaning is expressed in English with the phrases such as *I wonder..., What can be...?* and the like.

The conditional tense expresses the same meaning in the past. This tense is frequently expressed by one of the several meanings of the verb *would*. (In English *would* can indicate a variety of other time frames, such as past, or provisional actions.) For example, *He would go when he had the time.*

The conditional tense in Spanish is also used to communicate probability or conjecture in the past. Its meanings correspond to the future of probability, except in the past instead of the present tense.

For example:

> *¿Qué hora será?* (What time can it be?/I wonder what time it is?)
> *¿Qué hora sería?* (What time could it be?/I wonder what time it was?)

The compound tenses are used to refer to a time frame immediately prior to a specified point in time. For example, the present perfect refers to a period of time immediately before the present, as in: *He has done his homework.* The pluperfect and pluscuamperfect (the imperfect and the preterit of *haber* + a past participle, respectively) refer to a period of time occurring before a specified point in time in the past.

For example:

> *Había hecho la tarea cuando sus amigos llegaron.* (He had done his work when his friends arrived.)

The future perfect corresponds to a time occurring before another referenced point of time in the future, but after the present.

For example:

> *Ellos se habrán ido cuando yo llegue.* (They will have gone by the time I arrive.) (My arrival will take place in the future, and they will go after that future time when I arrive.)

The Use of the Subjunctive

The conventions for using the subjunctive are changing; they vary according to location and who is using it, so there is a lot of variety in the way the subjunctive is used. The following guidelines for using the subjective are generally accepted as standard, if there is such a thing in Spanish grammar outside of the *Real Academia Española* in Spain.

The subjunctive mood expresses doubt, uncertainty, hypothetical situations, contrary to fact situations, and anything not considered by the speaker to be a fact. The subjunctive mood is used in **dependent** or **subordinate** clauses and some **independent** clauses.

In **independent** clauses the subjunctive is frequently used after *quizás* or *tal vez*, which can introduce either the indicative or the subjunctive, depending on the degree of conjecture or probability the speaker wishes to communicate. After the expression *Ojalá* the present or the past subjunctive is used. Often the past subjunctive is used as a softened request, a polite way to make a request of someone, such as in *¿Quisiera usted ?...* or *¿pudiera usted....?* The subjunctive is used in elliptical statements, clauses that begin with *que...* There are a variety of ways to translate these expressions.

For example:

> *¡Que se divierta esta noche!* (I hope you have a good time tonight.)
> *¡Que te vaya bien!* (May you have a good trip.)
> *¡Que duermas bien!* (Sleep tight. Get a good night's sleep.)

In subordinate clauses the subjunctive usually occurs in noun, adjective, or adverb clauses. As a rule, there is a change of subject; the subject of the verb in the main clause is different from the subject of the verb in the dependent clause. When there is no change of subject, an infinitive functions as the object of the verb.

For example:

> *Yo quiero leer el libro.* (I want to read the book.)
> *Yo quiero que tú leas el libro.* (I want you to read the book.)
> *Me alegro de estar aquí.* (I am glad to be here.)
> *Me alegro que estés aquí.* (I am glad you are here.)

In noun clauses the subjunctive is used when the verb in the main clause expresses a request, a wish, desire, approval, opposition, preference, suggestion, recommendation, advisability, necessity, obligation, or a command. Some common verbs of this type are: *querer, pedir, desear, prohibir, mandar, rogar, permitir, dejar, impedir, sugerir, recomendar, exigir, oponer, requerir, aconsejar, hacer* and *preferir.*

At times *decir* indicates volition (a request), and at other times it expresses facts. When it indicates a request, then the subjunctive is used. The other times, it is followed by the indicative.

For example:

> *Él dice que su hermano viene mañana.* (He says that his brother is coming tomorrow.)
> *Él le dice a su hermano que venga mañana.* (He tells his brother to come tomorrow.)

Notice that when the verb indicates a request, an indirect object pronoun is often used. The English translation of the sentence often uses an infinitive construction instead of the subjunctive.

After verbs that express an emotion, the subjunctive is used in the dependent clause. Some common verbs of this type are: *alegrarse de, estar contento, lamentar, molestar, parecerle extraño, sentir,* and *arrepentir.*

After verbs that express doubt or denial the subjunctive is used. Common verbs of this type are *negar, dudar, no estar seguro,* and *no estar cierto.*

For example:

> *Dudo que vengan.* (I doubt that they are coming.)
> *Niego que lo escriban.* (I deny that they are writing it.)

When the negative of the above verbs is used, however, a certainty is expressed and the indicative is used.

For example:

> *No dudo que vienen.* (I do not doubt that they are coming.)
> *No niego que lo escriben.* (I do not deny that they are writing it.)

After an impersonal expression (the verb *ser* + an adjective), the subjunctive is used. The verb *ser* can be used in any tense, but it is always in the third person singular form, meaning *it is, it was, it will be,* etc.

For example:

> *Será preciso que lean.* (It will be necessary for them to read.)
> *Puede ser que lo tengan.* (It could be that they have it.)

Often an infinitive construction can be used in place of a subordinate clause containing the subjunctive. When the infinitive is used, the verb *ser* is preceded by an indirect object pronoun that is the subject of the verb in the subordinate clause in English.

For example:

> *Les fue imposible asistir.* (It was impossible for them to come.)
> *Fue imposible que asistieran.* (It was impossible for them to come./It was impossible that they come.)

The only impersonal expressions that require the indicative mood are those that express a certainty, such as *es obvio, es evidente, es claro, es seguro, es verdad, es cierto,* and *no cabe duda.* (Remember that the verb *es* can be in any other tense also: *es, fue, era, será sería, ha sido, había sido, habrá sido* and *habría sido,* or even the present participle *siendo necesario.*)

For example:

Es obvio que les gusta leer. (It is obvious that they like to read.)
Fue obvio que les gustaba leer. (It was obvious that they liked to read.)

When any of the above impersonal expressions of certainty are negated, then the subjunctive is used since doubt is then implied.

For example:

No es obvio que les guste leer. (It is not obvious that they like to read.)

In adjective clauses, the subjunctive is used if the antecedent (the noun that the clause modifies) is indefinite, unknown to the speaker, uncertain, hypothetical, or nonexistent.

For example:

Buscan un apartamento que sea barato. (They are looking for an apartment that is inexpensive.)
Buscan un estudiante que pueda traducirlo. (They are looking for a student who can translate it.)
No encontraron ningún estudiante que pudiera leerlo. (They did not find any student who read it.)
No hay nadie que recuerde toda esa historia. (There is no one who remembers all of that story.)

When the antecedent is indefinite, the personal *a* is often omitted. The absence of a personal *a*, then frequently indicates the subjunctive is necessary.

For example:

Buscan un estudiante que sepa de ingeniería eléctrica. (They are looking for a student who knows electrical engineering.)
Buscan al estudiante que sabe de ingeniería eléctrica. (They are looking for the student who knows electrical engineering.)

The construction *por ... que* indicates the subjunctive. The phrase is expressed several ways in English.

For example:

Por rico que sea, no me casaré con él. (No matter how rich he may be, I will not marry him.)
Me quedaré hasta la conclusión, por tarde que sea. (I will stay until the end, however late that may be.)
Por mucho que se quejaran, los estudiantes hicieron el trabajo. (For all the complaining they did, the students still did the work.)

In adverbial clauses the kind of conjunction determines whether the subjunctive is used or not. After the following conjunctions, the subjunctive is always used, regardless of the tenses of the verbs: *para que, con tal que, a menos que, a ser que, a fin de que, antes de que, sin que, a no ser que,* and *en caso de que.* The preposition *de* in most of the above adverbial conjunctions is normally omitted. These conjunctions, except for *antes de que*, introduce clauses of concession, proviso, or purpose.

For example:

> *El chico hizo la tarea para que pudiera ir a la fiesta.* (The boy did the chores so that he could go to the park.)
> *Ella dijo que vendría con tal que viniera su compañera.* (She said she would come provided that her companion came.)
> *Salieron sin que los viéramos.* (They left without our seeing them.)

Notice the variety of ways that the subjunctive is expressed in English, especially the last example where English uses a gerund, and Spanish uses the subjunctive.

Two adverbial conjunctions that take either the subjunctive or the indicative depending on the meaning desired by the speaker are: *de manera que* and *de modo que.* The selection depends on the kind of information that is being communicated.

For example:

> *El conferenciante habló de manera que todos los delegados lo oyeron.* (The speaker spoke so that the delegates understood him./The speaker spoke in such a way that the delegates understood him.) (Whichever the meaning, the delegates understood him.)
> *El conferenciante hablo de manera que todos los delegados le oyeran.* (The speaker spoke in a way that the delegates could understand him.) (It is unknown whether the delegates understood him or not.)

Aunque and *a pesar de que* also can take either the subjunctive or the indicative according to what the speaker wishes to communicate. The selection of the subjunctive expresses uncertainty about the facts in the mind of the speaker, and the indicative expresses the opposite meaning.

For example:

> *Aunque lloverá mañana, iremos.* (Although it will rain tomorrow, we will go.) (The speaker is reasonably certain it will rain.)
> *Aunque llueva mañana, iremos.* (Although it may rain tomorrow, we will go.) (The speaker makes no statement about whether it will rain or not.)

In adverbial clauses of time, the sequence of tenses is especially important. After the following adverbial conjunctions, use the subjunctive if the verbs in the independent clause are in the future (the action has not yet taken place), and the subjunctive in the subordinate clause: *en cuanto, tan pronto como, cuando, después, hasta que, mientras, una vez que.* The subjunctive is used because since these events have not taken place yet, they cannot be considered factual.

For example:

> *Pídales que se queden hasta que volvamos.* (Ask them to remain until we return.)
> *Te veremos tan pronto como llegues.* (We will see you as soon as you get here.)
> *Lo agradecerá cuando venga.* (They will thank him when he comes.)

When the action or event takes place in the past, the indicative is used. When the above sentences, for example, are expressed in the past, notice that the subjunctive is not used, since once the event has occurred, it is a fact, or is perceived as fact by the speaker.

For example:

> *Les pidió que se quedaran hasta que volvimos.* (He asked them to stay until we returned. OR We did return.)

The subjunctive is still used in the dependent noun clause after *pedir*, but after the adverbial conjunction, *hasta que*, the indicative is used.

For example:

> *Te vimos tan pronto como llegaste.* (We saw you as soon as you arrived. OR We saw you return; it is a fact.)
> *Lo agradecí cuando vino.* (I thanked him when he came. OR He came; it is a fact.)

The use of the subjunctive after *si* depends upon the tense of the verb, also, and the construction in which it occurs. After *si,* the present subjunctive is so seldom used that it is not likely to appear on the exam. (The exception would be when *si* means *cuando.*) When the present or future indicative is used, *si* is followed by the present indicative, or future.

For example:

> *Le pago si hace el trabajo.* (I pay him if he works.) (The speaker does not know if he will work or not, but when he works he gets paid.)

Compare this sentence with:

> *Le pagaré cuando trabaje.* (I will pay him when he works.) (I will pay him when he works, but he has not worked yet. I have not paid him yet.)
> *Si hará el trabajo, le pagaré.* (If he will do the work, I will pay him.)

When the sentence structure indicates an *if-then* statement, then the **past** subjunctive is used in the *if* portion of the sentence, or in both clauses. The subjunctive is used in the *if* portion of the sentence because the information expressed in that kind of clause is contrary to fact, which requires the use of the subjunctive.

For example:

> *Le pagaría si trabajara.* (I would pay him if he would work.)

(This sentence structure using the conditional, implies very strongly that he will not work. The information communicated through the use of this grammar is that it is uncertain whether he will work or not. The meaning implied is *if he would work, which he probably would not do,* meaning that his working is contrary to fact.)

In the past perfect (pluperfect and pluscuamperfect), the helping verb *haber* is conjugated in the appropriate tenses.

For example:

> *Le habría pagado si hubiera trabajado.* (I would have paid him if he had worked.)

Look at the following sequence of tenses to help fix in mind the progression from what is perceived as fact by the speaker, to hypothetical statements (*if-then* sentences.)

Si tengo dinero, voy a la fiesta. (If I have money I will go to the party.)
Si he tenido dinero, he ido a la fiesta. (If I have had money, I have gone to the party.)
Si tuviera dinero, iría a la fiesta. (If I had the money, I would go ...)
Si hubiera tenido dinero, habría ido a la fiesta. (If I had had money, I would have gone....)

Another case where the past subjunctive is always used because it expresses contrary to fact information is after the expression *como si*, meaning *as if*. Even in English this structure uses the English equivalent of the subjunctive.
For example:

Les habló como si fueran niñitos. (He spoke to them as if they were children.)
Les habla como si fueran niñitos. (He speaks to them as if they were children.)
Les hablará como si fueran niñitos. (He will speak to them as if they were children.)
Les ha hablado como si fueran niños. (He has spoken to them as if they were children.)
Les había hablado como si hubieran sido niños. (He had spoken to them as if they had been children.)

The other instance in which the subjunctive is used is in imperative sentences—commands.

A command is really a portion of a sentence in which the speaker means *I want that...* or *I order that....* For example, in the following cases, notice how the part of the sentence that is in parentheses actually expresses what is the main clause, followed by the dependent noun clause, with the subjunctive used after the verb that expresses volition.

(Yo quiero que usted) Diga la verdad. (I want that you.......) Tell the truth.
(Yo mando que usted) No revele el secreto. (I order that you.......) Do not reveal the secret.
(Yo exijo que ustedes) Lean el libro. (I require that you......) Read the book.
(Yo pido que nosotros) Aceptemos su oferta. (I request that we........) Accept their offer.

The one difference between the simple declarative sentence that uses the subjunctive in the dependent noun clause, and the imperative sentence is that the location of pronouns is different for imperative sentences.
For example:

Dígamelo. (Tell it to me.)

The pronouns are added to the end of the verb since it is a command form:

(Yo quiero que usted) me lo diga. (I want that you ....) tell it to me.

There is a command form for every person and number except the first person singular. The subjunctive is used for commands in all forms except for the second person singular and plural affirmative commands. The following chart shows which verb form to use for which command.

<u>Second Person, Singular, **Tú**</u>:

Affirmative form: the third person singular **present indicative**
For example:

Entrega (tú) los papeles. (Turn in the papers.)

Negative form: the second person, singular **present subjunctive**
For example:

No entregues (tú) los papeles. (Do not turn in the papers.)

<u>Third Person, Singular, **Usted**</u>:

Affirmative and negative forms: the third person singular, **present subjunctive**
For example:

Entregue Ud. los papeles. (Turn in the papers.)
No entregue Ud. los papeles. (Do not turn in the papers.)

<u>First Person Plural, **Nosotros, Nosotras**</u>:

Affirmative and negative forms: the first person plural, **present subjunctive**
For example:

Entreguemos los papeles. (Let's turn in the papers.)

When the reflexive pronoun, **nos**, is added to affirmative forms, the final *s* of the ending is dropped.
For example:

Sentémonos. (Let's sit down.)

Frequently the expression *Vamos a + infinitive* is used in place of the subjunctive command form. The one exception to this rule for formation of the *nosotros* command is the verb *irse* in the affirmative, which is simply *Vámonos.* (The negative form conforms to the rule: *No nos vayamos.*)

<u>Second Person Plural, **Vosotros, Vosotras**</u>:

Affirmative form: the infinitive with *d* in place of *r* of the infinitive ending
For example:

Entregad los papeles. (Turn in the papers.)

(When the reflexive pronoun is added to the affirmative form, the *d* is not used. Simply take off the *r* from the infinitive and add the pronoun, *os.*
For example:

Acostaos. (Go to bed.)

When the infinitive is an **-ir** verb, an accent is written over the **i** of the infinitive ending when the pronoun is attached.
For example:

Servíos. (Serve yourselves.)

The exception to this rule is the verb *ir*, whose second person plural form, affirmative, is **Idos.**)

Negative form: the second person plural of the **present subjunctive**
For example:

No entreguéis los papeles. (Do not turn in the papers.)

Third Person Plural, **Ustedes**:

Affirmative and negative forms: the third person, plural, **present subjunctive**
For example:

Entreguen Uds. los papeles. (Turn in the papers.)
No entreguen Uds. los papeles. (Do not turn in the papers.)

All of the above mentioned forms are for regular, stem changing, and spelling change verbs. There are, however, different forms for some irregular verbs.
For the second person singular irregular verbs, the affirmative and negative forms are:

Infinitive	Affirmative	Negative
decir	*di*	*no digas*
hacer	*haz*	*no hagas*
ir	*vé*	*no vayas*
poner	*pon*	*no pongas*
salir	*sal*	*no salgas*
ser	*sé*	*no seas*
tener	*ten*	*no tengas*
valer	*val*	*no valgas*
venir	*ven*	*no vengas*

For the third person singular and plural commands, the irregular forms are derived from the first person, singular, present indicative. That means that the only forms that cannot be determined from the present tense are those irregular first person singular forms that end in **-oy**. The irregular third person forms for these kinds of verbs are:

dar	*doy*	*dé usted, den ustedes*
estar	*estoy*	*esté usted, estén ustedes*
ir	*voy*	*vaya usted, vayan ustedes*
saber	*sé*	*sepa usted, sepan ustedes*
ser	*soy*	*sea usted, sean ustedes*

THE PAST PARTICIPLE

When the past participle functions verbally, the ending is invariable; it always ends in **-o**. It will always follow the verb *haber* when it functions as a part of a verbal form. When the past participle functions as an adjective, however, after the verbs *ser, estar*, or any other verb, then the ending must agree in gender and in number with the noun to which it refers.

Some verbs have irregular past participles. They are:

abrir	*abierto*
cubrir	*cubierto*
decir	*dicho*
escribir	*escrito*
hacer	*hecho*
imprimir	*impreso*
morir	*muerto*
poner	*puesto*
soler	*suelto*
ver	*visto*
volver	*vuelto*

Any of the compound forms of these verbs will take an irregular past participle form, such as *descubrir, desdecir, predecir, describir, deshacer, proponer, componer, satisfacer, devolver, envolver, revolver, prever*, etc.

Past participles also commonly function as absolutes. This use is found mainly in written language.

For example:

> *Determinada la ruta que había de seguir, salieron.* (Having decided on the route they were to follow, they left.)

In conversation the past participle can follow the verb *tener* to indicate that something is done.

For example:

> *Tengo hecha la tarea para mañana.* (I have the chores for tomorrow done.)

The Passive Voice

The structure of the passive voice is almost a formula. The agent in the true passive voice is either expressed or strongly implied. Sometimes the difference between the selection of the true passive and the substitute for the passive depends on what the speaker wishes to emphasize—either the fact that the act was done **by** someone, or some aspect of the action itself.

The structure for the true passive is:

TO BE + PAST PARTICIPLE + POR + THE AGENT

For example:

> *La tienda fue cerrada por el gerente.* (The store was closed by the manager.)

The agent is the person acting upon the subject; the agent does the action.

Notice that in Spanish the object comes before the verb. Also notice that the past participle agrees in gender and number with the noun to which it refers: *la tienda* is the antecedent for *cerrada*.

When the agent is not emphasized, or when the subject is a nonspecific subject (often expressed as *one, they,* or *you* in English), it is possible to use the pronoun **se** and the third person singular or plural of the verb instead of the true passive construction.

For example:

Se cierran las tiendas a las cinco. (The stores are closed at five o'clock. or They close the stores at five o'clock.)

Another way to express this in Spanish is with the third person plural. For example:

Dicen que el español es fácil. (They say that Spanish is easy.)
Se dice que el español es fácil. (They say that Spanish is easy. OR It is said that Spanish is easy.)

This construction is not to be confused with the use of the past participle with the verb *estar*, which indicates resultant action. In this case the past participle also agrees in gender and number with the noun it modifies.

For example:

La tienda estaba cerrada cuando llegué y tuve que volver a casa. (The store was closed when I arrived and I had to return home.)

Present Participles

When the present participle is used as an adverb in Spanish, it is called a *gerundio*. The term has not been used in this book to avoid any confusion about what precisely is meant by a *gerundio*, or a present participle. Remember that in English a gerund is a present participle that functions as a noun. (For example: Running is good for your health.) Remember that in Spanish the present participle, or *gerundio*, can never function as a noun. In its place an infinitive is used. (*El correr es muy saludable.*) The present participle is formed by removing the infinitive ending and adding **-ando** for **-ar** verbs and **-iendo** for **-er** and **-ir** verbs. For verbs that end in **-er** or **-ir**, the **i** changes to **y** when the unstressed **i** comes between two other vowels.

For example:

leer	*leyendo*
creer	*creyendo*
construir	*construyendo*
traer	*trayendo*
ir	*yendo*

Class II and III stem changing verbs have a change in the stem in the present participle. These verbs will change the **e** or **u** to an **i** or **u**, respectively.

For example:

dormir	*durmiendo*
morir	*muriendo*
sentir	*sintiendo*
reír	*riendo*
vestir	*vistiendo*
pedir	*pidiendo*

Verbally, the only use of the present participle is as a part of the progressive forms. *Estar* followed by the present participle is the progressive form. (See below.)

When this part of speech functions verbally, the ending in invariable; it always ends in **-o**. The present participle never functions as an adjective (it can never modify a noun). Even when the present participle is used adverbially, it is invariable.

For example:

Estábamos jugando al fútbol ayer. (We were playing soccer yesterday.)

In the adverbial usage, the present participle tells how something is being done.

For example:

El chico salió corriendo porque ya era tarde. (The boy left running because it was already late.)

The present participle frequently follows verbs of perception, such as *oír, ver, percibir, sentirse, mirar, escuchar,* etc. In these cases the word describes more about the verb.

For example:

Oí al gato maullando fuera de la puerta cerrada. (I heard the cat mewing outside the closed door.)

The verbs *continuar* and *seguir* take the present participle normally to complete their meaning.

For example:

Los chicos siguieron cantando dulcemente. (The boys continued singing sweetly.)
Continuamos divirtiéndonos toda la noche. (We continued to have a good time all night.)

At times the present participle can also provide explanatory or parenthetical information.

For example:

Temí que mi hermano, no estando yo presente, cometiera algún disparate. (I feared that my brother, I not being present, would commit some blunder.)
Pasando ayer por el mercado, encontré a mi antigua novia. (Going through the market yesterday, I met my former girlfriend.)

Progressive Forms   The progressive forms are always expressed with *estar* + *the present participle*.

 The verb *estar* is conjugated in any desired tense and the present participle is added. These forms are not used as much in Spanish normally as they are in English because the simple tenses in Spanish are translated into the progressive as one of the meanings. The progressive forms are used to underscore the fact that something is actually in the process of taking place.

 For example:

> *Estoy leyendo este libro en este momento.* (I am reading this book at this moment.)
> *Estaba leyendo cuando entraron los chicos.* (He was reading when the children came in.)
> *Estará volando a la Florida mientras tú manejarás.* (He will be flying to Florida while you will be driving.)

 The one instance where the Spanish will not use the progressive form where English does is in a time expression using *hacer*. What in English is the present perfect progressive becomes a simple tense in Spanish.

 For example:

> *Hace unos meses que* **estudio** *el español.* (I **have been studying** Spanish for a few months.)
> **Hacía** *unos meses que estudiaba el español.* (He **had been studying** Spanish for a few months.)

ADVERBS

Adverbs modify verbs, adjectives, or other adverbs. The ending **-mente** is added to the adjectives that end with **-e** or any consonant.

 For example:

> *general—generalmente*
> *frecuente—frecuentemente*

When the adjective ends with **-o**, then the ending **-mente** is added to the feminine form of the adjective.

 For example:

> *rápido—rápidamente*

When two adverbs are used together, the first adverb in the feminine form of the word and the ending is added to the second adverb only.

 For example:

> *Los rayos solares del amanecer se abrieron paso lenta y brillantemente al este.*

Frequently adverbs are replaced by prepositional phrases.

 For example:

generalmente	*por lo general*
cuidadosamente	*con cuidado*
cortésmente	*con cortesía*

Spanish-English Dictionary

A

abajo under, underneath, below, down
  para abajo downward
abandonar to leave, to forsake, to give up, to abandon
abarcar to include, to embrace, to take in
abastecer to supply, to purvey
abatir to throw down, to overthrow
abdicar to abdicate, to leave
la **abeja** bee
ablandarse (el corazón) to soften, to mellow, to relent
abogado lawyer
abolir to abolish
abonar to subscribe to, to pay
abrazar to hug, to embrace
el **abrazo** hug, embrace
abreviar to abbreviate
abrigado sheltered, protected, clothed warmly
el **abrigo** coat, overcoat
  el abrigo de piel fur coat
abrir to open
abrochar to button up, to button down, to buckle up
abrumar to crush, to overwhelm, to oppress
absorber to absorb, to soak up
abuelo, -a grandfather, grandmother
aburrirse to get bored, to become bored
acá y allá here and there
acabar(se) to finish
  acabar con to end with
  acabar de to have just + inf.
acalorado, -a hot, heated

acaramelado, -a caramel covered
acaso perhaps, maybe, by chance
  por si acaso just in case
acatar to respect, to heed
acceder to agree, to consent
el **accidente** accident
la **acción** action
accionar to work, to act
las **acciones** stocks
el **aceite** oil
la **aceituna** olive
acentuar(se) to accentuate
aceptar to accept
la **acequia** irrigation ditch
la **acera** sidewalk, pavement
acercarse to approach, to go near
el **acero** steel
acertar (ie) to ascertain, to be right, to guess
aclarar to clarify
acoger to welcome, to make welcome
acomodado comfortable
acomodar to accommodate
acompañar to accompany
aconsejar to advise
acontecer to happen, to occur, to take place
el **acontecimiento** event, happening
acordarse de to remember
acorralar to enclose, to corner
acostarse to go to bed
acostumbrar to be accustomed to
la **actitud** attitude
la **actividad** activity
la **actuación** action, conduct
actual present, modern
la **actualidad** present time

  en la actualidad at the present moment
actuar to act, to behave
acudir to come
  acudir a to come to, to aid, to heed
el **acuerdo** agreement, understanding
  de acuerdo con, a in accordance with
  de mutuo acuerdo in mutual agreement
  estar de acuerdo con to be in agreement with
  ponerse de acuerdo to bring to an agreement
el **acumulador** battery (car)
acusar to accuse
el **adagio** adage
adaptar to adapt
adelantar to move forward, to progress
¡adelante! Go on! Come in!
  en adelante from now on, henceforth, in the future
adelgazar(se) to get thin, to slim down
además moreover, in addition
  además de besides
adentro inside
adiestrar to train, to instruct, to guide
el **adiós** goodbye
la **adivinanza** riddle, prediction
adivinar to guess, to divine
el **adivino** magician, fortune-teller, sage
admirar to admire
adoctrinar to indoctrinate
adornarse to adorn oneself
el **adorno** ornament, adornment
adosar to lean, to attach

adquirir to acquire

el **advenedizo** upstart

el **advenimiento** coming, arrival, advent

advertencia warning, piece of advice

advertir to advise, to warn

el **afán** hard work, industry, zeal

afectar to affect

el **afecto** affection, fondness

afianzar to guarantee, to strengthen, to reinforce

el **aficionado** amateur

afirmar to affirm

afrontarse to confront, to face up to

las **afueras** outskirts, outside, out-of-doors, suburbs

agacharse to lean over, to bend down, to duck

agarrar to grasp, to seize

agasajar to treat kindly, to regale

el **agente publicitario** publicity agent

agitar to shake, to wave, to excite, to rouse

agitarse to get excited

agobiar to burden

agonizar to agonize

agotarse to become exhausted

agraciado pretty, attractive, graceful

agradable agreeable

agradar to please

agradecer to thank

agregar to add

agrícola farming, agricultural

agruparse to form a group, to crowd together

el **agua** water

   hacerse agua la boca to make one's mouth water

el **aguacate** avocado

aguantar to put up with, to stand, to tolerate, to bear

aguardar to wait for, to await

agudo sharp

el **águila** eagle

la **aguja** needle

el **agujero** hole

aguzar to sharpen

ahí there

   de ahí from there

el **ahijado** godchild, adopted child

ahogar to drown

ahorcar to hang

ahorrar(se) to save

airoso ventilated, windy, graceful, elegant

aislar to isolate

el **ajedrez** chess

ajeno other people's

el **ajo** garlic

el **ajonjolí** sesame

ajustar to adjust

el **ala** wing

alabar to praise

la **alabanza** praise

el **alambrado** wire netting, wire fencing

el **álamo** poplar tree

alargar to lengthen, to prolong

el **alarido** howl, yell, shriek

el **alba** dawn

albergar to lodge, to stay

el **alboroto** uproar, disturbance

la **alcachofa** artichoke

el **alcalde** mayor

el **alcance** reach

   al alcance de within reach of

   tener al alcance to have within reach

la **alcancía** money box, piggy bank

alcanzar to reach, to achieve

   alcanzar la felicidad to find happiness

la **alcoba** bedroom

la **aldea** village, town

alegrar to allege, to claim

alegrarse to be happy

la **alegría** happiness

alejado, -a faraway

el **alejamiento** estrangement, removal, absence

alejar(se) de to back away from, distance oneself from

el **alemán** German

alentar to encourage, to inspire

el **alero** eaves (house), fender (of a car)

la **alfarería** pottery, ceramic

el **alfil** bishop (chess)

la **algazara** uproar

algunas cuantas some, few

la **alhaja** jewel, gem, piece of jewelry

la **alhambrada** wire fencing, wire netting

el **aliento** breath

alimentar(se) to nourish

el **alimento** food

aliviar to relieve, to ease, to alleviate

el **alma** soul

el **almacén** department store, shop, warehouse

la **almendra** almond

el **almíbar** syrup (not medicine)

la **almohada** pillow

el **almuerzo** lunch

alojar to house, to lodge, to stay a night

el **alpinismo** mountain climbing

alquilar to rent

el **alquiler** rent

alrededor de around, about, encircling

los **alrededores** the outskirts, the out-of-doors

el **altavoz** speaker

alto high, tall, stop

la **altura** height

aludir to allude

el **alumbrado** light

alumbrar to light, to enlighten

alusivo allusive, referring to

el **alza** rise

el **alzamiento** lifting, raising

alzar to raise, to lift

allá there

   el **más allá** the beyond

más allá farther on, beyond

el **ama de casa** housewife

amable pleasant, agreeable

el **amaestrador** tamer

amanecer to get daylight

la **amapola** poppy (flower)

amar to love

amargo bitter

el **amargor**, la **amargura** bitterness

amarillo yellow

amarrar to tie up, to make fast, to moor

la **amatista** amethyst

ambicionar to aspire, to strive for, to seek

ambiental environmental

el **ambiente** environment

el **medio ambiente** natural environment

ambos both

la **amenaza** threat

amenazar to threaten

la **ametralladora** machine gun

amigable friendly

la **amistad** friendship

amontonarse to add up, to amass

amortizar to amortize, to pay off

amparar to help, to aid

ampliar to enlarge

amplio wide, large

la **ampolleta** hourglass, electric bulb

el **analfabetismo** illiteracy

analizar to analyze

ancho wide

el **anciano** old man

anclar to moor, to anchor

andar to walk

andar angustiado to worry, to stew about

el **anfiteatro** amphitheater

el **ángulo** angle

la **angustia** anxiety

anhelante yearning, longing

anhelar to long for, to pine for, to yearn for

el **anillo** ring

animar to animate, to encourage

animarse a to take heart, to regain courage

el **ánimo** spirit, will, heart

el **anochecer** to become night

el **ansia** anxiety, worry

ansioso anxious

anteayer day before yesterday

el **antepasado** ancestor

anterior before, anterior

anticuado antiquated

antiguo old, ancient

antojar(se) to fancy, to feel like

anular to repeal, to revoke, to invalidate

anunciar to announce

el **anuncio** ad, news, announcement

añadir to add to, to increase

el **añil** indigo

el **año** year

año tras año year after year

antaño long ago

apaciguar to pacify

apagado put out, extinguished

apagar to put out, to turn off

el **aparato** machine

aparecer to appear, to turn up

apartar(se) to depart from, to forsake, to go away a distance

aparte de aside from

apático apathetic, listless

el **apellido** father's name, family name

apenas scarcely

la **apertura** opening, hole

apetecer to appeal to, to look tasty

aplastar to smash

aplaudir to applaud

aplicar(se) to apply oneself

apodar to nickname

apoderarse de to seize, to take power

apolillado moth-eaten

apoltronado idle, lazy

aporrear to hit, to give a beating

la **aportación** contribution

aportar to contribute, to provide

apoyar to support

el **apoyo** support

apreciar(se) to appreciate

aprender to learn

el **aprendiz** apprentice

el **aprendizaje** apprenticeship

aprestarse a to get ready, to make up

apresurar to hurry

apretar to squeeze, to clasp, to bring together

el **apretón** squeeze, difficulty

aprisionar to imprison

aprobar to approve, to pass (a course, a bill)

el **aprovechamiento** benefit, gain, betterment

aprovechar(se) to take advantage of

aproximarse to get close, to go up to, to near

apuntar to aim, to sharpen, to point

apurar(se) to be in a hurry, to hurry

el **apuro** hurry, difficulty

el **árbol** tree

arcano arcane, secret

el **archivo** archive, library

arder to burn

ardiente burning

el **arecife** reef

la **arena** sand

el **argumento** plot

el **armario** cupboard, wardrobe

la **armonía** harmony

el **arquitecto** architect

la **arquitectura** architecture

la **artesanía** craft, craftwork

el **artículo de fondo**   lead article, editorial

arrancar   to tear off, to pluck out, to start up

arrastrar   to drag, to trail, to pull, to haul

arrebatar   to snatch away

arreglar   to arrange, to fix

el **arrendamiento**   lease

arrepentir(se)   to repent, to be sorry

arriba   above

arriesgar   to risk

arrimar   to bring close, to dock

arrodillar(se)   to kneel, to kneel down

arrojar   to throw, to toss

el **arrozal**   rice field

el **ascenso**   ascent, raise

asegurar   to assure, to insure, to ensure

asemejar   to resemble, to seem like

asequible   available, obtainable

asesinar   to assassinate, to murder, to kill

asiduo   industrious, hard working

el **asiento**   seat

   asiento delantero   back seat (in a car)

   asiento trasero   front seat (in a car)

   asiento de ventanilla   window seat (on an airplane)

la **asignatura**   course

asimilarse   to assimilate, to become one of a group

la **asistencia**   attendance

asistir   to attend (school)

asomar(se)   to show up, to appear at

asombroso   surprising

asqueroso   awful, vile, nasty

asustar   to surprise, to scare

atacar   to attack

atar   to tie, to tie up

atemorizar   to terrify

atender   to attend to (patients, business)

atenerse   to abide, to stick to, to hold

el **aterrizaje**   landing (of an airplane)

el **aterrizaje forzoso**   emergency landing

aterrizar   to land

el **atleta**   athelete

la **atmósfera**   atmosphere, environment

atónito   astonished, amazed

atormentar   to torment

el **atraco**   mugging, attack

atraer   to attract

atrancar   to bar, to block, to clog up

atrapar   to catch

atrás   behind

atrasar   to get behind, to retard

atravesar   to cross

atrever(se)   to dare, to venture

   atrevimiento   daring, boldness

atribuir   to attribute to, to ascribe

atropellar   to run over

el **auge**   peak

aumentar   to augment, to increase

aun   even

   aun cuando   even when

aún   still, yet

aunque   even though

auscultar   to auscultate

la **ausencia**   absence

el **auxilio**   help

   pedir auxilio   to ask for help

avanzar   to advance

avergonzar   to be ashamed, to shame

averiguar   to verify, to check

el **avión**   airplane

avisar   to advise, to warn, to inform

el **aviso**   notice, warning

la **ayuda**   help

ayudar   to help

el **ayuntamiento**   city hall

la **azafata**   stewardess

el **azar**   chance, accident

azotar   to whip, to beat

la **azotea**   flat roof, terrace roof

azteca   Aztec

el **azúcar**   sugar

B

el **bachillerato**   diploma

bailar   to dance

el **baile**   dance

bajar   to take down, to come down

   bajar de   to take, come down from

bajo   short, low

el **baloncesto**   basketball

balbucear   to stutter, to stammer, to babble

bancario   bank (adj.)

   giro bancario   bank draft

el **banco**   bank, park bench

la **bandera**   flag

el **banquero**   banker

bañar(se)   to bathe

la **bañera**   bathtub

el **baño**   bathroom

barato   cheap, inexpensive

la **barbilla**   chin

el **barco**   ship

   por barco   by ship

la **barra**   bar, rod, lever, ingot

barrer   to sweep

el **barril**   barrel

el **barrio**   neighborhood, suburb

la **base**   base, basis, foundation

basta con   suffice with, enough with

bastar   to be enough, to suffice

la **basura**   trash, garbage

el **batidor**   mixer

batir   to beat

el **baúl**   trunk, chest

bautizar   to baptize

el **bautizo**   baptism

la **baza** trick (in cards)

la **bebida** drink

la **beca** scholarship

el **bejuco** liana, rattan, reed, vine

Belén Bethlehem

bélico warlike

la **belleza** beauty

el **beneficio** benefit

besar to kiss

la **biblioteca** library

el **bibliotecario** librarian

la **bicicleta** bicycle

los **bienes** goods

   los **bienes muebles** personal property

el **bienestar** well-being

la **bienvenida** welcome

   dar la bienvenida to welcome

   ¡Bienvenido! Welcome!

la **blusa** blouse

la **boca** mouth

   boca abajo face down

   boca arriba face up

el **bocadillo** snack, bite

la **bocina** horn (mechanical)

la **boda** wedding

la **bola** ball

el **boletín de noticias** news bulletin, announcement

el **boleto** ticket

   boleto de ida y vuelta round trip ticket

el **boliche** bowling, small grocery shop

la **bolsa** bag, purse, pocket

el **bolsillo** pocket

la **bomba** bomb

el **bombero** fireman

el **bombín** bowler (hat), derby (hat), bicycle pump

los **bombones** bon bons

bordar to embroider

el **borde** side (of the road), edge

el **borracho** drunk, intoxicated person

el **borrador** eraser

borrar to erase

la **borrasca** storm, squall, flurry

bostezar to yawn

las **botas** boots

el **bote** boat

la **botella** bottle

el **botín** loot, booty

el **botiquín** medicine chest

el **botones** buttons, bellhop

el **brazo** arm

el **bribón** rascal, rogue

brincar to jump

brindar to toast (one's health)

el **brindis** toast

la **brisa** breeze

el **broche** brooch, pin

la **broma** joke

broncear(se) to tan, to get a suntan

brotar to sprout, to bud, to spring up

la **bruma** mist, fog

bruñir to polish, to burnish

bucear to dive

la **buhardilla** attic

el **búho** owl

la **bulla** uproar, noise

el **bulto postal** package

burlarse de to laugh at, to make fun of

el **burócrata** civil servant

buscar to search for, to look for

la **búsqueda** search

C

caber to fit

   no cabe duda there is no doubt

la **cabeza** head

la **cabina de teléfono** telephone booth

el **cabo** cape (land), corporal

   al fin y al cabo at last, finally

el **cacto** cactus

cada each

la **cadena** chain

caer(se) to fall (down)

la **cafetera** coffeepot

la **caja** box

el **cajero** teller (in a bank)

la **cal** lime (mineral)

calabaza gourd

calado soaked

el **calamar** squid

la **calavera** skull

los **calcetines** socks

calmar(se) to calm down, to be quiet

calvo bald

calzar to put on shoes

los **calzoncillos** underpants

la **calle** street

callejero in, of the street

la **cama** bed

la **cámara** chamber

la **Cámara de Diputados** chamber of deputies

el **camarero** waiter

cambiar to change

el **cambio** change

   casa de cambio de moneda foreign money exchange

la **camilla** stretcher, small bed

caminar to walk

la **camisa** shirt

la **campana** bell

el **campesino** farmer

el **campo** countryside, field

el **canal** channel, tunnel

la **canasta** basket

la **cancha** court (for sports), playing field

la **canción** song

la **cantidad** quantity

canoso white-haired, gray-haired

cansarse to get tired

el **cansancio** weariness, fatigue

el, la **cantante** singer

la **caña** cane, reed, rattan

la **caoba** mahogany

capacitado talented, able, capable

el **capital** capital, capital sum

la **capital** capital city

el **capitalista** capitalist

el **capó**   hood (of a car)

el **capricho**   whim

la **cara**   face

  la **cara de pocos amigos**
  long-faced (irritated)

el **caracol**   snail, sea shell

la **cárcel**   jail, cell

carecer   to be lacking, to need

el **cargador**   loader

el **cariño**   affection, love

cariñoso   affectionate, loving

el **carnaval**   carnival

la **carne**   meat

  carne de res   beef

  carne de ternera   veal

  carne de cerdo   pork

el **carnet**   card

  carnet de identidad
  identification card

la **carnicería**   butcher shop

el **carnicero**   butcher

caro   expensive

la **carrera**   career, race

la **carretera**   highway,
  interstate, road

la **carroza**   float (in a parade)

la **carta**   letter (mail)

el **cartel**   poster

la **cartera**   wallet

el **cartero**   mailman

la **casa**   house

  casa de coreos   post office

casado   married

casar(se)   to marry, to get
  married

la **cascada**   cascade, waterfall

la **cáscara**   shell (of eggs,
  nuts), husk, peel (of fruit)

el **casco**   helmet

casero   pertaining to a
  household

casi   almost

castigar   to punish

la **casualidad**   chance,
  occasion

  por casualidad   by chance

la **catarata**   cataract, waterfall

el **catarro**   cold (illness)

el **catedrático**   tenured
  professor, endowed chair

el **caucho**   rubber

caudal   wealth, volume, flow

la **causa**   cause

  a causa de   because of

cautelosamente   cautiously,
  warily

cavilar   to wonder

la **cebolla**   onion

ceder   to transfer to, to give
  up

las **cejas**   eyebrows

celoso   jealous

el **cementerio**   cemetery

cenar   to dine

la **censura**   censorship

el **centro**   downtown, center

  centro comercial
  commercial center

ceñir   to encircle, to surround

cepillar(se)   to brush

el **cepillo**   brush

  cepillo de dientes
  toothbrush

cerca   near

la **cercanía**   neighborhood

el **cerdo**   pig

el **cerebro**   brain

cesar   to stop, to cease

la **ciencia**   science

  ciencia ficción   science
  fiction

el **científico**   scientist

cierto   sure, certain

la **cifra**   figure (numerical)

la **cigarra**   cicada, cricket

el **cilindro**   cylinder

el **cine**   movie theater, movies

la **cinta**   tape, ribbon

la **cinturón**   waist, belt

la **cifra**   figure, number

el **círculo**   circle

circular   to circulate, to go
  around, to run

la **cita**   appointment, date

la **ciudad**   city

el **ciudadano**   citizen

las **claras**   egg-whites

claro   clear

  ¡Claro que sí!   Certainly!
  Clearly! Surely!

clavar   to nail

la **clave**   key

el **clavo**   nail

el **cliente**   client

el **club**   club, association

la **cobardía**   cowardice

cobrar   to charge, to cost

la **cocina**   kitchen

cocinar   to cook

el **coche**   car

  coche-cama   sleeping car
  (on a train)

  coche-comedor   dining car
  (on a train)

codiciar   to covet

el **codo**   elbow

el **cojín**   cushion

la **col**   cabbage

la **cola**   tail

  hacer cola   to wait in line

la **colcha**   bedspread

el **colchón**   mattress

el **colega**   colleague

colgar   to hang up

el **colibrí**   hummingbird

colocar   to place

colorado   colored, reddish

la **comadre**   kinswoman,
  friend (female)

la **comarca**   region, area

el **comedor**   dining room, cafe

el **comentarista**   commentator

comenzar   to start, to begin

comercial   commercial

la **cometa**   bite

cometer   to commit

cómico   comical, funny

la **comida**   food, meal

como   like, as

  ¿cómo?   what? how?

  ¡cómo!   how!

la **cómoda**   wardrobe, dresser

cómodo   comfortable

el **compañero**   companion,
  friend

  compañero de cuarto
  roommate

la **compañía**   company

compartir   to share

el **compatriota**   countryman

la **competencia** competition, race, contest

comportar(se) to behave

el **comprador** buyer

comprar to buy, to purchase

ir de compras to go shopping

comprometerse to compromise, to promise

comprometerse a to promise to

la **computadora** (Latin America) computer

comulgar to share, to partake of communion

la **comunidad** community

con with

con tal (de) que provided that

concebir to conceive, to think of

conceder to concede, to give in

concretar to express explicitly

el **concurso** race, competition

conducir to drive, to lead to

el **conductor** driver, leader

el **conejo** rabbit

conejo de Pascua Easter rabbit

confiar to entrust, to trust

conformarse to agree to, to comply, to put up with

confortable comfortable

la **confusión** confusion

congelar to freeze

la **congestión** congestion, cold (illness)

la **conjetura** conjecture

conjugar to conjugate

conjurar to conjure, to evoke

conmemorar commemorate

conocer to know (people), to meet

conseguir to obtain, to get

el **consejo** advice

consentir to agree, to consent

conservador conservative

conservar to preserve

conspirar to conspire

la **constitución** constitution

construir to build, to construct

consultar to consult

el **consultorio** doctor's office, waiting room

el **consumo** consumption, use

contado cash

al contado in cash

el **contador** bookkeeper, accountant

la **contaminación ambiental** environmental pollution

contaminar to contaminate

contagiar to transmit a disease

contar to count, to tell

contemplar to contemplate

contestar to answer, to respond

continuo continuous

a continuación below, following, immediately after

el **contrabajo** double bass (instrument)

el **contrabando** smuggled goods, contraband

el/la **contrabandista** smuggler

contratar to hire

contravenir to infringe

contribuir to contribute

convenir to agree upon, to arrange

convertir to convert

convertirse en to change into

la **convivencia** coexistence

la **convocatoria** examination session

la **copa** drink, small glass

copiar to copy

copioso abundant, plentiful, copious

el **corazón** heart

la **corbata** necktie

la **cordillera** mountain range

el **coro** choir

coronar to crown

el **corredor** runner

corregir to correct

el **correo** mail

oficina de correos post office

correo aéreo air mail

correo ordinario regular mail, surface mail

correo certificado registered mail

correr to run

correr las cortinas to close the curtains

correr las olas to surf

la **correspondencia** mail, correspondence

corresponder to correspond

corriente running

la **corriente** current

cortar to cut

cortés courteous

la **cortesía** courtesy

corto short

la **cosedora** seamstress

coser to sew

la **costa** coast

costar to cost

las **costillas** ribs

costoso costly, dear, expensive

la **costumbre** custom

cotidiano daily, everyday

crecer to grow, to grow up

el **crédito de vivienda (la hipoteca)** mortgage

la **creencia** belief

creer to believe

criar to raise

el **crimen** crime, criminal

el **cristal** glass, windowpane

el **crucero** crossing, cruise

crujir to creak

cruzar to cross

el **cruce de camino** intersection

cuadra city block

cuadro painting

a cuadros plaid

cual(es) which

  ¿cuál(es)? which one(s)?

cualquier whichever

cuando when

  ¿cuándo? when?

¿cuánto? how many, how much

el **cuarto** room

el **cuello** neck

la **cuenta** bill

  a fin de cuentas all things considered

  cuenta corriente checking account

  cuenta de ahorros savings account

  darse cuenta de to realize

el **cuento** story

el **cuero** leather

el **cuerpo** body

cuesta arriba uphill

cuestionar to question

cuidar(se) de to take care of

cuidado care

culpable guilty

el **cumpleaños** birthday

cumplir to fulfill

  cumplir... años to be ... years old

la **cuota** quota

el **cupón** coupon, ticket

curso course, subject; course, direction flow

CH

el **chaleco** vest

la **chamarra** jacket

chamuscar to singe, to char, to burn

la **chaqueta** jacket

la **charla** chat, talk

charlar to chat

chequear to check on

chillar to scream, to shriek

el **chisme** gossip

la **chispa** spark, glimmer of fire

chisporrotear to sizzle, to crackle

el **chiste** joke

chocar to hit against, to crash

el **chofer** driver

el **chorizo** sausage

chupar to suck

D

dactilar dactyl, referring to a finger

los **dados** dice

dañar(se) to injure, to harm

los **daños** harm, dangers

dar to give

  dar fin a to finish

  dar a luz to give birth

  dar la bienvenida to welcome

  dar una clase to give a class

  dar una paliza to give a beating to

  dar una película to show a movie

  dar una vuelta to turn around

  darse cita con to meet with

  darse cuenta de to realize

  dárselo a to give to

el **dátil** date (fruit)

de of, from, by

  ¿de dónde? from where

deber ought to, to owe

débil weak, frail

el **decano** dean

decidir decide

  decidirse a to decide to

decir to say, to tell

  querer decir to mean, to want to say

  es decir that is to say

la **declaración** statement

dedicar to dedicate

  dedicarse a to dedicate oneself to

el **dedo** finger, toe

deducir to deduct

defectuoso defective

defender to defend

dejar to leave, to let, to stop

  dejar de to stop

  dejárselo a to permit, to let

delante de in front of

deleitar to delight, to please

el **deleite** delight, pleasure

el **delfín** dolphin

delirar hallucinate

el **delito** crime

la **demanda** demand, request

demás the rest

  lo, los demás the rest, the others

demonios devils

  ¿dónde demonios? where in the devil?

demorar to delay

  la **demora** delay, layover

demostrar to demonstrate, to show how

el/la **dentista** dentist

el/la **dependiente** clerk

deplorar to deplore

el **deporte** sport

el, la **deportista** sportsman, sportswoman

deportivo sport, sporty, sporting

deprimir to depress

derecho right

  a la derecha to the right

  derechos de aduana duty (customs tax)

derramar to spill

derribar to knock down, to overthrow

derrocar to bring down, to pull down

la **derrota** defeat

derrumbar to tumble down

el **desacuerdo** disagreement

desafiar to defy

desahogar to comfort

desamparado helpless, sad

desanimar to depress, to discourage

desarrollar to develop

desasosegar to unsettle, disturb

el **desasosiego** uneasiness, anxiety, restlessness

desatinar to exasperate, to bewilder

desayunar(se) to have breakfast

el **desayuno** breakfast

descalzo barefooted

descansar to rest, to relax

el **descanso** rest, break

descender to descend, to come down from

descifrar to read, to decode

descolgar to take down

descompuesto broken

descongelar to defrost

describir to describe

el **descuento** discount

descuidar to neglect

desde from, since

desdeñar to disdain, to scorn

desdibujar to blur, to get blurred

desdichado unhappy, unfortunate

desdoblar to unfold

desear to wish, to want

es de desear to be hoped

desechable disposable

desembolsar to pay out

desempeñar to carry out, to fulfill, to play a role

el **desempleo** unemployment

el **deseo** wish

el **desfile** parade

desgraciadamente unfortunately

deshabitado uninhabited

deshilar to unravel, to fray

el **desierto** desert

desilusionar to disillusion, to deceive

desinflado flat

la **deslealtad** loyalty

deslizar to slip

desmayarse to faint

el **desmayo** fainting

desnudar to undress

la **desnutrición** malnutrition

desobedecer disobey

el **despacho** office, den

la **despedida** goodbye

despedir to fire

despedirse to say goodbye

despegar to take off

el **despegue** take-off (an airplane)

despejar to clear off

la **despenalización** legalization

despeñar to hurl, to throw

despertar to awaken

despertarse to wake up

desplegar to spread out, to fan out, to unfurl

desplomar to topple over, to collapse

desprender to turn off

desproveer to deprive

destacar to stand out

destapar to uncover, to uncork

desteñido discolored

el **destinatario** addressee

el **destornillador** screwdriver

destrozar to destroy

destruir to destroy

el **desván** attic

desvelarse to stay awake

la **desventaja** disadvantage

desvestir(se) to undress, to get rid of

el **detalle** detail

detenerse to stop

determinado certain, determined

detrás de behind

devolver to give back, to return

el **día** day

el **diablo** devil

el **diagnóstico** diagnosis

el **diario** newspaper

diariamente daily

dibujar to draw

el **dibujo** drawing

dibujos animados comic strip

la **dictadura** dictatorship

dictar to dictate, to give

dictar una conferencia to give a lecture

el **diente** tooth

difícil difficult

difundir to diffuse, to divulge

dilatar to expand

el **dilema** dilemma

diligencia diligence, speed, dispatch

diminuto small

el **diputado** deputy, representative

la **dirección** address

dirigir(se) to go toward, to direct toward

la **discoteca** discotheque

discriminado discriminated

la **disculpa** excuse, apology, plea

el **discurso** speech, discussion

el **diseño** design

el **disfraz** mask, disguise

disfrazar to mask, to cover up

disfrutar to enjoy

disimular to hide, to conceal

disminuir to diminish, to lessen

disparar to shoot, to fire a weapon

dispersar to disperse, to spread out

disponer to make available

la **disponibilidad** availability

disponible available, disposable

la **disposición** arrangement, provision, disposal

dispuesto a available for

la **disputa** dispute, argument

distinto different

distrito district

la **diversión** diversion, entertainment

divertido funny, enjoyable

divertirse to have fun, to enjoy

divisar to see, to glance, to make out

divorciado divorced

el **divorcio** divorce

divulgar to divulge, to reveal

doblar to fold over, to turn

doble   double
  habitación doble   double room
la **docena**   dozen
la **doctrina**   doctrine
el **documental**   documentary
doler   to hurt, to ache
el **dolor**   ache, pain
doloroso   painful
el **domicilio**   house
el **dominó**   dominoes
la **doncella a caballo**   horseback girl
donde   where
  ¿dónde?   where?
  ¿adónde?   to where?
dorado   golden
dormir   to sleep
  dormirse   to go to sleep
el **dormitorio**   bedroom
la **droga**   drug
la **ducha**   shower
ducharse   to take a shower
el **dueño**   owner
el **dulce**   sweet
los **dulces**   candy
durar   to last

E

echar   to throw, to toss
  echar al buzón   to mail
la **edad**   age
el **educador**   educator, teacher
el **efectivo**   cash
el **efecto**   effect
efectuar   to effect, to perform, to carry out
eficaz   efficient, effective
egresar   to leave, to exit, to graduate
el **eje**   axis, axle
ejecutar   to execute, to accomplish
el **ejecutivo**   executive
el **ejemplo**   example
el **ejercicio**   exercise
el **ejército**   army
elaborar   to elaborate, to embellish, to work out

elegir   to elect
elogiar   to praise
embarazada   pregnant
embarcar   to set out, to set sail, to get on board
el **embotellamiento**   bottleneck, traffic jam
la **emoción**   emotion
empapar(se)   to soak, to get wet
empeñarse en   to commit, to begin, to get involved
empezar   to begin, to start
el **empleado**   employee
el **empleo**   work, job
emprender   to begin
la **empresa**   company
empujar   to push
el **enamorado**   lover
enamorarse de   to fall in love with
encadenar   to chain, to shackle, to link up
encajar   to join, to insert, to fit
encantado   delighted
encantar   to delight, to enchant
encarar   to face
el **encarcelamiento**   jail, imprisonment
el **encargado**   one responsible for
encargar   to take charge of, to be responsible for
encariñarse con   to become fond of
encarnar   to embody
encender   to turn on, to light
encerrar   to enclose
encima de   over, on top of
encinta   pregnant
encomendar   to entrust
encontrar   to find, to meet up with
el **encuentro**   meeting
la **encuesta**   survey
endosar   to endorse
enfadado   angry
enfadar(se)   to get angry

enfermar(se)   to get sick
la **enfermedad**   illness, sickness
la **enfermera**   nurse
el **enfermo**   sick man, patient
enfocar   to focus
el **enfoque**   focus
enfrentarse   to confront
enfriar   to chill
engañar   to deceive, to cheat
engordar(se)   to get fat
engrasar   to grease
engreído   conceited
engrudar   to paste (papers)
enlatar   to can, to preserve
enlazar   to tie together
enloquecer   to go crazy
enojarse   to get angry
enriquecer   to get rich
ensayar   to test, to try out
la **enseñanza**   instruction, learning
enseñar   to learn, to show
  enseñar a   to teach to
el **ensimismamiento**   pensiveness, absorption
ensordecedor   deafening
ensuciar   to get dirty
entablar   to begin, to start
entender   to understand
enterarse de   to learn about
enterrar   to bury
entibiar   to warm
entonar   to intone, to chant
entornar   to leave ajar
entrañable   dear, beloved
las **entrañas**   entrails, insides
entrar (en)   to enter
entre   between, among
entregar   to hand in
entrenarse   to train, to practice
entretejer   to weave
entretenido   entertaining
el **entretenimiento**   entertainment
la **entrevista**   interview
entusiasmado   enthusiastic
enumerar   to list, to ennumerate

envasar   to can, to preserve
enviar   to send
envolver   to wrap up
envuelto   wrapped, enclosed
enyesado   plastered
   estar enyesado   in a plaster cast
la **época**   age, epoch
equilibrio   equilibrium, balance
el **equipaje**   equipment, luggage
el **equipo**   team
equivocado   mistaken
equivocar(se)   to mistake
erguir   to raise, to lift up
erigir   to erect, to build
erizar   to bristle
errar   to wander, to make mistakes
la **escala**   scale, stopover
la **escalera**   stairs
escampar   to clear up (weather)
escandalizar   to scandalize
escapar   to escape
el **escaparate**   store window
escaso   scarce
la **escena**   scene
el **escenario**   setting
la **escenificación**   planning, setting, staging
la **esclavitud**   slavery
la **escoba**   broom
escoger   to choose
los **escombros**   rubble
esconder   to hide
escribir   to write
el **escritor**   writer
escudriñar   to scrutinize, to look over
esforzarse   to make an effort
eslabonar   to link together, to connect
la **espada**   sword
la **espalda**   back
espantoso   frightful, scary
los **espárragos**   asparagus
la **especialización**   specialty
el **espectáculo**   show, performance

el **espejo**   mirror
la **espera**   wait
espesar   to thicken
las **espinacas**   spinach
el **espíritu**   spirit
el **esposo**   husband
el **esqueleto**   skeleton
la **esquina**   corner
establecer   to establish
la **estación**   season, station
la **estadística**   statistic
el **estado**   state
   estado civil   civil state
estallar   to break out, to explode
la **estancia**   estate, large landholding
el **estaño**   tin
estar   to be
   estar dispuesto a   to be willing
   estar en onda   to be in style
   estar por   to be for
estatal   of the state
el **este**   east
estirar   to stretch
el **estómago**   stomach
estorbar   to bother, to trouble
estornudar   to sneeze
la **estrategia**   strategy
estrechar   to bring together, to make close
estrecho   narrow
la **estrella**   star
estrellarse   to crash
estremecer   to shake
estrenar   to show (for the first time)
el **estreno**   opening night of a show
estricto   strict
estropear   to damage, to spoil, to ruin
el **estruendo**   roar, din
el **estudiante**   student
estudiantil   student (adj.)
estupendo   great, fantastic, stupendous
la **etapa**   stage
la **etiqueta**   label

europeo   European
evitar   to avoid
el **examen**   exam, test
examinar(se)   to examine
la **exigencia**   need, requirement
exigir   to require
el **éxito**   success
expender   to spend, to circulate
la **experiencia**   experience
experimentar   to experience, to experiment
explicar   to explain
exponer   to talk about, to present
extender   to extend, to lengthen
extinguir   to extinguish
extrañar   to miss, to seem strange
extraño   strange, odd

F
la **fábrica**   factory
fabricar   to manufacture, to make
la **fábula**   fable
fácil   easy
la **facilidad**   talent, ability
la **factura**   bill, invoice
facturar el equipaje   to check baggage, to bill, to invoice
la **facultad**   faculty
la **faena**   chore, duty
la **falda**   skirt, lap
faltar   to be lacking, to need
fallar   to fail, to give way
fallecer   to fail, to die
familiar   familiar, familial
el **farmacéutico**   druggist
la **farmacia**   pharmacy, drugstore
fastidiado   tired, worn out, bored
el **fastidio**   weariness
fastidiar   to wear out, to run ragged
fatigar   to get tired
la **fecha**   date (time)

felicitar to congratulate
¡Felicitaciones!
Congratulations!
¡Feliz cumpleaños! Happy
Birthday!
la **feria** carnival, fair
el **feriado** holiday
el **ferrocarril** railroad
festejar to celebrate
la **festividad** festivity
la **fibra** fiber
la **ficha** token, index card,
filing card
el **fichero** file, filing cabinet,
record
la **fiebre** fever
la **fiesta** party
figurar(se) to imagine
fijar(se) to notice, to take
note of
filmar to film
la **filosofía** philosophy
el **filósofo** philosopher
el **fin** end
a fines de at the end
por fin at last
fin de año end of the year
fin de semana weekend
financiero financial
la **firma** signature
la **flecha** arrow
flojo slack, loose, weak
la **flor** flower
florecer to flower
fluir to flow
folklórico folk *(adj.)*
los **fondos** funds
la **forma** shape, form
en forma in shape, in form
la **fórmula** formula
el **formulario** form (for an
application)
fortalecer to fortify
la **foto** photo
fracasar to fail
fracturar(se) to fracture, to
crack
la **franja** strip, band
franquear to stamp
el **franqueo** postage

la **franqueza** frankness,
candor
con franqueza openly
el **frasco** bottle, vial
la **frazada** blanket
la **frecuencia** frequency
con frecuencia frequently
el **fregadero** kitchen sink
fregar to rub, to scrub
frenar to brake, to stop
el **freno** brake (on a car)
la **frente** front, forehead
fresco fresh
el **frigorífico** refrigerator
los **frijoles** beans
frotar to rub, to stir
la **fruición** fulfillment,
completion
la **frutería** fruitstand
el **fuego** fire
los **fuegos artificiales**
fireworks
fuera outside, out-of-doors
fuerte strong
fuerza laboral labor force
fulgir to shine
fumar to smoke
la **función** show, role,
function
funcionar to work (a
machine), to run (a
machine)
el **funcionario** bureaucrat
la **funda** pillowcase
fundar to found, to set up, to
establish
fundir to melt, to blend, to
found
furioso angry
furtivo furtive, sneaky, sly
fusilar to shoot
el **fútbol** soccer

G
el **gabinete** closet, office,
cupboard
gallardo elegant, brave
el **gallo** rooster
la **gana** desire, will
tener gana de to feel like,
to desire

la **ganadería** ranching
el **ganadero** cattle rancher
el **ganado** cattle
las **ganancias** earnings,
winnings
ganar to win, to earn
la **ganga** bargain, deal
el **garaje** garage
garantizar to guarantee
la **garganta** throat
la **gasa** gauze
la **gaseosa** carbonated
beverage
la **gasolina** gasoline, gas
gastado spent, wasted
gastar to spend, to waste
el **gato** cat
a gatas on all fours
el **gemelo** twin
el **general** general
por lo general in general
el **gerente** agent, manager
el **gimnasio** gymnasium
la **gira** tour, trip
girar to spin, to revolve
girar un cheque to write a
check
el **girasol** sunflower
el **globo** balloon, globe
el **gobernador** governor
gobernar to govern
el **golpe** hit, strike
golpe de estado military
takeover
golpear to hit, to strike
el **gorro** cap, hat
la **gota** drop
gotear to drip
gozar de to enjoy
grabar to tape
gracias thanks
gracioso delightful, graceful
graduarse to graduate
el **grafista** graphic artist
el **granjero** rancher
la **grasa** grease, fat
gratis free
gratuito free
la **gravedad** severity, gravity
la **grieta** crack, aperture
el **grillo** cricket

la **gripe**   cold (illness)
gritar   to shout, to yell
el **grito**   shout, yell, scream
gruñir   to snarl, to grumble
los **guantes**   gloves
el **guardarropa**   closet
la **guardería infantil**
   childcare, nursery
la **guerra**   war
el, la **guía**   guide
   la **guía telefónica**
   telephone book
guiñar   to wink
el **guión**   script
la **guitarra**   guitar
gustar   to be pleasing to
el **gusto**   pleasure, enjoyment
   mucho gusto en conocerle
   very nice to meet you

H

haber   to have (auxiliary verb
   only)
las **habas**   beans
las **habichuelas**   beans
hábil   able, talented
la **habilidad**   talent, skill
la **habitación**   room
   habitación doble   room for
   two
   habitación sencilla   single
   room
habitar   to live
hablar   to speak, to talk
   ¡ni hablar!   you don't say!
hacer   to do, to make
   hacerse   to become
el **hada**   fairy
halar   to pull
hallar   to find, to discover
el **hallazgo**   discovery
el **hambre**   hunger
   tener hambre   to be hungry
harto   fed up with, full
   estar harto   to be fed up
   with, to be full
hasta que   until
   hasta pronto   see you soon
hay   there is, there are
   no hay de qué   you are
   welcome

hay que   one must, it is
necessary
la **hazaña**   exploit, deed
hechizar   to entrance, to
   charm, to cast a spell
el **hecho**   fact
   de hecho   in fact
el **helado**   iced, ice cream
helar   to freeze
el **hielo**   ice
heredar   to inherit
herido   injured, hurt
herir   to wound, to hurt
hervir   to boil
el/la **hermano, -a**
   brother/sister
la **herramienta**   tool
la **hierba**   grass
el **hierro**   iron
el **hígado**   liver
el/la **hijo, -a**   son/daughter
   hijo de vecino   neighbor
   child
el **hilo**   thread, fiber, strand
el **himno**   hymn, anthem
hinchar   to swell, to swell up
la **hipoteca**   mortgage on a
   house
hispánico   hispanic
hispano   hispanic
las **historietas**   comics
el **hito**   milestone
el **hogar**   home
la **hoja**   leaf, sheet of paper
la **hojalata**   tinplate
hojear   to leaf through (pages)
el **hombre**   man
el **hombro**   shoulder
los **hongos**   mushrooms
la **hora**   time, hour
   ¿qué hora es?   what time is
   it?
   ya es hora   it is time
   es hora de   it is time to
el **horario**   schedule
la **hormiga**   ant
hormiguear   to swarm, to
   teem
hornear   to bake
el **horno**   oven

hospedar   to lodge, to stay
hospitalizar   to hospitalize
hubo   there was, there were
el **hueco**   hole, cavity, hollow
la **huelga**   strike, work action
   (labor union)
la **huella**   track
el **hueso**   bone
el **huésped**   guest
el **huevo**   egg
huir   to flee
humillado   humilliated
hundir   to sink, to submerge,
   to collapse
el **huracán**   hurricane
hurtar   to steal, to cheat, to
   rob

I

ida   going, departure
   ida y vuelta   round trip
el **idioma**   language
el **ídolo**   idol
ignorar   to be unaware of, to
   ignore
igual   equal
la **igualdad**   equality,
   evenness
la **imagen**   image
imaginar(se)   to imagine
el **imperio**   empire
el **impermeable**   raincoat
imponer   to impose
importar   to matter, to import
   importarle a uno   to matter
   to oneself
el **importe**   value, cost, total
impresionar   to impress, to
   move
impreso   printed (past
   participle of imprimir)
el **impreso**   printed form
el **impuesto**   tax
inca   Inca
incauto   unwary, gullible
el **incendio**   fire
inclinarse   to be inclined, to
   lean toward
inconsciente   unconscious,
   unaware, thoughtless

inconstante fickle,
changeable, variable
el **inconveniente**
inconvenience
incorporarse to sit up in bed
inculcar to instill, to teach
incurrir to incur
indagar to investigate
la **indagación** investigation
el **indígena** native,
indigenous
indignarse to get angry
el **individuo** individual *(n.
and adj.)*
indudable undoubtedly
ineludible inescapable
inesperado unexpected
inferir to infer
infestar to infest
el **informe** report
la **informática** data
processing
infundir to inspire, to instill
la **ingeniería** engineering
el **ingeniero** engineer
ingresar to enter, to go in, to
enroll
los **ingresos** income
iniciar to initiate, to start
inmediato immediately
de inmediato immediately
inmigrar to immigrate
inolvidable unforgetable
inoportuno untimely,
unfortunate
la **inquietud** anxiety,
restlessness
inscribirse to register, to
enroll
insensato foolish, senseless
insolente insolent,
disrespectful
insólito unusual,
unaccustomed
el **insomnio** insomnia
inspirar to inspire
el **instituto** institute
el **instrumento** instrument
integrar to join

íntegro whole, entire,
complete
intentar to attempt, to try
intercalar to insert
intercambiar to exchange
interesarse en to be
interested in
el **interés** interest
tasa de interés rate of
interest
el **interlocutor** interviewer
internar to enroll, to board,
to admit
interponer to put between, to
interject
el **intérprete** player,
performer
interpretar el papel de to act
a part
interrogar to ask, to
interrogate
interrumpir to interrupt
intervenir to intervene
introducir to introduce, to
stick in
la **inundación** flood
inundar to flood
invertir to invest
involuntario involuntary,
reflex
la **inyección** injection, shot
poner una inyección to
give an injection
ir to go
ir de compras to go
shopping
irse to go away
irritarse to get annoyed
la **isla** island
el **itinerario** itinerary
izquierdo left
a la izquierda to the left

J

el **jabón** soap
jactarse to brag, to boast
jadear to pant, to breathe
hard
el **jamón** ham
el **jarabe** syrup (medicine)

el **jardín** garden
el **jardinero** gardener
la **jaula** cage
el **jefe** boss, chief, leader
la **jornada** day's work, day's
journey
media jornada part-time
work
jornada completa full-
time work
la **joya** jewel
la **joyería** jewelry store
jubilarse to retire
judío Jew, Jewish
el **juego** game
el **juez** judge
el **jugador** player
jugar to play
el **juguete** toy
jurar to swear
justificar to justify
justo just, exact, correct,
equitable
la **juventud** youth
juzgar to judge

L

el **labio** lip
labrar to carve, to chisel, to
farm, to till
lacerar to slash, to scar, to
cut
el **ladrón** thief, robber
el **lago** lake
lamentar to lament, to be
sorry
lamer to lick
la **lámpara** lamp
la **lana** wool
lanzar (se) to throw, to send
up
el **lápiz** pencil
largar (se) to let go, to release
largo long
a lo largo lengthwise,
throughout
a largo plazo in
installments
larga distancia long
distance

la **lástima** pity

lastimar to hurt

la **lata** can (tin can)

el **latido** beat (of heart)

el **lavabo** washbasin

la **lavadora** washing machine

el **lavaplatos** dishwasher

lavar to wash

  lavarse to wash oneself

el **lecho** bed

la **lechuga** lettuce

la **lechuza** owl

la **lectura** reading

la **lengua** language, tongue

  sacar la lengua stick out one's tongue

el **lenguaje** language

lentamente slowly

las **letras** letters (of the alphabet)

el **letrero** sign (on a store, on a wall)

levantar to raise

  levantarse to get up

la **ley** law

la **leyenda** legend

la **liana** vine

liberar to free

la **libertad de expresión** freedom of expression

la **libra** pound

libre free

la **libreta (talonario) de cheques** checkbook

la **licenciatura** degree (educational degree)

la **licuadora** blender

licuar to liquify, to melt

el **líder** leader

la **liebre** hare

la **liga** league

ligar to tie, to bind together

ligeramente lightly

ligero light

el **límite** limit

el **limón** lemon

la **limosna** alms, charity

el **limpiaparabrisas** windshield wiper

limpio clean

la **línea** line

liso smooth, flat, plain

lisonjero flattering, pleasing

la **lista** list

  lista de espera waiting list

  pasar lista to call roll

listo ready, clever, witty

  estar listo to be ready

liviano light, slight

loco crazy

el **lodo** mud

lograr to achieve, to attain

la **lombriz** worm

el **loro** parrot

la **lotería** lottery

lozano lush, luxurious; self-assured

lucir to shine, to appear

luchar to fight

luego then

el **lugar** place, site

el **lujo** luxury

el **lustrabotas** shoeshine boy

lustrar to shine, to polish

el **luto** mourning

la **luz** light

LL

la **llama** flame

la **llamada** call

  llamada equivocada wrong number

llamar to call

  llamarse to call oneself, to be named

el **llano** plain, prairie

la **llanta** inner tube (on a car). Mexico: tire

la **llanura** plains

la **llave** key

la **llegada** arrival

llegar to arrive

llenar to fill

llevar to carry, take

  llevarse bien to get along with

llover to rain

la **llovizna** drizzle

la **lluvia** rain

M

la **madera** wood

la **madre** mother

la **madrugada** dawn

madrugar to get up at the crack of dawn

maduro ripe, mature

la **maestría** mastery, teaching profession

el **mago** magician

el **mal** evil

mal(-o,-a) bad

  mal aliento bad breath

maldecir to curse

la **maleta** suitcase, bag

el **maletín** briefcase

maltratar to mistreat

el **mamífero** mammal

manchar to stain, to spot

mandar to order, to command

el **mando** order, command

mandón bossy, pushy

manejar to drive, to manage

la **manga** sleeve, cuff

el **manglar** mangrove swamp

manifestar to demonstrate, to declare

una **manisfestación** a demonstration

la **mano** hand

la **manta** blanket, spread, cape

mantener to maintain, to keep up

  mantenerse en forma to stay in shape

el **mantenimiento** maintenance

la **manzana** apple, city block

el **mañana** future

  la **mañana** morning

el **mapa** map

maquillar(se) makeup (cosmetics)

la **máquina** machine

  la **máquina de afeitar** electric razor

  la **máquina de escribir** typewriter

el **maratón**   marathon, race
la **maravilla**   wonder, marvel
maravillar(se)   to wonder
la **marca**   brand name, trade name
marcar   to mark, to dial
marcharse   to go away, to set in motion
marear   to get seasick
el **mareo**   dizziness, seasickness
los **mariachis**   Mexican musicians
la **marioneta**   marionette
los **mariscos**   shellfish
el **martillo**   hammer
la **masa**   mass, dough
masticar   to chew
la **materia**   matter, subject matter, material
materia prima   raw material
la **maternidad**   maternity, motherhood
matinal   morning
la **matrícula**   registration
el **matrimonio**   matrimony, married couple
maya   Maya
mayor   greater, older
la **mayoría**   the majority, the greatest part
la **mayúscula**   upper case, capital letters
el **mecánico**   mechanical
la **mecedora**   rocking chair
el **medicamento**   medication, drug, medicine
el **médico**   doctor
la **medida**   measure
a medida que   at the same time as
medio en broma   half in jest
los **medios**   means, methods
medios de comunicación   means of communication
medir   to measure
la **mejilla**   cheek
mejor   better
a lo mejor   perhaps, maybe

mejorar   to get better
el **mendigo**   beggar
menester   necessary
menor   younger
menor de edad   underage
el **mensaje**   message
mensual   monthly
menudo   small
a menudo   often
mero   mere, simple
la **mercadería**   merchandise, commodity, goods
el **mercado**   market
la **mercancía**   goods, merchandise
mero   mere, simple
el **mes**   month
la **mesa**   table
el **mestizo**   half-caste, mixed breed (half Indian, half Spanish)
la **meta**   goal, objective
el **miedo**   fear
tener miedo   to be afraid
la **miel**   honey
mientras (que)   while
la **miga**   crumb
mimado   spoiled
la **mina**   mine
el **mineral**   mineral
la **minería**   mining
minero   miner
la **minifalda**   miniskirt
mirar   to look at
la **misa**   mass (church service)
misa de gallo   midnight mass
el **misionero**   missionary
la **mitad**   half
el **mito**   myth
la **mochila**   backpack, bookbag, knapsack
la **moda**   fashion, trend
estar de moda   to be in fashion
estar pasado de moda   out of date, dated
el **modelo**   model
modificar   to modify
la **mofeta**   skunk

mojar(se)   to get wet
moler   to grind, to mill
molestar   to bother
la **moneda**   coin, money, currency
el **monje**   monk
el **mono**   monkey
la **montaña**   mountain
montar   to ride
montar a caballo   to ride a horse
montar en bicicleta   to ride a bicycle
montar en moto   to ride a motorcycle
la **moraleja**   moral (of a story)
moreno   dark-skinned, dark-haired
mortificar   to mortify, to embarrass
mosquitero   mosquito net
mosquito   mosquito
el **mostrador**   counter (in a store), showcase
mostrar   to show
la **moto(cicleta)**   motorcycle
moverse   to move
la **muchedumbre**   multitude
mudar   to change
mudarse   to move (change residence)
el **mueble**   piece of furniture
los **muebles**   furniture
la **muela**   molar, tooth
el **muelle**   dock, pier
la **muerte**   death
el **muerto**   dead man
la **mujer**   woman
la **muleta**   crutch
la **multa**   fine
el **mundo**   world
la **muñeca**   doll, wrist
el **muñeco**   puppet, doll
la **música**   music
el **músculo**   muscle

N

el **Nacimiento**   Nativity
el **nacimiento**   birth
nada   nothing
de nada   you are welcome

nadie no one, nobody
las **nalgas** buttocks
la **naranja** orange
el **narcotraficante** drug
  dealer
el **narcotráfico** drug traffic
la **nariz** nose
narrar to tell, to narrate
la **natación** swimming
natal by birth, natal
  ciudad natal native city,
  city of origin
naufragar to shipwreck
el **náufrago** shipwrecked
  person
la **náusea** nausea
la **nave** ship
navegar to navigate, to sail
la **Navidad** Christmas
el **necio** fool
nefasto ill-fated, dreadful
negar to deny
negociar to negotiate
los **negocios** business
  hombre/mujer de negocios
  businessman,
  businesswoman
el **negro** African American,
  black
nevar to snow
la **nevera** refrigerator
el **neumático** tire (in a car)
ni ... ni neither ... nor
el **nieto** grandson
la **nieve** snow
ningún (-o, -una) none, no
  one (adj.)
no más (México) no more,
  nothing more
nocivo noxious, harmful
la **noche** night
nocturno evening, nightly
el **norte** north
la **nota** grade, note
la **noticia** news
la **novena** novena (prayer)
el/la **novio, -a** boy/girlfriend
nuevo new
la **nuez** nut
el **número** number

O

obligar to force, to require
obligatorio obligatory,
  imperative
el **obrero** worker
obtener to get
el **ocaso** sunset
el **océano** ocean
ocultar to hide, to cover up
la **ocupación** job, occupation
ocupado busy
odiar to hate
el **oeste** west
la **oferta** offering, offer
la **oficina** office
el **oficio** vocation, calling,
  duty, job
ofrecer to offer
el **oído** ear (inner)
ojear to eye, to stare at
el **ojo** eye
la **ola** wave
oler to smell
olfatear to sniff, to smell
el **olor** smell
olvidar to forget
la **olla** pot, cooking vessel,
  ceramic pot
opinar to think, to have an
  opinion
opresivo oppressive
optativo choice, alternative
óptico optical
el **orden** order (general)
la **orden** command, order
  (specific)
el **ordenador** (Spain)
  computer
la **oreja** ear (external)
el **orgullo** pride
orgulloso proud
la **orilla** shore, bank (of a
  river)
oscilar to waver, to fluctuate
oscurecer to get dark
el **oso** bear
las **ostras** oysters
otorgar to grant, to authorize,
  to give

P

el **paciente** patient
padecer to suffer from
pagar to pay
el **pago** pay, wages
el **país** country
el **pájaro** bird
la **palabra** word
la **paliza** thrashing
la **paloma** dove
la **palomita de maíz** popcorn
palpar to touch
la **pampa** region of Argentina
el **pan** bread
  pan de molde soft, thin-
  crusted bread
la **panadería** bakery
el **panadero** baker
los **pantalones** pants
la **pantalla** screen
la **pantorrilla** calf (of a leg)
el **pañuelo** handkerchief
la **papa, patata** potato
Papá Noel Santa Claus
el **papel** paper, role (in a
  play)
  papel de Navidad
  Christmas wrapping paper
  papel higiénico toilet
  paper
el **paquete** package
el **par** pair
para for, in order to
  ¿para qué? what for?
la **parada** stop (bus)
el **paraguas** umbrella
parar(se) to stop
parecer to seem
  parecerse to resemble, to
  seem like
la **pared** wall
la **pareja** pair, couple
el **pariente** relative, kin
el **paro** work stoppage,
  unemployment
parpardear to blink
partidario fan, partisan of
el **partido** party (political);
  match, game (sport)
el **párrafo** paragraph

el **pasaje** passage

el **pasajero** passenger

pasar to pass, to happen

   pasar lista to call roll

   pasar de moda to go out of style

   pasar por to come/go by

la **Pascua** Easter

pasearse to stroll, to walk

el **paso** step, pace

la **pasta** paste

   pasta dentífrica toothpaste

el **pastel** dessert, pie

la **pastelería** bakery shop

la **pastilla** pill

   pastilla para dormir sleeping pill

el **pastor** shepherd, pastor

la **pata** foot (animals)

la **patente** license

las **patillas** sideburns

el **patinador** skater

la **patria** native land, fatherland

el **patrocinador** sponsor

paulatinamente slowly, little by little

el **pavo** turkey

el **payaso** clown

la **paz** peace

el **peatón** pedestrian

pecar to sin, to err

el **pecho** chest, breast

pedir to ask for, to order

   pedir prestado to borrow

pegar to hit, to strike (a blow)

peinar(se) to comb

pelar to peel

el **peldaño** step (of a stair)

pelear to fight

la **película** film, movie

el **peligro** danger

el **pelo** hair

la **pelota** ball

la **peluquería** barbershop

la **pena** pain, bother

   valer la pena to be worthwhile

pena de muerte death penalty

el **pendiente** earring, pendant

penetrante penetrating

el **pensamiento** thought

pensar to think

   pensar de to think about, have an opinon

   pensar en to think about, to ponder

   pensar + inf. to intend

peor worse

el **pepino** cucumber

la **pera** pear

el **percance** misfortune

la **percusión** percussion

perder to lose

   perder el vuelo to miss a flight

   perderse to get lost

las **pérdidas** losses

perdurable eternal, everlasting

perdurar to last

la **peregrinación** pilgrimage

el **perfume** perfume

el **periódico** newspaper

el **periodista** reporter (newspaper)

el **periodismo** journalism

el **perjuicio** prejudice, damage

la **permanencia** permanence, stay

permeable permeable

el **permiso** permission

pero but

perseguir to follow, to pursue

el **personaje** character (in a book)

personal personal

perspicuo clear, intelligible

las **pertenencias** possessions

perturbar disturb

pesar to weigh

   a pesar de in spite of

la **pescadería** fishing

el **pescado** fish (out of water)

pescar to fish

el **peso** weight

la **pestaña** eyelash

la **pestilencia** pestilence, plague

la **picadura** sting, bite (of an insect)

picar to bite, to peck at, to pierce

el **pie** foot

   a pie on foot

   de pie standing

la **piedra** rock, stone

la **piel** skin, fur

la **pierna** leg

la **pieza** piece, room

la **píldora** pill

el **piloto** pilot, driver (of a motorcycle)

la **piratería aérea** air piracy

la **piscina** swimming pool

el **piso** floor

la **pista** track

   pista de aterrizaje landing strip

la **placa** license plate

el **placer** pleasure

la **plancha** iron

   a la plancha grilled

planchar to iron

planear to plan

plano flat, even, level

la **planta** plant

la **planta baja** ground floor

plantear to set forth, to expound, to state

la **plata** silver

el **plátano** plantain

platicar to chat, to talk

el **plato** dish

la **playa** beach

la **plaza** public square, marketplace, room

el **plazo** period of time

   comprar a plazos buy in installments

el **pleito** lawsuit, case

pleno full

la **pluma** fountain pen

la **población** population

la **pobreza** poverty

poco few, little
  por poco que if ... at all
  por mucho que however much ...
podar to prune, to trim
poder to be able
podrido rotten
el **policía** police, policeman
  la **mujer policía** policewoman
el **político** politician
la **póliza** policy (insurance)
el **polvo** dust, powder
el **pollo** chicken, chick
poner to put
  poner atención to pay attention
  poner una inyección to give a shot
  poner la mesa to set the table
  ponerse to become
  ponerse en cola to get in line
el **poniente** west
popular popular
el **póquer** poker
por by, through, on behalf of, for
  por fin finally
  por lo menos at least
  por poco barely
  ¿por qué? why?
  por supuesto of course
los **pormenores** details
los **posadas** bullfighting, guesthouse
la **posesión** posession
posponer, postergar to postpone
el **postulante** candidate
postular to postulate, to request
potente powerful, strong
preceder to precede
el **precio** price
precisar to specify
predecir to foretell, to forecast
la **predilección** preference

preferir to prefer
pregonar to shout, to proclaim
la **pregunta** question
  hacer preguntas to ask questions
preguntar to ask, to question
el **prejuicio racial** racial prejudice
premiar to award
la **prenda** pledge, security
  prenda interior underwear
la **prensa** press
preocupar to worry
la **preparación** preparation, training
preparar(se) to get ready
las **preparativos** preparations
presenciar to witness
presentar to present
  presentarse al examen to take an exam
  me gustaría presentarle(te) a ... I would like to present to you...
el **presentimiento** foreboding
presentir to have a premonition
preservar to protect, to preserve
la **presión** pressure
  presión alta high pressure
el **préstamo** loan
prestar to lend
  prestar atención to pay attention
el **presupuesto** budget
prevenir to prevent
prever to foresee
primer (-o, -a) first
el **primo** cousin
el **principio** beginning
  a principios de at the beginning of
la **prisa** rush, hurry
  tener prisa to be in a hurry
probar to try, to test
la **procedencia** origin, source

procedente de coming from
el **procedimiento** method, procedure, proceeding
el **proceso** process
el **producto** product
el **proeza** exploit
el **profesor** teacher, professor
el **programador** computer programmer
el **promedio** middle, average
prometer promise
la **promoción** promotion
pronosticar to foretell
el **pronóstico** prediction, forecast, omen
pronto soon
  tan pronto como as soon as
la **propaganda** propaganda
  la **propaganda comercial** ads, commercials
propagar to propagate, to generate
la **propina** tip, gratuity
propio own, proper
  propiamente dicho strictly speaking
proponer to propose, to suggest
proporcionar to furnish, to provide
el **propósito** purpose
  a propósito by the way
proteger to protect
proveer to provide
la **provisión** provision
provocar to provoke
proyectar to project
el **proyecto** project
la **prueba** test, trial (run)
el **psicólogo** psychologist
la **publicidad** publicity
pudrir to rot
la **puerta** door
el **puesto** position
  el **puesto de periódicos** newsstand
pulir to polish
el **pulmón** lung
pulular to swarm, to infest

pulverizar to smash, to pulverize

la **puntería** aim, marksmanship

el **punto** point

punto de vista point of view

a puntillas on tiptoe

Q

que that, than

¿qué? what?

¿por qué? why?

¿qué tal? how are you?

¡qué lata! what a mess!

¡qué lástima! what a pity!

¡qué lío! what a mess!

¡qué tontería! what foolishness!

quebrar to break

quedar to stay, to remain

quedarse con to be left with

el **quehacer** chore, small task

quejarse to complain

quemar to burn

querer to wish, to want, to love

querer decir to mean to say

querido dear, beloved

el **queso** cheese

la **quiebra** bankruptcy

quien who, whom

¿quién? who? whom?

la **química** chemistry, chemical

la **quinceañera** girl celebrating her fifteenth birthday

quisiera I would like...

quitar(se) to take off

quizá, quizás perhaps

R

el **racimo** bouquet

la **ración** serving

la/el **radio** radio (set)

la **ráfaga** gust, burst

la **raíz** root

la **rama** branch

el **ramo** bouquet, bunch

la **rana** frog

el **rascacielos** skyscraper

rascar to scratch

rasgar to tear

rasguear to strum (a guitar)

raspar to scrape

el **rastro** trail

la **rata** rat

el **rato** while, time, period

la **raya** line

a rayas striped (design)

el **rayo** ray, lightning

rayos equis x-rays

la **rayuela** hopscotch

la **raza** race (of people), ethnic group

la **razón** reason

realizar to fulfill, to accomplish

realmente really, actually, truly

la **rebaja** discount

en rebaja on sale

rebajar to lower the price, to discount

el **rebozo** shawl

el **recado** message

la **recámara** chamber, dressing room

la **receta** prescription, recipe

recetar to prescribe

rechazar to reject, to refuse

recibir to receive

reciclado recycled

reclamar to demand, to petition

reclutar to recruit, to round up, to conscript

recobrar to recover

recoger to collect, to pick up

recoger la mesa to clear the table

recompensar to reward, to pay

recordar to remember

recorrer to go around, to tour

el **rector** director

el **recuerdo** memory, token, souvenir

recuperar to recuperate, to get back

la **red** net, network

redactar to edit

reembolsar to repay

reemplazar to replace

referirse a to refer to

reflejar reflect

el **refrán** refrain, saying

el **refugio** refuge

refutar to dispute, to refute

regalar to give as a gift

el **regalo** gift

regañar to quarrel

regar to water

regatear to bargain, to haggle

el **régimen militar** military regime

regir to govern

registrar to register, to record, to search (in an investigation)

el **reglón** ruler (measuring stick)

regocijar to delight, to cheer, to amuse

rehusar to decline, to refuse

relajar to relax

el **relámpago** lightning

releer reread

el **reloj** clock, watch (timepiece)

el **remedio** remedy

no tener más remedio there is no other way

el **remitente** sender

remitir to send

remontarse to go back to, to date from

rendido exhausted

la **rendija** crack, rip

rendir to exhaust, to tire out

rendirse to surrender

renunciar to renounce, to turn one's back on

reñir to quarrel

el **reo** convicted criminal

reparar to repair

repartir to deliver

repasar to review

repentinamente suddenly

de repente suddenly

repetir to repeat

repicar las campanas to ring the bells

reprimir to repress

reponer to replace

el **reportaje** report

representar to represent, to play a role

reprobar to condemn

repugnar to repel

requerir to request, to require

el **requisito** requirement

la **resaca** undertow, undercurrent, hangover

resaltar to project, to stand out

resbalar to slip

rescatar to rescue

el **resfriado,** el **resfrío** cold (illness)

coger un resfriado to catch a cold

resolver to solve

respaldar to back, to endorse

respirar to breathe

resplandecer to shine, to gleam

la **respuesta** answer

restar to subtract

el **resultado** result

resultar to end in, to result in

resumir to summarize

retirar to remove, to draw back, to leave

el **retraso** setback

retratar to portray

retumbar to resound, to thunder

reunir to get together, to unite, to join

la **reunión** meeting

revelar reveal

el **revendedor** reseller

reventar to burst, to give way

revisar to revise

la **revista** magazine

revolver to revolve, to stir

los **Reyes Magos** the Wise Men

rezar to pray

el **riesgo** risk

rifar to raffle

riguroso rigorous, severe

el **rincón** corner

el **riñón** kidney

el **río** river

el **ritmo** rhythm

robar to rob

el **robo** theft

rociar to sprinkle

el **rocío** dew

rodar to film, to roll

rodear to surround

la **rodilla** knee

roer to nibble, to gnaw

rogar to beg

la **romería** pilgrimage

romper to break

la **ropa** clothes, clothing

el **ropero** closet, wardrobe

rozar to rub against, to graze

la **rueda** wheel

el **ruido** noise

el **ruiseñor** nightingale

rumbo a toward, in the direction of

la **ruta** route

S

la **sábana** sheet

saber to know

el **sabor** taste

saborear to taste

sacar to take out

sacar notas to get grades

sacudir to shake, to tremble

la **sala** room, living room

sala de espera waiting room

salado salty

el **salario** salary

la **salida** exit

salir leave

salivar to salivate, to drool

salobre brackish, salty

el **salón** room, salon

salón de actos assembly hall

salpicar to splatter

saltar to jump

el **salto** jump

la **salud** health

saludar to greet

el **salvavidas** life preserver, lifeguard

salvar to save

salvo except

la **sandalia** sandal

la **sandía** watermelon

la **sangre** blood

el **santo** saint

saquear to loot, to rob, to steal

la **sartén** frying pan

la **secadora** clothes dryer

secar to dry

la **sed** thirst

tener sed to be thirsty

la **seda** silk

la **sede** headquarters

seguir to follow, to keep on

segundo second

la **seguridad** safety, security

seguro sure

estar seguro to be sure

el **seguro** insurance

seleccionar to choose

el **sello** stamp

la **selva** forest, jungle

el **semáforo** traffic light

la **Semana Santa** Holy Week

sembrar to sow

la **semilla** seed

sencillo simple, plain, one-way ticket or token

habitación sencilla single room

el **sendero** path

sentarse to sit down

el **sentimiento** feeling

sentir to feel, to regret

sentirse mal/bien to feel bad/good

la **sequía** drought

la **señal**   the sign
  señales del tránsito   traffic signs
la **serpiente**   snake
el **servicio**   service
servir   to serve
sigilosamente   quietly
el **siglo**   century
siguiente   following
silbar   to whistle
la **silla**   chair, seat
la **silla de ruedas**   wheelchair
el **sillón**   large chair
silvicultura   forestry
sin   without
  sin cesar   without end
  sin embargo   nevertheless
el **sindicato**   union
la **sinfonía**   symphony
sino   rather
el **síntoma**   symptom
la **soberanía**   sovereignty
sobornar   to bribe
sobrar   to have left over, to have more than enough
el **sobre**   envelope
sobre   about, on top of
sobregirar   to overdraw an account
sobrepasar   to exceed
sobresaltar   to startle, to scare
el **sobreviviente**   survivor
el, la **socialista**   socialist
el **socio**   associate, partner
socorro   help
  pedir socorro   to call for help
el **soldado**   soldier
soler   to be accustomed
el **solicitante**   applicant
solicitar un empleo   apply for a job
la **solicitud**   application
sollozar   to sob, to weep
sólo   only, just
solo   lone, alone
el **soltero**   bachelor
someter   to put down, to subdue
sonar   to ring, to sound

sonreír   to smile
soñar   to dream
  soñar con   to dream about
soplado a mano   hand-blown
soplar   to blow
soportar   to tolerate, to stand
sordo   deaf
sorprender   to surprise
la **sorpresa**   surprise
sortear   to draw in a lottery, to draw lots
sosegar   to calm, to quiet down
sospechoso   suspicious
subir   to go up
subir a   to climb
subrayar   to underline, to emphasize
el **subsidio**   subsidy, grant, aid
la **subvención**   subsidy, grant
suceder   to happen, to take place
el **suceso**   event, happening
sucio   dirty
sucumbir   to succumb, to submit
la **sucursal**   branch
el **sudor**   sweat
la **suegra**   mother-in-law
el **sueldo**   salary, pay
suele ser   it usually is
el **suelo**   floor
el **sueño**   dream
la **suerte**   luck
sufrir   to suffer
sugerir   to suggest
sumamente   extremely, highly
sumar   to add (math)
suministrar   to supply, to provide, to furnish
superar   to overcome, to exceed
suponer   to suppose
supuesto   supposed
  por supuesto   of course
el **sur**   south
el **surtido**   supply, stock
suspender   to fail (a course)

suspirar   to sigh
sustituir   to substitute

T

el **tablón de anuncios**   bulletin board
tacaño   miserly, stingy, cheap
el **tacón**   heel (of a shoe)
tal   such
  ¿qué tal?   how are you?
tallado   carved
tallar   to carve
el **taller**   shop, place of business
el **tallo**   stem
el **tamaño**   size
tampoco   neither
el **tanque de gasolina**   gas tank
tanto   so much, as much
  estar al tanto   to be up on
  por lo tanto   therefore
  tanto ... como   as much ... as
las **tapas**   snacks, appetizers
la **taquilla**   ticket window
tardar en   to be late in ..., to delay
la **tarea**   homework, work, chore
la **tarifa**   fare
la **tarjeta**   card
  tarjeta de crédito   credit card
  tarjeta postal   postcard
la **tasa de interés**   interest rate
la **taza**   cup
el **teatro**   theater
la **tecnología**   technology
tejer   to weave
tejido   weaving
la **tela**   cloth
la **televisión**   television
la **telenovela**   soap opera
el **televidente**   television viewer
el **televisor**   television set
el **telón**   curtain
el **temor**   fear
la **tempestad**   storm

la **temporada**   season (of sports, weather, events)

tenderse   to stretch out

tener   to have

tener lugar   to take place

teñir   to tint

terminar   to end

el **término**   end, term

la **ternera**   calf (animal)

la **ternura**   tenderness, care, love

la **tertulia**   gathering, get-together

la **terraza**   terrace

el **terremoto**   earthquake

el **terreno**   land, piece of land

el **tesoro**   treasure

el **testigo**   witness

el **testigo ocular**   eyewitness

tibio   tepid, lukewarm

el **tiburón**   shark

el **tiempo**   time, weather

tieso   rigid, stiff

las **tijeras**   scissors

la **tina**   bathtub

el **tinte**   dye, coloring agent

tinto   colored

vino tinto   red wine

el/la **tío, -a**   uncle/aunt

la **tira**   strip

tira cómica   comic strip

la **tirada**   throw

tirar   to throw, to toss

titular   to title

el **título**   title

la **toalla**   towel

el **tobillo**   ankle

tocar   to knock, to touch, to play an instrument

todo   all, everything

ante todo   before everything else

sobre todo   above all

tomar   to take, to have

tomar apuntes   to take notes

tomar asiento   to take a seat

la **tontería**   foolishness

¡qué tontería!   what stupidity!

el **topacio**   topaz

el **torbellino**   whirlwind, tornado

torcer   to twist, to wring

la **tormenta**   storm, tempest

la **torta**   cake

la **tortilla**   tortilla

tortilla española   Spanish tortilla

la **tortuga**   turtle

la **tos**   cough

toser   to cough

la **tostadora**   toaster

el **trabajador**   worker

tragar   to swallow

el **traje**   suit

el **trámite**   procedure

la **trampa**   trap, trick

tranquilo   calm, tranquil

transitar   to travel

el **tránsito**   traffic, passage

transmitir   transmit

transmutar   to transmute, to change radically

el **transporte**   transportation

el **trapo**   rag, piece of cloth

transtrocar   to change, to transform

tratar   to try, to be about

tratar con   to deal with

tratar de   to try, to attempt

la **travesura**   mischief

el **tren**   train

el **trigo**   wheat

el **tripulante**   crew

trotar   to jog

el **trueno**   thunder

el **tuerto**   one-eyed, blind in one eye

la **tumba**   tomb, grave

tutear   to speak using "tú" verb forms

U

último   last

único   only, singular

único hijo   only son

uniforme   uniform

el **universitario**   university student

la **uña**   fingernail

la **urraca**   crow

útil   useful

la **uva**   grape

V

la **vaca**   cow

vaciar   to empty

vacilar   to hesitate, to waiver

vagar   to wander

la **vajilla de plata**   silverware

el **valor**   worth

el **valle**   valley

el **vaquero**   cowboy

los **vaqueros**   jeans

la **variedad**   variety

el **varón**   male

el **vaso**   glass (for drinking)

el **vecino**   neighbor

el **vehículo**   vehicle

velar   to stay awake

la **velocidad**   speed

velozmente   rapidly

la **vena**   vein

el **vencimiento**   due

fecha de vencimiento   due date (for payment)

venir   to come

la **venta**   sale

la **ventaja**   advantage

la **ventanilla**   window (for selling)

el **verano**   summer

la **verbena**   carnival, fair

verde   green

la **verdulería**   market for vegetables

la **verdura**   greens, vegetables

verificar   to verify, authenticate

vespertino   evening (adj.)

el **vestido**   dress

la **vestimenta**   clothing, garments

vestirse   to get dressed

la **vez**   time (in a series)

otra vez   again

a veces   at times

el **viaje**   trip

el **viajero**   traveler

la **vida**   life

la **videocasetera** videorecorder

el **vidrio** glass

el **viento** wind

el **Viernes Santo** Good Friday

vigilar to watch over, to guard

el **villancico** Christmas carol

villanos lowly, common

el **vínculo** tie, bond

el **vino** wine

la **viña** vineyard

virar to veer, to turn, to curve

la **vista** view

 por lo visto apparently

la **viuda** widow

la **vivienda** housing

el **voceador** announcer (shouter, yeller)

vociferar to yell, to scream, to shout

el **volante** steering wheel

volcar to knock over

voltear to swing around, to sling, to turn

la **voluntad** will, volition

volver to return

 volver en sí to come to, to come around

 volverse to become, to go (crazy)

el **voto** vote

la **voz** voice

 voz en cuello shouting

el **vuelo** flight

la **vuelta** return, a spin around

el **vuelto** change (money)

Z

el **zafiro** sapphire

zambullir to plunge, to dip

la **zanahoria** carrot

el **zancudo** mosquito, gnat

el **zapato** shoe

zarpar to sail

la **zona** zone

la **zona postal** zip code

zozobra anxiety

zumbar to buzz

el **zumo** juice

Bibliography

Part Two, Chapter Two (Short Narratives)
Group One
    Narrative One.   Mikes, George: *Los Norteamericanos en su Salsa.* Translator, Juan G. de Luaces. Buenos Aires: Editorial Borocaba, 1953, p. 123.
    Narrative Two.   "Vuelven las Mujeres Toreras," *Mundo Hispánico*, Año XXVII, No. 320, noviembre 1974, p. 36.

Group Two
    Narrative One.   "José Guadalupe Posada," *Américas*, diciembre 1965, pp. 28-35.*
    Narrative Two.   Kelemen, Pal: "El Arte del Tejido," *Américas*, enero 1967, p. 2.*

Group Three
    Narrative One.   Regato, J.A. del: "Rebelde sin Odios: Jose Martí," *Américas*, febrero 1967, pp. 29-30.*
    Narrative Two.   Bareiro Saguier, Rubén: "El Guaraní: Certificado de Patria del Paraguayo," *Américas*, abril 1964, p. 7.*

Group Four
    Narrative One.   Goff, Charles W.: "Las Huesas de Machu Picchu" (abridged), *Américas*, septiembre 1966, pp. 9-18.*
    Narrative Two.   Zuleta Alvarez, Enrique: "1967: Año de Ruben Darío. Poeta de América" (abridged), *Américas*, marzo 1967, pp. 10-18.*

Group Five
    Narrative One.   Ward, Catherine: "La Epopeya del Gaucho," *Américas*, diciembre 1965, p. 8.*
    Narrative Two.   Stirling, Marion W.: "Los Olmecas" (abridged), *Américas*, diciembre 1969–enero 1970, pp. 3-10.*

Group Six
    Narrative One.   Macaya, Margarita O. de: "CIM" (abridged), *Américas*, septiembre 1966, pp. 37-41.*
    Narrative Two.   Zendegui, Guillermo de: "Cuando la Florida Era Española," *Américas*, octubre 1974, pp. 25-33.*

Group Seven
    Narrative One.   Johnson, Beverly Edna: "Popol Vuh," *Américas*, octubre 1974, pp. 8-10.*
    Narrative Two.   Zalamea, Luís: "La Quinta de Bolívar," *Américas*, enero 1966, p. 21.*

Group Eight
    Narrative One.   Cowes, Roberto A.: "El Hallazgo de Cocle," *Américas*, 1966, p. 19.*
    Narrative Two.   Nicolle, Edgar A.: "Café al Instante," *Américas*, febrero 1975, p. 26.*

Group Nine
    Narrative One.   Stoetzer, Carlos: "Alejandro von Humboldt," *Américas*, agosto 1972, p. S-19.*
    Narrative Two.   Gussinyer Alfonso, José: "Salvamiento Arqueológico" (abridged), *Américas*, abril 1971, pp. 15-19.*

Part Two, Chapter Three (Longer Listening Selections)
    Narrativa número 1:   *Puerta del Sol*, enero 1990, p. 4. Edited by Roger L. Ott. Nashville: Champs-Elysées, Inc.

---

*Reprinted from *Américas,* a bimonthly magazine published by the General Secretariat of the Organization of American States in English and Spanish.

Narrativa número 2:   *Puerta del Sol*, mayo 1990, p. 2. Edited by Roger L. Ott. Nashville: Champs-
        Elysées, Inc.

Narrativa número 3:   *Puerta del Sol*, febrero 1991, p. 5. Edited by Roger L. Ott. Nashville:
        Champs-Elysées, Inc.

Narrativa número 4:   *Puerta del Sol*, diciembre 1989, p.1. Edited by Roger L. Ott. Nashville:
        Champs-Elysées, Inc.

Narrativa número 5:   *Puerta del Sol*, abril 1991, p. 4. Edited by Roger L. Ott. Nashville: Champs-
        Elysées, Inc.

Entrevista número 1:   *Puerta del Sol*, abril 1991, p. 4. Edited by Roger L. Ott. Nashville: Champs-
        Elysées, Inc.

Entrevista número 2:   *Puerta del Sol*, enero 1991, p. 4. Edited by Roger L. Ott. Nashville: Champs-
        Elysées, Inc.

Entrevista número 3:   *Puerta del Sol*, enero 1991, p. 5. Edited by Roger L. Ott. Nashville: Champs-
        Elysées, Inc.

Entrevista número 4:   *Puerta del Sol*, marzo 1990, p. 5. Edited by Roger L. Ott. Nashville:
        Champs-Elysées, Inc.

Entrevista número 5:   *Puerta del Sol*, febrero 1990, p. 5. Edited by Roger L. Ott. Nashville:
        Champs-Elysées, Inc.

Entrevista número 6:   *Puerta del Sol*, marzo 1991, p. 5. Edited by Roger L. Ott. Nashville:
        Champs-Elysées, Inc.

Part Three, Chapter Four (Vocabulary and Grammatical Structures)

Selección 1.   González, Fernando: "Soda Stereo," *El Nuevo Herald*, Miami, 8 de marzo de 1996,
        p. 11D.

Selección 2.   Niurka, Norma: "El Ballet Nacional de España," *El Nuevo Herald*, Miami, viernes 8,
        1996, p. 9D.

Selección 3.   Waters, Gaby, and Round, Graham: *Crimen en el Vuelo Nocturno,* E. G. Anaya,
        Madrid, 1986. p. 22.

Selección 4.   Haney, Daniel Q.: "El Estrés," *El Nuevo Herald*, Miami, 28 de enero de 1996, p. 9A.

Selección 5.   "Manuel Pellegrini Fue Confirmado en la UC," *La Época Internet*, 16 de mayo de
        1996, hhtp://www.reuna.cl.

Selección 6.   Hervas, Mercedes: "El Propuesto *V-Chip*," *El Periódico*, Barcelona, 19 de diciembre
        de 1995, p. 61.

Selecicón 7.   Alvarez Bravo, Armando: "La Vida Seria de Luis Rodríguez", *El Nuevo Herald*,
        Miami, 28 de enero de 1996, pp. 1-2E.

Selección 8.   Rojas, Manuel: "Hijo de Ladrón," Zig-Zag, Santiago, Chile, 1964, pp. 101-102.

Selección 9.   Díaz-Plaja, Fernando: "El Español y los Siete Pecados Capitales," Alianza Editorial,
        Madrid, 1986, pp. 95-96.

Selección 10. Rojas, Manuel: "Hijo de Ladrón," Zig-Zag, Santiago, Chile, 1964, p. 103.

Selección 11. Búfalo, Enzo del: "Estado, Sociedad y Pobreza en América Latina,"*Reforma y
        Democracia*, Centro Latinoamericano de Administración para el Desarrollo, N°5,
        Caracas, Venezuela, enero de 1996, pp. 9-10.

Selección 12. Marías, Julián: "Tercera: ¿Excesiva Originalidad?," ABC, hhtp://www.abc.es, 16 de
        mayo de 1996.

Part Three, Chapter Six (Reading Strategies)

Selection One.   Díaz-Plaja, Fernando: *El Español y los Siete Pecados Capitales.* Madrid: Editorial
        Alianza, 1986, p. 302.

Selection Two.   Paz, Octavio: *Libertad bajo la Palabra.* México: Fondo de Cultura Económica,
        1960, p. 159.

Selection Three. Rulfo, Juan: "¡Diles que no me Maten!" in *El Llano en Llamas*. México: Fondo de Cultura Económica, 1953, p. 91.

Selection Four. Reproducido con autorización de ABC de Madrid, domingo 31 de mayo de 1992, p. 81.

Setting and/or Origin

Selection One. Cortázar, Julio: "Reunión" in *Todos los Fuegos el Fuego*. Editorial Sudamericana, 1975, p. 67.

Selection Two. Reproducido con autorización de ABC de Madrid, domingo 31 de mayo de 1992, p. 121.

Selection Three. Matute, Ana María: *Primera Memoria*. Barcelona: Ediciones Destino, 1960, p. 81.

Time

Passage One. Reproducido con autorización de ABC de Madrid, domingo 31 de mayo de 1992, p. 100.

Character, Object Definition and Identification

Passage One. Matute, Ana María: "La Consciencia" in *Historias de Artamila*. Barcelona: Ediciones Destino, 1961, p. 120.

Passage Two. Reproducido con autorización de ABC de Madrid, domingo 31 de mayo de 1992, p. 100.

Purpose and Reason

Passage One. Cortázar, Julio: "La Isla a Mediodía" in *Todos los Fuegos el Fuego*. Editorial Sudamericana, 1975, p. 118.

Passage Two. Fuentes, Carlos: "Chac Mool" in *Los Días Enmascarados*. México: Fondo de Cultura Económica, 1954, p. 16.

Interpretation

Passage One. "Prefectura Naval Argentina," *Información Argentina*, agosto 1973, p. 27.

Passage Two. Matute, Ana María: "El Arbol de Oro" in *Historias de Artamila*. Barcelona, Ediciones Destino, 1961, p. 157.

Parallel Structures

Passage One. Unamuno, Miguel de: "Verdad y Vida" in *Mi Religión y Otros Ensayos*. Madrid: Espasa-Calpe, p. 16. Reprinted by courtesy of the Heirs of Miguel de Unamuno.

Passage Two. Rulfo, Juan. "¡Diles que no me Maten!" in *El Llano en Llamas*. México: Fondo de Cultura Económico, 1953, p. 83.

Tone or Attitude

Passage One. Mikes, George: *Los Norteamericanos en su Salsa*. Buenos Aires: Editorial Borocaba, 1953, p. 51.

Passage Two. Arreola, Juan José: "En Verdad os Digo" in *Confabulario*. México: Joaquín Mortíz, 1971, p. 19.

Intended Reader

Passage One. Ott, Ernst: *Supérese Pensando*. Bilbao: Ediciones Mensajero, 1987, pagina preliminar.

Part Three, Chapter Six (Practice Reading Comprehension Passages)

Primer Grupo

Selección Uno. Amicis, Edmundo de: *Corazón (Diario de un Niño)*. Buenos Aires, publisher unknown, n.d., p. 62.

Selección Dos. Matute, Ana María: *Primera Memoria*. Barcelona: Editorial Destino, 1960, p. 200.

Selección Tres. *El País*, domingo 9 de junio de 1991, p. 45.

Selección Cuatro. Díaz-Plaja, Fernando: El Español y los siete Pecados Capitales. Madrid: Editorial Alianza, 1986, pp. 126-127.

Segundo Grupo
  Selección Uno. Delgado, Jaime: "Siqueiros," *Mundo Hispano*, febrero 1974, p. 52.
  Selección Dos. *El Informador Hispano*, Ft. Worth, TX, 7 de enero de 1993, p. 27.
  Selección Tres. Denevi, Marcos: *Rosaura a las Diez*. New York: Scribner's, 1964, p. 92.
  Selección Cuatro. *El Periódico U.S.A.*, McAllen, TX, 14 de abril de 1993, p. 1.
Tercer Grupo
  Selección Uno. Tome Bona, Javier María, *Mundo Hispánico*, diciembre 1973, p. 50.
  Selección Dos. LACSA ticket.
  Selección Tres. Letter from the Junta de Castilla y León (author's private correspondence).
  Selección Cuatro. Unamuno, Miguel de: *Tres Novelas Ejemplares y Un Prólogo*. Madrid:
    Espasa-Calpe. Reprinted by courtesy of the Heirs of Miguel de Unamuno.
Cuarto Grupo
  Selección Uno. Fuentes, Carlos: *Tiempo Mexicano*. México: Joaquín Mortíz, 1973, pp. 82-83.
  Selección Dos. *Cambio 16*, 19 de marzo de 1984, p. 642. Reprinted with permission of
    Cambio 16.
  Selección Tres. Alsasr, Collin, McCormick: "Tres Balsas en el Pacífico," *Mundo Hispánico*,
    agosto 1973, p. 40.
  Selección Cuatro. Arreola, Juan: "Baltasar Gerard" in *Confabulario*. México: Joaquín Mortíz,
    1971, p. 75.
Quinto Grupo
  Selección Uno. Menasche, Marcelo: *Y Van Dos...* Buenos Aires: Editorial Samet, 1931, p. 100.
  Selección Dos. Menasche, Marcelo: *Y Van Dos...* Buenos Aires: Editorial Samet, 1931, p. 62.
  Selección Tres. Ingenieros, José: *La Simulación en la Lucha por la Vida*. Buenos Aires: Editorial
    Tor, 1955, p. 164.
  Selección Cuatro. Lindemann, Hans A.: *Pláticas Filosóficas*, Zig-Zag, Santiago, 1940,
    pp. 147–148.

Part Four, Chapter Seven (Free-response Grammatical Structures)
  Group One. Linares, Luis G. de: "Tiempo Presente," *Semana*, 1 de junio de 1992, p. 19.
  Group Two. Matute, Ana María: *Primera Memoria*. Barcelona: Ediciones Destino, 1960, p. 14.
  Group Three. *Semana,* 24 de junio de 1992, p. 98.
  Group Four. *Semana,* 24 de junio de 1992, p. 78.
  Group Five. 1993 Olympics advertisement.
  Group Six. *Semana,* 1 de junio de 1992, p. 27.
  Group Seven. *El País. Semanal*, domingo 9 de junio de 1991, p. 123.
  Group Eight. *El País. Semanal*, 6 de septiembre de 1991, p. 56.
  Group Nine. *El País. Semanal*, domingo 9 de junio de 1991, p. 25.
  Group Ten. Montero, Rosa, *El País. Semanal*, domingo 9 de junio de 1991, p. 8.
  Group Eleven. *El País,* domingo 9 de junio de 1991, p. 128.
  Group Twelve. Mikes, George: *Otras Personalidades que he conocido*. Buenos Aires, Ediciones
    Peuser, 1946, p. 95.
  Group Thirteen. Castellano, Rosario: *Los Convidados de Agosto*. México: Ediciones Era, 1975,
    p. 158.
  Group Fourteen. Gómez-Quintero, Ela: *Al Día en los Negocios* (adaptation). New York: McGraw-
    Hill, Inc., 1984, p. 285. Reproduced with permission of McGraw-Hill, Inc.
  Group Fifteen. Valdés, Carlos, *Diario Las Americas,* Miami, sábado 6 de noviembre 1993, p. 2B.
  Group Sixteen. Hamill, Pete: "Bilingue...Monolingue," *Más*, Vol. 1, No. 1, otoño 1989, p. 62.
  Group Seventeen. Russell, Bertrand: *Ensayos Impopulares*. México: Editorial Hermes, 1952,
    p. 179.
  Group Eighteen. Russell, Bertrand: *Ensayos Impopulares*. México: Editorial Hermes, 1952, p. 45.

Group Nineteen.   Amicis, Edmundo de: *Corazón (Diario de un Niño)*. Buenos Aires: Publisher unknown, n.d., p. 63.

Group Twenty.   Amicis, Edmundo de: *Corazón (Diario de un Niño)*. Buenos Aires: Publisher unknown, n.d., p. 28.

Part Six, Model Exam

Reading (Vocabulary and Grammatical Structures in Context)

    Ejercicio 1: "Una demora sin sentido," *La nación*, edición electrónica, San José, Costa Rica, 10 de mayo de 1996.

    Ejercicio 2: Walsh, Rodolfo: "Cuento para tahures," *Cuentos argentinos de misterio,* E. Dale Carter, Jr and Joe Bas eds. Appleton-Century-Crofts, New York, 1968, p. 35.

    Ejercicio 3: Author's personal file.

Reading Comprehension

    Selection Number One.   Quiroga, Horacio: "El Sueño" in *El Salvaje*. Buenos Aires: Hemisferio, 1953, p. 9.

    Selection Number Two.   *La Voz de Houston*, adapted from an advertisement for Continental.

    Selection Number Three.   Lizardi, Fernández de: "El Periquillo Sarmiento" in Hespelt: *An Anthology of Spanish American Literature*, New York: Appleton-Century-Crofts, 1946, p. 148.

Writing (Section II, Part A)

    Alarcón, Pedro Antonio de: *El Escándalo,* Mexico: Editorial Novaro, 1958, p. 85.

Listening Comprehension

    Short Narrative One.   Soldao, Juan: "El Cura y el Muchacho Tonto" in *Cuentos Folklóricos de Argentina*. Buenos Aires: Editorial Universitaria de Buenos Aires, 1962, p. 122.

    Short Narrative Two.   "Pablo Casals," *Mundo Hispánico*, No. 309, diciembre 1973, p. 12.

    Longer Selection One.   Amicis, Edmundo de: *Corazón (Diario de un Niño)*. Buenos Aires: Publisher unknown, n.d., p. 296.

    Longer Selection Two.   *Puerta del Sol*, octubre 1990, p. 3.

Index